Fodor's 2011

SAN FRANCISCO

Fodor's Travel Publications   New York, Toronto, London, Sydney, Auckland
www.fodors.com

Be a Fodor's Correspondent

Your opinion matters. It matters to us. It matters to your fellow Fodor's travelers, too. And we'd like to hear it. In fact, we *need* to hear it.

When you share your experiences and opinions, you become an active member of the Fodor's community. That means we'll not only use your feedback to make our books better, but we'll publish your names and comments whenever possible. Throughout our guides, look for "Word of Mouth" excerpts of your unvarnished feedback.

Here's how you can help improve Fodor's for all of us.

Tell us when we're right. We rely on local writers to give you an insider's perspective. But our writers and staff editors—who are the best in the business—depend on you. Your positive feedback is a vote to renew our recommendations for the next edition.

Tell us when we're wrong. We're proud that we update most of our guides every year. But we're not perfect. Things change. Hotels cut services. Museums change hours. Charming cafés lose charm. If our writer didn't quite capture the essence of a place, tell us how you'd do it differently. If any of our descriptions are inaccurate or inadequate, we'll incorporate your changes in the next edition and will correct factual errors at fodors.com *immediately.*

Tell us what to include. You probably have had fantastic travel experiences that aren't yet in Fodor's. Why not share them with a community of like-minded travelers? Maybe you chanced upon a beach or bistro or B&B that you don't want to keep to yourself. Tell us why we should include it. And share your discoveries and experiences with everyone directly at fodors.com. Your input may lead us to add a new listing or highlight a place we cover with a "Highly Recommended" star or with our highest rating, "Fodor's Choice."

Send your nominations, comments, and complaints by mail to San Francisco Editor, Fodor's, 1745 Broadway, New York, NY 10019. Or e-mail editors@fodors.com with the subject line "San Francisco Editor."

You and travelers like you are the heart of the Fodor's community. Make our community richer by sharing your experiences. Be a Fodor's correspondent.

Happy traveling!

Tim Jarrell, Publisher

FODOR'S SAN FRANCISCO 2011

Editor: Maria Teresa Hart

Editorial Contributors: Denise M. Leto, Fiona G. Parrott, Sharron Wood, Sura Wood

Production Editor: Carrie Parker

Maps & Illustrations: David Lindroth, Mark Stroud, *cartographers;* Bob Blake, Rebecca Baer, *map editors;* William Wu, *information graphics*

Design: Fabrizio La Rocca, *creative director;* Guido Caroti, Siobhan O'Hare, *art directors;* Tina Malaney, Chie Ushio, Ann McBride, Jessica Walsh, *designers;* Melanie Marin, *senior picture editor*

Cover Photo: Chinatown: Westend61/age fotostock

Production Manager: Angela L. McLean

COPYRIGHT

Copyright © 2011 by Fodor's Travel, a division of Random House, Inc.

Fodor's is a registered trademark of Random House, Inc.

All rights reserved. Published in the United States by Fodor's Travel, a division of Random House, Inc., and simultaneously in Canada by Random House of Canada, Limited, Toronto. Distributed by Random House, Inc., New York.

No maps, illustrations, or other portions of this book may be reproduced in any form without written permission from the publisher.

ISBN 978–1–4000–0474–4

ISSN 1525–1829

SPECIAL SALES

This book is available at special discounts for bulk purchases for sales promotions or premiums. Special editions, including personalized covers, excerpts of existing books, and corporate imprints, can be created in large quantities for special needs. For more information, write to Special Markets/Premium Sales, 1745 Broadway, MD 6-2, New York, New York 10019, or e-mail specialmarkets@randomhouse.com.

AN IMPORTANT TIP & AN INVITATION

Although all prices, opening times, and other details in this book are based on information supplied to us at press time, changes occur all the time in the travel world, and Fodor's cannot accept responsibility for facts that become outdated or for inadvertent errors or omissions. So **always confirm information when it matters,** especially if you're making a detour to visit a specific place. Your experiences—positive and negative— matter to us. If we have missed or misstated something, **please write to us.** We follow up on all suggestions. Contact the San Francisco editor at editors@fodors.com or c/o Fodor's at 1745 Broadway, New York, NY 10019.

PRINTED IN SINGAPORE

10 9 8 7 6 5 4 3 2 1

CONTENTS

Fodor's Features

CONTENTS

ABOUT THIS BOOK

Our Ratings

Sometimes you find terrific travel experiences and sometimes they just find you. But usually the burden is on you to select the right combination of experiences. That's where our ratings come in.

As travelers we've all discovered a place so wonderful and also so locally unique that superlatives don't do it justice: you just have to be there to know. These sights, properties, and experiences get our highest rating, **Fodor's Choice,** indicated by orange stars throughout this book.

Black stars highlight sights and properties we deem **Highly Recommended,** places that our writers, editors, and readers praise again and again for consistency and excellence.

By default, there's another category: any place we include in this book is by definition worth your time, unless we say otherwise. And we will.

Disagree with any of our choices? Care to nominate a place or suggest that we rate one more highly? Visit our feedback center at www.fodors.com/feedback.

Budget Well

Hotel and restaurant price categories from ¢ to $$$$ are defined in the opening pages of each chapter. For attractions, we always give standard adult admission fees; reductions are usually available for children, students, and senior citizens. Want to pay with plastic? **AE, D, DC, MC, V** following restaurant and hotel listings indicate if American Express, Discover, Diners Club, MasterCard, and Visa are accepted.

Restaurants

Unless we state otherwise, restaurants are open for lunch and dinner daily. We mention dress only when there's a specific requirement and reservations only when they're essential or not accepted—it's always best to book ahead.

Hotels

Hotels have private bath, phone, TV, and air-conditioning and operate on the European Plan (aka EP, meaning without meals), unless we specify that they use the Continental Plan (CP, with a continental breakfast), Breakfast Plan (BP, with a full breakfast), or Modified American Plan (MAP, with breakfast and dinner), or are all-inclusive (AI, including all meals and most activities). We

always list facilities but not whether you'll be charged an extra fee to use them, so when pricing accommodations, find out what's included.

Listings	
★	Fodor's Choice
★	Highly recommended
⊠	Physical address
✛	Directions or Map coordinates
⌂	Mailing address
☎	Telephone
🖷	Fax
⊕	On the Web
✍	E-mail
☒	Admission fee
☉	Open/closed times
Ⓜ	Metro stations
▭	Credit cards
Hotels & Restaurants	
🏨	Hotel
⇆	Number of rooms
⚲	Facilities
⦿|	Meal plans
✕	Restaurant
⚲	Reservations
🜂	Dress code
⤡	Smoking
🍸	BYOB
Outdoors	
🏌	Golf
⛺	Camping
Other	
♨	Family-friendly
⇨	See also
⊠	Branch address
☞	Take note

Experience
San Francisco

SAN FRANCISCO TODAY

The quintessential boomtown, San Francisco has been alternately riding high and crashing since the gold rush. Those bearish during the heady days of the dot-com bubble had barely finished dancing on the grave of the Internet economy when biotech rode into town, turning bust to boom once again before the housing market downturn brought the city's previously stratospheric median home price almost down to earth. So which San Francisco will you find when you come to town? A reversal of fortune is always possible, but here's a snapshot of what the city's like—for now, anyway.

Today's San Francisco:

. . . is just as liberal as you've heard. Baghdad by the Bay, Sodom by the Sea: prudish types have been pegging San Francisco as a bastion of sexy liberalism since the town first rolled out the welcome mat. And we do tend to espouse a pretty live-and-let-live attitude here. Health insurance for city employees has covered gender-reassignment surgery since 2001. We voted in 2005 to ban handguns; we have a female fire chief, Joanne Hayes-White; and our biggest bash of the year is June's gay pride celebration, when roughly a million people descend on the city to party.

Our dashing young Mayor Gavin Newsom, himself a raging metrosexual, won the eternal devotion of gay San Franciscans when he decided to issue marriage licenses to same-sex couples in 2004, helping to shove the issue onto the supreme court docket as well as the ballot. And in this town he's considered a moderate. Newsom enjoys the city's tolerance as well. Following the 2007 revelation that he had a fling with his social secretary—who was also the wife of his good friend and campaign manager—and Newsom's admission that he has a drinking problem, his approval rating topped 70% and he went on to win a second term virtually unopposed.

. . . embraces its eccentrics. If a 6-foot-tall transvestite in evening wear doesn't merit a second look, just what does it take to stand out in this town? If history serves, it takes quirkiness and staying power. For instance, back in the 19th century a San Francisco businessman declared himself Norton I, Emperor of the United States and Protector of Mexico. Instead of shipping him off to a nice, quiet place, San Franciscans became his willing subjects, police officers saluted him, and newspapers printed his proclamations (among

WHAT WE'RE TALKING ABOUT

Curious about the state of the city? Hear about it in great detail (except that unpleasantness about a budget deficit) in Mayor Newsom's 7½-hour speech on his YouTube channel. And while you're at it, become one of the mayor's 50,000-plus Facebook friends

and check out his latest tweets on Twitter (where he broke the news of his wife's pregnancy).

You know the economy is bad when San Franciscans start curbing their dining-out expenditures. Sure, we still eat out, but we're spending less when we do. For the practice

of ordering appetizers to share instead of entrées, waiters have dubbed us "non'trées." Ouch.

We love to hate Muni. Grousing about Muni's slow service and accident rates is a rite of passage. Commuters unite on Web sites like munioutrage.

them that the Democrats and Republicans be abolished for bickering).

Today the Brown Twins, ladies of a certain age who dress alike in eye-catching outfits and are always together, have their own place on the list of San Francisco icons. There's also Pink Man, who rides on a unicycle wearing a hot pink unitard and cape. (He says you can tell someone's a local when "they don't balk at Pink Man.")

One of the most celebrated eccentrics is Frank Chu, a middle-aged guy in a frumpy suit who's been faithfully carrying a picket sign around the Financial District since the 1990s. He accuses various politicians of being in cahoots and keeping millions of dollars from him and the population of the "12 galaxies." The city's response? Politicians buy ad space on the back of his sign and fans named a Mission District bar 12 Galaxies in tribute. Chu eats and drinks on the house there.

. . . is losing residents. At 46 square mi, San Francisco is twice the size of Manhattan but has only half the population: about 799,000—only 24,000 more than in 1950—and dropping. The city maintained its population until the dot-com boom of the 1990s drove young families to the East Bay in search of lower housing prices. When the bubble burst, there was a second purge as many of those high-tech Johnny-come-latelies scrambled for cheaper ground out of town.

. . . is reshaping its downtown. Limited by its geography, San Francisco simply has nowhere to go but up. The sprawling area south of Market Street was long an industrial center, but since that industry has dried up, new high-rise developments are under way. Plot the nascent high-rises on a map and you can see a radical shift southward, stretching from Mission Street to Mission Bay (where UCSF's 43-acre medical and biotech campus is rising). More than 20 towers are in the works, several of which will eclipse the city's current tallest building, the 853-foot Transamerica Pyramid.

Got your bearings? Then join the locals as they constantly check the pulse of the city. Although the frenzied adrenaline rush of the dot-com era has died down, a new wave of energy is gathering.

com and grumble on blogs like The SF Muni Grouch ⊕ munig-rouch.blogspot.com.

There's lots of hand-wringing and gnashing of teeth in the Bay Area these days over the slipping housing market, and though the city hasn't been hit nearly as hard as most other Bay Area towns, the median home price is finally coming into range for most mere mortals: $552,000 (and climbing).

Pier 39 has suddenly become much quieter. The cacopho-nous sea lions that used to sun themselves here have suddenly moved on. Marine scientists have listed a variety of reasons why the sea lions split and some speculate they moved to Oregon. But one thing is certain: their frolicking and barking is missed by tour-ists and locals alike.

SAN FRANCISCO PLANNER

When to Go

You can visit San Francisco comfortably any time of year. Possibly the best time to visit San Francisco is September and October, when the city's summerlike weather brings outdoor concerts and festivals. The climate here always feels Mediterranean and moderate—with a foggy, sometimes chilly bite. The temperature rarely drops below 40°F, and anything warmer than 80°F is considered a heat wave. Be prepared for rain in winter, especially December and January. Winds off the ocean can add to the chill factor. That old joke about summer in SF feeling like winter is true at heart, but once you move inland, it gets warmer. (And some locals swear the thermostat has inched up in recent years.)

SAN FRANCISCO
TEMPERATURES

How's the Weather?

Thanks to its proximity to the Pacific Ocean, San Francisco has remarkably consistent weather throughout the year. The average high is 63°F and the average low is 51°F. Summer comes late in San Francisco, which sees its warmest days in September and October. On average, the city gets 20 inches of rainfall a year, most of it in the December–March period.

Getting Around

Walking: San Francisco dearly rewards walking, and the areas that most visitors cover are easy (and safe) to reach on foot. However, many neighborhoods have steep—make that *steep*—hills. In some areas the sidewalk is carved into steps; a place that seems just a few blocks away might be a real hike, depending on the grade. When your calves ache, you're that much closer to being a local. Check the Safety section (*see below*) for a summary on areas through which it may be best to avoid walking.

By Subway: BART is San Francisco's subway, limited to one straight line through the city. Within the city, it's a handy way to get to the Mission or perhaps Civic Center. BART is most useful for reaching the East Bay or the airport. There are no special visitor passes for BART; within town a ticket runs $1.75.

On Muni: Muni includes the city's extensive system of buses, electric streetcars, nostalgic F-line trolleys, and cable cars. The trolleys and cable cars are a pleasure for the ride alone, and they run in well-traveled areas like Market Street and, in the case of the cable cars, the hills from Union Square to Fisherman's Wharf. Basic fare for the bus, streetcars, and trolleys is $2; cable-car tickets cost $5 one-way. At $11, a one-day Muni Passport that includes cable car rides is a great deal.

By Car or Taxi: Considering its precipitous hills, one-way streets, and infuriating dearth of parking, San Francisco is not a good place to drive yourself. Taxis, however, can come in very handy. Call one or hail one on the street; they tend to cluster around downtown hotels.

Safety

Like any large city, San Francisco has its share of sketchy or downright troubled areas, but overall it's a relatively safe urban area. If you use common sense and follow basic precautions (sticking to well-lighted streets after dark, holding on to your bags rather than leaving them next to you), all should be well.

Even with forewarning, some visitors are taken aback by the high number of homeless people in the city's central areas. There's also a certain residual counterculture effect—the lingering visions of the 1960s scene bring in a few thousand street kids every summer. (These teens and twenty-somethings tend to hang out in the Haight and camp in the city's parks.) Although most homeless people are no threat, some panhandle aggressively. If you feel uncomfortable, simply don't engage them and move away.

Below is a list of the central city areas that you may want to avoid for safety's sake. Other parts of town, like the Haight, may look a bit scuzzy with graffiti or litter, but are basically safe during the day.

The Tenderloin. Named for a cut of steak, this neighborhood west of Union Square and above Civic Center can be a seedy part of town, with drug dealers, homeless people, hustlers, and X-rated joints. It's roughly bordered by Taylor, Polk, Geary, and Market streets. Avoid coming here after dark, especially if you're walking.

Western Addition. Gang activity makes this a sketchy neighborhood, even in daytime, with occasional outbreaks of gun violence. Don't stray too far off Fillmore Street.

Civic Center. After a show here, walk west to Gough Street; don't head north, east, or south from the Civic Center on foot, and avoid Market Street between 6th and 10th.

Parts of the Mission District. The flat blocks of the Mission range from a bit scruffy to edgy to truly sketchy, with some gang activity. Steer clear of the areas east of Mission Street and south of 24th Street, especially after dark. If you're walking between 16th and 24th streets, head west to Valencia, which runs parallel to Mission.

Some areas in Golden Gate Park. These include the area near the Haight Street entrance, where street kids often smoke and deal pot, and around the pedestrian tunnels on the far west end of the park.

Parts of SoMa: Drift a few blocks south of Market and you'll either be near the ballpark, in a high-rise jungle, or exploring the slow transformation of formerly industrial neighborhoods.

5 Helpful SF Web Sites

Check out these online options—besides our own www.fodors.com.www.onlyinsanfrancisco.com for the San Francisco visitors bureau.

www.sfgate.com/chronicle from the major daily newspaper, especially www.sfgate.com/traveler (for Bay Area travel) and www.sfgate.com/eguide (for entertainment articles and listings).

www.sfist.com for a daily feed of local news, gossip, and preoccupations.

http://mistersf.com for a passionate local's rundown on favorite local spots and city FAQs.

www.sfstation.com for daily listings on all sorts of events, restaurants, clubs, etc. Want to find a high volume of local comments on these places? Try www.yelp.com.

. . . and three more just for ha-has

www.burritoeater.com for opinionated reviews of Bay Area burritos.

http://munihaiku.com for poetic plaints about the Muni system.

www.lizhickok.com for photos of a model of SF made from Jell-O.

WHAT'S WHERE

1 Union Square. Home to a tourism trifecta: hotels, public transportation, and shopping. There are more hotel beds here than in any other neighborhood in the city; several transit options converge, including the cable cars. The square itself is dominated by flagship stores—but if you're not a shopper, this area may bore you.

2 Chinatown. Live fish flopping around on ice; the scent of incense, cigarettes, and vanilla; bargains announced in myriad Chinese dialects... you'll feel like you should have brought your passport.

3 SoMa. Anchored by SFMOMA and Yerba Buena Gardens, SoMa is a once-industrial neighborhood that's in transition. Luxury condos are going up and there are several cool dance clubs and restaurants, but some parts are still quite gritty.

4 Civic Center. Monumental city government buildings and performing arts venues, but also a chronic homeless magnet. Locals love Hayes Valley, the chic little neighborhood to the west.

5 Nob Hill. Topped by staid and elegant behemoths, hotels that ooze reserve and breeding, Nob Hill is old-money San Francisco.

6 Russian Hill. These steep streets hold a vibrant, classy neighborhood that's very au courant. Locals flock to Polk and Hyde streets, the hill's main commercial avenues, for excellent neighborhood eateries and fantastic window-shopping.

7 North Beach. The city's small Italian neighborhood makes even locals feel like they're on holiday. In the morning fresh focaccia beckons, and there are few better ways to laze away an afternoon than in one of North Beach's cafés.

8 The Embarcadero. The city's northeastern waterfront is anchored at the foot of Market Street by the exquisitely restored Ferry Building. The promenade that starts in back has great views of the bay and the Bay Bridge.

9 The Northern Waterfront. Wandering the shops and so-called attractions of Fisherman's Wharf, Pier 39, and Ghirardelli Square, the only locals you'll meet will be the ones with visitors in tow. Everything here is designed for tourists, so if you're looking for a souvenir shop...

10 Jackson Square. For history buffs and antiques lovers, this upscale corner of the Financial District is a pleasant diversion.

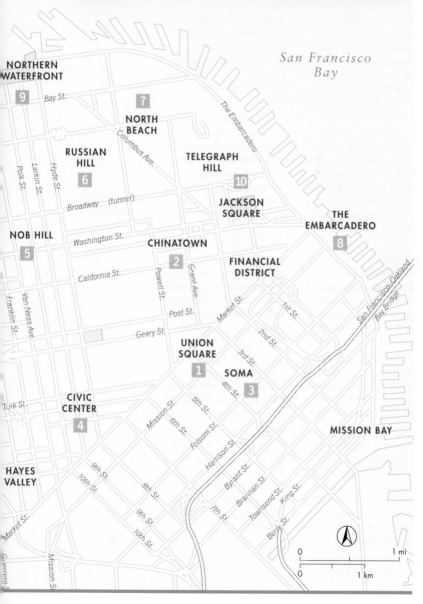

NORTHERN WATERFRONT

9

Bay St.

7

NORTH BEACH

The Embarcadero

Columbus Ave.

RUSSIAN HILL

6

TELEGRAPH HILL

10

Polk St.
Larkin St.
Hyde St.

Broadway   (tunnel)

JACKSON SQUARE

THE EMBARCADERO

8

NOB HILL

5

Washington St.

CHINATOWN

2

FINANCIAL DISTRICT

Van Ness Ave.
Franklin St.

California St.

Powell St.

Grant Ave.

Post St.

Market St.

1st St.

San Francisco–Oakland Bay Bridge

Geary St.

UNION SQUARE

1

2nd St.

3rd St.

SOMA

3

Turk St.

CIVIC CENTER

4

Mission St.
5th St.
6th St.

4th St.

Folsom St.

MISSION BAY

HAYES VALLEY

Harrison St.

9th St.
10th St.

8th St.

Bryant St.

Brannan St.

7th St.

Townsend St.

King St.

9th St.

10th St.

Berry St.

Market St.

Mission St.

Guerrero St.

0   1 mi

0   1 km

WHAT'S WHERE

11 The Marina. With fine-wine shops, trendy boutiques, fashionable cafés and restaurants, and pricey waterfront homes, the Marina is San Francisco's yuppiest neighborhood. It's also home to the exquisite 1915 Palace of Fine Arts.

12 The Presidio. Locals come to the Presidio, the wooded shoreline park just west of the Marina, for a quick in-town getaway, the spirit-lift only an amble on the sand in the shadow of the Golden Gate Bridge can provide.

13 Golden Gate Park. Covering more than 1,000 acres of greenery, with sports fields, windmills, museums, gardens, and a few buffalo thrown in for good measure, Golden Gate Park is San Francisco's backyard.

14 The Western Shoreline. A natural gem underappreciated by locals and visitors alike, the city's windswept Pacific shore stretches for miles.

15 The Haight. If you're looking for '60s souvenirs, you can find them here, along with some of the loveliest Victorians in town (and aggressive panhandling). Hip locals come for the great secondhand shops, cheap brunch, and low-key bars and cafés.

16 The Castro. Even with its rainbow-flag-waving,

in-your-face style, the Castro is a friendly neighborhood that welcomes visitors of all stripes. Shop the trendy boutiques, and catch a film at the truly noteworthy Castro Theatre.

17 Noe Valley. A cute, pricey neighborhood favored by young families. The main strip, 24th Street, is lined with coffee shops, eateries, and boutiques selling fancy bath products and trendy children's clothing.

18 The Mission District. When the sun sets, people descend on the Mission from all over the Bay Area for destination restaurants, excellent bargain-price ethnic eateries, and the hippest bar scene around.

19 Pacific Heights. This neighborhood has some of San Francisco's most opulent real estate—but in most cases you'll have to be content with an exterior view.

20 Japantown. A tight-knit Japanese-American population supports this area, of interest to outsiders mostly for the ethnic shopping and dining opportunities of the Japan Center and the small streets just north.

Golden Gate
National
Recreation
Area

MARINA
11

NORTHERN
WATERFRONT

Bay St.

Lombard St.

THE
PRESIDIO
12

PACIFIC
HEIGHTS
19

Steiner St.
Fillmore St.

Broadway

Washington St.

Hyde St.
Larkin St.
Polk St.

Sacramento St.

California St.

NOB HILL

Pine St.

Bush St.

S. Van Ness Ave.
Franklin St.
Gough St.
Laguna St.

Lake St.

EACLIFF

Clement St.

eary Blvd.

lboa St.

25th Ave.

19th Ave.

Park Presidio Blvd.

8th Ave.

Arguello Blvd.

Presidio Ave.

Geary St.

JAPANTOWN
20

Turk St.

Turk St.

Masonic Ave.

Golden Gate Ave.

Fulton St.

Divisadero St.

WESTERN
ADDITION

Hayes St.
Fell St.

RICHMOND

Fulton St.

Golden Gate
Park

Stow
Lake

iddle Dr.

13

Haight St.

HAIGHT
15

Buena
Vista
Park

Duboce Ave.

Market St.

S. Van Ness Ave.
Mission St.

Lincoln Way

Stanyan St.

Clayton St.

Judah St.

19th Ave.

Funston Ave.

7th Ave.

Clarendon Ave.

CASTRO
16

Castro St.

17th St.
Mission
Dolores
Park
20th St.

Guerrero St.
Dolores St.

MISSION
18

Lawton St.

Noriega St.

Ortega St.

28th Ave.

Twin Peaks

NOE VALLEY
17

SUNSET

Quintara St.

14th Ave.

25th St.

Diamond St.

Cesar Chavez St.

McCoppin
Square

araval St.

icente St.

Larsen
Park

Portola Dr.

Stern Grove

oat Blvd.

Bosworth St.

Southern Fwy.

TONESTOWN

Monterey Blvd.

Silver Ave.

Junipero Serra Blvd.

Miramar Ave.

San Jose Ave.

Alemany Blvd.
Mission St.
Excelsior Av.

GLEN
PARK

Felton St.

Harding
Park

Ocean Ave.

Balboa
Park

SAN FRANCISCO'S TOP ATTRACTIONS

Alcatraz

(A) Considering how many movies have been set here, you might feel like you've already "been there, done that"—but you really shouldn't miss a trip to America's most infamous federal pen. Husky-throated onetime inmates and grizzled former guards bring the Rock to life on the wonderful audio tour; you'll hear yarns about desperate escape attempts and notorious crooks like Al Capone while you walk the cold cement cellblock. But it's not all doom and gloom: you'll enjoy stunning views of the city skyline on the ferry ride to and from the island.

Golden Gate Bridge

(B) San Francisco's signature International Orange entryway is the city's majestic background, and about 10 million people a year head to the bridge for an up-close look. Walking the 1.7 mi to Marin County—inches from roaring traffic, steel shaking beneath your feet, and a far-too-low railing between you and the water 200 feet below—is much more than a superlative photo op (though it's that, too).

Fisherman's Wharf

(C) Once part of a thriving fishing industry, Fisherman's Wharf has deteriorated into a giant harpoon aimed straight at your wallet. Throngs from all over the world come to try and spot a remaining sea lion; buy cheap T-shirts; and chow down on overpriced, mediocre food. It's all an utter mystery to locals, who don't come here. Ever. See the magnificent historic ships at the Hyde Street Pier, then take your money and run.

Golden Gate Park

(D) It may be world famous, but first and foremost the park is the city's backyard. Come here any day of the week and you'll find a microcosm of San Francisco, from the Russian senior citizens feeding the pigeons at Stow Lake and the moms pushing strollers through the botanical gardens to science fans exploring the fabulous California Academy of Sciences and arts boosters checking out the latest at the de Young Museum. Be sure to visit the park's iconic treasures, including the serene Japanese Tea Garden and the beautiful Victorian Conservatory of Flowers. If you have the time to venture farther into this urban oasis, you'll discover less accessible gems like the Beach Chalet and the wild western shores of Ocean Beach.

Palace of Fine Arts

(E) Perched on a swan-filled lagoon near the Marina's yacht harbor, this stirringly beautiful terra-cotta-color dome has an otherworldly quality about it. Built for the 1915 Panama-Pacific International Exhibition, the palace is a San Francisco architect's version of a Roman ruin, and it's been eliciting gasps for almost a century. Try to see it from the water.

Coit Tower

(F) Most people assume that this stubby white tower atop Telegraph Hill is supposed to look like a fire hose. And considering that a fire truck–chasing, cross-dressing 19th-century socialite donated the funds to build it in honor of firefighters, maybe it is. The tower itself is of vague interest—it does house the history of San Francisco in murals—but the "park"(ing lot) at its base has fantastic views of the city and the bay. The tower sits at the top of Telegraph Hill's Filbert Steps, a steep stairway through glorious gardens with vistas of transcendent beauty, an only-in-San Francisco spot locals cherish.

Cable Cars

(G) You've already seen them (on the big screen, in magazines, and, admit it, on the Rice-a-Roni box). And considering a ticket costs $5 a pop, do you really need to ride a cable car? Yes, you do, at least once during your visit. Flag down a Powell–Hyde car along Powell Street, grab the pole, and clatter and jiggle up mansion-topped Nob Hill. Crest the hill, and hold on for the hair-raising descent to Fisherman's Wharf, with sun glittering off the bay and Alcatraz bobbing in the distance. Don't deny it—this would be a deal at twice the price.

AT&T Park

(H) One of the finest examples of modern "retro" ballparks, the Giants coastal digs are the perfect place to spend a sunny afternoon enjoying the national pastime. Grab a dog and some garlic fries, and revel in the bay views. If you're lucky, you'll get to see someone drill a splash hit into McCovey Cove.

Ferry Building

(I) Foodies rejoice! The historic Ferry Building is stuffed to the brim with all things tasty, including cafés, restaurants, a farmers' market, and merchants peddling

everything from wine and olive oil to oysters and mushrooms. The building backs up to the bay, so the views are great—but they're even better from the decks of the departing ferries.

Wine Country

(J) You don't need to be a connoisseur to enjoy a trip to Napa or Sonoma . . . or both (hey, you're on vacation). But there's more to a Wine Country visit than vineyard tours and tastings: landmark restaurants, breathtaking scenery, fantastic artwork, hot-air balloon rides, and secluded boutique hotels. And when you're ready for a break, a great glass of wine is never that far out of reach.

LOCAL FOR A DAY

Want to get a slice of local life by just hanging out, skipping the sightseeing? These experiences will let you pretend you're a San Franciscan, without a whopping rent check.

Shop the Ferry Plaza Farmers' Market
Roll out of bed and make your way to the Ferry Building—preferably on a Saturday—to join locals and celebrity chefs on a taste bud–driven raid. Out front, farmer-run stands showcase the Bay Area's finest organic, free-range, low-food-mile goods. The indoor stalls will keep your mouth watering with artisanal cheeses, chocolates, and luscious pastries. Snag some takeaway food plus some perfectly ripe fruit for a picnic.

Stretch Your Legs in the Presidio
Spend a few hours wandering around this former military base at the foot of the Golden Gate Bridge. The park is redeveloping the old military buildings, along with ball fields and other rec areas. Join people walking their dogs on the wooded hiking trails, or amble the paths along the sand of Crissy Field, then get in line for a cocoa at the Warming Hut.

Hang Out in Hayes Valley
Long beloved of artsy, cutting-edge locals, this quarter of cool cafés and high-design boutiques is either coming into its own or getting too big for its britches, depending on whom you ask. The renovation of Octavia Boulevard, one of this neighborhood's main arteries, makes Hayes Valley even busier. Grab a coffee from local cult microroasters Blue Bottle Coffee and check out the latest temporary art installation in Patricia's Green, the petite community park.

Find a Quiet Beach
Leave the beach near Fisherman's Wharf far behind and seek out these two instead. Breezy Baker Beach, tucked against the cliffs just south of the Golden Gate Bridge, is known for its bridge and ocean views—and its nudists, those hardy souls. A bit farther south, nestled in ultrapricey Seacliff, is China Beach, a smaller, more secluded spot that's never crowded.

Linger Over Breakfast
Notoriously food-centric San Franciscans are big on the most important meal of the day. The lines at popular breakfast places can be just as long as those at the hottest nightspots. Some longtime favorites include:

Mama's tried-and-true diner, where the line forms early (✉ *1701 Stockton St., at Filbert St., North Beach* ☎ *415/362–6421*).

Kate's Kitchen, where heaping plates of Southern-inspired fare take the edge off a hairy-tongued Lower Haight morning-after (✉ *471 Haight St., near Fillmore St., Lower Haight* ☎ *415/626–3984*).

Ella's, where oatmeal and chicken hash are served alongside gussied-up standbys like brandied French toast (✉ *500 Presidio Ave., at California St., Pacific Heights* ☎ *415/441–5669*).

Nurse a Coffee
Spend a few hours in the right independent café or coffeehouse and you'll feel like you're in a neighborhood living room. Come for a jolt of java, sometimes a reasonably priced meal, and usually Wi-Fi. Stay all afternoon—nobody minds—and you'll see the best reflection of a microcommunity.

SAN FRANCISCO WITH KIDS

On the Move

Cable Cars. This one's a no-brainer. But don't miss the **Cable Car Terminus** at Powell and Market streets, where conductors push the iconic cars on giant turntables, and the **Cable Car Museum,** where you can see how cable cars work.

Adventure Cat Sailing. Them: playing on the trampoline at the bow of this 55-foot catamaran. You: enjoying a drink and the bay sunset on the stern deck.

F-Line Trolleys. Thomas the Tank Engine fan in tow? Hop on one of the F-line's neat historic streetcars. ■TIP→ Bonus: this line connects other kid-friendly sights, like Fisherman's Wharf and the Ferry Building.

Sneak in Some Culture

Stern Grove Festival. Enjoying a delicious picnic in a eucalyptus grove, your kids might not even complain that they're listening to—gasp—classical music.

ODC/San Francisco. Best known for their holiday production of *The Velveteen Rabbit,* the dance troupe also holds other performances throughout the year.

San Francisco Mime Troupe. We know, it sounds lame. But these aren't your father's mimes. In fact, they're a vocal political theater troupe that gives family-friendly outdoor performances.

The Great Outdoors

Muir Woods. If these massive trees look tall to you, imagine seeing them from two or three feet lower.

Stow Lake. When feeding bread to the ducks gets old (like that's ever going to happen), you can rent a rowboat or paddleboat.

Golden Gate Promenade. If your kids can handle a 3.3-mi walk, this one's a beauty—winding from Aquatic Park Beach, through the Presidio, to Fort Point Pier near the base of the Golden Gate Bridge.

Aquatic Park Beach. Does your brood include a wannabe Michael Phelps? Then head to this popular beach, one of the few places around the city where it's safe to swim. ■TIP→ Many other Bay Area beaches have powerful currents that make swimming dangerous.

Just Plain Fun

AT&T Park. Emerald grass, a sun-kissed day, a hot dog in your hand . . . and suddenly, you're 10 again, too.

Dim Sum. A rolling buffet for which kids point and pick—likely an instant hit.

Fisherman's Wharf, Hyde Street Pier, Ghirardelli Square, and Pier 39. The phrase "tourist trap" may come to mind, but in this area you can get a shrimp cocktail, clamber around old ships, snack on chocolate, and laugh at the sea lions (if they're around).

Musée Mécanique. What did people do before Wii? Come here to find out.

Rooftop @ Yerba Buena Gardens. Head here for ice-skating, bowling, a carousel, a playground, and Zeum, an interactive arts and technology center.

San Francisco Zoo. Between Grizzly Gulch, Lemur Forest, and Koala Crossing, you can make a day of it.

Learn a Thing or Two

California Academy of Sciences. Dinosaurs, penguins, free-flying rainforest butterflies, giant snakes . . . what's not to like?

Exploratorium. A very hands-on science museum, including the full-immersion Tactile Dome.

TOP WALKING TOURS

■ **All About Chinatown** (☎415/982–8839 ⊕ *www.allaboutchinatown.com*). A delightful "behind-the-scenes" look at the neighborhood. Owner Linda Lee and her guides stop in Ross Alley and at a Buddhist temple. At herbal and food markets you'll learn the therapeutic yield of fish stomachs and ponder uses for live partridges.

■ **Chinatown Alleyway Tours** (☎415/984–1478 ⊕ *www.chinatownalleywaytours. org*). To learn about the modern Chinatown community, join up with one of these young guides. Tour leaders, who all grew up here, discuss not only Chinatown's history but also current social issues.

■ **Don Herron's Dashiell Hammett Tour** (⊕ *www.donherron.com*). Brush up on your noir slang and join trench-coated guide Herron for a walk by the mystery writer's haunts and the locations from some of Hammett's novels.

■ **Foot! Comedy Walking Tours** (☎415/793–5378 ⊕ *www.foottours.com*). You'll likely find yourself breathless with laughter, not just gasping after a steep hill. The tour leaders are all moonlighting pro comedians; they've got offerings like "Nude, Lewd and Crude" North Beach.

■ **Local Tastes of the City Tours** (☎415/665–0480 or 888/358–8687 ⊕ *www.localtastesofthecitytours.com*). If you want to aggressively snack your way through a neighborhood as you walk it, consider hanging with cookbook author Tom Medin. You'll learn why certain things just taste better in San Francisco—like coffee and anything baked with sourdough—and you'll get tips about how to find good food once you get back home. Along the way, you'll gradually gorge yourself into oblivion: the North Beach

tour, for instance, might include multiple stops for coffee and baked goods.

■ **Precita Eyes Mural Walks** (☎415/285–2287 ⊕ *www.precitaeyes.org*). For an insider's look at the vibrant murals in the Mission District, this is the place to call. The nonprofit organization has nurtured this local art form from the get-go, and they stay on top of all the latest additions. *See the Mission District Chapter 11 for more details.*

■ **San Francisco City Guides** (☎415/557–4266 ⊕ *www.sfcityguides.org*). An outstanding free service supported by the San Francisco Public Library. Walking-tour themes range from individual neighborhoods to local history (the gold rush, the 1906 quake, ghost walks) to architecture. Each May and October additional walks are offered. Although the tours are free and the knowledgeable guides are volunteers, it's appropriate to make a $5 donation for these nonprofit programs. Tour schedules are available at library branches and at the **San Francisco Visitor Information Center** (✉ *Hallidie Plaza, lower level, Powell and Market Sts., Union Sq.* ☎415/391–2000, 415/392–0328 TDD ⊕ *www.sfvisitor.org*).

■ **Wok Wiz Chinatown Tour** (☎650/355–9657 ⊕ *www.wokwiz.com*). Cookbook author Shirley Fong-Torres and her team lead these walks. Conversation topics include folklore and, of course, food. One version called "I Can't Believe I Ate My Way Through Chinatown!" includes breakfast and lunch.

A BEATNIK WALK THROUGH NORTH BEACH

Beyond the aroma of cappuccino and focaccia, the café tables spilling onto the sidewalk, and the convivial air, North Beach is alive with the spirit of the Beatniks, those revolutionary artists who electrified San Francisco and shocked the country in the 1950s and '60s. Listen for the rhythm of Beat poetry, of Jack Kerouac, Allen Ginsberg, and Lawrence Ferlinghetti, which still pulses in the city's Italian neighborhood.

City Lights Books: The Heart of the Beats

At **City Lights,** wander three stories of books but linger by the poetry, where you're bound to see at least one serious, budding Ginsberg or Ferlinghetti (or even Ferlinghetti himself). Along the store runs **Jack Kerouac Alley,** inlaid with the words of Kerouac, Maya Angelou, and Confucius. You'll also find poetry crawling right up the muraled walls, on **Vesuvio,** the art-splashed saloon. Peruse the Beat relics, order a Kerouac, and picture that night in 1960 when the *On the Road* author blew off an invitation from Arthur Miller, lingering here instead. The poetry continues across Broadway, where a flock of books flutters in the air, and words such as "soar over" and "of whoop" engrave the sidewalk below.

The Beat Museum, Ginsberg's Digs, and Lenny Bruce's Dive

On bawdy Broadway, pass the strip joints and today's relocated and x-rated version of **the hungry i** nightclub. Back in the day, Beat comic genius Lenny Bruce rocked the house, occasionally landing in jail for obscenity. He also landed on the pavement, naked, after falling (or jumping) from the second floor of the Swiss American Hotel; look for the mural of neighborhood life on the building's Romolo Place side. Around front, duck into the **Beat Museum.** Browse bookshelves and clothing racks—$20 Beat beret, anyone?—on your way to the exhibit space. You probably won't find a Jack Kerouac bobble-head anywhere else, even in San Francisco. Another block down Broadway brings you to Montgomery; Allen Ginsberg wrote "Howl" while living at **no. 1010.**

The Classic Coffee and Bagels

Continue down Montgomery and turn left on Vallejo for the venerable, still-boho **Caffè Trieste,** favorite perch of Kerouac, Ginsberg, and Charles Bukowski. Head north up Grant to **no. 1398,** where the **Co-Existence Bagel Shop** served as the living room of the Beat generation in the days when cops arrested kids for sandal-wearing. Today Grant Avenue's excellent boutiques sell edgy couture and vintage botanical prints. Photo op: shoot south down Grant for the culture collision of North Beach with Chinatown.

Beyond North Beach

True Beats will make the pilgrimage a mile west to 29 Russell Street, where Kerouac wrote part of *On the Road* while staying with his friends the Cassadys. Another mile west, at the long-defunct Six Gallery (3119 Fillmore), Kerouac shouted encouragement during Ginsberg's first reading of "Howl," in 1955; he later called it "The night of the birth of the San Francisco poetry renaissance."

—Denise M. Leto

Where to Start:	In front of City Lights Books, the heart of Beatnik San Francisco.
Time/Length:	3 hours, including time to peruse the bookstore and museum and imbibe at either Vesuvio or Caffè Trieste. About half a mile.
Where to Stop:	Caffè Trieste; or, if you choose the full-city Beat tour, the site of the Six Gallery, on Fillmore Street in the Marina, possibly the city's least Beat-y 'hood.
Best Time to Go:	On sunny weekend afternoons you'll feel like you've been transported to Italy, but browsing City Lights at night and downing a nightcap at Vesuvio will take you back to the Beat days.
Worst Time to Go:	Rainy days can take the holiday right out of North Beach, though happily bookstores and cafés were made for times like these.
Hightlights:	Saturday afternoon opera at Caffè Trieste; a postcard view of Francis Ford Coppola's green-patinaed Sentinel Building on Columbus; Grant Avenue's glorious jumble of boutiques.

GREAT ITINERARIES

Bring Your Appetite

Start the day at the Ferry Building, which is stuffed with tempting produce, cafés, and artisanal treats. Nab a little something for breakfast, then take the California line cable car uphill to Chinatown. Walk along Grant Avenue and Stockton Street, peeking into mysterious herb apothecaries, live-seafood stores, and sweet-smelling tea shops before having a dim sum lunch or a steamed-bun snack.

Then head to North Beach for an espresso and pastry at one of the classic outdoor cafés. The Italian delis, bakeries, and pasta houses are worth visiting even if you can't eat another bite. Get your appetite back by making your way uphill to Coit Tower for sweeping views of the bay. (Climbing the steep stairways is a tough but scenically stunning way to do this.)

At the end of the day, either head back to North Beach's Columbus Avenue and let one of the restaurant hawkers talk you into coming in for pasta, or make the trip to the Mission District for fantastic, inexpensive ethnic food.

Work the Wharf

Fisherman's Wharf and the surrounding attractions may be touristy with a capital T, but there are some fun experiences to be had. With your pre-reserved ticket in hand (do this in advance, since tours frequently sell out), set out for Alcatraz. When the ferry docks back at Pier 33, head north along the waterfront to Pier 39. If you're on a kitschy-souvenir hunt, browse through the pier's overpriced stores. Otherwise, see if you can spot sea lions basking on floating platforms next to the pier. Take a step back in time to early-20th-century San Francisco at delightful Musée Mécanique, then grab an Irish coffee at the Buena Vista.

As tempting as it might be to dine on the water, most Fisherman's Wharf restaurants have less-than-spectacular food (Gary Danko is an exception). A better and cheaper option is to pick up some to-go Dungeness crab from one of the outdoor vendors and eat as you stroll along the waterfront. Or hop the Powell–Hyde or Powell–Mason cable-car line for better dining in Russian Hill and North Beach, respectively.

Art and Retail Therapy

Beat the crowds in the morning at SFMOMA (remember that it's closed Wednesday). The modern art collection is SoMa's main magnet, but there are several other museums to consider, too, such as the new Contemporary Jewish Museum, the Museum of the African Diaspora, and the San Francisco Craft and Folk Art Museum.

Take a break from exhibits across the street from SFMOMA in the expansive Yerba Buena Gardens. If you have kids in tow, drop by the game- and gadget-heavy Metreon. Otherwise, head up 4th Street and join the masses at the Bloomingdale's-anchored Westfield San Francisco Shopping Centre and the shops around Union Square. This area isn't known for great restaurants, so when you get peckish, head to Belden Place. This bistro-lined alley (many places here are closed Sunday) is one of the few places around Union Square where locals dine.

To top off the evening, gaze down on the city lights from one of the square's skyview lounges like Harry Denton's Starlight Lounge.

Golden Gate Park

Golden Gate Park is better than usual on Sunday, when its main arteries are closed to cars (a more limited closure occurs on

Saturday from April to September). Start your day at the glorious Conservatory of Flowers (closed Monday). Be sure to take in the scenes ingeniously rendered in flowers out front. Pace the wooden bridges and stone pathways of the Japanese Tea Garden before hitting the San Francisco Botanical Garden at Strybing Arboretum. Next up: the striking, controversial de Young Museum (closed Monday) and the glorious reopened California Academy of Sciences. Make your way west, stopping at Stow Lake, where you can rent a boat and paddle near Strawberry Hill. Back on land, continue west toward Ocean Beach and the endless Pacific. Cap off your tour by kicking back with a pint to enjoy the sunset ocean view at the Beach Chalet.

Find the Funky Neighborhoods

Ride the antique trolleys to the western end of the F-line in the Castro. Stroll down Castro Street, past the art-deco Castro Theatre, window-shopping and stopping at any café that tempts you. Head east on 16th Street to Dolores Street and Mission Dolores, and wander rows of centuries-old gravestones in its tiny cemetery.

Then hit the "Valencia Corridor" (Valencia Street between 16th and 20th streets), dipping into independent bookstores, hipster cafés, and quirky shops. Seek out the area's vibrant, often politically charged murals, either on your own or on a tour with the Precita Eyes organization. Stay in the Mission for dinner and drinks; this is one of the city's best neighborhoods for restaurants and watering holes.

Take It to the Bridge

Start with a stroll and a search for picnic supplies in the Marina, before heading to the gorgeous Palace of Fine Arts. If you're traveling with kids, be sure to visit the Exploratorium (closed Monday) next door. Don't miss its bizarre-but-cool Tactile Dome.

Continue west into the Presidio and make for Crissy Field, the marshland and sandy beach along the northern shore, for your picnic. With the Golden Gate Bridge view to inspire you, head onto or over the bridge itself. Be sure to wear comfortable shoes; the bridge is 1.7 mi across. Save this for a sunny day—and don't forget your jacket!

Bay Views and Real Estate Envy

Start at terraced Ina Coolbrith Park on Russian Hill for broad vistas of the bay. Ascend the Vallejo Steps and you're within easy reach of many of Russian Hill's hidden lanes. Explore famous Macondray Lane; then head around the corner to Leavenworth Street just north of Union Street and look left for the steps to equally lovely but virtually unknown Havens Place. Continue north to zigzag down crooked Lombard Street. If you still have some stamina, head west to Pacific Heights, where you can check out the Haas-Lilienthal House, a Queen Anne treasure, and scads of other Victorians. Want to snap a picture of that iconic row of "painted ladies" with the city's skyline in the background? You'll need to head to Alamo Square in the Western Addition (Hayes and Steiner streets). Finally, head back to Hyde Street for dinner at one of Russian Hill's trendy eateries.

FREE AND ALMOST FREE

Despite—or perhaps because of—the astronomical cost of living here, San Francisco offers loads of free diversions. Here are our picks for the best free things to do in the city, in alphabetical order. (That is, in addition to the free theater that is life in San Francisco's neighborhoods, parks, beaches, churches, and other public spaces.)

Museums and Galleries That Are Always Free

- Chinese Culture Center
- Creativity Explored
- Fort Point National Historic Site
- Museo Italo-Americano
- Octagon House
- Randall Museum
- San Francisco Cable Car Museum
- San Francisco Railway Museum
- SFMOMA Artists Gallery
- Tattoo Art Museum
- Walter & McBean Galleries at the San Francisco Art Institute
- Wells Fargo History Museum

Free Museum Times

The first week of every month brings a bonanza of free museum times.

- Asian Art Museum, first Sunday of every month
- Cartoon Art Museum, first Tuesday of every month is pay-what-you-wish
- Chinese Historical Society of America, first Thursday of every month
- de Young Museum, first Tuesday of every month
- Exploratorium, first Wednesday of every month

- Legion of Honor, first Tuesday of every month
- Museum of Craft and Folk Art, first Tuesday of every month
- San Francisco Museum of Craft + Design, first Thursday of every month, 5–7 PM
- San Francisco Museum of Modern Art, first Tuesday of every month
- Yerba Buena Center for the Arts (galleries), first Tuesday of every month

Free Concerts

- The Golden Gate Park Band plays free public concerts on Sunday afternoon, April through October, on the Music Concourse in the namesake park. You might hear anything from Sousa marches to show tunes.
- The San Francisco Conservatory of Music offers frequent free recitals year-round.
- Stern Grove Festival concerts, held on Sunday afternoon from June through August, are a longstanding city tradition. Performances range from opera to jazz to pop music. The amphitheater is in a beautiful eucalyptus grove, so come early and picnic before the show.
- Yerba Buena Gardens Festival hosts many concerts and performances from May through October (sometimes almost daily), including Latin jazz, global music, dance, even puppet shows.

Free Tours

- The San Francisco City Guides walking tours are easily one of the best deals going. Knowledgeable, enthusiastic guides lead walks that focus on a particular neighborhood, theme, or historical period, like Victorian architecture in Alamo Square or the bawdy days of the

Barbary Coast. The tours are free, though a $5 donation is welcome.

■ City Hall offers free tours of its grandiose HQ on weekdays.

More Great Experiences for $5 or Less

■ See some baseball at AT&T Park, for free! Go to the stadium's Portwalk, beyond the outfield wall, and you'll have a standing-room view of the game through the open fence. The fans who watch here are known as the Knothole Gang. BYO peanuts.

■ Visit the Golden Gate Fortune Cookie Factory in Chinatown. This is technically free, although you'll have to resist the temptation to take photos (a 50¢ fee) and buy cookies. There are several nearby spots where you can get a delicious snack for just a dollar or two, like the custard tarts at Golden Gate Bakery. Stop in one or two of Chinatown's incense-filled temples, too—it's best to give a small donation, but you'll feel a world away.

■ Do your own walking tour of the Mission District's fantastic outdoor murals, then grab a bite at a taquería or taco truck.

■ Walk across the Golden Gate Bridge—an obvious but breathtaking choice.

■ Choose a perfect treat at the Ferry Building's fabulous marketplace—maybe a scoop of Ciao Bello gelato or a croissant from Miette—and stroll the waterfront promenade toward the Bay Bridge to Cupid's Span, the giant bow-and-arrow sculpture impaling Rincon Park.

■ Visit the Diego Rivera mural at the San Francisco Art Institute, then sip a cuppa at the school's café and check out the million-dollar view from its North Beach perch.

■ Tour the grounds around the Palace of Fine Arts, circling its swan-filled lagoon. Next, walk through the Presidio to the Letterman Digital Arts Center campus. Visit the Yoda fountain, then peek inside the building beyond to see a life-size Darth Vader figure. To further explore the Presidio, you can hop the free PresidiGo shuttle. (The Presidio also has lots of free parking.)

■ Check out the offerings at lively El Rio bar in the Mission District. They often have free live music and very cheap drink specials.

■ Hike up to the top of Telegraph Hill for sweeping city and bay views. Since the surrounding trees aren't trimmed back, the view isn't quite as terrific as the one from the hill's Coit Tower, but it's still a knockout.

■ If you're in town on the second Thursday of the month between April and October, head to the Mission for Dolores Park Movie Night. Screenings, which start at dusk, are free—check the schedule at ⊕ *www.doloresparkmovie.org.* Saturday screenings happen at Dolores Park, Union Square, and Washington Square Park; see ⊕ *www.sfntf.org.*

■ Ride a cable car. We hate to harp on this, but you gotta do it at least once.

OFFBEAT SF

Looking for an unusual San Francisco experience that'll give you bragging rights? Try one of these quirky choices—even a local would be impressed.

■ **ATA.** Dedicated to getting anyone's art in front of an audience, Artists' Television Access has been showing films by local artists for more than 20 years. An open-minded crowd comes to ATA's tiny space, where $5–$10 gets you a peek at what might be the next groundbreaker. ⊕ *www. atasite.org*

■ **Audium.** Billed as a "theater of sound-sculptured space," Audium is an experience like no other. Every Friday and Saturday a few dozen participants sit in concentric circles in a completely sound-proofed room in utter darkness, and music plays over the 169 speakers strategically placed, well, everywhere. ⊕ *www. audium.org*

■ **Mt. Davidson.** Ask most San Franciscans what the highest point in town is and they'll likely say Twin Peaks, but it's actually this "mountain," the next hill over. Visible from all over town but rarely visited, Mt. Davidson is topped with a eucalyptus-filled park. Finding the road up here is tricky (entrance at Dalewood and Myra ways), but once you get there you'll have amazing views—while all those tourists are still waiting for a parking space on Twin Peaks.

■ **Qoöl at 111 Minna.** The granddaddy of the gallery-cum-house-party scene, this hip SoMa loft is packed to the gills on Wednesday with a friendly, artsy crowd. The art is edgy, the DJ sets are potent, the drinks are stiff, and the party kicks off at 5 PM. ⊕ *www.qoolsf.com*

■ **16th Avenue Steps.** Just standing at the base of this glorious mosaic of a stairway in the Inner Sunset is a treat: its underwater theme gives way to daytime dragonflies and butterflies, eventually transitioning to a starry, bat-studded night sky. Hike to the top, and you may have tiny Grand View Park all to yourself. The view is, well, grand. (⊠ *Moraga St., between 15th and 16th Aves.*)

■ **Slides at AT&T Park.** The massive Coke bottle looming over the AT&T ballpark is a familiar sight, but most people don't know that you can slide inside. The Coca-Cola Superslide has a series of slides twisting and turning down the bottle's contours. Kids aren't the only ones who get a kick out of the 56-foot "Guzzlers" and the 20-foot "Twist-Offs." It's open for free on some nongame days.

■ **The Tamale Lady.** It's impossible to pin down her location, but if you're out and about in the Mission of an evening, keep an eye peeled for this San Francisco legend. Her tamales are terrific, but the real reason that she's revered is her supernatural ability to show up in a bar and provide protein at the critical moment in a bender.

■ **Thursday Night at the Cal Academy of Sciences.** Supersize snakes, waddling penguins, and taxidermy are cool anytime, but throw in a cash bar and a DJ and this science club gets even cooler. Join an in-the-know crowd knocking back drinks and getting up close and personal with wild animals (with help from the academy's staffers) from 6 PM to 10 PM. ⊕ *www. calacademy.org*

GET OUTTA TOWN

Marin County

Marin County beckons from the other side of the Golden Gate Bridge—the ultimate playground for anyone who likes being outdoors. Hordes of visitors crane their necks at the huge redwoods in Muir Woods National Monument; mountain bikers zoom down Mt. Tamalpais; and scenery buffs head to the Marin Headlands, Stinson Beach, and the Point Reyes National Seashore to gaze at the vast Pacific. Over 40% of Marin County is parkland, so there are plenty of places to hike and reconnect with nature.

The towns in Marin are small and low-key, with varying degrees of chic. There's Sausalito with its yachts and boutiques; Tiburon with its gallery-lined Main Street; and Mill Valley with its redwood groves and reclusive rock stars. Places like Stinson Beach and Bolinas, meanwhile, are for those who truly want to get away from anything urban. Lots of bed-and-breakfasts and hotels in Marin are geared for weekend retreats—it's the perfect place to drop out of sight for a few days. Taking a ferry here from San Francisco will make your getaway all the more romantic.

East Bay (Berkeley and Oakland)

To San Franciscans, the East Bay is shorthand for Berkeley and Oakland, both across the Bay Bridge from the city. Berkeley is defined by its University of California campus and its liberal-to-radical politics. Ever since the Free Speech Movement ignited at the Cal campus in the 1960s, Berkeley has been the place for renegade spirits, bursting bookstores, and caffeine-fueled debates. It's not all intellectual-politico jargon, though; there are plenty of creature comforts, too. Most famously, there's Chez Panisse, the restaurant that embodies seasonal, simple, local cooking—but there are countless tasty treasures to be sampled in Berkeley's Gourmet Ghetto. Or you could shop for indie tracks at Amoeba Music, academic tomes at Moe's Books, and the perfect bottle of Sancerre at Kermit Lynch Wine Merchant.

Oakland is grittier and even more diverse, with a buzzing arts scene. Small pockets of the city are pretty dodgy, so it's important to know where you're going. Old Oakland has a concentration of evocative Victorian buildings, now full of cafés and shops; the Rockridge neighborhood is home to lovely Market Hall, a European-style market. Jack London Square may be the best place to get a sense of Oakland's role as a major port, but it feels pretty sterile. Head to a jazz joint like Yoshi's or a gallery-bar like Café van Kleef, though, and you'll feel the city's indomitable energy.

Wine Country

With rolling, vine-covered hills, warm weather, and incredibly good restaurants, hotels, and spas, the Sonoma and Napa valleys are the places to indulge yourself. Whether you're passionate about wine or a curious newcomer, you'll find dozens upon dozens of tasting rooms and wineries that are right for you. Some of the world's most high-profile vintners work here, but there are also plenty of under-the-radar local stars to discover. Don't overlook the towns in your rush to the vineyards, though. Places like Napa, Sonoma, Healdsburg, Glen Ellen, and Calistoga have lovely, historic centers, farmers' markets, and tempting shops. You can get to the Wine Country in less than two hours by car—but the experience does not come cheap.

FESTIVALS AND PARADES

San Francisco's major parades and festivals are notoriously creative, energetic, and often off-the-wall. Among the hundreds of events on the city's annual calendar, here are the ones that are especially characteristic and fun.

■ **Chinese New Year, February.** This celebration in North America's largest Chinatown lasts for almost three weeks. The grand finale is the spectacularly loud, crowded, and colorful Golden Dragon Parade, which rocks with firecrackers. If you don't want to wait on the sidewalk for hours in advance, buy bleacher seats. Contact the Chinese Chamber of Commerce (☎ 415/982–3071 ⊕ www.chineseparade.com) for more info.

■ **St. Patrick's Day, March.** Held on the Saturday closest to March 17, the festival (⊕ www.sfsaintpatricksdayparade.com) includes snake races and a parade through downtown. Local bars get in the spirit by selling green-tinted beer (urp).

■ **St. Stupid's Day Parade, April.** The First Church of the Last Laugh (⊕ www.saintstupid.com) holds this fantastically funny event on—when else—April 1. It wanders through the Financial District, with hundreds of people dressed up in elaborate costumes (although there are fewer drag queens than on Halloween). Parade-goers toss socks at the Stock Exchange, throw pennies at the angular sculpture in front of the Bank of America building called the "banker's heart," and sing their way down Columbus Avenue.

■ **San Francisco International Film Festival, April–May.** The country's longest-running film festival packs in audiences with premieres, international films, and rarities. Check their listings (☎ 415/561–5000 ⊕ www.sfiff.org) well in advance for tickets.

■ **Cinco de Mayo Festival, May.** On the Sunday closest to May 5, the Mission District boils with activity, including a vibrant parade, Mexican music, and dancing in the streets.

■ **Lesbian, Gay, Bisexual, and Transgender Pride Celebration, June.** More than half a million people come to join the world's largest pride event, with a downtown parade roaring to a start by leather-clad Dykes on Bikes. If you're visiting around this time, book your hotel *far* ahead (☎ 415/864–0831 ⊕ www.sfpride.com).

■ **San Francisco Open Studios, October.** More than 700 artists open their studios to the public. It's a great window into the local fine arts scene (☎ 415/861–9838 ⊕ www.artspan.org).

■ **Dance-Along Nutcracker, December.** This fabulous holiday tradition, part spoof and part warmhearted family event, was started by the San Francisco Lesbian/Gay Freedom Band (⊕ www.sflgfb.org). You can join the dancers onstage for some free-form choreography, or simply toss snowflakes from the audience.

CABLE CARS

The moment it dawns on you that you severely underestimated the steepness of the San Francisco hills will likely be the same moment you look down and realize those tracks aren't just for show—or just for tourists.

Sure, locals rarely use the cable cars for commuting these days. (That's partially due to the recent fare hikes—hear that, Muni?) So you'll likely be packed in with plenty of fellow sightseers. You may even be approaching cable-car fatigue after seeing its image on so many souvenirs. But if you fear the magic is gone, simply climb on board, and those jaded thoughts will dissolve. Grab the pole and gawk at the view as the car clanks down an insanely steep grade toward the bay. Listen to the humming cable, the clang of the bell, and the occasional quip from the gripman. It's an experience you shouldn't pass up, whether on your first trip or your fiftieth.

HOW CABLE CARS WORK

The mechanics are pretty simple: cable cars grab a moving subterranean cable with a "grip" to go. To stop, they release the grip and apply one or more types of brakes. Four cables, totaling 9 miles, power the city's three lines. If the gripman doesn't adjust the grip just right when going up a steep hill, the cable will start to slip and the car will have to back down the hill and try again. This is an extremely rare occurrence—imagine the ribbing the gripman gets back at the cable car barn!

Gripman: Stands in front and operates the grip, brakes, and bell. Favorite joke, especially at the peak of a steep hill: "This is my first day on the job folks..."

Conductor: Moves around the car, deals with tickets, alerts the grip about what's coming up, and operates the rear wheel brakes.

❶ **Cable:** Steel wrapped around flexible sisal core; 2 inches thick; runs at a constant 9½ mph.

❷ **Bells:** Used for crew communication; alerts other drivers and pedestrians.

❸ **Grip:** Vice-like lever extends through the center slot in the track to grab or release the cable.

❹ **Grip Lever:** Left-hand lever; operates grip.

❺ **Car:** Entire car weighs 8 tons.

❻ **Wheel Brake:** Steel brake pads on each wheel.

❼ **Wheel Brake Lever:** Foot pedal; operates wheel brakes.

❽ **Rear Wheel Brake Lever:** Applied for extra traction on hills.

❾ **Track Brake:** 2-foot long sections of Monterey pine push down against the track to help stop the car.

❿ **Track Brake Lever:** Middle lever; operates track brakes.

⓫ **Emergency Brake:** 18-inch steel wedge, jams into street slot to bring car to an immediate stop.

⓬ **Emergency Brake Lever:** Right-hand lever, red; operates emergency brake.

ROUTES

Powell–Hyde line: Most scenic, with classic Bay views. Begins at Powell and Market streets, then crosses Nob Hill and Russian Hill before a white-knuckle descent down Hyde Street, ending near the Hyde Street Pier.

Powell–Mason line: Also begins at Powell and Market streets, but winds through North Beach to Bay and Taylor streets, a few blocks from Fisherman's Wharf.

California line: Runs from the foot of Market Street, at Drumm Street, up Nob Hill and back. Great views (and aromas and sounds) of Chinatown on the way up. Sit in back to catch glimpses of the Bay. ■TIP→ Take the California line if it's just the cable-car experience you're after—the lines are shorter, and the grips and conductors say it's friendlier and has a slower pace.

Cars run at least every 15 minutes, from around 6 AM to about 1 AM.

RULES OF THE RIDE

Tickets. A whopping $5 each way. There are ticket booths at all three turnarounds, or you can pay the conductor after you board (they can make change). Try not to grumble about the price—they're embarrassed enough as it is.

■TIP→ If you're planning to use public transit a few times, or if you'd like to ride back and forth on the cable car without worrying about the price, consider a one-day Muni passport ($11). You can get passports online, at the Powell Street turnaround, the TIX booth on Union Square, or the Fisherman's Wharf cable-car ticket booth at Beach and Hyde streets.

All Aboard. You can board on either side of the cable car. It's legal to stand on the running boards and hang on to the pole, but keep your ears open for the gripman's warnings. ■TIP→ Grab a seat on the outside bench for the best views.

Most people wait (and wait) in line at one of the cable car turnarounds, but you can also hop on along the route. Board wherever you see a white sign showing a figure climbing aboard a brown cable car; wave to the approaching driver, and wait until the car stops.

Riding on the running boards can be part of the thrill.

CABLE CAR HISTORY

HALLIDIE FREES THE HORSES

In the 1850s and '60s, San Francisco's streetcars were drawn by horses. Legend has it that the horrible sight of a car dragging a team of horses downhill to their deaths roused Andrew Smith Hallidie to action. The English immigrant had invented the "Hallidie Ropeway," essentially a cable car for mined ore, and he was convinced that his invention could also move people. In 1873, Hallidie and his intrepid crew prepared to test the first cable car high on Russian Hill. The anxious engineer peered down into the foggy darkness, failed to see the bottom of the hill, and promptly turned the controls over to Hallidie. Needless to say, the thing worked . . . but rides were free for the first two days because people were afraid to get on.

SEE IT FOR YOURSELF

The **Cable Car Museum** is one of the city's best free offerings and an absolute must for kids. (You can even ride a cable car there, since all three lines stop between Russian Hill and Nob Hill.) The museum, which is inside the city's last cable-car barn, takes the top off the system to let you see how it all works.

Eternally humming and squealing, the massive powerhouse cable wheels steal the show. You can also climb aboard a vintage car and take the grip, let the kids ring a cable-car bell (briefly), and check out vintage gear dating from 1873.

✉ *1201 Mason St., at Washington St., Nob Hill* ☎ *415/474–1887* ⊕ *www. cablecarmuseum.com* ☑ *Free* ⊙ *Oct.– Mar., daily 10–5; Apr.–Sept., daily 10–6*

■ TIP→ The gift shop sells cable car paraphernalia, including an authentic gripman's bell for $600 (it'll sound like Powell Street in your house every day). For significantly less, you can pick up a key chain made from a piece of worn-out cable.

CHAMPION OF THE CABLE CAR BELL

Each June the city's best and brightest come together to crown a bell-ringing champion at Union Square. The crowd cheers gripmen and conductors as they stomp, shake, and riff with the rope. But it's not a popularity contest; the ringers are judged by former bell-ringing champions who take each ping and gong very seriously.

Union Square and Chinatown

WORD OF MOUTH

"Chinatown is all that it's reputed to be, especially if you go beyond the first part designed for tourists. I've never been to China, but my daughter-in-law, who has been there, swears it's almost like being in Asia."

—rose_bud

GETTING ORIENTED

TOP 5 REASONS TO GO

Ross Alley, Chinatown: Breathe deep as you watch the nimble hands at Golden Gate Fortune Cookie Factory, then relax with a cocktail at Li Po around the corner, rumored to be haunted by the ghost of an opium junkie still looking to score.

Return to noir San Francisco: Have a late martini lunch under the gaze of the Maltese Falcon at John's Grill, then swing through the lobby of the Flood Building and nod to the other Maltese Falcon there.

Shop the Square: Prime your credit cards and dive right in, from Bloomie's to the boutiques of Maiden Lane.

Tin How Temple: Climb the narrow stairway to this space with hundreds of red lanterns, then step onto the tiny balcony and take in the alley scene below.

Elevator at the St. Francis: Ride a glass elevator to the sky (or the 32nd floor) for a gorgeous view of the cityscape, especially in the evening when the lights come up.

QUICK BITES

Upstairs in the San Francisco Centre, the treasures in the display cases at shiny, European-style **Cocola Bakery** (⊠ 845 Market St., Union Square ☎ 415/543–2207) can make pastry lovers commence their happy dance.

Eastern Bakery (⊠ 720 Grant Ave., Chinatown ☎ 415/433–7973) claims to be the oldest bakery in Chinatown. The packed little space has become a must-stop on the tourist trail. But it's not just a tourist trap, since the dirt-cheap steamed pork buns make a terrific quick lunch on the go.

If you're after a substantial bite to eat, duck into the **Irish Bank** (⊠ 10 Mark La., Union Square ☎ 415/788–7152), across from the Chinatown Gate, for fish-and-chips.

GETTING THERE

In these two neighborhoods, cars equal hassle. Traffic is slow and parking is pricey. Save yourself the frustration and take advantage of the confluence of public transit at Powell and Market streets; buses, BART (Powell Street Station), cable cars, and F-line streetcars run here.

For the love of Buddha, don't drive in Chinatown! The steep, narrow, one-way streets are notoriously difficult to navigate by car. Both Powell lines of the cable-car system pass through. You can also take the 30—Stockton bus; this route is a virtual "Chinatown Express," running from Fisherman's Wharf down Stockton Street through Chinatown to Union Square.

MAKING THE MOST OF YOUR TIME

Set aside at least an hour to scope out the stores and sights in and around Union Square—or most of the day if you're a shopper—but don't bother arriving before 10 AM, when the first shops open. Sunday is a bit quieter.

Give yourself at least two hours to see compact Chinatown. If possible, come on a weekday (less crowded) and before lunchtime (busiest with locals). You won't need more than 15 or 20 minutes at any of the sights themselves, but exploring the shops and alleys is, indeed, the whole point.

2

Sightseeing
★★★
Nightlife
★
Dining
★★★
Lodging
★★★★
Shopping
★★★★★

The Union Square area bristles with big-city bravado, while just a stone's throw away is a place that feels like a city unto itself, Chinatown. The two areas share a strong commercial streak, although manifested very differently. In Union Square the crowds zigzag among international brands, trailing glossy shopping bags. A few blocks north, people dash between small neighborhood stores, their arms draped with plastic totes filled with groceries or souvenirs.

Updated by
Denise M. Leto

In Union Square the city's finest department stores put on their best faces, along with such exclusive emporiums as Tiffany & Co. and Prada, and such big-name franchises as Niketown, Apple Store, H&M, and Barney's. Visitors lay their heads at several dozen hotels within a three-block walk of the square, and the downtown theater district and many fine-arts galleries are nearby. By any measure, Union Square is shop-centric; if you're not that into shopping, you can find little beyond buildings of vague historical interest to entice you here.

A few blocks uphill is the abrupt beginning of dense and insular Chinatown—the oldest such community in the country. When the street signs have Chinese characters, produce stalls crowd pedestrians off the sidewalk, and folks scurry by with telltale pink plastic shopping bags, you'll know you're there. (The neighborhood huddles together in the 17 blocks and 41 alleys bordered roughly by Bush, Kearny, and Powell streets and Broadway.) Chinatown has been attracting the curious for more than 100 years, and no neighborhood in the city absorbs as many tourists without seeming to forfeit its character. Join the flow and step into another world. Good-luck banners of crimson and gold hang beside dragon-entwined lampposts and pagoda roofs, while honking cars chime in with shoppers bargaining loudly in Cantonese or Mandarin.

WHAT TO SEE IN UNION SQUARE

American Conservatory Theater. The 1906 earthquake destroyed all eight of downtown San Francisco's theaters, and this one, a neoclassical stunner, stepped up to the plate a year later. Today it's inextricably linked with its eponymous repertory company, known for award-winning productions by major playwrights such as Tony Kushner (*Angels in America*) and Tom Stoppard (premieres of *Indian Ink*, *The Invention of Love*), and cutting-edge works such as *The Black Rider* by Tom Waits, William S. Burroughs, and Robert Wilson. Damaged heavily in the 1989 earthquake, the building has been beautifully restored. ⊠ *415 Geary St., box office at 405 Geary St., Union Square* ☎ *415/749–2228.*

CABLE CAR TERMINUS

Two of the three cable-car lines begin and end their runs at Powell and Market streets, a couple of blocks south of Union Square. These two lines are the most scenic, and both pass near Fisherman's Wharf, so they're usually clogged with first-time sightseers. The wait to board a cable car at this intersection is longer than at any other stop in the system. If you'd rather avoid the mob, board the less-touristy California line at the bottom of Market Street, at Drumm Street. ⇨ *For more info on the cable cars, see the Experience San Francisco chapter.*

Hallidie Building. Named for cable-car inventor Andrew S. Hallidie, this 1918 structure is best viewed from across the street. Willis Polk's revolutionary glass-curtain wall—believed to be the world's first such facade—hangs a foot beyond the reinforced concrete of the frame. The reflecting glass, decorative exterior fire escapes that appear to be metal balconies, and Venetian Gothic cornice are notably lovely. ⊠ *130 Sutter St., between Kearny and Montgomery Sts., Union Square*

Lotta's Fountain. Saucy gold rush–era actress, singer, and dancer Lotta Crabtree so aroused the city's miners that they were known to shower her with gold nuggets and silver dollars after her performances. The peculiar, rather clunky fountain was her way of saying thanks to her fans. Given to the city in 1875, the fountain became a meeting place for survivors after the 1906 earthquake. (The last known survivor of the quake passed away in 2009.) Each April 18, the anniversary of the quake, San Franciscans gather at this quirky monument. You can see an image of Lotta herself in one of the Anton Refregier murals in Rincon Center. ⊠ *Traffic triangle at intersection of 3rd, Market, Kearny, and Geary Sts., Union Square.*

Maiden Lane. Known as Morton Street in the raffish Barbary Coast era, this former red-light district reported at least one murder a week during the late 19th century. Things cooled down after the 1906 fire destroyed the brothels, and these days Maiden Lane is a chic, boutique-lined pedestrian mall stretching two blocks, between Stockton and Kearny streets. Wrought-iron gates close the street to traffic most days between 11 and 5, when the lane becomes a patchwork of umbrella-shaded tables.

The epicenter of high-end shopping, Union Square is lined with department stores.

At **140 Maiden Lane** you can see the only Frank Lloyd Wright building in San Francisco. Walking through the brick archway and recessed entry feels a bit like entering a glowing cave. The interior's graceful, curving ramp and skylights are said to have been his model for the Guggenheim Museum in New York. Xanadu Tribal Arts, a gallery showcasing Baltic, Latin-American, and African folk art, now occupies the space. ⊠ *Between Stockton and Kearny Sts., Union Square.*

San Francisco Museum of Craft + Design. You could be forgiven for walking by this museum, thinking that it's a private office or boutique. No one expects a front garden—a garden!—in this pack-in-every-square-foot neighborhood. It's a serene welcome to this stark three-room space, which opened in 2004. Quarterly exhibits focus on modern design of all sorts, from fanciful furniture to designer toys to wine labels. Whether you should visit depends entirely on the exhibit: if the theme grabs you, it's well worth coming by. ⊠ *550 Sutter St., Union Square* ☎ *415/773–0303* ⊕ *www.sfmcd. com* ✉ *$3 donation* ☉ *Tues., Wed., Fri., and Sat. 10–5, Thurs. 10–7, Sun. noon–5.*

San Francisco Visitor Information Center. A multilingual staff operates this facility below the cable-car terminus. Staffers answer questions and provide maps and pamphlets. You

FANTASY FOUNTAIN

In front of the Grand Hyatt hotel at 345 Stockton Street gurgles an intricate bronze fountain depicting San Francisco. It's one of many local public works by Ruth Asawa, the city's "fountain lady." Look closely at this one and you can find an amorous couple behind one of the Victorian bay windows.

can also pick up discount coupons—the savings can be significant, especially for families—and hotel brochures here. If you're planning to hit the big-ticket stops like the California Academy of Sciences, the Exploratorium, and SFMOMA, and ride the cable cars, consider picking up a CityPass here (or at any of the attractions it covers). ■ TIP➔ The CityPass ($59, $39 ages 5–12), good for nine days including seven days of transit, will save you about 50%. Also buy your Muni Passport here. ⊠ *Hallidie Plaza, lower level, Powell and Market Sts., Union Square* ☎ *415/391–2000 or 415/283–0177* ⊕ *www.onlyinsanfrancisco.com* ◷ *Weekdays 9–5, Sat. 9–3; also Sun. 9–3 in May–Oct.*

Union Square. The heart of San Francisco's downtown since 1850, a 2½-acre square surrounded by department stores and the St. Francis Hotel, is about the only place you can sit for free in this part of town. The public responded to Union Square's 2002 redesign with a resounding shrug. With its pretty landscaping, easier street access, and the addition of a café (welcome, but nothing special), it's certainly an improvement over the old concrete wasteland, but no one's beating a path downtown to hang out here. Four globular lamp sculptures by the artist R. M. Fischer preside over the space; there's also an open-air stage, a visitor information booth, and a front-row seat to the cable car tracks. And there's a familiar kaleidoscope of characters: office workers sunning and brown-bagging, street musicians, shoppers taking a rest, kids chasing pigeons, and a fair number of homeless people.

LITTLE SAIGON

The best Vietnamese food in the city is west of Union Square, along Larkin Street between Eddy and O'Farrell streets, where 80% of the businesses are owned by Vietnamese-Americans. Marketing types call this corridor Little Saigon; locals call it the Tenderloin, AKA the hood. If working girls and drug dealers can't come between you and your *pho* (beef-broth noodle soup), you can find cheap, often fantastic food here. Check out Turtle Tower for pho, Saigon Sandwiches for *bánh mì* (unsurprisingly, Vietnamese sandwiches), and Pagolac for excellent everything. And if you come for dinner, take a cab.

The square takes its name from the violent pro-Union demonstrations staged here before the Civil War. At center stage, Robert Ingersoll Aitken's *Victory Monument* commemorates Commodore George Dewey's victory over the Spanish fleet at Manila in 1898. The 97-foot Corinthian column, topped by a bronze figure symbolizing naval conquest, was dedicated by Theodore Roosevelt in 1903 and withstood the 1906 earthquake. After the earthquake and fire of 1906, the square was dubbed Little St. Francis because of the temporary shelter erected for residents of the St. Francis Hotel. Actor John Barrymore (grandfather of actress Drew Barrymore and a notorious carouser) was among the guests pressed into volunteering to stack bricks in the square. His uncle, thespian John Drew, remarked, "It took an act of God to get John out of bed and the United States Army to get him to work."

On the eastern edge of Union Square, **TIX Bay Area** (☎ *415/433–7827 info only* ⊕ *www.theatrebayarea.org*) provides half-price day-of-

Where can I find . . . ?

PARKING	Sutter-Stockton Garage 444 Stockton St. Reasonable prices and not too crowded.	North Beach Parking Garage 735 Vallejo St. Relatively clean and roomy.
A DRUGSTORE	Walgreens 459 Powell St. Open 24 hours.	Walgreens 776 Market St. Open from 7 AM to 9 PM.
A NIGHTCAP	The Hidden Vine Wine Bar 620 Post St. A quiet spot that pours mostly California wines.	Bourbon & Branch 501 Jones St. Worth calling ahead to sip such outstanding cocktails.

performance tickets to all types of performing-arts events, as well as regular full-price box-office services. Union Square covers a convenient four-level garage, allegedly the first underground garage in the world. ✉ *Bordered by Powell, Stockton, Post, and Geary Sts., Union Square.*

Westin St. Francis Hotel. The second-oldest hotel in the city, established in 1904, was conceived by railroad baron and financier Charles Crocker and his associates as a hostelry for their millionaire friends. Swift service and sumptuous surroundings have always been hallmarks of the property. After the hotel was ravaged by the 1906 fire, a larger, more luxurious Italian Renaissance–style residence was opened in 1907 to attract loyal clients from among the world's rich and powerful. The hotel's checkered past includes the ill-fated 1921 bash in the suite of the silent-film comedian Fatty Arbuckle, at which a woman became ill and later died. Arbuckle endured three sensational trials for rape and murder before being acquitted, by which time his career was kaput. In 1975 Sara Jane Moore, standing among a crowd outside the hotel, attempted to shoot then-president Gerald Ford. As might be imagined, no plaques in the lobby commemorate these events. ■ TIP→ One of the best views in the city is from the glass elevators here—and best of all, a ride is free. Zip up to the 32nd floor for a bird's-eye view; the lights of the nighttime cityscape are particularly lovely. Don't be shy if you're not a guest: some visitors make this a stop every time they're in town. Every November the hotel's pastry chef creates a spectacular, rotating 12-foot gingerbread castle, on display in the grand lobby—a fun holiday treat for families. ✉ *335 Powell St., at Geary St., Union Square* ☎ *415/397–7000* ⊕ *www.westinstfrancis.com.*

WHAT TO SEE IN CHINATOWN

Chinatown Gate. This is the official entrance to Chinatown. Stone lions flank the base of the pagoda-topped gate; the lions, dragons, and fish up top symbolize wealth, prosperity, and other good things. The four Chinese characters immediately beneath the pagoda represent the philosophy of Sun Yat-sen (1866–1925), the leader who unified China in the early 20th century. Sun Yat-sen, who lived in exile in San Francisco for a few years, promoted the notion of friendship and peace among all nations based on equality, justice, and goodwill. The vertical characters under the left pagoda read "peace" and "trust," the ones under the right pagoda "respect" and "love." The whole shebang usually telegraphs the internationally understood message of "photo op." ⊠ *Grant Ave. at Bush St., Chinatown.*

> ### PUT YOUR HANDS TOGETHER
>
> For a rockin' gospel concert and inclusive, feel-good vibe, head to **Glide Memorial Church** (⊠ *Ellis and Taylor Sts., Tenderloin*) on the edge of the sketchy Tenderloin, Sunday morning at 9 and 11. Reverend Cecil Williams, a bear of a man, is a local celeb do-gooder who leads a hand-clapping, shout-it-out, get-on-your-feet "celebration" that attracts a diverse and enthusiastic crowd. Visitors—gay and straight, all colors of the rainbow, religious or not—are welcome (and plentiful). You might recognize the church from the film *The Pursuit of Happyness.*

Chinese Culture Center. Mostly a place for the community to gather for calligraphy and Mandarin classes, the center also houses a gallery with occasionally interesting temporary exhibits by Chinese and Chinese-American artists. Heritage walks ($18; make reservations a day ahead) focus on the history of the Chinese in San Francisco; four participants required. ⊠ *Hilton, 750 Kearny St., 3rd fl., Chinatown* ☎ *415/986–1822* ⊕ *www.c-c-c.org* ⊠ *Free* ☉ *Tues.–Sat. 10–4.*

Chinese Historical Society of America Museum and Learning Center. This airy, light-filled gallery has displays about the Chinese-American experience from 19th-century agriculture to 21st-century food and fashion trends, including a poignant collection of racist games and toys. A separate room hosts rotating exhibits by contemporary Chinese-American artists. ⊠ *965 Clay St., Chinatown* ☎ *415/391–1188* ⊕ *www.chsa.org* ⊠ *$3, free 1st Thurs. of month* ☉ *Tues.–Fri. noon–5.*

Chinese Six Companies. Once the White House of Chinatown, this striking building has balconies and lion-supported columns. Begun as an umbrella group for the many family and regional *tongs* (mutual-aid and fraternal organizations) that sprang up to help gold-rush immigrants, the Chinese Six Companies functioned as a government within Chinatown, settling disputes among members and fighting against anti-Chinese laws. The business leaders who ran the six companies (which still exist) dominated the neighborhood's political and economic life for decades. The building is closed to the public. ⊠ *843 Stockton St., Chinatown.*

Golden Gate Fortune Cookie Factory. Follow your nose down Ross Alley to this tiny but fragrant cookie factory. Workers sit at circular motorized

Chinatown bursts into color and light on Chinese New Year.

griddles and wait for dollops of batter to drop onto a tiny metal plate, which rotates into an oven. A few moments later out comes a cookie that's pliable and ready for folding. It's easy to peek in for a moment, and hard to leave without a few free samples. A bagful of cookies—with mildly racy "adult" fortunes or more-benign ones—costs about $3. You can also purchase the cookies "fortuneless" in their waferlike unfolded state, which makes snacking that much more efficient. Being allowed to photograph the cookie makers at work will set you back 50¢. ⊠ 56 *Ross Alley, west of and parallel to Grant Ave., between Washington and Jackson Sts., Chinatown* ☎ *415/781–3956* ▢ *Free* ☉ *Daily 9–8.*

Kong Chow Temple. This ornate temple sets a somber, spiritual tone right away with a sign warning visitors not to touch *anything*. The god to whom the members of this temple pray represents honesty and trust. Chinese stores and restaurants often display his image because he's thought to bring good luck in business. Chinese immigrants established the temple in 1851; its congregation moved to this building in 1977. Take the elevator up to the fourth floor, where incense fills the air. You can show respect by placing a dollar or two in the donation box and by leaving your camera in its case. Amid the statuary, flowers, and richly colored altars (red wards off evil spirits and

LOOK UP!

When wandering around Chinatown, don't forget to look up! Above the chintziest souvenir shop might loom an ornate balcony or a curly pagoda roof. The best examples are on the 900 block of Grant Avenue (at Washington St.) and at Waverly Place.

Chinatown Tongs

If you take it from Hollywood, Chinese *tongs* (secretive fraternal associations) rank right up there with the Italian Mafia and the Japanese yakuza. The general public perception is one of an honor-bound brotherhood with an impenetrable code of silence; fortunes amassed through prostitution and narcotics; and disputes settled in a hail of gunfire, preferably in a crowded restaurant. In fact, the tongs began as an innocent community service—but for roughly a century there's been more than a little truth to the sensational image.

When Chinese immigrants first arrived in San Francisco during the gold rush, they made a beeline for an appropriate tong. These benevolent organizations welcomed people from specific regions of China, or those with certain family names, and helped new arrivals get a foothold. For thousands of men otherwise alone in the city, these tongs were a vital social connection. It didn't take long, however, until offers of protection services ushered in a new criminal element, casting a sinister shadow over all the tongs, legitimate or not.

As gambling parlors, illegal lotteries, opium dens, and brothels took root, many tongs became the go-to sources for turf protection and retribution. Early on, the muscles behind the tongs became known as "hatchet men" for their weapons of choice. (They believed guns made too much noise.)

"Tong wars" regularly broke out between competing groups, with especially blood-soaked periods in the 1920s and 1970s. Today the tongs are less influential than at the turn of the 20th century, but they remain a major part of Chinatown life, as they own large swaths of real estate and provide care for the elderly. The criminal side is alive and well, profiting from prostitution and drugs and doing a brisk business in pirated music and DVDs. Violence still erupts, too. In 2006 Allen Leung, a prominent community leader, was shot dead in his shop on Jackson Street. Among his activities, Leung was a very influential "dragon head" of the Hop Sing tong, a group involved in prostitution, the heroin trade, and other underground activities. And just as in the movies, no one's talking.

—Denise M. Leto

signifies virility, green symbolizes longevity, and gold connotes majesty), a couple of plaques announce that MRS. HARRY S. TRUMAN CAME TO THIS TEMPLE IN JUNE 1948 FOR A PREDICTION ON THE OUTCOME OF THE ELECTION . . . THIS FORTUNE CAME TRUE. The temple's balcony has a good view of Chinatown. ⊠ *855 Stockton St., Chinatown* ☏ *No phone* ✉ *Free* ⊙ *Mon.–Sat. 9–4.*

Old Chinese Telephone Exchange. After the 1906 earthquake, many Chinatown buildings were rebuilt in western style with pagoda roof and fancy balconies slapped on. This building—today the Bank of Canton—is the exception, an example of top-to-bottom Chinese architecture. The intricate three-tier pagoda was built in 1909. The exchange's operators were renowned for their prodigious memories, about which the San Francisco

Chamber of Commerce boasted in 1914: "These girls respond all day with hardly a mistake to calls that are given (in English or one of five Chinese dialects) by the name of the subscriber instead of by his number—a mental feat that would be practically impossible to most high-schooled American misses." ⊠ *Bank of Canton, 743 Washington St., Chinatown.*

> **FROM TIGER TO RABBIT**
>
> During Chinese New Year in February, Chinatown explodes with activity. The three-week festival peaks with the crazy-popular Chinese New Year's Parade, ushering in the Year of the Rabbit in 2011.

Old St. Mary's Cathedral. Dedicated in 1854, this served as the city's Catholic cathedral until 1891. The verse below the massive clock face beseeched naughty Barbary Coast boys: "Son, observe the time and fly from evil." Across the street from the church in **St. Mary's Square,** a statue of Sun Yat-sen towers over the site of the Chinese leader's favorite reading spot during his years in San Francisco. ■TIP➔ A surprisingly peaceful spot, St. Mary's Square also has a couple of small, well-kept playgrounds, perfect for a break from the hustle and bustle of Chinatown. ⊠ *Grant Ave. and California St., Chinatown.*

Portsmouth Square. Chinatown's living room buzzes with activity. The square, with its pagoda-shape structures, is a favorite spot for morning tai chi; by noon dozens of men huddle around Chinese chess tables, engaged in not-always-legal competition. Kids scamper about the square's two grungy playgrounds (warning: the bathrooms are sketchy). Back in the late 19th century this land was near the waterfront, and Robert Louis Stevenson, the author of *Treasure Island*, often dropped by, chatting up the sailors who hung out here. Some of the information he gleaned about life at sea found its way into his fiction. A bronze galleon sculpture, a tribute to Stevenson, is anchored in a corner of the square. ⊠ *Bordered by Walter Lum Pl. and Kearny, Washington, and Clay Sts., Chinatown .*

Tin How Temple. Duck into the inconspicuous doorway, climb three flights of stairs—on the second floor is a mah-jongg parlor whose patrons hope the spirits above will favor them—and be assaulted by the aroma of incense in this tiny, altar-filled room. Day Ju, one of the first three Chinese to arrive in San Francisco, dedicated this temple to the Queen of the Heavens and the Goddess of the Seven Seas in 1852. In the temple's entryway, elderly ladies can often be seen preparing "money" to be burned as offerings to various Buddhist gods or as funds for ancestors to use in the afterlife. Hundreds of red-and-gold lanterns cover the ceiling; the larger the lamp, the larger its donor's contribution to the temple. Gifts of oranges, dim sum, and money left by the faithful, who kneel mumbling prayers, rest on altars to various gods. Tin How presides over the middle back of the temple, flanked by one red and one green lesser god. Take a good look around, since taking photographs is not allowed. ⊠ *125 Waverly Pl., Chinatown* ☎ *No phone* ✉ *Free, donations accepted* ✆ *Daily 9–4.*

CHINATOWN

Chinatown's streets flood the senses. Incense and cigarette smoke mingle with the scents of briny fish and sweet vanilla. Rooflines flare outward, pagoda-style. Loud Cantonese bargaining and honking car horns rise above the sharp clack of mah-jongg tiles and the eternally humming cables beneath the street.

Most Chinatown visitors march down Grant Avenue, buy a few trinkets, and call it a day. Do yourself a favor and dig deeper. This is one of the largest Chinese communities outside Asia, and there is far more to it than buying a back-scratcher near Chinatown Gate. To get a real feel for the neighborhood, wander off the main drag. Step into a temple or an herb shop and wander down a flag-draped alley. And don't be shy: residents welcome guests warmly, though rarely in English.

Whatever you do, don't leave without eating something. Noodle houses, bakeries, tea houses, and dim sum shops seem to occupy every other storefront. There's a feast for your eyes as well: in the market windows on Stockton and Grant, you'll see hanging whole roast ducks, fish, and shellfish swimming in tanks, and strips of shiny, pink-glazed Chinese-style barbecued pork. (For the scoop on dim sum, *see* the Union Square and Chinatown spotlight in the Where to Eat chapter.)

CHINATOWN'S HISTORY

Sam Brannan's 1848 cry of "Gold!" didn't take long to reach across the world to China. Struggling with famine, drought, and political upheaval at home, thousands of Chinese jumped at the chance to try their luck in California. Most came from the Pearl River Delta region, in the Guangdong province, and spoke Cantonese dialects. From the start, Chinese businesses circled around Portsmouth Square, which was conveniently central. Bachelor rooming houses sprang up, since the vast majority of new arrivals were men. By 1853, the area was called Chinatown.

The Street of Gamblers (Ross Alley), 1898 (top).
The first Chinese telephone operator in Chinatown (bottom).

COLD WELCOME

The Chinese faced discrimination from the get-go. Harrassment became outright hostility as first the gold rush, then the work on the Transcontinental Railroad petered out. Special taxes were imposed to shoulder aside competing "coolie labor." Laws forbidding the Chinese from moving outside Chinatown kept the residents packed in like sardines,

with nowhere to go but up and down—thus the many basement establishments in the neighborhood. State and federal laws passed in the 1870s deterred Chinese women from immigrating, deeming them prostitutes. In the late 1870s, looting and arson attacks on Chinatown businesses soared.

The coup de grace, though, was the Chinese Exclusion Act, passed by the U.S.

Chinatown's Grant Avenue.

Women and children flooded into the neighborhood after the Great Quake.

Congress in 1882, which slammed the doors to America for "Asiatics." This was the country's first significant restriction on immigration. The law also prevented the existing Chinese residents, including American-born children, from becoming naturalized citizens. With a society of mostly men (forbidden, of course, from marrying white women), San Francisco hoped that Chinatown would simply die out.

OUT OF THE ASHES
When the devastating 1906 earthquake and fire hit, city fathers thought they'd seize the opportunity to kick the Chinese out of Chinatown and get their hands on that desirable piece of downtown real estate. Then Chinatown businessman Look Tin Eli had a brainstorm of Disneyesque proportions.

He proposed that Chinatown be rebuilt, but in a tourist-friendly, stylized, "Oriental" way. Anglo-American architects would design new buildings with pagoda roofs and dragon-covered columns. Chinatown would attract more tourists—the curious had been visiting on the sly

for decades—and add more tax money to the city's coffers. Ka-ching: the sales pitch worked.

PAPER SONS
For the Chinese, the 1906 earthquake turned the virtual "no entry" sign into a flashing neon "welcome!" All the city's immigration records went up in smoke, and the Chinese quickly began to apply for passports as U.S. citizens, claiming their old ones were lost in the fire. Not only did thousands of Chinese become legal overnight, but so did their sons in China, or "sons," if they weren't really related. Whole families in Chinatown had passports in names that weren't their own; these "paper sons" were not only a windfall but also an uncomfortable neighborhood conspiracy. The city caught on eventually and set up an immigration center on Angel Island in 1910. Immigrants spent weeks or months being inspected and interrogated while their papers were checked. Roughly 250,000 people made it through. With this influx, including women and children, Chinatown finally became a more complete community.

A GREAT WALK THROUGH CHINATOWN

■ Start at the Chinatown Gate and walk ahead on Grant Avenue, entering the souvenir gauntlet. (You'll also pass Old St. Mary's Cathedral.)

■ Make a right on Clay Street and walk to Portsmouth Square. Sometimes it feels like the whole neighborhood's here, playing chess and exercising.

■ Head up Washington Street to the elaborately pagodaed Old Chinese Telephone Exchange building, now the Bank of Canton. Across Grant, look left for Waverly Place. Here Republic of China flags flap over some of the neighborhood's most striking buildings, including Tin How Temple.

■ At the Sacramento Street end of Waverly Place stands the oddly beautiful brick First Chinese Baptist Church of 1908. Just across the way, the Clarion Music Center is chock-full of unusual instruments, as well as exquisite lion-dance sets.

■ Head back to Washington Street and check out the herb shops, like the Superior Trading Company (No. 839) and the Great China Herb Co. (No. 857).

■ Follow the scent of vanilla from Washington Street down Ross Alley (entrance across

from Superior Trading Company) to the Golden Gate Fortune Cookie Factory. Then head across the alley to Sam Bo Trading Co., where religious items are stacked chockablock in the narrow space. Tell the friendly owners your troubles and they'll prepare a package of joss papers, joss sticks, and candles, and tell you how and when to offer them up.

■ Turn left on Jackson Street; ahead is the real Chinatown's main artery, Stockton Street. This is where most residents do their grocery shopping; if it's Saturday, get ready for throngs (and their elbows). Look toward the back of stores for Buddhist altars with offerings of oranges and grapefruit. From here you can loop one block east back to Grant.

ALL THE TEA IN CHINATOWN

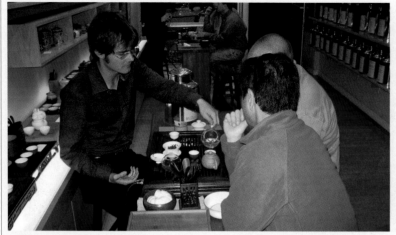

Preparing a perfect brew at Red Blossom Tea.

San Francisco's close ties to Asia have always made it more tea-conscious than other American burgs, but these days the city is in the throes of a tea renaissance, with new tasting rooms popping up in every neighborhood. Below are our favorite Chinatown spots for every tea under the sun.

Red Blossom Tea. A light and modern shop—the staff really know their stuff. It's a favorite among younger tea enthusiasts, who swear by its excellent bang-for-the-buck value. While Red Blossom doesn't do formal tastings or sell tea by the cup, they'll gladly brew up perfect samples of the teas you're interested in. ✉ *831 Grant Ave.* ☎ *415/395–0868.*

Vital Tea Leaf. Tastings here work like those for wine—one of the gregarious, knowledgeable servers chooses the teas and describes them as you sample. It's a great spot for tea newbies to get their feet wet without a hard sell, but local connoisseurs grumble about the high prices and the self-promotion. ✉ *1044 Grant Ave.* ☎ *415/981–2388.*

Imperial Tea Court. If you want to visit the most respected of traditional tea purveyors, you'll need to venture outside of Chinatown. Imperial Tea Court's serene Powell Street oasis closed unexpectedly in 2007, but you'll find the same great selection and expertise at their fancy new digs in the Ferry Building. ☎ *415/544–9830.*

WAITING FOR CUSTARD

As you're strolling down Grant Avenue, past the plastic Buddhas and yin/yang balls, be sure to stop at the **Golden Gate Bakery** (No. 1029) for some delicious eggy *dan tat* (custard tarts). These flaky-crusted treats are heaven for just a buck. There's often a line, but it's worth the wait.

DON'T-MISS SHOPS

Locals snap up flowers from an outdoor vendor.

If you're in the market for a pair of chirping metal crickets (oh you'll hear them, trust us), you can duck into any of the obvious souvenir-stuffed storefronts. But if you're looking for something special, head for these tempting sources. ■TIP→ Fierce neighborhood competition keeps prices within reason, but for popular wares like jade, it pays to shop around before making a serious investment. Many stores accept cash only.

Chinatown Kite Shop. Family-run shop selling bright, fun-shaped kites —dragons, butterflies, sharks—since the 1960s. ⊠ *717 Grant Ave.* ☎ *415/ 989–5182.*

Dragon House. A veritable museum: the store sells authentic, centuries-old antiques like ivory carvings. ⊠ *455 Grant Ave.* ☎ *415/421–3693.*

Jade Galore. Not the cheapest place to pick up jade figures and jewelry, but locals trust its quality and adore its

wide selection of Chinese bling. ⊠ *1000 Stockton St.* ☎ *415/982–4863.*

Old Shanghai. One of the largest selections of hand-painted robes, formal dresses, and jackets in Chinatown, plus chic Asian-inspired pieces. ⊠ *645 Grant Ave.* ☎ *415/986–1222.*

CHINATOWN WITH KIDS

It can be tough for the little ones to keep their hands to themselves, especially when all sorts of curios spill out onto the sidewalk at just the right height. To burn off some steam (in them) and relieve some stress (in you), take them to the small but spruce playground directly behind Old St. Mary's at Grant Avenue and California Street. If that setting's too tranquil, head to the more boisterous Willie Wong Playground, on Sacramento Street at Waverly Place.

3

SoMa and Civic Center

WORD OF MOUTH

"A hit in SF for our kids is Zeum in Yerba Buena Gardens. It's an arts and technology museum for kids. Our 7 year old actually passed on a big birthday party with her friends to take 1 friend to SF to visit Zeum."

—monterey123

GETTING ORIENTED

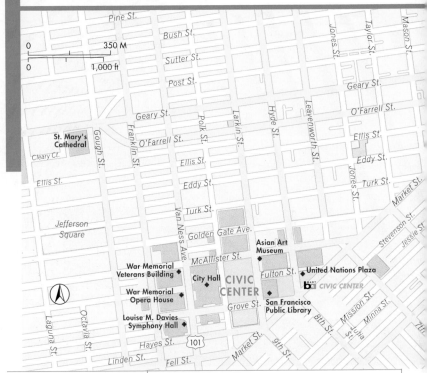

GETTING THERE

For most SoMa visitors, who stick close to SFMOMA and the Yerba Buena Gardens, getting here is a matter of walking roughly 10 minutes from Union Square, less from the Market Street transit.

It's best to reach Civic Center by BART, bus, or F-line. Hoofing it from Union Square requires walking through the unsavory Tenderloin area, and from SoMa it's a long, ugly haul.

After dark, safety concerns dictate a cab for both neighborhoods.

QUICK BITES

Above the Martin Luther King Jr. memorial in the Yerba Buena Gardens, the **Samovar Tea Lounge** (✉ *730 Howard St., SoMa* ☎ *415/227–9400*) is a serene retreat with glass walls overlooking an infinity pool. Especially on a blustery day, the organic and fair-trade teas hit the spot.

Metreon's **Taste of San Francisco** (✉ *101 4th St., between Mission and Howard Sts., SoMa*) is the perfect spot to grab all the fixings for an alfresco lunch. Choose wood-fired pizza from the Firewood Café or a generous burrito from Luna Azul and stake out a spot in the Yerba Buena Gardens.

If you see a clutch of people gathered around what looks like a garage in Hayes Valley, chances are you've stumbled upon **Blue Bottle Coffee** (✉ *315 Linden St., Hayes Valley* ☎ *415/252–7535*), a tiny stand selling what many claim is the best organic coffee on the planet. The "artisanal micro-roasting" philosophy says that all coffee should be brewed within 24 hours of roasting, and yes, they are Very Serious.

3

MAKING THE MOST OF YOUR TIME

You could spend all day museum-hopping in SoMa. Allow two hours to see SFMOMA; if there's a big show on, avoid the line by buying tickets online and arrive early to beat the throngs. An hour each should do it for the Museum of the African Diaspora, the Contemporary Jewish Museum, and the Center for the Arts, less than that for the minor museums.

SoMa after dark is another adventure entirely. More interested in merlot or megaclubs than Matisse? Start here around 8 PM for dinner, then move on to a bar or dance spot. *See the Where to Eat and Nightlife and the Arts chapters for our top recommendations.*

Don't be suckered by visions of grand architecture and "important" performing-arts venues in Civic Center. Unless you have tickets to the opera, ballet, or a concert, there's no good reason for you to spend much time here.

KEY
bä *BART station*

TOP 5 REASONS TO GO

SFMOMA: Big-name modern art exhibits in a durably cool building.

Asian Art Museum: Stand face-to-face with a massive gold Buddha in one of the world's largest collections of Asian art.

Club-hopping in SoMa: Shake it with the cool, friendly crowd that fills SoMa's dance clubs until the wee hours, and all weekend long at the EndUp.

Yerba Buena Gardens: Gather picnic provisions and choose a spot on the grass in downtown's oasis.

Hanging out at Patricia's Green: Grab a cup of coffee (Blue Bottle's just around the corner) and head to the narrow swath of park that serves as hopping Hayes Valley's living room. Check out the monumental temporary art exhibit—it always has an interactive element—and the little ones clambering on the fantastic climbing dome.

Sightseeing
★★★
Nightlife
★★★★
Dining
★★★
Lodging
★★
Shopping
★

To a newcomer, SoMa (short for "south of Market") and Civic Center may look like cheek-by-jowl neighbors—they're divided by Market Street. To locals, though, these areas are firmly separate entities, especially since Market Street itself is considered such a strong demarcation line. Both neighborhoods have a core of cultural sights but more than their share of sketchy blocks.

Updated by
Denise M. Leto

SoMa is less a neighborhood than it is a sprawling area of wide, traffic-heavy boulevards lined with office high-rises and pricey live-work lofts. Aside from the fact that many of them work in the area, locals are drawn to the cultural offerings, smattering of destination restaurants, and concentration of dance clubs. In terms of sightseeing, SoMa holds a few points of interest—SFMOMA and the museums of the Yerba Buena District top the list—and these are conveniently close together.

SoMa was once known as South of the Slot (read: the Wrong Side of the Tracks) in reference to the cable-car slot that ran up Market Street. Ever since gold-rush miners set up their tents in 1848, SoMa has played a major role in housing immigrants to the city. Industry took over much of the area when the 1906 earthquake collapsed most of the homes.

SoMa's emergence as a focal point of San Francisco's cultural life was more than three decades in the making. Huge sections of the then-industrial neighborhood were razed in the 1960s, and alternative artists and the gay leather crowd set up shop. A dozen bars and bathhouses frequented by the latter group cropped up; some survive today, and the legacy of that time is the still-raucous annual Folsom Street Fair. The neighborhood lost many artists to the far reaches of SoMa and to the Mission District when urban renewal finally began in earnest in the 1970s; still more fled when the dot-com heyday sent prices here skyrocketing.

Life in the SoMa of the mid- to late 1990s was what the gold rush must have felt like. Young prospectors flooded in to take their pick of well-paying jobs at high-tech startups. Companies with hot (or not)

ideas filled their $100-plus-per-square-foot offices with recent college grads, foosball tables, $1,000 ergonomic chairs, and free catered meals. Gaggles of gadget-toting twentysomethings spent their evenings wandering from launch party to marketing event, loading up on swag. Rents—commercial in SoMa and residential citywide—went through the roof, but the dot-commers could still pony up while waiting for the holy grail of the IPO. South Park, the green oval anchored by high-tech hangout Caffè Centro, briefly became the center of the universe.

The electric buzz of the dot-com boom, when venture capitalists couldn't give their money away fast enough, changed the face of the neighborhood forever. Today's post-boom SoMa is sobered up and on the rise; the thousands of kids rich on paper have been replaced with substantially wealthy people staking out luxury high-rises in striking residential towers, such as 62-story One Rincon Hill, the pencil-thin building at the end of the Bay Bridge, that will dwarf what are now the city's tallest buildings. The area may still have more than its share of seedy pockets, but even in earthquake town, the 60th-story penthouse at the chic, unfinished Millennium sold for $11 million in 2008 (and prices continued to hover around $850,000 on average in 2009).

Across Market Street from the western edge of SoMa is another of the city's patchy neighborhoods, the Civic Center, between McAllister and Grove streets and Franklin and Hyde streets. The optimistic "City Beautiful" movement of the early 20th century produced the Beaux Arts–style complex for which this area is named, including the War Memorial Opera House, the Veterans Building, and the old public library, now home of the Asian Art Museum. The centerpiece is the eye-catching, gold-dome City Hall. The current main library on Larkin Street between Fulton and Grove streets is a modern variation on the Civic Center's architectural theme.

The Civic Center area may have been set up on City Beautiful principles, but illusion soon gives way to reality. The buildings are grand, but there's a stark juxtaposition of the powerful and the powerless here. On the streets and plazas of Civic Center, many of the city's most destitute residents eke out an existence.

Despite the evidence of social problems, there are areas of interest on either side of City Hall. East of City Hall is United Nations Plaza, which hosts a poor man's version of the Ferry Building's glorious farmers'

HAYES VALLEY

Hayes Valley, right next door to the Civic Center, is an offbeat neighborhood with terrific eateries, cool watering holes, and great browsing in its funky clothing and home-decor boutiques. Swing down main drag Hayes Street, between Franklin and Laguna, and you can hit the highlights, including two very popular restaurants, Absinthe and Suppenküche. Comfy Place Pigalle (at Hayes and Octavia streets) is also a favorite for its living-room atmosphere, wines, and microbrews. Locals love this quarter, but without any big-name draws it remains off the radar for most visitors.

market twice weekly. On the west side of City Hall are the opera house, the symphony hall, and other cultural institutions. A few upscale restaurants in the surrounding blocks cater to the theater-symphony crowd. Tickets to a show at one of the grand performance halls are the main reason to venture here. Otherwise, unless you have a hankering to gawk at gray-stone, monumental structures, a glimpse of the gold-veined dome of City Hall as you drive down the street should be enough, especially for first-time visitors.

WHAT TO SEE IN SOMA

California Historical Society. If you're not a history buff, the CHS might seem like an obvious skip—who wants to look at fading old photographs and musty artifacts? If the answer is an indignant "I do!" or if you're just curious, these airy galleries are well worth a stop. A rotating selection draws from the society's vast repository of Californiana—hundreds of thousands of photographs, publications, paintings, and gold-rush paraphernalia.■TIP➔ From out front, take a look across the street: this is the best view of MoAD's three-story photo mosaic. ⊠ *678 Mission St., SoMa* ☏ *415/357–1848* ⊕ *www.californiahistoricalsociety.org* ◪ *$3* ☉ *Wed.–Sat. noon–4:30; galleries close between exhibitions.*

OFF THE
BEATEN
PATH

GLBT Historical Society Museum. Tucked away in a small exhibit space on the third floor, the Gay, Lesbian, Bisexual, and Transgender (GLBT) Historical Society Museum presents rotating multimedia exhibits on themes such as the Gay Olympics, Harvey Milk, and GLBT military service. Though perhaps not for the faint of heart (those offended by photos of lustily frolicking naked people may, well, be offended), this thoughtful display offers an inside look at these communities so integral to the fabric of San Francisco life. The upstairs location and tiny space mean you may well be the only visitor; a helpful docent from the GLBT Historical Society's office next door will gladly show you around and answer any questions. ⊠ *657 Mission St., 3rd fl., SoMa* ☏ *415/777–5455* ⊕ *www.glbthistory.org* ◪ *$4 donation* ☉ *Tues.–Sat. 1–5.*

Cartoon Art Museum. Krazy Kat, Zippy the Pinhead, Batman, and other colorful cartoon icons greet you at the Cartoon Art Museum, established with an endowment from cartoonist-icon Charles M. Schulz. The museum's strength is its changing exhibits, which explore such topics as America from the perspective of international political cartoons, and the output of women and African-American cartoonists. Serious fans of cartoons—especially those on the quirky underground side—will likely enjoy the exhibits; those with a casual interest may be disappointed. The museum store carries lots of cool books. ⊠ *655 Mission St., SoMa* ☏ *415/227–8666* ⊕ *www.cartoonart.org* ◪ *$6, pay what you wish 1st Tues. of month* ☉ *Tues.–Sun. 11–5.*

Contemporary Jewish Museum. Fascinating museum buildings are sprouting up all over the city, and this new, Daniel Liebeskind–designed CJM is a real coup for SoMa. It's impossible to ignore that diagonal blue cube. The all-new addition jutting into a painstakingly restored power substation is a physical manifestation of the Hebrew phrase *l'chaim* (to life). And even if the architectural philosophy behind the design seems

a bit esoteric, the blue, steel-clad cube—one of the most striking structures in town—creates a unique, light-filled space that merits a stroll through the lobby even if current exhibits don't entice you into the galleries. Be sure to check out the seam where old building meets new. ■TIP➔ "Seeing Gertrude Stein," an exhibit examining this cultural giant's role in 20th-century arts, is set to open in mid-2011. ⊠ *736 Mission St., between 3rd and 4th Sts., SoMa* ☎ *415/655–7800* ⊕ *www.thejcm.org* ⊠ *$10, $5 Thurs. after 5 PM* ⊙ *Thurs. 1–8, Fri.–Tues. 11–5.*

Metreon. Child's play meets the 21st century at this high-tech mall, adored by gearheads and teenage boys obsessed with tabletop games. Tilt, a high-tech interactive arcade, a 15-screen multiplex and IMAX theater, retail shops including local specialty publisher Chronicle Books, and outposts of some of the city's favorite restaurants are all part of the complex. It's a good place to pick up lunch for a picnic in the Yerba Buena Gardens, right outside; if you forgot your blanket, head to the patio tables outside Metreon's second floor. ⊠ *101 4th St., between Mission and Howard Sts., SoMa* ☎ *800/638–7366* ⊕ *www.metreon. com.* ⊙ *Sun.–Thurs. 10–9, Fri. and Sat. 10–10.*

Museum of the African Diaspora (MoAD). Dedicated to the influence that people of African descent have had all over the world, MoAD provokes discussion from the get-go with the question, "When did you discover you are African?" painted on the wall at the entrance. With no permanent collection, the museum is light on displays and heavy on interactive exhibits. For instance, you can sit in a darkened theater and listen to the moving life stories of slaves; hear snippets of music that helped create genres from gospel to hip-hop; and see videos about the Civil Rights movement or the Haitian Revolution. Some grumble that sweeping generalities replace specific information, but almost everyone can appreciate the museum's most striking exhibit, in the front window. The three-story mosaic, made from thousands of photographs, forms the image of a little girl's face. Walk up the stairs inside the museum and view the photographs up close—Malcolm X is there, Muhammad Ali, too, along with everyday folks—but the best view is from across the street. ⊠ *685 Mission St., SoMa* ☎ *415/358–7200* ⊕ *www.moadsf. org* ⊠ *$10* ⊙ *Wed.–Sat. 11–6, Sun. noon–5.*

OFF THE BEATEN PATH

Mint Plaza. Arising from what had long been a gritty, windswept cut-through behind the abandoned Old Mint, L-shape Mint Plaza is shaping up to be that vibrant mix that urban planners always aim for but often miss: stylish urban residences (that are actually occupied) cheek-by-jowl with thriving local businesses, all combining to produce a happening street scene. The secret, tucked-away feel of the alley—which is mere feet from Mission Street—will make you feel like an insider when you visit. Stop by Blue Bottle Café for coffee and a nosh or grab a table at Chez Papa, one of the city's favorite French bistros. Betting pools are forming now to wager how long those orange chairs—meant to encourage the public-space feel—will survive. Even the mint itself is being reinvented: the Museum of San Francisco is slated to open inside the structure in 2011. ⊠ *Jessie and Mint Sts., near Mission and 5th Sts., SoMa.*

The glass-domed Garden Court contributes to the majestic feel of the Palace Hotel.

Museum of Craft and Folk Art. If you're in the area, this one-room museum is a great way to spend a half-hour. Its bright space hosts five rotating exhibits per year showcasing American folk art, tribal art, and contemporary crafts. One exhibit saw the museum transformed into a forest of plants, trees, and a river, all created from paper by an artisan in Japan. Another was devoted entirely to the art of the ukulele. Its tiny front space houses a shop with high-end, sometimes whimsical crafts from around the world. ✉ *51 Yerba Buena La., SoMa* ☎ *415/227–4888* ⊕ *www.mocfa.org* ⬚ *$5, free 1st Tues.* ⊙ *Mon., Tues., Thurs., and Fri. 11–6, weekends 11–5, 1st Thurs. of month until 7:30.*

Palace Hotel. The city's oldest hotel, a Sheraton property, opened in 1875. Fire destroyed the original Palace after the 1906 earthquake, despite the hotel's 28,000-gallon reservoir; the current building dates from 1909. President Warren Harding died at the Palace while still in office in 1923, and the body of King Kalakaua of Hawaii spent a night here after he died in San Francisco in 1891. The managers play up this ghoulish past with talk of a haunted guest room. **San Francisco City Guides** (☎ *415/557–4266* ⊙ *Tours Tues. and Sat. at 10, Thurs. at 2*) offers free guided tours of the Palace Hotel's grand interior. You see the glass-dome Garden Court restaurant, mosaic-tile floors in Oriental rug designs, and Maxfield Parrish's wall-size painting *The Pied Piper*, the centerpiece of the Pied Piper Bar. Glass cases off the main lobby contain memorabilia of the hotel's glory days. ✉ *2 New Montgomery St., SoMa* ☎ *415/512–1111* ⊕ *www.sfpalace.com.*

Rincon Center. The only reason to visit what is basically a modern office building is the striking Works Project Administration mural by

Anton Refregier in the lobby of the streamlined moderne–style former post office on the building's Mission Street side. The 27 panels depict California life from the days when Native Americans were the state's sole inhabitants through World War I. Completion of this significant work was interrupted by World War II (which explains the swastika in the final panel) and political infighting. The latter led to some alteration in Refregier's "radical" historical interpretations; they exuded too much populist sentiment for some of the politicians who opposed the artist. A permanent exhibit below the murals contains photographs and artifacts of life in the Rincon area in the 1800s. A sheer five-story column of water resembling a mini-rainstorm is the centerpiece of the indoor arcade around the corner from the mural. ✉ *Bordered by Steuart, Spear, Mission, and Howard Sts., SoMa.*

WORD OF MOUTH

"One cannot compare the SF MOMA with the size and scope of [the] collection at the NYC MoMA or Tate Modern; but … [it] has a good representation of [the] 'cream of the crop,' so to speak."

—yk

FodorsChoice ★ **San Francisco Museum of Modern Art** *(SFMOMA)*. With its brick facade and a striped central tower lopped at a lipstick-like angle, architect Mario Botta's SFMOMA building fairly screams "modern-art museum." Indeed it is. The stripes continue inside, from the black marble and gray granite of the floors right up the imposing staircase to the wooden slats on the ceiling. ■TIP➔ **Taking in all of SFMOMA's four exhibit floors can be overwhelming, so having a plan is helpful. Keep in mind that the museum's heavy hitters are on floors 2 and 3.** Floor 2 gets the big-name traveling exhibits and collection highlights such as Matisse's *Woman with the Hat,* Diego Rivera's *The Flower Carrier,* and Georgia O'Keeffe's *Black Place 1.* Photography buffs should hustle up to floor 3, with its works by Ansel Adams and Alfred Stieglitz. The large-scale contemporary exhibits on floors 4 and 5 can usually be seen quickly (or skipped). If it's on display, don't miss sculptor Jeff Koons' memorably creepy, life-size gilded porcelain *Michael Jackson and Bubbles,* on the fifth floor at the end of the Turret Bridge, a vertiginous catwalk dangling under the central tower. The window at the bridge's other end offers a great view over the Yerba Buena Gardens below. In 2009, the museum's new fifth-floor, garage-top sculpture garden opened.

Seating in the museum can be scarce, so luckily Caffè Museo, accessible from the street, provides a refuge for quite good, reasonably priced drinks and light meals. It's easy to drop a fortune at the museum's large store, chockablock with fun gadgets, artsy doodads of all kinds, very modern furniture, and possibly the best selection of kids' books in town. ■TIP➔ **No ticket is required to visit the lobby, so if it's the architecture you're interested in, save yourself the admission and have a gander for free.** ✉ *151 3rd St., SoMa* ☎ *415/357–4000* ⊕ *www.sfmoma.org* ✉ *$15, free 1st Tues. of month, ½ price Thurs. 6–9* ☽ *Labor Day–Memorial Day, Fri.–Tues. 11–5:45, Thurs. 11–8:45; Memorial Day–Labor Day, Fri.–Tues. 10–5:45, Thurs. 10–8:45.*

Above the Yerba Buena Gardens, SF MOMA's striped "eye" can be spotted.

Yerba Buena Center for the Arts. If MOMA's for your parents, the Center is for you. You never know what's going to be on at this facility in the Yerba Buena Gardens, but whether it's an exhibit of Mexican street graphics (graffiti to laypeople), innovative modern dance, or baffling video installations, it's likely to be memorable. The productions here tend to draw a young, energetic crowd, and lean hard toward the cutting edge. ⊠ *701 Mission St., SoMa* ☎ *415/978–2787* ⊕ *www.ybca.org* ⊠ *Galleries $7, free 1st Tues. of month* ☉ *Thurs. and Fri. 2–8, Sat. noon–8, Sun. noon–6, 1st Tues. of the month noon–8.*

☾
★ **Yerba Buena Gardens.** There's not much south of Market that encourages lingering outdoors, or indeed walking at all, with this notable exception. These two blocks encompass the **Center for the Arts, Metreon, Moscone Convention Center,** and the convention center's rooftop **Zeum,** but the gardens themselves are the everyday draw. Office workers escape to the green swath of the East Garden. The memorial to Martin Luther King Jr. is the focal point here. Powerful streams of water surge over large, jagged stone columns, mirroring the enduring force of King's words that are carved on the stone walls and on glass blocks behind the waterfall. Moscone North is behind the memorial, and an overhead walkway leads to Moscone South and its rooftop attractions. ■TIP→ The gardens are liveliest during the week and especially during the **Yerba Buena Gardens Festival** (May–October, www.ybgf.org), when free performances run from Latin music to Balinese dance.

Atop the Moscone Convention Center perch a few lures for kids. The historic **Looff carousel** ($3 for two rides) twirls daily 11 to 6. South of the carousel is **Zeum** (☎ *415/820–3320* ⊕ *www.zeum.org*), a high-tech, interactive arts-and-technology center (adults, $10; kids 3–18, $8) geared to children ages eight and over. Kids can make Claymation videos, work in a computer lab, and view exhibits and performances. Zeum is open 1 to 5 Wednesday through Friday and 11 to 5 weekends during the school year and Tuesday through Sunday 11 to 5 when school's out. Also part of the rooftop complex are gardens, an ice-skating rink, and a bowling alley. ⊠ *Bordered by 3rd, 4th, Mission, and Folsom Sts., SoMa* ☏ *No phone* ⊕ *www.yerbabuena.org* ▢ *Free* ⊙ *Daily sunrise–10* PM.

WORD OF MOUTH

"I wouldn't hesitate to visit the buildings in the San Francisco Civic Center (City Hall and surrounding buildings) or to take a cab or bus to the Golden Gate or Orpheum theaters on performance nights or matinees…but I would avoid them at other times."
—JBC411

WHAT TO SEE IN CIVIC CENTER

★ **Asian Art Museum.** Expecting a building full of Buddhas and jade? Well, yeah, you can find plenty of that here. Happily, though, you don't have to be a connoisseur of Asian art to appreciate a visit to this splendidly renovated museum, whose monumental exterior conceals a light, open, and welcoming space. The fraction of the museum's items on display (about 2,500 pieces from a 15,000-plus-piece collection) is laid out thematically and by region, making it easy to follow developments.

Begin on the third floor, where highlights of Buddhist art in Southeast Asia and early China include a large, jewel-encrusted, exquisitely painted 19th-century Burmese Buddha and clothed rod puppets from Java. On the second floor you can find later Chinese works, as well as pieces from Korea and Japan. Look for a cobalt tiger jauntily smoking a pipe on a whimsical Korean jar and delicate Japanese tea implements. The ground floor displays rotating exhibits, including contemporary and traveling shows. ■TIP→ If you'd like to attend one of the occasional tea ceremonies and tastings at the Japanese Teahouse, call ahead, since preregistration is required. ⊠ *200 Larkin St., between McAllister and Fulton Sts., Civic Center* ☏ *415/581–3500* ⊕ *www.asianart.org* ▢ *$12, free 1st Sun. of month; $5 Thurs. 5–9; tea ceremony $20, includes museum* ⊙ *Tues., Wed., and Fri.–Sun. 10–5, Thurs. 10–9.*

City Hall. This imposing 1915 structure with its massive gold-leaf dome—higher than the U.S. Capitol's—is about as close to a palace as you're going to get in San Francisco. (The metal detectors take something away from the grandeur, though.) The classic granite-and-marble behemoth was modeled after St. Peter's Cathedral in Rome. Architect Arthur Brown Jr., who also designed Coit Tower and the War Memorial Opera House, designed an interior with grand columns and a sweeping central staircase. San Franciscans were thrilled, and probably a bit surprised, when his firm built City Hall in just a few years. The building it replaced, dubbed "the new City Hall ruin," had lined the pockets of corrupt builders and politicians during its 27 years of construction. That 1899 structure collapsed in about 27 seconds in the 1906 earthquake, revealing trash and newspapers mixed into the building materials.

WORD OF MOUTH

"City Hall is one of the most beautiful public buildings I have ever seen. Open to the public and the free tour is worth an hour of your time."   —QC

City Hall was spruced up and seismically retrofitted in the late 1990s, but the sense of history remains palpable. Some noteworthy events that have taken place here include the marriage of Marilyn Monroe and Joe DiMaggio (1954); the hosing—down the central staircase—of civil-rights and freedom-of-speech protesters (1960); the murders of Mayor George Moscone and openly gay supervisor Harvey Milk (1978); the torching of the lobby by angry members of the gay community in response to the light sentence given to the former supervisor who killed both men (1979); and the registrations of scores of gay couples in celebration of the passage of San Francisco's Domestic Partners Act (1991). February 2004 has come to be known as the Winter of Love: thousands of gay and lesbian couples responded to Mayor Gavin Newsom's decision to issue marriage licenses to same-sex partners, turning City Hall into the site of raucous celebration and joyful nuptials for a month before the state Supreme Court ordered the practice stopped. That celebratory scene replayed during 2008, when scores of couples were wed between the court's June ruling that everyone enjoys the civil right to marry and the November passage of California's ballot proposition banning same-sex marriage. (Stay tuned . . .) Free tours are offered weekdays at 10, noon, and 2.

The South Light Court houses a modest, rotating display from the collection of the **Museum of the City of San Francisco** (⊕ *www.sfmuseum. org*), including historical items, maps, and photographs. That enormous, 700-pound iron head once crowned the *Goddess of Progress* statue, which topped the old City Hall building when it crumbled during the 1906 earthquake. Unlike the building, the statue survived the earthquake in one piece, but the subsequent removal proved too much for it.

Across Polk Street is **Civic Center Plaza,** with lawns, walkways, seasonal flower beds, a playground, and an underground parking garage. This sprawling space is generally clean but somewhat grim. A large part of the city's homeless population hangs out here, despite frequently being shunted away, so the plaza can feel dodgy. ⊠ *Bordered by Van Ness Ave. and Polk, Grove, and McAllister Sts., Civic Center* ☎ *415/554–6023* ⊕ *www.sfgov.org/site/cityhall* ☒ *Free* ⊘ *Weekdays 8–8.*

NEED A BREAK?

Once exclusively a bakery and sandwich joint, star pastry chef Elizabeth Falkner's Citizen Cake (⊠ *399 Grove St., Civic Center* ☎ *415/861–2228*) is now a full-fledged restaurant, but it's still a very worthwhile detour. Choose a sweet to go—cookies, pastries, chocolates, even house-made ice cream—from the patisserie case, or stake out a table in the urban-industrial space.

Louise M. Davies Symphony Hall. Fascinating and futuristic looking, this 2,750-seat hall is the home of the San Francisco Symphony. The glass wraparound lobby and pop-out balcony high on the southeast corner

Where can I find . . . ?

PARKING	Civic Center Plaza Garage 355 McAllister St. Most convenient place to use if you're here for a performance.	Jesse Square Garage 223 Stevenson St. A SoMa secret with good rates and plenty of space.
A GAS STATION	76 390 1st St. Near I–80, with middling prices.	Chevron 1298 Howard St. In SoMa but relatively close to Civic Center.
PRETHEATER DRINKS	Hôtel Biron 45 Rose St. Have a glass of wine in this tiny, arty Hayes Valley spot.	Olive 743 Larkin St. Stylish cocktail bar/restaurant on the edge of the Tenderloin.

are visible from outside, as is the Henry Moore bronze sculpture that sits on the sidewalk at Van Ness Avenue and Grove Street. The hall's 59 adjustable Plexiglas acoustical disks cascade from the ceiling like hanging windshields. Concerts range from typical symphonic fare to more unusual combinations, such as performers like Al Green and Arlo Guthrie. Scheduled tours (75 minutes), which meet at the Grove Street entrance, take in Davies and the nearby opera house and Herbst Theatre. ⊠ *201 Van Ness Ave., Civic Center* ☎ *415/552–8338* ⊕ *www.sfwmpac.org* ✉ *Tours $5* ⊗ *Tours Mon. on the hr 10–2.*

San Francisco Public Library. Topped with a swirl like an art-deco nautilus, the library's seven-level glass atrium fills the building with light. Opened in 1996, the New Main (as Herb Caen dubbed it) is a modernized version of the old Beaux Arts–style library. Local researchers take advantage of centers dedicated to gay-and-lesbian, African-American, Chinese, and Filipino history, and everyone appreciates the basement-level café, Wi-Fi, and 15-minute Internet terminal access. On the sixth floor an exhibit inside the San Francisco History Center includes doo-dads from the 1894 Mid-Winter Fair and the 1915 Pan-Pacific Exhibition, as well as the "valuable emeralds" philanthropist Helene Strybing left to the city—alas merely green glass. ■ TIP➜ Noir fans should head to the back of the center; you can see "Maltese Falcon" statues in the Flood Building and at John's Grill, but this is the only place to see novelist Dashiell Hammett's typewriter. Free tours of the library are conducted the second Wednesday of the month at 2:30. ⊠ *100 Larkin St., at Grove St., Civic Center* ☎ *415/557–4400* ⊕ *sfpl.lib.ca.us* ⊗ *Mon. and Sat. 10–6, Tues.–Thurs. 9–8, Fri. noon–6, Sun. noon–5.*

United Nations Plaza. Locals know this plaza for two things: its Wednesday and Sunday farmers' market—cheap and earthy to the Ferry Building's pricey and beautiful—and its homeless population, which seems to return no matter how many times the city tries to shunt them aside. Brick pillars listing various nations and the dates of their admittance into the United Nations line the plaza, and its floor is inscribed with the goals and philosophy of the United Nations charter, which was signed at the War Memorial Opera House in 1945. ⊠ *Fulton St. between Hyde and Market Sts., Civic Center.*

War Memorial Opera House. During San Francisco's Barbary Coast days, operagoers smoked cigars, didn't check their revolvers, and expressed their appreciation with "shrill whistles and savage yells," as one observer put it. All the old opera houses were destroyed in the 1906 quake, but lusty support for opera continued. The San Francisco Opera didn't have a permanent home until the War Memorial Opera House was inaugurated in 1932 with a performance of *Tosca*. Modeled after its European counterparts, the building has a vaulted and coffered ceiling, marble foyer, two balconies, and a huge silver art-deco chandelier that resembles a sunburst. The San Francisco Opera performs here from September through December and in summer; the opera house hosts the San Francisco Ballet from February through May, with December *Nutcracker* performances. ⊠ *301 Van Ness Ave., Civic Center* ☏ *415/621–6600* ⊕ *www.sfwmpac.org.*

War Memorial Veterans Building. Performing- and visual-arts organizations occupy much of this 1930s structure. **Herbst Theatre** (☏ *415/392–4400*) hosts classical ensembles, dance performances, and City Arts and Lectures events. Past City Arts speakers have included author Salman Rushdie and comedian and author Al Franken. Also in the building are two galleries that charge no admission. The street-level **San Francisco Arts Commission Gallery** (☏ *415/554–6080* ⊒ *Free* ☾ *Wed.–Sat. noon–5*) displays the works of Bay Area artists. The **Museum of Performance & Design** (☏ *415/255–4800* ⊒ *Free* ☾ *Library Wed.–Sat. noon–5; gallery Tues.–Sat. noon–5*) occupies part of the fourth floor. A small gallery hosts interesting exhibitions, but the organization functions mainly as a library and research center for the San Francisco Bay Area's rich performing-arts legacy. ⊠ *401 Van Ness Ave., Civic Center* ⊕ *www.sfwmpac.org.*

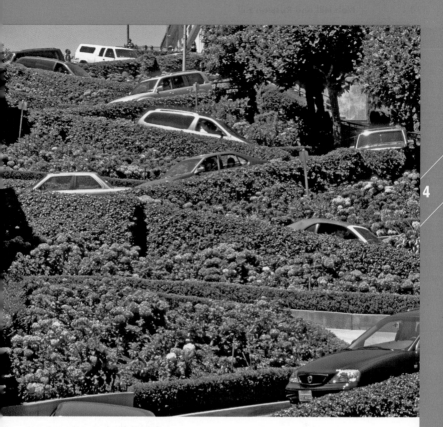

Nob Hill and Russian Hill

WORD OF MOUTH

"Rode the cable cars and what fun that is! . . . And a little scary when you are standing on the side that must squeeze past the cable car passing by in the opposite direction! Just couldn't believe the HILLS! Whose idea was it to build a city on all these hills? It's magnificent!"

—mwessel

GETTING ORIENTED

TOP 5 REASONS TO GO

Macondray Lane: Duck into this secret, lush garden lane and walk its narrow, uneven cobblestones.

Vallejo Steps area: Make the steep climb up to lovely Ina Coolbrith Park, then continue up along the glorious garden path of the Vallejo Steps to a spectacular view at the top.

San Francisco Art Institute: Contemplate a Diego Rivera mural and stop at the café for cheap organic coffee and a priceless view of the city and the bay. It may be the best way to spend an hour for a buck in town.

Cable Car Museum: Ride a cable car all the way back to the barn, hanging on tight as it clack-clack-clacks its way up Nob Hill, then go behind the scenes at the museum.

Play "Bullitt" on the steepest streets: For the ride of your life, take a drive up and down the city's steepest streets on Russian Hill. A trip over the precipice of Filbert or Jones will make you feel like you're falling off the edge of the world.

QUICK BITES

A harpist plays the classics and other tunes during afternoon tea at the **Ritz-Carlton, San Francisco** (✉ *600 Stockton St., at California St., Nob Hill* ☎ *415/296–7465* ⊕ *www.ritzcarlton.com*), served weekends 1–4:30. A holiday tradition, afternoon tea is served daily between Thanksgiving and Christmas.

Take a break from walking the hills at the original **Swensen's Ice Cream** (✉ *1999 Hyde St., at Union St., Russian Hill* ☎ *415/775–6818*), a neighborhood favorite since it opened in 1948. An antique sign still fronts the tiny shop, which has just a single counter inside, but concessions to the times include such ice-cream flavors as green tea and lychee.

GETTING THERE

The thing about Russian Hill and Nob Hill is that they're both especially steep hills. If you're not up for the hike, a cable car is certainly the most exciting way to reach the top. Take the California line for Nob Hill and the Powell–Hyde line for Russian Hill. There is some bus service as well, such as the 1–California bus for Nob Hill, but the routes only run east–west. Only the cable cars tackle the steeper north–south streets. Driving yourself is a hassle, since parking is a challenge on these crowded, precipitous streets.

MAKING THE MOST OF YOUR TIME

Since walking Nob Hill is (almost) all about gazing at exteriors, touring the neighborhood during daylight hours is a must. The sights here don't require a lot of visiting time—say a half hour each at the Cable Car Museum and Grace Cathedral—but allow plenty of time for the walk itself. An afternoon visit is ideal for Russian Hill, so you can browse the shops. You could cover both neighborhoods in three or four hours. If you time it just right, you can finish up with a sunset cocktail at one of the überswanky hotel lounges or the quirky Tonga Room.

4

Sightseeing
★★
Nightlife
★
Dining
★★★
Lodging
★★★
Shopping
★★

In place of the quirky charm and cultural diversity that mark other San Francisco neighborhoods, Nob Hill exudes history and good breeding. Topped with some of the city's most elegant hotels, Gothic Grace Cathedral, and private blue-blood clubs, it's the pinnacle of privilege. One hill over, across Pacific Avenue, is another old-family bastion, Russian Hill. It may not be quite as wealthy as Nob Hill, but it's no slouch—and it's known for its jaw-dropping views.

Updated by
Denise M. Leto

Nob Hill was officially dubbed during the 1870s when "the Big Four"—Charles Crocker, Leland Stanford, Mark Hopkins, and Collis Huntington, who were involved in the construction of the transcontinental railroad—built their hilltop estates. The lingo is thick from this era: those on the hilltop were referred to as "nabobs" (originally meaning a provincial governor from India) and "swells," and the hill itself was called Snob Hill, a term that survives to this day. By 1882 so many estates had sprung up on Nob Hill that Robert Louis Stevenson called it "the hill of palaces." But the 1906 earthquake and fire destroyed all the palatial mansions, except for portions of the Flood brownstone. History buffs may choose to linger here, but for most visitors, a casual glimpse from a cable car will be enough.

Essentially a tony residential neighborhood of spiffy pieds-à-terre, Victorian flats, Edwardian cottages, and boxlike condos, Russian Hill also has some of the city's loveliest stairway walks, hidden garden ways, and steepest streets—brave drivers can really have some fun here—not to mention those bay views. Several stories explain the origin of Russian Hill's name. One legend has it that Russian farmers raised vegetables here for Farallon Islands seal hunters; another attributes the name to a Russian sailor of prodigious drinking habits who drowned when he fell into a well on the hill. A plaque at the top of the Vallejo Steps gives credence to the version that says sailors of the Russian-American company were buried here in the 1840s. Be sure to visit the sign for yourself—its location offers perhaps the finest vantage point on the hill.

WHAT TO SEE IN NOB HILL

For details on the Cable Car Museum, see the Cable Cars feature in the Experience San Francisco chapter.

Fairmont San Francisco. The hotel's dazzling opening was delayed a year by the 1906 quake, but since then the marble palace has hosted presidents, royalty, movie stars, and local nabobs. Things have changed since its early days, however: on the eve of World War I you could get a room for as low as $2.50 per night, meals included. Nowadays, prices go as high as $8,000, which buys a night in the eight-room, Persian-art-filled penthouse suite that was showcased regularly in the 1980s TV series *Hotel.* Swing through the opulent lobby on your way to tea (served daily 2:30–4:30) at the **Laurel Court** restaurant. Don't miss an evening cocktail (a mai tai is in order) in the kitschy **Tonga Room,** complete with tiki huts, a sporadic tropical rainstorm, and a floating bandstand. ✉ *950 Mason St., Nob Hill* ☎ *415/772–5000* ⊕ *www.fairmont.com.*

LOOK FAMILIAR?

The grand Brocklebank Apartments, on the northeast corner of Sacramento and Mason streets across from the Fairmont hotel, might look eerily familiar. In 1958 the complex was showcased in Alfred Hitchcock's *Vertigo* (Jimmy Stewart starts trailing Kim Novak here) and in the 1990s it popped up in the miniseries *Tales of the City.*

Grace Cathedral. Not many churches can boast a Keith Haring sculpture and not one but two labyrinths. The seat of the Episcopal Church in San Francisco, this soaring Gothic-style structure, erected on the site of Charles Crocker's mansion, took 53 years to build, wrapping up in 1964. The gilded bronze doors at the east entrance were taken from casts of Lorenzo Ghiberti's incredible Gates of Paradise, which are on the Baptistery in Florence, Italy. A black-and-bronze stone sculpture of St. Francis by Beniamino Bufano greets you as you enter.

The 35-foot-wide labyrinth, a large, purplish rug with a looping pattern, is a replica of the 13th-century stone maze on the floor of Chartres Cathedral. All are encouraged to walk the ¼-mi-long labyrinth, a ritual based on the tradition of meditative walking. There's also a terrazzo outdoor labyrinth on the church's north side. The AIDS Interfaith Chapel, to the right as you enter Grace, contains a metal tryptich sculpture by the late artist Keith Haring and panels from the AIDS Memorial Quilt. ■TIP➔ Especially dramatic times to view the cathedral are during Thursday-night evensong (5:15) and during special holiday programs. ✉ *1100 California St., at Taylor St., Nob Hill* ☎ *415/749–6300* ⊕ *www.gracecathedral.org* ⊗ *Weekdays 7–6, Sat. 8–6, Sun. 7–7.*

InterContinental Mark Hopkins Hotel. Built on the ashes of railroad tycoon Mark Hopkins's grand estate (constructed at his wife's urging; Hopkins himself preferred to live frugally), this 19-story hotel went up in 1926. A combination of French château and Spanish Renaissance architecture, with noteworthy terra-cotta detailing, it has hosted statesmen, royalty, and Hollywood celebrities. The 11-room penthouse was turned into a glass-wall cocktail lounge in 1939: the **Top of the Mark** is

WALKING THE HILLS

Start a tour of Nob Hill and Russian Hill with a cable car ride up to **California and Powell streets** on Nob Hill (all lines go here). Walking two blocks east you can pass all the Big Four mansions-cum-hotels on the hill. Peek at the Keith Haring triptych in impressive **Grace Cathedral**; grab a Peet's coffee in the basement café if you need a lift. Next, head down to the **Cable Car Museum** to see the machinery in action. Then make your way to Russian Hill—a cable car is a fine way to reach the peak—to visit some of the city's loveliest hidden lanes and stairways. At **Mason** and **Vallejo streets,** head up the **Vallejo Steps,** passing contemplative, terraced **Ina Coolbrith Park** and beautifully tended private gardens. Take in the sweeping city and bay view from the top of the hill, then head right on **Jones Street** and duck right under the trellis to wooded and shady **Macondray Lane.** From here it's a six-block hike to crooked **Lombard Street.** If you've still got some steam, be sure to go another block to see **Diego Rivera's mural** and the surprise panoramic view from the **San Francisco Art Institute.**

remembered fondly by thousands of World War II veterans who jammed the lounge before leaving for overseas duty. Wives and sweethearts watching the ships depart gave the room's northwest nook its name—Weepers' Corner. With its 360-degree views, the lounge is a wonderful spot for a nighttime drink. ⊠ *999 California St., at Mason St., Nob Hill* ☎ *415/392–3434* ⊕ *www.markhopkins.net.*

Nob Hill Masonic Center. Erected by Freemasons in 1957, the hall is familiar to locals mostly as a concert and lecture venue, where such notables as Van Morrison and Al Gore have appeared. The recent Dan Brown–led spate of interest in the Masons and other secret fraternities unfortunately hasn't done anything to improve the sightlines or the seats here, but those interested in Masonic history can check out the impressive lobby mosaic. On the eve of his mosaic's renovation in 2005, artist Emile Norman wondered aloud, "How the hell did I do that?" Mainly in rich greens and yellows, the mosaic depicts the Masons' role in California history. There's also an intricate model of King Solomon's Temple in the lobby. ⊠ *1111 California St., Nob Hill* ☎ *415/776–4702* ⊕ *www.sfmasoniccenter.com* ⊗ *Lobby weekdays 8–5.*

Pacific Union Club. The former home of silver baron James Flood cost a whopping $1.5 million in 1886, when even a stylish Victorian like the Haas-Lilienthal House cost less than $20,000. All that cash did buy some structural stability. The Flood residence (to be precise, its shell) was the only Nob Hill mansion to survive the 1906 earthquake and fire. The Pacific Union Club, a bastion of the wealthy and powerful, purchased the house in 1907 and commissioned Willis Polk to redesign it; the architect added the semicircular wings and third floor. (The ornate fence design dates from the mansion's construction.) West of the house, Huntington Park is the site of the Huntington mansion, destroyed in 1906. Mrs. Huntington donated the land to the city for use as a park; the Crockers purchased the Fountain of the Tortoises, based on the original in Rome. ■TIP→ **The benches around the fountain offer a welcome break after climbing Nob Hill.** It's hard to get the skinny on the club itself; its 700 or so members allegedly follow the directive "no women, no Democrats, no reporters." Those who join usually spend decades on the waiting list and undergo a stringent vetting process, the rigors of which might embarrass the NSA. Needless to say, the club is closed to the public. ⊠ *1000 California St., Nob Hill.*

The Stanford Court Hotel. In 1876 trendsetter Leland Stanford, a California governor and founder of Stanford University, was the first to build an estate on Nob Hill. The only part that survived the earthquake was a basalt-and-granite wall that's been restored; check it out from the eastern side of the hotel. In 1912 an apartment house was built on the site of the former estate, and in 1972 the present-day hotel was constructed from the shell of that building. The lobby has a stained-glass dome and sepia-tone murals depicting scenes of early San Francisco. ⊠ *905 California St., Nob Hill* ☎ *415/989–3500* ⊕ *www.renaissancehotels.com.*

WHAT TO SEE IN RUSSIAN HILL

Feusier House. Octagonal houses were once thought to make the best use of space and enhance the physical and mental well-being of their occupants. A brief mid-19th-century craze inspired the construction of several in San Francisco. Only the Feusier House, built in 1857, and the Octagon House in Pacific Heights remain standing. A private residence, the Feusier House is easy to overlook unless you look closely— it's dwarfed by the large-scale apartments around it. Across from the Feusier House is the **1907 Firehouse** (⊠ *1088 Green St., Russian Hill*). Louise M. Davies, the local art patron for whom symphony hall is named, bought it from the city in 1957. The firehouse is closed to the public, but it's worth taking in the exterior. ⊠ *1067 Green St., Russian Hill.*

★ **Ina Coolbrith Park.** If you make it all the way up here, you may have the place all to yourself, or at least feel like you do. The park's terraces are carved from a hill so steep that it's difficult to see if anyone else is there or not. Locals love this park because it feels like a secret no one else knows about—one of the city's magic hidden gardens, with a meditative setting and spectacular views of the bay peeking out from among the trees. A poet, Oakland librarian, and niece of Mormon prophet Joseph Smith, Ina Coolbrith (1842–1928) introduced Jack London and Isadora Duncan to the world of books. For years she entertained literary greats in her Macondray Lane home near the park. In 1915 she was named poet laureate of California. ⊠ *Vallejo St. between Mason and Taylor Sts., Russian Hill.*

★ **Lombard Street.** The block-long "Crookedest Street in the World" makes eight switchbacks down the east face of Russian Hill between Hyde and Leavenworth streets. Residents bemoan the traffic jam outside their front doors, and occasionally the city attempts to discourage drivers by posting a traffic cop near the top of the hill, but the determined can find a way around. If no one is standing guard, join the line of cars waiting to drive down the steep hill, or avoid the whole mess and walk down

4

Where can I find . . . ?

PARKING	State Garage 818 Leavenworth St. Won't get you to the top of Nob Hill, but decent rates.	Lombardi Parking Garage 1600 Jackson St. Relatively close to the parking desert of Russian Hill.
A CUP OF COFFEE	Nook 1500 Hyde St. Coffee, chai tea, and healthy light meals.	Chameleon Café 1299 Pacific Ave. Retro Russian Hill spot with potent coffee and free Wi-Fi.
A DRUGSTORE	Walgreens 1300 Bush St. Grab a drink here if the hills are getting to you.	Walgreens 1524 Polk St. Open Mon.–Sat. until midnight, Sun. until 11 PM.

the steps on either side of Lombard. You take in super views of North Beach and Coit Tower whether you walk or drive—though if you're the one behind the wheel, you'd better keep your eye on the road lest you become yet another of the many folks who ram the garden barriers. ■TIP➔ **Can't stand the throngs? Thrill seekers of a different stripe may want to head two blocks south of Lombard to Filbert Street. At a gradient of 31.5%, the hair-raising descent between Hyde and Leavenworth streets is the city's steepest. Go slowly!** ⊠ *Lombard St. between Hyde and Leavenworth Sts., Russian Hill.*

Fodor'sChoice **Macondray Lane.** San Francisco has no shortage of impressive, grand
★ homes, but it's the tiny fairy-tale lanes that make most folks want to move here, and Macondray Lane is the quintessential hidden garden. Enter under a lovely wooden trellis and proceed down a quiet, cobbled pedestrian lane lined with Edwardian cottages and flowering plants and trees. ■TIP➔ **Watch your step—the cobblestones are quite uneven in spots.** A flight of steep wooden stairs at the end of the lane leads to Taylor Street—on the way down you can't miss the bay views. If you've read any of Armistead Maupin's *Tales of the City* books, you may find the lane vaguely familiar. It's the thinly disguised setting for part of the series' action. ⊠ *Between Jones and Taylor Sts., and Union and Green Sts., Russian Hill.*

★ **San Francisco Art Institute.** A Moorish-tile fountain in a tree-shaded courtyard draws the eye as soon as you enter the institute. The number-one reason for a visit is Mexican master Diego Rivera's *Making of a Fresco Showing the Building of a City* (1931), in the student gallery to your immediate left inside the entrance. Rivera himself is in the fresco—his broad behind is to the viewer—and he's surrounded by his assistants. They in turn are surrounded by a construction scene, laborers, and city notables such as sculptor Robert Stackpole and architect Timothy Pfleuger. *The Making of a Fresco* is one of three San Francisco murals painted by Rivera. The number-two reason to come here is the café, or more precisely the eye-popping, panoramic view from the café, which serves surprisingly decent food for a song.

The older portions of the Art Institute, including the lovely Mission-style bell tower, were erected in 1926. To this day, otherwise pragmatic people claim that ghostly footsteps can be heard in the tower

WORD OF MOUTH

"Wonderful stairways up though amazing garden areas with great views of the whole bay area and bridges. I huffed and puffed a bit but they were high points of the trip."   —suec1

at night. Ansel Adams created the school's fine-arts photography department in 1946, and school directors established the country's first fine-arts film program. Notable faculty and alumni have included painter Richard Diebenkorn and photographers Dorothea Lange, Edward Weston, and Annie Leibovitz. The **Walter & McBean Galleries** (☎ 415/749–4563 ☉ Tues.–Sat. 11–6) exhibit the often provocative works of established artists. ✉ 800 Chestnut St., North Beach ☎ 415/771–7020 ⊕ www.sfai. edu ✆ Galleries free ☉ Student gallery daily 8:30–8:30.

Vallejo Steps area. Several Russian Hill buildings survived the 1906 earthquake and fire and remain standing. Patriotic firefighters saved what's come to be known as the **Flag House** (✉ 1652–56 Taylor St., Russian Hill) when they spotted the American flag on the property and doused the flames with seltzer water and wet sand. The owner, a flag collector, fearing the house would burn to the ground, wanted it to go down in style, with "all flags flying."

The Flag House, at the southwest corner of Ina Coolbrith Park, is one of a number of California Shingle–style homes in this neighborhood, several of which were designed by Willis Polk. Polk also laid out the Vallejo Steps, which climb the steep ridge across Taylor Street from the Flag House. If the walk up the steps themselves is too steep for you, it's possible to park at the top of the steps by heading east on Vallejo from Jones. The **Polk-Williams House** (✉ Taylor and Vallejo Sts., Russian Hill) was designed by Polk, who lived in one of its finer sections. The architect also designed **1034–1036 Vallejo,** across the street from the Polk-Williams House. ✉ Taylor and Vallejo Sts., steps lead up toward Jones St., Russian Hill.

7–10 AM All available troops report to Mayor Eugene Schmitz and begin rescuing civilians.

10:30 AM "Ham and Egg Fire" is started by a family cooking breakfast. This fire destroys City Hall and advances south down Mission Street.

2:30 PM Soldiers begin dynamiting buildings around 5th and Mission streets to create firebreaks.

8:15 AM A major aftershock hits; many damaged buildings collapse.

1 PM The entire Financial District is in flames.

3 PM Mayor Schmitz issues "shoot to kill" order to police to quell looting and other crimes.

WEDNESDAY, APRIL 18, 1906

5:12 AM The brunt of the earthquake hits, with sharp shocks and violent shaking lasting up to a minute. Fifty-two fires start across the city.

EARTHQUAKE CITY

San Franciscans know that they are, quite literally, living on the edge. Multiple fault lines run through the Bay Area. Small, undetectable earthquakes rumble beneath the surface here every few days; a few each year are strong enough to feel. Yet residents are willing to tempt fate to live in this vibrant city, and usually the gamble pays off. But if you roll the dice often enough, eventually they come up snake eyes.

9 PM Firefighters attempt to stop fires from advancing up Nob Hill; they are unsuccessful.

5 AM Nob Hill mansions are engulfed in flames. Fire reaches Van Ness, where the army has dynamited mansions along the wide avenue to create a firebreak.

Firebreak at Van Ness is successful in the early morning, and the fire's westward movement is halted.

FRIDAY, APRIL 20

THURSDAY, APRIL 19

4 AM Secretary of War William Howard Taft orders rations, supplies, and "all the tents in the U.S. Army" sent to San Francisco.

SATURDAY, APRIL 21

Fire in the Mission is stopped at 20th and Dolores streets.

4

IN FOCUS EARTHQUAKE CITY

April 1906: A view of Sacramento Street looking east from Powell Street showing the destruction after the great earthquake.

1906: THE GREAT QUAKE AND FIRE

Looking down Sacramento Street as the fire rages.

It was dark at 5:12 AM on Wednesday, April 18, 1906—a peaceful midweek morning. A few early risers had just rolled out of bed to put a kettle on. High-society revelers, having attended the much-anticipated Metropolitan Opera of New York performance of *Carmen* Tuesday night, had only just shut their eyes. Night-shifters were still trudging home along the cobblestone avenues.

Seconds later, the face of San Francisco would change forever, after the most severe urban earthquake in known history and four days of uncontrollable fires ravaged the city. The toll would be massive: 28,188 buildings destroyed; $500 million in damages ($8–$12 billion in today's dollars); more than 3,000 dead; and, in a city of 400,000, approximately 225,000 residents left homeless.

Contrary to popular belief, the 1906 earthquake left many landmarks relatively unharmed—it was the subsequent fires that reduced San Francisco to rubble. Nearly all of the city's

"As soon as I reached the curb a second shock hit. . . . I was thrown flat and the cobblestones danced like corn in a popper."

—Thomas Jefferson Chase,
a Ferry Building ticket clerk

water mains were severed by the quake, leaving fires to rage unchecked for four days. By the time the flames subsided on Saturday, April 21, burned areas of the city extended more than 500 city blocks, from the bay west to Van Ness and south to 7th and Townsend streets. SoMa, the Financial District, North Beach, and other center-city neighborhoods were beyond repair. The death toll was estimated at just under 500 people—a number that stood until quite recently. But over the past 20 years, dogged research has upped that number to about 3,400. Most of the disaster's victims were consumed by the fires, buried in rubble, or were left uncounted because of their immigrant status.

BY THE NUMBERS

Magnitude: Estimated 7.9 on the moment magnitude scale. The energy unleashed was roughly the equivalent of 15 million tons of dynamite.

Area: Felt in an area of approximately 375,000 square miles, from Coquille, Oregon in the north (390 mi), to Los Angeles in the south (370 mi), to central Nevada in the east (340 mi).

Epicenter: 2 mi offshore, under the Pacific Ocean. **Speed:** Ruptures began at 14,000 mph, but slowed to 8,000 mph by the time they hit the city.

AREA DESTROYED BY FIRE

(top) Fire on Market Street.
(bottom) Clay Street in ruins.

LANDMARKS THAT REMAIN

Lotta's Fountain, at the intersection of Kearny and Market streets, was dedicated to the city in 1875; it's the oldest standing monument in San Francisco. A ceremony commemorating the Great Quake is held here every April 18 at 5:12 AM.

The 1889 **Audiffred Building** (Mission St. and the Embarcadero) was the only waterfront structure standing after the fires.

The exterior wall of the 42-room brownstone **Flood mansion** (1000 California St.), now the private Pacific Union Club, is the only intact pre-1906 building on Nob Hill.

The Italian renaissance palazzo–style **U.S. Post Office** (7th and Mission Sts.), completed in 1905, still stands.

Employees dramatically rescued the 1874 **Old U.S. Mint** (88 5th St.)—and the $300,000,000 in its vaults—from within, pumping water from an artesian well.

"The glass in our windows … melted down like butter; the sandstone and granite, of which the building was constructed, began to flake off with explosive noises like the firing of artillery."

—U.S. Mint Superintendent Frank Aleomon Leach

THE LITTLE HYDRANT THAT COULD

On Friday, April 20, 1906, fires raged through the Mission. The situation looked bleak, until locals alerted firemen to a working hydrant at 20th and Church streets. With help from refugees and "the Little Giant," firefighters were able to halt the fire's advance at 20th and Dolores streets, steps from the Mission Dolores. Each April, locals paint the hydrant gold in celebration.

Removing debris at Third, Kearney, and Market streets.

LOST TREASURES

The **Palace Hotel** (Market and Montgomery Sts.), built in 1876, was the city's most elegant and prestigious hotel, with 800 rooms, marble balconies, and elevators.

The huge, Beaux-Arts **City Hall**, finished in 1899, took 26 years and $6 million (about $130 million in today's dollars) to build. It collapsed in about a minute.

The most ostentatious displays of wealth in San Francisco were the **Nob Hill mansions** owned by railroad magnates Charles Crocker, Mark Hopkins, Leland Stanford, and Collis Huntington—San Francisco's "Big Four." Some considered the homes' destruction to be retribution for the millionaires' corrupt dealings.

REBUILDING

Grand plans to re-create San Francisco in the image of Paris or Washington were short-lived. Residents and business-owners, eager to erase the scars of the disaster, hastily rebuilt the city. Formerly opulent structures, such as City Hall, were reconstructed quickly, with simpler designs and cheaper materials. Graft scandals engulfed Mayor Schmitz, who was removed from office in summer 1907. By then, the last refugee houses were being pulled down. Two years later, about 20,000 new buildings had gone up.

LEARN MORE

The Bancroft Library, at UC Berkeley, has an excellent digital collection titled "The 1906 San Francisco Earthquake and Fire" (⊕ http://bancroft.berkeley.edu/collections/earthquakeandfire), with an interactive map and hundreds of photographs of the earthquake and fire.

The Virtual Museum of the City of San Francisco (⊕ www.sfmuseum.org) has the city's best collection of photographs and information about the event; it's available online only, except during special exhibitions.

The *San Francisco Chronicle's* coverage (⊕ www.sfgate.com/greatquake) includes first-person accounts, overview articles, and current-day assessments.

San Francisco City Guides (☎ 415/577–4266, ⊕ www.sfcityguides.org) gives earthquake and fire walking tours year-round.

> "They held on longest to their trunks, and over these trunks many a strong man broke his heart that night. The hills of San Francisco are steep, and up these hills, mile after mile, were the trunks dragged."
>
> —Jack London, for *Collier's* national weekly

1989: THE LOMA PRIETA QUAKE

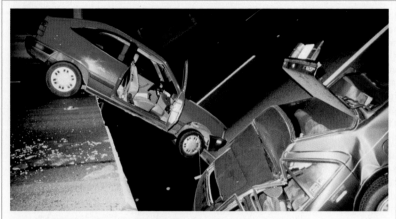

Smashed cars on the collapsed section of the Bay Bridge.

Excitement filled the Bay Area on October 17, 1989—it was Game 3 of the World Series between the Oakland Athletics and the San Francisco Giants. But as the players took the field of Candlestick Park, exhilaration turned to shock when, at 5:04 pm, a 6.9-magnitude earthquake shook the region.

At first, the thousands of fans in the ballpark thought it might be a joke, but then the field began to roll. The Giants' pitcher, Mike Krukow, said "It felt like a 600-pound gopher going underneath my feet at 40 miles an hour."

The Giants' stadium resisted damage, as did much of San Francisco, but the Marina district was not so lucky. It was built on filled-in marshland, which liquefied as it shook. (Liquefaction occurs when un-compacted soil is jolted and loosens, sinks, and shifts.) Parking garages below buildings collapsed. Fires broke out. To the east, a fifty-foot section of the Bay Bridge collapsed onto the lower deck, claiming one motorist's life. In Oakland, the top deck of the Cypress freeway crashed down, killing 42 drivers. In all, 62 people lost their lives in the earthquake, and 12,000 lost their homes.

The lack of damage from Loma Prieta was mainly due to luck. A blimp covering the World Series game filmed the Marina fires, alerting the fire chief to their existence since phone lines were down. Water lines were ruptured, but the Marina fires were put out by a fireboat that happened to be in the harbor. Winds were light, so the fires didn't spread. And traffic was light on the Bay Bridge, thanks to the World Series.

BY THE NUMBERS

Magnitude: 6.9 on the moment magnitude scale—about $\frac{1}{32}$ the force of the 1906 quake. The shaking lasted for about 15 seconds.

Area: Felt throughout central California and into western Nevada.

Epicenter: About 60 mi south-southeast of San Francisco, near Loma Prieta peak in the Santa Cruz Mountains.

Cost: Over $6 billion in damages (about $3 billion in San Francisco alone).

> "It was like something out of a Godzilla movie. There were people screaming, hollering, waving, every hellish sight you could imagine, every rescue you could imagine."
>
> —Oakland firefighter Mike Hill

4

IN FOCUS EARTHQUAKE CITY

SCIENTIFICALLY SPEAKING

Modern earthquake science was born after the 1906 quake. Geologists were stunned by the size and the massive north/south shift of the earth (nearly 20 feet in places), which could not be explained by the prevailing scientific belief that earthquakes themselves created faults. Subsequent studies led to the development of the theory of plate tectonics in the 1950s and 60s, now generally accepted as the cause of earthquakes.

THE NEXT BIG ONE

In 2002, the U.S. Geological Survey reported that there was a 62% chance that an earthquake of magnitude 6.7 or higher would hit the Bay Area before 2032, most likely occurring at the San Andreas Fault (which cuts the peninsula at its "neck") or at the Hayward Fault (which runs through Oakland and Berkeley).

Small quakes hit the Bay Area every few days, but are usually only magnitude 2 or 3, which most people don't even feel. Fewer than five quakes per year are large enough to be felt, but these are usually akin to the rumble of a tractor-trailer passing, and last only a few seconds. Since 1800, only four quakes have been categorized as "major," at a magnitude of 7.0 or higher.

Berkeley Digital Seismic Network, Northern California Seismic Network, USGS Low-Frequency Physical Network, and Parkfield High-Frequency Seismic Network all have instruments spread around the Bay Area: surface motion sensors, borehole geophones and accelerometers, tensor strain meters, GPS receivers, and ocean-bottom observatories are monitoring the area's shaky ground.

WHAT HAVE WE LEARNED?

Every earthquake teaches engineers a bit more, and modern building codes are such that it's unlikely that a new building would topple in an earthquake. In the Loma Prieta quake, newer up-to-code structures like the Transamerica Pyramid survived with barely a scrape. Unfortunately, modern building codes don't apply to older buildings unless they undergo renovation.

BART tunnels under the bay are not strong enough to withstand a major quake. The new, earthquake-ready eastern section of the Bay Bridge isn't scheduled for completion until 2013—more than 20 years after the Loma Prieta quake. Water pipeline upgrades are a work in progress, but are far from done. About 85% of the city's hospitals are not retrofitted. The entire Sunset neighborhood is on unstable ground and could collapse in a major quake, as buildings did in 1989. And an earthquake on the Hayward fault could destroy the Delta levee system, which supplies water to at least a third of the state of California.

Progress is being made, albeit slowly. Schools have been retrofitted for the most part, and other public buildings, like hospitals, have deadlines for retrofitting. By 2030, all hospitals must be fully functional in an earthquake.

The U.S. Geological Survey posts real-time earthquake maps and 24-hour forecasts on its Web site (⊕ http://quake.wr.usgs.gov/recent/index.html).

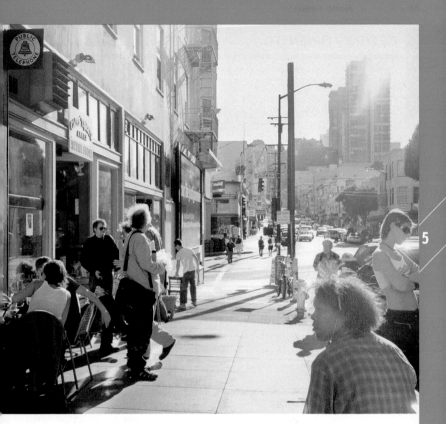

North Beach

WORD OF MOUTH

"We took the bus up Telegraph Hill and went to the top of Coit Tower . . . but the part I was really looking forward to was walking down the hill and looking for parrots. I'd seen the movie *The Wild Parrots of Telegraph Hill,* and the neighborhood was one of the things that meant 'San Francisco' to me. The neighborhood itself was beautiful, and we did indeed see parrots."   —sunny16

GETTING ORIENTED

0   350

0   1,000 ft

Pier 43

Pier 41

Pier 39

Pier 35

San Francisco Bay

Pier 33

Pier 31

Pier 29

◆ Fisherman's Wharf

Beach St.

NORTH BEACH

North Point St.

The Embarcadero

Taylor St. Cable Car

Mason St.

Powell St.

Stockton St.

Bay St.

Kearny St.

Pfeiffer St.

Chestnut St.

Chestnut St.

TELEGRAPH HILL

Lombard St.

Lombard St.

◆ Telegraph Hill

Greenwich Step

Tattoo Art Museum ◆

◆ Coit Tower

Napier La.

Greenwich St.

Saints Peter and Paul Catholic Church ◆

Medau Pl.

Filbert Steps

Levi Strau Headquar ◆

Genoa Pl.

1360 Montgomery St.

Mason St.

Filbert St.

Washington Square ◆

Columbus Ave.

Union

Jones St.

Union St.

Green St.

Grant Ave.

Kearny St.

Montgomery St.

Green St.

Sansome St.

Macondray La.

Taylor St.

Green St.

Vallejo St.

Romolo Pl.

Tunnel

Broadway

Cable Car

Stockton St.

City Lights Bookstore ◆

◆ Beat Museum

Kerouac Al.

◆ Sentinel Building

Jackson Square Historic District

Pacific Ave.

John St.

Cable Car

Jackson St.

CHINATOWN

Cable Car Museum ◆

Washington St.

Portsmouth Square

M. Twain Pl.

Clay St.

Commercial St.

TOP 5 REASONS TO GO

Espresso, espresso, espresso: Or cappuccino, Americano, mocha—however you take your caffeine, this is the neighborhood for it. Hanging out in a café constitutes sightseeing here, so find a chair and get to work.

Colorful watering holes: The high concentration of bars with character, like Tosca Café, makes North Beach the perfect neighborhood for a pub crawl.

Filbert Steps: Walk down this dizzying stairway from Telegraph Hill's Coit Tower, past lush private gardens and jaw-dropping bay views—and listen for the hill's famous screeching parrots.

Grant Avenue: Check out vanguard boutiques, rambling antiques shops, and cavernous old-time bars, all chockablock on narrow Grant Avenue. The best stuff is crowded into the four blocks between Columbus Avenue and Filbert Street.

Browsing books at City Lights: Illuminate your mind at this Beat-era landmark. Its great book selection, author events, and keen staff make it just as cool as ever.

QUICK BITES

Many consider the fresh-from-the-oven focaccia from **Liguria Bakery** (✉ *1700 Stockton St., at Filbert St., North Beach* ☎ *415/421–3786*) to be the best in the neighborhood. Get there early, before noon—when the focaccia is gone, the place usually closes.

The friendly *paesans* behind the counter at **Molinari Delicatessen** (✉ *373 Columbus Ave., North Beach* ☎ *415/421–2337*) serve up the most delicious, and quite possibly the biggest, sandwiches in town. Take a number, grab your bread from the bin, and gaze upon the sandwich board. If you want to eat in, say a prayer to the patron saint of table nabbing—there are all of three tables, outside. Fortunately, Washington Square park is close by.

GETTING THERE

The Powell–Mason cable-car line can drop you within a block of Washington Square park, in the heart of North Beach. The 30–Stockton and 15–3rd Street buses run to the neighborhood from Market Street. Once you're here, North Beach is a snap to explore on foot. It's mostly relatively flat—but climbing Telegraph Hill to reach Coit Tower is another story entirely.

MAKING THE MOST OF YOUR TIME

There's no bad time of day to visit this quarter. The cafés buzz morning to night, the shops along main drags Columbus Avenue and Broadway tend to stay open until at least 6 or 7 PM, and late-night revelers don't start checking their watches until about 2 AM. Sunday is quieter, since some shops close (though City Lights is open daily, until midnight).

Plan to spend a few hours here—it's all about lingering and the only major "sightseeing" spot is Coit Tower. The walk up to the tower is strenuous but rewarding; if you can tough it, make time for it. If you're driving, keep in mind that parking is difficult, especially at night.

5

Sightseeing
★★
Nightlife
★★★★
Dining
★★★
Lodging
★
Shopping
★★★

San Francisco novelist Herbert Gold calls North Beach "the longest-running, most glorious American bohemian operetta outside Greenwich Village." Indeed, to anyone who's spent some time in its eccentric old bars and cafés, North Beach evokes everything from the Barbary Coast days to the no-less-rowdy Beatnik era. Italian bakeries appear frozen in time, homages to Jack Kerouac and Allen Ginsberg pop up everywhere, and the modern equivalent of the Barbary Coast's "houses of ill repute," strip joints, do business on Broadway. With its outdoor café tables, throngs of tourists, and holiday vibe, this is probably the part of town Europeans are thinking of when they say San Francisco is the most European city in America.

Updated by
Denise M. Leto

The neighborhood truly was a beach at the time of the gold rush—the bay extended into the hollow between Telegraph and Russian hills. Among the first immigrants to Yerba Buena during the early 1840s were young men from the northern provinces of Italy. The Genoese started the fishing industry in the newly renamed boomtown of San Francisco, as well as a much-needed produce business. Later, Sicilians emerged as leaders of the fishing fleets and eventually as proprietors of the seafood restaurants lining Fisherman's Wharf. Meanwhile, their Genoese cousins established banking and manufacturing empires.

Once almost exclusively Italian-American, today North Beach is a mixture of Italian (many of them elderly), Chinese, and San Francisco yuppie, the last among the few able to afford moving here after neighborhood real estate prices began their steep ascent in the late 1990s. But walk down narrow Romolo Place (off Broadway east of Columbus) or Genoa Place (off Union west of Kearny) or Medau Place (off Filbert west

A NORTH BEACH WALK

To hit the highlights of the neighborhood, start off with a browse at Beat landmark **City Lights Bookstore**. For cool boutique shopping, head north up **Grant Avenue**. Otherwise, it's time to get down to the serious business of hanging out. Make a left onto **Columbus Avenue** when you leave the bookstore and walk the strip until you find a café table or pastry display that calls your name.

Fortified, continue down Columbus to **Washington Square**, where

you can walk or take the 39 bus up **Telegraph Hill** to Coit Tower's views. Be sure to take in the gorgeous gardens along the **Filbert Steps** on the way down. Finally, reward yourself by returning to **Columbus Avenue** for a drink at one of the atmosphere-steeped watering holes like Tosca, which is run by a woman Sean Penn calls "the last of the great saloon mistresses."

5

of Grant) and you can feel the immigrant Italian roots of this neighborhood. Locals know that most of the city's finest Italian restaurants are elsewhere, but North Beach is the place that puts folks in mind of Italian food, and there are many decent options to choose from. Bakeries sell focaccia fresh from the oven; eaten warm or cold, it's the perfect portable food. Many other aromas fill the air: coffee beans, deli meats and cheeses, Italian pastries, and—always—pungent garlic. ⇨ *For more on the North Beach food scene, see the Where to Eat chapter.*

WHAT TO SEE

Beat Museum. It's hard to tell whether the folks who opened this small museum in 2006 are serious—what would the counterculture say about the $18 "Beat beret"? But if you're truly Beat-curious, stop by. Check out the "Beat pad," a mockup of one of the cheap, tiny North Beach apartments the writers and artists populated in the 1950s, complete with bongos and bottle-as-candleholder. Memorabilia includes the shirt Neal Cassady wore while driving Ken Kesey's Merry Prankster bus, "Further." An early photo of the legendary bus is juxtaposed with a more current picture showing it covered with moss and overgrowth, labeled "Nothing lasts." Indeed. There are also manuscripts, letters, and early editions by Jack Kerouac, Allen Ginsberg, and Lawrence Ferlinghetti. The gift store has a good selection of Beat philosophy, though it's nothing you won't find across the street at City Lights. ⊠ *540 Broadway, North Beach* ☎ *415/399–9626* ⊕ *www.thebeatmuseum.org* ⌨ *$5* ⊙ *Mon. and Tues 10–6, Wed.–Sun. 10–10.*

★ **City Lights Bookstore.** Take a look at the exterior of the store: the replica of a revolutionary mural destroyed in Chiapas, Mexico, by military forces; the poetry in the windows; and the sign that says "Turn your sell [sic] phone off. Be here now." This place isn't just doling out best sellers. Designated a city landmark, the hangout of Beat-era writers—Allen Ginsberg and store founder Lawrence Ferlinghetti among them—remains a vital part of San Francisco's literary scene. Browse the three

False rumors persist that Coit Tower was made in the image of a fire hose nozzle.

levels of sometimes haphazardly arranged poetry, philosophy, politics, fiction, history, and local 'zines, to the tune of creaking wood floors. ■TIP➜ Be sure to check their calendar of literary events.

Back in the day, the basement was a kind of literary living room, where writers like Ginsberg and Kerouac would read and even receive mail. Ferlinghetti cemented City Lights' place in history by publishing Ginsberg's *Howl and Other Poems* in 1956. The small volume was ignored in the mainstream . . . until Ferlinghetti and the bookstore manager were arrested for corruption of youth and obscenity. In the landmark First Amendment trial that followed, the judge exonerated both, saying a work that has "redeeming social significance" can't be obscene. *Howl* went on to become a classic.

Kerouac Alley, branching off Columbus Avenue next to City Lights, was rehabbed in 2007. Embedded in the pavement are quotes from Lawrence Ferlinghetti, Maya Angelou, Confucius, John Steinbeck, and of course, the namesake himself. ✉ *261 Columbus Ave., North Beach* ☎ *415/362–8193* ⊕ *www.citylights. com* ☉ *Daily 10* AM*–midnight.*

★ **Coit Tower.** Whether you think it resembles a fire hose or something more, ahem, adult, this 210-foot tower is among San Francisco's most distinctive skyline sights. Although the monument wasn't

WORD OF MOUTH

"One of my favorite things to do in North Beach is to have a picnic in Washington Square Park. Pick up a panini on Columbus Ave. and then sit in the park and eat it. On a nice day, this is some of the best people watching in town."

—erin74

3 Reasons To Love the Espresso in North Beach

Cafés are a way of life in North Beach, and if you're serious about your coffee as the average San Franciscan (or Fodor's editor), you might want to stop in at all three of these spots.

The Giotta family celebrates the art of a good espresso as well as a good tune at **Caffè Trieste** (✉ *601 Vallejo St., at Grant Ave., North Beach* ☎ *415/392–6739*). Every Saturday (as they have since 1971) from noon to 2 PM, the family presents a weekly musical. Arrive early to secure seats. The program ranges from Italian pop and folk music to operas, and patrons are encouraged to participate. If you're one of the few people in creation who haven't gotten started on a screenplay, you may take inspiration from the fact that Francis Ford Coppola reportedly wrote the screenplay for *The Godfather* here.

Intimate, triangular **Mario's Bohemian Cigar Store** (✉ *566 Columbus Ave., North Beach* ☎ *415/362–0536*) serves up great hot focaccia sandwiches and North Beach–worthy

espresso at its few tables and beautiful antique oak bar under old-time posters. On sunny days, take your order across the street to Washington Square for a classic San Francisco picnic.

A glance at the menu board— "Espresso: $1.80, Espresso with lemon: $10"—will clue you in that **Caffè Roma** (✉ *526 Columbus Ave., North Beach* ☎ *415/296–7942*) takes its coffee a lot more seriously than it takes itself. And if you've got a problem with that, owner Tony Azzollini will convince you, from his refusal to make your coffee extra hot to his insistence that you drink your espresso the moment it's brewed. Airy and decidedly undistracting—black and white marble is the predominant theme—Roma is a no-nonsense coffee drinker's pit stop for a hot cup as well as coffee drinks, pastries, and wine. Spot the massive red roaster in the window and you'll know you're here. And if you insist on the lemon twist, you deserve to pay.

---

intended as a tribute to firemen, it's often considered as such because of the donor's special attachment to the local fire company. As the story goes, a young gold rush–era girl, Lillie Hitchcock Coit (known as Miss Lil), was a fervent admirer of her local fire company—so much so that she once deserted a wedding party and chased down the street after her favorite engine, Knickerbocker No. 5, while clad in her bridesmaid finery. She became the Knickerbocker Company's mascot and always signed her name "Lillie Coit 5." When Lillie died in 1929 she left the city $125,000 to "expend in an appropriate manner . . . to the beauty of San Francisco."

You can ride the elevator to the top of the tower—the only thing you have to pay for here—to enjoy the view of the Bay Bridge and the Golden Gate Bridge; due north is Alcatraz Island. ■TIP➔ The views from the base of the tower are also expansive—and free. Parking at Coit Tower is limited; in fact, you may have to wait (and wait) for a space. Save yourself some frustration and take the 39 bus which goes all the way up to

Where can I find . . . ?

PARKING	North Beach Garage	Vallejo Street Garage
	735 Vallejo St.	766 Vallejo St.
	Open 24 hours and each space is printed with a fortune.	Bonus: great view from the top floor.

SOMETHING SWEET	Stella Pastry & Café	Victoria Pastry Co.
	446 Columbus Ave.	1362 Stockton St.
	It's all about the creamy sacripantina cake.	Look for the custardy St. Honoré cake, cooked in a brick oven.

A NIGHTCAP	Tosca Café	Vesuvio
	242 Columbus Ave.	255 Columbus Ave.
	A time-warp saloon, with brandy-spiked cappuccino.	A true 1960s boho hangout.

the tower's base or, if you're in good shape, hike up. ⇨ *For more details on the lovely stairway walk, see the Telegraph Hill listing.*

Inside the tower, 19 Depression-era murals depict California's economic and political life. The federal government commissioned the paintings from 25 local artists, and ended up funding quite a controversy. The radical Mexican painter Diego Rivera inspired the murals' socialist-realist style, with its biting cultural commentary, particularly about the exploitation of workers. At the time the murals were painted, clashes between management and labor along the waterfront and elsewhere in San Francisco were widespread. ⊠ *Telegraph Hill Blvd. at Greenwich St. or Lombard St., North Beach* ☏ *415/362–0808* 🖃 *Free; elevator to top $5* ⊘ *Daily 10–6.*

OFF THE
BEATEN
PATH
Tattoo Art Museum. Legendary tattoo artist and historian Lyle Tuttle's collection of tattoo memorabilia fills half this crowded tattoo parlor on the edge of North Beach. Exhibits, including equipment, photographs, newspaper clippings, and a stuffed bat, cover everything from primitive tattooing in Samoa (where the bat comes in) to tattooing in San Francisco in the 1960s. ⊠ *841 Columbus Ave., near Lombard St., North Beach* ☏ *415/775–4991* 🖃 *Free* ⊘ *Daily noon–8.*

Grant Avenue. Originally called Calle de la Fundación, Grant Avenue is the oldest street in the city, but it's got plenty of young blood. Here dusty bars such as the Saloon and perennial favorites like the Savoy Tivoli mix with hotshot boutiques, odd curio shops like the antique jumble that is Aria, atmospheric cafés such as the boho haven Caffè Trieste, and authentic Italian delis. While the street runs from Union Square through Chinatown, North Beach, and beyond, the fun stuff in this neighborhood is crowded into the four blocks between Columbus Avenue and Filbert Street. ⊠ *North Beach.*

Levi Strauss headquarters. The carefully landscaped complex appears so collegiate that it's affectionately known as LSU—short for Levi Strauss

The Birds

While on Telegraph Hill, you might be startled by a chorus of piercing squawks and a rushing sound of wings. No, you're not about to have a Hitchcock bird-attack moment. These small, vivid green parrots with cherry-red heads number in the hundreds; they're descendants of former pets that escaped or were released by their owners. (The birds dislike cages and they bite if bothered...must've been some disillusioned owners along the way.)

The parrots like to roost high in the aging cypress trees on the hill, chattering and fluttering, sometimes taking wing en masse. They're not popular with most residents, but they did find a champion in local bohemian Mark Bittner, a former street musician. Bittner began chronicling their habits, publishing a book and battling the homeowners who wanted to cut down the cypresses. A documentary, *The Wild Parrots of Telegraph Hill*, made the issue a cause célèbre. In 2007 City Hall, which recognizes a golden goose when it sees one, stepped in and brokered a solution to keep the celebrity birds in town. The city will cover the homeowners' insurance worries and plant new trees for the next generation of wild parrots.

—Denise M. Leto

University. Lawns complement the redbrick buildings, and gurgling fountains drown out the sounds of traffic, providing a perfect environment for brown-bag and picnic lunches. The lobby visitor center has six displays focusing on the history of the company, including a vintage ad exhibit and the latest Levi products. The Filbert Steps to Coit Tower are across the street. ⊠ *Levi's Plaza, 1155 Battery St., North Beach*.

Saints Peter and Paul Catholic Church. Camera-toting visitors focus their lenses on the Romanesque splendor of what's often called the Italian Cathedral. Completed in 1924, the church has Disneyesque stone-white towers that are local landmarks. Mass reflects the neighborhood; it's given in English, Italian, and Chinese. (It's one of the few churches in town where you can hear mass in Italian.) Following their 1954 City Hall wedding, Marilyn Monroe and Joe DiMaggio had their wedding photos snapped here. ■TIP→ On the first Sunday of October a mass followed by a parade to Fisherman's Wharf celebrates the Blessing of the Fleet. Another popular event is the Columbus Day pageant in North Beach, with a parade that ends at the church. ⊠ *666 Filbert St., at Washington Sq., North Beach* ☎ 415/421–0809 ⊕ *www.stspeterpaul.san-francisco. ca.us/church*.

Sentinel Building. A striking triangular shape and a gorgeous green patina make this 1907 building at the end of Columbus Avenue a visual knockout. In the 1970s local filmmaker Francis Ford Coppola bought the building to use for his production company. The ground

WORD OF MOUTH

"One strong point is that [North Beach] is often sunny and warm when other parts of SF are cold and/or foggy. It is low-keyed and casual. Well, maybe not low-key on weekend nights, but it is fun."

—LoveItaly

floor is now Coppola's stylish wine bar, **Café Zoetrope.** Stop in for wines from the Coppola vineyards in Napa and Sonoma, simple Italian dishes, and foodie gifts. ⊠ *916 Kearny St., at Columbus Ave., North Beach.*

Fodor's Choice ★

Telegraph Hill. Hill residents have some of the best views in the city, as well as the most difficult ascents to their aeries. The hill rises from the east end of Lombard Street to a height of 284 feet and is capped by Coit Tower (*see above*). Imagine lugging your groceries up that!

O PIONEERS!

The corner of Broadway and Columbus Avenue witnessed an unusual historic breakthrough. Here stood the Condor Club where, in 1964, Carol Doda became the country's first dancer to break the topless barrier. A bronze plaque honors the milestone (only in SF). And Doda, naturally, now owns a lingerie store in Cow Hollow.

If you brave the slope, though, you can be rewarded with a "secret treasure" SF moment. Filbert Street starts up the hill, then becomes the Filbert Steps when the going gets too steep. You can cut between the Filbert Steps and another flight, the Greenwich Steps, on up to the hilltop. As you climb, you can pass some of the city's oldest houses and be surrounded by beautiful, flowering private gardens. In some places the trees grow over the stairs so they feel like a green tunnel; elsewhere, you'll have wide-open views of the bay. And the telegraphic name? It comes from the hill's status as the first Morse code signal station back in 1853. ⊠ *Bordered by Lombard, Filbert, Kearny, and Sansome Sts., North Beach.*

OFF THE BEATEN PATH

1360 Montgomery Street. In the 1947 film *Dark Passage* Humphrey Bogart plays an escaped prisoner from San Quentin convicted of killing his wife. His real-life wife, Lauren Bacall, befriends him and lets him hole up in her apartment, inside this fantastic art-deco building. From the street you can view the etched-glass gazelles and palms counterpointing a silvered fresco of a heroic bridge worker. ⊠ *Montgomery St. between Union and Filbert Sts., near top of Filbert Steps, North Beach.*

Washington Square. Once the daytime social heart of Little Italy, this grassy patch has changed character numerous times over the years. The Beats hung out in the 1950s, hippies camped out in the 1960s and early '70s, and nowadays you're just as likely to see kids of Southeast Asian descent tossing a Frisbee as Italian men or women chat about their children and the old country. In the morning elderly Asians perform the motions of tai chi, but by mid-morning groups of conservatively dressed Italian men in their 70s and 80s begin to arrive. Any time of day, the park may attract a number of homeless people, who stretch out to rest on the benches and grass, and young locals sunbathing or running their dogs. Lillie Hitchcock Coit, in yet another show of affection for San Francisco's firefighters, donated the statue of two firemen with a child they rescued. ■TIP→ The North Beach Festival, the city's oldest street fair, celebrates the area's Italian culture here each June. ⊠ *Bordered by Columbus Ave. and Stockton, Filbert, and Union Sts., North Beach.*

On the Waterfront

WORD OF MOUTH

"In San Francisco locals don't go to Fisherman's Wharf . . . in New York City they don't go to The Statue of Liberty, etc. Fisherman's Wharf is tacky. So what? It's famous. Check it out and decide for yourself."

—happytrailstoyou

GETTING ORIENTED

← Angel Island

KEY
b BART statio

San Francisco Bay

Hyde Street Pier
Pier 45
Pier 47
Pier 41
Pier 35
Pier 33
Aquatic Park
Fisherman's Wharf
Pier 39
Pier 31
San Francico National Maritime Museum
Jefferson St.
Pier 29
NORTH BEACH
Beach St.
North Point St.
Pier 27
Ghirardelli Square
Bay St.
Bay St.
Francisco St.
Pier 23
Chestnut St.
Pier 19
Lombard St.
Pier 17
Lombard St.
TELEGRAPH HILL
Coit Tower
Pier 15
Greenwich St.
Pier 9
Filbert St.
Washington Sq.
Union St.
Pier 7
Union St.
Green St.
Pier 5
Green St.
Vallejo St.
Vallejo St.
Pier 3
Broadway
Pier 1
RUSSIAN HILL
Tunnel
San Francisco Brewing Company
Broadway
Pacific Ave.
Pacific Ave.
Jackson Square
Justin Herman Plaza
Jackson St.
Washington St.
Ferry Building
Washington St.
Transamerica Pyramid
Clay St.
Hyatt Rengency
Cable Car Museum
Sacramento St.
San Francisco Railway Museum
California St.
Wells Fargo Bank History Museum
EMBARCADERO
NOB HILL
Pine St.
Bush St.
Sutter St.
DOWNTOWN
Market Street Buildings
Post St.
MONTGOMERY ST.
Union Sq.
Geary St.
O'Farrell St.
Ellis St.
UNION SQUARE
MONTGOMERY ST.
Eddy St.
Turk St.
Yerba Buena Gardens
Golden Gate Ave.
Old U.S. Mint
CIVIC CENTER
Grove St.
Main Post Office
SOMA
CIVIC CENTER
Pier 34
Pier 38
Pier 40
Pier 42
Pacific Bell Park
South Be Harbo
S.F. Tennis Club
Caltrain Depot
Hall Of Justice And Co. Jail
Pier 48
Pier 50
Hover Port
0   500

0   1,50

GETTING THERE

The Powell–Hyde and Powell–Mason cable-car lines both end near Fisherman's Wharf. The walk from downtown through North Beach to the northern waterfront is lovely, and if you stick to Columbus Avenue, the incline is relatively gentle. F-line trolleys, often packed to capacity, run all the way down Market to the Embarcadero, then north to the Wharf.

TOP 5 REASONS TO GO

Ferry Building: Join locals eyeing luscious produce and foods prepared by some of the city's best chefs at San Francisco's premier farmers' market on Saturday morning.

Hyde Street Pier: Sing sea chanteys and raise the sails aboard the gorgeously restored 19th-century square-rigged ship *Balclutha*, then head to the Buena Vista for an Irish coffee.

Alcatraz: Go from a scenic bay tour to "the hole"—solitary confinement in absolute darkness—while inmates and guards tell you stories about what life was really like on the Rock.

F-line: Grab a polished wooden seat aboard one of the city's lovingly restored vintage streetcars and clatter down the tracks toward the Ferry Building's spire.

Musée Mécanique: Take a pocketful of quarters and step through the gaping mouth of Laffing Sal to this arcade of vintage machines.

QUICK BITES

The Ferry Building is everyone's favorite spot for a bite on the Embarcadero. Gather bread, cheese, and fruit for a picnic, or grab something to go from **Out the Door** (⊠ *1 Ferry Plaza, Embarcadero* ☎ *415/321–3740*), beloved Vietnamese restaurant Slanted Door's takeout counter. If you need a sweet treat, head to pink **Miette** (⊠ *1 Ferry Plaza, Embarcadero* ☎ *415/837–0300*), where the cakes and pastries are absolute organic perfection.

MAKING THE MOST OF YOUR TIME

If you're planning to go to Alcatraz, be sure to buy your tickets in advance, as tours frequently sell out. Alcatraz ferries now leave from Pier 33—so there isn't a single good reason to suffer Pier 39's tacky, overpriced attractions. If you're a sailor at heart, definitely spend an hour with the historic ships of Hyde Street Pier.

FERRIES

The bay is a huge part of San Francisco's charm, and getting out on the water gives you an attractive and unique (though windy) perspective on the city. Keep in mind that a ride on a commuter ferry is cheaper than a cruise, and just as lovely. The **Red and White Fleet** (⊠ *Pier 43½, Fisherman's Wharf* ☎ *415/673–2900* ⊕ *www.redandwhite.com*) has the widest range of tour options, including sunset cruises from April to October. The **Blue & Gold Fleet** (⊠ *Pier 41, Fisherman's Wharf* ☎ *415/705–5555* ⊕ *www.blueandgoldfleet.com*) is essentially a ferry company, with service to Oakland, Alameda, Tiburon, Sausalito, Vallejo, and Angel Island.

6

Sightseeing
★★
Nightlife
–
Dining
★★★
Lodging
★★★★
Shopping
★★

San Francisco's waterfront neighborhoods have fabulous views and utterly different personalities. Kitschy, overpriced Fisherman's Wharf struggles to maintain the last shreds of its existence as a working wharf, while Pier 39 is a full-fledged consumer circus. The Ferry Building draws well-heeled locals with its culinary pleasures, firmly reconnecting the Embarcadero to downtown. Between the Ferry Building and Pier 39 a former maritime no-man's land is filling in a bit—especially near Pier 33, where the perpetually booked Alcatraz cruises depart—with a waterfront restaurant here and a restored pedestrian-friendly pier there.

Updated by
Denise M. Leto

Today's shoreline was once Yerba Buena Cove, filled in during the latter half of the 19th century, when San Francisco was a brawling, extravagant gold-rush town. Jackson Square, now a genteel and upscale corner of the inland Financial District, was the heart of the Barbary Coast, bordering some of the roughest wharves in the world. Below Montgomery Street (in today's Financial District), between California Street and Broadway, lies a remnant of these wild days: more than 100 ships abandoned by frantic crews and passengers caught up in gold fever lie under the foundations of buildings here.

WHAT TO SEE

Angel Island. For an outdoorsy adventure, consider a day at this island northwest of Alcatraz. Discovered by Spaniards in 1775 and declared a U.S. military reserve 75 years later, the island was used as a screening ground for Asian immigrants—who were often held for months, even years, before being granted entry—from 1910 until 1940. Since 2009 you can visit the restored Immigration Station; from the dock where detainees landed to the barracks where you can see the poems in Japanese script they etched onto the walls. In 1963 the government designated Angel Island a state park. Today people come for picnics, hikes along the scenic 5-mi path that winds around the island's perimeter, and tram tours that explain the park's history; venture inland and you'll likely see evidence of the 2008 fire that swept more than half of the island's 740 acres. Twenty-five bicycles are permitted on the ferry on a first-come, first-served basis, and you can rent mountain bikes for $10 an hour or $35 a day at the landing (daily April–October; call during other times). There are also a dozen primitive campsites. Blue and Gold Fleet is the only Angel Island ferry service with departures from

F-LINE TROLLEYS

The F-line, the city's system of vintage electric trolleys, gives the cable cars a run for their money as San Francisco's best-loved mode of transportation. These beautifully restored streetcars—some dating from the 19th century—run from the Castro all the way down Market Street to the Embarcadero, then north to Fisherman's Wharf. Each car is unique, restored to the colors of its city of origin, from New Orleans and Philadelphia to Moscow and Milan. Purchase tickets on board; exact change is required. ⊕ *www.streetcar.org* ⊠ *$2.*

6

San Francisco. Boats leave from Pier 41 and the Ferry Building. ⊠ *Pier 41, Fisherman's Wharf* ☎ *415/435–1915 park information and ferry schedules, 415/705–5555, 800/426–8687 tickets* ⊕ *www.angelisland. org* ⊠ *$18* ☉ *Daily 8 AM to sunset.*

NEED A BREAK?   Even locals love the cheery **Buena Vista Café** (⊠ *2765 Hyde St., Fisherman's Wharf* ☎ *415/474–5044*), which claims to be the first place in the United States to have served Irish coffee. The café opens at 9 AM weekdays (8 AM weekends) and dishes up a great breakfast. They serve about 2,000 Irish coffees a day, so it's always crowded; try for a table overlooking nostalgic Victorian Park and its cable-car turntable.

Fodor's Choice ★   **Ferry Building.** Renovated in 2003, the Ferry Building is the jewel of the Embarcadero. The beacon of the port area, erected in 1896, has a 230-foot clock tower modeled after the campanile of the cathedral in Seville, Spain. On the morning of April 18, 1906, the tower's four clock faces, powered by the swinging of a 14-foot pendulum, stopped at 5:17—the moment the great earthquake struck—and stayed still for 12 months.

Today San Franciscans flock to the street-level Market Hall, stocking up on supplies from local favorites such as Acme Bread, Scharffen Berger Chocolate, and Cowgirl Creamery. Lucky diners claim a coveted table at Slanted Door, the city's beloved high-end Vietnamese restaurant. The seafood bars at Hog Island Oyster Company and Ferry Plaza Seafood have fantastic city panoramas—or you can take your purchases around to the building's bay side, where benches face views of the Bay Bridge. Saturday mornings the plaza in front of the building buzzes with an upscale, celebrity-chef-studded farmers' market. Extending from the piers on the north side of the building south to the Bay Bridge, the waterfront promenade is a favorite among joggers and picnickers,

with a front-row view of the sailboats slipping by. The Ferry Building also serves actual ferries: from
behind the building they sail to Sausalito, Larkspur, Tiburon, and the
East Bay. ⊠ *Embarcadero at foot of
Market St., Embarcadero* ⊕ *www.
ferrybuildingmarketplace.com.*

WORD OF MOUTH

"Went to Musee Mecanique and
got a huge kick out of all of the
antique arcade machines from an
era gone by.... Our kids thought
this place was an absolute
scream!" —mwessel

Fisherman's Wharf. It may be one of
the city's best-known attractions,
but the wharf is a no-go zone for most locals, who shy away from the
difficult parking, overpriced food, and cheesy shops at third-rate shopping centers like the Cannery at Del Monte Square. If you just can't
resist a visit here, come early to avoid the crowds and get a sense of the
wharf's functional role—it's not just an amusement park replica.

Most of the entertainment at the wharf is schlocky and overpriced, with
one notable exception: the splendid **Musée Mécanique** (☎ *415/346–
2000* ⊙ *Weekdays 10–7, weekends 10–8*), a time-warped arcade with
antique mechanical contrivances, including peep shows and nickel-
odeons. Some favorites are the giant and rather creepy "Laffing Sal"
(you enter the museum through his gaping mouth), an arm-wrestling
machine, the world's only steam-powered motorcycle, and mechanical
fortune-telling figures that speak from their curtained boxes. Note the
depictions of race that betray the prejudices of the time: stoned Chinese
figures in the "Opium-Den" and clown-faced African-Americans eating
watermelon in the "Mechanical Farm." Admission is free, but you'll
need quarters to bring the machines to life.

Among the two floors of exhibits at **Ripley's Believe It or Not! Museum**
(⊠ *175 Jefferson St., Fisherman's Wharf* ☎ *415/771–6188* ⊕ *www.
ripleysf.com* 🖃 *$14.99* ⊙ *Late June–Labor Day, Sun.–Thurs.* 9 AM–11
PM, *Fri. and Sat.* 9 AM–*midnight; Labor Day–early June, Sun.–Thurs.*
10–10, *Fri. and Sat.,* 10 AM–*midnight*) is a tribute to San Francisco—an
8-foot-long scale model of a cable car, made entirely of matchsticks.
Notables from local boy Robin Williams to Jesus await at the **Wax
Museum** (⊠ *145 Jefferson St., Fisherman's Wharf* ☎ *415/202–0400 or
800/439–4305* ⊕ *www.waxmuseum.com*), open weekdays 10–9, weekends 9 AM–11 PM. Admission is $14.

The USS *Pampanito* (⊠ *Pier 45, Fisherman's Wharf* ☎ *415/775–1943*
⊕ *www.maritime.org/pamphome.htm* ⊙ *Oct.–Memorial Day, Sun.–
Thurs.* 9–6, *Fri. and Sat.* 9–8; *Memorial Day–Sept., Thurs.–Tues.* 9–8,
Wed. 9–6) provides an intriguing if mildly claustrophobic glimpse into
life on a submarine during World War II. The sub sank six Japanese
warships and damaged four others. Admission is $10; the family pass
is a great deal at $20 for two adults and up to four kids. ⊠ *Jefferson St.
between Leavenworth St. and Pier 39, Fisherman's Wharf.*

**OFF THE
BEATEN
PATH**

S.S. *Jeremiah O'Brien.* A participant in the D-day landing in Normandy
during World War II, this Liberty Ship freighter is one of two such
vessels (out of 2,500 built) still in working order. To keep the 1943
ship in sailing shape, the steam engine—which appears in the film

Titanic—is operated dockside seven times a year on special "steaming weekends." Cruises take place several times a year between May and October, and the vessel is open to visitors daily. ⊠ *Pier 45, Fisherman's Wharf* ☎ *415/544–0100* ⊕ *www.ssjeremiahobrien.org* ☞ *$10* ☉ *Daily 9–4.*

Ghirardelli Square. Most of the red-brick buildings in this early-20th-century complex were once part of the Ghirardelli factory. Now tourists come here to pick up the famous chocolate, but you can purchase it all over town and save yourself a trip to what is essentially a mall.

ALCATRAZ'S FUTURE

Alcatraz is currently undergoing an extensive restoration, and funds are being raised to renovate and reopen outbuildings that have been closed for years. The jail cells' vintage locks are also slated to be repaired. Tours of the island once included briefly locking members into cells—but this hasn't been a part of the program since corroded lock mechanisms began sticking, *really* locking some people in!

(If you're a shopaholic, though, it definitely beats the Cannery.) There are no fewer than three Ghirardelli stores here, as well as gift shops and a couple of restaurants—including Ana Mandara—that even locals love. Fairmont recently opened an upscale urban time-share directly on the square. Placards throughout the square describe the factory's history. ⊠ *900 N. Point St., Fisherman's Wharf* ☎ *415/775–5500* ⊕ *www. ghirardellisq.com.*

Hyatt Regency. John Portman designed this hotel noted for its 17-story hanging garden, a delightful interior green space you'd never expect from the unwelcoming, imposing exterior. The garden glows at Christmas, when strands of tiny white lights dangle over the cavernous atrium lobby. The four glass elevators facing the lobby are fun to ride, unless you suffer from vertigo. ⊠ *5 Embarcadero Center, Embarcadero* ☎ *415/788–1234* ⊕ *sanfranciscoregency.hyatt.com.*

☼ ★ **Hyde Street Pier.** Cotton candy and souvenirs are all well and good, but if you want to get to the heart of the Wharf—boats—there's no better place to do it than at this pier, by far one of the Wharf area's best bargains. Depending on the time of day, you might see boat builders at work or children pretending to man an early-1900s ship.

Don't pass up the centerpiece collection of historic vessels, part of the **San Francisco Maritime National Historic Park,** almost all of which can be boarded. The newly restored *Balclutha,* an 1886 full-rigged three-masted sailing vessel that's more than 250 feet long, sailed around Cape Horn 17 times; kids especially love the *Eureka,* a side-wheel passenger and car ferry, for her onboard collection of vintage cars; the *Hercules* is a steam-powered tugboat. The *C. A. Thayer,* a three-masted schooner, recently underwent a painstaking restoration and is back on display. Across the street from the pier and almost a museum in itself is the San Francisco Maritime National Historic Park's **Visitor Center** (⊠ *499 Jefferson St., at Hyde St., Fisherman's Wharf* ☎ *415/447–5000* ☉ *Memorial Day–Sept., daily 9:30–6; Oct.–Memorial Day, daily 9:30–5*), happily free of mind-numbing, text-heavy displays. Instead, fun, large-scale exhibits, such as a huge First Order Fresnel lighthouse lens and a shipwrecked boat, make this an engaging and relatively quick stop. ✉ *Hyde and Jefferson Sts., Fisherman's Wharf* ☎ *415/561–7100* ⊕ *www.nps.gov/safr* ⛴ *Ships $5* ☉ *Memorial Day–Sept., daily 9:30–6; Oct.–Memorial Day, daily 9:30–5.*

WORD OF MOUTH

"Alcatraz is truly amazing.... I think it's one of the best sites I've seen and I've been all over the world and I live in San Francisco. I always take people there."

—galaxygrrl200

Jackson Square. This was the heart of the Barbary Coast of the Gay '90s (the 1890s, that is). Although most of the red-light district was destroyed in the fire that followed the 1906 earthquake, old redbrick buildings and narrow alleys recall the romance and rowdiness of San Francisco's early days. The days of brothels and bar fights are long gone—now Jackson Square is a genteel, quiet corner of the Financial District. It's of interest to the historically inclined and antiques-shop browsers, but otherwise safely skipped.

Some of the city's first business buildings, survivors of the 1906 quake, still stand between Montgomery and Sansome streets. After a few decades of neglect, these old-timers were adopted by preservation-minded interior designers and wholesale-furniture dealers for use as showrooms. In 1972 the city officially designated the area—bordered by Columbus Avenue on the west, Broadway and Pacific Avenue on the north, Washington Street on the south, and Sansome Street on the east—San Francisco's first historic district. When property values soared, many of the fabric and furniture outlets fled to Potrero Hill. Advertising agencies, attorneys, and antiques dealers now occupy the Jackson Square–area structures. Restored 19th-century brick buildings line Hotaling Place, which connects Washington and Jackson streets. The lane is named for the head of the **A. P. Hotaling Company whiskey distillery** (✉ *451 Jackson St., at Hotaling Pl.*), which was the largest liquor repository on the West Coast in its day. (Hotaling whiskey is still made in the city, by the way; look for their single malts for a sip of truly local flavor.)

It takes a bit of conjuring to evoke the wild Barbary Coast days when checking out the now-gentrified gold rush–era buildings in the 700 block of **Montgomery Street.** But this was an especially colorful block. Author Mark Twain was a reporter for the spunky *Golden Era* newspaper, which occupied No. 732 (now part of the building at No. 744). From 1959 to 1996 the late ambulance-chaser extraordinaire, lawyer Melvin Belli, had his headquarters there. There was never a dull moment in Belli's world; he represented clients from Mae West to Gloria Sykes (who in 1964 claimed that a cable-car accident turned her into a nymphomaniac) to Jim and Tammy Faye Bakker. Whenever he won a case, he fired a cannon and raised the Jolly Roger. Belli was also known for receiving a letter from the never-caught Zodiac killer. It seems fitting that the building sat for years, deteriorating and moldering, while the late attorney's sons fought wife number five (joined with Belli in holy matrimony just three months before his death). She eventually won, but today the dilapidated building is for sale. ✉ *Jackson Sq. district* *bordered by Broadway and Washington, Kearny, and Sansome Sts., Financial District.*

Market Street buildings. The street, which bisects the city at an angle, has consistently challenged San Francisco's architects. One of the most intriguing responses to this challenge sits diagonally across Market Street from the Palace Hotel. The tower of the **Hobart Building** (No. 582) combines a flat facade and oval sides and is considered one of Willis Polk's best works in the city. East on Market Street is

> ## WHISKEY RHYME
>
> The Italianate Hotaling building survived the disastrous 1906 quake and fire—a miracle considering the thousands of barrels of inflammable liquid inside. A plaque on the side of the structure repeats a famous query: IF, AS THEY SAY, GOD SPANKED THE TOWN FOR BEING OVER FRISKY, WHY DID HE BURN THE CHURCHES DOWN AND SAVE HOTALING'S WHISKEY?

Charles Havens's triangular **Flatiron Building** (No. 540–548), another classic solution. At Bush Street, the **Donahue Monument** holds its own against the skyscrapers that tower over the intersection. This homage to waterfront mechanics, which survived the 1906 earthquake (a famous photograph shows Market Street in ruins around the sculpture), was designed by Douglas Tilden, a noted California sculptor. The plaque in the sidewalk next to the monument marks the spot as the location of the San Francisco Bay shoreline in 1848. Telltale nautical details such as anchors, ropes, and shells adorn the gracefully detailed **Matson Building** (No. 215), built in the 1920s for the shipping line Matson Navigation. ✉ *Between New Montgomery and Beale Sts., Financial District.*

Pier 39. The city's most popular waterfront attraction draws millions of visitors each year who come to browse through its vertiginous array of shops and concessions hawking every conceivable form of souvenir. The pier can be quite crowded, and the numerous street performers may leave you feeling more harassed than entertained. Arriving early in the morning ensures you a front-row view of the sea lions, but if you're here to shop—and make no mistake about it, Pier 39 wants your money—be aware that most stores don't open until 9:30 or 10 (later in winter).

Pick up a buckwheat hull–filled otter neck wrap or a plush sea lion to snuggle at the **Marine Mammal Store** (☎ 415/289–7373), whose proceeds benefit Sausalito's respected wild-animal hospital, the Marine Mammal Center. Sales of the excellent books, maps, and collectibles—including a series of gorgeous, distinctive art-deco posters for Alcatraz, the Presidio, Fort Point, and the other members of the Golden Gate National Recreation Area—at the **National Park Store** (☎ 415/433–7221) help to support the National Park Service. Brilliant colors enliven the double-decker **San Francisco Carousel** (✉ $3 per ride), decorated with images of such city landmarks as the Golden Gate Bridge and Lombard Street.Follow the sound of barking to the northwest side of the pier to view the sea lions that remain after the majority of them migrated. At **Aquarium of the Bay** (☎ 415/623–5300 or 888/732–3483 ⊕ *www.aquariumofthebay.org* ✉ $15.95) moving walkways transport you through a space surrounded on three sides by water filled with indigenous San Francisco Bay marine life, from fish and plankton to

Where can I find . . . ?

PARKING	Beach and Hyde Garage 655 Beach St. Steps away from Fisherman's Wharf attractions.	Embarcadero Center Battery St., near Broadway Four hours free on nights and weekends with validation.
A DRUGSTORE	Walgreens 320 Bay St. Stop in for sunscreen on your way to your Alcatraz cruise.	Safeway 145 Jackson St. Need some aspirin after walking the Embarcadero?
A DRINK	Harrington's 245 Front St. Irish saloon with a good selection of imported beers.	Hog Island Oyster Bar Ferry Building Wine and oysters with a bay view.

sharks. Many find the aquarium overpriced; if you can, take advantage of the family rate ($39.95 for two adults and two kids under 12). The aquarium is open June through September daily 9–8; during the rest of the year it's open Monday through Thursday 10–6 and Friday through Sunday 10–7.

The **California Welcome Center** (☎ 415/981–1280 ⊕ www.visitcwc. com ☉ Daily 10–6), on Pier 39's second level, includes an Internet café. Parking (free with validation from a Pier 39 restaurant) is at the Pier 39 Garage, off Powell Street at the Embarcadero. ⊠ Beach St. at Embarcadero, Fisherman's Wharf ⊕ www.pier39.com.

San Francisco Brewing Company. Built in 1907, this pub looks like a museum piece from San Francisco's Barbary Coast days. An old upright piano sits in the corner under the original stained-glass windows. Take a seat at the mahogany bar, where you can look down at the white-tile spittoon. An adjacent room holds the handmade copper brewing kettle used to produce a dozen beers—with names such as Pony Express—by means of old-fashioned gravity-flow methods. ⊠ 155 Columbus Ave., North Beach ☎ 415/434–3344 ⊕ www.sfbrewing.com ☉ Mon.–Thurs. and Sun. 11:30–1 AM, Fri. and Sat. 11 AM –2 AM.

San Francisco National Maritime Museum. You'll feel as if you're out to sea when you step aboard, er, inside this sturdy, round, ship-shaped structure dubbed the Bathhouse. Part of the **San Francisco Maritime National Historical Park,** the museum has three floors that exhibit intricate ship models, beautifully restored figureheads, photographs of life at sea, and other artifacts chronicling the maritime history of San Francisco and the West Coast. The views from the top floor are stunning, and be sure to step onto the first-floor balcony, which overlooks the beach, and check out the lovely WPA-era tile designs on your way to the steamships exhibit. At this writing the museum was open but empty; exhibitions are expected to return mid-2010 (call ahead to check before visiting). ⊠ Aquatic Park foot of Polk St., Fisherman's

BRAVING THE WATERS

Federal prison officials liked to claim that it was impossible to escape Alcatraz, and for the most part, that assertion was true. For seasoned swimmers, though, the trip has never posed a problem—in fact, it's been downright popular.

In the 1930s, in an attempt to dissuade the feds from converting Alcatraz into a prison, a handful of schoolgirls made the swim to the city. At age 60, native son Jack LaLanne did it (for the second time) while shackled and towing a 1,000-pound rowboat. Every year a couple of thousand participants take the plunge during the annual Escape from Alcatraz Triathlon. Heck, a dog made the crossing in 2005 and finished well ahead of most of the (human) pack. And in 2006 seven-year-old Braxton Bilbrey became the youngest "escapee" on record. Incidentally, those reports of shark-infested waters are true—but the sharks aren't a dangerous species.

Wharf ☎ *415/447–5000* ⊕ *www.nps.gov/safr* ✉ *Donation suggested* ⊙ *Daily 10–5.*

San Francisco Railway Museum. A labor of love brought to you by the same vintage-transit enthusiasts responsible for the F-line's revival, this one-room museum and store celebrates the city's storied streetcars and cable cars with photographs, models, and artifacts. The permanent exhibit will eventually include the (replicated) end of a streetcar with a working cab for kids to explore. In the meantime, little ones will have to content themselves with operating the cool, antique Wiley birdcage traffic signal and viewing (but not touching) models and display cases. Right on the F-line track, just across from the Ferry Building, this is a great quick stop. ⊠ *77 Steuart St., Embarcadero* ☎ *415/974–1948* ⊕ *www.streetcar.org* ✉ *Free* ⊙ *Tues.–Sun. 10–6.*

Transamerica Pyramid. It's neither owned by Transamerica nor is it a pyramid, but this 853-foot-tall obelisk *is* the most photographed of the city's high-rises. Excoriated in the design stages as "the world's largest architectural folly," the icon was quickly hailed as a masterpiece when it opened in 1972. Today it's probably the city's most recognized structure after the Golden Gate Bridge. A fragrant redwood grove along the east side of the building, replete with benches and a cheerful fountain, is a placid patch in which to unwind. ⊠ *600 Montgomery St., Financial District* ⊕ *www.transamerica.com.*

Wells Fargo Bank History Museum. There were no formal banks in San Francisco during the early years of the gold rush, and miners often entrusted their gold dust to saloon keepers. In 1852 Wells Fargo opened its first bank in the city, and the company soon established banking offices in mother-lode camps throughout California. Stagecoaches and pony-express riders connected points around the burgeoning state, where the population boomed from 15,000 to 200,000 between 1848 and 1852. The museum displays samples of nuggets and gold dust from mines, a mural-size map of the Mother Lode, mementos of the poet bandit Black Bart (who signed his poems "Po8"), and an old telegraph

Native Land

In the 1960s Native Americans attempted to reclaim Alcatraz, citing an 1868 treaty that granted Native Americans any surplus federal land. Their activism crested in 1969, when several dozen Native Americans began a 19-month occupation, supported by public opinion and friendly media.

The group offered to buy the island from the government for $24 worth of beads and other goods—exactly what Native Americans had been paid for Manhattan in 1626. In their Proclamation to the Great White Father and His People, the group laid out the 10 reasons why Alcatraz would make an ideal Indian reservation, among them: "There is no industry and so unemployment is very great," and "The soil is rocky and nonproductive, and the land does not support game." The last holdouts were removed by federal agents in 1971, but today's visitors are still greeted with the huge graffitied message: "Indians Welcome. Indian Land."

machine on which you can practice sending codes. The showpiece is a red Concord stagecoach, the likes of which carried passengers from St. Joseph, Missouri, to San Francisco in just three weeks during the 1850s. ✉ *420 Montgomery St., Financial District* ☎ *415/396–2619* ⊕ *www. wellsfargohistory.com* 🎟 *Free* ⊙ *Weekdays 9–5.*

ALCATRAZ

"They made that place purely for punishment, where men would rot. It was designed to systematically destroy human beings . . . Cold, gray, and lonely, it had a weird way of haunting you—there were those dungeons that you heard about, but there was also the city . . . only a mile and a quarter away, so close you could almost touch it. Sometimes the wind would blow a certain way and you could smell the Italian cooking in North Beach and hear the laughter of people, of women and kids. That made it worse than hell."

—Jim Quillen, former Alcatraz inmate

Gripping the rail as the ferryboat pitches gently in the chilly breeze, you watch formidable Alcatraz rising ahead. Imagine making this trip shackled at the ankle and waist, the looming fortress on the craggy island ahead, waiting to swallow you whole. Thousands of visitors come every day to walk in the footsteps of Alcatraz's notorious criminals. The stories of life and death on "the Rock" may sometimes be exaggerated, but it's almost impossible to resist the chance to wander the cellblock that tamed the country's toughest gangsters and saw daring escape attempts of tremendous desperation.

LIFE ON THE ROCK

The federal penitentiary's first warden, James A. Johnston, was largely responsible for Alcatraz's (mostly false) hell-on-earth reputation. A tough but relatively humane disciplinarian, Johnston strictly limited the information flow to and from the prison when it opened in 1934. Prisoners' letters were censored, newspapers and radios were forbidden, and no visits were allowed during a convict's first three months in the slammer. Understandably, imaginations ran wild on the mainland.

A LIFE OF PRIVILEGE

Monotony was an understatement on Alcatraz; the same precise schedule was kept daily. The rulebook stated, "You are entitled to food, clothing, shelter, and medical attention. Anything else you get is a privilege." These privileges, from the right to work to the ability to receive mail, were earned by following the prison's rules. A relatively minor infraction meant losing privileges. A serious breach, like fighting, brought severe punishments like time in the Hole (a.k.a. the Strip Cell, since the prisoner had to strip) or the Oriental (an absolutely dark, silent cell with a hole in the ground for a toilet).

THE SPAGHETTI RIOT

Johnston knew that poor food was one of the major causes of prison riots, so he insisted that Alcatraz serve the best chow in the prison system. But the next warden at Alcatraz slacked off, and in 1950, one spaghetti meal too many sent the inmates over the edge. Guards deployed tear gas to subdue the rioters.

A PRISONER'S DAY

6:30 AM: Wake-up call. Prisoners get up, get dressed, and clean cells.

6:50 AM: Prisoners stand at cell doors to be counted.

7:00 AM: Prisoners march single-file to mess hall for breakfast.

7:20 AM: Prisoners head to work or industries detail; count.

9:30 AM: 8-minute break; count.

11:30 AM: Count; prisoners march to mess hall for lunch.

12:00 PM: Prisoners march to cells; count; break in cells.

12:20 PM: Prisoners leave cells, march single-file back to work; count.

2:30 PM: 8-minute break; count.

4:15 PM: Prisoners stop work, two counts.

4:25 PM: Prisoners march into mess hall and are counted; dinner.

4:45 PM: Prisoners return to cells and are locked in.

5:00 PM: Prisoners stand at their doors to be counted.

8:00 PM: Count.

9:30 PM: Count; lights out.

12:01 AM—5 AM: Three counts.

INFAMOUS INMATES

Fewer than 2,000 inmates ever did time on the Rock; though they weren't necessarily the worst criminals, they were definitely the worst prisoners. Most were escape artists, and others, like Al Capone, had corrupted the prison system from the inside with bribes.

Name Al "Scarface" Capone

On the Rock 1934–1939

In for Tax evasion

Claim to fame Notorious Chicago gangster and bootlegger who arranged the 1929 St. Valentine's Day Massacre.

Hard fact Capone was among the first transfers to the Rock and arrived smiling and joking. He soon realized the party was over. Capone endured a few stints in the Hole and Warden Johnston's early enforced-silence policy; he was also stabbed by a fellow inmate. The gangster eventually caved, saying "it looks like Alcatraz has got me licked," thus cementing the prison's reputation.

Name Robert "The Birdman" Stroud

On the Rock 1942–1959

In for Murder, including the fatal stabbing of a prison guard

Claim to fame Subject of the acclaimed but largely fictitious 1962 film *Birdman of Alcatraz*.

Hard fact Stroud was actually known as the "Bird Doctor of Leavenworth." While incarcerated in Leavenworth prison through the 1920s and 30s, he became an expert on birds, tending an aviary and writing two books. The stench and mess in his cell discouraged the guards from searching it—and finding Stroud's homemade still. His years on the Rock were birdless.

Name George "Machine Gun" Kelly

On the Rock 1934–1951

In for Kidnapping

Claim to fame Became an expert with a machine gun at the urging of his wife, Kathryn. Kathryn also encouraged his string of bank robberies and the kidnapping for ransom of oilman Charles Urschel. Insert "ball and chain" joke here . . . While stashed in Leavenworth on a life sentence, Kelly boasted that he would escape and then free Kathryn. That got him a one-way ticket to Alcatraz.

Hard fact Was an altar boy on Alcatraz and was generally considered a model prisoner.

NO ESCAPE

Alcatraz was a maximum-security federal penitentiary with one guard for every three prisoners. The biggest deterrent to escape, though, was the 1.4-mi of icy bay waters separating the Rock from the city. Only a few prisoners made it off the island, and only one is known to have survived. And that story about the shark-infested waters? There are sharks in the bay, but they're not the man-eating kind.

Bloodiest Attempt: In 1946, six prisoners hatched a plan to surprise a guard, seize weapons, and escape through the recreation yard. They succeeded up to a point, arming themselves and locking several guards into cells, but things got ugly when the group couldn't find the key that opened the door to the prison yard. Desperate, they opened fire on the trapped guards. Warden Johnston called in the Marines, who shelled the cell house for two days in the so-called Battle of Alcatraz. Three ringleaders were killed in the fighting; two were executed for murder; and one, who was just 19 years old, got 99 years slapped on to his sentence.

Craftiest Attempt: Over six months, three convicts stole bits and pieces from the kitchen and machine shop to make drills and digging pieces. They used these basic tools to widen a vent into the utility corridor. They also gathered bits of cardboard, toilet paper, and hair from the prison's barbershop to make crude models of their own heads. Then, like teenagers sneaking out, they put the decoy heads in their cots and walked away—up the pipes in the utility corridor to the roof, then down a drainpipe to the ground. They apparently swam for it, equipped with life vests made from prison raincoats, and are officially presumed dead.

Most Anticlimactic: In 1962, one prisoner spent an entire year loosening the bars in a window. Then he slipped through and managed to swim all the way to Fort Point, near the Golden Gate Bridge. He promptly fell asleep there and was found an hour later by some teenagers.

6 TIPS FOR ESCAPING TO ALCATRAZ

"Broadway," once the cell blocks' busiest corridor.

1. Buy your ticket in advance. Visit the Web site for Alcatraz Cruises (☎415/981–7625 ⊕ www.alcatrazcruises.com) to scout out available departure times for the ferry. Prepay by credit card—the ticket price covers the boat ride and the audio tour—and print your ticket at home. Bring it to Pier 33 up to an hour before sailing and experience just a touch of schadenfreude as you overhear attendants tell scores of too-late passengers that your tour is sold out.

2. Dress smart. Bring that pullover you packed to ward off the chill from the boat ride and Alcatraz Island. Also: sneakers. Some Alcatraz guides are fanatical about making excellent time.

3. Go for the evening tour. You'll get even more out of the experience if you do it at night. The evening tour has programs not offered during the day, the bridge-to-bridge view of the city twinkles at night, and your "prison experience" will be amplified as darkness mournfully falls while you shuffle around the cell block.

4. Unplug and go against the flow. If you miss a cue on the excellent audio tour and find yourself out of synch, don't sweat it—use it as an opportunity to switch off the tape and walk against the grain of the people following the tour. No one will stop you if you walk back through a cell block on your own, taking the time to listen to the haunting sound of your own footsteps on the concrete floor.

5. Be mindful of scheduled and limited-capacity talks. Some programs only happen once a day (the schedule is posted in the cell house). Certain talks have limited capacity seating, so keep an eye out for a cell house staffer handing out passes shortly before the start time.

6. Talk to the staff. One of the island's greatest resources is its staff, who practically bubble over with information. Pick their brains, and draw them out about what they know.

PRACTICALITIES

Visitors at the Alcatraz dock waiting to depart "Uncle Sam's Devil's Island."

GETTING THERE

All cruises are operated by Alcatraz Cruises, the park's authorized concessionaire.

✉ *Pier 33, Fisherman's Wharf* ☎ *415/981–7625* 🎫 *$26, including audio tour; $33 evening tour, including audio* ⏱ *Ferry departures every 30–45 mins Sept.–late May, daily 9:30–2:15, 4:20 for evening tour Thurs.–Mon. only; late May–Aug., daily 9:30–4:15, 6:10 and 6:45 for evening tour* ⊕ *www.nps.gov/alca, www.parksconservancy.org/visit/alcatraz, www.alcatrazcruises.com*

TIMING

The boat ride to Alcatraz is only about 15 minutes long, but you should allow about three hours for your entire visit. The delightful F-line vintage streetcars are the most direct public transit to the dock; on weekdays the 10-Townsend bus will get you within a few blocks of Pier 33.

FOOD

The prisoners might have enjoyed good food on Alcatraz, but you won't—unless you pack a picnic. Food is not available on the island, so be sure to stock up before you board the boat. The Ferry Building's bounty is just a 20-minute walk from Pier 33. In a pinch, you can also pony up for the underwhelming snacks on the boat.

KIDS ON THE ROCK

Parents should be aware that the audio tour, while engaging and worthwhile, includes some startlingly realistic sound effects. (Some children might not get a kick out of the gunshots from the Battle of Alcatraz—or the guards' screams, for that matter.) If you stay just one minute ahead in the program, you can always fast forward through the violent moments on your little one's audio tour.

STORM TROOPER ALERT!

When he was filming *Star Wars,* George Lucas recorded the sound of Alcatraz's cell doors slamming shut and used the sound bite in the movie whenever Darth Vader's star cruiser closed its doors.

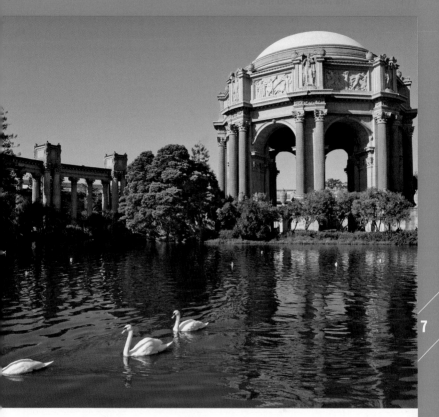

The Marina and the Presidio

WORD OF MOUTH

"I think the prettiest section to walk is along Crissy field from the St Francis yacht club to Ft Point. At Ft Point, you'll be directly under the GG bridge. If you climb up to the ramparts at Ft Point, you'll be rewarded with fabulous views of the Golden Gate (entrance to the Bay), and also back towards downtown."

— StuDudley

GETTING ORIENTED

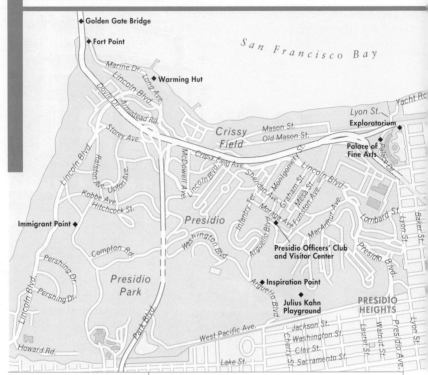

MAKING THE MOST OF YOUR TIME

Allow two hours for the Exploratorium, plus a half-hour to stroll around the Palace of Fine Arts. Walking across the Golden Gate Bridge takes about 30 minutes, but leave some time to take in the view on the other side. If you aren't in a hurry, plan to spend at least two to three hours in the Presidio. In a pinch, make a 30- to 45-minute swing-through for the views. Shoppers can burn up an entire day browsing the Marina's Chestnut Street and Cow Hollow's Union Street. Weekends are liveliest, while Mondays are quiet since some shops close.

TOP 5 REASONS TO GO

Golden Gate Bridge: Get a good look at the iconic span from the Presidio, then bundle up and walk over the water.

Shop Cow Hollow and the Marina: Browse hip boutiques and lavish antiques shops on Union Street, Cow Hollow's main drag. Then head north across Lombard Street to the Marina's shopping hot spot, Chestnut Street.

Exploratorium and the Palace of Fine Arts: The hands-on Exploratorium is a perennial kids' fave. Just outside is the stunning, Romanesque Palace of Fine Arts.

Crissy Field: Try to spot egrets and herons from the bayside wooden boardwalk over this restored tidal marshland under the Golden Gate Bridge.

Presidio wanderings: Lace up your walking shoes and follow one of the wooded trails; the city will feel a hundred miles away. If you've got a car, take a meandering drive, stopping at any and all ocean lookouts—Inspiration Point and Immigrant Point will take your breath away.

GETTING THERE

The only public transportation that operates to this part of town is the bus, so if you don't have your own wheels, take the 30–Stockton to Chestnut and Laguna in the Marina, two blocks south of Fort Mason.

The Marina and the Presidio are great for biking (though the Presidio has some hills) and easily reached along the Embarcadero.

The Presidio, vast and with plenty of free parking, is one area where it pays to have a car. If you're driving to either the Marina or the Presidio, parking isn't too bad—the Exploratorium and the Palace of Fine Arts, and Crissy Field all have free lots; parking at Fort Mason is free for one hour.

For those without wheels, the free year-round shuttle Presi-diGo, which loops through the Presidio every half-hour, is a dream; ride the whole route for a good 45-minute overview. Pick it up at the transit center, at Lincoln Boulevard and Graham Street. For a map and schedule, check ⊕ *www.presidio.gov/directions/presidigo*.

7

QUICK BITES

Greens to Go (⊠ *Fort Mason, Bldg. A, Marina* ☎ *415/771–6330*), the take-out wing of the famous Greens vegetarian restaurant, carries mouthwatering premade salads, sandwiches, and soups. There aren't any seats, but a steep flight of stairs leads up to a grassy picnicking area with splendid views of the Marina.

If you're after something sweet, look for the periwinkle awning at **La Boulange** (⊠ *1909 Union St., Cow Hollow* ☎ *415/440–4450*), which serves tartines (open-faced sandwiches) in addition to perfect pastries and cakes. Free refills of organic coffee and a welcoming interior encourage lingering.

Sightseeing
★★★★
Nightlife
★★
Dining
★★★
Lodging
★★★
Shopping
★★★★

Yachts bob at their moorings, satisfied-looking folks jog along the Marina Green, and multimillion-dollar homes overlook the bay in this picturesque, if somewhat sterile, neighborhood. Does it all seem a bit too perfect? Well, it got this way after the hard knock of Loma Prieta—the current pretty face was put on after hundreds of homes collapsed in the 1989 earthquake. Just west of this waterfront area is a more natural beauty: the Presidio. Once a military base, this beautiful, sprawling park is mostly green space, with hills, woods, and the marshlands of Crissy Field.

Updated by
Denise M. Leto

It's often said that the Marina's 1989 disaster was literally built on the legacy of the Great Quake. Local legend has it that rubble from the 1906 catastrophe was used to fill in the area—unstable landfill that then liquefied when the Loma Prieta temblor struck. That story was disproved in 2004, but regardless of the origin of Marina land, its shaky character stays the same. The district suffered the worst damage in the city from the 1989 quake, and many residents fled in search of more solid ground. Others stayed put. "I realize that we're sitting on Jell-O," said one local. "[But] how many areas are as beautiful as the Marina? At some point, you just have to pick your poison. . . ."

Well-funded postcollegiates and the nouveau riche quickly replaced those who left, changing the tenor of this formerly low-key neighborhood. The number of yuppie coffee emporiums skyrocketed, a bank became a Williams-Sonoma, and the local grocer gave way to a Pottery Barn. On weekends a young, fairly homogeneous, well-to-do crowd floods the cafés and bars. (Some things don't change—even before the quake, the Marina Safeway was a famed pickup place for straight singles, hence the nickname "Dateway.") One unquestionable improvement has been the influx of contemporary cuisine into this former bastion of outdated Italian fare. South of Lombard Street is the Marina's affluent neighbor, Cow Hollow, whose main drag, Union Street, has some of the city's best boutique shopping and a good selection of fun, fine restaurants and cafés. Joggers and kite-flyers head to the Marina Green, the strip of lawn between the yacht club and the mansions of Marina Boulevard.

The Presidio, meanwhile, is going through some shakeups, too. In 1996 President Clinton signed a bill placing the Presidio in the hands of a trust corporation as part of a novel money-generating experiment. The trust manages most of the Presidio land, leasing buildings and allowing limited development with the goal of making enough money to cover the Presidio's operating costs. The National Park Service oversees the coastal sections. Whether this arrangement is a worthy model for national parks of the future, or the first step in the crass commercialization of a public resource, remains to be seen. Whatever the outcome, the Presidio will still have superb views and the best hiking and biking areas in San Francisco; a drive through the lush area is also a treat.

> ### DON'T LOOK DOWN
>
> Armed only with helmets, safety harnesses, and painting equipment, a full-time crew of 38 painters keeps the Golden Gate Bridge clad in International Orange. Contrary to a favorite bit of local lore, they don't actually sweep on an entire coat of paint from one end of the bridge to the other, but instead scrape, prime, and repaint small sections that have rusted from exposure to the elements.

WHAT TO SEE IN THE MARINA

Exploratorium. Walking into this fascinating "museum of science, art, and human perception" is like visiting a mad scientist's laboratory. Most of the exhibits are supersize, and you can play with everything. You can feel like Alice in Wonderland in the distortion room, where you seem to shrink and grow as you walk across the slanted, checkered floor. In the shadow room, a powerful flash freezes an image of your shadow on the wall; jumping is a favorite pose. "Pushover" demonstrates cow-tipping, but for people: stand on one foot and try to keep your balance while a friend swings a striped panel in front of you (trust us, you're going to fall).

More than 650 other exhibits focus on sea and insect life, computers, electricity, patterns and light, language, the weather, and much more. "Explainers"—usually high-school students on their days off—demonstrate cool scientific tools and procedures, like DNA sample-collection and cow-eye dissection. One surefire hit is the pitch-black, touchy-feely Tactile Dome. In this geodesic dome strewn with textured objects, you crawl through a course of ladders, slides, and tunnels, relying solely on your sense of touch. Not surprisingly, lovey-dovey couples sometimes linger in the "grope dome," but be forewarned: the staff will turn on the lights if they have to. ■TIP➔ Reservations are required for the Tactile Dome and will get you 75 minutes of access. You have to be at least seven years old to go through the dome, and the space is not for the claustrophobic. ✉ *3601 Lyon St., at Marina Blvd., Marina* ☎ *415/561–0360 general information, 415/561–0362 Tactile Dome reservations* ⊕ *www.*

exploratorium.edu ✉ *$14, free 1st Wed. of month; Tactile Dome $3 extra* ⊙ *Tues.–Sun. 10–5.*

Wave Organ. Conceived by environmental artist Peter Richards and fashioned by master stonecutter George Gonzales, this unusual wave-activated acoustic sculpture gives off subtle harmonic sounds produced by seawater as it passes through 25 tubes. The sound is loudest at high tide. The granite and marble used for walkways, benches, and alcoves that are part of the piece were salvaged from a gold rush–era cemetery. ✉ *North of Marina Green at end of jetty by Yacht Rd., park in lot north of Marina Blvd. at Lyon St., Marina.*

EXHIBITS IN THE SUNSHINE

Dotting the shoreline along Fort Mason are 20 outdoor exhibits, revealed in 2009, that together make up San Francisco's first Outdoor Exploratorium site. The creative folks at the city's stellar, hands-on science museum are moving outside, using a series of flags to create a wind observatory, bringing nature to your tongue with drinking fountains designed to simulate the varying salinity of the bay, and using the Golden Gate Bridge as a thermometer.

Fort Mason Center. Originally a depot for the shipment of supplies to the Pacific during World War II, the fort was converted into a cultural center in 1977. Here you can find the vegetarian restaurant Greens and shops, galleries, and performance spaces, most of which are closed Monday. There's also plentiful free parking—a rarity in the city.

You have to be seriously into Italian-American culture to appreciate the text- and photograph-heavy exhibits at the **Museo Italo-Americano** (✉ *Bldg. C* ☎ *415/673–2200* ⊙ *Tues.–Sun. noon–4*), but depending on the exhibit, it might be worth a glance if you're already at Fort Mason. Plus, it's free. The temporary exhibits downstairs at the free **SFMOMA Artists Gallery** (✉ *Bldg. A* ☎ *415/441–4777*) can be great, but head upstairs and check out the paintings, sculptures, prints, and photographs for sale and for rent. It's a fun scene, with folks flipping through the works like posters. You won't find a Picasso or a Rembrandt here, but you can find works of high quality by emerging Northern California artists—and where else can you get a $50,000 work of art to hang on your wall for $400 (a month)? It's open Tuesday through Saturday 11:30–5:30. ✉ *Buchanan St. and Marina Blvd., Marina* ☎ *415/345–7500 event information* ⊕ *www.fortmason.org.*

Fodor's Choice
★

Palace of Fine Arts. At first glance this stunning, rosy rococo palace seems to be from another world, and indeed, it's the sole survivor of the many tinted-plaster structures (a temporary classical city of sorts) built for the 1915 Panama-Pacific International Exposition, the world's fair that celebrated San Francisco's recovery from the 1906 earthquake and fire. The expo buildings originally extended about a mile along the shore. Bernard Maybeck designed this faux–Roman Classic beauty, which was reconstructed in concrete and reopened in 1967.

A victim of the elements, the Palace completed a piece-by-piece renovation in 2008, though the pseudo-Latin language adorning the exterior urns continues to stump scholars. The massive columns (each topped with four "weeping maidens"), great rotunda, and swan-filled lagoon have been used in countless fashion layouts, films, and wedding photo shoots. After admiring the lagoon, look across the street to the house at 3460 Baker Street. If the maidens out front look familiar, they should—they're original casts of the lovely "garland ladies" you can see in the Palace's colonnade. The house was on the market in 2007; if you'd had a cool $8 million, it could've been yours. ⊠ *Baker and Beach Sts., Marina* ☎ *415/561–0364 Palace history tours* ⊕ *www. exploratorium.edu/palace* ☞ *Free* ☉ *Daily 24 hrs.*

WORD OF MOUTH

"I would highly recommend a bike ride over the Golden Gate Bridge and down into Sausalito. It is a tough ride in some spots but it was amazing. The view from the bridge was incredible! The hill down into Sausalito is steep and long but very fun!"   —Kerry392

WHAT TO SEE IN THE PRESIDIO

Fort Point. Dwarfed today by the Golden Gate Bridge, this brick fortress constructed between 1853 and 1861 was designed to protect San Francisco from a Civil War sea attack that never materialized. It was also used as a coastal-defense fortification post during World War II, when soldiers stood watch here. This National Historic Site is now a sprawling museum filled with military memorabilia, surrounding a lonely, windswept courtyard. The building has a gloomy air and is suitably atmospheric. (It's usually chilly and windy, too, so bring a jacket.) On days when Fort Point is staffed, guided group tours and cannon drills take place. The top floor affords a unique angle on the bay. ■TIP➜ Take care when walking along the front side of the building, as it's slippery and the waves have a dizzying effect. Though it's only open Friday through Sunday, Fort Point may soon be open during the week; call ahead for hours. The fort's popular guided candlelight tours, available only in winter, sell out in advance, so be sure to book ahead. Southeast of this structure is the **Fort Point Mine Depot,** an army facility that functioned as the headquarters for underwater mining operations throughout World War II. Today it's the Warming Hut, a National Park Service café and bookstore. ⊠ *Marine Dr. off Lincoln Blvd., Presidio* ☎ *415/556–1693* ⊕ *www.nps.gov/fopo* ☞ *Free* ☉ *Fri.–Sun. 10–5.*

Fodor's Choice ★ **Golden Gate Bridge.** The suspension bridge that connects San Francisco with Marin County has long wowed sightseers with its simple but powerful art-deco design. Completed in 1937 after four years of construction, the 2-mi span and its 750-foot towers were built to withstand winds of more than 100 mph. It's also not a bad place to be in an earthquake: designed to sway up to 27.7 feet, the Golden Gate Bridge, unlike the Bay Bridge, was undamaged by the 1989 Loma Prieta quake. (If you're on the bridge when it's windy, stand still and you can feel it swaying a bit.) Though it's frequently gusty and misty—always bring a jacket, no matter what the weather's like—the bridge provides unparalleled views of the Bay Area. Muni buses 28 and 29 make stops at the Golden Gate Bridge toll plaza, on the San Francisco side. However,

Where can I find . . . ?

PARKING	Marina Green Park Marina Blvd. The price is right: free!	Lombard Street Garage 2055 Lombard St. City-owned, with reasonable rates.
A DRUGSTORE	Walgreens 3201 Divisadero, at Lombard St. Open 24 hours.	Safeway 15 Marina Blvd. The infamous "Dateway" has a pharmacy.
A BAR	MatrixFillmore 3138 Fillmore St. On the prowl and looking fabu- lous? Stop in for a martini.	Bus Stop 1901 Union St. Not dressed up? Drop by this Cow Hollow sports bar.

drive to fully appreciate the bridge from multiple vantage points in and around the Presidio; you'll be able to park at designated areas.

From the bridge's eastern-side walkway—the only side pedestrians are allowed on—you can take in the San Francisco skyline and the bay islands; look west for the wild hills of the Marin Headlands, the curving coast south to Land's End, and the Pacific Ocean. On sunny days, sailboats dot the water, and brave windsurfers test the often-treacherous tides beneath the bridge. ■TIP➜ A vista point on the Marin side gives you a spectacular city panorama.

But there's a well-known, darker side to the bridge's story, too. The bridge is perhaps the world's most popular suicide platform, with an average of about 20 jumpers per year. (The first leaped just three months after the bridge's completion, and the official count was stopped in 1995 as the 1,000th jump approached.) Signs along the bridge read "There is hope. Make the call," referring the disconsolate to the special telephones on the bridge. Bridge officers, who patrol the walkway and watch by security camera to spot potential jumpers, successfully talk down two-thirds to three-quarters of them each year. Documentary filmmaker Eric Steel's controversial 2006 movie *The Bridge* once again put pressure on the Golden Gate Bridge Highway and Transportation District to install a suicide barrier; various options are being considered, with most locals supporting an unobtrusive net. ⊠ *Lincoln Blvd. near Doyle Dr. and Fort Point, Presidio* ☎ *415/921–5858* ⊕ *www.goldengatebridge.org* ☉ *Pedestrians Mar.–Oct., daily 5 AM–9 PM; Nov.–Feb., daily 5 AM–6 PM; hrs change with daylight saving time. Bicyclists daily 24 hrs.*

★ **Presidio.** When San Franciscans want to spend a day in the woods, they head here. The Presidio has 1,400 acres of hills and majestic woods, two small beaches, and—the one thing Golden Gate Park doesn't have—stunning views of the bay, the Golden Gate Bridge, and Marin County. Famed environmental artist Andy Goldsworthy's new sculpture greets visitors at the Arguello Gate entrance. Erected at the end of 2008, the

100-plus-foot *Spire,* made of 37 cypress logs reclaimed from the Presidio, looks like a rough, natural version of a church spire. ■TIP➔ The best lookout points lie along Washington Boulevard, which meanders through the park.

Part of the **Golden Gate National Recreation Area,** the Presidio was a military post for more than 200 years. Don Juan Bautista de Anza and a band of Spanish settlers first claimed the area in 1776. It became a Mexican garrison in 1822, when Mexico gained its independence from Spain; U.S. troops forcibly occupied the Presidio in 1846. The U.S. Sixth Army was stationed here until October 1994, when the coveted space was transferred into civilian hands.

Today the area is being transformed into a self-sustaining national park with a combination of public, commercial, and residential projects. In 2005 Bay Area filmmaker George Lucas opened the **Letterman Digital Arts Center,** his 23-acre digital studio "campus," along the eastern edge of the land. Seventeen of those acres are exquisitely landscaped and open to the public, but not even landscaping this perfect can compete with the wilds of the Presidio.

The battle over the fate of the rest of the Presidio is ongoing. Many older buildings have been reconstructed; the issue now is how to fill them. The original plan described a nexus for arts, education, and environmental groups. Since the Presidio's overseeing trust must make the park financially self-sufficient by 2013, which means generating enough revenue to keep afloat without the federal government's monthly $20 million checks, many fear that money will trump culture. The Asian-theme SenSpa and a new Walt Disney museum have opened, and a lodge at the Main Post is in the planning stages. With old military housing now repurposed as apartments and homes with rents up to $10,000 a month, there's some concern that the Presidio will become an incoherent mix of pricey real estate. Still, the $6 million that Lucas shells out annually for rent does plant a lot of saplings. . . .

The Presidio also has two beaches, a golf course, a visitor center, and picnic sites; the views from the many overlooks are sublime.

★ Especially popular is **Crissy Field,** a stretch of restored marshlands along
☾ the sand of the bay. Kids on bikes, folks walking dogs, and joggers share the paved path along the shore, often winding up at the Warming Hut, a combination café and fun gift store at the end of the path, for a hot chocolate in the shadow of the Golden Gate Bridge. Midway along the Golden Gate Promenade that winds along the shore is the Gulf of the Farallones National Marine Sanctuary Visitor Center, where kids can get a close-up view of small sea creatures and learn about the rich ecosystem offshore. Toward the promenade's eastern end, Crissy Field Center offers great children's programs and has cool science displays. West of the Golden Gate Bridge is sandy **Baker Beach,** beloved for its spectacular views and laid-back vibe (read: you'll see naked people here). This is one of those places locals like to show off to visitors. ✉ *Between Marina and Lincoln Park, Presidio* ⊕ *www.nps.gov/prsf and www.presidio.gov.*

The Presidio with Kids

If you're in town with children (and you have a car), the sprawling, bayside Presidio offers enough kid-friendly diversions for one very full day. Start off at **Julius Kahn Park**, on the Presidio's southern edge, which has a disproportionate number of structures that spin. Swing by George Lucas's **Letterman Digital Arts Center** to check out the Yoda fountain; then head to the **Immigrant Point Lookout** on Washington Boulevard, with views of the bay and the ocean. Children love the pet cemetery, with its sweet, leaning headstones; it's near the stables, where you might glimpse some of the park police's equestrian members. The last stop is **Crissy Field**, where kids can ride bikes, skate, or run along the beach and clamber over the rocks; the view of the Golden Gate Bridge from below is captivating. Two nature centers here have fun, hands-on exhibits for kids. Finally, stop by the **Warming Hut**, at the western end of Crissy Field, for sandwiches and hot chocolate. You can also do a version of this day using the PresidiGo shuttle, but you'll need to adapt your route according to the shuttle stops.

Presidio Officers' Club and Visitor Center. A remnant of the days when the Presidio was an army base, this Mission-style clubhouse now doubles as a temporary visitor center and exhibit space. Hit the visitor center for maps, schedules of the walking and biking tours, recaps of the Presidio's history, and a good selection of Bay Area books and souvenirs.

The club's temporary art exhibitions explore the unique cultural identity of the American West and the Pan-Pacific, such as Japanese wood-block prints. The space also sometimes offers dance performances, lectures, and theater. And a bonus that's rare in San Francisco: ample free parking. In one of the Presidio's most exciting projects, the parade ground parking lot (on what's known as the Main Post) is slated to become a lodge—most likely a swank and green one—and a swath of restored habitat that will stretch all the way to Crissy Field. ⊠ *50 Moraga Ave., Presidio* ☎ *415/561–4323 visitor center, 415/561–5500 for exhibits* ⊕ *www.presidio.gov* ⊗ *Visitor center daily 9–5; exhibit space Wed.–Sun. 11–5.*

The Western Shoreline

WORD OF MOUTH

"Wow! What a magnificent setting! The [Legion of Honor] is majestic, but the grounds are even lovelier, with great views of the ocean and Golden Gate Bridge."

—yk

GETTING ORIENTED

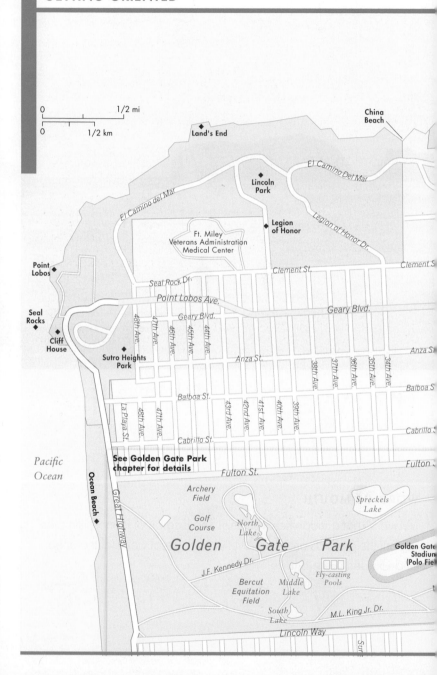

0 _____ 1/2 mi

0 _____ 1/2 km

China Beach

Land's End

El Camino Del Mar

Lincoln Park

Legion of Honor

El Camino del Mar

Legion of Honor Dr.

Ft. Miley Veterans Administration Medical Center

Point Lobos

Clement St.

Clement S

Seal Rock Dr.

Point Lobos Ave.

Geary Blvd.

Seal Rocks

Geary Blvd.

48th Ave.
47th Ave.
46th Ave.
45th Ave.
44th Ave.

Cliff House

Anza St.

Anza S

38th Ave.
37th Ave.
36th Ave.
35th Ave.
34th Ave.

Sutro Heights Park

Balboa St.

43rd Ave.
42nd Ave.
41st Ave.
40th Ave.
39th Ave.

Balboa S

48th Ave.
47th Ave.

La Playa St.

Cabrillo St.

Cabrillo S

Pacific Ocean

See Golden Gate Park chapter for details

Fulton St.

Fulton

Ocean Beach

Great Highway

Archery Field

Golf Course

North Lake

Spreckels Lake

Golden   Gate   Park

Golden Gate Stadium (Polo Fiel

J.F. Kennedy Dr.

Fly-casting Pools

Bercut Equitation Field

Middle Lake

South Lake

M.L. King Jr. Dr.

Lincoln Way

MAKING THE MOST OF YOUR TIME

Despite low-lying fog and often biting chill, the premier sights of the Western Shoreline are outdoors—gorgeous hiking trails and sandy stretches of coastline. Bundle up and start off on the Coastal Trail, which passes by the Legion of Honor; time it to arrive at the museum in the afternoon to avoid buses of schoolchildren. Continue west to catch the sunset from the Cliff House or the Beach Chalet. If you don't want to do the entire 3-mi hike, you can spend an hour touring the museum, catch the stunning views just below it, and head to the beach.

TOP 5 REASONS TO GO

Lands End: Head down the freshly restored Coastal Trail near the Cliff House; you'll quickly find yourself in a forest with unparalleled views of the Golden Gate Bridge.

Toast the sunset at the Beach Chalet: Top off a day of exploring with a cocktail overlooking Ocean Beach.

Legion of Honor: Tear yourself away from the spectacular setting and eye-popping view and travel back to 18th-century Europe through the paintings, drawings, and porcelain collected here.

Ocean Beach: Wrap up warm and stroll along the strand on a brisk, cloudy day and you'll feel like a gritty local. Then thaw out over a bowl of steaming pho in the Richmond.

Old-time San Francisco: Wandering among the ruins of the Sutro Baths below the Cliff House, close your eyes and imagine vintage San Francisco: the monumental baths, popular amusement park Playland at the Beach, and that great old teetering, Victorian Cliff House of days gone by.

GETTING THERE

To reach the Western Shoreline from downtown by bus, nab the 38–Geary, which runs all the way to 48th and Point Lobos avenues, just east of the Cliff House. Along the Western Shoreline, the 18–46th Avenue bus runs between the Legion of Honor and the zoo (and beyond).

WORD OF MOUTH

"Undeniably, the best meal during our trip was at Cliff House. I [resisted] eating there, thinking that it's probably a tourist trap... Since we were at Legion of Honor, it seems reasonable to go there for lunch. We got a table next to the window with a commanding view of the beach and ocean... Despite me living in Boston, I have never had clams this good."   —yk

QUICK BITES

The gorgeous setting often overshadows the upscale comfort food at the **Beach Chalet** and **Park Chalet** (⊠ *1000 Great Hwy.* ☎ *415/386–8439*), across from Ocean Beach, on the western edge of Golden Gate Park. With its plain-wrap storefront, mom-and-pop shop **Hunan Café 2** (⊠ *4450 Cabrillo St., Outer Richmond* ☎ *415/751–1283*) may not look like much, but the friendly folks here serve super fresh, delicious Chinese food; favorites include the ginger and onion chicken, Mongolian beef, and hot and sour soup.

8

Sightseeing
★ ★ ★
Nightlife
–
Dining
★
Lodging
–
Shopping
–

Few American cities provide a more intimate and dramatic view of the power and fury of the surf attacking the shore than San Francisco does along its wild Western Shoreline. From Lincoln Park in the north, along Ocean Beach from the Richmond south to the Sunset, a different breed of San Franciscan chooses to live in this area: surfers who brave the heaviest fog to ride the waves; writers who seek solace and inspiration in this city outpost; dog lovers committed to giving their pets a good workout each day.

Updated by
Denise M. Leto

From Lands End in Lincoln Park you have some of the best views of the Golden Gate (the name was given to the opening of San Francisco Bay long before the bridge was built) and the Marin Headlands. From the historic Cliff House south to the sprawling San Francisco Zoo, the Great Highway and Ocean Beach run along the western edge of the city. (If you're here in winter or spring, keep your eyes peeled for migrating gray whales.) The wind is often strong along the shoreline, summer fog can blanket the ocean beaches, and the water is cold and usually too rough for swimming. Don't forget your jacket!

WHAT TO SEE

Cliff House. A meal at the Cliff House isn't about the food—the spectacular ocean view is what brings folks here. The vistas, which include offshore Seal Rock (the barking marine mammals who reside there are actually sea lions), can be 30 mi or more on a clear day—or less than a mile on foggy days. ■ TIP➜ Come for drinks just before sunset; then head back into town for dinner.

Three buildings have occupied this site since 1863. The current building dates from 1909; a 2004 renovation has left a strikingly attractive restaurant and a squat concrete viewing platform out back. The complex, owned by the National Park Service, includes a gift shop.

Sitting on the observation deck is the **Giant Camera,** a cute yellow-painted wooden model of an old-fashioned camera with its lens pointing skyward. Built in the 1940s and threatened many times with demolition, it's now on the National Register of Historic Places. Step into the dark, tiny room inside (for a rather steep $5 fee); a fascinating 360-degree image of the surrounding area—which rotates as

WORD OF MOUTH

"The Legion of Honor is in the most terrific setting with its views to the Golden Gate Bridge and the headlands. The porcelain on the lower level is beautifully displayed—sort of like being at Gump's except you can't buy anything!"   —dovima

the "lens" on the roof rotates—is projected on a large, circular table. ■TIP➜ In winter and spring, you may also glimpse migrating gray whales from the observation deck.

To the north of the Cliff House are the ruins of the once-grand glass-roof **Sutro Baths,** which you can explore on your own (they look a bit like water-storage receptacles). Adolf Sutro, eccentric onetime San Francisco mayor and Cliff House owner, built the bath complex, including a train out to the site, in 1896, so that everyday folks could enjoy the benefits of swimming. Six enormous baths (some freshwater and some seawater), more than 500 dressing rooms, and several restaurants covered 3 acres north of the Cliff House and accommodated 25,000 bathers. Likened to Roman baths in a European glass palace, the baths were for decades the favorite destination of San Franciscans in search of entertainment. The complex fell into disuse after World War II, was closed in 1952, and burned down (under officially questionable circumstances, wink wink) during demolition in 1966. ✉ *1090 Point Lobos Ave., Outer Richmond* ☎ *415/386–3330* ⊕ *www.cliffhouse.com* ✉ *Free* ☉ *Weekdays 9* AM–*9:30* PM, *weekends 9* AM–*10* PM.

Fodor'sChoice ★ **Legion of Honor.** The old adage of real estate—location, location, location—is at full force here. You can't beat the spot of this museum of European art—situated on cliffs overlooking the ocean, the Golden Gate Bridge, and the Marin Headlands. A pyramidal glass skylight in the entrance court illuminates the lower-level galleries, which exhibit prints and drawings, English and European porcelain, and ancient Assyrian, Greek, Roman, and Egyptian art. The 20-plus galleries on the upper level display the permanent collection of European art (paintings, sculpture, decorative arts, and tapestries) from the 14th century to the present day.

The noteworthy Auguste Rodin collection includes two galleries devoted to the master and a third with works by Rodin and other 19th-century sculptors. An original cast of Rodin's *The Thinker* welcomes you as you walk through the courtyard. As fine as the museum is, the setting and view outshine the collection and make a trip here worthwhile.

The **Legion Café,** on the lower level, serves tasty light meals (soup, sandwiches, grilled chicken) inside and on a garden terrace. (Unfortunately, there's no view.) Just north of the museum's parking lot is George Segal's *The Holocaust,* a stark white installation that evokes life in

8

Where can I find . . . ?

A CUP OF COFFEE	Java Beach Café 1396 La Playa St. Strong, organic coffee and outdoor tables.	Trouble Coffee Company 4033 Judah St. Rich, not-too-strong joe and cinnamon toast.
A GAS STATION	Sunset 76 1700 Noriega St. Head here to get a flat patched, or to gas up.	19th Ave. 76 Station 1401 19th Ave. Stop by for gas and auto repairs.
A DRUGSTORE	Walgreens 25 Point Lobos Ave., near 43rd Ave. Open until midnight.	Walgreens 199 Parnassus Ave. Just two blocks from Golden Gate Park's southeast corner.

concentration camps during World War II. It's haunting at night, when backlighted by lights in the Legion's parking lot. ■ TIP→ Admission to the Legion also counts as same-day admission to the de Young Museum. ⊠ *34th Ave. at Clement St., Outer Richmond* ☎ *415/750–3600* ⊕ *www. thinker.org* ✉ *$10, $2 off with Muni transfer, free 1st Tues. of month* ⊙ *Tues.–Sun. 9:30–5:15.*

★ **Lincoln Park.** Although many of the city's green spaces are gentle and welcoming, Lincoln Park is a wild 275-acre park with windswept cliffs and panoramic views. The newly renovated Coastal Trail, the park's most dramatic, leads out to **Lands End**; pick it up west of the Legion of Honor (at the end of El Camino del Mar) or from the parking lot at Point Lobos and El Camino del Mar. Time your hike to hit Mile Rock at low tide, and you might catch a glimpse of two wrecked ships peeking up from their watery graves. ⚠ Do be careful if you hike here; landslides are frequent, and many people have fallen into the sea by standing too close to the edge of a crumbling bluff top.

On the tamer side, large Monterey cypresses line the fairways at Lincoln Park's 18-hole golf course, near the Legion of Honor. At one time this land was the Golden Gate Cemetery, where the dead were segregated by nationality; most were indigent and interred without ceremony in the potter's field. In 1900 the Board of Supervisors voted to ban burials within city limits, and all but two city cemeteries (at Mission Dolores and the Presidio) were moved to Colma, a small town just south of San Francisco. When digging has to be done in the park, bones occasionally surface again. ⊠ *Entrance at 34th Ave. at Clement St., Outer Richmond.*

Ocean Beach. Stretching 3 mi along the western side of the city from the Richmond to the Sunset, this sandy swath of the Pacific coast is good for jogging or walking the dog—but not for swimming. The water is so cold that surfers wear wet suits year-round, and riptides are strong. As

Visitors enjoy the rough beauty of the Pacific from the Cliff House.

for sunbathing, it's rarely warm enough here; think meditative walking instead of sun worshipping.

Paths on both sides of the Great Highway lead from Lincoln Way to Sloat Boulevard (near the zoo); the beachside path winds through landscaped sand dunes, and the paved path across the highway is good for biking and in-line skating. (Though you have to rent bikes elsewhere.) The **Beach Chalet** restaurant and brewpub is across the Great Highway from Ocean Beach, about five blocks south of the Cliff House. ⊠ *Along Great Hwy. from Cliff House to Sloat Blvd. and beyond.*

San Francisco Zoo. Awash in bad press since one of its tigers escaped its enclosure and killed a visitor on Christmas day 2007, the city's zoo is struggling to polish its image, raise its attendance numbers, scrounge up funds to update its habitats, and restore its reputation with animal welfare organizations. Nestled onto prime oceanfront property, the zoo—which some have accused of caring more about human entertainment than the welfare of its wards—is touting its metamorphosis into the "New Zoo," a wildlife-focused recreation center that inspires visitors to become conservationists. Integrated exhibits group different species of animals from the same geographic areas together in enclosures that don't look like cages. More than 250 species reside here, including endangered species such as the snow leopard, Sumatran tiger, and grizzly bear.

The zoo's superstar exhibit is **Grizzly Gulch,** where orphaned sisters Kachina and Kiona enchant visitors with their frolicking and swimming. When the bears are in the water, the only thing between you and them is (thankfully thick) glass. Grizzly feedings are 11 AM daily.

The **Lemur Forest** has five varieties of the bug-eyed, long-tailed primates from Madagascar. You can help hoist food into the lemurs' feeding towers and watch the fuzzy creatures climb up to chow down. African Kikuyu grass carpets the circular outer area of **Gorilla Preserve,** one of the largest and most natural gorilla habitats of any zoo in the world. Trees and shrubs create communal play areas.

Ten species of rare monkeys—including colobus monkeys, white ruffed lemurs, and macaques—live and play at the two-tier **Primate Discovery Center,** which contains 23 interactive learning exhibits on the ground level.

Magellanic penguins waddle about the rather sad concrete **Penguin Island,** splashing and frolicking in its 200-foot pool. Feeding time is 2:30. Koalas peer out from among the trees in **Koala Crossing,** and kangaroos and wallabies headline the **Australian Walkabout** exhibit. The 7-acre **Puente al Sur** (Bridge to the South) re-creates habitats in South America, replete with giant anteaters and capybaras.

An **African Savanna** exhibit mixes giraffes, zebras, kudus, ostriches, and many other species, all living together in a 3-acre section with a central viewing spot, accessed by a covered passageway.

The 6-acre **Children's Zoo** has about 300 mammals, birds, and reptiles, plus an insect zoo, a meerkat and prairie-dog exhibit, a nature trail, a nature theater, a restored 1921 Dentzel carousel, and a mini–steam train. A ride on the train costs $4, and you can hop astride one of the carousel's 52 hand-carved menagerie animals for $2. ⊠ *Sloat Blvd. and 47th Ave., Sunset ⌖ Muni L–Taraval streetcar from downtown* ☎ *415/753–7080 ⊕ www.sfzoo.org ⊠ $15, $1 off with Muni transfer* ☉ *Daily 10–5. Children's zoo 10–4:30.*

Sutro Heights Park. Crows and other large birds battle the heady breezes at this cliff-top park on what were once the grounds of the home of Adolph Sutro, an eccentric mining engineer and former San Francisco mayor. An extremely wealthy man, Sutro may have owned about 10% of San Francisco at one point, but he couldn't buy good taste: a few remnants of his gaudy, faux-classical statue collection still stand (including the lions at what was the main gate). Monterey cypresses and Canary Island palms dot the park, and photos on placards depict what things looked like before the house burned down in 1896, from the greenhouse to the ornate carpet-bed designs.

All that remains of the main house is its foundation. Climb up for a sweeping view of the Pacific Ocean and the Cliff House below (which Sutro owned), and try to imagine what the perspective might have been like from one of the upper floors. San Francisco City Guides (☎ 415/557–4266) runs a free Saturday tour of the park that starts at 2 (meet at the lion statue at 48th and Point Lobos avenues). ⊠ *Point Lobos and 48th Aves., Outer Richmond.*

Golden Gate Park

WORD OF MOUTH

"My husband and I are visiting [with our kids] . . . and I want to see Golden Gate Park . . . hear JFK Dr. is closed to cars on Sundays— will this make it hard to get to the things we want to see?"

—dimpi213

"You might consider renting bikes with a kid trailer in order to avoid the whole search for parking. This is how many locals with small kids enjoy the park on Sundays."

—SAB

A GREEN RETREAT

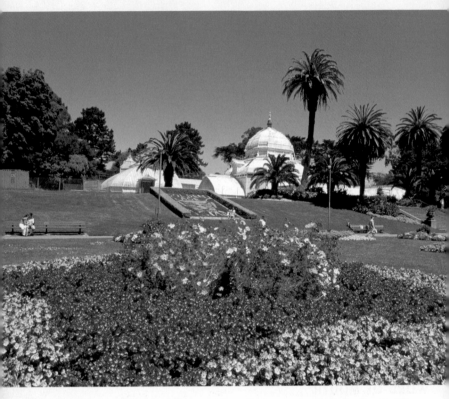

Stretching more than 1,000 acres from the ocean to the Haight, Golden Gate Park is a place to slow down and smell the eucalyptus. Stockbrokers and gadget-laden parents stroll the Music Concourse, while speedy tattooed cyclists and wobbly, training-wheeled kids cruise along shaded paths. Stooped seniors warm the garden benches, hikers search for waterfalls, and picnickers lounge in the Rhododendron Dell. San Franciscans love their city streets, but the park is where they come to breathe.

PLANNING A PARK VISIT

ORIENTATION

The park breaks down naturally into three chunks. The eastern end attracts the biggest crowds with its cluster of blockbuster sights. It's also the easiest place to dip into the park for a quick trip. Water hobbyists come to the middle section's lake-speckled open space, home to fly-casting pools and the Model Yacht Club. Sporty types head west to the coastal end for its soccer fields, golf course, and archery range. This windswept western end is the park's least visited and most naturally landscaped part. ☉ Daily 6 am–10pm ⊕ www.parks.sfgov.org

WALKING TOURS

San Francisco Botanical Garden (☏ 415/661–1316) has free botanical tours every day. Tours start at the bookstore weekdays at 1:30 PM, weekends at 10:30 AM and 1:30 PM. Meet at the Friend Gate (at the northern entrance) Wednesday, Friday, and Sunday at 2 PM.

San Francisco Parks Trust (☏ 415/263–0991) offers historically minded tours of the Japanese Tea Garden Monday at 9:30 AM and

Wednesday and Sunday at 1. The hour-long tours are free but don't include garden admission.

BEST TIMES TO VISIT

Time of day: It's best to arrive early at the Conservatory of Flowers, the de Young Museum, and the Japanese Tea Garden to avoid crowds. At sunset, the only place to be is the park's western end, watching the sun dip into the Pacific.

Time of year: Come to the eastern end of the park on a sunny weekend, and you'll think the whole Bay Area is here with you—visit during the week if you can. The long, Indian summer days of September and October are the warmest times to visit, and many special weekend events are held then.

Blooms: The rhododendrons burst into billowy bloom between February and May. The Queen Wilhelmina Tulip Garden blossoms in February and March. Cherry trees in the Japanese Tea Garden bloom in April, and the Rose Garden is at its best from mid-May to mid-June, in the beginning of July, and during September.

(opposite) Conservatory of Flowers. (top left) The Strybing Arboretum in bloom.

IN FOCUS GOLDEN GATE PARK

9

TIPS

■ Carry a map—the park's sightlines usually prevent you from using city landmarks as reference points. Posted maps in the park are few and far between, and they're often out of date. Paths aren't always clear, so stick to well-marked trails.

■ In Golden Gate Park, free public restrooms are fairly common and mostly clean, especially around the eastern end's attractions. The San Francisco Botanical Garden has numerous facilities, including inside each gate. Enter the de Young Museum at the sculpture garden and café patio and you can use the public restrooms there. Farther west, behind Stow Lake's boathouse and near the Koret Children's Quarter are facilities.

BEST WAYS TO SPEND YOUR TIME

The park stretches 3 mi east to west and is a half-mile wide, so it's possible to cover the whole thing in a day—by car, public transportation, bike, or even on foot. But to do so might feel more like a forced march than a pleasure jaunt. Weigh your time and your interests, choose your top picks, then leave at least an extra hour to just enjoy being outdoors.

Two hours: Swing by the exquisite Conservatory of Flowers for a 20-minute peek, then head to the de Young Museum. Spend a few minutes assessing its controversial exterior and perhaps glide through some of the galleries before heading to the observation tower for a panoramic view of the city. Cross the music concourse to the spectacular Academy of Sciences.

Half day: Spend a little extra time at the sights described above, then head to the nearby Japanese Tea Garden to enjoy its perfectionist landscape. Next, cross the street to the San Francisco Botanical Garden at Strybing Arboretum and check out the intriguing Primitive Garden. If you brought supplies, this is a great place for a picnic; you can also grab lunch at the de Young Café.

Full day: After the half-day (above) continue on to the children's playground if you have kids in tow. Once your little ones see the playground's tree house–like play structures and climbing opportunities, you may be here for the rest of the day. Alternatively, make your way to the serene National AIDS Memorial Grove. Then head west, stopping at Stow Lake to climb Strawberry Hill. Wind up at the Beach Chalet for a sunset drink.

(top) Amateur musicians entertain passersby. (middle) Sundays are ideal biking days. (bottom) The meandering paths are perfect for strolling.

GETTING AROUND THE PARK

WALKING

The most convenient entry point is on the eastern edge at Stanyan and Kezar streets, which points you directly toward the Conservatory of Flowers. It's a 10-minute walk there; allow another 10–15 minutes to reach the California Academy of Sciences, de Young Museum, Japanese Tea Garden, and San Francisco Botanical Garden. Stow Lake is another 10 minutes west from these three sights.

BY BIKE

The park is fantastic for cycling, especially on Sunday when cars are barred from John F. Kennedy Drive. Biking the park round trip is about a 7-mi trip, which usually takes 1–2 hours. The route down John F. Kennedy Drive takes you past the prettiest, well-maintained sections of the park on a mostly flat circuit. The most popular route continues all the way to the beach. Keep in mind that the ride is downhill toward the ocean, uphill heading east.

BY CAR

If you have a car, you'll have no trouble hopping from sight to sight. (But remember, the main road, John F. Kennedy Drive, is closed to cars on Sunday and, April–September, on Saturday.) Parking within the park is often free and is usually easy to find, especially beyond the eastern end. On Sundays or anytime the eastern end is crowded, head for the residential streets north of the park or the underground parking lot; enter on 10th and Fulton (northern edge of the park) or MLK and Concourse (in the park).

BY SHUTTLE

If you're visiting on a weekend between May and October, you can ride the free Golden Gate Park shuttle. This loops through the park every 15 minutes, roughly between 10 AM and 6 PM, stopping at 15 sights from McLaren Lodge to the Beach Chalet. Maps are posted at each stop.

WHERE TO RENT

Golden Gate Park Bike & Skate (✉ 3038 Fulton St. ☎ 415/668–1117).
On the northern edge of the park; has good deals on rentals.

Blazing Saddles (✉ 1095 Columbus Ave., North Beach ☎ 415/202–8888). The biggest rental outfit in town. Although their branches aren't close to the park, the company is worth considering since they have tons of bikes in good condition. They're very helpful when it comes to route recommendations, too.

BEST PLACES TO PICNIC

■ Lawn in front of the Conservatory of Flowers.

■ By the pond in the San Francisco Botanical Garden.

■ The benches overlooking the Rustic Bridge at Stow Lake.

■ Rhododendron Dell.

(top) Water lilies adorn the Japanese Tea Garden.

DON'T-MISS SIGHTS

← see overview map

Map labels: 29th Ave. · 27th Ave. · 25th Ave. · 23rd Ave. · 21st Ave. · 19th Ave. · 15th Ave. · Park Presidio Blvd · 12th Ave. · Cabrillo St. · Fulton St. · Rose Garden · Cross Over Dr. · Marx Meadow · Portals of the Past · Boat House · de Young Museum · Strawberry Hill · Beach Chalet · Dutch Windmill · Speedway Meadow · Cross Over Dr. · Japanese Tea Garden · Stow Lake · Friend Gate · Middle Dr. · Metson Lake · Mallard Lake · S.F. Botanical Garden at Strybing Arboretum · Lincoln Way · 30th Ave. · 23rd Ave. · 21st Ave. · 9th Ave. · 15th Ave. · 13th Ave. · 11th Ave.

0 — 1/4 mile
0 — 400 meters

Conservatory of Flowers

✉ John F. Kennedy Dr. at Conservatory Dr.

☎ 415/666–7001

💲 $7, free 1st Tues. of month

🕐 Tues.–Sun. 9–5

🌐 www.conservatoryof flowers.org

CONSERVATORY OF FLOWERS

Whatever you do, be sure to at least drive by the Conservatory of Flowers—it's just too darn pretty to miss. The gorgeous, white-framed, 1878 glass structure is topped with a 14-ton glass dome. Stepping inside the giant greenhouse is like taking a quick trip to the rainforest; it's humid, warm, and smells earthy. The undeniable highlight is the Aquatic Plants section, where lily pads float and carnivorous plants dine on bugs to the sounds of rushing water. On the east side of the conservatory (to the right as you face the building), cypress, pine, and redwood trees surround the **Dahlia Garden,** which blooms in summer and fall. To the west is the **Rhododendron Dell,** which contains 850 varieties, more than any other garden in the country. It's a favorite local Mother's Day picnic spot.

STOW LAKE

Russian seniors feed the pigeons, kids watch turtles sunning themselves, and joggers circle this placid body of water, Golden Gate Park's largest lake. Early park superintendent John McLaren may have snarked that manmade Stow Lake was "a shoestring around a watermelon," but for more than a century visitors have come to walk its paths and bridges, paddle boats, and climb Strawberry Hill (the "watermelon"). Cross one of the bridges—the 19th-century stone bridge on the southwest side is lovely—and ascend the hill; keep your eyes open for the waterfall and an elaborate Chinese Pavilion.

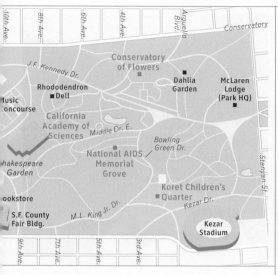

SAN FRANCISCO JAPANESE TEA GARDEN

As you amble through the manicured landscape, past Japanese sculptures and perfect miniature pagodas, over ponds of carp that have been there since before the 1906 quake, you may be transported to a more peaceful plane. Or maybe the shrieks of kids clambering over the almost vertical "humpback" bridges will keep you firmly in the here and now. Either way, this garden is one of those tourist spots that's truly worth a stop (a half-hour will do). And at 5 acres, it's large enough that you'll always be able to find a bit of serenity, even when the tour buses drop by. ■TIP→ The garden is especially lovely in April, when the cherry blossoms are in bloom.

KORET CHILDREN'S QUARTER

The country's first public children's playground reopened in 2007 after a spectacular renovation, with wave-shaped climbing walls, old-fashioned cement slides, and a 20-plus-foot rope climbing structure that kids love and parents fear. Thankfully, one holdover is the beautiful, handcrafted 1912 Herschell-Spillman Carousel. The lovely stone Sharon Building, next to the playground, offers kids' art classes. Bring a picnic or pick up grub nearby on 9th Avenue and you could spend the entire day here. Be aware that the playground, which has separate areas for toddlers and bigger kids, is unenclosed and sightlines can be obstructed.

Stow Lake

✉ Off John F. Kennedy Dr.

☎ Boat rental 415/752–0347; surrey and bike rental 415/668–6699

🕐 Boat rentals daily 10–4, surrey and bicycle rentals daily 9–dusk.

San Francisco Japanese Tea Garden

✉ Hagiwara Tea Garden Dr.

☎ 415/752-4227

💲 $7, free Mon., Wed., and Fri. 9 AM–10 AM

🕐 Mar.–Oct., daily 9–6; Nov.–Feb., daily 9–4:45.

Koret Children's Quarter

✉ Bowling Green Dr., off Martin Luther King Jr. Dr

☎ 415/831-2700

💲 Playground free, carousel $2, kids 6–12 $1

🕐 Playground daily dawn–dusk; carousel Memorial Day–Labor Day, daily 10–4:30, Labor Day–Memorial Day, Fri.–Sun. 10–4:30.

DE YOUNG MUSEUM

✉ 50 Hagiwara Tea Garden
Dr.

☎ 415/750–3600

🌐 www.famsf.org/deyoung

💳 $10; free 1st Tues. of
month

🕙 Tues.–Sun. 9:30–5:15

TIPS

■ Admission at the de Young
is good for same-day admission to the Legion of Honor
and vice-versa.

■ The de Young is famous
these days first and foremost
for its striking and controversial new building and
tree-topping tower. These
are accessible to the public
for free, so if it's not the art
you're interested in seeing,
save the cost of admission
and head up the elevator to
360-degree views from the
glass-walled observation floor.

■ When it's time for a nosh,
head to the de Young Café
and dine in the lovely outdoor sculpture garden on
tableware fit for MOMA.

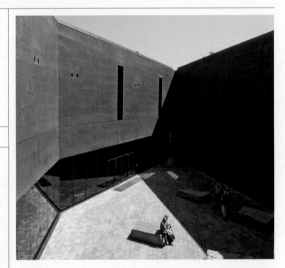

Everyone in town has a strong opinion about the new de Young.
Some adore the striking copper façade, while others grimace and
hope that the green patina of age will mellow the effect. The
building almost overshadows the museum's respected collection
of American, African, and Oceanic art. However, the courts may
decide whether or not the museum keeps its priceless collection
of art from Papua New Guinea, whose owner used the collection
as collateral in a legal dispute. An emergency court order is keeping the work in the de Young ... for now.

HIGHLIGHTS

Head through the sprawling concourse level and begin your visit on
the upper level, where you'll find textiles; art from Africa, Oceana,
and New Guinea; and highlights of the 20th-century American
painting collection (such as Wayne Thiebaud, John Singer Sargent,
Winslow Homer, and Richard Diebenkorn). These are the don't-miss
items, so take your time. Then head back downstairs to see art from
the Americas and contemporary work.

CALIFORNIA ACADEMY OF SCIENCES

✉ 55 Music Concourse Dr.

☎ 415/379-8000

🌐 www.calacademy.org

💲 $24.95, free 3rd Wed. of month

🕐 Mon.–Sat. 9:30–5, Sun. 11–5

TIPS

■ The academy often hosts gaggles of schoolchildren. Arrive early and allow plenty of time to wait in line.

■ Plan ahead: check Planetarium show times, animal feeding times, etc, before you arrive.

■ Visitors complain about the high cost of food here; consider bringing a picnic.

■ Free days are tempting, but the tradeoff includes extremely long lines and the possibility that you won't get in.

■ With antsy kids, visit Early Explorers Cove and use the academy's in-and-out privileges to run around outside.

■ Take time to examine the structure itself, from denim insulation to weather sensors.

With its native plant–covered living roof, retractable ceiling, three-story rainforest, gigantic planetarium, living coral reef, and frolicking penguins, the Cal Academy is one of the city's most spectacular treasures. Dramatically designed by Renzo Piano, it's an eco-friendly, energy-efficient adventure in biodiversity and green architecture. The roof's large mounds and hills mirror the local topography, and Piano's audacious design completes the dramatic transformation of the park's Music Concourse. Moving away from a restrictive role as a backward-looking museum that catalogued natural history, the new academy is all about sustainability and the future, but you'll still find those beloved dioramas in African Hall.

HIGHLIGHTS

By the time you arrive, hopefully you've decided which shows and programs to attend, looked at the academy's floorplan, and designed a plan to cover it all in the time you have. And if not, here's the quick version: Head left from the entrance to the wooden walkway over otherworldly leopard rays in the Philippine Coral Reef, then continue to the Swamp to see the famous albino alligator. Swing through African Hall and gander at the penguins, take the elevator up to the living roof, then return to the main floor and get in line to explore the Rainforests of the World, ducking free-flying butterflies and watching for other live surprises. You'll end up below ground in the Amazonian Flooded Rainforest, where you can explore the academy's other aquarium exhibits. Phew.

IN FOCUS GOLDEN GATE PARK

9

ALSO WORTH SEEING

San Francisco Botanical Garden at Strybing Arboretum

SAN FRANCISCO BOTANICAL GARDEN AT STRYBING ARBORETUM

One of the best picnic spots in a very picnic-friendly park, the 55-acre arboretum specializes in plants from areas with climates similar to that of the Bay Area. Walk the Eastern Australian garden to see tough, pokey shrubs and plants with cartoon-like names, such as the hilly-pilly tree. Kids gravitate toward the large shallow fountain and the pond with ducks, turtles, and egrets. ✉ *Enter the park at 9th Ave. at Lincoln Way* ☎ *415/661–1316* ⊕ *www.sfbotanicalgarden.org* ✒ *Free* ☉ *Weekdays 8–4:30, weekends 10–5.*

NATIONAL AIDS MEMORIAL GROVE

This lush, serene 7-acre grove was conceived as a living memorial to the disease's victims. Coast live oaks, Monterey pines, coast redwoods, and other trees flank the grove. There are also two stone circles, one recording the names of the dead and their loved ones, the other engraved with a poem. Free 20-minute tours are available some Saturdays. ✉ *Middle Dr. E, west of tennis courts* ☎ *415/765–0497* ⊕ *www.aidsmemorial.org.*

Beach Chalet

BEACH CHALET

Hugging the park's western border, this 1925 Willis Polk–designed structure houses gorgeous depression-era murals of familiar San Francisco scenes, while verses by local poets adorn niches here and there. Stop by the ground-floor visitors center on your way to indulge in a microbrew upstairs, ideally at sunset. ✉ *1000 Great Hwy.* ☎ *restaurant 415/386–8439* ⊕ *http://beachchalet.com* ☉ *Restaurant Mon.–Thurs. 9 AM–10 PM, Fri. 9 AM–11 PM, Sat. 8 AM– 11 PM, Sun. 8 AM–10 PM.*

Dutch Windmill

DUTCH WINDMILL

It may not pump water anymore, but this carefully restored windmill, built in 1903 to irrigate the park, continues to enchant visitors. The Queen Wilhelmina Tulip Garden here is a welcoming respite, particularly lovely during its February and March bloom. Fund-raising is underway to restore the Murphy Windmill, just south; swing by for an interesting comparison. ✉ *Northwest corner of the park* ☎ *No phone* ☉ *Dawn–dusk.*

The Haight, the Castro, and Noe Valley

WORD OF MOUTH

"I have a suggestion. When you get to SF, take the street car to the Castro with the whole family. It's a fun ride and it ends up at the Castro. Once you see the giant rainbow flag, you know you're there."

—MikeT

GETTING ORIENTED

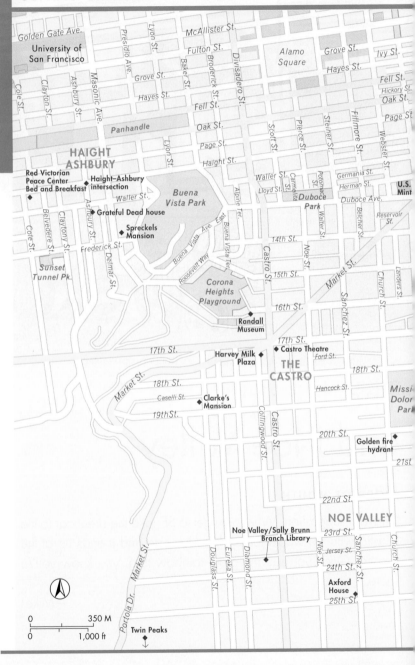

University of San Francisco

Golden Gate Ave.

McAllister St.

Fulton St.

Alamo Square

Grove St.

Ivy St.

Presidio Ave.

Lyon St.

Grove St.

Hayes St.

Baker St.

Broderick St.

Divisadero St.

Hayes St.

Fell St.

Masonic Ave.

Ashbury St.

Clayton St.

Cole St.

Panhandle

Oak St.

Scott St.

Pierce St.

Steiner St.

Fillmore St.

Fell St.

Hickory St.

Oak St.

Page St.

Webster St.

HAIGHT ASHBURY

Lyon St.

Page St.

Haight St.

Red Victorian Peace Center Bed and Breakfast

Haight–Ashbury intersection

Waller St.

Waller St.

Carmelita St.

Potomac St.

Germania St.

Herman St.

U.S. Mint

Belvedere St.

Clayton St.

Cole St.

Ashbury St.

Grateful Dead house

Buena Vista Park

Lloyd St.

Alpine Ter.

Buena Vista Ave. East

Buena Vista Ter.

Duboce Park

Waller St.

Duboce Ave.

Belcher St.

Reservoir St.

Spreckels Mansion

Frederick St.

Delmar St.

Buena Vista Ave.

Roosevelt Way

14th St.

Castro St.

Noe St.

Sunset Tunnel Pk.

Corona Heights Playground

15th St.

16th St.

Sanchez St.

Church St.

Landers St.

Market St.

Randall Museum

17th St.

17th St.

Harvey Milk Plaza

♦ Castro Theatre

Ford St.

THE CASTRO

18th St.

18th St.

Market St.

Caselli St.

Clarke's Mansion

Hancock St.

Missi Dolor Park

19th St.

Castro St.

Collingwood St.

20th St.

Golden fire hydrant

21st

22nd St.

NOE VALLEY

Noe Valley/Sally Brunn Branch Library

23rd St.

Sanchez St.

Church St.

Douglass St.

Eureka St.

Diamond St.

Noe St.

Jersey St.

24th St.

Market St.

Portola Dr.

Axford House

25th St.

0   350 M

0   1,000 ft

Twin Peaks

MAKING THE MOST OF YOUR TIME

The Upper Haight is only a few blocks long, and although there are plenty of shops and amusements, an hour or so should be enough. Many restaurants here cater to the morning-after crowd, so this is a great place for brunch. With the prevalence of panhandling in this area, you may be most comfortable here during the day.

The Castro, with its fun storefronts, invites unhurried exploration; allot at least 60 to 90 minutes. Visit in the evening to check out the lively nightlife, or in the late morning—especially on weekends—when the street scene is hopping.

A loop through Noe Valley takes about an hour. With its popular breakfast spots and cafés, this neighborhood is a good place for a morning stroll. After you've filled up, browse the shops along 24th and Castro streets.

TOP 5 REASONS TO GO

Castro Theatre: Take in a film at this gorgeous throwback and join the audience shouting out lines, commentary, and songs. Come early and let the Wurlitzer set the mood.

Sunday brunch in the Castro: Recover from Saturday night (with the entire community) at one of the Castro's top three brunch destinations: Lime (⌧ *2247 Market*), 2223 (⌧ *2223 Market*), and Caffè Luna Piena (⌧ *558 Castro St.*).

Vintage shopping in the Haight: Find the perfect chiffon dress at La Rosa, a pristine faux-leopard coat at Held Over, or the motorcycle jacket of your dreams at Buffalo Exchange.

24th Street stroll: Take a leisurely ramble down loveable Noe Valley's main drag, lined with unpretentious cafés, comfy eateries, and cute one-of-a-kind shops.

Cliff's Variety: Stroll the aisles of the Castro's "hardware" store (⌧ *479 Castro St.*) for lightbulbs, hammers, and pipes (as well as false eyelashes, tiaras, and feather boas) to get a feel for what makes this neighborhood special.

QUICK BITES

Lovejoy's Antiques & Tea Room (⌧ *1351 Church St., at Clipper St., Noe Valley* ☎ *415/648–5895*) is a homey jumble, with its lace-covered tables, couches, and mismatched chairs set among the antiques for sale. High tea and cream tea are served, along with traditional English-tea-room "fayre."

Get a jolt of organic fair-trade caffeine and a bit of revolutionary spirit at book-filled **Coffee to the People** (⌧ *1206 Masonic Ave., Haight* ☎ *415/626–2435*).

The aroma alone might lure you into **Philz Coffee** (⌧ *4023 18th St., Castro* ☎ *415/875–9656*), just off the main drag of Castro Street. Its fedora-hung, cramped space gives off a casual vibe, but don't be fooled: the city's second most-popular place for the über-serious coffee drinker (after Blue Bottle) serves up the strongest handcrafted cup of joe in town.

GETTING THERE

The Castro is the end of the line for the F-line, and both the Castro and Noe Valley are served by the J–Church Metro. The only public transit that runs to the Haight is the bus; take the 7–Haight from Civic Center or the 6–Parnassus from Polk and Market. If you're on foot, keep in mind that the hill between the Castro and Noe Valley is very steep.

10

Sightseeing
★

Nightlife
★★★

Dining
★★★

Lodging
★

Shopping
★★★

These distinct neighborhoods are where the city's soul resides. They wear their personalities large and proud, and all are perfect for just strolling around. Like a slide show of San Franciscan history, you can move from the Haight's residue of 1960s counterculture to the Castro's connection to 1970s and '80s gay life to 1990s gentrification in Noe Valley. Although historic events thrust the Haight and the Castro onto the international stage, both are anything but stagnant—they're still dynamic areas well worth exploring.

Updated by
Denise M. Leto

During the 1960s the siren song of free love, peace, and mind-altering substances lured thousands of young people to the Haight, a neighborhood just east of Golden Gate Park. By 1966 the area had become a hot spot for rock artists, including the Grateful Dead, Jefferson Airplane, and Janis Joplin. Some of the most infamous flower children, including Charles Manson and People's Temple founder Jim Jones, also called the Haight home.

Today the '60s message of peace, civil rights, and higher consciousness has been distilled into a successful blend of commercialism and progressive causes: the Haight Ashbury Free Medical Clinic, founded in 1967, survives at the corner of Haight and Clayton, while throwbacks like Bound Together Books (the anarchist book collective), the head shop Pipe Dreams, and a bevy of tie-dye shops all keep the Summer of Love alive in their own way. The Haight's famous political spirit—it was the first neighborhood in the nation to lead a freeway revolt, and it continues to host regular boycotts against chain stores—survives alongside some of the finest Victorian-lined streets in the city. And the kids continue to come: this is where young people who end up on San Francisco's streets most often gather. Visitors tend to find the Haight either edgy and exhilarating or scummy and intimidating (the panhandling here can be aggressive).

DID YOU KNOW?

The Haight-Ashbury inter-section retains some of its hippie counterculture past, but these days it also shares street space with global businesses, mixing corporate vibes with flower power.

Hippie History

The eternal lure for twentysome-things, cheap rent, first helped spawn an indelible part of SF's history and public image. In the early 1960s, young people started streaming into the sprawling, inexpensive Victorians in the area around the University of San Francisco. The new Haight locals earnestly planned a new era of communal living, individual empowerment, and expanded consciousness.

Golden Gate Park's Panhandle, a thin strip of green on the Haight's northern edge, was their public gathering spot—the site of protests, concerts, food giveaways, and general hanging out. In 1967 George Harrison strolled up the park's Hippie Hill, borrowed a guitar, and played for a while before someone finally recognized him. He led the crowd, Pied Piper–style, into the Haight.

At first, the counterculture was all about sharing and taking care of one another—a good thing, considering most hippies were either broke or had renounced money. They hadn't renounced food, though, and the daily free "feeds" in the Panhandle were a staple for many. The Diggers, an anarchist street-theater group, were known for handing out bread shaped like the big coffee cans they baked it in. (The Diggers also gave us immortal phrases such as "Do your own thing.")

At the time, the U.S. government, Harvard professor Timothy Leary, a Stanford student named Ken Kesey, and the kids in the Haight were all experimenting with LSD. Acid was legal, widely available, and usually given away for free. At Kesey's all-night parties, called "acid tests," a buck got you a cup of "electric" Kool-Aid, a preview of psychedelic art, and an earful of

the house band, the Grateful Dead. LSD was deemed illegal in 1966, and the kids responded by staging a Love Pageant Rally, where they dropped acid tabs en masse and rocked out to Janis Joplin and the Dead.

Things crested early in 1967, when between 10,000 and 50,000 people ("depending on whether you were a policeman or a hippie," according to one hippie) gathered at the Polo Field in Golden Gate Park for the Human Be-In of the Gathering of the Tribes. Allen Ginsberg and Timothy Leary spoke, the Dead and Jefferson Airplane played, and people costumed with beads and feathers waved flags, clanged cymbals, and beat drums. A parachutist dropped onto the field, tossing fistfuls of acid tabs to the crowd. America watched via satellite, gape-mouthed—it was every conservative parent's nightmare.

Later that year, thousands heeded Scott McKenzie's song "San Francisco," which promised "For those who come to San Francisco, Summertime will be a love-in there." The Summer of Love swelled the Haight's population from 7,000 to 75,000; people came both to join in and to ogle the nutty subculture. But degenerates soon joined the gentle people, heroin replaced LSD, crime was rampant, and the Haight began a fast slide.

Hippies will tell you the Human Be-In was the pinnacle of their scene, while the Summer of Love came from outside—a media creation that turned their movement into a monster. Still, the idea of that fictional summer still lingers, and to this day pilgrims from all over the world come to the Haight to search for a past that never was.

Just over Buena Vista Hill from Haight Street, nestled at the base of Twin Peaks, lies the brash and sassy Castro District—the social, political, and cultural center of San Francisco's thriving gay (and, to a lesser extent, lesbian) community. This neighborhood is one of the city's liveliest and most welcoming, especially on weekends. Streets teem with folks out shopping, pushing political causes, heading to art films, and lingering in bars and cafés. Hard-bodied men

WORD OF MOUTH

"I climbed to the top of Buena Vista Park which is near the old Haight-Ashbury area, then dipped down and then up again to Corona Heights. Talk about the seven hills of Rome! Someone should mention the seven hills of San Francisco.... Then there's the absolutely fantastic view up on Twin Peaks."   —easytraveler

in painted-on tees cruise the cutting-edge clothing and novelty stores, and pairs of all genders and sexual persuasions hold hands. Brightly painted, intricately restored Victorians line the streets here, making the Castro a good place to view striking examples of the architecture San Francisco is famous for.

Still farther south lies Noe Valley—also known as Stroller Valley for its relatively high concentration of little ones—an upscale but relaxed enclave that's one of the city's most desirable places to live. Church Street and 24th Street, the neighborhood's main thoroughfares, teem with laid-back cafés, kid-friendly restaurants, and comfortable, old-time shops. You can also see remnants of Noe Valley's agricultural beginnings: Billy Goat Hill (at Castro and 30th streets), a wild-grass hill often draped in fog, is named for the goats that grazed here right into the 20th century.

WHAT TO SEE IN THE HAIGHT

Buena Vista Park. If you can manage the steep climb, this eucalyptus-filled park has great city views. Be sure to scan the stone rain gutters lining many of the park's walkways for inscribed names and dates; these are the remains of gravestones left unclaimed when the city closed the Laurel Hill cemetery around 1940. You might also come across used needles and condoms; definitely avoid the park after dark, when these items are left behind. ⊠ *Haight St. between Lyon St. and Buena Vista Ave. W, Haight.*

Grateful Dead house. On the outside, this is just one more well-kept Victorian on a street that's full of them—but true fans of the Dead may find some inspiration at this legendary structure. The three-story house (closed to the public) is tastefully painted in sedate mauves, tans, and teals (no bright tie-dye colors here). ⊠ *710 Ashbury St., just past Waller St., Haight.*

Haight-Ashbury intersection. On October 6, 1967, hippies took over the intersection of Haight and Ashbury streets to proclaim the "Death of Hip." If they thought hip was dead then, they'd find absolute confirmation of it today, what with the only tie-dye in sight on the Ben & Jerry's storefront on the famed corner.

10

Everyone knows the Summer of Love had something to do with free love and LSD, but the drugs and other excesses of that period have tended to obscure the residents' serious attempts to create an America that was more spiritually oriented, more environmentally aware, and less caught up in commercialism. The Diggers, a radical group of actors and populist agitators, for example, operated a free shop a few blocks off Haight Street. Everything really was free at the free shop; people brought in things they didn't need and took things they did. (The group also coined immortal phrases like "Do your own thing.")

> ### SISTER ACT!
>
> If you're lucky enough to happen upon a cluster of cheeky cross-dressing nuns while in the Castro, meet the legendary Sisters of Perpetual Indulgence. They're decked out in white face-paint, glitter, and fabulous jewels. Renowned for their wit and charity fund-raising bashes, the Sisters—Sister Mary MaeHimm, Sister Bea Attitude, Sister Farrah Moans, and the gang—are the pinnacle of Castro color.

Among the folks who hung out in or near the Haight during the late 1960s were writers Richard Brautigan, Allen Ginsberg, Ken Kesey, and Gary Snyder; anarchist Abbie Hoffman; rock performers Marty Balin, Jerry Garcia, Janis Joplin, and Grace Slick; LSD champion Timothy Leary; and filmmaker Kenneth Anger. If you're keen to feel something resembling the hippie spirit these days, there's always Hippie Hill, just inside the Haight Street entrance of Golden Gate Park. Think drum circles, guitar players, and whiffs of pot smoke.

WHICH HAIGHT The Haight is actually composed of two distinct neighborhoods: the Lower Haight runs from Divisadero to Webster; the Upper Haight, immediately east of Golden Gate Park, is the part people tend to call Haight-Ashbury (and the part that's covered here). San Franciscans come to the Upper Haight for the myriad vintage clothing stores concentrated in its few blocks, bars with character, restaurants where huge breakfast portions take the edge off a hangover, and Amoeba, the best place in town for new and used CDs and vinyl. The Lower Haight is a lively, grittier stretch with several well-loved pubs and a smattering of niche music shops.

Red Victorian Peace Center Bed & Breakfast. By even the most generous accounts, the Summer of Love quickly crashed and burned, and the Haight veered sharply away from the higher goals that inspired that fabled summer. In 1977 Sami Sunchild acquired the Red Vic, built as a hotel in 1904, with the aim of preserving the best of 1960s ideals. She decorated her rooms with 1960s themes—one chamber is called the Flower Child Room—and opened the Peace Art Center on the ground floor. Here you can buy her paintings, T-shirts, and "meditative art," along with books about the Haight and prayer flags. Simple, cheap vegan and vegetarian fare is available in the Peace Café, and there's also a meditation room. ⊠ *1665 Haight St., Haight* ☎ *415/864–1978* ⊕ *www.redvic.com.*

A colorful mosaic mural in the Castro.

NEED A BREAK?

Boisterous Cha Cha Cha (✉ *1801 Haight St., at Shrader St., Haight* ☎ *415/386–7670*) serves island cuisine, a mix of Cajun, Southwestern, and Caribbean influences. The decor is Technicolor tropical plastic, and the food is hot and spicy. Try the fried calamari or chili-spiked shrimp, and wash everything down with a pitcher of Cha Cha Cha's signature sangria. Reservations are not accepted, so expect a wait for dinner.

Spreckels Mansion. Not to be confused with the Spreckels Mansion of Pacific Heights, this house was built for sugar baron Richard Spreckels in 1887. Jack London and Ambrose Bierce both lived and wrote here, while more recent residents included musician Graham Nash and actor Danny Glover. The boxy, putty-color Victorian—today a private home—is in mint condition. ✉ *737 Buena Vista Ave. W, Haight.*

WHAT TO SEE IN THE CASTRO

★ **Castro Theatre.** Here's a classic way to join in the Castro community: grab some popcorn and catch a flick at this gorgeous, 1,500-seat art-deco theater; opened in 1922, it's the grandest of San Francisco's few remaining movie palaces. The neon marquee, which stands at the top of the Castro strip, is the neighborhood's great landmark. The Castro was the fitting host of 2008's red-carpet preview of Gus Van Sant's film *Milk,* starring Sean Penn as openly gay San Francisco supervisor Harvey Milk. The theater's elaborate Spanish baroque interior is fairly well preserved. Before many shows the theater's pipe organ rises from the orchestra pit and an organist plays pop and movie tunes, usually ending

Children of the Rainbow Revolution

San Francisco's gay community has been a part of the city since its earliest days. As a port city and a major hub during the 19th-century gold rush, it became known for its sexual openness along with all its other liberalities. But a major catalyst for the rise of a gay community was World War II.

During the war, hundreds of thousands of servicemen cycled through "Sodom by the Sea," and for most San Francisco's permissive atmosphere was an eye-opening experience. The army's "off-limits" lists of forbidden establishments unintentionally (but effectively) pointed the way to the city's gay bars. When soldiers were dishonorably discharged for homosexual activity, many stayed on.

Scores of these newcomers found homes in what was then called Eureka Valley. When the war ended, the predominantly Irish-Catholic families in that neighborhood began to move out, heading for the 'burbs. The new arrivals snapped up the Victorians on the main drag, Castro Street.

The establishment pushed back. In the 1950s San Francisco's police chief vowed to crack down on "perverts," and the city's gay, lesbian, bisexual, and transgender residents lived in fear of getting caught in police raids. (Arrest meant being outed in the morning paper.) But harassment helped galvanize the community. The Daughters of Bilitis lesbian organization was founded in the city in 1955; the gay male Mattachine Society, started in Los Angeles in 1950, followed suit with an SF branch.

By the mid-1960s these clashing interests gave the growing gay population a national profile. The police upped their policy of harassment, but overplayed their hand. In 1965 they dramatically raided a New Year's benefit event, and the tide of public opinion began to turn. The police were forced to appoint the first-ever liaison to the gay community. Local gay organizations began to lobby openly. As one gay participant noted, "We didn't go back into the woodwork."

The 1970s—thumping disco, raucous street parties, and gay bashing—were a tumultuous time for the gay community. Thousands from across the country flocked to San Francisco's gay scene. Eureka Valley had more than 60 gay bars, the bathhouse scene in SoMa (where the leather crowd held court) was thriving, and graffiti around town read "Save San Francisco—Kill a Fag." When the Eureka Valley Merchants Association refused to admit gay-owned businesses in 1974, camera shop owner Harvey Milk founded the Castro Valley Association, and the neighborhood's new moniker was born. Milk was elected to the city's Board of Supervisors in 1977, its first openly gay official (and the inspirational figure for the Oscar-winning film *Milk*).

San Francisco's gay community was getting serious about politics, civil rights, and self-preservation, but it still loved a party: 350,000 people attended the 1978 Gay Freedom Day Parade, where the rainbow flag debuted. But on November 27, 1978, Milk and Mayor George Moscone were gunned down in City Hall by enraged former city council member Dan White. Thousands marched in silent tribute out of the Castro down to City Hall.When the killer got a relatively light conviction of manslaughter, the next march was not silent. Another

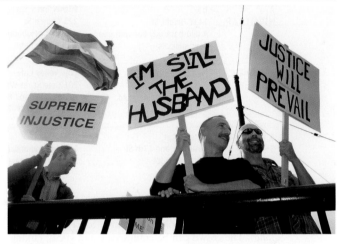

crowd of thousands converged on City Hall, this time smashing windows, burning 12 police cars, and fighting with police in what became known as the White Night Riot. The police retaliated by storming the Castro.

The gay community recovered, even thrived—especially economically—but in 1981 the first medical and journalistic reports of a dangerous new disease surfaced. A notice appeared in a Castro pharmacy's window warning people about "the gay cancer," later named AIDS. By 1983, the populations most vulnerable to the burgeoning epidemic were publicly identified as gay men in San Francisco and New York City.

San Francisco gay activists were quick to mobilize, starting foundations as early as 1982 to care for the sick, along with public memorials to raise awareness nationwide. By 1990 the disease had killed 10,000 San Franciscans. Local organizations lobbied hard to speed up drug development and FDA approvals. In the past decade the city's network of volunteer organizations and public outreach has been recognized as one of the best global models for combating the disease.

Today the Castro is still the heart of San Francisco's gay life—though many young hetero families have also moved in. As the ur-gay mecca starts to get diluted, new neighborhood coalitions are forming to debate its character and future. In the meantime, a Harvey Milk bust was unveiled in City Hall on May 22, 2008, Milk's birthday.

10

Where can I find . . . ?

A NIGHTCAP	Trax 1437 Haight St. A laid-back gay bar with good beer specials.	Pilsner Inn 225 Church St. A casual neighborhood joint with a nice patio.
A CUP OF COFFEE	Peet's 2257 Market St. One cup, and you could become a Peetnik.	Cole Valley Café 701 Cole St., at Waller St. Good coffee and free Wi-Fi. What's not to like?
A PARKING SPACE	Metered Lot Castro St. and 17th St. City-owned lot.	Metered Lot Collingwood and 18th Sts. Another city-owned lot.

with the Jeanette McDonald standard "San Francisco" (go ahead, sing along). The crowd can be enthusiastic and vocal, talking back to the screen as loudly as it talks to them. Classics such as *Who's Afraid of Virginia Woolf?* take on a whole new life, with the assembled beating the actors to the punch and fashioning even snappier comebacks for Elizabeth Taylor. Head here to catch classics, a Fellini film retrospective, or the latest take on same-sex love. ⊠ *429 Castro St., Castro* ☎ *415/621–6120.*

Clarke's Mansion. Built for attorney Alfred "Nobby" Clarke, this 1892 off-white baroque Queen Anne home was dubbed Clarke's Folly. (His wife refused to inhabit it because it was in an unfashionable part of town—at the time, anyone who was anyone lived on Nob Hill.) The greenery-shrouded house (now apartments) is a beauty, with dormers, cupolas, rounded bay windows, and huge turrets topped by gold-leaf spheres. ⊠ *250 Douglass St., between 18th and 19th Sts., Castro.*

NEED A BREAK? Sometimes referred to as Café Floorshow because it's such a see-and-be-seen place, Café Flore (⊠ *2298 Market St., Castro* ☎ *415/621–8579*) serves coffee drinks, beer, and café fare. It's a good place to catch the latest Castro gossip.

Harvey Milk Plaza. An 18-foot-long rainbow flag, the symbol of gay pride, flies above this plaza named for the man who electrified the city in 1977 by being elected to its Board of Supervisors as an openly gay candidate. In the early 1970s, Milk had opened a camera store on the block of Castro Street between 18th and 19th streets. The store became the center for his campaign to open San Francisco's social and political life to gays and lesbians.

The liberal Milk hadn't served a full year of his term before he and Mayor George Moscone, also a liberal, were shot in November 1978 at City Hall. The murderer was a conservative ex-supervisor named Dan

CASTRO AND NOE WALK

The Castro and Noe Valley are both neighborhoods that beg to be walked—or ambled through, really, without time pressure or an absolute destination. Hit the Castro first, beginning at **Harvey Milk Plaza** under the gigantic rainbow flag. If you're going on to Noe Valley, first head east down **Market Street** for the cafés, bistros, and shops, then go back to **Castro Street** and head south, past the glorious art-deco **Castro Theatre**, checking out boutiques and cafés along the way (Cliff's Variety, at 479 Castro St., is a must). To tour Noe Valley, go east down **18th Street** to Church (at Dolores Park), and then either strap on your hiking boots and head south over the hill or hop the J–Church to **24th Street**, the center of this rambling neighborhood.

White, who had recently resigned his post and then became enraged when Moscone wouldn't reinstate him. Milk and White had often been at odds on the board, and White thought Milk had been part of a cabal to keep him from returning to his post. Milk's assassination shocked the gay community, which became infuriated when the infamous "Twinkie defense"—that junk food had led to diminished mental capacity—resulted in a manslaughter verdict for White. During the so-called White Night Riot of May 21, 1979, gays and their sympathizers stormed City Hall, torching its lobby and several police cars.

Milk, who had feared assassination, left behind a tape recording in which he urged the community to continue the work he had begun. His legacy is the high visibility of gay people throughout city government; a bust of him was unveiled at City Hall on his birthday in 2008, and the 2008 film *Milk* gives insight into his life. A plaque at the base of the flagpole lists the names of past and present openly gay and lesbian state and local officials. ⊠ *Southwest corner of Castro and Market Sts., Castro.*

OFF THE BEATEN PATH

Branching out from its small, third-floor exhibit space in the Mission, the Gay, Lesbian, Bisexual and Transgender (GLBT) Historical Society finally has a toehold in the Castro, half a block from the site of Harvey Milk's camera shop. Swing by the corner of Castro and 18th to see displays on the community's history, but do it quickly: the society may only have this space through 2010. Admission is $3.

10

Randall Museum. The best thing about visiting this free nature museum for kids may be its tremendous views of San Francisco. Younger kids who are still excited about petting a rabbit, touching a snakeskin, or seeing a live hawk will enjoy a trip here. (Many of the creatures here can't be released into the wild due to injury or other problems.) The museum sits beneath a hill variously known as Red Rock, Museum Hill, and, correctly, Corona Heights; hike up the steep but short trail for great, unobstructed city views. ■ TIP➔ It's a great resource for local families, but if you're going to take the kids to just one museum in town, make it the Exploratorium. ⊠ *199 Museum Way, off Roosevelt Way, Castro* ☎ *415/554–9600* ⊕ *www.randallmuseum.org* ⊠ *Free* ☉ *Tues.–Sat. 10–5.*

WHAT TO SEE IN NOE VALLEY

Axford House. This mauve house was built in 1877, when Noe Valley was still a rural area, as evidenced by the hayloft in the gable of the adjacent carriage house. The house is perched several feet above the sidewalk. Various types of roses grow in the well-maintained garden that surrounds the house, which is a private home. ⊠ *1190 Noe St., at 25th St., Noe Valley.*

TWIN PEAKS

Windswept and desolate Twin Peaks yields sweeping vistas of San Francisco and the neighboring East and North Bay counties. You can get a real feel for the city's layout here; arrive before the late-afternoon fog turns the view into pea soup during the summer. To drive here, head west from Castro Street up Market Street, which eventually becomes Portola Drive. Turn right (north) on Twin Peaks Boulevard and follow the signs to the top. Muni Bus 37–Corbett heads west to Twin Peaks from Market Street. Catch this bus above the Castro Street Muni light-rail station on the island west of Castro at Market Street.

PINK TRIANGLE PARK

On a median near the Castro's huge rainbow flag stands this memorial to the gays, lesbians, and bisexual and transgender people whom the Nazis forced to wear pink triangles. Fifteen triangular granite columns, one for every 1,000 gays, lesbians, bisexual, and transgender people estimated to have been killed during and after the Holocaust, stand at the tip of a pink-rock-filled triangle—a reminder of the gay community's past and ongoing struggle for civil rights. ⊠ *Corner of Market, Castro, and 17th Sts., Castro.*

Golden fire hydrant. When all the other fire hydrants went dry during the fire that followed the 1906 earthquake, this one kept pumping. Noe Valley and the Mission District were thus spared the devastation wrought elsewhere in the city, which explains the large number of pre-quake homes here. Every year on April 18 (the anniversary of the quake) the famous hydrant gets a fresh coat of gold paint. ⊠ *Church and 20th Sts., southeast corner, across from Dolores Park, Noe Valley.*

Noe Valley/Sally Brunn Branch Library. In the early 20th century philanthropist Andrew Carnegie told Americans he would build them elegant libraries if they would fill them with books. A community garden flanks part of the yellow-brick library Carnegie financed (completely renovated and reopened in 2008), and there's a deck (accessed through the children's book room) with picnic tables where you can relax and admire Carnegie's inspired structure. ⊠ *451 Jersey St., Noe Valley* ☎ *415/355–5707* ⊙ *Tues. 10–9, Wed. 1–9, Thurs. and Sat. 10–6, Fri. 1–6, Sun. 1–5.*

Mission District

WORD OF MOUTH

"Totally fascinated and captivated with the Mission District. Walked along 'The Heart of the Mission' on 24th Street to Balmy Street where we took in all the murals there. Just absolutely enchanting and beautiful."

—mwessel

GETTING ORIENTED

TOP 5 REASONS TO GO

Bar-hop: Embrace your inner (or not-so-inner) hipster. Start off at Medjool's rare rooftop deck, then move up to the stylish Nihon Whisky Lounge or pull up a chair in pretension-free Truck. Round the night off in the company of the 100 beers available at the Monk's Kettle.

Chow down on phenomenal, cheap ethnic food: Keen appetites and thin wallets will meet their match here. Just try to decide between deliciously fresh burritos, garlicky falafel, thin-crust pizza, savory crepes, and more.

One-of-a-kind shopping: Barter for buried treasure at 826 Valencia and its Pirate Supply Store, then hop next door and say hello to the giraffe's head at the mad taxidermy-cum-garden store hodgepodge that is Paxton Gate.

Vivid murals: Check out dozens of energetic, colorful public artworks in alleyways and on building exteriors.

Hang out in Dolores Park: Join Mission locals and their dogs on this hilly expanse of green with a glorious view of downtown and, if you're lucky, the Bay Bridge.

QUICK BITES

Latin-American pastries are the specialty at **La Victoria** (⊠ 2937 24th St., at Alabama St., Mission ☎ 415/642–7120). You can also pick up a coffee, piñatas, and votive candles.

For an old-fashioned soda or homemade ice cream, stop into the **St. Francis Fountain and Candy Store** (⊠ 2801 24th St., at York St., Mission☎ 415/826–4200).

Muddy Waters (⊠ 521 Valencia St., at 16th St., Mission ☎ 415/863–8006) is a welcome stop near the 16th Street Mission BART station. You'll get an eyeful of the neighborhood culture here—some oddball characters and very casual housekeeping—but the coffee, chai, and wireless crackle at full capacity.

GETTING THERE

After climbing the hills downtown, you'll find the Mission to be welcomingly flat. BART's two Mission District stations drop you right in the heart of the action. Get off at 16th Street for Mission Dolores, shopping, nightlife, and restaurants, or 24th Street to see the neighborhood murals. The busy 14–Mission bus runs all the way from downtown into the neighborhood, but BART is a much faster and more direct route. Parking can be a drag, especially on weekend evenings. If you're heading out in the evening, your safest bet would be taking a cab, since some blocks are sketchy.

MAKING THE MOST OF YOUR TIME

A walk that includes Mission Dolores and the neighborhood's murals takes about two hours. If you plan to go on a mural walk with the Precita Eyes organization or if you're a window-shopper, add at least another hour. The Mission is a neighborhood that sleeps in. In the afternoon and evening the main drags really come to life.

Sunday through Tuesday is relatively quiet here, especially in the evening—a great time to get a café table with no wait. If you're getting bummed out by fog elsewhere in the city, come here—the Mission wins out in San Francisco's system of microclimates.

Sightseeing
★★

Nightlife
★★★★★

Dining
★★★★★

Lodging
–

Shopping
★★★

The Mission has a number of distinct personalities: it's the Latino neighborhood, where working-class folks raise their families and where gangs occasionally clash; it's the hipster hood, where tattooed and pierced twenty- and thirtysome-things hold court in the coolest cafés and bars in town; it's a culinary epicenter, with the strongest concentration of des-tination restaurants and affordable ethnic cuisine; and it's the artists' quarter, where murals adorn literally blocks of walls. It's also the city's equivalent of the Sunshine State—this neighborhood's always the last to succumb to fog.

Updated by
Denise M Leto

The eight blocks of Valencia Street between 16th and 24th streets—what's come to be known as the Valencia Corridor—typify the neigh-borhood's diversity. Businesses on the block between 16th and 17th streets, for instance, include an upscale Peruvian restaurant, the Bombay Ice Cream parlor (try a scoop of the zesty cardamom ice cream) and adjacent Indian grocery and sundries store, a tattoo parlor, the yuppie-chic bar Blondie's, a handful of funky home-decor stores, a pizzeria, a taquería, a Turkish restaurant, a sushi bar, bargain and pricey thrift shops, and the Puerto Alegre restaurant, a hole-in-the-wall with pack-a-punch margaritas locals revere. On the other hand, Mission Street itself, three blocks east, is mostly a down-at-the-heels row of check-cashing places, dollar stores, and residential hotels—but there are more than a few great taquerías. And the farther east you go, the sketchier the neighborhood gets.

Italian and Irish in the early 20th century, the Mission became heavily Latino in the late 1960s, when immigrants from Mexico and Central America began arriving. An influx of Chinese, Vietnamese, Arabic, and other immigrants, along with a young bohemian crowd enticed by cheap rents and the burgeoning arts-and-nightlife scene, followed in the 1980s and early 1990s. The skyrocketing rents of the late 1990s have leveled off and the district is yet again in transition. The Mission

BETHANY

DID YOU KNOW?

San Francisco is chockablock with murals—about 600 by recent count—and the Mission District is the epicenter of all that artistic fervor.

Murals with a Mission

San Francisco fairly teems with murals. Since the 1970s, groups of artists have worked to transform the city's walls into canvases, art accessible to everyone. Muralists here fall into two loose categories: those in the Latin American tradition of addressing political and social justice issues through art, and everyone else (those who simply paint on a large scale and like lots of people to see it).

Rediscovering the work of Mexican liberal artist and muralist Diego Rivera in the 1960s, Latino muralists began to address public issues on the community's walls. Heavily Latino since the 1970s, the Mission District became the collective canvas for these artists. The Precita Eyes Mural Arts Center emerged to support those artists and galvanize collaborative projects in the neighborhood. Early on, the San Francisco Arts Commission hired the center to create murals all over town. Of the 800-plus murals that adorn city surfaces, a good quarter of them were painted by muralists associated with Precita Eyes.

Bright Sunbelt colors reflect the medium's historical geography; in contemporary work, look for anime and woodblock cuts along with traditional Latino symbols. Murals are considered permanent, and aren't painted over without consulting the artist. Keep your eyes peeled as you wander the city and you'll begin to discover art everywhere. Here are the best and brightest of the Mission District:

■ **826 Valencia.** Fans of graphic novelist Chris Ware will want to take a good look at the facade here. Ware designed the intricate mural for the storefront, a meditation on the evolution of human communication.

■ **Balmy Alley.** The most famous of the Mission's murals—a vivid sweep from end to end. This group series began in 1971 and still gets new additions.

■ **Clarion Alley.** A new generation of muralists is creating a fresh alley-cum-gallery here, between Valencia and Mission streets and 17th and 18th streets. The loosely connected artists of the Clarion Alley Mural Project (CAMP) represent a broad range of style and imagery. Carpet-draped Indonesian elephants plod calmly down the block; kung fu movie-style headlines shout slogans. The works here offer a dense glimpse at the Mission's contemporary art scene.

■ **Shotwell Street grocery.** A bit off the beaten path but well worth the detour is Brian Barneclo's gigantic *Food Chain*. This adorns the grocery store on Shotwell Street between 14th and 15th streets. It's a retro, 1950s-style celebration of the city's many neighborhoods (and the food chain), complete with an ant birthday party and worms finishing off a human skull. But in a cute way. Barneclo fans can see more of his work at cool watering hole Rye and hipster restaurant Nopa.

■ **24th Street.** Several murals in the Mexican political tradition adorn the buildings along 24th Street, including St. Peter's (at Alabama Street) and even McDonald's (at Mission Street).

■ **Women's Building.** *Maestrapeace*—the impressive, towering mural that seems to enclose this building—celebrates women around the world who work for peace.

—Denise M. Leto

Where can I find . . . ?

A CAFÉ WITH FREE WI-FI	Philz Coffee 3101 24th St. Potent joe with a loyal following.	Ritual Roasters 1026 Valencia St. Strong coffee, very sceney.
A GAS STATION	Arco 1798 Mission St. Close to the neighborhood core.	Potrero Hill 76 401 Potrero Ave. Average prices; near the 101.
A DRUGSTORE	Community Pharmacy 2462 Mission St. All the OTC standbys.	Walgreens 1979 Mission St. Right by the 16th Street BART station.

is still quite scruffy in patches, so as you plan your explorations take into account your comfort zone. ■TIP→ If raucous barhoppers are a bit intimidating to you, an afternoon trip to the Valencia Corridor may be your best bet.

WHAT TO SEE

Balmy Alley. Mission District artists have transformed the walls of their neighborhood with paintings, and Balmy Alley is one of the best-executed examples. Murals fill the one-block alley, with newer ones continually filling in the blank spaces. Local children working with adults started the project in 1971. Since then dozens of artists have steadily added to it, with the aim of promoting peace in Central America, as well as community spirit and AIDS awareness. ■TIP→ Be alert here: the 25th Street end of the alley adjoins a somewhat dangerous area. ⊠ *24th St. between and parallel to Harrison and Treat Sts., alley runs south to 25th St., Mission.*

Creativity Explored. Joyous, if chaotic, creativity pervades the workshops of this art-education center and gallery for developmentally disabled adults. Several dozen adults work at the center each day—guided by a staff of working artists—painting, working in the darkroom, producing videos, and crafting prints, textiles, and ceramics. On weekdays you can drop by and see the artists at work. The art produced here is striking, and some of it is for sale; this is a great place to find a unique San Francisco masterpiece to take home. ⊠ *3245 16th St., Mission* ☎ *415/863–2108* ⊕ *www.creativityexplored.org* ☜ *Free* ☉ *Mon.–Wed. and Fri. 10–3, Thurs. 10–7, Sat. 1–6.*

Galería de la Raza. San Francisco's premier showcase for contemporary Latino art, the gallery exhibits the works of mostly local artists. Events include readings and spoken word by local poets and writers, screenings of Latin American and Spanish films, and theater works by local

Vivid public art provides a backdrop for the Mission District.

minority theater troupes. Just across the street, amazing art festoons the 24th Street/York Street Minipark, a tiny urban playground. A mosaic-covered Quetzalcoatl serpent plunges into the ground and rises, creating hills for little ones to clamber over, and mural-covered walls surround the space. ⊠ *2857 24th St., at Bryant St., Mission* ☎ *415/826–8009* ⊕ *www.galeriadelaraza.org* ☉ *Gallery Tues. 1–7, Wed.–Sat. noon–6.*

OFF THE
BEATEN
PATH

Vermont Street. With a similar series of switchbacks, this Potrero Hill street is a kind of blue-collar Lombard Street, but minus the throngs (and the spectacular gardens and views). It's on the east side of the 101 from the Mission. To check it out, head down 24th Street to the end, go left on Vermont, right on 23rd Street past the freeway, left on Rhode Island Street, left on 20th Street, and finally head left down the curvy stretch of Vermont. Bring a city map along! ⊠ *Between 20th and 22nd Sts., Potrero Hill.*

★ **Mission Dolores.** Two churches stand side by side at this mission, including the small adobe **Mission San Francisco de Asís,** the oldest standing structure in San Francisco. Completed in 1791, it's the sixth of the 21 California missions founded by Father Junípero Serra in the 18th and early 19th centuries. Its ceiling depicts original Ohlone Indian basket designs, executed in vegetable dyes. The tiny chapel includes frescoes and a hand-painted wooden altar. There's a hidden treasure here, too. In 2004 an archaeologist and an artist crawling along the ceiling's rafters opened a trap door behind the altar and rediscovered the mission's original mural, painted with natural dyes by Native Americans in 1791. The centuries have taken their toll, so the team photographed the 20-by-22-foot mural and began digitally restoring the photographic

Reel-Life San Francisco

11

With its spectacular cityscape, atmospheric fog, and a camera-ready iconic bridge, it's little wonder that San Francisco has been the setting for hundreds of films. While you're running around town, you might have the occasional sense of déjà vu, sparked by a scene from a Hitchcock or Clint Eastwood thriller. Below are a few of the city's favorite cinematic sites:

■ *Zodiac,* a 2007 drama about a legendary Bay Area serial killer, filmed scenes at the real-life locations where victims were gunned down. It also re-created the San Francisco Chronicle offices, but down south in L.A.

■ City Hall shows up in the Clint Eastwood cop thrillers *Dirty Harry* and *Magnum Force,* and is set aflame in the James Bond flick *A View to a Kill.* Its domed interior became a nightclub for Robin Williams' *Bicentennial Man* and a courthouse in *Tucker: The Man and His Dream.*

■ Streets in Russian Hill, Potrero Hill, and North Beach were used for the supreme car-chase sequence in *Bullitt.* The namesake detective, played by Steve McQueen, lived in Nob Hill at 1153–57 Taylor Street. And the "King of Cool" did much of his own stunt driving, thank you very much.

■ Brocklebank Apartments, at Mason and Sacramento streets in Nob Hill,

appears in several films, most notably as the posh residence of Kim Novak in Alfred Hitchcock's *Vertigo.* Other key *Vertigo* locations include the cemetery of Mission Dolores and the waterfront at Fort Point.

■ The great Bogie-and-Bacall noir film *Dark Passage* revolves around the art-deco apartment building at 1360 Montgomery Street and the nearby Filbert Steps.

■ Dashiell Hammett's "Thin Man" characters, Nick and Nora Charles, do much of their sleuthing in the city, especially in films like *After the Thin Man,* in which the base of Coit Tower stands in as the entrance to the Charles' home.

■ North Beach's Tosca Café, at 242 Columbus Avenue, is the bar where Michael Douglas unwinds in *Basic Instinct.*

■ The Hilton Hotel at 333 O'Farrell Street became the "Hotel Bristol," the scene of much of the mayhem caused by Barbra Streisand in *What's Up, Doc?*

■ At 2640 Steiner Street in Pacific Heights is the elegant home that Robin Williams infiltrates while disguised as a nanny in *Mrs. Doubtfire.*

■ The Castro of the 1970s comes alive in *Milk,* Gus Van Sant's film starring Sean Penn as slain San Francisco supervisor Harvey Milk.

■ And, of course, there are plenty of movies about the notorious federal prison on Alcatraz Island, including Burt Lancaster's redemption drama *Birdman of Alcatraz,* Clint Eastwood's suspenseful *Escape from Alcatraz,* the goofy *So I Married an Axe Murderer,* and the Sean Connery and Nicolas Cage action flick, *The Rock.*

—Jim Van Buskirk

version. Among the images is a dagger-pierced Sacred Heart of Jesus. There's a small museum covering the mission's founding and history, and the pretty little mission cemetery (made famous by a scene in Alfred Hitchcock's *Vertigo*) maintains the graves of mid-19th-century European immigrants. (The remains of an estimated 5,000 Native Americans lie in unmarked graves.) Services are held in both the Mission San Francisco de Asís and next door in the handsome multi-dome basilica. ⊠ *Dolores and 16th Sts., Mission* ☎ *www. missiondolores.org* ✉ *$5 donation, audio tour $7* ⊙ *Nov.–Apr., daily 9–4; May–Oct., daily 9–4:30.*

Precita Eyes Mural Arts and Visitors Center. Founded by muralists, this nonprofit arts organization designs and creates murals. The artists themselves lead informative guided walks of murals in the area. Most tours start with a 45-minute slide presentation. The bike and walking trips, which take between one and three hours, pass several dozen murals. May is Mural Awareness Month, with visits to murals-in-progress and presentations by artists. You can pick up a map of 24th Street's murals at the center and buy art supplies, T-shirts, postcards, and other mural-related items. Bike tours are available by appointment; Saturday's 11 AM walking tour meets at Cafe Venice, at 24th and Mission streets. (All other tours meet at the center.) ⊠ *2981 24th St., Mission* ☎ *415/285–2287* ⊕ *www.precitaeyes.org* ✉ *Center free, tours $10–$12* ⊙ *Center weekdays 10–5, Sat. 10–4, Sun. noon–4; walks weekends at 11 and 1:30 or by appointment.*

Women's Building. The cornerstone of the female-owned and -run businesses in the neighborhood, this place has held workshops and conferences of particular interest to women since 1979. The exterior is the reason to visit: its two stories are completely covered with an impressive mural, *Maestrapeace*, depicting women's peacekeeping efforts over the centuries. Inside are offices for many social and political organizations; the center also sponsors talks and readings by writers such as Alice Walker and Angela Davis. Head inside to pick up a key to the murals' figures and symbols. ⊠ *3543 18th St., Mission* ☎ *415/431–1180* ⊕ *www.womensbuilding.org* ⊙ *Mon.–Thurs. 9–5, Fri. 10–6.*

SAFETY IN THE MISSION

The Mission is a vibrant area, but it does have dodgy zones. The safest area is bordered by Mission, Dolores, 16th, and 20th streets—where everything is happening anyway. Even here, plenty of homeless people crash in doorways, and robberies and assaults are not uncommon. After dark, the areas east of Mission Street and south of 24th Street can feel unsafe, with empty stretches or groups of loitering toughs. If you're in this area after dark, stick to main drags like Mission and 24th streets. If you keep your wits about you and stick to well-lighted areas, you're unlikely to run into trouble.

Pacific Heights
and Japantown

WORD OF MOUTH

"[There's a] crazy photo booth shop [in the Japan Center] called PicaPica where . . . a photo booth takes a series of photos of you. Then you go back and choose your six favorites and decorate the photos with their computer graphics. Fun and silly and our girls LOVED it! Apparently it's all the rage in Japan."

—mwessel

GETTING ORIENTED

Gashouse Cove

Fort Mason

North Point St.

Beach St.

Cervantes Blvd.

Beach St.

North Point St.

Bay St.

Capra Way

Avila St.

George R. Moscone Rec. Center

Francisco St.

Chestnut St.

Toledo Way

Lombard St.

Magnolia St.

101

FILLMORE

RUSSIAN HILL

Lombard St.

Moulton St.

Greenwich St.

Greenwich St.

Pixley St.

Filbert St.

101

Polk St.

Larkin St.

Filbert St.

Wedding Houses ◆

Green St.

Vedanta Society ◆

Laguna St.

Octavia St.

◆ Octagon House

Vallejo St.

Union St.

Gough St.

Franklin St.

Van Ness Ave.

Green St.

Scott St.

Pierce St.

Steiner St.

Fillmore St.

Webster St.

Buchanan St.

PACIFIC HEIGHTS

Broadway

Broadway

Broadway and Webster Street estates

Whittier Mansion ◆

Pacific Ave.

Jackson St.

Haas-Lilienthal House ◆

NOB HILL

Spreckels Mansion ◆

Washington St.

Clay St.

WEBSTER ST. HISTORIC DISTRICT

Lafayette Park

Franklin Street ◆ buildings

Alta Plaza Park ◆

Clay St.

Sacramento St.

California St.

◆ Noteworthy Victorians

Pine St.

Perine Pl.

California St.

Laguna St.

Octavia St.

Austin St.

Bush St.

Pine St.

Wilmot St.

Webster St.

Divisadero St.

Bush St.

Gough St.

Franklin St.

Van Ness Ave.

Fern St.

Sutter St.

Hemlock St.

JAPANTOWN

Cedar St.

Sutter St.

Geary St.

Post St.

Kabuki Springs and Spa ◆

◆ Japan Center Mall

◆ Japan Center

Geary Blvd.

Starr King Way

Myrtle St.

O'Farrell St.

St. Francis Square

Olive St.

Ellis St.

Steiner St.

Fillmore St.

Ellis St.

Willow St.

Laguna St.

Gough St.

Franklin St.

101

Willow St.

Eddy

O'Farrell St.

Jefferson Square

Larch St.

Ellis St.

Elm St.

Broderick

Scott St.

Pierce St.

Turk St.

Elm St.

Golden Gate Ave.

McAllister St.

0   1/4 mile

0   400 m

12

TOP 5 REASONS TO GO

Chic shopping on Fillmore Street: Browse the superfine shops along Pacific Heights' main drag.

Picnic with a view at Lafayette Park: Gather supplies along Fillmore Street and climb to the top of this park. It's surrounded by grand homes and has a sweeping view of the city.

Asian food galore in the Japan Center: Graze your way through the mall, from sushi boat offerings at Isobune to quick bean-paste snacks at May's Coffee Stand, decked out like an open-air Japanese restaurant.

Spa serenity at Kabuki Springs: Enter the peaceful lobby and prepare to be transported at the Japanese-style communal baths.

See how the other half lives: Check out the grand, historic homes along the tree-lined streets of Pacific Heights.

QUICK BITES

Swing by **Boulangerie Bay Bread** (⊠ *2325 Pine St., at Fillmore St., Pacific Heights* ☎ *415/440–0356*), an oh-so-French bakery and patisserie whose patrons swoon for its perfect baguettes, rounds, croissants, and tartlets. Flaky-crust savory tarts filled with veggies and cheese or leeks and prosciutto make perfect picnic fare for Lafayette Park.

Red-and-white lanterns adorn the room at the Japan Center's **Isobune** (⊠ *Kintetsu Bldg., 1737 Post St., Japantown* ☎ *415/563–1030*), where "sushi boats" float around the counter. Crowds of customers take what they want and pay per dish at the end of the meal.

GETTING THERE

Steep streets in Pacific Heights make for impressive views and rough walking; unless you're in decent shape, consider taking a car or taxi to this neighborhood.

The only public transit that runs through the area is the bus. For Pacific Heights proper, take the 12–Folsom to the area just north of Lafayette Park. For shopping on Union Street in Cow Hollow (lower Pacific Heights), catch the 41– or the 45–Union bus.

Buses that run to Japantown from downtown include the 2–Clement, 3–Jackson, and 4–Sutter to Sutter Street and the very busy 38–Geary.

MAKING THE MOST OF YOUR TIME

Give yourself an hour to wander Fillmore Street, more if you're planning to have a meal here or picnic in Lafayette or Alta Plaza parks. Checking out the stunning homes in Pacific Heights is best done by car, unless you have serious stamina; a half hour should be enough.

Since the Japan Center is the only real highlight of Japantown, plan a daytime visit for a meal and some window-shopping; lunchtime is ideal.

Sightseeing
★★

Nightlife
★★

Dining
★★★

Lodging
★

Shopping
★★★

Pacific Heights and Japantown are something of an odd couple: privileged, old-school San Francisco and the workaday commercial center of Japanese-American life in the city, stacked virtually on top of each other. The sprawling, extravagant mansions of Pacific Heights gradually give way to the more modest Victorians and unassuming housing tracts of Japantown. The most interesting spots in Japantown huddle in the Japan Center, the neighborhood's two-block centerpiece, and along Post Street. You can find plenty of authentic Japanese treats in the shops and restaurants, if you have a special interest in these.

Updated by
Denise M. Leto

Pacific Heights defines San Francisco's most expensive and dramatic real estate. Grand Victorians line the streets, mansions and town houses are priced in the millions, and there are magnificent views from almost any point in the neighborhood. Old money and new, personalities in the limelight, and those who prefer absolute media anonymity live here, and few outsiders see anything other than the pleasing facades of Queen Anne charmers, English Tudor imports, and baroque bastions. Nancy Pelosi and Dianne Feinstein, Larry Ellison, and Gordon Getty all own impressive homes here, but not even pockets as deep as those can buy a large garden—space in the city is simply at too much of a premium. The boutiques and restaurants along Fillmore, which range from glam to funky, have become a draw for the whole city.

Japantown, on the other hand, feels somewhat adrift. (Also called Nihonmachi, it's centered on the southern slope of Pacific Heights, north of Geary Boulevard between Fillmore and Laguna streets.) The Japan Center mall, for instance, comes across as rather sterile. Where Chinatown is densely populated and still largely Chinese, Japantown struggles to retain its unique character.

The Japanese community in San Francisco started around 1860; after the 1906 earthquake and fire many of these newcomers settled in the Western Addition. By the 1930s they had opened shops, markets, meeting halls, and restaurants and established Shinto and Buddhist temples. But during World War II the area was virtually gutted, when many of its residents, including second- and third-generation Americans, were forced into so-called relocation camps. During the 1960s and '70s redevelopment further eroded the neighborhood, and most Japanese-Americans now live elsewhere in the city.

Still, when several key properties in the neighborhood were sold in 2007, a vocal group rallied to "save Japantown," and some new blood may finally be infusing the neighborhood with energy: Robert Redford's Sundance corporation turned the venerable Kabuki Theatre into a destination cinema-restaurant combo, local hotel group Joie de Vivre took over the Hotel Kabuki, and the new J-Pop Center NEW PEOPLE brings Japanese pop culture to the neighborhood. ■ TIP➔ Japantown is a relatively safe area, but the Western Addition, south of Geary Boulevard, can be dangerous even during the daytime. Avoid going too far west of Fillmore Street on either side of Geary.

WHAT TO SEE IN PACIFIC HEIGHTS

🕐 **Alta Plaza Park.** Golden Gate Park's fierce longtime superintendent, John McLaren, designed Alta Plaza in 1910, modeling its terracing on that of the Grand Casino in Monte Carlo, Monaco. From the top you can see Marin to the north, downtown to the east, Twin Peaks to the south, and Golden Gate Park to the west. Kids love the many play structures at the large, enclosed playground at the top; everywhere else is dog territory. ⊠ *Bordered by Clay, Steiner, Jackson, and Scott Sts., Pacific Heights.*

Broadway and Webster Street estates. Broadway uptown, unlike its garish North Beach stretch, has plenty of prestigious addresses. The three-story palace at 2222 Broadway, which has an intricately filigreed doorway, was built by Comstock silver-mine heir James Flood and later donated to a religious order. The Convent of the Sacred Heart purchased the **Grant House** at 2220 Broadway. These two buildings, along with a Flood property at 2120 Broadway, are used as school quarters. A gold-mine heir, William Bourn II, commissioned Willis Polk to build the nearby brick mansion at 2550 Webster Street.

Franklin Street buildings. What at first looks like a stone facade on the **Golden Gate Church** (⊠ *1901 Franklin St. Pacific Heights*) is actually redwood painted white. A Georgian-style residence built in the early 1900s for a coffee merchant sits at 1735 Franklin. On the northeast corner of Franklin and California streets is a **Christian Science church**; built in the Tuscan revival style, it's noteworthy for its terra-cotta detailing. The **Coleman House** (⊠ *1701 Franklin St., Pacific Heights*) is an impressive twin-turret Queen Anne mansion that was built for a gold-rush mining and lumber baron. Don't miss the large, brilliant-purple stained-glass window on the house's north side. ⊠ *Franklin St. between Washington and California Sts., Pacific Heights.*

A PACIFIC HEIGHTS WALK

Start at **Broadway and Webster Street**, where four notable estates stand within a block of one another. Two are on the north side of Broadway to the west of the intersection, one is on the same side to the east, and the last is half a block south on Webster Street. Head south down Webster and hang a right onto Clay to **Alta Plaza Park**, or skip the park and turn left on Jackson to the **Whittier Mansion**, on the corner of Jackson and Laguna streets. Head south down Laguna and cross Washington Street to **Lafayette Park**. Walk on Washington along the edge of Lafayette Park, past the formal French **Spreckels Mansion** at the corner of Octavia Street, and continue east two more blocks to Franklin Street. Turn left (north); halfway down the block stands the handsome **Haas-Lilienthal House**. Head back south on Franklin Street, stopping to view several **Franklin Street buildings**. At California Street, turn right (west) to see more **noteworthy Victorians** on that street and Laguna Street. Beyond Laguna, continue three blocks west back to Fillmore Street.

Haas-Lilienthal House. A small display of photographs on the bottom floor of this elaborate, gray 1886 Queen Anne house makes clear that despite its lofty stature and striking, round third-story tower, the house was modest compared with some of the giants that fell victim to the 1906 earthquake and fire. The Foundation for San Francisco's Architectural Heritage operates the home, whose carefully kept rooms provide an intriguing glimpse into late-19th-century life through period furniture, authentic details (antique dishes in the kitchen built-in), and photos of the family who occupied the house until 1972. Volunteers conduct one-hour house tours three days a week and informative two-hour walking tours ($8) of the Civic Center, Broadway, and Union Street areas on Saturday afternoon, and of the eastern portion of Pacific Heights on Sunday afternoon (call or check Web site for schedule). ⊠ *2007 Franklin St., between Washington and Jackson Sts., Pacific Heights* ☎ *415/441–3004* ⊕ *www.sfheritage.org* ⊠ *Entry $8* ⊙ *1-hr tour Wed. and Sat. noon–3, Sun. 11–4; 2-hr tour Sun. at 12:30.*

Lafayette Park. Clusters of trees dot this four-block-square oasis for sunbathers and dog-and-Frisbee teams. On the south side of the park, squat but elegant **2151 Sacramento,** a private condominium, is the site of a home occupied by Sir Arthur Conan Doyle in the late 19th century. Coats of arms blaze in the front stained-glass windows. The park itself is a lovely neighborhood space, where Pacific Heights residents laze in the sun or exercise their pedigreed canines while gazing at downtown's skyline in the distance. ⊠ *Bordered by Laguna, Gough, Sacramento, and Washington Sts., Pacific Heights.*

Noteworthy Victorians. Two **Italianate Victorians** (⊠ *1818 and 1834 California St., Pacific Heights*) stand out on the 1800 block of California. A block farther is the Victorian-era **Atherton House** (⊠ *1990 California St., Pacific Heights*), whose mildly daffy design incorporates Queen Anne, Stick-Eastlake, and other architectural elements. Many claim

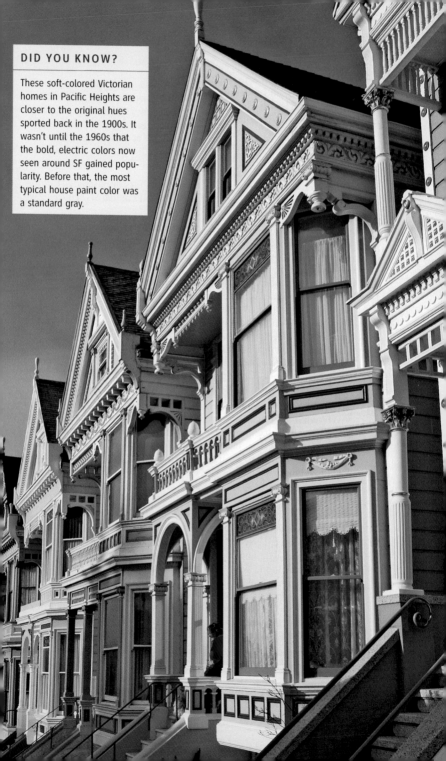

DID YOU KNOW?

These soft-colored Victorian homes in Pacific Heights are closer to the original hues sported back in the 1900s. It wasn't until the 1960s that the bold, electric colors now seen around SF gained popularity. Before that, the most typical house paint color was a standard gray.

the house—now apartments—is haunted by the ghosts of its 19th-century residents, who regularly whisper, glow, and generally cause a mild fuss. The oft-photographed **Laguna Street Victorians**, on the west side of the 1800 block of Laguna Street, cost between $2,000 and $2,600 when they were built in the 1870s. No bright colors here

WORD OF MOUTH

"Fillmore Street (farther up the hill toward Pacific Heights) is an interesting neighborhood—not as yuppy as the Marina/Cow Hollow, but not as counterculture as the Haight."   —waldrons

though—most of the paint jobs are in soft beiges or pastels. ⊠ *California St. between Franklin and Octavia Sts., and Laguna St. between Pine and Bush Sts., Pacific Heights.*

Octagon House. This eight-sided home sits across the street from its original site on Gough Street; it's one of two remaining octagonal houses in the city (the other is on Russian Hill), and the only one open to the public. White quoins accent each of the eight corners of the pretty blue-gray exterior, and a colonial-style garden completes the picture. Inside, it's full of antique American furniture, decorative arts (paintings, silver, rugs), and documents from the 18th and 19th centuries. A deck of Revolutionary-era hand-painted playing cards takes an antimonarchist position: in place of kings, queens, and jacks, the American upstarts substituted American statesmen, Roman goddesses, and Indian chiefs. ⊠ *2645 Gough St., Pacific Heights* ☎ *415/441-7512* 🎫 *Free, donations encouraged* ☉ *Feb.–Dec., 2nd Sun. and 2nd and 4th Thurs. of month noon–3; group tours weekdays by appointment.*

Spreckels Mansion. Shrouded behind tall juniper hedges at the corner of lovely winding, brick Octavia Street, overlooking Lafayette Park, the estate was built for sugar heir Adolph Spreckels and his wife Alma. Mrs. Spreckels was so pleased with her house that she commissioned George Applegarth to design another building in a similar vein: the Legion of Honor. One of the city's great iconoclasts, Alma Spreckels was the model for the bronze figure atop the Victory Monument in Union Square. Today this house belongs to prolific romance novelist Danielle Steel. ⊠ *2080 Washington St., at Octavia St., Pacific Heights.*

Vedanta Society. A pastiche of colonial, Queen Anne, Moorish, and Hindu opulence, lavender with turrets battling red-top onion domes, and Victorian detailing everywhere, this 1905 structure was the first Hindu temple in the West. Vedanta, an underlying philosophy of Hinduism, maintains that all religions are paths to one goal. Although the Vedanta Society's main location is the temple at Vallejo and Fillmore streets (closed Tuesday), *this* temple (open only Friday evening from 8 to 9) is the organization's heart. ⊠ *2963 Webster St., Pacific Heights* ☎ *415/922-2323* ⊕ *www.sfvedanta.org.*

Wedding Houses. These identical white double-peak homes (joined in the middle) were erected in the late 1870s or early 1880s by dairy rancher James Cudworth as wedding gifts for his two daughters. These days the buildings house businesses and an English-style pub. ⊠ *1980 Union St., Pacific Heights.*

Where can I find . . . ?

A DRUGSTORE	Walgreens 1899 Fillmore St. Open until 10 PM Mon.–Sat., 9 PM on Sun.	Safeway 1335 Webster St., at Geary St. Open daily until midnight.
A COFFEE SHOP	Peet's Coffee and Tea 2197 Fillmore St. The Berkeley Peet's was the inspiration for Starbucks.	White Crane Tea Company 1737 Post St., #337 Japanese tea that's actually from Japan.
A PARKING SPACE	Japan Center Garage 1610 Geary Blvd. Validation available through many Japan Center proprietors.	California and Steiner 2450 California St. Outdoor parking lot with metered spaces.

12

Whittier Mansion. With a Spanish-tile roof and scrolled bay windows on all four sides, this is one of the most elegant 19th-century houses in the state. Unlike other grand mansions lost in the 1906 quake, the Whittier Mansion was built so solidly that only a chimney toppled over during the disaster. ⊠ *2090 Jackson St., Pacific Heights.*

WHAT TO SEE IN JAPANTOWN

★ **Japan Center.** Cool and curious trinkets, noodle houses and sushi joints, a destination bookstore, and a peek at Japanese culture high and low await at this 5-acre complex, designed in 1968 by noted American architect Minoru Yamasaki. Architecturally, the development hasn't aged well, and its Peace Plaza, where seasonal festivals are held, is an unwelcoming sea of cement. The Japan Center includes the shop- and restaurant-filled Kintetsu and Kinokuniya buildings; the excellent Kabuki Springs & Spa; the Hotel Kabuki; and the Sundance Kabuki, Robert Redford's fancy, reserved-seating cinema/restaurant complex.

The Kinokuniya Bookstores, in the Kinokuniya Building, have an extensive selection of Japanese-language books, *manga* (graphic novels), books on design, and English-language translations and books on Japanese topics. Just outside, follow the Japanese teenagers to Pika Pika, where you and your friends can step into a photo booth and then use special effects and stickers to decorate your creation. On the bridge connecting the center's two buildings, check out Shige Antiques for *yukata* (lightweight cotton kimonos) for kids and lovely silk kimonos, and Asakichi and its tiny incense shop for tinkling wind chimes and display-worthy teakettles. Continue into the Kintetsu Building for a selection of Japanese restaurants.

Between the Miyako Mall and Kintetsu Building are the five-tier, 100-foot-tall **Peace Pagoda** and the Peace Plaza. The pagoda, which draws on the 1,200-year-old tradition of miniature round pagodas dedicated to eternal peace, was designed in the late 1960s by Yoshiro Taniguchi to convey the "friendship and goodwill" of the Japanese people to the people of the United States. The plaza itself is a shadeless, unwelcoming stretch of cement with little seating. Continue into the Miyako Mall to Ichiban Kan, a Japanese dollar store where you can pick up fun Japanese kitchenware, tote bags decorated with hedgehogs, and erasers shaped like food. ⊠ *Bordered by Geary Blvd. and Fillmore, Post, and Laguna Sts., Japantown* ☎ *No phone.*

Japan Center Mall. The buildings lining this open-air mall are of the shoji school of architecture. The mall's many good restaurants draw a lively crowd of nearby workers for lunch, but the atmosphere remains weirdly hushed. The shops are geared more toward locals—travel agencies, electronics shops—but there are some fun Japanese-goods stores. Arrive early in the day and you may score some fabulous mochi (a soft, sweet Japanese rice treat) at **Benkyodo** (⊠ *1747 Buchanan St., Japantown* ☎ *415/922–1244*). It's easy to spend hours among the fabulous origami and craft papers at **Paper Tree** (⊠ *1743 Buchanan St., Japantown* ☎ *415/921–7100*), open since the 1960s. Be sure to swing around the corner, just off the mall, to **Super 7** (⊠ *1628 Post St., Japantown* ☎ *415/409–4700*), home of many large plastic Godzillas, glow-in-the-dark robots, and cool graphic tees. You can have a seat on local artist Ruth Asawa's twin origami-style fountains, which sit in the middle of the mall; they're squat circular structures made of fieldstone, with three levels for sitting and a brick floor. ⊠ *Buchanan St. between Post and Sutter Sts., Japantown* ☎ *No phone.*

★ **Kabuki Springs & Spa.** This serene spa is one Japantown destination that draws locals from all over town, from hipster to grandma, Japanese-American or not. Balinese urns decorate the communal bath area of this house of tranquillity, and you're just as likely to hear soothing flute or classical music as you are Kitaro.

The massage palette has also expanded well beyond traditional Shiatsu technique. The experience is no less relaxing, however, and the treatment regimen includes facials, salt scrubs, and mud and seaweed wraps. You can take your massage in a private room with a bath or in a curtained-off area. The communal baths ($22 weekdays, $25 weekends) contain hot and cold tubs, a large Japanese-style bath, a sauna, a steam room, and showers. Bang the gong for quiet if your fellow bathers are speaking too loudly.

The clothing-optional baths are open for men only on Monday, Thursday, and Saturday; women bathe on Wednesday, Friday, and Sunday. Bathing suits are required on Tuesday, when the baths are coed. Men and women can reserve private rooms daily. An 80-minute massage-and-bath package with a private room costs $130; a package that includes a 50-minute massage and the use of the communal baths costs $100. ⊠ *1750 Geary Blvd., Japantown* ☎ *415/922–6000* ⊕ *www.kabukisprings.com* ☉ *Daily 10–10.*

EYE ON ARCHITECTURE

San Francisco's architecture scene has been going through a dramatic growth spurt—with the growing pains to match. Boldface international architects seem to be everywhere, spearheading major projects like the de Young Museum (Herzog & de Meuron of Switzerland), the California Academy of Sciences (Renzo Piano of Italy), and the Contemporary Jewish Museum (Polish New Yorker Daniel Libeskind). As the hard hats multiply, so do the heated local debates.

The development flurry is thrown into relief by the previous decades spent carefully preserving the city's historic buildings. Genteel Victorian homes are a city signature, and this residential legacy has been fiercely protected. But some critics complain of the lack of a current, strong, homegrown style and the trend for "imported talent."

Residents aren't shy about voicing opinions on the "starchitect" plans, either. As high-profile designs unfold and new condo neighborhoods break ground, criticism will surely escalate. (One thing that gratifies everyone: The impressive advances made in eco-friendly building practices.) As *Chronicle* columnist John King put it, SF is getting "a crash course in contemporary architecture. One that is long, long overdue."

San Francisco Museum of Modern Art (SFMOMA)

SAN FRANCISCO'S SIGNATURE BUILDINGS

Octagonal Houses

❶ OCTAGONAL HOUSES
c. 1850–60s

Only a few examples of this fad remain; the preserved home on Gough Street is a prime specimen. The style was promoted as being particularly healthy, as it would bring in more light and fresh air. Inside the Gough Street house (open to the public) are square rooms divided by triangular storage spaces. The builder, William McElroy, hid a "time capsule" letter under its stairway.

❷ QUEEN ANNE HOUSES
c. 1885–1890s

The most richly decorated, over-the-top style for Victorian town houses. Known for steep, shingled roofs, slanted bay windows, gingerbread adornments, and "witch's-cap" towers. (The ornamentation was mostly mass-produced, then added to façades.) One of the best is the Haas-Lilienthal home in Pacific Heights, now a public museum.

Haas-Lilienthal House

❸ PAINTED LADIES
c. 1870–1900, paint jobs in the 1960s

The nickname for Victorian houses with vivid, polychrome paint jobs. The original colors were neutrals, but hippies slathered on buttercup yellow, purple, fuschia, you name it. Examples of all the Victorian architectural variations have gotten the Easter-egg treatment, from the pointed arches of the Gothic Revival to the angular bay windows of the Stick-Eastlake look. The most scenic collection of painted ladies can be found along "Postcard Row," a stretch of six candy-colored homes on Steiner Street opposite Alamo Square.

Painted Ladies

WALKING TOURS

For architecture-centric walking tours, check out the offerings from **San Francisco Architectural Heritage** (☎ 415/441–3000 ⊕ www.sfheritage. org). San Francisco City Guides (☎ 415/557–4266 ⊕ www.sfcityguides. org) has some cool tours focusing on specific buildings, like the Ferry Building or the Yerba Buena Complex.

Transamerica Pyramid

❹ TRANSAMERICA PYRAMID
c. 1972

At 853 feet, this tapering skyscraper, long synonymous with San Francisco, is the tallest building in the city (though Sutro Tower, topping 981 feet, is the tallest *structure*). Initially the pyramid, designed by William Pereira, ignited a storm of protest, with then-Assemblyman John Burton claiming it would "rape the skyline."

Now it's considered an icon. Although the building isn't open to the public, you can walk among the redwood trees on the east side of the tower.

❺ SAN FRANCISCO MUSEUM OF MODERN ART (SFMOMA)
c. 1995

SFMOMA

Renowned Swiss architect Mario Botta's first shot at designing a museum. The sturdy, geometric, symmetrical forms have become his characteristic style. Here a black-and-white striped cylindrical tower anchors the brick building. Botta called the huge, slanted skylight the city's "eye, like the Cyclops."

❻ DE YOUNG MUSEUM OF FINE ART
c. 2005

de Young Museum of Fine Art

Love it or hate it, the structure is a must-see destination in Golden Gate Park. After the original Egyptian-revival edifice was deemed seismically unsafe following the Loma Prieta quake in 1989, the Pritzker prize–winning Swiss team Herzog & de Meuron won the commission to rebuild. Their design's copper façade and, in particular, the 144-foot observation tower—a twisted parallelogram grazing the treetops—drew fire from critics, who compared the design to a "rusty aircraft carrier." But the copper hue is mellowing with age, and the panoramic view from the ninth-floor observation deck is a hit—shifting any controversy to the museum's internal politics.

WORD OF MOUTH

"At what time of day are the Painted Ladies at their best? Many of the photos that I see appear to have the houses in partial shade or dusk with the city behind in late sunshine or with lights on in the buildings. Is late afternoon/ early evening the best time to view this sight?"—kiwi_rob

"The views are best in the late afternoon—since the Queen Anne Victorians all face west. That series of Victorians is called Postcard Row."—StuDudley

NEW STARS AND COMING ATTRACTIONS

❼ MISSION BAY, RINCON HILL, AND THE TRANSBAY DISTRICT
Ongoing

Tremendous changes are coming to San Francisco's cityscape, especially moving south from Market Street along the waterfront. Don't expect old-school ginger-bread. Instead, glass-sheathed, condo-crammed high-rises are taking over what was a working-class area of warehouses and lofts, studded by the AT&T Ballpark. A new University of California, San Francisco (UCSF) campus is springing up in Mission Bay, with a blocky Campus Community Center by Mexican architect Ricardo Legorreta now open for business.

❽ PRESIDIO
Ongoing

The development of this parkland continues at a relatively slow pace. Its historic military-base buildings are being put to new uses—everything from a printing press to a spa. Filmmaker George Lucas built a digital arts center here, and a Walt Disney museum opened in October 2009.

❾ CONTEMPORARY JEWISH MUSEUM
Opened June 2008

Architect Daniel Libeskind, known for his work on the World Trade Center site, designed this new arrival in the vibrant Yerba Buena Arts corridor. The multi-use building retains original features of Willis Polk's 1907 power substation—exposed brick, skylights, trusses, exterior arches, and moldings—while incorporating a dramatic two-storey gallery space and blue-steel panels forming rectangle-like structures.

❿ CALIFORNIA ACADEMY OF SCIENCES
Opened September 2008

An eco-friendly, energy-efficient adventure in biodiversity, Renzo Piano's audacious design for this natural history museum comes equipped with a rain forest, a planetarium, skylights, and a retractable ceiling over the central courtyard. But it's the "living roof," covered in native plants, that's generating comment. Dotted with large mounds and hills (Piano's tribute to local topography) the roof looks like an alien launchpad.

The UCSF Community Center

Contemporary Jewish Museum

California Academy of Sciences

ARCHI-FEST

Are you craving more? The American Institute of Architects' SF chapter organizes an **Architecture and the City festival** each September. The event includes tours, lectures, films, and what's been called "domestic modernist porn," a home-tour weekend. Check www.aiasf.org for details.

For an incredibly rich trove of architecture and design publications, head to **William Stout Architectural Books** (⇨ the Shopping chapter).

Where to Eat

WORD OF MOUTH

"Know some easy, tasty, won't-break-the-bank places to eat?"
—mwessel

"Dim sum, Swan's, the takeout at Slanted Door, all the spots on Belden—all places you won't find at home."
—Stu Dudley

Updated by
Sharon Silva
and Sura
Wood

You can find just about any food in San Francisco, a place where trends are set and culinary diversity rules. Since the 1849 gold rush flooded the city with foreign flavors, residents' appetites for exotic eats haven't diminished by even one bite.

Today San Francisco remains a vital culinary crossroads, with nearly every ethnic cuisine represented, from Afghan to Vietnamese. You don't just go out for Chinese here: regional offerings range from the classic Cantonese to the obscure Hakka cuisine of southern China. And although locals have long headed to the Mission District for Latin food, Chinatown for Asian food, and North Beach for Italian food, they also know that every part of the city offers dining experiences beyond the neighborhood tradition.

As for restaurant trends, small plates—à la Spanish tapas—have become the eating experience *du jour*. Now a slew of Italian, Asian, Latin, Mediterranean, and even American restaurants, as well as Spanish spots, are satisfying locals' hunger for myriad small tastes in a single sitting. At the same time, Italian restaurants, which once typically put dishes from all over the boot on their menus, are now focusing on the traditions of just one region, such as Liguria, Lazio, Campania, or Sardinia.

Diners also have grown increasingly serious about what they're sipping. In response, restaurateurs are offering more sophisticated wine lists, emphasizing new vintners, lesser-known varietals, and emerging winemaking regions. And "cocktailians" have been treated to an explosion of innovative drinks that are keeping mixologists busy pouring, stirring, and shaking from one end of town to the other.

San Francisco Bay

MARINA
busy bar scene, upscale eats

NORTHERN WATERFRONT

NORTH BEACH
red-sauce eateries

Bay St.

The Embarcadero

Columbus Ave.

Lombard St.

Polk St.

Larkin St.

Hyde St.

RUSSIAN HILL

TELEGRAPH HILL

FILLMORE

Broadway (tunnel)

CHINATOWN
dim-sum palaces, noodle shops, Asian bakeries

Broadway

Washington St.

FINANCIAL DISTRICT

PACIFIC HEIGHTS

NOB HILL
deluxe dining rooms

California St.

Powell St.

Grant Ave.

1st St.

Sacramento St.

ne St.

Laguna St.

Gough St.

Franklin St.

Van Ness Ave.

Post St.

2nd St.

ush St.

JAPANTOWN
Ramen shops and sushi restaurants

Geary St.

UNION SQUARE
Posh noshing

3rd St.

4th St.

Geary St.

Steiner St.

Turk St.

CIVIC CENTER

Market St.

5th St.

HAYES VALLEY

Mission St.

6th St.

Folsom St.

Harrison St.

1st St.

den Gate Ave.

Fulton St.

SOMA

Bryant St.

Brannan St.

Townsend St.

King St.

WESTERN ADDITION

Hayes St.

Fell St.

8th St.

7th St.

Berry St.

Divisadero St.

AIGHT

Haight St.

HAYES VALLEY
hipster hangouts, great brunch spots

9th St.

10th St.

ena sta rk

Duboce Ave.

Market St.

Mission St.

Van Ness Ave.

CASTRO
swanky lounges, lively bistros

17th St.

Dolores St.

Guerrero St.

Harrison St.

Potrero Ave.

Mariposa St.

POTRERO HILL

Castro St.

Mission Dolores Park

20th St.

MISSION
burrito joints and trendy eateries

0   1 mi

0   1 km

NOE VALLEY

WHERE TO EAT PLANNER

Eating Out Strategy

Where should we eat? With hundreds of San Francisco eateries competing for your attention, it may seem like a daunting question. But don't worry. Our expert writers and editors have done most of the legwork. The 130-plus selections here represent the best this city has to offer. Search the Best Bets section for top recommendations by price, cuisine, and experience. Sample local flavor in the neighborhood features. Delve in, and enjoy!

Hours

Unless otherwise noted, the restaurants listed in this guide are open daily for lunch and dinner. Prime time for dinner is around 7:30 or 8 PM, and although places for night owls to fuel up are plentiful, most restaurants stop serving around 10 PM. Restaurants, along with bars and clubs, may serve alcohol between the hours of 6 AM and 2 AM. The legal age to buy alcoholic beverages in California is 21.

Smoking

Smoking is banned in all city restaurants and bars.

What to Wear

In general, San Franciscans are neat but casual dressers; only at the top-notch dining rooms do you see a more formal style. But the way you look can influence how you're treated—and where you're seated. Generally speaking, jeans will suffice at most table-service restaurants in the $ to $$ range. Moving up from there, many pricier restaurants require jackets, and some insist on ties. In reviews, we mention dress only when men are required to wear a jacket or a jacket and tie. Note that shorts, sweatpants, and sports jerseys are rarely appropriate. When in doubt, call the restaurant and ask.

Reservations

Currently, reservations are a bit easier to get than in the past, but it's still a good idea to plan ahead if you're determined to snag a table at a restaurant with lots of buzz. If you neglected to plan ahead, however, you can get lucky at the last minute if you're flexible—and friendly. Most restaurants keep a few tables open for walk-ins and VIPs. Show up for dinner early (5:30 PM) or late (after 9 PM) and politely inquire about any last-minute vacancies or cancellations. If you're calling a few days ahead of time, ask if you can be put on a waiting list. Occasionally, an eatery may ask you to call the day before your scheduled meal to reconfirm: don't forget, or you could lose out.

Wine

Some of the city's top restaurants still automatically stock historic French vintages, but most wine lists respect the origin of the cuisine being served, such as Italian restaurants primarily pouring Italian labels. Of course, California wines are commonly in the mix, too, with those from limited-production, lesser-known wineries on the better lists. Some restaurants even deliberately keep their wine lists small, so they can change them frequently to match the season and the menu. Half bottles are becoming more prevalent, and good wines by the glass are everywhere.

Tipping and Taxes

In most restaurants, tip the waiter 16%–20%. (To figure out a 20% tip quickly, just move the decimal spot one place to the left and double that)

Bills for parties of six or more sometimes include the tip. Tip at least $1 per drink at the bar. Tipping the maître d' is not necessary unless you're trying to pave your way to being a regular. Also be aware that many restaurants, now required to fund the city's new universal health-care ordinance, are passing these costs along to their customers—usually in the form of a 3%–4% surcharge or a $1–$1.50-per-head charge. (SF sales tax has climbed to 9.5%, too.)

Parking

Most upper-end restaurants offer valet parking—worth considering in crowded neighborhoods such as North Beach, Union Square, and the Mission. There's often a nominal charge and a time restriction on validated parking.

Prices

If you're watching your budget, be sure to ask the price of daily specials. The charge for these dishes can sometimes be out of line with the menu. And always review your bill. If you eat early or late you may be able to take advantage of a prix-fixe deal not offered at peak hours. Many upscale restaurants offer lunch deals with special menus at bargain prices. Credit cards are widely accepted, but some restaurants (particularly smaller ones) accept only cash. If you plan to use a credit card, it's a good idea to double-check its acceptability when making reservations or before sitting down to eat. Also, keep in mind that a restaurant listed as $$$ may actually have a good deal or two, such as an early prix-fixe dinner or a great bar scene and good, reasonably priced bar food to go with it.

WHAT IT COSTS

	¢	$	$$	$$$	$$$$
Restaurants	under $10	$10–$14	$15–$22	$23–$30	over $30

Prices are per person for a typical main course or equivalent combination of smaller dishes. Note: If a restaurant offers only prix-fixe (set-price) meals, it has been given the price category that reflects the full prix-fixe price.

In This Chapter

13

Children

Dining with youngsters in the city does not have to mean culinary exile. Many of the restaurants reviewed in this chapter are excellent choices for families and are marked with a ⏲ symbol.

Using the Maps

Throughout the chapter, you'll see mapping symbols and coordinates (✚ 3:F2) after property names or reviews. To locate the property on a map, turn to the San Francisco Dining and Lodging Atlas at the end of the chaper. The first number after the ✚ symbol indicates the map number. Following that is the property's coordinate on the map grid.

BEST BETS FOR SAN FRANCISCO DINING

With thousands of restaurants to choose from, how will you decide where to eat? Fodor's writers and editors have selected their favorite restaurants by price, cuisine, and experience in the Best Bets lists below. In the first column, Fodor's Choice designations represent the "best of the best" in every price category. You can also search by neighborhood for excellent eats—just peruse the following pages.

MEXICAN

Los Jarritos, $, p. 219
Mijita Cocina Mexicana, ¢, p. 206

SEAFOOD

Aqua, $$$$, p. 208
Hog Island Oyster Company, $$, p. 206
Plouf, $$, p. 210
Swan Oyster Depot, $$, p. 234
Woodhouse Fish Co., $$, p. 200

STEAK HOUSE

Acme Chophouse, $$$, p. 226
Epic Roasthouse, $$$$, p. 205
Harris', $$$$, p. 233

VIETNAMESE

Bodega Bistro, $$, p. 232
Pagolac, $, p. 233
Slanted Door, $$$, p. 207

By Experience

BAR MENU

Absinthe, $$$, p. 201
Epic Roasthouse, $$$$, p. 205
Farallon, $$$$, p. 230
Kokkari, $$$, p. 209

BAY VIEWS

Epic Roasthouse, $$$$, p. 205
Greens, $$, p. 204

Slanted Door, $$$, p. 207
Waterbar, $$$$, p. 208

BRUNCH

Foreign Cinema, $$$, p. 218
Rose's Café, $$, p. 204
Suppenküche, $$, p. 202

BUSINESS DINING

Boulevard, $$$$, p. 205
One Market, $$$, p. 207

CHILD-FRIENDLY

Burger Joint, ¢, p. 216
Capp's Corner, $$, p. 221
Mijita Cocina Mexicana, ¢, p. 206
Park Chow, $, p. 230
San Tung, $, p. 230
Tommaso's, $$, p. 223
Yank Sing, $$, p. 211

COMMUNAL TABLE

Bocadillos, $$, p. 209
Nopa, $$, p. 213
Salt House, $$$, p. 228
Tommaso's, $$, p. 223

HISTORIC INTEREST

Boulevard, $$$$, p. 205
Swan Oyster Depot, $$, p. 234
Tadich, $$, p. 211
Tommaso's, $$, p. 223

HOT SPOTS

A16, $$$, p. 203
Foreign Cinema, $$, p. 218
Nopa, $$, p. 213
SPQR, $$, p. 223
Spruce, $$$$, p. 224

HOTEL DINING

Ame, $$$$, p. 226
Canteen, $$$, p. 230
Ducca, $$$, p. 227
O Izakaya Lounge, $$, p. 215

LATE-NIGHT BITES

Absinthe, $$$, p. 201
Chow, $, p. 200
Nopa, $$, p. 213
Zuni Café, $$$, p. 203

PRETHEATER MEAL

Farallon, $$$$, p. 230
Le Colonial, $$$$, p. 231
Scala's Bistro, $$$, p. 232

QUIET MEAL

Acquerello, $$$$, p. 232
Bodega Bistro, $$, p. 232

Coi, $$$$, p. 222
Fleur de Lys, $$$$, p. 231

SINGLES SCENE

Laïola, $$, p. 204
Nopa, $$, p. 213
Poleng, $, p. 213
Salt House, $$$, p. 228

SMALL PLATES

Bocadillos, $$, p. 209
Coco500, $$, p. 227
Laïola, $$, p. 204
O Izakaya Lounge, $$, p. 215
Poleng, $, p. 213

SPECIAL OCCASION

Boulevard, $$$$, p. 205
Gary Danko, $$$$, p. 213
Jardinière, $$$$, p. 202
Michael Mina, $$$$, p. 231

UNION SQUARE, FINANCIAL DISTRICT, AND CHINATOWN

Fashion, business, and history collide in this broad swatch of the city, where you can eat for pennies or spend your rent in a single sitting.

Around Union Square, *pictured above*, department stores and boutiques rule, and hotels—from Campton Place to the Sir Francis Drake to the Hilton with its **Urban Tavern** (⊠ *333 O'Farrell St.* ☎ *415/923–4400* ✛ *4:E5*), a savvy mix of country charm and city elegance—pull diners in for pricey lunches and pricier dinners. Here and in the nearby Financial District, CEOs find a bounty of old-school dining rooms, including **Alfred's Steak House** (⊠ *659 Merchant St.* ☎ *415/781–7058* ✛ *1:E4*) and Dashiell Hammett's one-time haunt, the atmospheric **John's Grill** (⊠ *63 Ellis St.* ☎ *415/986–3274* ✛ *4:F5*).

But budget-minded locals know to slip into sandwich shops that line the alleys off Kearny, Montgomery, and Bush streets, or to head to Sutter and Post streets, where modest storefronts dish up well-priced Burmese, Japanese, Thai, and Indonesian plates. Or you can hotfoot it over to the narrow lanes of Chinatown, where a bowl of wonton soup or a rice plate in dozens of storefront eateries along Jackson, Clay, or Washington streets will bring change from a five-dollar bill.

EURO FLAVOR

San Franciscans like to brag about their city's European atmosphere, citing Belden Alley as evidence of that claim. The charming pedestrians-only street is anchored by the historic **Sam's Grill** (⊠ *374 Bush St.* ☎ *415/421–0594* ✛ *1:E5*), a seafood institution for more than 70 years. Beyond Sam's, the possibilities are a delicious mix of European tables, with French favorites like **Plouf** (⊠ *40 Belden Pl.* ☎ *415/986–6491* ✛ *1:E5*) and **Café Bastille** (⊠ *22 Belden Pl.* ☎ *415/986–5673* ✛ *4:H1*), the Italian **Brindisi Cucina di Mare** (⊠ *88 Belden Pl.* ☎ *415/593–8000* ✛ *4:H2*), and the Spanish **B44** (⊠ *44 Belden Pl.* ☎ *415/986–6287* ✛ *4:H2*).

DIVING INTO DIM SUM

The popular Cantonese midday custom of going out for dim sum—small dishes, both savory and sweet, hot and cold—can be explored on nearly every block in Chinatown. In big restaurants, servers push dish-laden carts around the dining room, and diners select what they want. Smaller places dispense with the carts in favor of more easily managed trays. You won't always know what you're choosing, so embrace the mystery.

New Asia (✉ 772 Pacific Ave. ☎ 415/391–6666 ✛ 1:D3) is perfect for dim sum newbies—English is spoken here, and the sprawling room means you won't stick out like a sore thumb. For the best selection, try for a table near the kitchen; by the time the carts make their way upstairs, they're picked over.

For more adventurous spirits, **Dol Ho** (✉ 808 Pacific Ave. ☎ 415/392–2828 ✛ 1:D3) is a hole-in-the-wall serving up good dim sum at great prices. Neighborhood regulars fill the small space, snapping up the best items from the single cart. There's not much English spoken here, but the authenticity and low tab make any sign-language efforts pay off.

When you walk downstairs into **Hang Ah** (✉ 1 Pagoda Pl., at Stockton St. ☎ 415/982–5686 ✛ 4:G1), you'll feel like you've discovered a long-hidden gem, where you can fill up on conventional dim sum for a song. If you're in a rush, stop at friendly You's (✉ 675 Broadway ☎ 415/788–7028 ✛ 1:D3), a busy takeout spot famous for its barbecued pork buns.

Many locals like **Great Eastern** (✉ 649 Jackson St. ☎ 415/986–2500 ✛ 1:D4) because they can check off what they want on dim sum menus instead of waiting for a cart. Others, especially Financial District workers on weekdays and families on weekends, migrate to **City View Restaurant** (✉ 622 Commercial St. ☎ 415/398–2838 ✛ 1:E4) for its relatively quiet dining room, ample choices, and atmospheric location on one of the neighborhood's quaint cobblestone blocks. —*Denise Leto*

AND FOR DESSERT

13

The chameleon **Sugar Café** (✉ 679 Sutter St., near Taylor St. ☎ 415/441–5678 ✛ 4:D3) is a smart breakfast and lunch spot by day and a sleek cocktail lounge and dessert destination by night. In the luxe bar, complete with film screenings, customers sip a ginger martini or Bacardi mojito while enjoying a slice of chocolate espresso cake or roasted baby bananas with rum raisin–caramel and vanilla ice cream. If your sweet tooth strikes midday, you can still get the decadent desserts without the libation. Chinatown's **Eastern Bakery** (✉ 720 Grant Ave., near Sacramento St. ☎ 415/982–5157 ✛ 1:D4) is the neighborhood's oldest bakery and best-known outpost for traditional mooncakes, in some two dozen styles, from winter melon to yellow bean to coconut. If you're not tempted by mooncakes, try the tiny egg custard tartlets or the coffee crunch cake, with coffee-flavor pastry cream between the sponge-cake layers and crunchy toffee on top.

SOMA, CIVIC CENTER, AND HAYES VALLEY

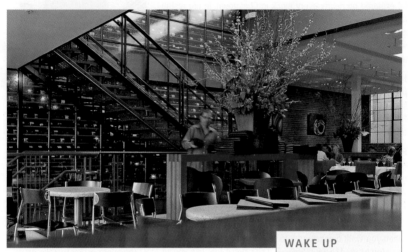

These areas prove that terrific restaurants can spring up in gritty surroundings—and often, they'll help spur a general neighborhood improvement. This serving of gentrification comes with tempting menus and stylish dining rooms.

The hip SoMa once was a warehouse district punctuated by blue-collar households. Nowadays, the same streets are chockablock with residential lofts, trendy bars and clubs, and scores of restaurants that fuel the mostly young and single local crowd.

The Civic Center is heavy with government buildings and grand performance spaces. Its dining scene is geared for people grabbing a bite before or after *La Bohème* or Mahler.

Hayes Valley is sprouting several hip and haute dining destinations along its main stem, Hayes Street. The low-key vibe in its wine bars and cafés makes it easy to feel like a local.

WAKE UP

Ask locals to describe Hayes Valley in one word and they usually respond with "sophisticated" or "pricey." So **Stacks'** (✉ *501 Hayes St., at Octavia St.* ☎ *415/241–9011* ✛ *3:E2*), an all-American breakfast-and-lunch spot, right down to the ketchup bottle on the table, looks out of place. But that doesn't seem to bother the crowd that piles into the big, bright dining room every morning for three-egg scrambles, super omelets with potatoes, eight kinds of pancakes, frittatas, crepes, waffles, and more. Be prepared to wait for a table on weekends. The portions would satisfy a sumo wrestler, so don't show up unless you're hungry.

EAT CHEAP OR DINE CHIC

SNACKING AROUND . . .

SoMa: Tree-lined South Park is a charming green oasis. The park is bordered by 2nd and 3rd streets, and Brannan and Bryant streets. One of our favorite cafés is **The Butler & the Chef** (✉ 155 S. Park St. ☎ 415/896–2075 ✛ 3:H3), which offers organic breakfast and lunch items, including croissants and *croque monsieurs* that will make you think you're in Paris. Closer to Market Street, the takeaway-only **Sentinel** sandwich shop (✉ 35 New Montgomery St. ☎ 415/284–9960 ✛ 1:E5), with Canteen's star chef Dennis Leary at the helm, builds and wraps the city's best Reuben.

Civic Center: For something quick before a show at the symphony hall or opera house, head to **Arlequin** (✉ 384 Hayes St., near Gough St. ☎ 415/626–1211 ✛ 3:E2), the café offshoot of the classy Absinthe restaurant. Arlequin is famous for its grilled ham-and-Gruyère-cheese sandwich on *pain levain*. Nearby, East Coast transplants stop into **Max's in Opera Plaza** (✉ 601 Van Ness Ave. ☎ 415/771–7300 ✛ 3:A1) for pastrami sandwiches or a bowl of soul-satisfying matzo-ball soup.

Hayes Valley: At **Frjtz** (✉ 581 Hayes St., near Laguna St. ☎ 415/864–7654 ✛ 3:E2) you can opt for Belgian fries with a wild array of dips or six different kinds of Belgian waffles.

SOMA SOPHISTICATES

Around Brannan and 4th streets and nearby South Park, several classy restaurants dish up eats, including the wine-savvy **Bacar** (✉ 448 Brannan St. ☎ 415/904–4100 ✛ 1:E6), the lively small-plates **Coco500** (✉ 500 Brannan St. ☎ 415/543–2222 ✛ 4:H6), and the very French **South Park Café** (✉ 108 S. Park St. ☎ 415/495–7275 ✛ 1:F6).

AND FOR DESSERT

13

For high-style desserts in Hayes Valley, head to **Citizen Cake** (✉ 399 Grove St., at Gough St. ☎ 415/861–2228 ✛ 3:E2), where star pastry chef Elizabeth Falkner turns out such creative concoctions as upside-down pineapple parfait and rosebud crème brûlée. For a quick sweets fix, cruise the small pastry counter next door and then grab a seat and enjoy your cookie, cupcake, brownie, or wedge of cake with a potent coffee. If you don't have time to sit, head to the nearby **Miette Confiserie** (✉ 449 Octavia St., near Hayes St. ☎ 415/626–6221 ✛ 1:G4) and sample their ladylike cakes—try the best-selling gingerbread cupcakes topped with a swirl of cream-cheese frosting, or get a couple of their cream-filled macaroons to nibble as you stroll. SoMa's **Patisserie Philippe** (✉ 655 Townsend St., between 7th and 8th Sts. ☎ 415/558–8016 ✛ 1:E6), good for both walkabout and sit-down, is no slouch either when it comes to perfect French macaroons—or to tarts, cakes, pastries, and more, for that matter.

THE WATERFRONT

Locals and visitors alike flock here for gorgeous bay views, a world-class waterfront esplanade, and a ferry building that is much better known for its food than its boat rides.

Not surprisingly, both restaurateurs and diners appreciate proximity to the water, and a slew of restaurants, including the award-winning **Boulevard** (⊠ *1 Mission St.* ☎ *415/543–6084* ✢ *1:G4*), Hotel Vitale's sleek **Americano** (⊠ *8 Mission St.* ☎ *415/278–3777* ✢ *1:G4*), the splashy **Waterbar** (⊠ *399 Embarcadero* ☎ *415/284–9922* ✢ *1:H5*), the meat-driven **Epic Roasthouse** (⊠ *369 Embarcadero* ☎ *415/369–9955* ✢ *1:H5*), and the Zen-tranquil **Ozumo** (⊠ *161 Steuart St.* ☎ *415/882–1333* ✢ *1:G4*), are just steps from the shore.

To the north of the Ferry Building lies Fisherman's Wharf, a jumbled mix of seafood dining rooms, sidewalk vendors, and trinket shops that visitors religiously trudge through and San Franciscans invariably dismiss as a tourist trap. But even disdainful locals are sometimes seen making their way home from the Wharf with a cracked crab tucked under one arm and a loaf of sourdough bread under the other.

DUNGENESS CRAB

The local Dungeness season runs from November through June, which is when San Franciscans descend on the more than half-dozen crab stands at the wharf. Buy an expertly cracked Dungeness at the century-old **Guardino's** (⊠ *corner of Jefferson and Taylor Sts.* ☎ *415/775–3669* ✢ *1:B1*), pick up a loaf of sourdough bread, and feast on a true San Francisco tradition.

If you happen to be in town in February, you're in for a treat: events honoring the celebrated crustacean occur throughout the month at restaurants citywide, as part of the annual San Francisco Crab Festival. Check local listings.

A MOVABLE FEAST

The **Ferry Building Marketplace** (✉ *1 Ferry Bldg., Embarcadero* ✛ *1:G4*) is located at the foot of Market Street on the Embarcadero, with a magnetic pull that makes even the most jaded foodies go weak in the knees. It has just about everything: you can sit down to a three-course meal at **Marketbar** (☎ *415/434–1100*), snack on tacos at **Mijita** (☎ *415/399–0814*) or beluga caviar at **Tsar Nicoulai** (☎ *415/288–8630*), or stock up on amazing fresh ingredients.

Hungry for Asian fare? The Japan-based **Delica rf1** (☎ *415/834–0344*) offers an irresistible daily bento. Looking for a panino packed with house-made salami, sweet basil, roasted peppers, and creamy mozzarella? **Boccalone Salumeria** (☎ *415/433–6500*) will build it for you. Happy with a cheese sandwich? Stop in at **Cowgirl Creamery** (☎ *415/362–9354*) for a wedge of artisanal blue, and then grab a crusty baguette at the **Acme Bread Company** (☎ *415/288–2978*) a few steps away. Or order a burger at **Gott's Roadside Tray Gourmet** (☎ *415/328–3663*), a bowl of clam chowder at **Hog Island** (☎ *415/391–7117*), a Vietnamese spring roll at **Out the Door** (☎ *415/321–3740*), or a glass of vintage cabernet at the **Wine Merchant** (☎ *415/391–9400*).

Have a sweet tooth? There are chocolates at **Recchiuti Confections** (☎ *415/834–9494*), cupcakes at **Miette** (☎ *415/837–0300*), and creamy gelato at **Ciao Bella** (☎ *415/834–9330*).

LOCAL FAVORITE: BOULETTE'S LARDER
Long before you get to **Boulette's Larder** (✉ *Ferry Bldg.* ☎ *415/399–1155*), you know something is cooking. The aromas that rise from this retail food shop and daytime dining spot waft through the Ferry Building Marketplace, drawing people to the southern end of the complex. Breakfast might be poached eggs and Dungeness crab, or piping-hot beignets, while lunch is whatever is on the stove that day—chard and squash gratin, chicken ragout with Indian spices, homey lamb stew, guinea hen … it's all delicious.

AND FOR DESSERT

13

If you're a fan of cupcakes and the color pink—pink walls, take-out boxes, frosting—you'll find a rosy spot at **Kara's Cupcakes** (✉ *900 N. Point St., Ghirardelli Sq.* ☎ *415/351–2253* ✛ *1:A1*), where a long glass case holds about a dozen flavors, including chocolate velvet (chocolate cake with chocolate buttercream), java (chocolate cake with espresso buttercream), coconut (vanilla or chocolate cake with coconut cream-cheese frosting), and sweet vanilla (vanilla cake with vanilla frosting). To accompany your cupcakes: cold milk or hot French-press coffee. Or, go traditional and stop at the **Ghirardelli Ice Cream and Chocolate Shop** (✉ *900 N. Point St., Ghirardelli Sq.* ☎ *415/474–3938* ✛ *1:A1*), where you can first see equipment that was used to make chocolate in 19th-century San Francisco and then sit down to a luscious hot fudge sundae, banana split, or cup of hot cocoa topped with whipped cream.

NORTH BEACH, NOB HILL, AND RUSSIAN HILL

One of the city's oldest neighborhoods, North Beach continues to speak Italian, albeit in fewer households than it did when Joe DiMaggio was hitting home runs at the local playground. But the Italian presence in the markets and cafés is deliciously unmissable.

For great people-watching, snag a sidewalk table at Calzone's, a pizza eatery at 430 Columbus Avenue, near Vallejo Street.

Columbus Avenue, North Beach's primary commercial artery, and nearby side streets boast dozens of moderately priced Italian restaurants and coffee bars that San Franciscans flock to for a dose of strong community feeling.

Nob Hill, the most famous hill in a city of hills, is known for its iconic hotels—the Fairmont, the Mark, the Ritz-Carlton, the Huntington—though only the Ritz-Carlton is a destination for serious diners nowadays.

Nearby Russian Hill, which rises from Columbus Avenue, has few restaurants on its peak and higher slopes, but packs in scores of kitchens and cafés, especially around Polk and Larkin streets, as it descends to Van Ness Avenue.

BOB'S DONUTS

OK, doughnuts aren't the healthiest food, but if you're gonna splurge, why not make it count with the award-winning dough rings at the no-frills **Bob's Donuts** (⊠ 1621 Polk St., near Clay St. ☎ 415/776–3141 ✥ 1:H5). However you like 'em—cake, glazed, raised, sugared, or apple-studded—Bob's makes them 24 hours a day. They're fried in small batches, guaranteeing that every bite is fresh and delicious.

ON THE CHEAP: BIG FLAVORS IN . . .

LITTLE ITALY

The casual bites in this neighborhood are almost always first-rate. The century-old **Molinari's** (✉ *373 Columbus Ave., at Vallejo St.* ☎ *415/421–2337* ✛ *1:D3*) makes delicious Italian sandwiches to order—mortadella, salami, prosciutto—that are great for toting to a bench in nearby Washington Square Park. So, too, does the aptly named **Petite Deli** (✉ *752 Columbus Ave., between Filbert and Greenwich Sts.* ☎ *415/398–1682* ✛ *3:C2*), a one-woman operation where the customers rave about the egg-salad sandwich and the turkey club. If you prefer to eat indoors, grab a table at the modest **Mario's Bohemian Cigar Store** (✉ *566 Columbus Ave., at Union St.* ☎ *415/362–0536* ✛ *1:D3*), which no longer sells cigars but does offer a legendary meatball sandwich on focaccia.

For good coffee, take a seat at the more than half-century-old **Caffè Trieste** (✉ *609 Vallejo St., at Grant Ave.* ☎ *415/982–2605* ✛ *1:D3*), where you may also be serenaded by local opera singers; the jukebox-outfitted **Caffè Puccini** (✉ *411 Columbus Ave., between Green and Stockton Sts.* ☎ *415/989–7033* ✛ *1:D3*), where big sandwiches, soups, and even pasta are served; or grab a sidewalk table at **Caffè Greco** (✉ *423 Columbus Ave., near Vallejo St.* ☎ *415/397–6261* ✛ *1:D3*), pictured below, to enjoy espresso and one of the best versions of tiramisu in the neighborhood.

LITTLE SAIGON

The northern edge of Nob Hill bleeds into the mean streets of the Tenderloin. But hidden here are some Vietnamese culinary gems, especially on Larkin Street. That's where you can find **Bodega Bistro** (✉ *607 Larkin St.* ☎ *415/921–1218* ✛ *4:A6*), the neighborhood's best Vietnamese restaurant, along with **Pagolac** (✉ *655 Larkin St.* ☎ *415/776–3234* ✛ *4:A6*), **Turtle Tower** (✉ *631 Larkin St.* ☎ *415/409–3333* ✛ *4:A6*), and the bright yellow **Baguette Express** (✉ *668 Larkin St.* ☎ *415/345–8999* ✛ *4:A6*), with a dozen different sandwiches on offer.

AND FOR DESSERT

13

Jacqueline Margulis makes only one thing at her small, charming **Café Jacqueline** (✉ *1454 Grant Ave., between Union and Green Sts.* ☎ *415/981–5565* ✛ *1:D3*): tall, airy, gorgeous soufflés, both savory and sweet. She changes the menu regularly, offering such irresistible classics as bittersweet-chocolate, strawberry, or Grand Marnier, all of them with creamy centers. For more creamy goodness, grab a buttery scoop of gelato at the venerable **Gelato Classico** (✉ *576 Union St., between Stockton St. and Grant Ave.* ☎ *415/391–6667* ✛ *1:D3*), a slim spot with just a counter and no place to sit. Every flavor—and there are many—looks delicious, and the patient staff hands over a taste to curious customers—which, face it, is everyone. The coppa mista, a wild swirl together of vanilla, chocolate, pistachio, and rum gelatos, is a house specialty, and a good way to satisfy the craving for multiple flavors.

THE MISSION, THE CASTRO, AND NOE VALLEY

You'll never go hungry here, in some of San Francisco's most jam-packed restaurant neighborhoods. From dirt-cheap taquerías to hip tapas joints, city dwellers know this sector as the go-to area for a great meal.

The city's best Mexican food can be found in the Mission. A pile of hot, salty chips and fiery salsa often arrives gratis with your meal. A filling burrito meal goes for about $5.

Head over to the Mission to dig into Mexican and Latin American menus. In recent years the Latino community has been sharing the neighborhood with legions of twenty- and thirtysomethings who pack the dozens of eateries along Valencia Street, between 16th and 24th streets, and Mission Street, from 19th to 24th streets. East of the Mission, Potrero Hill is home to a cluster of casual dining rooms in the blocks around Connecticut and 18th streets.

The Castro neighborhood, the epicenter of the city's gay community, is chockablock with restaurants and bars. Market Street between Church and Castro streets is a great stretch for people-watching and restaurant-hopping. Just south, in Noe Valley, everyone seems to be pushing a baby carriage, but they're all eating out too, mostly along 24th Street from Church to Castro streets, and on Church Street from 24th to 30th streets.

WAKE UP

A placard at the door says to sign in and wait to be seated at homey **Chloe's Café** (✉ 1399 Church St., between 26th and Clipper Sts. ✛ 1:D6). That wait for your croissant French toast or avocado and cheese scramble is bound to be long on weekends—hey, everyone else has the same delicious idea—so come with your patience. Come with cash in your pocket, too, as no credit cards are taken.

MISSION DINING TWO WAYS

	MEXICAN:	ITALIAN:
Grab-and-go	Two silver **El Toyanese Taco Trucks** (✉ 19th St. and Harrison St.; 22nd St. and Harrison St. ✛ 3:G6) serve up the city's most authentic tacos, stuffed with pork or beef and sizzling salsa.	The no-frills **Arinell** (✉ 509 Valencia St., near 16th St. ☎ 415/255–1303 ✛ 3:E5) is famous for its floppy New York–style slices handed across a walk-up counter.
Cheap eats	**Pancho Villa Taqueria** (✉ 3071 16th St., between Mission and Valencia Sts. ☎ 415/864–8840 ✛ 3:E5) is a Mission institution. The bulging burritos, heavy with beans, rice, meat, and salsa, are just $5.	The super-busy **Little Star** (✉ 400 Valencia St., at 15th St., ☎ 415/551–7827 ✛ 3:F4) doles out cornmeal-crusted pizzas, deep-dish or thin, with toppings like spinach and feta, pesto, and chicken.
Casual chic	**Velvet Cantina** (✉ 3349 23rd St., at Bartlett St. ☎ 415/648–4142 ✛ 3:F6) offers a modern take on Mexican cuisine, in a dimly lighted, bordello-theme room filled with hipsters. Try the avocado-cactus enchiladas with cilantro pesto, washed down with a memorable margarita.	Stop in at **Pizzeria Delfina** (✉ 3611 18th St., at Guerrero St. ☎ 415/437–6800 ✛ 3:E6), the casual offshoot of upscale Delfina, for classic Neapolitan pies, antipasto (eggplant caponata, fresh-stretched mozzarella), and some 15 wines by the glass.

MEXICAN VS. ITALIAN

For years the Mission was where San Franciscans went to eat burritos and tacos, enchiladas, and tamales. But in the mid-1990s new Italian eateries began to open up in this Mexican stronghold, with Parmesan and pasta threatening to outshine queso fresco and frijoles. The culinary turf struggle continues today. Thankfully for diners, there are plenty of tasty choices on both sides of the menu.

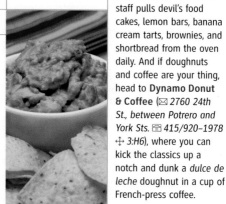

AND FOR DESSERT

13

The Mission has ice cream in every flavor imaginable. **Bombay Ice Creamery** (✉ *552 Valencia St., near 16th St.* ☎ *415/861–3995* ✛ *3:F5*) dishes out dreamy cardamom or pistachio. **Bi-Rite Creamery** (✉ *3692 18th St., near Valencia St.* ☎ *415/626–5600* ✛ *3:E6*) balances orbs of salted caramel or coffee toffee in organic cones. And the venerable **Mitchell's** (✉ *668 San Jose St., at 29th St.* ☎ *415/648–2300* ✛ *3:E6*) has been scooping out creamy lemon custard and Mexican chocolate for over 50 years. For something baked, hit **Tartine Bakery** (✉ *600 Guerrero St., at 18th St.* ☎ *415/487–2600* ✛ *3:E6*), where the staff pulls devil's food cakes, lemon bars, banana cream tarts, brownies, and shortbread from the oven daily. And if doughnuts and coffee are your thing, head to **Dynamo Donut & Coffee** (✉ *2760 24th St., between Potrero and York Sts.* ☎ *415/920–1978* ✛ *3:H6*), where you can kick the classics up a notch and dunk a *dulce de leche* doughnut in a cup of French-press coffee.

PACIFIC HEIGHTS, THE MARINA, AND JAPANTOWN

One of the city's best public transit rides is on the 22–Fillmore trolley, from the edge of Japantown at Geary Boulevard and Fillmore Street, up through mansion-lined Pacific Heights, then down to Cow Hollow and the Marina. We recommend jumping on and off the trolley, stopping for treats along the way.

In Japantown, which covers about six city blocks, start with a green tea latte at the pillbox-size **Café Tan Tan** in the Japan Center (⊠ *Kinokuniya Bldg.* ☎ *415/346–6260* ✢ *2:F6*), or an ice-cream-and-fruit-filled crepe next door at **Sophie's Crepes** (☎ *415/929–7732* ✢ *2:F6*).

Up the hill, Lower Pacific Heights is all about shopping. But growling stomachs can find relief in a baguette sandwich at **Bay Bread Boulangerie** (⊠ *2325 Pine St.* ☎ *415/440–0356* ✢ *2:F5*). Climb back on the trolley for a spectacular view as it crests the hill on Broadway. On your way down, you'll travel past upscale restaurants and no-frills diners, and dimly lighted bars along Union, Lombard, and Chestnut streets.

ITALIAN WINE BAR

A simple bite and a glass of Dolcetto d'Alba may be all you want after a long day of scaling San Francisco's hills. The small, delightfully rustic **Ottimista Enoteca** (⊠ *1838 Union St.* ☎ *415/674–8400* ✢ *2:G3*), *pictured at upper right*, offers just that, with more than two-dozen wines by the glass and small plates like saffron-scented *arancine* (deep-fried, fontina-stuffed rice balls) and a trio of crostini with three different toppings. For something more substantial, try the braised pork with rosemary-mascarpone polenta. If you're out late, end on a sweet note with a glass of *vin santo* and biscotti, served until 2 AM on weekends.

TASTE OF TOKYO, WEST-COAST STYLE

At San Francisco's three-building Japan Center mall, bordered by Geary Boulevard and Post, Fillmore, and Laguna streets, you can eat as they do in Tokyo, stopping in at the sleek **Juban** (✉ *Kinokuniya Bldg.* ☎ *415/776–5822* ⊹ *2:F6*) for *yaki-niku*, meat grilled at your table, including prized Wagyu beef at $60 a serving; at the homey **Izumiya** (✉ *Kinokuniya Bldg.* ☎ *415/441–6867* ⊹ *2:F6*), where *okonomiyaki*, a design-your-own savory pancake studded with pork or squid, is the draw; or at the refined **Ino Sushi** (✉ *Mikyako Bldg.* ☎ *415/922–3121* ⊹ *2:F6*), with its 10-seat sushi bar and handful of tables.

Noodle aficionados will want to try the house-made ramen at **Sapporo-ya** (✉ *Kinokuniya Bldg.* ☎ *415/563–7400* ⊹ *2:F6*) or the soba and udon at **Mifune** (✉ *Kintetsu Bldg.* ☎ *415/922–0337* ⊹ *2:F6*). If your group wants a mix of specialties, wend your way to **Taraka** (✉ *Miyako Bldg.* ☎ *415/921–2000* ⊹ *2:F6*), a *shokuji dokoro*, or Japanese bistro, which offers a mix of choices, from sushi to tempura. But even Taraka has a specialty: a traditional sukiyaki prepared at your table, just as it would be in Japan.

BRUNCHING LIKE A LOCAL

Don't be surprised on weekend mornings to find San Franciscans of all ages waiting in line—rain or shine—at eateries around town. Like attending church or watching Sunday football, going out to brunch is a revered weekend ritual here, a time for friends and family to gather and gab. And, of course, to eat.

For corned-beef hash on toasted biscuits and cinnamon-scented French toast, head to **Elite Café** (✉ *2049 Fillmore St.* ☎ *415/673–5483* ⊹ *2:F5*). The wildly popular **Ella's** (✉ *500 Presidio Ave.* ☎ *415/441–5669* ⊹ *2:C6*) is home to some of the city's best sticky buns and chicken hash with eggs. For classic diner flavor, grab a seat at **Home Plate** (✉ *2274 Lombard St.* ☎ *415/922–4663* ⊹ *2:E3*), where the scones are free and the atmosphere is low-key.

AND FOR DESSERT

13

It seems like everything at the utterly French **Pâtisserie Delanghe** (✉ *1890 Fillmore St., at Bush St.* ☎ *415/923–0711* ⊹ *2:H6*) is wonderfully light, buttery, and/or crispy—the croissants, the Danishes, the macaroons, the strawberry cakes with whipped-cream frosting, the éclairs. You can't linger here—there's only a chair or two—so nab something portable. Or, if you want to rest your feet, continue up Fillmore Street to **Bittersweet** (✉ *2123 Fillmore St., between Sacramento and California Sts.* ☎ *415/346–8715* ⊹ *2:F5*), where you can sit and enjoy a drink, a pastry, or a confection, all with a healthy dose of chocolate. You can also get a chocolate fix at the lively **Mamacita** (✉ *2317 Chestnut St., near Scott St.* ☎ *415/346–8494* ⊹ *2:D3*), a modern Mexican restaurant that serves a rich *budin de cocoa ahogado en cajeta* (chocolate pudding with candied peanuts, caramel sauce, and dulce de leche gelato) and cinnamon-and-sugar-dusted churros with hot chocolate.

HAIGHT, RICHMOND, AND SUNSET

The Haight-Ashbury was home base for the country's famed 1960s counterculture, and its café scene still reflects that colorful past. For ethnic flavors, go to the neighborhoods on either side of Golden Gate Park.

Over time, the Haight has become two distinct neighborhoods. The Upper Haight is an energetic commercial stretch from Masonic Ave. to Stanyan St., where head shops and tofu-burger joints still thrive. A few upscale boutiques and restaurants, like the sizzling Caribbean kitchen of **Cha Cha Cha** (⌧ *1801 Haight St.* ☎ *415/386–5758* ✛ *3:A4*), *pictured below right,* give the blocks a whiff of class. Meanwhile, the modestly gritty Lower Haight has emerged as a lively bohemian quarter of sorts, with hip, mostly ethnic eateries lining the blocks between Webster and Pierce streets.

The Richmond and Sunset neighborhoods encompass the land on both sides of Golden Gate Park, running all the way to the ocean's edge. Both districts have welcomed a dramatic increase in Asian families. And not surprisingly, scores of Asian restaurants have opened to serve them.

HAUTE PIES

The shoebox-size **Pizzetta 211** (⌧ *211 23rd Ave., near Clement St., Richmond* ☎ *415/379–9880* ✛ *3:B1*) puts together thin-crust pies topped with the kinds of ingredients that will make you swoon. The selection changes daily—the tomato, basil, and mozzarella pizza is the only constant—but our favorites include the pancetta, Gorgonzola, and fig pizza, and the Sardinian cheese, pine nut, and rosemary pie. Pizzetta 211 is open for lunch and dinner Wednesday through Sunday, and doesn't take reservations. Go early to avoid a long wait.

EXPLORING THE RICHMOND DISTRICT

NEW CHINATOWN

Since the early 20th century the Richmond District has been a desirable family address. Today, those families are primarily Asian, and the neighborhood has been dubbed New Chinatown, though its dining choices go far beyond the People's Republic. Locals in search of a meal head to three main areas: Clement Street from Arguello Boulevard to 26th Avenue; Geary Boulevard from Masonic Avenue to 26th Avenue, and Balboa Street from 33rd to 39th avenues. Clement Street is a sea of temptation. If you'd like to try the complex curries and salads at the always-busy **Burma SuperStar** (✉ *309 Clement St., near 3rd Ave.* ☎ *415/387–2147* ✛ *2:A6*), put your name and cell phone number on the waiting list as soon as you get to the neighborhood. A cluster of plain-Jane storefronts fire up smoky charcoal braziers on Geary Boulevard between Arguello Boulevard and 10th Avenue, including the **Wooden Charcoal Barbecue House** (✉ *4611 Geary Blvd.* ☎ *415/751–6336* ✛ *3:B1*), which serves up Korean *bulkogi*, or grilled beef ribs.

OLD RUSSIA

Nostalgia hangs heavy in the dining room of the half-century-old **Cinderella Bakery and Restaurant** (✉ *436 Balboa St., near 5th Ave.* ☎ *415/751–9690* ✛ *3:B1*), where diners tuck into borscht and cabbage rolls while sipping *kvass*, or beer brewed from bread. Be sure to stop at the bakery counter on your way out for a flaky napoleon or cheese pastries. Not far away, at **Moscow and Tblisi Bakery** (✉ *5540 Geary Blvd., near 19th Ave.* ☎ *415/668–6959* ✛ *3:B1*), locals line up for some of those same old-country tastes, including *piroshki* (meat- and vegetable-filled pastries) and poppy-seed rolls that will both turn back the clock and recharge your batteries for the touring ahead.

AND FOR DESSERT

13

Out in the Richmond, you would be hard pressed to find a longtime resident who didn't spend some of his or her youth in the truly kitschy **Toy Boat Dessert Cafe** (✉ *401 Clement St., between 5th and 6th Aves.* ☎ *415/751–7505* ✛ *2:A6*), where Double Rainbow ice cream competes with a battalion of vintage toys. No toys compete with the scoops at the funky **Joe's Ice Cream** (✉ *5351 Geary Blvd., at 18th Ave.* ☎ *415/751–1950* ✛ *3:B1*), and no Joe is there now, either. But Mutsuhiko and Aki Murashige have been keeping Joe's name honest since 1979, when they bought the business. They fashion thick milk shakes, make a mean banana split, and put together their own It's-It, San Francisco's iconic ice-cream sandwich—all with their house-made ice cream.

RESTAURANT REVIEWS

Alphabetical by Neighborhood

THE CASTRO AND NOE VALLEY

THE CASTRO

$ ✕ **Chow.** Wildly popular and consciously unpretentious, Chow is a
AMERICAN funky yet savvy diner where soporific standards like hamburgers, piz-
🍂 zas, and spaghetti and meatballs are treated with culinary respect. A
magnet for penny-pinchers, the restaurant has built its top-notch reputation on honest fare made with fresh local ingredients priced to sell.
Salads, pastas, and mains come in two sizes to accommodate big and
small appetites, there's a daily sandwich special, and kids can peruse
their mini-menu. Because reservations are restricted to large parties,
folks hoping to snag seats usually surround the doorway. Come early
(before 6:30) or late (after 10) to reduce the wait, and don't even think
about leaving without trying the ginger cake with caramel sauce. ✉ *215
Church St., Castro* ☎ *415/552–2469* ▭ *MC, V* ✛ *3:C5.*

$$ ✕ **Woodhouse Fish Co.** New Englanders hungry for a lobster-roll fix need
SEAFOOD look no further than this superfriendly spot, where the utterly authentic
lobster rolls, properly served on a buttered top-loaded bun and accom-
panied with slaw and fries, come in two sizes, a three-ouncer and a
"mega" six-ouncer. You'll also find fried Ipswich clams, crab cakes, fish
and chips, clam chowder, and plenty more to keep East Coast seafood
partisans smiling. The restaurant's V-shape storefront, which stands on
a busy Market Street corner, is all worn wood and paint and comfort-
ably funky. On Tuesdays, from 4 PM on, oysters are just a buck apiece
and a pint of draft beer is only four bucks. It seems like everyone in
the neighborhood turns out for this delicious bargain, so be prepared
to wait for a table. A second branch has now opened in Lower Pacific
Heights. ✉ *2073 Market St., Castro* ☎ *415/437–2722* ✍ *Reservations
not accepted* ▭ *AE, MC, V* ✛ *3:D4.*

NOE VALLEY

$$ ✕ **Incanto.** The people who run Incanto are thoughtful. They filter, chill,
ITALIAN and carbonate the very good local tap water and serve it in eco-friendly
reusable glass carafes. They use sustainably grown and harvested ingredients produced by local farmers. They even grow many of their own
herbs in their rooftop garden. They are also adventurous, putting invariably tasty dishes not found at any other restaurant in town on their
daily-changing menu: acorn soup with duck livers and sage; corzetti
("stamped" pasta disks) with pig's trotter, foie gras, and dates; shaved
tripe salad with Meyer lemon, chili, and parsley; braised veal breast
with wild mushrooms; bay leaf panna cotta. The consciously rustic interior—faux stone walls, tile floors, dark-wood tables and sideboards—is
the perfect setting for the inspired fare, while the wine list of obscure
Italian labels makes everything taste even better. ✉ *1550 Church St.,
at Duncan St., Noe Valley* ☎ *415/641–4500* ▭ *AE, MC, V* ⊘ *Closed
Tues. No lunch* ✛ *3:D6.*

$$$ ✕**La Ciccia.** Chef Massimiliano Conti quickly won a loyal following
ITALIAN after opening this charming neighborhood trattoria serving Sardinian
food. The island's classics are all represented—seafood salad dressed
with olive oil and lemon, seared lamb chops, pasta with *bottarga* (salted
mullet roe), and *fregola* (pebble-shape pasta) with an aromatic tomato
sauce—and recommended. The space came with a pizza oven, so Conti
also turns out a pair of respectable thin-crust pies. The wine list, which
boasts nearly 200 labels, looks no further than Italy, and one-fourth of
the choices are Sardinian. The staff is both friendly and efficient, and
Conti regularly circles the room to make sure everyone is happy. ✉ *291
30th St., Noe Valley* ☎ *415/550–8114* ▭ *AE, MC, V* ☉ *Closed Mon.
No lunch* ✛ *3:D6.*

13

CHINATOWN

$$ ✕**Great Eastern.** Don't be tempted to order a Szechuan or Beijing dish
CHINESE here or you'll leave unhappy. This is a Cantonese restaurant, and that
☯ means fresh, simply prepared seafood, quickly cooked vegetables and
meats, clear soups, and no fiery chilies. Tanks filled with crabs, black
bass, catfish, shrimp, and other freshwater- and saltwater creatures
occupy a corner of the street-level main dining room. Look to them for
your meal, but check prices, as swimming seafood isn't cheap. Kids will
find their Chinese-restaurant favorites here: stir-fried noodles, cashew
chicken, fried rice. Avoid the basement dining room, which is brightly
lighted but also claustrophobic. Toward midnight, Chinese night owls
drop in for a plate of noodles or a bowl of *congee* (rice porridge). ✉ *649
Jackson St., Chinatown* ☎ *415/986–2500* ▭ *AE, MC, V* ✛ *1:D4.*

$$ ✕**R&G Lounge.** The name conjures up an image of a dark, smoky bar
CHINESE with a piano player, but this Cantonese restaurant is actually as bright
☯ as a new penny. On the lower level (entrance on Kearny Street) is a no-
tablecloth dining room that's packed at lunch and dinner. The classy
upstairs space (entrance on Commercial Street) is a favorite stop for
Chinese businessmen on expense accounts and special-occasion ban-
quets. The street-level room on Kearny is a comfortable spot to wait
for a table to open. A menu with photographs helps you pick from
the many wonderful, sometimes pricey, always authentic dishes, such
as salt-and-pepper Dungeness crab, roast squab, and shrimp-stuffed
tofu. You can sip a lychee- or watermelon-flavor martini while wait-
ing for your table. ✉ *631 Kearny St., Chinatown* ☎ *415/982–7877 or
415/982–3811* ▭ *AE, D, DC, MC, V* ✛ *1:E4.*

CIVIC CENTER/HAYES VALLEY

$$$ ✕**Absinthe.** In 2007 this restaurant's long-notorious namesake could
FRENCH once again be poured legally in the United States, after nearly a century
in exile. Not surprisingly, regular customers turned up in big numbers to sample the legendary Green Fairy, and then stayed on to enjoy
Absinthe's brasserie-inspired fare of onion soup, cold seafood platters,
grilled lamb loin, and braised beef cheeks, all served in an upscale
dark wood–lined, white-tablecloth dining room The bar, reminiscent

of a Belle Époque Parisian café, offers a late-night bar menu—oysters, *croque monsieur* (grilled ham-and-cheese sandwich), grass-fed-beef burgers, *steak frites, addictive spicy fried chickpeas*—that fuels neighborhood night owls. ✉ *398 Hayes St., Hayes Valley* ☎ *415/551–1590* ▤ *AE, DC, MC, V* ☉ *Closed Mon. No lunch weekends* ✛ *3:E2.*

$$$ ✕ **Bar Jules.** An open kitchen, a counter lined with red-topped stools,
FRENCH a dozen or so small tables, and a generally young crowd are tucked into this cozy, bright eatery on the edge of trendy Hayes Valley. The daily-changing blackboard menu is small and invariably appealing, with dishes like butternut squash soup with pumpkin seed, cauliflower and sunchoke gratin with Gruyère and thyme, and wood-grilled steak with caper butter sauce. Desserts range from plum tart to butterscotch pudding to strawberry fool. Sunday brunch draws a neighborhood crowd to the sunny storefront. On the downside: service can be slow and sketchy, and the sea of hard surfaces can make quiet conversation impossible. ✉ *609 Hayes St., Hayes Valley* ☎ *415/621–5482* ⚄ *Reservations not accepted* ▤ *AE, MC, V* ☉ *Closed Mon. No lunch Tues. No dinner Sun.* ✛ *3:E2.*

$$$ ✕ **Hayes Street Grill.** Arrive here just as local music lovers are folding
SEAFOOD their napkins and heading off for the 8 PM curtain at the nearby opera house and you'll snag a table and some perfectly fresh seafood. Much of the fish—sea bass, yellowfin tuna, swordfish—is simply grilled and served with a choice of sauces from beurre blanc to tomato salsa. A pile of crisp, thin Belgian frites rides alongside the grilled offerings. Brass coat hooks, white tablecloths, a long bar, and a mix of banquettes and tables define the traditional San Francisco look of this three-decades-old seafood stronghold. Folks who eschew water-based fare will be happy to know grass-fed-beef steak and thick pork chops are on the menu. Anyone on a budget will want to come after 7:30 Sunday through Thursday for the three-course prix-fixe menu priced at just $33. ✉ *320 Hayes St., Hayes Valley* ☎ *415/863–5545* ▤ *AE, D, MC, V* ☉ *No lunch weekends* ✛ *3:F2.*

$$$$ ✕ **Jardinière.** A special anniversary? An important business dinner? A
NEW AMERICAN fat tax refund? These are the reasons you book a table at Jardinière.
Fodor'sChoice The restaurant takes its name from its chef-owner, Traci Des Jardins,
★ and the sophisticated interior, with its eye-catching oval atrium and curving staircase, fills nightly with locals and out-of-towners alike. The equally sophisticated French-cum-Californian dining-room menu, served upstairs in the atrium, changes daily, but regularly includes such high-priced adornments as caviar, foie gras, and truffles. Downstairs, the lounge menu, with smaller plates and smaller prices ($8 to $25), is ideal for when you want to eat light while visiting with friends or tame your hunger before or after the nearby opera or symphony. Cheese lovers will appreciate the wide variety of choices—both Old World and New—housed in the glassed-in cheese-aging chamber in the rear of the restaurant. ✉ *300 Grove St., Hayes Valley* ☎ *415/861–5555* ⚄ *Reservations essential* ▤ *AE, DC, MC, V* ☉ *No lunch* ✛ *3:F2.*

$$ ✕ **Suppenküche.** Nobody goes hungry—and no beer drinker goes
GERMAN thirsty—at this lively, hip outpost of simple German cooking in the trendy Hayes Valley corridor. When the room gets crowded, which

it regularly does, strangers sit together at unfinished pine tables. The food—bratwurst and red cabbage, potato pancakes with house-made applesauce, meat loaf, braised beef, pork loin, schnitzel, strudel—is tasty and kind to your pocketbook, and the imported brews are first-rate. There's also a popular Sunday brunch, with appealing fare such as gravlax with mustard-dill sauce and pancakes with brandied raisins. ⊠ *601 Hayes St., Hayes Valley* ☎ *415/252–9289* ▭ *AE, MC, V* ☾ *No lunch* ✛ *3:E2.*

$$$ ✕ **Zuni Café.** After one bite of chef Judy Rodgers' succulent brick-oven-
MEDITERRANEAN roasted whole chicken with Tuscan bread salad, you'll understand
Fodor'sChoice why she's a national star. Food is served here on two floors; the rabbit
★ warren of rooms on the second level includes a balcony overlooking the main dining room. The crowd is a disparate mix that reflects the makeup of the city: casual and dressy, young and old, hip and staid. At the long copper bar, trays of briny-fresh oysters on the half shell are dispensed along with cocktails and wine. The southern French–Italian menu changes daily (though the signature chicken, prepared for two, is a fixture). Rotating dishes include house-cured anchovies with Parmigiano-Reggiano, deep-fried squid and lemons, nettle and onion soup with a poached egg, and brick-oven squab with polenta. Desserts are simple and satisfying, and include crumbly crusted tarts and an addictive cream-laced coffee granita. The lunchtime burger on rosemary focaccia with a side of shoestring potatoes is a favorite with locals. ⊠ *1658 Market St., Hayes Valley* ☎ *415/552–2522* ▭ *AE, MC, V* ☾ *Closed Mon.* ✛ *3:F3.*

13

COW HOLLOW/MARINA

$$$ ✕ **A16.** Marina residents—and, judging from the crowds, everybody
ITALIAN else—gravitate to this lively trattoria, named for the autostrada that
Fodor'sChoice winds through Italy's sunny south. The kitchen serves the food of
★ Naples and surrounding Campania, such as *burrata* (cream-filled mozzarella) with olive oil and crostini and crisp-crust pizzas, including a classic Neapolitan Margherita (mozzarella, tomato, and basil). Among the regularly changing mains are chicken meatballs with fennel and salsa verde (green sauce) and rock cod, scallops, and clams in acqua pazza (literally, "crazy water"). A big wine list of primarily southern Italian with some California wines suits the fare perfectly. The long space includes an animated bar scene near the door; ask for a table in the quieter alcove at the far end. Reservations are easier to snag mid-week. ⊠ *2355 Chestnut St., Marina* ☎ *415/771–2216* ▭ *AE, MC, V* ☾ *No lunch Sat.–Tues.* ✛ *2:D2.*

$$ ✕ **Betelnut.** Most of the primarily young, hip crowd that packs this
ASIAN Union Street landmark probably don't know what a betel nut is (the seed of an Asian palm, chewed for the mild high it delivers). But they do know they like the Pan-Asian cuisine and adventurous drinks (everything from martinis to house-brewed rice beer and sake flights). The menu, divided into big and small plates, noodles, dumplings, and salads, includes chili-crusted calamari, spicy Chinese green beans, firecracker shrimp with a sizzling sambal dip, and Korean short ribs with Asian pear kimchi. Lacquered walls, bamboo ceiling fans, and period posters

create a comfortably exotic mood that matches the food. Patience is required to cope with long wait times and the occasional sluggish service. Smokers find acceptance on the outdoor patio. ⊠ *2030 Union St., Cow Hollow* ☎ *415/929–8855* ▭ *AE, D, DC, MC, V* ✛ *2:F3.*

$$ ✕ **Greens Restaurant.** Owned and operated by the San Francisco Zen
VEGETARIAN   Center, this nonprofit vegetarian restaurant gets some of its fresh produce from the center's famous Green Gulch organic farm. Floor-to-ceiling windows give diners a sweeping view of the Marina and the Golden Gate Bridge. Despite the lack of meat, hearty dishes like the Vietnamese yellow curry with cashew jasmine rice are designed to satisfy. Other standouts include thin-crust pizza with three types of mushrooms, leeks, and cave-aged Gruyère; and pasta with roasted tomatoes, grilled red onion and fennel, pine nuts, and olives. An à la carte menu is offered on Sunday and weeknights, but on Saturday a $49 four-course prix-fixe dinner is served. Sunday brunch is a good time to watch boaters on the bay. A small counter just inside the front door stocks sandwiches, soups, and sweets for easy takeout. ⊠ *Bldg. A, Fort Mason, enter across Marina Blvd. from Safeway, Marina* ☎ *415/771–6222* ▭ *AE, D, MC, V* ☾ *No lunch Sun. and Mon.* ✛ *2:G1.*

$$ ✕ **Isa.** A tiny storefront dining room, a talented chef, and a heated,
FRENCH   candlelighted patio—Isa has all the trappings of a great night out, whether it's the first date or the 50th. The menu of French-inspired tapas changes seasonally but regularly offers such crowd-pleasers as seared foie gras, flatiron steak topped with Cognac–green peppercorn demi-glace, potato-wrapped halibut, and saffron paella cooked in lobster broth. Portions are sometimes petite, so hearty appetites can run up a sizable tab. A good way to keep your costs down is to opt for the two-course prix-fixe menu offered Monday through Thursday for just $24. The wine list, smartly crafted and including plenty of by-the-glass choices, complements the food. ⊠ *3324 Steiner St., Marina* ☎ *415/567–9588* ▭ *MC, V* ☾ *Closed Sun. No lunch* ✛ *2:E3.*

$$ ✕ **Laïola.** San Franciscans never seem to tire of tapas, as the crowds—
SPANISH   mostly young—at this smart, compact Marina outpost of Spanish small plates prove. Try for a seat at the long copper-top bar or at a window table, and then contemplate the seasonally shifting menu that boasts some two dozen tempting tapas, such as braised pork meatballs, Brussels sprouts flecked with bacon, potatoes with pepper-spiked aioli, chickpea croquettes, and slow-roasted piglet. Most regulars seem to skip the four large plates but save room for a creamy chocolate pudding sprinkled with sea salt and olive oil. On Monday nights you can fill up on a big plate of chicken and seafood paella, churros and hot chocolate, and a glass of wine for just $30. If you are hard of hearing or don't want to speak in a raised voice, this is not the restaurant for you, unless you go on a very slow weeknight. ⊠ *2031 Chestnut St., Marina* ☎ *415/346–5641* ▭ *AE, D, MC, V* ☾ *No lunch* ✛ *2:E2.*

$$ ✕ **Rose's Café.** Sleepy-headed locals turn up at Rose's for the break-
ITALIAN   fast pizza of ham, eggs, and fontina; house-baked pastries and breads;
☾   poached eggs with Yukon Gold potatoes and chanterelles, or soft polenta with mascarpone and jam. Midday is time for a roasted chicken and fontina sandwich; pizza with mushrooms, feta, and thyme; or pasta

13

with clams. Evening hours find customers eating their way through more pizza and pasta if they are on a budget, and sirloin steak and roasted sea bass if they aren't. The ingredients are top-notch, the service is friendly, and the seating is in comfortable booths, at tables, and at a counter. At the outside tables, overhead heaters keep you toasty when the temperature dips. Expect long lines for Sunday brunch. ⊠ *2298 Union St., Cow Hollow* ☎ *415/775–2200* ▭ *AE, D, DC, MC, V* ✛ *2:E3.*

$$$
MEDITERRANEAN

✕ **Terzo.** With its zinc tapas bar, fireplace, big communal table, and mix of leather banquettes and oak tables, Terzo has what it takes to pull in the neighborhood social set and everyone else who appreciates expertly prepared Mediterranean fare. Although the restaurant debuted with a small-plates menu, it has since added entrées to the mix. On the compact, seasonally shifting menu you might find creamy hummus and pita, chanterelles with crisp polenta and pecorino, mussels steamed in sherry, chicken spiedini, and sea bass with garbanzos and charmoula sauce (spicy Moroccan sauce). But a plate of seriously addictive onion rings is available year-round. The pricey wine list is loaded with interesting vintners and varietals. Choosing from a handful of aperitifs—Lillet, Dubonnet, sherry, vermouth—is a good way to start your meal. ⊠ *3011 Steiner St., Cow Hollow* ☎ *415/441–3200* ▭ *AE, D, DC, MC, V* ☻ *No lunch* ✛ *2:E3.*

EMBARCADERO

$$$$
AMERICAN
Fodor'sChoice
★

✕ **Boulevard.** Two of San Francisco's top restaurant celebrities—chef Nancy Oakes and designer Pat Kuleto—are responsible for this high-profile, high-priced eatery in the magnificent 1889 Audiffred Building, a Parisian look-alike and one of the few downtown structures to survive the 1906 earthquake. Kuleto's Belle Époque interior and Oakes's sophisticated American food with a French accent attract well-dressed locals and flush out-of-towners. The menu changes seasonally, but count on generous portions of dishes like roasted quail stuffed with sweetbreads, chanterelle bisque with pan-seared ricotta gnocchi, and wood-grilled extra-thick pork chop with roasted Lady apples. Save room (and calories) for one of the dynamite desserts, such as butterscotch-almond apple tart Tatin with cinnamon ice cream. There's counter seating for folks too hungry to wait for a table, and a Kobe beef burger at lunchtime that lets you eat with the swells without raiding your piggybank. ⊠ *1 Mission St., Embarcadero* ☎ *415/543–6084* ☜ *Reservations essential* ☎ *AE, D, DC, MC, V* ☻ *No lunch weekends* ✛ *1:G4.*

$$$$
STEAK HOUSE

✕ **Epic Roasthouse.** "Epic" describes it all: the outsized dining room, the seven-foot flywheel and pulley that sits in the middle of it (an homage to old bayside pump houses), the mile-wide bay view, the huge metal fireplace, the hearty slabs of meat, and, alas, the prices. This is the latest venture, along with the seafood-theme Waterbar right next door, of famed restaurant architect-owner Pat Kuleto. Chef Jan Birnbaum, who made his name first in San Francisco and later in the Napa Valley, is in charge of putting $54 porterhouses and $25 burgers on the fire. For sides, he has opted for sautéed spinach with garlic confit over classic creamed spinach, and truffled cauliflower over scalloped potatoes. If you don't have a Texas-size wallet but still want an Epic experience, head upstairs to the Quiver bar and graze from the bar menu, served only until 9 PM. ⊠ *369 Embarcadero, between Folsom and Harrison Sts., Embarcadero* ☏ *415/369–9955* ▭ *AE, D, DC, MC, V* ⊙ *No lunch weekends* ✛ *1:H5.*

$$
AMERICAN
☙

✕**Fog City Diner.** This fully chromed destination is a far cry from the no-frills diner of Edward Hopper's *Nighthawk*s. Fog City has all the trappings of a luxurious railroad car: wood paneling, huge windows, comfortable booths, and attentive staff. The menu is both classic and contemporary and includes memorable mac-and-cheese made with Gouda, ham, and peas; fried salt-and-pepper squid with chili-lime sauce; hanger steak with mashed potatoes; a half-pound burger with a choice of cheese; and a peanut-butter-cup dessert that will make you forget the famous candy bar. Locals complain of too many out-of-towners, but plenty of folks who call San Francisco home fill the booths at lunch and dinner. ⊠ *1300 Battery St., Embarcadero* ☏ *415/982–2000* ▭ *AE, D, DC, MC, V* ✛ *1:E2.*

$$
SEAFOOD

✕**Hog Island Oyster Company.** Hog Island, a thriving oyster farm in Tomales Bay, north of San Francisco, serves up its harvest at this attractive raw bar and retail shop in the busy Ferry Building. The U-shape counter and a handful of tables seat no more than three-dozen diners, who come here for impeccably fresh oysters (from Hog Island and elsewhere) or clams (from Hog Island) on the half shell. Other mollusk-centered options include a first-rate oyster stew, clam chowder, and Manila clams with white beans. The bar also turns out what is arguably the best grilled-cheese sandwich (with three artisanal cheeses on artisanal bread) this side of Wisconsin. You need to eat early, however, as the bar closes at 8 on weekdays and 6 on weekends. Happy hour, 5 to 7 on Monday and Thursday, is an oyster lover's dream and jam-packed: sweetwaters for a buck apiece and beer for $3.50. ⊠ *Ferry Bldg., Embarcadero at Market St., Embarcadero* ☏ *415/391–7177* ▭ *AE, MC, V* ⊙ *Closed Sun.* ✛ *1:G4.*

$$$
LATIN AMERICAN

✕**La Mar Cebicheria Peruana.** This casually chic restaurant, set right on the water's edge, is divided into three areas: a lounge with a long ceviche bar where diners watch chefs put together their plates; the savvy Pisco Bar facing the Embarcadero, where mixologists make a dozen different cocktails based on Peru's famed Pisco brandy; and a bright blue and whitewashed dining room overlooking an outdoor patio and the bay. The waiter starts you out with a pile of potato and plantain chips with three dipping sauces, but then you're on your own, choosing from a long list of ceviches, causas (cubed potatoes topped with a choice of fish, shellfish, or vegetable salads), and everything from crisp, light deep-fried fish and shellfish to soups and stews and rice dishes. The original La Mar is in Lima, Peru. San Francisco is the first stop in its campaign to open a string of cebicherias across the United States and Latin America. ⊠ *Pier 1½ between Washington and Jackson Sts., Embarcadero* ☏ *415/397–8880* ▭ *AE, D, MC, V* ✛ *1:F3.*

¢
MEXICAN
☙

✕**Mijita Cocina Mexicana.** Famed local chef Traci Des Jardins is the culinary powerhouse behind two of the city's best-known white-tablecloth restaurants, Jardinière and Acme Chophouse. But to honor her Latin roots, she chose Mexican hot chocolate over martinis when she opened this casual taquería and weekend brunch spot. The tacos feature hand-made corn tortillas and fillings like *carnitas* (slow-cooked pork), mahi-mahi, and *carne asada* (grilled strips of marinated meat). The superb meatball soup and Oaxacan chicken tamales are served daily, and the weekend brings such favorites as *huevos rancheros,* fried corn tortillas topped with fried eggs and salsa. Kid-size burritos (beans and cheese) and quesadillas will keep your niños happy. Ingredients are purchased from suppliers whose foods are produced in a sustainable manner, making prices here a bit higher than at many Mexican eateries, but you can feel good about where those pennies go. Seating is simple—wooden tables and benches—but a perfect perch for watching gulls on the bay. Plan to eat dinner early; Mijita closes at 7 on weekdays, 8 on weekends. ✉ *Ferry Bldg., Embarcadero at Market St., Embarcadero* ☎ *415/399–0814* ⊟ *AE, MC, V* ☻ *No dinner Sun.* ✢ *1:G4.*

$$$ ✕ **One Market.** A giant among American chefs, Bradley Ogden runs an
AMERICAN upscale mini–restaurant chain that stretches from Marin County to San Diego. This large space with a bay view and a grown-up ambience is his well-known San Francisco outpost. (He also boasts a steak house in the downtown Westfield Centre.) The two-tier dining room seats 170—many of them suits brokering deals—and serves a seasonal, wonderfully homey yet imaginative menu that might include tender bacon-wrapped pork tenderloin with dandelion greens, olive oil–poached black cod, and braised beef cheeks with black-pepper spaetzle. Folks who want only a small sweet to finish can choose from a half-dozen mini-desserts, such as chocolate toffee almond cake, a mint chip ice-cream bar, or butterscotch pudding. The wine list includes the best California labels, many by the glass. Hearty appetites will appreciate the three-course market menu for just $45. Business types on a budget can opt for the two-course lunch for $23. And the weekday happy hour from 4:30 to 7 PM delivers $3 beers on tap, $5 cocktails, and bar snacks at prices for the people. ✉ *1 Market St., Embarcadero* ☎ *415/777–5577 AE, DC, MC, V* ☻ *Closed Sun. No lunch Sat.* ✢ *1:F4.*

$$$ ✕ **Piperade.** Longtime San Francisco chef Gerald Hirogoyen serves a
SPANISH French Basque menu full of the rustic dishes of his childhood. Among them are *piquillo* peppers stuffed with salt cod, poached foie gras with apple compote, *pipérade* (cooked peppers and tomatoes served with serrano ham and poached egg), warm sheep's milk cheese–and-ham terrine, and lamb chops with white beans. Try a Basque wine from the impressive list and don't miss the featherweight orange-blossom beignets or the pastry cream–filled gâteau basquaise with cherry preserves. Service in the typically packed dining room is professional without being stuffy. Hirogoyen also operates a small café and take-out operation around the corner and the small-plates Bocadillos in the Financial District. ✉ *1015 Battery St., Embarcadero* ☎ *415/391–2555* ⊟ *AE, D, MC, V* ☻ *Closed Sun. No lunch Sat.* ✢ *1:E3.*

$$$ ✕ **Slanted Door.** If you're looking for homey Vietnamese food served in
VIETNAMESE a down-to-earth dining room at a decent price, *don't* stop here. Celebrated chef-owner Charles Phan has mastered the upmarket, Western-accented Vietnamese menu. To showcase his cuisine, he chose a big space with sleek wooden tables and chairs, white marble floors, a

cocktail lounge, a bar, and an enviable bay view. Among his popular dishes are green papaya salad, cellophane crab noodles, chicken clay pot, and shaking beef (tender beef cubes with garlic and onion). Alas, the crush of fame means that no one speaking in a normal voice can be heard. To avoid the midday and evening crowds (and to save some bucks), stop in for the afternoon-tea menu (spring rolls, grilled pork over rice noodles), or visit Out the Door, Phan's take-out counter around the

WORD OF MOUTH

"I'd plan (definitely make reservations) lunch at The Slanted Door on a Saturday. Spend the morning wandering around the Embarcadero, Ferry Building, and the Ferry Building Farmers Market (which closes at 2:00), then have lunch. It's a great spot, with great food. The ginger limeade cocktail is really really good."   —dmlove

corner from the restaurant. A second Out the Door, complete with table service, is in the Westfield Centre downtown, and a third one, again with table service, is now open in the Lower Pacific Heights. ✉ *Ferry Bldg., Embarcadero at Market St., Embarcadero* ☎ *415/861–8032* ⚇ *Reservations essential* ▭ *AE, MC, V* ✛ *1:G4.*

$$$$ ✕ **Waterbar.** When you walk in the door of Waterbar, there's no mistaking
SEAFOOD   what's on the menu. The 200-seat dining room is dominated by sky-high aquariums filled with candidates—or at least cousins of candidates (the kitchen has its own aquariums)—for your dinner plate. Every fin and shell is sustainably sourced, so there's no guilt in sitting down to a plate of poached petrale sole, wood oven–roasted striped bass, or seared haddock. Waterbar, like its next-door neighbor, Epic Roasthouse, is part of the steadily expanding empire of high-energy architect-restaurateur Pat Kuleto. Chef Parke Ulrich, who spent a decade at the city's celebrated seafood palace Farallon, dishes up the catch raw, cured, and cooked in dozens of ways, while nationally acclaimed pastry chef Emily Luchetti handles the sweet end of the menu. If you want to experience this watery world and not pay $60 (ouch!) for a whole lobster, grab a seat in the bar, where you can snack off the bar menu and take in the drop-dead bay view. ✉ *399 Embarcadero, between Folsom and Harrison Sts., Embarcadero* ☎ *415/284–9922* ▭ *AE, D, DC MC, V* ✛ *1:H5.*

FINANCIAL DISTRICT

$$$$ ✕ **Aqua.** Quietly elegant, heavily mirrored and bouqueted, and playing
SEAFOOD   mostly to a society crowd, this spot is among the city's most lauded seafood restaurants and among the most expensive. The kitchen, known for using exquisite ingredients, assembles beautiful preparations that are seriously fancy but not too fussy: tuna tartare with Moroccan spices, sturgeon and veal-cheek bourguignon, ahi tuna and squab breast. Lunch offers an à la carte menu, a three-course business lunch ($45), and a six-course tasting menu ($60), but dinner is a strictly prix-fixe affair, with three courses for $75. Lottery winners can opt for the seven-course tasting menu for $130. Service is as smooth as silk, desserts are showy, and the wine list is as high-class as the clientele. And if you find the house olive oil particularly tasty, Aqua sells it by the bottle. ✉ *252 California*

St., Financial District ☎ 415/956–9662 ♨ Reservations essential ▤ AE, D, DC, MC, V ☾ No lunch ✢ 1:F4.

$$$ ✕ **B44.** Going to restaurant-lined Belden Place is like visiting your favor-
SPANISH ite candy store: there are just too many choices. But this spare, modern
Spanish restaurant, which draws locals and visitors alike with its Cata-
lan tapas and paellas, won't disappoint. The open kitchen sends out
appealing small plates: white anchovies with pears and Idiazábal cheese,
grilled sardines with fennel salad, warm octopus with tiny potatoes,
and blood sausage with white beans. The paellas, individually served
in an iron skillet, bring together inviting combinations such as chicken,
rabbit, and mushrooms, or mixed seafood with squid ink. ✉ 44 Belden
Pl., Financial District ☎ 415/986–6287 ▤ AE, DC, MC, V ☾ No lunch
weekends ✢ 4:H2.

$$ ✕ **Bocadillos.** The name means "sandwiches," but that's only half the
SPANISH story here. You'll find 11 bocadillos at lunchtime: plump rolls filled
with everything from serrano ham to Catalan sausage with arugula to
a memorable lamb burger. But at night chef-owner Gerald Hirigoyen,
who also owns the high-profile Piperade, focuses on tapas, offering
some two-dozen choices, including a delicious grilled quail, an equally
superb pig's trotters with herbs, and calamari with *romesco* sauce (a
thick combination of red pepper, tomato, almonds, and garlic). His wine
list is well matched to the food. A youngish crowd typically piles into
the modern, red-brick-wall dining space, so be prepared to wait for a
seat. A large communal table is a good perch for singles. If you're in the
neighborhood at breakfast time, there is plenty here to keep you happy,
including a scrambled eggs and cheese bocadillo or house-made chorizo
and eggs. ✉ 710 Montgomery St., Financial District ☎ 415/982–2622
♨ Reservations not accepted ▤ AE, D, DC, MC, V ☾ Closed Sun. No
lunch Sat. ✢ 1:E4.

$$ ✕ **Café Claude.** If you think this place looks like it could be in Paris,
FRENCH you're right. Nearly everything, from the zinc bar and the banquettes to
the light fixtures and cinema posters, was shipped from a defunct café in
the City of Light to this atmospheric downtown alley. Order a *croque
monsieur* or niçoise salad at lunchtime. The francophone kitchen sends
out even more French staples for dinner, like escargots, steak tartare,
coquilles Saint-Jacques, and roast lamb. Grab a table outdoors (heat
lamps keep you warm on cool nights) and pretend you are in Paris at a
sidewalk café. Stop by Thursday, Friday, and Saturday nights to enjoy
live music along with your meal. ✉ 7 Claude La., Financial District
☎ 415/392–3515 ▤ AE, D, DC, MC, V ☾ No lunch Sun. ✢ 4:H2.

$$$ ✕ **Kokkari.** The interior of this classy restaurant won't recall homey
GREEK tavernas just steps from the Acropolis. But its menu will satisfy your
craving for good Greek taverna food—albeit at steak-house prices.
Most savvy diners start off with a trio of dips—eggplant, yogurt, and
cucumber—and *taramasalata,* fish roe puréed with olive oil and bread
crumbs. Main courses showcase such Athenian standards as moussaka,
a mixed seafood grill, braised lamb shank, lemon-oregano chicken, and
grilled lamb chops. A bar menu of small plates—crispy smelts, feta-
stuffed phyllo, grilled octopus—satisfies weekday afternoon customers. Desserts like semolina custard wrapped in phyllo, and yogurt with

walnuts and honey, make for a light, sweet finish. ⊠ *200 Jackson St., Financial District* ☏ *415/981–0983* ▭ *AE, D, DC, MC, V* ☉ *Closed Sun. No lunch Sat.* ✢ *1:E3.*

$$$
AMERICAN
✕ **Midi.** The small, stylish Galleria Park Hotel, a favorite address of savvy business travelers, harbors this sleek but casual restaurant with the talented Michelle Mah wearing the top toque. Mah's menu is New American with contemporary French bistro touches, and all the dishes—warm seafood salad with fried artichokes, pork rillette with pickled radishes, panfried skate with lemon brown-butter sauce and haricots verts—draw on the agricultural riches of the Bay Area. The space, with access from the street, combines a lively bar downstairs, popular with the after-work crowd, and dining on two levels upstairs. For the quietest meal, ask for a table on the mezzanine level, to avoid the chatter that can drift up from the bar below. Or, join the fun downstairs and pair your cocktail with popcorn flavored with white truffle oil and sea salt, chickpea fries, harissa-and-honey-roasted pistachios, a grass-fed beef burger on a sesame-seed bun, or steak tartare from the bar menu. ⊠ *Galleria Park Hotel, 191 Sutter St., Financial District* ☏ *415/781–3060* ▭ *AE, D, DC, MC, V* ☉ *Closed Sun.* ✢ *1:E5.*

¢
INDIAN
✕ **Naan 'N' Curry.** You will find no frills here—and minimal service and housekeeping—but you will find food fresh off the fire at rock-bottom prices. This is just one location in a local mini-chain of Indian-Pakistani eateries that cater primarily to starving students, poorly paid office workers, local South Asians, and anyone else who likes spicy food but doesn't give a damn about ambience. The tandoor-fired chicken *tikka masala,* bhindi (okra with onion and spices), garlic naan, and tongue-scorching tandoori lamb chops are favorites. The Bollywood music is too loud, but the naan is the size of a hubcap and the chai (milk) tea is free. ⊠ *533 Jackson St., Financial District* ☏ *415/693–0499* ▭ *MC, V* ✢ *1:D4.*

$$$
ITALIAN
✕ **Perbacco.** With its long marble bar and open kitchen, this brick-lined two-story space oozes big-city charm. The arrival of skinny, brittle bread sticks is the first sign that the kitchen understands the cuisine of northern Italy, specifically Piedmont. And if the breadbasket doesn't convince you, try the antipasto of house-made cured meats (the chef owns a Northern California pig farm to ensure you get only the finest *salumi*) or *burrata* (cream-filled mozzarella) with peppers and anchovies, the delicate *agnolotti dal plin* (veal-stuffed pasta with a cabbage-laced meat sauce), or *pappardelle* with full-flavored short rib *ragù*. The clientele, a mix of business types and Italian food aficionados, appreciates the big, smart wine list along with the superb food. ⊠ *230 California St., Financial District* ☏ *415/955–0663* ▭ *AE, DC, MC, V* ☉ *Closed Sun. No lunch Sat.* ✢ *1:E4.*

$$
SEAFOOD
✕ **Plouf.** This French-friendly spot is a gold mine for mussel lovers, with six preparations to choose from, plus a mussels and clams combo, all at a modest price. Among the best are *marinière* (white wine, garlic, and parsley) and one combining coconut milk, lime juice, and chili. Add a side of the skinny fries and that's all most appetites need. The menu changes seasonally and includes grilled rack of lamb and roasted duck to satisfy any unrepentant carnivores. Many of the appetizers—oysters

on the half shell, calamari with fennel tempura, tuna tartare—stick to seafood, as well. The tables are squeezed together in the bright, lively dining room, so you might overhear neighboring conversations. On temperate days and nights, try for one of the outdoor tables. ⊠ *40 Belden Pl., Financial District* ☎ *415/986–6491* ▭ *AE, MC, V* ☻ *Closed Sun. No lunch Sat.* ⊹ *1:E5.*

$$ ✕ **Tadich Grill.** Locations and owners have changed more than once since
SEAFOOD   this old-timer started as a coffee stand on the waterfront in 1849, but the crowds keep coming. Generations of regulars advise that simple grills, sautés, and panfries are the best choices. Try the cioppino during crab season (November to May), the Pacific halibut between January and May, and iconic San Francisco sand dabs year-round. Happily, the old-fashioned house-made tartar sauce doesn't change with the seasons. There's counter seating, a few tables, and private booths (complete with a bell to summon the waiter), and a long line of business types at noon is inevitable. The crusty, white-coated waiters are a throwback to another time, and the old-school bartenders serve up martinis as good as the mollusks. ⊠ *240 California St., Financial District* ☎ *415/391–1849* ⌂ *Reservations not accepted* ▭ *MC, V* ☻ *Closed Sun.* ⊹ *1:F4.*

$$ ✕ **Yank Sing.** This is the granddaddy of the city's dim sum teahouses. It
CHINESE   opened in a plain-Jane storefront in Chinatown in 1959, but left its Can-
☾   tonese neighbors behind for the high-rises of downtown by the 1970s. This brightly decorated location on quiet Stevenson Street (there's also a big, brassy branch in the Rincon Center) serves some of San Francisco's best dim sum to office workers—bosses and clerks alike—on weekdays and to big, boisterous families on weekends. The kitchen cooks up some 100 varieties of dim sum on a rotating basis, offering 60 different types daily. These include both the classic (steamed pork buns, shrimp dumplings, egg custard tartlets) and the creative (scallion-skewered prawns tied with bacon, lobster and tobiko roe dumplings, basil seafood dumplings). A take-out counter makes a meal on the run a satisfying and penny-wise compromise when office duties—or touring—won't wait. (You can also seek out the Embarcadero branch at 101 Spear St.) ⊠ *49 Stevenson St., Financial District* ☎ *415/541–4949* ▭ *AE, DC, MC, V* ☻ *No dinner* ⊹ *1:E5.*

$$$ ✕ **Zinnia.** When chef Sean O'Brien left his last post, at the now-closed
AMERICAN   Myth, his fan club went into mourning. And when Zinnia opened its doors in late 2008 with O'Brien at the stove, his fans filled the tables immediately. They were there for some of his signature dishes—seared sweetbreads, potato gnocchi, fish and pasta dishes offered in two sizes, his legendary grilled burger on focaccia with crisp Kennebec fries—and for whatever new tricks he had in his modern American cuisine bag. The space, with its brick exterior and hardwood and marble floors, tables and banquettes, and four large multicolor light fixtures, suits O'Brien's trendy but not studied fare, including roasted black cod with shiitakes, fresh rigatoni with foie-gras cream, and pork chops with cranberry beans. The bar is a good place to perch and sample an appetizer or two chased with one of the talented bartender's snazzy cocktails. ⊠ *500 Jackson St., Financial District* ☎ *415/956–7300* ▭ *AE, D, MC, V* ☻ *Closed Sun. and Mon. No lunch* ⊹ *1:E3.*

Eating with Kids

Kids can be fussy eaters, but parents can be, too, so picking places that will satisfy both is important. Fortunately, there are plenty of excellent possibilities all over town.

If you're downtown for breakfast, stop at the venerable **Sears Fine Foods** (✉ *439 Powell St., near Post St.*☎ *415/986–0700* ⊹ *4:F3*), home of "the world-famous Swedish pancakes." Eighteen of the silver-dollar-size beauties cost less than a movie ticket. Nearby in Chinatown, **City View Restaurant** (✉ *662 Commercial St., near Kearny St.*☎ *415/398–2838* ⊹ *1:E4*) serves a varied selection of dim sum, with tasty pork buns for kids and more exotic fare for adults.

If you found yourself dragging the kids through SFMOMA, you can win them back with lunch at the nearby **Crêpe O Chocolate** (✉ *75 O'Farrell St., between Stockton St. and Grant Ave.* ☎ *415/362–0255* ⊹ *4:G4*), where they can fill up on a turkey and cheese sandwich and a crepe filled with peanut butter and chocolate— and you can, too. Try **Pluto's** (✉ *627 Irving St., between 7th and 8th Sts.* ☎ *415/753–8867* ⊹ *2:A6*) after a visit to Golden Gate Park. Small kids love the chicken nuggets, which arrive with good-for-you carrot and celery sticks, whereas bigger kids will likely opt for one of the two-fisted sandwiches. Everyone will want a double fudge brownie for dessert. **Barney's Gourmet Burgers** (✉ *3344 Steiner St., near Union St.*☎ *415/563–0307* ⊹ *3:C6*), not far from Fort Mason and the Exploratorium, caters to older kids and their parents with mile-high burgers and giant salads. But Barney's doesn't forget "kids under 8," who have their own menu featuring

a burger, an all-beef frank, chicken strips with ranch dressing, and more.

Nearly everybody loves pasta, and **Pasta Pomodoro** (✉ *655 Union St., near Powell St.*☎ *415/399–0300* ⊹ *2:F3*) in North Beach offers a kids'-only menu that lets youngsters match up any one of three pasta shapes with five different sauces.

The Mission has dozens of no-frills taco-and-burrito parlors; especially worthy is the bustling **La Corneta** (✉ *2731 Mission St., between 23rd and 24th Sts.*☎ *415/252–9560* ⊹ *2:F6*), which has a baby burrito. Banana splits and hot fudge sundaes are what **St. Francis Fountain** (✉ *2801 24th St., at York St.* ☎ *415/826–4200* ⊹ *3:H6*) is known for, along with its vintage decor. Opened in 1918, it recalls the early 1950s, and the menu, with its burgers, BLT, grilled-cheese sandwich, and chili with corn bread, is timeless. In Lower Haight, the small **Rosamunde Sausage Grill** (✉ *545 Haight St., between Steiner and Fillmore Sts.*☎ *415/437–6851* ⊹ *3:D3*) serves just that—a slew of different sausages, from Polish to duck to Weisswurst (Bavarian veal). Grilled onions, sauerkraut, and chili are extra, and since there are only six stools, plan on takeout. Hint: head to nearby Duboce Park, with its cute playground.

Finally, both kids and adults love to be by the ocean, and the **Park Chalet** (✉ *1000 Great Hwy., at Fulton St.*☎ *415/386–8439* ⊹ *3:A3*), hidden behind the two-story Beach Chalet, offers pizza, a juicy burger, sticky ribs, a big banana split, and, on sunny days, outdoor tables and a wide expanse of lawn where kids can play.

—Sharon Silva

FISHERMAN'S WHARF

$$$$ ✕**Gary Danko.** Be prepared to wait your turn for a table behind chef
NEW AMERICAN Gary Danko's legion of loyal fans, who typically keep the reservation
Fodor'sChoice book chock-full here (plan on reserving two months in advance). The
★ cost of a meal ($66–$98) is pegged to the number of courses, from
three to five. The menu, which changes seasonally, may include pancetta-wrapped frogs' legs, seared foie gras with Fuji apples, shellfish
with Thai red curry, and quail stuffed with foie gras and pine nuts. A
diet-destroying chocolate soufflé with two sauces is usually among the
desserts. So, too, is a "no-cholesterol" Grand Marnier soufflé with rasp-
berry sorbet, perfect for diners with a conscience or a heart problem.
The wine list is the size of a small-town phone book, and the banquette-
lined room, with beautiful wood floors and stunning (but restrained)
floral arrangements, is as memorable as the food. ✉ *800 N. Point St.,*
Fisherman's Wharf ☎ *415/749–2060* ✍ *Reservations essential* ▭ *D,*
DC, MC, V ✆ *No lunch* ✛ *1:A1.*

13

THE HAIGHT

$$ ✕**Indian Oven.** This Victorian storefront draws diners from all over
INDIAN the city who come for the tandoori specialties—chicken, lamb, breads.
The *saag paneer* (spinach with Indian cheese), aloo gobbi (potato, cau-
liflower, and spices), and *bengan bartha* (roasted eggplant with onions
and spices) are also excellent. The chef wants to keep his clientele
around for the long haul, too, and puts a little "heart healthy" icon
next to some of the menu items. On Friday and Saturday nights fam-
ished patrons overflow onto the sidewalk as they wait for open tables.
If you try to linger over a mango *lassi* or an order of the excellent kheer
(rice pudding) on one of these nights, you'll probably be hurried along
by a waiter. For better service, come on a slower weeknight. ✉ *233*
Fillmore St., Lower Haight ☎ *415/626–1628* ▭ *AE, D, DC, MC, V*
✆ *No lunch* ✛ *3:D3.*

$$ ✕**Nopa.** In the mid-2000s, North of the Panhandle became the city's
AMERICAN newest talked-about neighborhood in part because of the big, bustling
Nopa, which is cleverly named after it. This casual space, with its high
ceilings, concrete floor, long bar, and sea of tables, suits the high-energy
crowd of young suits and neighborhood residents that fills it every night.
They come primarily for the rustic fare, like an irresistible flatbread
topped with fennel sausage and chanterelles; creamy cauliflower soup
with almonds and mint; smoky, crisp-skinned rotisserie chicken; a juicy
grass-fed hamburger with thick-cut fries; and dark ginger cake with
caramelized pears and cream. But they also love the lively spirit of the
place. Unfortunately, that buzz sometimes means that raised voices are
the only way to communicate with fellow diners. A big community table
eases the way for anyone dining out on his or her own. ✉ *560 Divisa-*
dero St., Haight ☎ *415/864–8643* ▭ *AE, MC, V* ✆ *No lunch* ✛ *3:B3.*

$ ✕**Poleng Lounge.** At once a restaurant, nightclub, and tearoom, this cap-
ASIAN tivating space hosts a young, diverse crowd that is happy to graze on
Poleng's two-dozen modern Pan-Asian small plates. The food delivers
a satisfying mix that keeps you ordering more: sweet-potato fries with

banana ketchup, Thai basil eggplant, poached beef marrow with coconut bread, garlic crab noodles, and crispy salt-and-pepper squid with green chili sauce. No one goes thirsty here, with dozens of cocktails, teas (including alcohol-infused teas), sakes, and wines to choose from. The dining space, with a communal table, batik accents, and water gently flowing down a limestone-tile wall, is comfortably separated from the nightclub, which doesn't tune up until 10. Happy hour, from 4 to 7 weekdays, is a good option for budget-watchers. ⊠ *1751 Fulton St., Haight* ☎ *415/441–1751* ▭ *AE,MC, V* ⊘ *Closed Mon. No lunch Sun. and Mon.* ✛ *3:A2.*

$$$ ✕ **RNM.** A small, glamorously lighted bar, a big LCD screen, and table-
NEW AMERICAN fuls of well-heeled hipsters make RNM look more like a cozy dinner house in New York's SoHo than in the endearingly scruffy Lower Haight. The menu, which changes seasonally, is divided into "small" and "larger" plates and delivers American food with French and Italian accents. In cooler months you might find grilled hearts of romaine with Fuji apples and blue cheese, black cod on gypsy pepper coulis, and boudin blanc on creamy polenta. The pizzas ($14) are generally good, as are the molten chocolate cake and Meyer lemon tart. Portions can be petite, so plan on at least two small plates per person. Folks watching their pennies know to come before 7 for the $28 three-course prix-fixe dinner, and folks who like cocktails know this place knows how to mix them. ⊠ *598 Haight St., Lower Haight* ☎ *415/551–7900* ▭ *MC, V* ⊘ *Closed Sun. and Mon. No lunch* ✛ *3:D3.*

$$ ✕ **Thep Phanom.** Long ago, local food critics and restaurant-goers began
THAI singing the praises of Thep Phanom. The tune hasn't stopped, except for an occasional sour note on rising prices. Duck is deliciously prepared in several ways—atop a mound of spinach, in a fragrant curry, minced for salad. Seafood (in various guises) is another specialty, along with warm eggplant salad, fried tofu with peanut sauce, spicy beef salad, fried quail, and rich Thai curries. The lengthy regular menu is supplemented by a list of daily specials, which only makes it harder to make a decision. At least you'll be pondering your choices in comfortable surroundings: the cozy dining room is lined with Thai art and artifacts that owner Pathama Parikanont has collected over the years. ⊠ *400 Waller St., Lower Haight* ☎ *415/431–2526* ▭ *AE, D, DC, MC, V* ⊘ *No lunch* ✛ *3:D3.*

$ ✕ **Uva Enoteca.** A marble counter, a handful of banquettes, tables for
ITALIAN two and four, a long brick wall, a young, savvy staff—Uva has all the trappings of the perfectly casual Italian wine bar. It's a brand-new style for the hip but somewhat sketchy Lower Haight, where it caught on immediately with the neighborhood denizens and everyone else. The menu is straightforward: assortments of Italian cured meats and cheeses, about ten salads and vegetable dishes, a trio of pizzas, and a quartet of bruschette. The grilled panini—prosciutto, caponata, and bitter greens; mortadella, onions, and monstasio cheese—are both delicious and priced right at eight bucks each. Italian wine aficionados are contented with some 20 wines by the glass, available in two sizes, assaggio (2 ounces) and quartino (8 ounces), and a long list of bottles. Many of the vini are from small vineyards and all of them are carefully chosen.

Even the coffee beans are special here: they come from the acclaimed Ritual Coffee Roasters in the Mission. ⊠ *568 Haight St., Lower Haight* ☎ *415/829–2024* ▭ *D, MC, V* ⊗ *No lunch* ✛ *3:D3.*

JAPANTOWN

$$ ✕ **Maki.** *Wappa-meshi,* rice topped with meat or fish and steamed in a
JAPANESE bamboo basket, is the specialty at this diminutive restaurant featuring the refined Kansai cuisine of Osaka and Kyoto. The sashimi, sukiyaki, udon, tempura soba, and freshwater eel on rice in a lacquer box are also first-rate. Everything is served on beautiful tableware, from the smallest *sunomono* salad to a big lunchtime *donburi,* protein-topped rice. Maki stocks an impressive assortment of sakes, which it serves in exquisite decanters. If you don't know your sake, the helpful staff will lead you in the right direction. ⊠ *Japan Center, Kinokuniya Bldg., 1825 Post St., Japantown* ☎ *415/921–5215* ▭ *MC, V* ⊗ *Closed Mon. No lunch Tues.–Fri.* ✛ *2:F6.*

$$ ✕ **Mifune.** Thin brown soba and thick white udon are the stars at this
JAPANESE long-popular North American outpost of an Osaka-based noodle
⟳ empire. A line regularly snakes out the door, but the house-made noodles, served both hot and cold and with a score of toppings, are worth the wait. Seating is at wooden tables, where diners of every age can be heard slurping down big bowls of such traditional Japanese combinations as *nabeyaki udon,* wheat noodles topped with tempura, chicken, and fish cake; and *tenzaru,* cold noodles and hot tempura with gingery dipping sauce served on lacquered trays. The noodle-phobic can choose from a few rice dishes. ⊠ *Japan Center, Kintetsu Bldg., 1737 Post St., Japantown* ☎ *415/922–0337* ▭ *AE, D, MC, V* ✛ *2:F6.*

$$ ✕ **O Izakaya Lounge.** San Francisco has been hit by a mini-tsunami of
JAPANESE izakaya spots, Japanese-style pubs where folks gather to drink and share small plates. The good-looking O Izakaya delivers that tradition plus big flat-screen TVs so that no one misses an inning. The walls are covered with oversize baseball cards, and seating is a mix of booths and tall communal tables. The menu is a wild ride of noodles (soba, yam), skewers (pork belly, beef loin, duck heart), tempura, dumplings, salads, raw and cooked fish—even burgers. Sake aficionados will find plenty to choose from, including a trio of flights, plus there's lots of beer, shochu (a distilled spirit made from sweet potato, rice, or barley; similar to vodka), and cocktail choices to ensure no one goes thirsty. ⊠ *Hotel Kabuki,1625 Post St., Japantown* ☎ *415/614–5431* ▭ *AE, D, DC, MC, V* ⊗ *No lunch. No dinner Mon. and Tues.* ✛ *2:G6.*

$$$ ✕ **Yoshi's.** San Franciscans were long envious of Oakland jazz lovers who
JAPANESE had Yoshi's restaurant and nationally known jazz club at their doorstep. But with the late 2007 opening of Yoshi's in San Francisco's slowly rising jazz district on the edge of Japantown, that envy quickly became history. While talented musicians do their thing in a separate space, the equally talented chef Shotaro Kamio serves some of the city's finest—and priciest—Japanese food: exquisite sashimi, memorable robata, crisp tempura, exotic maki-sushi (rolls), pristine nigiri sushi. A wood-burning oven delivers hamachi (yellowtail) collar with chile-ponzu sauce, cedar

13

paper–wrapped vegetables, lamb chops, and more. The big, handsome restaurant harbors stylish booths, a sushi bar, small tables, a tatami room, a mezzanine lounge, and a bar, ensuring a comfortable perch for every diner. When funds are tight, order from the pub menu in the bar to sample Kamio's fine culinary hand. ⊠ *1300 Fillmore St., Japantown* ☎ *415/655–5600* ⊟ *AE, D, DC, MC, V* ⊗ *No lunch* ⊹ *3:D1.*

THE MISSION

¢   ✕ **Angkor Borei.** Aromatic Thai basil, lemongrass, and softly sizzling
CAMBODIAN   chilies perfume this modest neighborhood restaurant, opened by Cambodian refugees in the late 1980s. The menu includes an array of curries; salads of squid or cold noodles with ground fish; a crisp, pork-and-sprout-filled crepe; and lightly curried fish mousse cooked in a banana leaf. Chicken grilled on skewers and served with mild pickled vegetables is a house specialty, as are the green papaya salad and the panfried catfish. Vegetarians will be happy to discover two full pages of selections. Service is friendly though sometimes languid, so don't stop here when you're in a hurry. ⊠ *3471 Mission St., Mission* ☎ *415/550–8417* ⊟ *MC, V* ⊹ *3:F6.*

$$ ✕ **Beretta.** The formula here works: great cocktails, great antipasti, great
ITALIAN   pizzas, great risottos, great piatti del giorno (daily mains), and great late hours. The mixologists are both serious and friendly, smiling when they detail the ten or so gins you can choose from for your martini. The pizzas respect their Italian heritage (thin crusts, traditional and contemporary toppings) and the antipasti are an appealing mix of vegetables (charred radicchio, broccolini with chile and garlic), fish (a light fritto misto of marinated sardines), and locally made artisanal salumi (cured meats). A quartet of first-rate risottos and the single daily main, including an excellent Friday-night cioppino, satisfy folks with bigger appetites. The long, ascetically outfitted room—tin ceiling, white walls, bare wood tables—is casual and smart, and typically filled with a crowd that was too young to drink the year Jerry Garcia died. What doesn't work here? Conversation, unless you speaking pretty loudly or read lips, and vertiginous high heels, unless you stay away from those dynamite cocktails. ⊠ *1199 Valencia St., Mission* ☎ *415/695–1199* ⊠ *Reservations accepted for groups of 6 or more only* ⊟ *AE, D, MC, V* ⊗ *No lunch weekdays* ⊹ *3:F6.*

¢   ✕ **Burger Joint.** Cross the threshold here and you're back in the days
BURGER   of sock hops and big Chevy sedans. Dressed in red and turquoise,
☺   with checkered floors and comfy booths, the retro Burger Joint serves Niman Ranch beef burgers, ridiculously good thick and creamy milk shakes, big root beer floats, and crisp, stocky fries. Every burger comes with tomatoes, lettuce, onion, and pickles, a toasted sesame bun, and a pile of fries. A petite appetite? The mini-cheeseburger and fries fit the bill. Cheeseburger partisans can dress up their patties with American, cheddar, Swiss, or Monterey Jack. Non–beef eaters can opt for a gardenburger or chicken-breast burger. ⊠ *807 Valencia St., Mission* ☎ *415/824–3494* ⊟ *No credit cards* ⊹ *4:A6.*

$$ ✕ **Charanga.** It's hard to resist the tropical vibe that weaves its way
LATIN AMERICAN through this animated tapas depot, with its eclectic mix of Caribbean-inspired flavors. Some tapas stay true to their Spanish ancestry, like *patatas bravas,* which are twice-fried potatoes with roast-tomato sauce. Others, like fried yucca with chipotle aioli, are a mix of both the Old and the New World, and some, like Cuban *picadillo,* a minced-beef dish studded with green olives and raisins, and Costa Rican–style arroz con pollo, chicken and rice with peas, cilantro, and olives, are firmly rooted on this side of the Atlantic. All of the dishes are bigger than typical tapas—more like *raciones,* tapas' traditional big brothers—which means healthy appetites will be satisfied here. The dining room, with walls of exposed brick and soothing green and accents of gold, is small and friendly, so grab—or make—some friends, order a pitcher of sangria or a round of margaritas, and enjoy yourself. ⊠ *2351 Mission St., Mission* ☎ *415/282–1813* 🖒 *Reservations not accepted* ▤ *AE, D, MC, V* ⊘ *Closed Mon.* ✛ *3:F6.*

$$ ✕ **Chez Papa.** France arrived on Potrero Hill with Chez Papa, which
FRENCH delivers food, waiters, and charm that would be right at home in Provence. The modest corner restaurant, with a Mediterranean blue awning, big windows overlooking the street, and a small heated patio, caters to a lively crowd that makes conversation difficult. Small plates include mussels in wine, *brandade de morue* (salt-cod gratin), and caramelized onion tart with anchovies. Big plates range from rack of lamb and salmon with braised endives to homey lamb daube. Leave space for a typically Gallic crème brûlée or wedge of lemon tart. The $31.95 prix fixe is also a good deal for the penny wise. To accommodate the overflow of Hill residents who have packed this place since Day One, the owners opened the tiny (and more casual) Chez Maman (crepes, burgers with blue cheese, salads) halfway down the block. ⊠ *1401 18th St., Potrero Hill* ☎ *415/824–8205* ▤ *AE, D, DC, MC, V* ⊘ *No lunch Sun.* ✛ *3:H6.*

$$$ ✕ **Chez Spencer.** A semi-industrial neighborhood, with an OfficeMax
FRENCH outlet a nearby neighbor, is an unlikely location for an upmarket French restaurant. Yet that's where you'll find Chez Spencer. Tucked into a former warehouse, it boasts arching beam ceilings, polished concrete floors, a wood-burning oven, and a steady flow of devotees from all over the city. The menu—foie-gras torchon, grilled steak with morels and truffled butter, smoked duck-breast salad with a poached egg at its center, warm chocolate pudding cake—is meticulously prepared. The wine list, small and mostly French, is carefully crafted to match the food. There's patio dining, too, with plenty of heaters to keep you warm. The downside of Chez Spencer? The chef needs to tinker with the menu occasionally to keep regulars interested. ⊠ *82 14th St., Mission* ☎ *415/864–2191* ▤ *AE, D, DC, MC, V* ⊘ *No lunch* ✛ *3:G4.*

$$$ ✕ **Delfina.** "Irresistible." That's how countless die-hard fans describe
ITALIAN Craig and Anne Stoll's Delfina. Such wild enthusiasm has made patience
Fodor's Choice the critical virtue for anyone wanting a reservation here. The interior
★ is comfortable, with hardwood floors, aluminum-top tables, a tile bar, and a casual, friendly atmosphere. The menu changes daily, and among the usual offerings are salt cod *mantecato* (whipped with olive oil) with

fennel flatbread and grilled squid with warm white bean salad. If Piedmontese fresh white truffles have made their way to San Francisco, you are likely to find hand-cut tagliarini dressed with butter, cream, and the pricey aromatic fungus on the menu alongside dishes built on more prosaic ingredients. On warm nights, try for a table on the outdoor heated patio. The storefront next door is home to pint-size Pizzeria Delfina. And for folks who can't get to the Mission, the Stolls have opened a second pizzeria on California Street in lively Lower Pacific Heights. ⊠ *3621 18th St., Mission* ☎ *415/552–4055* ⊜ *Reservations essential* ▤ *MC, V* ⊘ *No lunch* ✛ *3:E6.*

$
INDIAN

✕ **Dosa.** Like Indian food but crave more than tandoori chicken and naan? Dosa is your answer. This temple of South Indian cuisine, done in cheerful tones of tangerine and turmeric, serves not only the large, thin savory pancake for which it is named, but also curries, uttapam (open-face pancakes), and various starters, breads, rice dishes, and chutneys. You can select from about 10 different dosa fillings, ranging from traditional potatoes, onions, and cashews to nontraditional cheddar, mozzarella, and onion. Each comes with tomato and fresh coconut chutneys and sambar (lentil curry) for dipping. Lamb curry with fennel and potatoes and prawn coconut masala are popular, as are starters like Chennai chicken (chicken marinated in yogurt and spices and lightly fried), fried chili-dusted prawns, and mung sprout salad. The wine and beer lists are top drawer, and both include some Indian labels. Queues for this Mission District spot convinced the owners to open a second branch on the corner of Fillmore and Post in Japantown. ⊠ *995 Valencia St., at 21st St., Mission* ☎ *415/642–3672* ▤ *AE, D, MC, V* ⊘ *No lunch* ✛ *3:F6.*

$$$
ITALIAN

✕ **Farina.** Locals shed a tear when the longtime Anna's Danish Cookies closed in this spot, and cookie lovers are still mourning. But anyone who craves the Ligurian fare of northern Italy—the home of pesto, focaccia, and delicate pastas—is still cheering the arrival of Farina. Here they fill up on such iconic dishes as focaccia di Recco (paper-thin pizzalike focaccia sandwiching melted stracchino cheese), "handkerchief" pasta dressed with pesto, corzetti ("stamped" pasta rounds) with tomato meat sauce, and raviolini stuffed with borage and ricotta. Those with slim pocketbooks should stay away from the very pricey secondi and instead choose from the regularly changing array of Ligurian carbs and small dishes of sautéed greens, roasted peppers, or other vegetables. Weekend brunch offerings sometimes include eggs sunny-side up topped with shards of fresh black truffle or scrambled eggs with fresh porcini. ⊠ *3560 18th St., at Dearborn St., Mission* ☎ *415/565–0360* ▤ *AE, D, DC, MC, V* ⊘ *No lunch* ✛ *3:E6.*

$$$
NEW AMERICAN
☾

✕ **Foreign Cinema.** Forget popcorn. In this hip, loftlike space, "dinner and a movie" become one joyous event. Classic films like René Clément's noirish 1960 *Purple Noon* and Krzysztof Kieslowski's 1990 *Blue* are projected on a wall in a large inner courtyard while you're served oysters on the half shell, house-cured sardines, grilled squid with roasted peppers, or steak with Argentine salsa from the dinner menu; or a crab panino or chicken-liver pâté from the café menu. Fussy filmgoers should call ahead to find out what's playing and arrive in time for a good seat.

Kids aren't forgotten, with celery and carrot sticks, pasta with butter and cheese, and two scoops of ice cream for just $7. The adjacent two-level Laszlo Bar has a serious DJ, and the weekend brunch brings big crowds. ⊠ *2534 Mission St., Mission* ☎ *415/648–7600* ⊟ *AE, MC, V* ✆ *No lunch* ✚ *3:F6.*

$ ✕ **La Santaneca de la Mission.** Lots of El Salvadorans live in the Mission,
LATIN AMERICAN and here they find the *pupusa,* a stuffed cornmeal round that is more
☻ or less the hamburger of their homeland. It usually comes filled with beans, cheese, or meat—sometimes in combination—and is eaten with seasoned shredded cabbage. The kitchen at this friendly, family-run place also makes the more unusual rice-flour pupusa, as well as other dishes popular in Central America, including fried plantains, seafood soup, tamales filled with chicken or pork, *chicharrones* (fried pork skins), and yucca. Accompany your meal with *horchata,* a cooling rice-base drink flavored with cinnamon. Service is sometimes a bit slow, so don't come here when you want a quick bite. ⊠ *2815 Mission St., Mission* ☎ *415/285–2131* ⊟ *No credit cards* ✚ *3:F6.*

$ ✕ **Limón Rotisserie.** The kid sister of Limón, this cheery but modest dining
LATIN AMERICAN room, outfitted with dark-wood tables and brightened with splashes of
☻ yellow, orange, and lime-green, is just a 10-minute walk from its classier sibling. The neighborhood is a bit bleak, but the friendly prices and even friendlier staff quickly help you forget the street scene. An order of the crisp-skinned citrusy chicken, which is typically fresh off the rotisserie, comes with a pair of salsas and a choice of two sides, including rice-and-bean cakes called tacu-tacu, green salad, grilled vegetables, french fries, and yucca fries. Or, you can opt for one of the three ceviches; a mixed fry of shellfish and rock fish; lomo saltado; deep-fried chicken chunks flavored with soy, garlic, and yellow chilies; or a big bowl of chicken-rice soup. You won't go thirsty, either. The list of beverages includes about four dozen wines, half a dozen beers, and even some sakes—a smart list for a small, easy-on-the-budget place. ⊠ *1001 S. Van Ness Ave., Mission* ☎ *415/821–2134* ⌲ *Reservations not accepted* ⊟ *MC, V* ✆ *Closed Sun.* ✚ *3:F6.*

$ ✕ **Los Jarritos.** A *jarrito* is an earthenware cup used for drinking tequila
MEXICAN and other beverages in Mexico. You'll see plenty of these small tradi-
☻ tional mugs hanging from the ceiling and decorating the walls in this old-time, sun-filled, family-run restaurant. At brunch, try the hearty *chilaquiles,* made from day-old tortillas cut into strips and cooked with cheese, eggs, chilies, and sauce. Or order eggs scrambled with cactus or with chicharrones (crisp pork skins) and served with freshly made tortillas. Soup offerings change daily, with Tuesday's *albondigás* (meatballs) comfort food at its best. On weekend evenings adventurous eaters may opt for *birria,* a spicy goat stew, or *menudo,* a tongue-searing soup made from tripe, calf's foot, and hominy. The latter is a time-honored hangover cure. Bring plenty of change for the jukebox loaded with Latin hits. ⊠ *901 S. Van Ness Ave., Mission* ☎ *415/648–8383* ⊟ *AE, MC, V* ✚ *3:F6.*

$$ ✕ **Luna Park.** It can be a tight fit on weekend nights in this clangorous
AMERICAN American bistro in the trendy Mission District. The youngish crowd is here to sip mojitos and Long Islands and nosh on steamed mussels or

goat-cheese fondue with apple wedges. Most of the mains are homey—mac-and-cheese, barbecued spareribs with fries and slaw, grilled salmon, breaded pork cutlet—and priced to sell (except for a grass-fed rib eye at $27). An order of s'mores includes cups of melted chocolate and marshmallows and a handful of house-made graham crackers to customize the campfire classic. On weekends a slew of popular brunch dishes are added to the weekday lunch list of salads and sandwiches. ⊠ *694 Valencia St., Mission* ☎ *415/553–8584* ▭ *AE, MC, V* ✛ *3:F6.*

$$$ ✕ **Range.** The name sounds strictly down-home, but the place looks and
AMERICAN feels big city. Just across the threshold is a full bar stocked with the best bottles—and plenty of people to appreciate them. An open kitchen with a line of tables opposite comes next, and then the dining room furnished with roomy banquettes. The compact, changing menu is a nice mix of high-end and homey, with raw yellowfin with pickled beets sharing space with coffee-rubbed pork shoulder on creamy hominy and greens. On the sweeter side, you'll find a bittersweet chocolate–espresso soufflé with cinnamon–caramel swirl ice cream that will make you forget your diet. For the more ascetic, there's buckwheat crepes with huckleberries and crème fraîche. Service is smooth—informative but not gushy—in both the dining room and the bar. Adventurous cocktail-drinkers will want to dip into the specialty drinks menu before dinner. ⊠ *842 Valencia St., Mission* ☎ *415/282–8283* ▭ *MC, V* ☯ *No lunch* ✛ *3:F6.*

$ ✕ **Ti Couz.** Big, thin, square buckwheat crepes just like those found
FRENCH in Brittany are the specialty here, filled with everything from ham to
☺ Gruyère to ratatouille to sausage to scallops. You can begin with a green salad, oysters on the half shell, a plate of charcuterie, or a bowl of soup. Then, order a savory crepe from the long list of possibilities—you can create your own filling combination—and end with a divine white chocolate or chestnut crepe. Or, you can skip the sweet crepe and order a gelato doused with espresso or liqueur. The self-consciously rustic dining room—sturdy wood tables, mismatched cutlery, whitewashed walls—welcomes an eclectic crowd late into the night. A full bar serves mixed drinks, but the best—and the traditional—beverage is French hard cider, served in pottery bowls. ⊠ *3108 16th St., Mission* ☎ *415/252–7373* ▭ *MC, V* ✛ *3:E5.*

NOB HILL

$$$$ ✕ **Masa's.** Although the toque has been passed to several chefs since
FRENCH the death of founding chef Masataka Kobayashi, this 25-year-old restaurant, with its chocolate-brown walls, white fabric ceiling, and red-silk-shaded lanterns, is still one of the country's most celebrated food temples. Chef Gregory Short, who worked alongside Thomas Keller at the famed French Laundry for seven years, is at the helm these days, and his tasting menus of six and nine courses, including a vegetarian option, are pleasing both diners and critics. The fare is dubbed New French, and all the dishes are laced with fancy ingredients, leaving diners struggling to choose between foie gras au torchon with poached Seckel pears and foie gras *en sous vide* with Agen prunes. In fall, when northern Italy's exquisite white truffles are in season, Short typically puts together a tasting menu that tucks them into every course, including dessert, which in

Coffee with a Shot of Local Flavor

North Beach may have the highest coffee profile, but fantastic brews can be found all over town. Tear yourself away from Columbus Avenue and head to Hayes Valley's **Blue Bottle Coffee** (✉ 315 Linden St., near Gough St.☎ 415/252–7535 ⊕ 3:E2), a modest kiosk where the organic beans (no more than two days from the roaster) are ground for each cup and the espresso is automatically *ristretto*—a short shot. (Although traditionalists stick to the quirky kiosk, in early 2008 Blue Bottle opened a "proper café" downtown in the newly minted Mint Plaza.) In the Mission District, the owners of the inviting **Ritual Coffee Roasters** (✉ 1026 Valencia St., between 21st and 22nd Sts. ☎ 415/641–1024 ⊕ 3:E6) have plunked their roaster in the middle of the café, so you know where your beans—usually single-origin, rather than a blend—were roasted when you order your cap or latte. While you're sipping your inky strong cup at friendly **Farley's** (✉ 1315 18th St., at Texas St. ☎ 415/648–1545 ⊕ 3:H5), a neighborhood institution on sunny Potrero Hill, you can play chess, check out the eclectic magazine selection,

or catch up on the local gossip. If you are a serious bicyclist and serious about coffee, the funky **Mojo Bicycle Café** (✉ 639A Divisadero St., between Grove and Hayes Sts.☎ 415/440–2338 ⊕ 3:B3), in the increasingly hip North of the Panhandle neighborhood, is the place for you. You can down an espresso made from locally roasted fair-trade beans, tuck into a great sandwich, and either buy or admire a beautiful new bike or get the one you are riding fixed. In the Lower Haight, sun seekers grab an outside table at **Café du Soleil** (✉ 200 Fillmore St., at Waller St. ☎ 415/934–8637 ⊕ 3:D3.) and sip bowls of café au lait brewed from organic beans with their morning croissant. And anyone looking for a real cup of joe in a bare-bones pine shack should join the savvy dock workers, carpenters, and young suits at the more than 80-year-old **Red's Java House** (✉ Pier 30, between Embarcadero and Bryant St. ☎ 415/777–5626 ⊕ 1:H6), where the coffee typically follows a cheeseburger and a Bud and the gorgeous view of the East Bay is priceless.

—Sharon Silva

13

a past season featured white-truffle ice cream perched next to an apple tartlet. Wine drinkers are bound to find something that suits them, with 900 bottles on the list. Be prepared for a decidedly stuffy, though not suffocating, atmosphere (a jacket is preferred for gentlemen). ✉ *Hotel Vintage Court, 648 Bush St., Nob Hill* ☎ *415/989–7154* ⌘ *Reservations essential* ▭ *AE, D, DC, MC, V* ☉ *Closed Sun. and Mon. No lunch* ⊕ *4:F2.*

NORTH BEACH

$$ ✕ **Capp's Corner.** One of North Beach's last family-style trattorias, Capp's
ITALIAN is steadfastly old-fashioned. The men at the bar still roll dice for drinks,
☙ celebrity photos line the walls, and diners sit elbow-to-elbow at long,
oilcloth-covered tables. The fare is packaged in bountiful five-course dinners for $20.50, with the roast lamb a good choice for the main (the

tasty osso buco and polenta is $5 more). The food isn't award-winning, but a meal here won't break the bank either. A three-course option, good for smaller appetites—and smaller budgets ($18)—includes minestrone, salad, and choice of pasta. For $4 more, you can finish with an order of spumoni. Kids under 10 will be happy with their own menu priced at $13. ⊠ *1600 Powell St., North Beach* ☎ *415/989–2589* ▭ *AE, D, DC, MC, V* ✢ *1:C3.*

$$$$
NEW AMERICAN
Fodor'sChoice
★

✕ **Coi.** Daniel Patterson, who has made a name for himself both as a chef and as a pundit on contemporary restaurant trends, has had a restless career, but seems to have settled in at this intriguing 50-seat spot on the gritty end of Broadway. Coi (pronounced *kwa*) is really two restaurants. One is a 30-seat formal dining room—ascetic gold-taupe banquettes on two walls—that offers an 11-course tasting menu ($120). The food matches the space in sophistication, with such inspired dishes as chilled piquillo pepper soup, smoked and seared bone marrow with pomegranate and Asian pear, seared bison with gold turnips, and Monterey Bay abalone with escarole. The menu in the more casual—and more casually priced—lounge is à la carte, with less than a dozen items, including a crisp-skinned roast chicken, a bowl of udon noodles, and a grilled Gruyère cheese sandwich. ⊠ *373 Broadway, North Beach* ☎ *415/393–9000* ⚠ *Reservations not accepted for lounge* ▭ *AE, MC, V* ☻ *Closed Sun. and Mon. No lunch* ✢ *1:E3.*

$
ITALIAN
Fodor'sChoice
★
☺

✕ **L'Osteria del Forno.** A staff chattering in Italian and seductive aromas drifting from the open kitchen make customers who pass through the door of this modest storefront, with its sunny yellow walls and friendly waitstaff, feel as if they've stumbled into a homey trattoria in Italy. Each day the kitchen produces small plates of simply cooked vegetables (grilled radicchio, roasted carrots and fennel), a few pastas, a daily special or two, milk-braised pork, a roast of the day, creamy polenta, and thin-crust pizzas—including a memorable "white" pie topped with porcini mushrooms and mozzarella. Wine drinkers will find a good match for any dish they order on the all-Italian list, which showcases gems from limited-production vineyards. At lunch try one of North Beach's best focaccia sandwiches. ⊠ *519 Columbus Ave., North Beach* ☎ *415/982–1124* ▭ *No credit cards* ☻ *Closed Tues.* ✢ *1:D3.*

$$
MIDDLE EASTERN

✕ **Maykadeh.** Although it sits in an Italian neighborhood, this authentic Persian restaurant has a large and faithful following of homesick Iranian émigrés. Lamb dishes with rice are the specialties, served in an attractive but not showy dining room. Among the many appetizers are traditional dishes such as eggplant with mint sauce, pickled vegetables, and saffron-and-lime-spiced lamb tongue. Along with the requisite—and tasty—kebabs, the restaurant serves a variety of poultry and meats marinated in olive oil, lime juice, and herbs. Anyone looking for a hearty, traditional main dish should order *ghorme sabzee,* lamb shank braised with a bouquet of Middle Eastern spices, or baghali polo, lamb shank with fava beans and rice. Give yourself plenty of time here, as service occasionally slows to a crawl. ⊠ *470 Green St., North Beach* ☎ *415/362–8286* ▭ *MC, V* ✢ *1:D3.*

$$$
ITALIAN

✕ **Rose Pistola.** This busy spot is named for one of North Beach's most revered barkeeps, while the food celebrates the neighborhood's early

Ligurian settlers. The menu changes daily, but a large assortment of antipasti—grilled octopus with fennel and arugula; bruschetta with figs and prosciutto—and pizzas from the wood-burning oven are favorites, as are the cioppino and the fresh fish of the day, served in various ways. A big bar area opens onto the sidewalk, and an exhibition kitchen lets you keep an eye on your order. Even though the kitchen has had trouble holding on to a good chef, the service sometimes arrives with attitude, and the tab can shoot up pretty fast, the crowds keep coming. ⊠ *532 Columbus Ave., North Beach* ☎ *415/399–0499* ⊟ *AE, D, DC, MC, V* ✛ *1:D3.*

$$ ✕ **Tommaso's.** This is the site of San Francisco's first wood-fire pizza

PIZZA oven, installed in 1935 when the restaurant opened. The oven is still

☺ here, and the restaurant, with its coat hooks, boothlike dining nooks, and communal table running the length of the basement dining room, has changed little since those early days. The pizzas' delightfully chewy crusts, creamy mozzarella, and full-bodied house-made sauce have kept legions of happy eaters returning for decades. Pair one of the hearty pies with a salad of grilled sweet peppers, green beans, or broccoli dressed in lemon juice and olive oil and a bottle of the house wine. If you have room—and you may not if you ordered a small pizza for yourself—treat yourself to tiramisu. ⊠ *1042 Kearny St.,North Beach* ☎ *415/398–9696* ⌂ *Reservations not accepted* ⊟ *AE, D, MC, V* ☾ *Closed Mon. No lunch* ✛ *1:D3.*

PACIFIC HEIGHTS

$$$ ✕ **Florio.** San Franciscans have always had a weakness for little French

FRENCH bistros, which helped make Florio a hit from the day it opened. It had all the elements: a space that looked like a Paris address, classic charcuterie and roast chicken, and reasonably priced French wines. Since then, this neighborhood favorite has picked up a thick Italian accent, with marinated sardines with bufala mozzarella, chicken-liver crostini, and bigoli with tomatoes and pancetta lining up next to duck confit on wispy torn frisée, steamed mussels, and *steak frites* on the menu. Save room for the kitchen's crème caramel, a neighborhood favorite. The room can get noisy, so don't come here hoping for a quiet tête-à-tête. You can eat at the bar, too, a nice plus if you're out on the town on your own. ⊠ *1915 Fillmore St., Lower Pacific Heights* ☎ *415/775–4300* ⊟ *AE, MC, V* ☾ *No lunch* ✛ *2:F6.*

$$ ✕ **SPQR.** If you know your Italian history, you know this acronym

ITALIAN roughly translates to the senate and people of Rome—and in this case, the food, too. Brought to you by the same team that operates the Marina's wildly popular A16, SPQR is a casual, friendly spot—bare-topped tables, open kitchen, old travel posters on the walls—with a dedicated neighborhood following of all ages. Of course, that dedication usually means a long wait for a table, unless you turn up after 9 or on a slow Monday. Singles can opt for a seat at the counter. The loyalists come here for the nearly 20 antipasti (hot, cold, and fried), nine pastas, and quartet of mains. Share a selection of antipasti (three for $18, five for $28), move on to spaghetti carbonara (eggs, bacon, and pecorino) or amatriciana (tomatoes and bacon), and finish with almond-milk granita and you'll feel like the Colosseum could be just outside. ✉ *1911 Fillmore St., Lower Pacific Heights* ☎ *415/771–7779* ⌕ *Reservations not accepted* ▭ *AE, MC, V* ☺ *No lunch weekends* ✛ *2:F6.*

$$$$

NEW AMERICAN

✕ **Spruce.** One of the hottest reservations in town from the day it opened, Spruce caters to the city's social set, with the older crowd sliding into the mohair banquettes in the early hours and the younger set taking their places after eight. The large space, a former 1930s auto barn, shelters a high-style dining room and a more casual bar-cum-library lounge, and the menu, which boasts burgers and foie gras, beer and Champagne, is served in both. Charcuterie, bavette steak with bordelaise sauce and duck-fat fries, and sweetbreads and chanterelles reflect the French slant of the modern American menu. If you can't wrangle a table, stop in at the take-out café next door, which carries not only sandwiches, salads, and pastries but also anything from the dining room menu to go. And if you are watching your pocketbook, you can graze off the bar menu and watch the swells come and go. ✉ *3640 Sacramento St., Pacific Heights* ☎ *415/931–5100* ⌕ *Reservations essential* ▭ *AE, D, DC, MC, V* ☺ *No lunch weekends* ✛ *2:B5.*

$$

ITALIAN

✕ **Vivande Porta Via.** The secret of how this Italian delicatessen-restaurant, operated by well-known chef and cookbook author Carlo Middione, has outlasted many of its competitors for more than a quarter of a century is simple: authentic, carefully made trattoria dishes served by an engaged staff. The regularly changing menu includes simple fare at lunchtime—frittatas, sandwiches, pastas—and classier plates at night—prosciutto with figs, grilled Belgian endive wrapped in pancetta with lemon vinaigrette, fresh fettuccine with house-made fennel sausage, and risotto with shrimp and lemon. Counter seating lets you enjoy an antipasto and a glass of wine, or one of the excellent house-made desserts—lemon tart, cannoli, biscotti—and an espresso before or after a movie at the nearby Clay Theater. ✉ *2125 Fillmore St., Lower Pacific Heights* ☎ *415/346–4430* ▭ *AE, D, DC, MC, V* ✛ *2:F5.*

RICHMOND DISTRICT

$$

MOROCCAN

✕ **Aziza.** Chef-owner Mourad Lahlou's Moroccan food boasts a healthy dose of modernity that keeps locals coming back for his unique flavors. Diners enjoy first courses like spicy lamb sausage with goat's-milk yogurt dipping sauce or a trio of luscious spreads (eggplant, pomegranate-almond, and yogurt-cucumber) with flatbread. The main courses, such as quail with a cumin-orange glaze accompanied with a bread salad, and a fork-tender lamb shank with spiced prunes, tend to be more audacious. The attractive three-room dining area, done in blue, saffron, and white, is a warm, inviting sea of tiles, arches, and candlelight. The wine list is skillfully geared to North African flavors (waiters can advise on the best choices), while cocktail enthusiasts can pick from more than two-dozen inspired potions. ✉ *5800 Geary Blvd., Richmond* ☎ *415/752–2222* ▭ *AE, MC, V* ☺ *Closed Tues. No lunch* ✛ *3:B1.*

$$

RUSSIAN

✕ **Katia's.** This bright Richmond District gem serves Russian food guaranteed to make former Muscovites smile. Order the deep-purple borscht, crowned with a dollop of sour cream. Small dishes of eggplant caviar, marinated mushrooms, blini and smoked salmon, and meat- or vegetable-filled *piroshki* are delicious ways to start a meal. Follow up with hearty beef Stroganoff, delicate chicken cutlets, or homey *pelmeni*, meat-filled dumplings in broth. You can sip a Russian beer—the porter is good—or a cup of Russian tea (Assam and Keemun blend) with milk or lemon. If you can put together a group, make a reservation for one of Katia's afternoon tea parties, complete with sweets and savories and tea dispensed from a handsome samovar. ⊠ *600 5th Ave., Inner Richmond* ☏ *415/668–9292* ▭ *AE, D, MC, V* ⊙ *Closed Mon. and Tues. No lunch weekends* ⊕ *3:A2.*

¢ ✕ **Pho Hoa Clement.** The menu at this homey Formica-and-linoleum spot
VIETNAMESE is big and remarkably cheap. You can order everything from sandwiches and salads to rice dishes and noodle plates. But the soups are what shine, from the two-dozen varieties of *pho*, rice noodles in beef broth, to a dozen types of *hu tieu*, seafood and pork noodle soups. All of them are served in three sizes—small, medium, and large—usually separated by just 75¢ and no bowl is skimpy. Regulars, many of whom hail from Southeast Asia, favor the shrimp, fish ball, and pork slices soup with clear noodles and the special combo *pho* with rare steak, well-done brisket, tendon, and tripe. ⊠ *239 Clement St., Inner Richmond* ☏ *415/379–9008* ▭ *MC, V* ⊕ *2:A6.*

$$ ✕ **Ton Kiang.** This restaurant introduced the lightly seasoned Hakka cui-
CHINESE sine of southern China, rarely found in this country and even obscure
ⓒ to many Chinese. Salt-baked chicken, stuffed bean curd, steamed fresh bacon with dried mustard greens, chicken in wine sauce, and clay pots of meats and seafood are among the hallmarks of the Hakka kitchen, and all of them are done well here, as the tables packed with local Chinese families and others prove. Don't overlook the excellent seafood offerings like salt-and-pepper shrimp, catfish in black-bean sauce, or stir-fried crab with ginger and scallions. Some of the finest dim sum in the city—delicate dumplings of pea shoots and shrimp, scallops and shrimp, pork and greens—brings in the noontime rush (a small selection is available at night, too). ⊠ *5821 Geary Blvd., Richmond* ☏ *415/387–8273* ▭ *AE, D, MC, V* ⊕ *3:B1.*

RUSSIAN HILL

$$ ✕ **Antica Trattoria.** The dining room—pale walls, dark-wood floors, a
ITALIAN partial view of the kitchen—reflects a strong sense of restraint. The same no-nonsense quality characterizes the authentic Italian food of owner-chef Ruggero Gadaldi, who also operates the flashier Beretta in the Mission. A small, regularly shifting, honestly priced menu delivers archetypal dishes such as carpaccio with capers and Parmesan, *pappardelle* (wide flat noodles) with wild boar, *tagliata di manzo* (beef fillet slices) with arugula, and tiramisu. The wine list is fairly priced, and the genial service is polished but not stiff. ⊠ *2400 Polk St., Russian Hill* ☏ *415/928–5797* ▭ *DC, MC, V* ⊙ *Closed Mon. No lunch* ⊕ *2:H3.*

$$$$ ✕ **La Folie.** This small, *très* Parisian establishment, has long been a favor-
FRENCH ite of Francophiles (and anyone who loves foie gras). The restaurant, outfitted in warm woods and white linens, is smartly designed to let the cuisine take center stage. Choose from well-apportioned prix-fixe

menus of three, four, or five courses ($75, $85, and $95, respectively). The dishes, such as squab with pistachio-crusted foie-gras torchon and butter-poached lobster on a butternut squash ravioli, are artfully presented and always delicious. Vegetarians will be happy to discover a menu of their own ($75). Such rarefied preparation is costly, of course, so you may want to save La Folie for a special occasion. ⊠ *2316 Polk St., Russian Hill* ☎ *415/776–5577* ▭ *AE, D, DC, MC, V* ☾ *Closed Sun. No lunch* ⊹ *2:H3.*

SOMA

$$$ ✕ **Acme Chophouse.** Dine here and you'll agree that cows shouldn't eat
STEAKHOUSE   corn. Grass-fed beef, served up as a filet mignon and tartare, is the specialty at this old-style chophouse next door to the Giants baseball park. The kitchen stocks only naturally raised local meats and poultry, including a 22-ounce rib eye that's sized to satisfy a sumo wrestler and priced for an emperor. All the familiar chophouse sides—creamed spinach, crisp onion rings, creamy mac-and-cheese—will keep traditionalists smiling. The setting is suitably casual, with lots of wood; TV monitors in the bar area mean no inning is missed. The lunch menu is more casual, with burgers, a crab-and-shrimp salad, pastrami on rye, and a flatiron steak that won't break the bank. Open hours vary on game days, so check before the first pitch. ⊠ *24 Willie Mays Plaza, SoMa* ☎ *415/644–0240* ▭ *AE, D, DC, MC, V* ☾ *Closed Sun. and Mon. No lunch Sat.* ⊹ *1:F6.*

$$$$ ✕ **Ame.** America and Japan, along with France and Italy, converge in
ECLECTIC   high style on the plates of chef Hiro Sone. Indeed, his food, from *chawan mushi* (egg custard) with matsutake mushrooms and Manila clams and smoked trout with caviar and Asian pear–celery root salad to sake-marinated black cod, is almost too beautiful to eat. He serves it in an equally stunning, modern space in the handsome St. Regis, which shelters both hotel guest rooms and condominium residences, including one that Al Gore makes his West Coast home. Not surprisingly, the space and the plates attract members of the local—and, some would say, stuffy—elite who know food and have the means to pay a lofty price for it. ⊠ *St. Regis Hotel, 689 Mission St., SoMa* ☎ *415/284–4040* ▭ *AE, D, DC, MC, V* ☾ *No lunch* ⊹ *1:E6.*

$$$ ✕ **Chez Papa Resto.** Downtown's newish Mint Plaza, tucked behind the
FRENCH   city's long-decommissioned 1874 federal mint, is home to Blue Bottle Café, the über-hip Mezzanine music venue, and this utterly urban 70-seat restaurant, with its exposed concrete, bare-wood-topped tables, and high black ceiling. The contemporary French menu—charcuterie du jour, grilled lamb chops with lavender salt, New York steak with a velvety béarnaise and frites, poached halibut with fennel and artichokes, profiteroles filled with vanilla ice cream and drizzled with warm chocolate sauce—will have you dreaming of the Left Bank. Three-course prix-fixe dinners ($34.95) and a three-course prix-fixe lunch ($22.95), all with multiple choices in each category, are available. And for the impecunious after-work crowd, happy hour delivers six-buck cocktails and delicious nibbles from 5 to 7 PM weekdays. ⊠ *4 Mint Plaza, SoMa* ☎ *415/546–4134* ▭ *AE, D, DC, MC, V* ☾ *Closed Sun.* ⊹ *4:E6.*

$$$
NEW AMERICAN

✕**Coco500.** Chef-owner Loretta Keller knows how to change with the times. She shuttered her long-admired Bizou restaurant and reopened in the same spot with this up-to-the-minute small-plates and not-so-small-plates venue. Menu categories like "small starts," "leaf (salads)," and "California dirt (local organic vegetables)" reflect Keller's modern outlook, as do dishes like the COCOmole taco, which pairs tortilla triangles with beef cheeks

WORD OF MOUTH

"Boudin Bakery at Fisherman's Wharf has good sandwiches, clam chowder in a bread bowl, etc. In the Ferry Building, you could assemble a picnic—cheese from Cowgirl Creamery, bread from Acme, etc. Don't forget the many inexpensive dim sum places in Chinatown."   —Elendilpickle

13

and a chili-chocolate sauce. You'll also find duck-liver terrine, truffled flatbread, grilled quail, braised pork belly with fennel and apples, and a signature *vacherin* (crème anglaise, Swiss meringue, coffee ice cream, and chocolate sauce) from Bizou days. For a simpler and smaller sweet ending, order the chocolate-dipped frozen banana. That delicious menu mix pulls in young hipsters and sophisticated oldsters, all cheerfully grazing the menu. Keller is also busy, in partnership with Slanted Door chef Charles Phan, at The Moss Room in the California Academy of Sciences in Golden Gate Park. ✉ *500 Brannan St., SoMa* ☎ *415/543–2222* ▭ *AE, D, DC, MC, V* ☺ *Closed Sun. No lunch Sat.* ✛ *4:H6.*

$$$
ITALIAN

✕**Ducca.** Nowadays some of the city's best restaurants are in hotel dining rooms, and Ducca, resting smartly in a busy neighborhood of museums, movie houses, and theater spaces, is part of that welcome trend. Start off right with an aperitif and little fried rice balls concealing truffled cheese, or a handful of fried green olives stuffed with Gorgonzola. Follow that up with chef Richard Corbo's dreamy lobster sformato (a custardy soufflé) or rustic—and delicious—whole-wheat pasta tossed with sardines and caramelized fennel. Mains are split nearly evenly between meats and fish, including chicken riding alongside polenta flecked with chanterelles and peas. Alas, service is unforgivably ragged at times. Just looking to rest your feet? Join the after-work crowd in the handsome alfresco bar (wisely heated) for a drink and a snack. ✉ *Westin San Francisco Market Street, 50 3rd St., SoMa* ☎ *415/977–0271* ▭ *AE, D, DC, MC, V* ✛ *1:E6.*

$$$$
FRENCH

✕**Fifth Floor.** A clubhouse for well-off diners, this swanky spot is tucked away in the Palomar Hotel. It has seen toques come and go in the last few years, but consulting chef Laurent Manrique, who also oversees the Financial District's Aqua, and executive chef Jennie Lorenzo are now firmly at the helm. Dressed up in sandy beige walls, hardwood floors, sleek dark-wood tables, and modern club chairs, the dining room is the stylish setting for a regularly changing menu that celebrates the kitchens of southwest France, including such dishes as Moroccan-spiced black tiger prawns, parsley-crusted lamb loin with eggplant marmalade, and slow-roasted chicken thigh and butter-poached lobster with mushrooms and quince. For dessert, there might be a luscious Meyer lemon soufflé or an equally addictive gâteau Basque (almond custard tart with cherries and almond milk cream). Dining here is like a trip to France, so allow for plenty of time—and money. If you want to see how the other half eats, enjoy a grass-fed-beef burger or steak frites in the more casual—and more affordable—lounge next door to the dining room. ⊠ *Palomar Hotel, 12 4th St., SoMa* ☎ *415/348–1555* ⊟ *AE, D, DC, MC, V* ⊘ *Closed Sun. No lunch* ✛ *4:G5.*

$$$ ✕ **LuLu.** In its early years LuLu was a magnet for dot-commers, who
MEDITERRANEAN jammed the place every night. When the high-tech industry buckled, LuLu cooled, but never lost its appeal. Nowadays many of the same uncomplicated dishes—fried artichokes, fennel, and lemon slices; mussels roasted in an iron skillet; wood-oven roasted poultry, meats, and shellfish; a small selection of pizzas and pastas—fuel a more mixed clientele. There is a well-supplied raw bar, and main-course specials include a rotisserie-cooked option that changes daily; Friday brings a succulent suckling pig. Sharing dishes is the custom here, and portions are typically bountiful. Wine drinkers will appreciate the long list of choices by the glass. When LuLu is packed, service can suffer. ⊠ *816 Folsom St., SoMa* ☎ *415/495–5775* ⊟ *AE, DC, MC, V.* ✛ *1:F6.*

$$ ✕ **Orson.** Edgy California cuisine—that's what chef Elizabeth Falkner,
NEW AMERICAN who made eating cupcakes fashionable at her popular Citizen Cake in Hayes Valley, has dubbed the fare at her newly minted Orson. This self-proclaimed edginess translates into some intriguing dishes, such as bone marrow with garlic confit, short ribs with curry pappardelle, and snapper with maple-braised kale. The stunning two-story space, an old warehouse done up with a circular marble bar, an eclectic mix of dining spaces, soaring ceilings, and catwalks, would be right at home in TriBeCa. Uneven execution—food and service—plagued Orson for several months, forcing Falkner to make some changes, including retooling the regular menu to eliminate some unsuccessful quirkiness; turning Monday evening into pizza night, featuring half-a-dozen pies nicely crisp from the wood-burning oven; and lassoing the after-work crowd Monday to Friday with five-buck cocktails from 5 to 7. If you are short of cash, stop in for some duck-fat french fries and a snazzy cocktail or a fanciful Falkner dessert with coffee to enjoy the lively scene without blowing your paycheck. ⊠ *508 4th St., at Bryant, SoMa* ☎ *415/777–1508* ⊟ *AE, MC, V* ⊘ *Closed Sun. and Mon.* ✛ *4:H6.*

$$$ ✕ **Salt House.** A boisterous crowd—coworkers at the end of the day,
NEW AMERICAN folks in from the avenues, conventioneers from nearby Moscone Center—packs this high-ceiling, brick-lined dining space that once housed a printing press. Rusted girders, chandeliers fashioned from old postcard racks, and water poured from vintage milk bottles set a casual mood. The small plates, like crisp shrimp atop spicy green beans, almonds, and serrano ham and foie gras with sautéed quince, are so appealing that most diners find it hard to move to the mains. Such flawed logic means missing out on a first-rate roast chicken with fingerlings or Sonoma rabbit with Lady apples. Single diners can grab a seat at the big communal table. ⊠ *545 Mission St., SoMa* ☎ *415/543–8900* ⊟ *AE, D, MC, V* ⊘ *No lunch weekends* ✛ *1:E6.*

$$ ✕ **South food + winebar.** The young and stylish flock to San Francis-
AUSTRALIAN co's first restaurant from Down Under. Star Sydney chef Luke Mangan serves Aussie fare in a lively space decorated with New Zealand

gourdlike lights made of hoop-pine plywood. The menu offers a mix of traditional Australian ingredients with Asian influences, such as pan-roasted barramundi with burnt lime and New Zealand lamb chops with mint chimichurri. The wine list offers selections from small producers in Australia and New Zealand, and is divided into categories like crisp, silky, and spicy. ✉ *330 Townsend St., SoMa* ☎ *415/974–5599* 🖃 *AE, D, MC, V* �》 *Closed Sun. No lunch Sat.* ✛ *3:H3.*

$$
NEW AMERICAN

✕ **Town Hall.** Well-known chefs Mitchell and Steven Rosenthal are the culinary brains behind this way station for the city's powerbrokers and their acolytes. The fare is sophisticated American—roasted veal meatballs, spicy shrimp, slow-roasted duck with wild rice, rib-eye steak with roasted garlic white bean purée, butterscotch-and-chocolate *pot de crème*—with plenty of variety to satisfy nearly everyone. The converted-warehouse space, with dark-wood floors, exposed brick walls, white wainscoting, and contemporary art, comfortably blends old with new. You can cool your heels with a cocktail on the heated patio while you wait for your table. Locals travel across town for the lobster roll that occasionally turns up on the lunch menu. The decibel level here can wear down your vocal chords, so ask for a quiet table. ✉ *342 Howard St., SoMa* ☎ *415/908–3900* 🖃 *AE, MC, V* �》 *No lunch weekends* ✛ *1:F5.*

13

SUNSET DISTRICT

$$
VIETNAMESE

✕ **Dragonfly.** Refined Vietnamese fare draws droves of locals to this modestly decorated, bi-level restaurant each night. They return for intriguing dishes like shaking beef, fork-tender pork and egg in coconut juice, and crunchy lotus-root salad. Even the rice offerings go beyond the ordinary, with five types offered: coconut, Hainan (cooked in chicken stock with ginger and garlic), white, brown jasmine, or pineapple fried rice with prawns, chickens, cashews, and raisins. Wash down the meal with one of three refreshing Vietnamese beers, and cap it all off with a cup of slow-drip inky coffee or a coffee ice-cream float. Lunchtime brings more casual dishes, including *pho,* rice plates, and noodles. The service can take a bumpy turn, but the staff is always friendly. ✉ *420 Judah St., Inner Sunset* ☎ *415/661–7755* 🖃 *AE, MC, V* �》 *Closed Mon.* ✛ *3:A5.*

$$
MEDITERRANEAN

✕ **The Moss Room.** Two of San Francisco's leading chefs, Loretta Keller of Coco500 and Charles Phan of Slanted Door, have put their toques together at this destination restaurant in the California Academy of Sciences. You reach the coolly ascetic dining room by entering the museum and then descending a staircase lined with a moss-covered wall, a live reminder of the thoroughly green building. Although Phan is famous for his Vietnamese dishes, the menu sticks with the cuisine Keller is known for, an easy mix of Mediterranean and Californian: smoked-trout salad with fingerling potatoes and quail eggs; warm pita with hummus, peppers, and Manouri cheese; grilled squid with chickpeas and Swiss chard; mackerel cooked with tomatoes, mint, and preserved lemon; Kobe bavette steak with watercress. Save room for the tart Tatin with Calvados ice cream, and save your money for the wine list, which leans heavily on your pocketbook. During the day, a museum admission is the only way to enter The Moss; at night, when the museum is closed, a staffer stationed on the patio directs you through the only open door. It can be an inky, foggy trek to the entrance, so watch your step. ⊠ *California Academy of Sciences in Golden Gate Park, 55 Music Concourse Dr., Sunset* ☎ *415/876–6121* ⌘ *Reservations essential* ⊟ *AE, DC, MC, V* ✚ *3:A5.*

$
AMERICAN
☺

╳ **Park Chow.** What do spaghetti-and-meatballs, Thai noodles with chicken and shrimp, and big burgers have in common? They're all on the eclectic comfort-food menu at Park Chow, and offered at unbeatable prices. This neighborhood favorite is also known for its desserts: fresh-baked pies and ginger cake with pumpkin ice cream are standouts. Kids get their own menu, with items such as a burger, grilled-cheese sandwich, chicken, fish, and pizza to choose from. In cool weather there's a roaring fire in the dining-room fireplace; in warm weather, get there early to snag an outdoor table. Up early? You can sit down to breakfast on weekdays and brunch on weekends. The original location is in the Castro neighborhood. ⊠ *1240 9th Ave., Inner Sunset* ☎ *415/665–9912* ⊟ *AE, MC, V* ✚ *3:A5.*

$$
CHINESE
☺

╳ **San Tung.** Many of the best chefs in Beijing's imperial kitchens hailed from China's northeastern province of Shandong. San Franciscans, with or without imperial ancestry, regularly enjoy dishes of the same province at this bare-bones storefront restaurant. Specialties include steamed dumplings—shrimp and leek dumplings are the most popular—and hand-pulled noodles, in soup or stir-fried. Among the typical accompaniments are a salad of jellyfish, seaweed, or sliced cucumbers and a plate of cold, poached chicken marinated in Shaoxing wine. Parents and kids regularly fight over platters of dry-fried chicken wings. To get a table without a wait, come before or after the noon or dinner rush. ⊠ *1031 Irving St., Inner Sunset* ☎ *415/242–0828* ⊟ *MC, V* ◷ *Closed Wed.* ✚ *3:A5.*

UNION SQUARE

$$$
AMERICAN

╳ **Canteen.** Blink and you'll miss this place. Chef-owner Dennis Leary has transformed this narrow coffee shop into one of the most sought-after dinner reservations in town. The homey place has just 20 counter seats and a quartet of wooden booths. But that's all Leary, with a modest open kitchen and a single assistant, can handle. The dinner menu, which changes often, offers only four first courses, four mains, and three or four desserts. A typical meal might start with mussels soup spiked with chili paste, followed by bulgur-crusted sole or stuffed breast of guinea hen with a confit leg and lentils, and then a dreamy vanilla soufflé or pistachio tart. On Tuesday night a three-course prix-fixe menu is in force (no choices within each course) for $35. Because this is a one-man band, your food arrives at a leisurely pace. If a dinner reservation is elusive, try for lunch on weekdays or weekend brunch. ⊠ *Commodore Hotel, 817 Sutter St., Union Square* ☎ *415/928–8870* ⌘ *Reservations essential* ⊟ *AE, MC, V* ◷ *Closed Mon. No lunch Tues. or weekends* ✚ *4:C3.*

$$$$
SEAFOOD

╳ **Farallon.** Sculpted jellyfish chandeliers, kelp-covered columns, and sea-urchin lights give this swanky Pat Kuleto–designed restaurant a decidedly quirky look. But there's nothing quirky about chef Mark Franz's impeccable seafood, which reels in serious diners from coast to coast. The menu changes daily, but you might find stuffed Monterey squid, seared scallops and green-lipped mussels with caramelized onions, and ahi tuna with French lentils and picholine olives. Meat eaters aren't ignored, with such choices as grilled rack of lamb with butternut squash purée or stuffed chicken breast with foie-gras sausage. If you want to enjoy the surroundings but not pay the price, you can take a seat at the French-style oyster bar and fill up on oyster shooters, a shrimp cocktail, crab cakes, french fries with aioli, and more from the cheaper bar menu. ⊠ *450 Post St., Union Square* ☎ *415/956–6969* ➡ *AE, D, DC, MC, V* ⊘ *No lunch* ✛ *4:E3*.

$$$$ ✕ **Fleur de Lys.** The creative cooking of chef-owner Hubert Keller has
FRENCH brought every conceivable culinary award to this romantic spot. His three-, four-, and five-course prix-fixe menus (each course with many choices), priced from $70 to $92, include plenty of foie gras, squab, lobster, and truffles to satisfy palates geared to fancy French plates. Choosing some items will boost your tab, such as $25 extra for filet mignon with foie gras, $72 extra for an ounce of osetra caviar, and even $5 extra for chocolate soufflé. The dining room, with its dramatic tented ceiling of 900 yards of draped and swathed fabric, is as showy as the food. These days some regulars have grumbled that Keller is paying more attention to his growing gourmet burger-bar and steakhouse chain than his San Francisco dining room, citing less-than-stellar service and a stagnant menu as evidence of their claims. ⊠ *777 Sutter St., Union Square* ☎ *415/673–7779* ✍ *Reservations essential, jacket required* ➡ *AE, D, DC, MC, V* ⊘ *Closed Sun. No lunch* ✛ *4:D3*.

$$$$ ✕ **Le Colonial.** This is high-style Vietnamese food served up in a French-
VIETNAMESE colonial time machine: stamped-tin ceiling, period photographs, slow-moving fans, and tropical plants. Local society types come for the sea bass steamed in banana leaves, tiger prawns in coconut curry, and lamb chops with grilled eggplant salad. They also like to pick from among the big selection of fried or fresh appetizer rolls, filled with everything from shredded duck to Dungeness crab. Downstairs are two large and rather formal dining rooms. Anything goes upstairs in the lively lounge: you can eat (so-called Vietnamese street food at indoor prices—$3 to $12), you can dance (Wednesday through Saturday nights), or you can just sip a cocktail at the bar and unwind. Plenty of locals find the dining room stuffy—and expensive—but are quick to defend the lounge. ⊠ *20 Cosmo Pl., Union Square* ☎ *415/931–3600* ➡ *AE, D, DC, MC, V* ⊘ *No lunch* ✛ *4:D3*.

$$$$ ✕ **Michael Mina.** Decorated in celadon and ivory with stately columns
NEW AMERICAN and a vaulted ceiling, this elegant space, inside the Westin St. Francis Hotel, is a match for chef Michael Mina's highly refined fare. His
Fodor's Choice three-course prix-fixe (multiple choices for each course) includes a trio
★ of tastes on each plate—for example, three preparations of pork for a first (terrine with foie gras, belly pork with frisée and quail egg, short ribs bourguignon with forest mushrooms), or of chocolate for a dessert (white chocolate and rose panna cotta, s'mores, chocolate ice cream with lavender and shortbread). Folks who prefer one taste rather than triple bites can opt for one of Mina's signature dishes, such as black

mussel soufflé or lobster potpie. Deep-pocketed diners can splurge on a six-course tasting menu. Diners who want to taste Mina's food but not squander next month's rent can stop in at the swanky Clock Bar, across the lobby, where the same kitchen turns out lobster corn dogs, lamb panini, and black truffle popcorn, all nicely partnered with some of the best cocktails in town. ⊠ *Westin St. Francis Hotel, 335 Powell St., Union Square* ☎ *415/397–9222* ◈ *Reservations essential* ▤ *AE, D, DC, MC, V* ☉ *Closed Sun. and Mon. No lunch* ✚ *4:F3.*

$$$ ✕ **Millennium.** This big, wood-lined dining room in the Hotel California
VEGETARIAN   is *the* gourmet dining destination for visiting vegans. The seasonal menu of "animal-free" dishes made with organic ingredients includes flat bread with caramelized onion and cherry tomatoes, cornmeal-crusted oyster mushrooms with black-bean and Balinese pepper salsa, truffled tomato arancine (rice balls), and maple-glazed smoked tempeh (fermented soybean cake) with garlic-horseradish mashed potatoes. All dishes are dressed up with bold flavors that won't disappoint omnivores. Come dessert, you may find the chocolate almond midnight (mocha chocolate filling in an almond-cashew crust) hard to resist. A long list of organic wines is available, and a five-course tasting menu ($65) is offered for when your wallet is full. ⊠ *Hotel California, 580 Geary St., Union Square* ☎ *415/345–3900* ▤ *AE, D, DC, MC, V* ☉ *No lunch* ✚ *4:D4.*

$$$ ✕ **Scala's Bistro.** Smart leather-and-wood booths, a pressed-tin ceiling, a
ITALIAN   menu of Italian (and a few French) dishes, a steady hum of activity—it's hard not to like the big-city feel of this hotel dining room. Fritto misto of shrimp, squid, and fennel; gnocchi with lemon, parsley, and mushrooms; and salmon with buttermilk mashed potatoes are among the evening choices. The room is open late, making it a welcome dessert destination—with sweet successes like apple crostata with salted caramel gelato and chocolate I.V. (mousse, pecan crust, gelato, sauce)—after the theater. ⊠ *Sir Francis Drake Hotel, 432 Powell St., Union Square* ☎ *415/395–8555* ▤ *AE, D, DC, MC, V* ✚ *4:F3.*

VAN NESS/POLK

$$$$ ✕ **Acquerello.** For years, devotees of chef-owner Suzette Gresham-Tog-
ITALIAN   netti's Italian cooking have been swooning over what emerges from her kitchen: roasted peppers stuffed with tuna, short pasta with foie gras and truffles, pancetta-wrapped scallops over squash purée. Dinners are prix-fixe, with three ($60), four ($72), or five ($82) courses and at least six choices within each course. Tognetti also tempts with an eight-course tasting menu ($172, with wine pairings). Co-owner Giancarlo Paterlini oversees the service and the list of Italian wines, both of which are superb. The room, with its vaulted ceiling and terra-cotta and pale-ocher palette, suits the refined food. ⊠ *1722 Sacramento St., Van Ness/Polk* ☎ *415/567–5432* ▤ *AE, D, MC, V* ☉ *Closed Sun. and Mon. No lunch* ✚ *2:H5.*

$$ ✕ **Bodega Bistro.** With just one taste of his green papaya salad, you'll
VIETNAMESE   be hooked on the inspired cooking of North Vietnam–born Jimmy Kwok. His casual bistro, located on the mildly sketchy edge of the Tenderloin, brims at lunchtime with savvy eaters from Civic Center

offices who know that Kwok makes what may be the best bowl of pho in town. For dinner, come for his roast squab, *bun cha Hanoi* (broiled pork, herbs, rice vermicelli, and lettuce wrapped in rice paper), and salt-and-pepper Dungeness crab with garlic noodles, the latter priced for a special occasion. Kwok punctuates his Asian menu with a handful of French dishes. ⊠ *607 Larkin St., Van Ness/Polk* ☎ *415/921–1218* ▤ *MC, V* ✛ *4:A6.*

WORD OF MOUTH

"You want 'funky'? Try the Clement Street area, which abounds with great budget restaurants, at least two on every block. Vietnamese, Thai, Peruvian, Korean, Burmese, Chinese, Argentinean, Russian, Indian—you name it. Cool bars, too."   —LucieV

13

$$$$ ✕ **Harris'.** Red-meat connoisseurs will appreciate this old-school restaurant, home to some of the best dry-aged steaks in town, including pricey Kobe rib eye. Harris' ages all of its beef for 21 days; proof of the process is visible from the street through a window where large cuts can be seen hanging. There are a dozen steaks to choose from, plus grilled chops, chicken, and a couple of seafood dishes for anyone who wants to steer clear of beef. Don't overlook the classic sides: creamed spinach, caramelized onions, and sautéed mushrooms. If you're a martini drinker, take this opportunity to enjoy an artful example of the legendary cocktail. And if you want to try to cook this top-notch beef yourself, you can pick up raw steaks to go at the well-stocked beef counter. ⊠ *2100 Van Ness Ave., Van Ness/Polk* ☎ *415/673–1888* ▤ *AE, D, DC, MC, V* ☽ *No lunch* ✛ *2:H4.*

STEAK HOUSE

$$ ✕ **Helmand Palace.** In late 2007 this popular—and popularly priced—restaurant moved from a scruffy block of Broadway in North Beach to a smaller Van Ness address and added "Palace" to its name, but kept everything else—authentic Afghan cooking and a handsomely outfitted dining room—intact. Highlights of the reasonably priced menu include *aushak* (leek-filled ravioli served with yogurt and ground beef), pumpkin with yogurt-and-garlic sauce, and the half lamb rack with sautéed eggplant and rice served on Afghan flatbread. Basmati rice pudding, perfumed with cardamom and pistachio, is an exotic finish. ⊠ *2424 Van Ness Ave., Van Ness/Polk* ☎ *415/362–0641* ▤ *AE, MC, V* ☽ *No lunch* ✛ *2:F3.*

MIDDLE EASTERN

$ ✕ **Pagolac.** Savvy diners know that Pagolac serves a great "seven-way beef" dinner, the classic south Vietnamese feast of seven different beef dishes for an unbelievable $16 per person. This is also a good place for lotus-root salad with pink shrimp, all kinds of rolls, aromatic clay pots, and noodles or rice topped with protein—pork, beef, shrimp, chicken—in all forms—fried, shredded, grilled. The narrow space is decorated in dark-wood tables and chairs and a few nice pieces of Vietnamese art, and the service, though sometimes a little ragged, is always friendly. Of course, such low prices and good food haven't remained a secret, so come before 6 or after 9 to avoid a long wait. ⊠ *655 Larkin St., Van Ness/Polk* ☎ *415/776–3234* ▤ *No credit cards* ☽ *Closed Mon. No lunch* ✛ *4:A6.*

VIETNAMESE

$$ ✕ **Swan Oyster Depot.** Half fish market and half diner, this small, slim
SEAFOOD   seafood operation, open since 1912, has no tables, only a narrow mar-
Fodor'sChoice   ble counter with about a dozen-and-a-half stools. Most people come
★   in to buy perfectly fresh salmon, halibut, crabs, and other seafood to
take home. Everyone else hops onto one of the rickety stools to enjoy
a bowl of clam chowder—the only hot food served—a dozen oysters,
half a cracked crab, a big shrimp salad, or a smaller shrimp cocktail.
Come early or late to avoid a long wait. ⊠ *1517 Polk St., Van Ness/
Polk* ☎ *415/673–1101* ✍ *Reservations not accepted* ▭ *No credit cards*
☉ *Closed Sun. No dinner* ✛ *2:H5.*

Dining and
Lodging Atlas

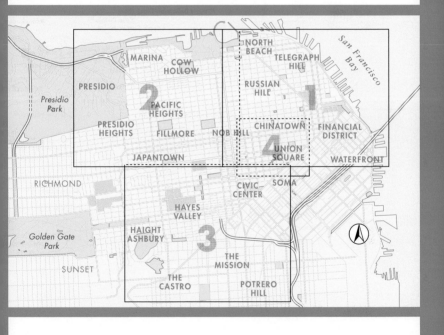

KEY	
□	Hotels
■	Restaurants
■	Restaurant in Hotel
Embarcadero	
b□	BART Station
	Bay Area Rapid Transit

A   **B**   **C**   **D**

Pier 47
Pier 45
Pier 39
Pier 35

FISHERMAN'S WHARF

Aquatic Park
Argonaut
Guardino's
Beach St.

1

MARITIME MUSEUM

Jefferson St.
Hyatt at Fisherman's Wharf
North Point St.
Kearny St.

Beach St.
Gary Danko
Best Western Tuscan Inn
Bay St.

Ghirardelli Square
North Point St.

Ghirardelli Ice Cream & Chocolate Shop
San Francisco Marriott Fisherman's Wharf

Russian Hill Park
Pfeiffer St.

Kara's Cupcakes
Francisco St.
San Remo

TELEGRAPH HILL

SAN FRANCISCO ART INSTITUTE

2

Chestnut St.

NORTH BEACH

COIT TOWER

Lombard St.

Petite Deli

Washington Square Inn
Washington Square

Greenwich St.

Grant Ave.

Van Ness Ave.
Polk St.
Larkin St.
Hyde St.
Leavenworth St.
Jones St.
Taylor St.
Columbus Ave.
Jansen St.

Filbert St.

Mario's Bohemian Cigar Store
Rose Pistola
Maykadeh

Union St.
Capp's Corner
Bohème

Macondray La.
L'Osteria del Forno

3

Green St.

RUSSIAN HILL

Caffè Greco
Caffè Puccini
Caffè Trieste
Molinari's

Vallejo St.

Broadway
Tommaso's

Tunnel
Dol Ho
New Asia

Broadway
Bernard St.
John St.
Great Eastern

Pacific Ave.
Naan 'N Curry

Jackson St.
Hilton San Francisco Financial District

CABLE CAR MUSEUM

4

NOB HILL
Washington St.

Portsmouth Square

Commercial St.

Eastern Bakery

See Map 4
Union Square area

Pleasant St.

CHINATOWN

Clay St.
Huntington Park
California St.

St. Mary's Sq.

Bob's Donuts

Sacramento St.
Cable Car
CHINATOWN GATE

5

California St.

Bush St.

Pine St.
Sutter St.

Franklin St.
Polk St.
Larkin St.
Hyde St.
Leavenworth St.
Jones St.
Taylor St.
Mason St.
Powell St.
Grant Ave.

Bush St.
Post St.

Fern St.
Union Square
Maiden Ln.

Sutter St.
Hemlock St.
Post St.

Cedar St.

6

Geary St.

UNION SQUARE

Myrtle St.
Geary St.

O'Farrell St.
O'Farrell St.

Olive St.
Ellis St.
POWELL ST.

Ellis St.
Eddy St.
4th St.

A   **B**   **C**   **D**

San Francisco Bay

Map 1

- Chinatown
- Downtown
- Financial District
- Nob Hill
- North Beach
- Russian Hill
- Telegraph Hill
- Union Square
- Waterfront

1

2

3

4

5

6

Pier 31
Pier 29
Pier 27

hestnut St.
ombard St.

Pier 23
Pier 19
Pier 17
Pier 15
Pier 9
Pier 7
Pier 5
Pier 3
Pier 1

■ Fog City Diner

Alta St.

Union St.
Green St.
■ Piperade

Sansome St.
Battery St.
Front St.
Davis St.
The Embarcadero

Montgomery St.

■ Coi

■ Quince
Pacific Ave. Walton Park
Jackson Square Historic District
innia
Jackson St. ■ Kokkari
■ La Mar Cebicheria Peruana

FINANCIAL DISTRICT

Washington St.
■ Bocadillos
□ Le Meridien
TRANSAMERICA PYRAMID
Clay St.
DOWNTOWN
Embarcadero Center
Drumm St.
Justin Herman Plaza
FERRY BUILDING

R&G Lounge
Sacramento St.
■ Tadich Grill
One Market ■
Vitale □

■ Perbacco
Aqua ■
Omni San Francisco Hotel
EMBARCADERO
bᴄ□
Boulevard ■
Ozumo ■
□ Harbor Court

Mandarin Oriental □
Pine St.
Midi ■
Galleria Park
■ Sam's Grill

The Embarcadero

Waterbar ■
Epic Roasthouse ■

Market St.
1st St.
Fremont St.
Mission St.
Howard St.
Spear St.
Steuart St.

San Francisco - Oakland Bay Bridge

Yank Sing ■
Ecker St.
Elim Al.
TRANSBAY TERMINAL
Town Hall ■
Main St.
Folsom St.
Harrison St.
Pier 26

bᴄ■ MONTGOMERY ST.
Salt House ■
Natoma St.
Beale St.
Pier 28

Palace □
New Montgomery St.
Minna St.
Tehama St.
Clementina St.
Pier 30

Sentinel ■
2nd St.
W Hotel □
Essex St.
Pier 32

Annie St.
3rd St.
■ Ame

Folsom St.
I-80
WATERFRONT
Pier 34

SFMOMA
Ducca ■ □
■ LuLu
South Park Café ■
Pier 32

Westin San Francisco Market Street
■ Bacar
■ Chaat Café
San Francisco Airport □
Acme Chophouse ■
1st St.
■ Oola
■ Patisserie Philippe

ERBA BUENA GARDENS

ssie St.
Mission St.
Kearny St.
Sacramento St.

0 ────── 350 M
0 ────── 1,000 ft

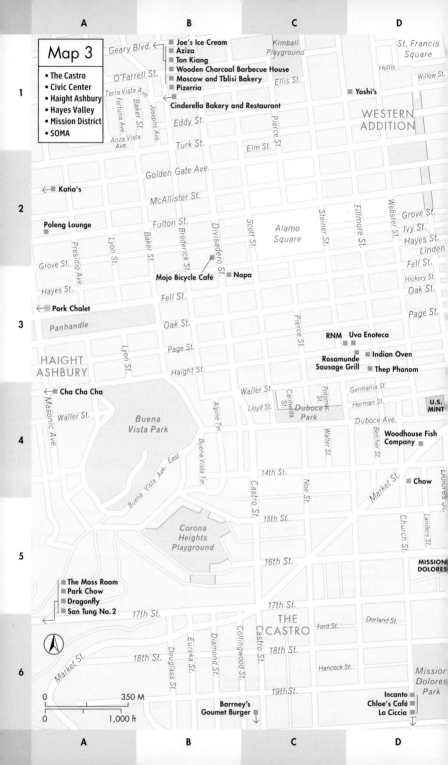

Map 3

- The Castro
- Civic Center
- Haight Ashbury
- Hayes Valley
- Mission District
- SOMA

A

Geary Blvd.

O'Farrell St.

Terra Vista Ave.

Fortuna Ave.

Anza Vista Ave.

Eddy St.

Turk St.

Golden Gate Ave.

←■ Katia's

McAllister St.

■ Poleng Lounge

Fulton St.

Presidio Ave.

Lyon St.

Baker St.

Grove St.

Hayes St.

Fell St.

←■ Park Chalet

Panhandle

Oak St.

Page St.

HAIGHT ASHBURY

Lyon St.

Haight St.

←■ Cha Cha Cha

Masonic Ave.

Waller St.

Buena Vista Park

Buena Vista Ave. East

Buena Vista Ter.

Corona Heights Playground

■ The Moss Room
■ Park Chow
■ Dragonfly
■ San Tung No. 2

17th St.

Market St.

18th St.

Douglass St.

Eureka St.

Diamond St.

Collingwood St.

0   350 M
0   1,000 ft

B

■ Joe's Ice Cream
■ Aziza
■ Ton Kiang
■ Wooden Charcoal Barbecue House
■ Moscow and Tblisi Bakery
■ Pizerria

← Cinderella Bakery and Restaurant

Eddy St.

Turk St.

Scott St.

Broderick St.

Baker St.

Divisadero St.

Mojo Bicycle Café ■ Nopa

Fell St.

Oak St.

Page St.

Alpine Ter.

Waller St.

Lloyd St.

Carmelita

Castro St.

Noe St.

14th St.

15th St.

16th St.

17th St.

18th St.

Barrney's Goumet Burger
↓

THE CASTRO

C

Kimball Playground

Ellis St.

Pierce St.

Elm St.

Steiner St.

Alamo Square

Scott St.

Pierce St.

RNM Uva Enoteca
■ ■

Rosamunde ■ Indian Oven
Sausage Grill ■ Thep Phanom

Germania St.

Potomac St.

Duboce Park

Herman St.

Duboce Ave.

Walter St.

Ford St.

Dorland St.

Hancock St.

19th St.

D

St. Francis Square

Hollis

Willow St.

■ Yoshi's

WESTERN ADDITION

Fillmore St.

Webster St.

Grove St.

Ivy St.

Hayes St.

Linden

Fell St.

Hickory St.

Oak St.

Page St.

U.S. MINT

Belcher St.

Woodhouse Fish Company ■

Market St.

■ Chow

Church St.

Landers St.

Dolores St.

MISSION DOLORES

Mission Dolores Park

Incanto ■
Chloe's Café ■
La Ciccia ■
↓

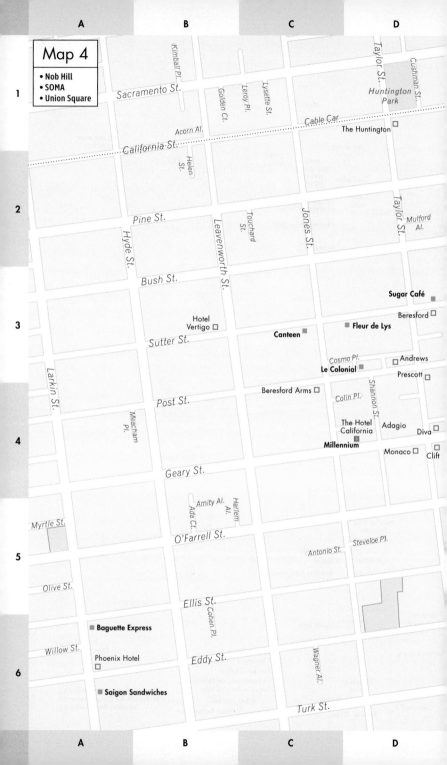

Map 4

- Nob Hill
- SOMA
- Union Square

Where to Stay

WORD OF MOUTH

"[We've] stayed at a number of places near Union Square, but on my last two visits we stayed at the Galleria Park and Le Meridien in the Financial District. I much prefer this location to the noisier Union Square area. It is close to a BART station and to the Ferry Building (can't miss the Farmer's Market)."

—enzian

Updated by
Sura Wood

San Francisco is one of the country's best hotel towns, offering a rich selection of properties that satisfy most tastes and budgets. Whether you're seeking a cozy inn, a kitschy motel, a chic boutique, or a grande-dame hotel, this city has the perfect room for you.

If you're searching for a centrally located, classy hotel, check out the dramatic Clift, a property with surrealistic flavor, conjured by maverick star-designer Philippe Starck, or Hotel Monaco, a sumptuous Beaux Arts beauty. Both are a few blocks from Union Square, a shopper's paradise.

Now is a great time to go: hotel deals are easier to come by, upgrades and renovations are taking place at properties throughout the city, and both new and established properties are trending toward the eco-friendly—SF hotels are "going green" in a big way. Although the Orchard Garden boasts San Francisco's first all-new green construction, many other local properties are installing ecological upgrades. Most of the city's hotels are no-smoking—or will be soon.

Wherever you stay, be sure to ask what's included in your room rate. And when you settle into your perfect room, remember this tip: When in doubt, ask the concierge. This holds true for almost any request, whether you have special needs or burning desires (if anyone can get you tickets to a sold-out show or reservations at a fully booked restaurant, it's the concierge). You'll likely be impressed by the lengths hoteliers are willing to go to please their guests.

Finally, consider timing: If you're flexible on dates, ask the reservationist if there's a cheaper time to stay in your preferred travel window.

WHERE SHOULD I STAY?

	NEIGHBORHOOD VIBE	PROS	CONS
By the Airport	Construction booms near San Francisco International Airport have added several luxury hotels to this rather prosaic area.	Rates are about 20% lower than in-town hotels, and weekend prices are often slashed because clients tend to be midweek business travelers.	The drive from the airport area to downtown San Francisco takes 20 to 30 minutes, so what you gain in value you may lose in convenience.
Civic Center/ Van Ness	A wide mix of lodgings scattered throughout this area.	Asian Art Museum, opera house, symphony hall, and government offices surround this central hub. Close to busy Fillmore Street and not far from Union Square.	Away from touristy areas, public transportation can sometimes be a challenge. There's a large homeless population in the Civic Center area.
Financial District	A mini-midtown Manhattan where properties cater to business travelers.	Excellent city and bay views, which are spectacular by night. Easy access to restaurants and nightclubs.	Some streets are iffy at night. Street parking takes some work. Hotels are on the pricey side.
Fisherman's Wharf/North Beach	Mostly chain hotels by the Wharf; lodgings get funkier and smaller in North Beach.	Near attractions like Ghirardelli Square, Pier 39, and the Cannery. Cable-car lines and piers for bay cruises are nearby.	City ordinances limit Wharf hotels to four stories, so good views are out. Very hilly area.
Nob Hill	Synonymous with San Francisco's high society, this area contains some of the city's best-known luxury hotels.	Many hotels boast gorgeous views and notable restaurants. Easy access to Union Square and Chinatown.	Hotels here will test your wallet, while the area's steep hills may test your endurance.
Pacific Heights/Cow Hollow/The Marina	A few tony accommodations in the quietly residential Pacific Heights. Mostly motels along Lombard Street, the major traffic corridor leading to the Golden Gate Bridge.	Away from the more tourist-oriented areas, visitors have a chance to explore where locals eat and shop. Lots of free parking.	Getting downtown can be challenging via public transportation. Some complain of the fraternity-like bar scene.
SoMa	The "new heart of the city," adjacent to the developing Mission Bay neighborhood, offers luxury high-rises, old classics, and a few bargains.	Near the cultural magnet of the San Francisco Museum of Modern Art and Yerba Buena Gardens, as well as a growing number of eateries.	Lots of construction may mean traffic snarls. As with many changing neighborhoods, street life takes many forms. Be cautious walking around at night.
Union Square/ Downtown	Union Square is Square One for visitors; you'll find a wide range of choices—and prices—for lodging.	Excellent shopping and dining. Home to the theater district, great transit access to other neighborhoods.	Often crowded and noisy. Close to Tenderloin, a still-seedy part of town. Take cabs at night.

14

WHERE TO STAY PLANNER

Strategy

Where should we stay? With hundreds of San Francisco hotels, it may seem like a daunting question. But fret not—our expert writers and editors have done most of the legwork. The 90-plus selections here represent the best this city has to offer—from the best budget motels to the sleekest designer hotels. Scan "Best Bets" on the following pages for top recommendations by price and experience. Or find a review quickly in the listings. Search by neighborhood, then alphabetically. Happy hunting!

Family Travel

San Francisco has gone to great lengths to attract family vacationers, and hotels have followed the family-friendly trend. Some properties provide diversions like in-room video games; others have suites with kitchenettes and fold-out sofa beds. Most full-service San Francisco hotels provide roll-away beds, babysitting, and stroller rentals, but be sure to make arrangements when booking the room, not when you arrive.

Reservations

Reservations are always advised, especially during the peak seasons—May through October and weekends in December. The San Francisco Convention and Visitors Bureau publishes a free lodging guide with a map and listings of San Francisco and Bay Area hotels. You can reserve a room, by phone or via the Internet, at more than 60 Bureau-recommended hotels. San Francisco Reservations, in business since 1986, can arrange reservations at more than 200 Bay Area hotels, often at special discounted rates. **Booking: San Francisco Convention and Visitors Bureau** (☎ 415/391–2000 general information, 415/283–0177, 888/782–9673 lodging service ⊕ www. onlyinsanfrancisco.com). **San Francisco Reservations** (☎ 800/677–1500 ⊕ www.hotelres.com). **Bed & Breakfast San Francisco** (☎ 415/899–0060 ⊕ www.bbsf.com).

Parking

Several properties on Lombard Street and in the Civic Center area have free parking (but not always in a covered garage). Hotels in the Union Square and Nob Hill areas almost invariably charge $23 to $50+ per day for a spot in their garages. Some hotel package deals include parking. Some B&Bs have limited free parking available, but many don't, and require you to park on the street. Depending on the neighborhood and the time, this can be easy or difficult, so ask for realistic parking information when you call. Some hotels with paid parking offer a choice of valet parking with unlimited in-out privileges or self-parking (where the fee is less expensive and there's no tipping).

Facilities

In each hotel review, we list what facilities are available, but we don't specify whether they cost extra. When pricing accommodations, always ask what's included and what entails an additional charge. All the hotels listed have private baths, central heating, and private phones unless otherwise noted. Many places don't have air-conditioning, but you probably won't need it. Even in September and October, when the city sees its warmest days, the temperature rarely climbs above 70°F.

Many hotels now have wireless Internet (Wi-Fi) available, although it's not always free. Larger hotels often have video or high-speed checkout capability, and many can arrange babysitting. Pools are a rarity, but most properties have gyms or health clubs, and sometimes full-scale spas; hotels without facilities usually have arrangements for guests at nearby gyms, sometimes for a fee.

Prices

San Francisco hotel prices, among the highest in the United States, may come as an unpleasant surprise. But as at most hotels, prices are starting to soften. Weekend rates for double rooms in high season average about $132 a night citywide. Rates may vary widely according to room availability; always inquire about special rates and packages when making reservations; call the property directly, but also check its Web site and try Internet booking agencies.

The lodgings we list are the cream of the crop in each price category. Assume that prices are based on the European Plan (EP, with no meals) unless we specify that hotels operate on the Continental Plan (CP, with a continental breakfast), Breakfast Plan (BP, with a full breakfast), Modified American Plan (MAP, with breakfast and dinner), or Full American Plan (FAP, with all meals).

WHAT IT COSTS

¢	$	$$	$$$	$$$$
under $90	$90–$149	$150–$199	$200–$250	over $250

Prices are for two people in a standard double room in high season, excluding 14% tax.

In This Chapter

14

Using the Maps

Throughout the chapter, you'll see mapping symbols and coordinates (✢ 3:F2) after property names or reviews. To locate the property on a map, turn to the San Francisco Dining and Lodging Atlas at the end of the dining chapter. The first number after the ✢ symbol indicates the map number. Following that is the property's coordinate on the map grid.

BEST BETS FOR SAN FRANCISCO LODGING

Fodor's offers a selective listing of quality lodging experiences at every price range, from the city's best budget motel to its most sophisticated luxury hotel. Here we've compiled our top recommendations by price and experience. The very best properties—in other words, those that provide a particularly remarkable experience in their price range—are designated in the listings with the Fodor's Choice logo.

JET-SETTING CLIENTELE

Clift, p. 273
Hotel Bohème, p. 258
Hotel Monaco, p. 277
Hotel Triton, p. 278
W San Francisco, p. 271

MOST KID-FRIENDLY

Hilton San Francisco, p. 274
Hotel del Sol, p. 265
Omni SF Hotel, p. 255
Seal Rock Inn, p. 253
Westin San Francisco Market Street, p. 272

MOST ROMANTIC

Fairmont, p. 259
Hotel Drisco, p. 261
Hotel Majestic, p. 261
Palace, p. 270
Queen Anne, p. 263

TOP B&BS

Golden Gate Hotel, p. 274
Hotel Drisco, p. 261
Washington Square Inn, p. 259

TOP SPAS

Mandarin Oriental, p. 254

Fodor's Choice ★

Argonaut Hotel, $$$, p. 255
Four Seasons, $$$$, p. 266
Hotel Adagio, $$$$, p. 275
Hotel Drisco, $$$, p. 261
Hotel Monaco, $$$$, p. 277
Hotel Nikko, $$$$, p. 277
InterContinental San Francisco, $$$$, p. 268
Mandarin Oriental, $$$$, p. 254
Orchard Hotel, $$$, p. 281
Palace Hotel, $$$$, p. 270
Queen Anne, $$, p. 263
Ritz-Carlton, $$$$, p. 260
San Remo Hotel, ¢, p. 258
Union Street Inn, $$$, p. 265

By Price

$

Cornell Hotel de France, p. 274
Cow Hollow Motor Inn, p. 265
Hotel des Arts, p. 276
Queen Anne, p. 263

$$

Beresford Arms, p. 276
Harbor Court, p. 267

$$$

Hotel Drisco, p. 261
Orchard Hotel, p. 281
Sofitel, p. 251

$$$$

Campton Place, p. 272
Hotel Adagio, p. 275
Hotel Monaco, p. 277
Hotel Nikko, p. 277
Hotel Palomar, p. 267
Mandarin Oriental, p. 254
Ritz-Carlton, p. 260

By Experience

BUSINESS TRAVELERS

Four Seasons, p. 266
Hilton SF Financial District, p. 254
Hotel Nikko, p. 277
Hotel Vitale, p. 268
Le Méridien, p. 254

GREAT CONCIERGE

Hilton San Francisco, p. 274
Hotel Triton, p. 278
JW Marriott, p. 279
Ritz-Carlton, p. 260

HISTORICAL FLAVOR

Fairmont, p. 259
Hotel Vertigo, p. 279
Hotel Whitcomb, p. 252
Palace, p. 270
Westin St. Francis, p. 283

LODGING REVIEWS

Alphabetical by neighborhood

BY THE AIRPORT

$$–$$$ **Embassy Suites San Francisco Airport, Burlingame.** This beige-and-orange California Mission–style hostelry is one of the most lavish hotels in the airport corridor. Set on the bay, with clear vistas of airplanes flying above San Francisco in the distance, the building's focal point is a nine-story atrium and tropical garden showcasing exotic towering palms, bamboo and banana plants, and koi-filled ponds all crowned by a waterfall. The property was renovated in 2007, and each suite has a living room with work area, flat-screen TVs, microwave, a sleeper sofa, and bedroom; kitchenettes are conveniently located between each suite's two rooms. Rates include a complimentary cooked-to-order breakfast, evening cocktails, and free access to the business center. **Pros:** low rates, luxurious accommodations. **Cons:** no standard rooms, no concierge. ⊠ *150 Anza Blvd., Burlingame* ☎ *650/342–4600 or 800/362–2779* ⊕ *www.sfoburlingame.embassysuites.com* ⇲ *340 suites* ⌂ *In-room: kitchen, refrigerator, Wi-Fi. In-hotel: restaurant, bar, pool, gym, laundry service, parking (fee), some pets allowed (fee), no-smoking rooms* ⊟ *AE, D, DC, MC, V* ⏹ *BP* ✛ *1:F6.*

$$$–$$$$ **Sofitel–San Francisco Bay.** Set on a lagoon in a business park near several big-name corporate headquarters, this hotel is a warm, inviting oasis in an otherwise sterile area. Parisian lampposts, a Métro sign, and a poster-covered kiosk lend an unexpected French ambience to the public spaces, while the light, expansive, luxurious rooms have a more modern feel. Done in pale earth tones, accommodations include fine linens, French bath products, complimentary turndown service, Evian water, and fresh orchids. Many staff members speak both French and English. Bay 223 restaurant and bar completes the experience with a fine menu of artfully presented, contemporary American cuisine. **Pros:** bilingual staff, stylish interior design, reasonable rates, airport shuttle. **Cons:** uninviting environs, a bit far from the city. ⊠ *223 Twin Dolphin Dr., Redwood City* ☎ *650/598–9000* ⊕ *www.sofitel-sanfrancisco-bay.com* ⇲ *421 rooms, 42 suites* ⌂ *In-room: safe, refrigerator (some), Wi-Fi. In-hotel: restaurant, room service, bar, pool, gym, laundry service, concierge, airport shuttle, parking (no fee), some pets allowed (fee), no-smoking rooms* ⊟ *AE, D, DC, MC, V* ✛ *1:F6.*

CIVIC CENTER/VAN NESS

¢–$ **Hayes Valley Inn.** Offering "European charm in the heart of Hayes Valley," the modest, clean rooms of this hotel come with sinks and vanities . . . but the bathroom is down the hall. The Opera House, Davies Symphony Hall, and a chic shopping and dining district are steps away on Hayes Street. Slightly larger, corner turret rooms overlook a busy intersection. **Pros:** inexpensive; free local calls; close to shopping, restaurants, and theater. **Cons:** no in-room bathroom, no elevator, some street noise. ⊠ *417 Gough St., Civic Center* ☎ *415/431–9131 or*

800/930–7999 ⊕ *www.hayesvalleyinn.com* ↘ *28 rooms* ♿ *In room: no a/c, Wi-Fi. In hotel: restaurant, laundry facilities, concierge, public Internet, Wi-Fi, parking (fee), some pets allowed, no-smoking rooms* ▭ *AE, MC, V* ⫟◎⫠ *CP* ✛ *3:E2.*

$$$ 🏨 **Hotel Kabuki.** This pagoda-style hotel, which underwent a $10-million face-lift in 2007, is next door to Japantown and two blocks from Fillmore Street and Pacific Heights. Rooms are located in the tower and the garden wing, which has a traditional Japanese garden and waterfall. Japanese-style rooms have futon beds with tatami mats, while the Western variety have traditional beds. All rooms are decorated with gorgeous Asian furniture and original artwork, and most have their own soaking rooms, which come with a bucket, stool, and a Japanese-style tub (1 foot deeper than Western tubs). The O Izakaya Lounge serves breakfast daily and dinner Wednesday through Sunday. A club level offers complimentary breakfast as well as free appetizers and cocktails during happy hour. **Pros:** Japanese style, serene environment. **Cons:** popular with the business crowd. ✉ *1625 Post St., at Laguna St., Japantown* ☎ *415/922–3200 or 800/533–4567* ⊕ *www.jdvhotels.com* ↘ *204 rooms, 14 suites* ♿ *In-room: safe, Internet, Wi-Fi. In-hotel: restaurant, bar, gym, laundry service, public Internet, parking (fee), no-smoking rooms* ▭ *AE, D, DC, MC, V* ✛ *2:G6.*

$–$$ 🏨 **Hotel Whitcomb.** Built in 1910, this historic hotel (formerly the Ramada Plaza) was the temporary seat of city government from 1912 to 1915 before becoming a hotel in 1916. (What was once the mayor's office now serves as the hotel's administrative offices, and the jail cells are still intact in the hotel basement.) The expansive, well-appointed lobby boasts marble balustrades and columns, carved wooden ceilings, rare Janesero paneling, Austrian crystal chandeliers, Tiffany stained glass, and a ballroom with one of the largest parquet dance floors in the city. Broad halls lead to spacious, newly refurbished rooms with flat-screen TVs and baths. Northeast corner suites offer views of Market Street and the gold-encrusted dome of City Hall. Stroll out the front door to find the Civic Center Muni and BART stations and the main public library; the Asian Art Museum, Opera House, Davies Symphony Hall, and Westfield Centre are close by. **Pros:** good location, rich architectural and historical legacy, opulent lobby, spacious rooms, airport shuttle. **Cons:** difficult to find street parking, area can be dodgy at night. ✉ *1231 Market St., Civic Center* ☎ *415/626–8000 or 800/227–4747* ⊕ *www. hotelwhitcomb.com* ↘ *447 rooms, 12 suites* ♿ *In room: Wi-Fi. In hotel: restaurant, room service, bar, gym,laundry service, concierge, meeting rooms, public Wi-Fi, parking (fee), no-smoking rooms* ▭ *AE, D, DC, MC, V* ✛ *3:G2.*

$$ 🏨 **Inn at the Opera.** Within walking distance of Davies Symphony Hall and the War Memorial Opera House, this homey boutique hotel caters to season-ticket holders for the opera, ballet, and symphony; it has been the venue of choice for stars of the music, dance, and opera worlds, from Luciano Pavarotti to Mikhail Baryshnikov. The genteel, newly refurbished, marble-floor lobby resembles the foyer of a finely appointed mansion, and the compact standard rooms feature dark-wood furnishings, queen-size pillow-top beds with 250-thread-count

sheets, and cozy terry robes. The sumptuous, romantically lit Ovation restaurant, with its Old World charm, is an intimate place for performers and audience members to congregate before and after shows.

WORD OF MOUTH

"I love the Phoenix. A whole lot of rock 'n' roll history happened in that pool." —Jason P

Rates include an expanded continental breakfast buffet, and complimentary cookies and apples are available at the front desk. An Internet kiosk in the lobby ($10 per hour) is equipped with its own printer. **Pros:** staff goes the extra mile, intimate restaurant. **Cons:** smallish rooms and bath, sold out far in advance during opera season. ⊠ *333 Fulton St., Van Ness/Civic Center* ☎ *415/863–8400 or 800/325–2708* ⊕ *www. shellhospitality.com* ⌑ *30 rooms, 18 suites* ⚇ *In-room: no a/c, refrigerator, Internet, Wi-Fi. In-hotel: restaurant, room service, bar, laundry service, concierge, parking (fee), no-smoking rooms* ▭ *AE, D, DC, MC, V* �‖‖ *CP* ✛ *3:E2.*

14

$–$$ ⌖ **Seal Rock Inn.** About as far west as you can go in San Francisco without falling into the Pacific, this hotel within easy walking distance of the Cliff House and Ocean Beach is a welcome refuge from the hubbub of downtown. A recreation area with a small pool, Ping-Pong table, and badminton court—plus large rooms with accordion-style dividers separating a queen bed from two twins—makes it a good choice for families with kids. Recent improvements include two ADA-compliant rooms; new furniture, carpets, curtains, and mattresses; renovated bathrooms; and a new patio. Second-story rooms enjoy ocean views, some have kitchenettes, and a little restaurant serves breakfast and lunch. **Pros:** close to the beach, lots of activities for kids. **Cons:** no a/c, no pets allowed. ⊠ *545 Point Lobos Ave., Lincoln Park* ☎ *415/752–8000 or 888/732–5762* ⊕ *www.sealrockinn.com* ⌑ *27 rooms* ⚇ *In-room: no a/c, kitchen (some), refrigerator, Internet, Wi-Fi. In-hotel: restaurant, pool, parking (no fee), no-smoking rooms* ▭ *AE, DC, MC, V* �‖‖ *EP* ✛ *2:A6.*

FINANCIAL DISTRICT

$$–$$$$ ⌖ **Galleria Park.** This boutique hotel, which has a dedicated clientele and is particularly packed on weekdays with corporate travelers, is close to BART, the Chinatown Gate, Union Square, and the high-end Crocker Galleria shopping complex. A recent $8-million renovation has updated and dramatically improved guest rooms (which are now decorated in chartreuse and sage), as well as modernized the meeting and fitness facilities. Complimentary morning coffee and tea and evening wine are served in the art-deco lobby in front of the pièce de résistance, a massive, hand-sculpted art-nouveau fireplace that looks like it leaped out of a fairy tale. Restored original 1911 skylights and artwork by local artists contribute to the inviting atmosphere. A new restaurant, Midi, a French-Californian brasserie headed by chef Michelle Mah, opened in 2009 with decor by Michael Guthrie, who contributed to the panache of Myth and Bix. **Pros:** can't beat the location, one block from BART, friendly management, quiet rooms. **Cons:** small rooms and baths.

✉ *191 Sutter St., Financial District/Union Square* ☎ *415/781–3060 or 800/792–9639* ⊕ *www.galleriapark.com* ➾ *169 rooms, 8 suites* △ *In-room: refrigerator, Internet, Wi-Fi. In-hotel: restaurant, room service, bar, gym, laundry service, public Internet, public Wi-Fi, parking (fee), some pets allowed, no-smoking rooms* ⊟ *AE, D, DC, MC, V* ⊹ *1:E5.*

$$$–$$$$ 🏨 **Hilton San Francisco Financial District.** A $45-million transformation has taken place at this stylish, luxurious hotel adjacent to Chinatown and the Financial District. The lobby's minimalist decor has a distinctly Asian flavor. The Seven Fifty restaurant, which serves breakfast only, is adjacent to the Grille, a recent addition that doubles as a sports bar and offers comfort food with a Northern California twist. The new wine bar called Flyte showcases local wines from Sonoma and Napa Valley paired with small food plates. A Tully's coffee bar is located in the lobby for your morning coffee fix. For personal pampering, sample the Tru day spa, which provides a range of packages. Tastefully decorated, airy rooms come with blond-wood Signature Serenity beds, Wi-Fi, flat-screen TVs, and large work desks with ergonomic chairs. **Pros:** abundant parking, bay and city views. **Cons:** congested area. ✉ *750 Kearny St., Financial District* ☎ *415/433–6600* ⊕ *www.sanfranciscohiltonhotel. com* ➾ *537 rooms, 7 suites* △ *In room: safe, Internet, Wi-Fi. In-hotel: room service, bar, laundry service, concierge, parking (fee), public Wi-Fi* ⊟ *AE, D, DC, MC, V* ⏏ *BP* ⊹ *1:D4.*

$$$$ 🏨 **Le Méridien.** Across Battery Street from the Embarcadero Center complex, this hotel (formerly the Park Hyatt) has completed renovating its lounge and lobby area, as well as a style-makeover of its standard rooms and suites in an effort to attract both leisure and business visitors. Australian lacewood paneling, polished granite sinks, stylish contemporary furniture, and fresh flowers outfit the spacious guest rooms. The in-room safes have interior outlets for recharging laptops and cell phones. The Park Grill serves excellent, high-end California cuisine (breakfast and lunch), and the popular Bar 333 off the lobby has a Mediterranean menu and an extensive list of wines and other libations. **Pros:** excellent service, ultraconvenient, spacious rooms, great views, top-notch concierge. **Cons:** New Age elevator soundtrack. ✉ *333 Battery St., Financial District* ☎ *415/296–2900* ⊕ *www.lemeridien.com/ sanfrancisco* ➾ *281 rooms, 79 suites* △ *In-room: safe, Internet, Wi-Fi. In-hotel: 2 restaurants, room service, bars, gym, laundry service, concierge, public Internet, parking (fee), no-smoking rooms* ⊟ *AE, MC, V* ⊹ *1:E4.*

$$$$ 🏨 **Mandarin Oriental, San Francisco.** Two towers connected by glass-enclosed sky bridges compose the top 11 floors of one of San Francisco's tallest buildings. Spectacular panoramas grace every room, and windows open so you can hear that trademark San Francisco sound: the "ding ding" of the cable cars some 40 floors below. The rooms, corridors, and lobby areas are decorated in rich hues of red, gold, and chocolate-brown. The Mandarin Rooms have extra-deep tubs next to picture windows, enabling guests to literally and figuratively soak up what one reader called "unbelievable views from the Golden Gate to the Bay Bridge and everything in between." Pamper yourself with luxurious Egyptian-cotton sheets, two kinds of robes (terry and waffle-

Fodor's Choice
★

weave), and cozy slippers. A lovely complimentary tea-and-cookie tray delivered to your room upon your arrival is one among many illustrations of the hotel's commitment to service. The pricey mezzanine-level restaurant, Silks, earns rave reviews for innovative American cuisine with an Asian flair. Special rate plans for families are available. Several top-floor suites have been recently revamped, as has the Mandarin Lounge. **Pros:** spectacular "bridge-to-bridge" views, attentive service. **Cons:** located in a business area that's quiet on weekends, restaurant is excellent but expensive (as is the hotel). ✉ *222 Sansome St., Financial District* ☏ *415/276–9600 or 800/622–0404* ⊕ *www.mandarinoriental. com/sanfrancisco* ↺ *151 rooms, 7 suites* ♿ *In-room: safe, DVD, Wi-Fi. In-hotel: restaurant, room service, bar, gym, laundry service, concierge, public Internet, public Wi-Fi, parking (fee), some pets allowed (fee), no-smoking rooms* ▣ *AE, D, DC, MC, V* ✛ *1:E4.*

\$\$\$–\$\$\$\$ 🏨 **Omni San Francisco Hotel.** Although the lobby's glittering crystal chandeliers, dark mahogany paneling, and iron-and-marble staircase may hark back to an old-fashioned gentility, this 1926 redbrick-and-stone building, a former bank, is now home to a modern luxury hotel. Rooms have updated bedding, flat-screen TVs, 9-foot-high ceilings with crown moldings, and carved-mahogany furniture; sliding doors open to reveal bathrooms with marble floors and green-and-black granite basins. Daylight floods the corner suites, each of which has six tall windows. More expensive Signature Rooms offer extra amenities such as complimentary fresh seasonal fruit daily, bottled water, and assorted business tools including color printer-copiers and a direct line to your room with its own phone number. The recently spruced up Bob's Steak and Chop House, which is more elegant than the name implies, is off the lobby. **Pros:** outstanding personalized service, cookies and milk for the kids, immaculately clean, historical flavor. **Cons:** so-so a/c, rooftop views are less than inspiring. ✉ *500 California St., Financial District* ☏ *415/677–9494* ⊕ *www.omnisanfrancisco.com* ↺ *347 rooms, 15 suites* ♿ *In-room: safe, DVD (some), Internet, Wi-Fi. In-hotel: restaurant, room service, bar, gym, laundry service, concierge, public Internet, public Wi-Fi, parking (fee), some pets allowed (fee), no-smoking rooms* ▣ *AE, D, DC, MC, V* ✛ *1:E4.*

14

FISHERMAN'S WHARF/NORTH BEACH

FISHERMAN'S WHARF

\$\$\$–\$\$\$\$ 🏨 **Argonaut Hotel.** When the four-story Haslett Warehouse was a fruit-
Ⓒ   and-vegetable canning complex in 1907, boats docked right up against
Fodor's Choice   the building. Today it's a hotel with a nautical decor—think anchors,
★   ropes, compasses, and a row of cruise-ship deck chairs in the lobby—
that reflects its unique partnership with the San Francisco Maritime National Historical Park. Spacious rooms, many with a sofa bed in the sitting area, have exposed-brick walls, wood-beam ceilings, and whitewashed wooden furniture reminiscent of a summer beach house. Windows open to the sea air and the sounds of the waterfront, and many rooms have views of Alcatraz and the Golden Gate Bridge. Suites come with extra-deep whirlpool tubs and telescopes for close-up views of passing ships. **Pros:** bay views, clean rooms, near Hyde Street cable

Mandarin Oriental

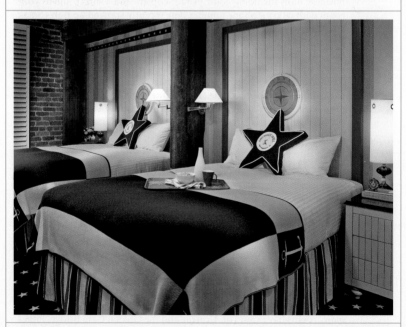

Argonaut Hotel

car, sofa beds, toys for the kids. **Cons:** nautical theme isn't for every-one, cramped public areas, service can be hit or miss, location is a bit of a hike from other parts of town. ✉ *495 Jefferson St., at Hyde St., Fisherman's Wharf* ☎ *415/563–0800 or 866/415–0704* ⊕ *www.argonauthotel.com* ➯ *239 rooms, 13 suites* ⏃ *In-room: safe, refrigerator, Internet, Wi-Fi. In-hotel: restaurant, room service, bar, gym, laundry service, concierge, public Wi-Fi, parking (fee), some pets allowed, no-smoking rooms* ▭ *AE, D, DC, MC, V* ✛ *1:A1.*

$$–$$$ 🏨 **Best Western Tuscan Inn.** Described by some Fodors.com users as a "hidden treasure," this hotel's redbrick facade barely hints at the Tuscan country villa that lies within. Each small, Italianate room has white-pine furniture, floral bedspreads and curtains, a completely mirrored wall, and a refurbished bathroom. Complimentary beverages and biscotti are laid out mornings near the fireplace in the oak-panel lobby, where a convivial wine hour is held nightly. There's free morning limousine service to the Financial District. Café Pescatore, the Italian seafood restaurant off the lobby, provides room service for breakfast. **Pros:** wine/beer hour, down-home feeling. **Cons:** congested touristy area, small rooms. ✉ *425 N. Point St., at Mason St., Fisherman's Wharf* ☎ *415/561–1100 or 800/648–4626* ⊕ *www.tuscaninn.com* ➯ *209 rooms, 12 suites* ⏃ *In-room: Wi-Fi. In-hotel: restaurant, room service, bar, laundry service, public Internet, parking (fee), some pets allowed, no-smoking rooms* ▭ *AE, D, DC, MC, V* ✛ *1:C1.*

$$$ 🏨 **Hyatt at Fisherman's Wharf.** The location is key to this hotel's popularity: it's within walking distance of tourist hot spots such as Ghirardelli Square, the Cannery, Pier 39, Aquatic Park, and Alcatraz ferries; bay cruises dock nearby; and it's across the street from a cable-car turnaround. The double-pane windows of the moderately sized rooms—which have flat-screen TVs and dark-wood furniture—keep out the considerable street noise. Each floor has a laundry room. In the North Point Lounge, a domed Tiffany skylight with a seashore motif crowns a large, comfy lounge area with a fireplace and fountain. Plans to renovate the restaurant and guest rooms, expand the fitness center, and redesign the lobby are in the works. **Pros:** primo sightseeing location, close to cable cars. **Cons:** street noise, crowds. ✉ *555 N. Point St., Fisherman's Wharf* ☎ *415/563–1234 or 800/233–1234* ⊕ *www.fishermanswharf.hyatt.com* ➯ *313 rooms, 8 suites* ⏃ *In-room: safe, refrigerator (some), Wi-Fi. In-hotel: restaurant, room service, bar, pool, gym, laundry facilities, laundry service, concierge, public Internet, parking (fee), no-smoking rooms* ▭ *AE, D, DC, MC, V* ✛ *1:B1.*

$$$ 🏨 **Marriott Fisherman's Wharf.** Behind the hotel's sand-color facade is a lavish, low-ceiling lobby with marble floors, a double fireplace, and English club–style furniture. Rooms—which are expected to be fully remodeled by mid-2009—have either a king-size bed or two double beds; all are triple-sheeted, and the abundance of extra pillows allows for lots of luxurious lounging. One hundred rooms, designed with business travelers in mind, have an extra-large desk, ergonomic chair, speakerphone, and two data ports. Restaurant Spada serves all three meals. **Pros:** near tourist hot spots, comfortable bedding. **Cons:** touristy area. ✉ *1250 Columbus Ave., Fisherman's Wharf* ☎ *415/775–7555* ⊕ *www.marriott.*

*com/hotels/travel/sfofw-sanfrancisco-marriott-fishermanswharf/ ⇨ 269
rooms, 16 suites ᗡ In-room: safe, refrigerator, Internet. In-hotel: restaurant, room service, bar, gym, laundry facilities, laundry service,
concierge, public Internet, parking (fee), some pets allowed (fee), no-
smoking rooms ▭ AE, D, MC, V ⊹ 1:B1.*

NORTH BEACH

$$ ⓣ **Hotel Bohème.** This small hotel in historic North Beach takes you
back in time with cast-iron beds, large mirrored armoires, and memo-
rabilia recalling the Beat generation—whose leading light, Allen Gins-
berg, often stayed here (legend has it that in his later years he could
be seen sitting in a window, typing away on his laptop computer).
Screenwriters toiling nearby at Francis Ford Coppola's dream factory,
American Zoetrope Studio, as well as sundry poets and artists, are fre-
quent patrons. Rooms have a bistro table, two chairs, and tropical-style
mosquito netting over the bed; bathrooms have cheerful yellow tiles
and tiny showers. Rooms in the rear are a refuge from the noisy crush,
especially on weekends. Complimentary sherry is served in the lobby.
Pros: North Beach location with literary pedigree. **Cons:** street parking
is scarce, lots of traffic congestion, no a/c. ⊠ *444 Columbus Ave., North
Beach* ☎ *415/433–9111* ⊕ *www.hotelboheme.com* ⇨ *15 rooms* ᗡ *In-
room: no a/c, Internet, Wi-Fi. In-hotel: no elevator, concierge, public
Wi-Fi, no-smoking rooms* ▭ *AE, D, DC, MC, V* ⊹ *1:D3.*

¢   ⓣ **San Remo Hotel.** A few blocks from Fisherman's Wharf, this three-
story 1906 Italianate Victorian—once home to longshoremen and
Beat poets—has a narrow stairway from the street leading to the front
desk and labyrinthine hallways. Rooms are small but charming, with
lace curtains, forest-green-painted wood floors, brass beds, and other
antique furnishings. The top floor is brighter, because it's closer to the
skylights that provide sunshine to the thriving population of potted
plants that line the brass-banistered hallways. About a third of the
rooms have sinks, and all share spotless black-and-white-tile bathroom
facilities with pull-chain toilets. A rooftop suite must be reserved three
to six months in advance. Fior D'Italia, "America's Oldest Italian Res-
taurant," occupies the building's entire first floor. **Pros:** inexpensive.
Cons: some rooms are dark, no private bath, spartan amenities. ⊠ *2237
Mason St., North Beach* ☎ *415/776–8688 or 800/352–7366* ⊕ *www.
sanremohotel.com* ⇨ *64 rooms with shared baths, 1 suite* ᗡ *In-room:
no a/c, no phone, no TV, Wi-Fi. In-hotel: laundry facilities, public Wi-Fi,
parking (fee), no-smoking rooms* ▭ *AE, D, MC, V* ⊹ *1:C2.*

$$ ⓣ **SW Hotel.** Opened in 1913 as the Columbo Hotel, this lodging on the
bustling border between Chinatown and North Beach has rooms and
suites decorated in a blend of Italian and Chinese styles, with Floren-
tine wall coverings and Ming-style furniture. Old-fashioned wooden
venetian blinds cover the windows, and baths have polished granite
countertops. Top-floor rooms have nice views of Coit Tower and North
Beach. Be warned: The smallest rooms have teensy closets and bathrooms, so ask for the most spacious accommodations available. A multilingual staff serves morning pastries and beverages in the mezzanine
area. **Pros:** top-floor views of Coit Tower, multilingual staff, self-serve
parking under building. **Cons:** cramped closets and bathrooms. ⊠ *615*

Fodor's Choice
★

Broadway, Chinatown/North Beach ☎ *415/362–2999 or 888/595–9188* ⊕ *www.swhotel.com* ⇨ *105 rooms, 2 suites* ☐ *In-room: no a/c (some), Wi-Fi. In-hotel: public Internet, public Wi-Fi, parking (fee), no-smoking rooms* ▭ *AE, DC, MC, V* ◎ *CP* ✛ *1:D3.*

$$–$$$$ ☒ **Washington Square Inn.** Overlooking the tree-lined park of its namesake and surrounded by fine shops and cafés, this gracious corner B&B sits at the foot of Telegraph Hill in the heart of North Beach. Both large and small rooms are individually decorated with Venetian and French accents; upgraded bathrooms are done in imported marble and tiles. Most rooms have gas fireplaces and beds with 400- to 600-thread-count sheets. The lobby, which has a gleaming mahogany fireplace and brass chandeliers, is the setting for free wine and antipasti in the evening. A complimentary continental breakfast is served by the front windows. **Pros:** nice rooms, fun location. **Cons:** some guests complain about gruff management, no a/c, street parking is difficult to come by. ✉ *1660 Stockton St., at Filbert St., North Beach* ☎ *415/981–4220 or 800/388–0220* ⊕ *www.wsisf.com* ⇨ *15 rooms* ☐ *In-room: no a/c, Wi-Fi. In-hotel: concierge, public Internet, public Wi-Fi, parking (fee), no-smoking rooms* ▭ *AE, D, DC, MC, V* ◎ *BP* ✛ *1:D2.*

14

NOB HILL

$$–$$$ ☒ **Executive Hotel Vintage Court.** This Napa Valley–inspired hotel two blocks from Union Square has inviting rooms named after California wineries. Some have sunny window seats, and all have large writing desks, dark-wood venetian blinds, and steam heat. Bathrooms are small; some have tub-showers, while others have stall showers. The Wine Country theme extends to complimentary local vintages served nightly in front of a roaring fire in the chocolate-hue lobby, where long couches encourage lingering. For a superior gastronomic experience, book a table at the adjoining Masa's, one of the city's most celebrated French restaurants. **Pros:** complimentary local wines. **Cons:** small bathrooms, far from downtown and many tourist spots. ✉ *650 Bush St., Nob Hill/Union Square* ☎ *415/392–4666 or 800/654–1100* ⊕ *www.executivehotels.net/vintagecourt* ⇨ *106 rooms, 1 suite* ☐ *In-room: safe, refrigerator, Internet, Wi-Fi. In-hotel: restaurant, bar, laundry service, concierge, public Internet, public Wi-Fi, parking (fee), no-smoking rooms* ▭ *AE, D, DC, MC, V* ◎ *CP* ✛ *4:F2.*

$$$$ ☒ **Fairmont San Francisco.** This hotel, which dominates the top of Nob Hill like a European palace, has a rich history that includes surviving the 1906 earthquake and hosting the signing of the United Nations Charter in 1945. Architect Julia Morgan's timeless 1907 lobby design includes alabaster walls and gilt-embellished ceilings supported by Corinthian columns. In the main building, gracious rooms done in conservative color schemes have high ceilings, fine dark-wood furniture, colorful Chinese porcelain lamps, wonderful new beds, flat-screen TVs, and marble bathrooms. Rooms in the Tower are generally larger and have better views. Amenities and special services (including free chicken soup if you're under the weather) keeps loyal guests coming back. Don't miss drinks at the recently spiffed up Tonga Room, an outsized Tiki lounge that serves blue tropical cocktails with umbrellas. **Pros:** huge bathrooms, stunning lobby, great location. **Cons:** some guests have complained about spotty service, hills can be challenging for those on foot. ✉ *950 Mason St., Nob Hill* ☎ *415/772–5000 or 800/257–7544* ⊕ *www.fairmont.com/sanfrancisco* ⟿ *591 rooms, 65 suites* ⚘ *In-room: safe, Internet, Wi-Fi. In-hotel: 2 restaurants, room service, bars, gym, spa, laundry service, concierge, public Wi-Fi, parking (fee), some pets allowed (fee), no-smoking rooms* ▭ *AE, D, DC, MC, V* ✛ *4:E1.*

$$$$
Fodor's Choice
★

Ritz-Carlton, San Francisco. A preferred destination for travel-industry honchos, movie stars, and visitors alike, this hotel—a stunning tribute to beauty and attentive, professional service—completed a $12.5-million renovation of its guest rooms and meeting spaces in 2006. Ionic columns grace the neoclassical facade; crystal chandeliers illuminate Georgian antiques and museum-quality 18th- and 19th-century paintings in the lobby. All rooms have flat-screen TVs, featherbeds with 300-thread-count Egyptian cotton Frette sheets, and down comforters. Club Level rooms include use of the upgraded Club Lounge, which has a dedicated concierge and several elaborate complimentary food presentations daily. The Dining Room has a seasonal menu with modern French accents. The delightful afternoon tea service in the Lobby Lounge, which overlooks the beautifully landscaped Terrace courtyard, is a San Francisco institution. **Pros:** terrific service, all-day food service on club level, beautiful surroundings. **Cons:** expensive, hilly location. ✉ *600 Stockton St., at California St., Nob Hill* ☎ *415/296–7465* ⊕ *www.ritzcarlton.com* ⟿ *276 rooms, 60 suites* ⚘ *In-room: safe, refrigerator, DVD, Wi-Fi. In-hotel: 2 restaurants, room service, bars, pool, gym, laundry service, concierge, public Internet, parking (fee), some pets allowed (fee), no-smoking rooms* ▭ *AE, D, DC, MC, V* ✛ *4:F1.*

$$$$

The Stanford Court, A Renaissance Hotel. A stained-glass dome and a sweeping 360-degree mural depicting scenes of early San Francisco and the gold rush dominate the lobby of this stately-but-comfortable Marriott-operated hotel. Rooms achieve understated elegance with warm tones, lounge chairs, and tasteful accessories. Nice touches include 300-thread-count Frette sheets, plush robes, heated towel racks, bathrooms with granite vanities, and nightly turndown service. A recent $35-million renovation of the entire hotel, from the guest rooms and lobby to a spanking new club lounge with a view of the bay, has made the place sparkle. The new Aurea Restaurant offers a seasonal menu of California cuisine. Complimentary coffee or tea is delivered to your room each morning upon request. **Pros:** focus on comfort, classic elegance. **Cons:** far from most popular tourist sights, some guests complain that rooms are small. ✉ *905 California St., Nob Hill* ☎ *415/989–3500* ⊕ *www.stanfordcourt.com* ⟿ *389 rooms, 4 suites* ⚘ *In-room: Internet, Wi-Fi. In-hotel: restaurant, room service, bar, gym, laundry service, concierge, public Internet, parking (fee), some pets allowed, no-smoking rooms* ▭ *AE, D, DC, MC, V* ✛ *4:F1.*

PACIFIC HEIGHTS/COW HOLLOW/THE MARINA

PACIFIC HEIGHTS

$$–$$$$
Fodor's Choice
★
🖼 **Hotel Drisco.** Pretend you're a resident of one of the wealthiest and most beautiful residential neighborhoods in San Francisco at this understated, elegant 1903 Edwardian hotel. The quiet haven, which feels like a secluded B&B, serves as a celebrity hideaway for the likes of Ethan Hawke and Ashley Judd. Genteel furnishings and luxurious amenities like flat-screen TVs grace pale yellow-and-white rooms, some of which have sweeping city views. Morning newspaper, plush robes, slippers, and nightly turndown service are included. A free breakfast is offered in a sunny, spacious room; wine is set out each evening in a lovely area off the lobby. Guests have commented on the helpful and incredibly friendly staff. Recent renovations added flat-screen TVs and new carpeting, furnishings, and bedding to the guest rooms. **Pros:** great service, comfortable rooms, quiet residential retreat. **Cons:** small rooms, far from downtown. ⊠ *2901 Pacific Ave., Pacific Heights* ☎ *415/346–2880 or 800/634–7277* ⊕ *www.hoteldrisco.com* ⇨ *29 rooms, 19 suites* ⚷ *In-room: no a/c, safe, refrigerator, DVD. In-hotel: laundry service, concierge, public Internet, no-smoking rooms* ⊟ *AE, D, DC, MC, V* ⁣|◯| *CP* ⊹ *2:D4.*

$$–$$$$ 🖼 **Hotel Majestic.** Built in 1902 as a private residence, this five-story white Edwardian building, the city's oldest continually operating hotel, turned into a residence club two years later—movie star sisters Joan Fontaine and Olivia de Havilland, symbols of Old Hollywood royalty, once lived here. Nicolas Cage, his uncle August Coppola, and the crew of *Sweet November* are among the more contemporary moviemakers who have visited the hotel's elegant lobby, appointed with antique chandeliers, plush Victorian chairs, and hundreds of antiquarian French books. Most rooms—which have either hand-painted four-poster or two-poster twin beds—have gas fireplaces and claw-foot tubs. The hotel, which survived both of San Francisco's major 20th-century earthquakes, is legendary for its friendly ghost, the lovely Butterfly Bar, and the largest collection of exotic butterflies in Northern California—on display at the café bar, where you can also order light fare. The hotel planned to upgrade all rooms in early 2009. **Pros:** quintessential SF hotel, destination café, Victorian flavor, quiet neighborhood, spacious rooms, perfect for a romantic getaway. **Cons:** you'll need a cab to get downtown or to tourist hot spots. ⊠ *1500 Sutter St., Pacific Heights* ☎ *415/441–1100 or 800/869–8966* ⊕ *www.thehotelmajestic.com* ⇨ *47 rooms, 9 suites* ⚷ *In-room: refrigerator (some), Wi-Fi. In-hotel: restaurant, room service, bar, laundry service, concierge, public Internet, parking (fee), no-smoking rooms* ⊟ *AE, D, DC, MC, V* |◯| *CP* ⊹ *2:G6.*

$$$ 🖼 **Laurel Inn.** The blue-and-tan Googie-style facade of this stylish inn
☾ suggests its 1963 urban-motel origins. Rooms, decorated in black and taupe, are spacious and clean; all have ceiling fans, some have desks and fold-out sofas, and 18 offer convenient kitchenettes. Adjoining rooms can be connected to create a kid-friendly suite. Accommodations in the rear have cityscape views and tend to be quieter. Day passes are available to the extensive exercise facilities at the Jewish Community Center of San Francisco, located directly across the street. Diverse shops

14

CLOSE UP

A Concierge's Top Tips

Concierges can be the Great Finesser of your trip: finding hard-to-get reservations or tickets, helping with business matters, and generally making your stay easier. Here's the inside scoop from a former concierge.

Be specific. When soliciting help in choosing a restaurant, focus on what you like, not what you don't. Avoid unhelpful statements such as "Where should I eat? I don't like fish, I don't like steak, and I don't like Chinese." Instead, tell the concierge what you do like and reveal your tastes, as in, "I love candlelit French bistros, but tonight I feel like something livelier, more casual, maybe Italian." You'll always get better results.

Do your homework. Nothing drives a concierge crazier than a guest who arrives at the desk and says, "I'm in San Francisco for two weeks, and I've never been here before. What should I do?" (Fortunately you're already one step ahead by having consulted Fodor's first!)

Save big at biz hotels. If you're a weekend traveler on a mid-range budget, you can sometimes get great deals at high-end hotels that cater primarily to business travelers. The opposite is true at tourist hotels, which spike their rates on weekends.

"Block" your room. If you want to book a particular room or room type, call the hotel on the morning of your arrival and reconfirm the arrangements with the front-office manager. Ask the manager to "block" (preassign) your room. This is especially important when the hotel is sold out and you're arriving late at night; otherwise you'll get the "last-sell" room—the least popular room reserved for the last-to-arrive guest.

Call ahead for your car. When you're ready to retrieve your car from valet parking, don't expect simply to arrive in the lobby, hand over your ticket, and instantly get your vehicle. Always call at least 10 minutes beforehand, lest you be left standing in the driveway, late for dinner.

Timing is everything. If you have a complicated request, or need to have a personal conversation with the concierge, call or stop by the desk in the late morning, mid-afternoon, or evening. Concierges are busiest in the morning at check-out time, when business travelers need the most assistance, and in the late afternoon and early evening at check-in time, when guests want dinner reservations. The ideal times to chitchat are usually between noon and 4 PM and 8 PM and 10 PM.

Tip early and often. For the best service, don't wait to tip your concierge: give half the money up front, then the other half once your request has been fulfilled. If the staff knows you're a good tipper, they'll work extra hard to ensure that you get what you want, when you want it.

Tip your concierge based on the time spent arranging your request. For simple matters that require only one phone call, such as an airport shuttle, tip $2. For restaurant recommendations and reservations that require discussion and opinion, $5 to $20, the latter for harder-to-book tables. For itinerary planning, tip $20 to $100, depending on how complicated and time-consuming the arrangements are.

—John Vlahides

and restaurants are one block away on Sacramento Street. The hotel also offers complimentary continental breakfast and, in the afternoon, a cookie tray and lemonade. **Pros:** clean, spacious, kid-friendly rooms; close to Sacramento Street. **Cons:** no a/c, far from downtown. ⊠ *444 Presidio Ave., Pacific Heights* ☎ *415/567–8467 or 800/552–8735* ⊕ *the-laurelinn.com* ⤴ *49 rooms* ⌂ *In-room: no a/c, kitchen (some), refrigerator (some), Wi-Fi. In-hotel: bar, laundry service, concierge, public Wi-Fi, parking (fee), some pets allowed, no-smoking rooms* ⊟ *AE, D, DC, MC, V* ⦿ *CP* ⊹ *2:C3.*

14

$–$$ ⊞ **Pacific Heights Inn.** One of the most genteel-looking motels in town, this two-story motor court near the busy intersection of Union and Van Ness is dressed up with wrought-iron railings and benches, hanging plants, and pebbled exterior walkways facing the parking lot. Rooms, with floral bedspreads and brass beds, are on the small side; however, about half have kitchenettes, and several units are two-bedroom suites. Two rooms come with special Duxiana beds, which are especially kind to weary backs. Complimentary morning pastries and coffee are served in the lobby, along with a free newspaper. **Pros:** kitchenettes, reasonable rates. **Cons:** small rooms, noisy, crowded parking area. ⊠ *1555 Union St., Pacific Heights* ☎ *415/776–3310 or 800/523–1801* ⊕ *www.pacificheightsinn.com* ⤴ *35 rooms, 5 suites* ⌂ *In-room: no a/c, kitchen (some), refrigerator, Wi-Fi. In-hotel: parking (no fee), some pets allowed (fee), no-smoking rooms* ⊟ *AE, DC, MC, V* ⦿ *CP* ⊹ *2:H3.*

$$–$$$
Fodor's Choice
★
⊞ **Queen Anne.** Built in the 1890s as a girls' finishing school and located in fashionable Pacific Heights, this Victorian mansion has a large comfortable parlor done up in red brocade, lace, and heirloom antiques. Original stained glass, inlaid wood floors throughout its elegant hallways, and 14 fireplaces combine "the romantic charm of the past with present day comfort." Complimentary amenities include a continental breakfast, daily newspaper, weekday courtesy car service downtown, and afternoon tea and sherry. The versatile parlor, salon, boardroom, library, and small covered outdoor courtyard make this a popular spot for weddings. Recent renovations added new beds, linens, and paint to the guest rooms. **Pros:** free weekday car service, character. **Cons:** far from downtown. ⊠ *1590 Sutter St., Pacific Heights* ☎ *415/441–2828 or 800/227–3970* ⊕ *www.queenanne.com* ⤴ *41 rooms, 7 suites* ⌂ *In-room: Wi-Fi. In-hotel: laundry service, concierge, public Wi-Fi, parking (fee)* ⊟ *AE, D, DC, MC, V* ⦿ *CP* ⊹ *2:G6.*

COW HOLLOW

¢–$ ⊞ **Coventry Motor Inn.** Among the many motels on busy Lombard Street, this is one of the cleanest, friendliest, and quietest—especially the rooms that don't face Lombard. The oak-panel lobby is decorated with leather furniture and photographs of historic San Francisco, and the unusually spacious rooms have cheery yellow wallpaper, gold drapes, oak furniture, and well-lit dining and work areas. Many rooms have bay windows, and some on the upper floors have views of the Golden Gate Bridge. **Pros:** clean, friendly, good value, lots of eateries nearby, free parking in building. **Cons:** busy street, few amenities. ⊠ *1901 Lombard St., Cow Hollow* ☎ *415/567–1200* ⊕ *www.coventrymotorinn.com*

The Ritz-Carlton, San Francisco

Hotel Drisco

Queen Anne Hotel

Union Street Inn

69 rooms ⚄ In-room: Wi-Fi. In-hotel: public Wi-Fi, parking (no fee), no-smoking rooms ▭ AE, MC, V ✛ 2:F3.

$$$–$$$$ 🆃 **Union Street Inn.** Precious family antiques and unique artwork helped
Fodor's Choice British innkeepers Jane Bertorelli and David Coyle (former chef for the
★ Duke and Duchess of Bedford) transform this green-and-cream 1902
Edwardian into a delightful B&B. Equipped with candles, fresh flowers,
wineglasses, and fine linens, rooms are popular with honeymooners and
those looking for a romantic getaway. The newly renovated Carriage
House, separated from the main house by an old-fashioned English
garden planted with lemon trees, is equipped with a double Jacuzzi,
refinished hardwood floors, and upgraded bathrooms. An elaborate
breakfast, which many guests rave about, is included, as are afternoon
tea and evening hors d'oeuvres. **Pros:** personal service, excellent full
breakfast, romantic setting. **Cons:** congested neighborhood, no a/c, no
elevator. ✉ 2229 Union St., Cow Hollow ☎ 415/346–0424 ⊕ www.
unionstreetinn.com 6 rooms ⚄ In-room: no a/c, Wi-Fi. In-hotel: no
elevator, parking (fee), no-smoking rooms ▭ AE, D, MC, V ¹⁰¹ BP
✛ 2:E3.

THE MARINA

$ 🆃 **Cow Hollow Motor Inn and Suites.** Suites at this large, family-owned
modern motel are more spacious than average, with sitting-dining areas,
dark-wood traditional furniture, and wallpaper with muted yellow,
brown, and green patterns. Resembling typical San Francisco apart-
ments, expansive rooms feature hardwood floors, Oriental rugs, antique
furnishings, marble wood-burning fireplaces, big living rooms, and fully
equipped kitchens; some have views of the Golden Gate Bridge. Huge,
lovely suites, overlooking the eclectic mix of shops, coffeehouses, and
neighborhood businesses on Chestnut Street, have one or two bedrooms
and baths. **Pros:** suites are the size of apartments, covered parking in
building. **Cons:** congested neighborhood has a fratty feeling. ✉ 2190
Lombard St., Marina ☎ 415/921–5800 ⊕ www.cowhollowmotorinn.
com 117 rooms, 12 suites ⚄ In-room: kitchen (some), Wi-Fi. In-hotel:
parking (no fee), no-smoking rooms ▭ AE, DC, MC, V ✛ 2:E3.

$$–$$$ 🆃 **Hotel Del Sol.** Go tropical in the Marina District at this colorfully
☺ restored three-story 1950s motor lodge. Summer barbecues by the
courtyard pool and the hotel's proximity to Funston Playground make
this place kid-friendly, as do free toys, games, a "pillow library," and
evening cookies and milk. Since the Del Sol is only two blocks from
Union Street shopping and restaurants, with easy access off Lombard
Street, it will please adults, too. **Pros:** kid-friendly, plenty of nearby
places to eat and shop. **Cons:** congested area, street parking is elu-
sive. ✉ 3100 Webster St., Marina ☎ 415/921–5520 or 877/433–5765
⊕ www.thehoteldelsol.com 42 rooms, 15 suites ⚄ In room: kitchen
(some), refrigerator (some), DVD, Wi-Fi. In hotel: pool, children's pro-
grams (ages toddler to 10), laundry service, concierge, parking (no fee),
no-smoking rooms ▭ AE, D, DC, MC, V ¹⁰¹ CP ✛ 2:F3.

¢–$ 🆃 **Marina Inn.** Five blocks from the Marina, this four-story 1924 build-
ing feels like a B&B but is priced like a motel. English country–style
rooms with vivid floral wallpaper and bedspreads are simply appointed
with queen-size two-poster beds, private baths, small pinewood writing

desks, and armoires. Some rooms have daybeds appropriate for a small child. The rooms facing Octavia and Lombard streets have bay windows with window seats, but they are noisier than the inside rooms. A simple continental breakfast is served in the central sitting room. **Pros:** affordable, daybed option for kids. **Cons:** street-side rooms can be noisy. ✉ *3110 Octavia St., at Lombard St., Marina* ☎ *415/928–1000 or 800/274–1420* ⊕ *www.marinainn.com* ➾ *40 rooms* ♿ *In-room: no a/c, dial-up, Wi-Fi. In-hotel: no-smoking rooms* ▭ *AE, DC, MC, V* ✛ *2:G2.*

$ 🏨**Marina Motel.** Reminiscent of the motor courts of yesteryear, this family-owned motel is an inexpensive lodging within walking distance of restaurants, bars, and shops in the Marina District and on the waterfront. Although some rooms are next to the street, others are tucked away inside a courtyard planted with flowers and trees. The individual enclosed garages are a nice feature, too, especially in a neighborhood notorious for its lack of street parking. The motel, located on the busy thoroughfare of Lombard Street, is of an older vintage, which translates to thin walls and no air-conditioning (though a/c is unnecessary on all but the hottest days). Some rooms have kitchenettes with eating areas and all have spotless baths and small shower stalls. Despite roaring traffic, the motel is a good value in a popular location. **Pros:** friendly staff that accommodates guests with pets; more character than the chain motels on the same strip. **Cons:** no a/c; located on a busy street; rooms can be noisy and stuffy. ✉ *2576 Lombard St., Marina* ☎ *415/921–9406 or 800/346–6118* ⊕ *www.marinamotel.com* ➾ *40 rooms* ♿ *In-room: no a/c, phone, kitchen (some), refrigerator, Wi-Fi. In-hotel: public Wi-Fi, parking (no fee), some pets allowed* ▭ *AE, D, MC, V* ✛ *2:D3.*

SOMA

$$$$ 🏨**Four Seasons Hotel San Francisco.** Occupying floors 5 through 17 of a
☺ skyscraper, this luxurious hotel, designated as the "heart of the city,"
Fodor'sChoice is sandwiched between multimillion-dollar condos, elite shops, and a
★ premier sports-and-fitness complex. Elegant rooms with contemporary artwork and fine linens have floor-to-ceiling windows overlooking either Yerba Buena Gardens or the historic downtown. All have deep soaking tubs, glass-enclosed showers, and flat-screen TVs. From the contemporary street-level lobby, take the elevator to the vast Sports Club/LA, where you have free access to the junior Olympic pool, full-size indoor basketball court, and the rest of the magnificent facilities, classes, and spa services. Seasons restaurant serves high-end California cuisine, with a strong focus on seasonal and local ingredients. Various packages offer focuses on art, shopping, and cooking. **Pros:** near museums, galleries, restaurants, and clubs; terrific fitness facilities. **Cons:** pricey. ✉ *757 Market St., SoMa* ☎ *415/633–3000, 800/332–3442, or 800/819–5053* ⊕ *www.fourseasons.com/sanfrancisco* ➾ *231 rooms, 46 suites* ♿ *In-room: safe, DVD, Internet, Wi-Fi. In-hotel: restaurant, room service, bar, pool, gym, spa, laundry service, concierge, public Internet, parking (fee), some pets allowed, no-smoking rooms* ▭ *AE, D, DC, MC, V* ✛ *4:H4.*

$$–$$$ ☷ **Harbor Court.** Exemplary service and a friendly staff earn high marks for this cozy hotel, which overlooks the Embarcadero and is within shouting distance of the Bay Bridge. Guest rooms are on the small side, but have double sets of soundproof windows and include nice touches such as wall-mounted 27-inch flat-screen TVs. Brightly colored throw pillows adorn beds with 320-thread-count sheets, and tub-showers have curved shower-curtain rods for more elbow room. Some rooms have views of the Bay Bridge and the Ferry Building. Complimentary evening wine and late-night cookies and milk are served in the lounge, where coffee and tea are available mornings. The hotel provides free use of the adjacent YMCA. **Pros:** convenient location, quiet, friendly service, cozy. **Cons:** small rooms. ⊠ *165 Steuart St., SoMa* ☏ *415/882–1300 or 866/792–6283* ⊕ *www.harborcourthotel.com* ⇲ *130 rooms, 1 suite* ☖ *In-room: Wi-Fi. In-hotel: bar, laundry service, concierge, public Internet, public Wi-Fi, parking (fee), some pets allowed, no-smoking rooms* ▭ *AE, D, DC, MC, V* ✛ *1:G4.*

14

$$ ☷ **Hotel Milano.** Adjacent to the new Westfield San Francisco Shopping Centre—whose tenants include Bloomingdale's and Nordstrom—and close to many of the museums and attractions south of Market Street, this hotel is a shopping and culture maven's delight. The eight-story hotel's stately 1913 neoclassical facade gives way to a warm, stylish lobby with a large Alexander Calder–style mobile over the lounge area. Warm earth tones complement the spacious, attractive guest rooms, which have contemporary Italian furnishings and softly illuminated bathrooms. Too much sightseeing or shopping? Ease your fatigue in the split-level fitness center on the seventh and eighth floors. **Pros:** good value, great location close to shopping/museums, comfy beds, responsive front desk, stylish arty environs. **Cons:** lots of hubbub and traffic, a/c is inconsistent, some rooms are dark. ⊠ *55 5th St., SoMa* ☏ *415/543–8555* ⊕ *www.hotelmilanosf.com* ⇲ *108 rooms* ☖ *In-room: safe, refrigerator, Internet, Wi-Fi. In-hotel: restaurant, room service, bar, gym, laundry service, concierge, parking (fee), no-smoking rooms* ▭ *AE, D, DC, MC, V* ✛ *4:F6.*

$$$$ ☷ **Hotel Palomar.** The top five floors of the green-tile 1908 Pacific Place Building offer a luxurious oasis above the busiest part of town. A softly lit lounge area with plush sofas gives way to the high-end, newly renovated Fifth Floor restaurant-café, renowned for its adventurous French cuisine. Rooms have muted alligator-pattern carpeting, drapes with bold navy-and-cream stripes, Frette linens, flat-screen TVs, and sleek furniture echoing a 1930s sensibility. Sparkling bathrooms provide a decadent "tub menu" of L'Occitane herbal/ botanical infusions for optimal relaxation. In-room spa services such as massage, manicures, and body wraps are facilitated through the Relax and Rejuvenate Spa. **Pros:** in-room spa service available, first-class restaurant, good location, refuge from downtown. **Cons:** pricey. ⊠ *12 4th St., SoMa* ☏ *415/348–1111 or 866/373–4941* ⊕ *www.hotelpalomar-sf.com* ⇲ *185 rooms, 13 suites* ☖ *In-room: safe, DVD, Wi-Fi. In-hotel: restaurant, room service, bar, gym, laundry service, concierge, public Internet, public Wi-Fi, parking (fee), some pets allowed, no-smoking rooms* ▭ *AE, D, DC, MC, V* ✛ *4:G5.*

$$$$ 🏨 **Hotel Vitale.** "Luxury, naturally,"
☾ the theme of this eight-story terraced bay-front hotel, is apparent in
every thoughtful detail: little vases
of aromatic herbs mounted outside
each room; the penthouse day spa
with soaking tubs set in a rooftop
bamboo forest; the aromatherapy
garden off the patio of restaurant
Americano, whose outdoor terrace
is packed Thursday and Friday;
the complimentary newspaper and
yoga-stretch classes available each
morning. Handsome rooms have
440-thread-count sheets, twice-
daily maid service, limestone-lined
baths, and views of the Bay Bridge,
Embarcadero, Treasure Island, or
the city skyline. Wi-Fi and LCD

WORD OF MOUTH

"We stayed at the Hotel Vitale
and LOVED the location. Breakfast
each morning in the ferry building across the road, drinks in the
evening at the ferry building or
in our hotel bar, across the road
from a great spot for our morning run along the waterfront,
complimentary yoga one morning,
great restaurants within walking
distance each evening and steps
from public transport. Without a
doubt, next time we stay in SF, we
would stay in this area again and
at the Vitale." —CaptCanuck

flat-screen TVs keep businesspeople in the loop, and spacious family studios have two sofa beds curtained off from the main sleeping
area. **Pros:** family-friendly studios, great views, recently renovated spa,
luxurious amenities throughout. **Cons:** cramped rooms can be noisy,
some guests report inconsistent service from staff and find the hotel
pricey. ⊠ *8 Mission St., Embarcadero* ☎ *415/278–3700 or 888/890–
8688* ⊕ *www.hotelvitale.com* ⌁ *190 rooms, 9 suites* ⌂ *In-room: safe,
refrigerator, Internet, Wi-Fi. In-hotel: restaurant, room service, bar,
gym, spa, laundry service, concierge, public Internet, public Wi-Fi,
parking (fee), some pets allowed, no-smoking rooms* ▤ *AE, D, DC,
MC, V* ⏻ *EP* ✦ *1:G4.*

$$$$ 🏨 **InterContinental San Francisco.** The arctic-blue glass exterior and sub-
Fodor'sChoice dued, Zen-like lobby of this sparkling new hotel may be as bland as
★ an airport concourse, but it's merely a prelude to the spectacularly
light, expansive, thoughtfully laid-out guest rooms, which have all the
ultramodern conveniences. Within shouting distance of the Moscone
Center, the hotel's business is geared toward convention and corporate travelers, which, depending on occupancy, can make for lower
rates on weekends. Bar 888 specializes in vintage grappas, and Luce
Restaurant, trimmed in iridescent black mosaic, serves Italian/Califor-
nia cuisine. The quiet Club Lounge offers hot breakfast, tasty snacks,
sandwiches, beverages, desserts, plus access to computer terminals and
a pleasant outdoor terrace. Be aware: the hotel, which opened February 2008, is located in a so-called transitional neighborhood. Stick to
4th Street and walk a couple of blocks to BART, shopping, or museums. **Pros:** a stone's throw from the Moscone Center, well-equipped
gym, near hip clubs and edgy eateries, perfect for a weekend getaway.
Cons: conservative decor is a bit short on character, borders a rough
neighborhood, a bit far from many major points of interest for tourists.
⊠ *888 Howard St., SoMa* ☎ *415/616–6500 or 888/811–4273* ⊕ *www.
intercontinentalsanfrancisco.com* ⌁ *536 rooms, 14 suites* ⌂ *In-room:*

InterContinental San Francisco

Palace Hotel

Hotel Adagio

safe, refrigerator, Wi-Fi. In hotel: restaurant, room service, bar, pool, gym, spa, laundry service, concierge, public Wi-Fi, parking (fee), some pets allowed, no-smoking rooms ⊟ *AE, D, DC, MC, V* ⊹ *4:H6.*

$–$$ ⊡ **The Mosser.** Originally built by patron of the arts Alice Phelan in 1913 as the Keystone, this property was purchased in 1981 by composer Charles W. Mosser and completely renovated in 2003. The result is a compatible pairing of contemporary decor and original Victorian architectural elements. Recent upgrades include the newly replaced elevator, double-pane windows, and flat-screen TVs. A musical motif extends throughout: Studio Paradiso, which offers state-of-the-art recording equipment and expert technical staff, is next door, and handsomely framed lithographs of recording equipment hang on the walls of the rooms. Tastefully decorated in geometrical patterns of either olive-green or dusty fuchsia, 75% of the rooms have tiled private baths with deep tubs, and 25% offer clean, convenient shared facilities on each floor. Annabelle's Bar & Bistro serves contemporary California-style cuisine for lunch and dinner. Ask for special rates at this convenient, stylish, family-owned hotel. **Pros:** convenient location. **Cons:** a quarter of the rooms are without private baths. ⊠ *54 4th St., SoMa* ☎ *415/986–4400 or 800/227–3804* ⊕ *www.themosser.com* ⟿ *166 rooms, 112 with private baths, 54 with shared bath* ⌂ *In-room: Wi-Fi (fee). In-hotel: restaurant, bar, laundry service, concierge, parking (fee), no-smoking rooms* ⊟ *AE, D, DC, MC, V* ⊹ *4:G5.*

$$$$ ⊡ **Palace Hotel.** "Majestic" is the word that best sums up this landmark
Fodor'sChoice hotel, which was the world's largest and most luxurious when it opened
★ in 1875. It was completely rebuilt after the 1906 earthquake and fire, and the carriage entrance reemerged as the grand Garden Court restaurant. Today the hotel is still graced with architectural details that recall a bygone era, like chandeliers; tall, mirrored glass doors; and eight pairs of turn-of-the-century, bronze-filigreed marble columns supporting a magnificent dome ceiling filtering natural light; it's a refined environment ideally suited for the high tea served on weekends and daily during holiday periods. Rooms, with twice-daily maid service and nightly turndown, have soaring 14-foot ceilings, traditional mahogany furnishings, flat-screen TVs, and marble bathrooms. The wood-panel Pied Piper Bar is named after the delightful 1909 Maxfield Parrish mural behind the bar. **Pros:** gracious service, close to Union Square, near BART. **Cons:** older design, small rooms with even smaller baths, many nearby establishments closed on weekends, west-facing rooms can be warm and stuffy. ⊠ *2 New Montgomery St., SoMa* ☎ *415/512–1111 or 888/627–7196* ⊕ *www.sfpalace.com* ⟿ *518 rooms, 34 suites* ⌂ *In-room: safe, refrigerator, Internet. In-hotel: 3 restaurants, room service, bar, pool, gym, laundry service, concierge, public Wi-Fi, parking (fee), no-smoking rooms* ⊟ *AE, D, DC, MC, V* ⊹ *1:E5.*

$$$ ⊡ **Pickwick.** This terra-cotta-clad neo-Gothic hotel, built in 1926, is decked out with a can't-miss-it, seven-story corner sign straight out of film noir. Next door to the Westfield San Francisco Centre, which houses Bloomingdale's and Nordstrom, and convenient to Moscone Center, Yerba Buena District, and Union Square, the hotel caters to both business and leisure travelers. Some rooms have flat-screen TVs.

Little Joe's offers Italian cuisine as well a traditional breakfast and lunch. Courteous multilingual staff and 24-hour concierge service offer welcome assistance. Café Venue next door serves breakfast and lunch. **Pros:** multilingual staff, helpful concierge, close to Yerba Buena District. **Cons:** not as opulent as some other options, some rooms dark and on the small side. ⊠ *85 5th St., SoMa* ☎ *415/421–7500 or 800/227–3282* ⊕ *www.thepickwickhotel.com* ⊅ *187 rooms, 2 suites* ♿ *In-room: refrigerator (some), Wi-Fi. In-hotel: restaurant, bar, laundry service, concierge, public Wi-Fi, parking (fee), no-smoking rooms* ⊟ *AE, D, DC, MC, V* ✛ *4:G6.*

$$$$ 🏨 **The St. Regis Hotel, San Francisco.** This may be the most luxurious hotel in the city. Guests often remark that it's hipper and more modern than other hotels in the St. Regis chain, though the decor is still conservative: Rooms have subdued cream-color, leather-texture walls and window seats, and 85% have views of the city. The 42-inch plasma-screen TVs and cordless remotes handle everything from raising the motorized window shades to controlling the entertainment systems to providing weather and other electronic information. Rooms also have Bose sound systems, a copier/fax/printer combo, and direct phone lines. Baths, with limestone tiling and TVs, have deep soaking tubs and separate showers with shower heads that rain straight down. All suites and some rooms have 24-hour butler service. The two-level spa has nine treatment rooms, and the area around the 50-foot lap pool, filled with natural light and bubbling water sounds, is a stunning essay in bright white: a Jacuzzi and sauna are in the immaculate dressing area. The showplace lobby has an elegant bar, restaurant, and a 16-foot-long, two-sided open fireplace. **Pros:** stunning, newly furnished rooms; good location; views. **Cons:** expensive, some guests report inconsistent service, hallway noise, long waits for room service and valet parking, some rooms and baths are on the small side. ⊠ *125 3rd St., SoMa* ☎ *415/284–4000* ⊕ *www.stregis.com/sanfrancisco* ⊅ *214 rooms, 46 suites* ♿ *In-room: safe, refrigerator, DVD, Internet, Wi-Fi. In-hotel: 2 restaurants, room service, bar, pool, gym, spa, laundry service, concierge, public Internet, public Wi-Fi, parking (fee), some pets allowed (fee), no-smoking rooms* ⊟ *AE, D, DC, MC, V* 🍽 *EP* ✛ *4:H4.*

$$$–$$$$ 🏨 **W San Francisco.** The epitome of cool urban chic and fashion forward in design and clientele, this swanky 31-story Starwood hotel owes some of its cachet to a prime location next door to the San Francisco Museum of Modern Art. The hotel is infused with hip energy: techno-pop pulses in the lobby and café, and otherworldly mobiles (which change with the seasons) hang overhead; add the mauve leather ottomans and blue velvet sofas to the mix, and you have a cross between a fashion-show runway and a stage set. Compact guest rooms, some of which have upholstered window seats, come with flat-screen TVs, luxurious beds, comfy pillow-top mattresses, and goose-down comforters and pillows. Sleek baths sport green glass countertops and shiny steel sinks. The glass-roof pool and hot-tub area, next to Bliss Spa, is open 24/7, as is the Whatever/Whenever concierge desk in the lobby. In the evening there's a lively bar scene, and the lobby, lit by candlelight, sets the mood for XYZ, the hotel's signature restaurant, an "in spot" which

14

attracts celebs such as Sharon Stone and Kanye West. Upper floors boast excellent views of the Museum of Modern Art, Yerba Buena Gardens, and/or the Bay Bridge. During the week the majority of the guests are businesspeople, but on weekends the hotel is kid-friendly, and pets are always welcome. The accommodating staff will help parents arrange for babysitting and will take your pup for a walk. Fragrances waft throughout the hotel and guest rooms, so sensitive noses should call ahead to request special preparations. **Pros:** hip energy, mod, sophisticated digs, in the heart of the cultural district. **Cons:** three blocks from BART, hotel's signature scents could pose a problem for sensitive noses. ⊠ *181 3rd St., SoMa* ☎ *415/777–5300* ⊕ *www.whotels.com/sf* ⟋ *404 rooms, 9 suites* ⌂ *In-room: safe, refrigerator, DVD, Internet, Wi-Fi. In-hotel: restaurant, room service, bar, pool, gym, spa, laundry service, concierge, public Internet, public Wi-Fi, parking (fee), some pets allowed (fee), no-smoking rooms* ▤ *AE, D, DC, MC, V* ✛ *1:F6.*

$$$$ 🖫 **Westin San Francisco Market Street.** Rising 36 stories over the bustling downtown and SoMa areas, this hotel (formerly the Argent) revels in its views. Bright, airy rooms have floor-to-ceiling windows. Floors 16 to 34 overlook Yerba Buena Gardens, the city, bay, and the hills beyond; others peer between the tall looming edifices of the Financial District (though some of these also glimpse the Golden Gate Bridge, the bay, or Alcatraz). Back on earth, the inlaid marble lobby is home to Ducca, a restaurant with an outdoor eating area adjacent to a landscaped piazza and the new Contemporary Jewish Museum. The hotel recently remodeled its guest rooms (adding Westin's Heavenly beds), expanded its meeting space, and added an outdoor dining and lounge space with fire pit. A room with a treadmill or stationary bike is available. **Pros:** good location, clean rooms. **Cons:** some street noise, lots of convention/corporate business. ⊠ *50 3rd St., SoMa* ☎ *415/974–6400 or 877/222–6699* ⊕ *www.westin.com* ⟋ *641 rooms, 26 suites* ⌂ *In-room: safe, refrigerator (some), Internet, Wi-Fi. In-hotel: restaurant, room service, bar, gym, laundry service, concierge, public Wi-Fi, parking (fee), no-smoking rooms* ▤ *AE, D, DC, MC, V* ✛ *1:E6.*

UNION SQUARE/DOWNTOWN

$ 🖫 **Andrews Hotel.** Two blocks west of Union Square, this Queen Anne–style abode began its life in 1904 as the Sultan Turkish Baths. The lobby is dominated by a huge Elliott grandfather clock and the original cage-style elevator. Rooms and bathrooms are small, but well decorated with Victorian reproductions, old-fashioned flower curtains with lace sheers, iron bedsteads, ceiling fans, and large closets. Complimentary wine is served each evening in the lobby. Fino, the hotel restaurant, has been praised for its pizza and spaghetti carbonara. **Pros:** intimate, decor has character, moderately priced. **Cons:** smallish rooms and baths. ⊠ *624 Post St., Union Square* ☎ *415/563–6877 or 800/926–3739* ⊕ *www. andrewshotel.com* ⟋ *48 rooms, 5 suites* ⌂ *In-room: no a/c, DVD, Wi-Fi. In-hotel: restaurant, laundry service, public Internet, parking (fee), no-smoking rooms* ▤ *AE, DC, MC, V* ⅋◎ *CP* ✛ *4:D3.*

$$$$ 🖫 **Campton Place.** Aesthetic beauty and highly attentive service remain the hallmarks of this exquisite jewel-like, top-tier hotel. Fresh-cut

orchids and Japanese floral arrangements bring natural beauty inside, where you'll feel sheltered from the teeming crowds on the street. Rooms can be small but are well laid out and elegantly decorated in a contemporary Italian style, with sandy earth tones and handsome pearwood paneling and cabinetry. Limestone baths have deep soaking tubs; double-pane windows keep city noises at bay, a plus in this active neighborhood. The Campton Place Restaurant, whose new East Indian chef serves French-infused contemporary cuisine at dinner, is famed for its lavish breakfasts. The lounge is a popular cocktail-hour hangout for the downtown crowd. **Pros:** attentive service, first-class restaurant, abundant natural light. **Cons:** smallish rooms, pricey (but worth it). ⊠ *340 Stockton St., Union Square* ☎ *415/781–5555 or 866/332–1670* ⊕ *www.camptonplace.com* ☞ *101 rooms, 9 suites* �110 *In-room: safe, DVD, Wi-Fi. In-hotel: restaurant, room service, bar, gym, laundry service, concierge, public Wi-Fi, parking (fee), some pets allowed (fee), no-smoking rooms* ▭ *AE, D, DC, MC, V* ✛ *4:G3.*

14

$–$$ **Chancellor Hotel on Union Square.** Built to accommodate visitors to the 1915 Panama Pacific International Exposition, this busy hotel is considered by many to be one of the best bets on Union Square for comfort without extravagance. Floor-to-ceiling windows in the modest lobby overlook cable cars on Powell Street. The moderate-size Edwardian-style rooms, some with huge walk-in closets, have high ceilings, and were recently remodeled. Though a bit dated, the small, clean bathrooms have deep tubs—rubber ducky included. The pleasant Restaurant Luques serves American breakfast and lunch, and complimentary coffee, tea, apples, and cookies are available round-the-clock in the lobby. **Pros:** huge walk-in closets, great value for Union Square, clean rooms. **Cons:** older building with dark hallways and rooms, small bathrooms, noise from cable cars. ⊠ *433 Powell St., Union Square* ☎ *415/362–2004 or 800/428–4748* ⊕ *www.chancellorhotel.com* ☞ *135 rooms, 2 suites* �110 *In-room: no a/c, safe, Wi-Fi. In-hotel: restaurant, room service, bar, laundry service, concierge, public Internet, public Wi-Fi, parking (fee), no-smoking rooms* ▭ *AE, D, DC, MC, V* ✛ *4:F3.*

$$$$ **Clift.** A favorite of hipsters, music industry types, and celebrities fleeing the media onslaught—security discreetly keeps photographers and other heat-seekers away—this sexy hotel, whose entrance is so nondescript you can walk right past it without a hint of what's inside, is the brainchild of entrepreneur Ian Schrager and artist-designer Philippe Starck, known for his collection of eccentric chairs. The moody, dramatically illuminated lobby is dominated by a gigantic Napoleonic chair that could accommodate Shrek, with room to spare. This theatrical staging is enhanced by surreal seating options like a leather love seat with buffalo tusks and a miniature "drink me" chair, all surrounding a floor-to-ceiling, pitch-black fireplace. Spacious rooms—as light as the lobby is darkly intriguing—have translucent orange Plexiglas tables, high ceilings, flat-screen TVs, and two huge "infinity" wall mirrors. Some visitors have remarked on the thin walls and advise booking a room on an upper-level floor to avoid street noise. The art-deco Redwood Room bar, paneled with wood from a 2,000-year-old tree, is known for its "beautiful people." Asia de Cuba restaurant prepares an

artful fusion of Asian and Latino cuisines. **Pros:** good rates compared to similar top-tier hotels in SF, surreal moody interior design, ideal location for shopping and theaters, close to public transportation, discreet and helpful staff. **Cons:** some guests note thin walls, street noise. ⊠ *495 Geary St., Union Square* ☎ *415/775–4700 or 800/606–6090* ⊕ *www.clifthotel.com* ⇨ *337 rooms, 26 suites* ⚭ *In-room: safe, Internet, Wi-Fi. In-hotel: restaurant, room service, bar, gym, laundry service, concierge, public Internet, parking (fee), some pets allowed (fee), no-smoking rooms* ▭ *AE, D, DC, MC, V* ✛ *4:D4.*

$　▦ **Cornell Hotel de France.** Discovering this French family-operated hotel is like finding a bit of Paris near Union Square. Charming hosts Claude and Micheline Lambert arrived from their native Orléans 40 years ago, and over the years have renovated and decorated each room with prints of paintings by Picasso, Chagall, and Gustav Klimt. Many savvy repeat visitors know to ask about special packages and discounted rates. Downstairs, Restaurant Jeanne d'Arc offers classic French cuisine in a medieval scene set off by stained-glass windows and artifacts depicting—who else?—Joan of Arc. **Pros:** special packages and discounts available upon request, a little bit of France in SF. **Cons:** several blocks from the center of things, surrounding area can be dodgy after dark. ⊠ *715 Bush St., Union Square* ☎ *415/421–3154 or 800/232–9698* ⊕ *www.cornellhotel.com* ⇨ *55 rooms* ⚭ *In-room: no a/c, safe, Wi-Fi. In-hotel: restaurant, public Wi-Fi, parking (fee), no-smoking rooms* ▭ *AE, D, DC, MC, V* � ⧉❙ *BP* ✛ *4:F2.*

$–$$　▦ **Golden Gate Hotel.** Families looking for accommodations in the Union
☾　Square area will delight in this homey, family-run B&B. Built in 1913, the four-story Edwardian building has front and back bay windows and an original "birdcage" elevator that transports you to hallways lined with nostalgic historical photographs. Freshly painted and carpeted guest rooms are decorated with antiques, wicker pieces, and Laura Ashley bedding and curtains. Fourteen rooms have private baths, some with claw-foot tubs. Sit in the cozy parlor by the fire and savor afternoon tea and homemade cookies. **Pros:** friendly staff, spotless rooms, comfortable bedding, good location if you're a walker. **Cons:** only half of the rooms have private baths. ⊠ *775 Bush St., Union Square* ☎ *415/392–3702 or 800/835–1118* ⊕ *www.goldengatehotel.com* ⇨ *25 rooms, 14 with bath* ⚭ *In-room: no a/c, Internet, Wi-Fi. In-hotel: concierge, public Internet, parking (fee), some pets allowed, no-smoking rooms* ▭ *AE, DC, MC, V* ⧉❙ *CP* ✛ *4:E2.*

$$$　▦ **Hilton San Francisco.** With 1,908 renovated rooms and suites, this is the largest hotel on the West Coast—its lobby can sometimes feel like downtown at rush hour. Its silvery tower rises 46 floors to a penthouse event space with awe-inspiring 360-degree panoramic views that rank among the finest in San Francisco. Handsome rooms, many with balconies and superlative views of their own, are either in the original 16-story building or in the tower, which was built in 1971. Accommodations on the 44th floor afford the most stunning views of the city and the bay. Seventy-eight ADA compliant rooms have roll-in showers. Thirty-five executive cabana-style rooms surround a sheltered courtyard by an outdoor heated swimming pool and whirlpool. "Sight and

Sound" guest rooms feature plasma televisions and custom connectivity panels for digital cameras, iPods, and video downloads. In 2008 the hotel added 13,600 square feet of event space; a Starbucks; and a new restaurant, Urban Tavern, a place to enjoy a community table, charcuterie, and a simple menu. A full-service spa, bars, and shops are also on the premises. As the hotel is located near the sometimes-dicey Tenderloin area, guests are directed toward Union Square (two blocks away) when venturing out on foot after dark. **Pros:** super views, excellent service, full-service spa. **Cons:** area is dodgy after dark, there can be a wait at check-in. ✉ *333 O'Farrell St., Union Square* ☎ *415/771–1400* ⊕ *www.hiltonsanfranciscohotel.com* ⌕ *1,824 rooms, 84 suites* ♿ *In-room: safe, refrigerator, DVD (some). In-hotel: restaurant, room service, bars, pool, gym, spa, laundry service, concierge, public Wi-Fi, parking (fee), no-smoking rooms* ⊟ *AE, D, DC, MC, V* ♦ *4:E5.*

14

$$ 🛏 **Hotel Abri.** The Larkspur Hotel Collection has renovated the former Monticello Inn into a stylish, affordable hotel near Union Square shops, theaters, and restaurants. Most rooms are small but well appointed, with flat-screen TVs, iPod docking stations, comfy bedding, and L'Occitane bath products. The lobby has a modern feel, with recessed fireplace, and warm wood and stainless steel accents. Puccini & Pinetti, an Italian restaurant next to the hotel, provides a lively bar scene. Free gym facilities are available a block away at Abri's sister hotel, Villa Florence. Despite its neighborhood designation, the hotel is closer to the seedy Tenderloin than the upscale Union Square. Free morning coffee and newspapers are available in lobby. **Pros:** free Wi-Fi; shouting distance from the cable-car turnaround, shops, and eateries. **Cons:** slightly sketchy area after dark, most rooms have showers only, on-street parking nearly impossible. ✉ *127 Ellis St., Union Square* ☎ *866/823–4669 or 415/392–8800* ⊕ *www.hotel-abri.com* ⌕ *63 rooms, 28 suites* ♿ *In-room: safe, refrigerator, DVD (some), Wi-Fi. In-hotel: restaurant, room service, bar, laundry service, public Internet, public Wi-Fi, parking (fee), some pets allowed* ⊟ *AE, D, DC, MC, V* ♦ *4:E5.*

$$$$ 🛏 **Hotel Adagio.** The gracious, Spanish-colonial facade of this 16-story,
Fodor's Choice theater-row hotel complements its chic, modern interior. Walnut furni-
★ ture, bronze light fixtures, and brown and deep orange hues dominate the decent-size, updated rooms, half of which have city views; two penthouse suites have terraces overlooking the neighborhood. The airy lobby lounge was newly redone. **Pros:** close to theater district, on a bus route, good on-site restaurant. **Cons:** street noise, side streets can be dodgy at night. ✉ *550 Geary St., Union Square* ☎ *415/775–5000 or 800/228–8830* ⊕ *www.thehoteladagio.com* ⌕ *169 rooms, 2 suites* ♿ *In-room: safe, refrigerator, Wi-Fi. In-hotel: room service, bar, gym, laundry service, public Internet, public Wi-Fi, parking (fee), no-smoking rooms* ⊟ *AE, D, DC, MC, V* ♦ *4:D4.*

$–$$ 🛏 **Hotel Beresford.** This relatively inexpensive hotel is less than two blocks from Union Square. Well-maintained rooms with traditional furniture have clean, bright bathrooms. The friendly staff assists with sightseeing arrangements, and the front desk has a large video library. **Pros:** reasonably priced, close to Union Square, friendly staff. **Cons:** no a/c, no in-room Internet access. ✉ *635 Sutter St., Union Square* ☎ *415/673–9900* *or 800/533–6533* ⊕ *www.beresford.com* ↘ *114 rooms* ᗘ *In-room: no a/c, refrigerator. In-hotel: bar, laundry service, concierge, public Internet, public Wi-Fi, parking (fee), some pets allowed, no-smoking rooms* ⊟ *AE, D, DC, MC, V* ⦿ *CP* ✢ *4:D3.*

$–$$ **Hotel Beresford Arms.** Surrounded by fancy molding and 10-foot-tall ⟳   windows, the red-carpet lobby of this ornate brick Victorian explains why the building is on the National Register of Historic Places. Rooms with dark-wood antique-reproduction furniture vary in size and setup: junior suites have sitting areas and either a wet bar or kitchenette; full suites have two queen beds, a Murphy bed, and a kitchen. All suites have a bidet in the bathroom. Continental breakfast, afternoon tea, and wine are served beneath a crystal chandelier in the lobby. **Pros:** moderately priced, suites with kitchenettes and Murphy beds are a plus for families with kids. **Cons:** no a/c. ⊠ *701 Post St., Union Square* ☎ *415/673–2600 or 800/533–6533* ⊕ *www.beresford.com* ↘ *83 rooms, 12 suites* ᗘ *In-room: no a/c, kitchen (some), refrigerator, VCR, Wi-Fi. In-hotel: laundry service, concierge, public Internet, public Wi-Fi, parking (fee), some pets allowed, no-smoking rooms* ⊟ *AE, D, DC, MC, V* ⦿ *CP* ✢ *4:C3.*

$–$$ **Hotel Bijou.** Dedicated to the city's cinematic history, this hotel's tasteful lobby is filled with black-and-white photographs of local movie houses and reproductions of Tamara De Lempicka's art-deco paintings. Each night the red-velvet curtains of the hotel's twenty-seat 1930s "movie palace," Le Petit Théâtre Bijou, open for guests-only shows, complimentary screenings of films shot on location in San Francisco; classic noirs such as *The Maltese Falcon* have been on the bill. Smallish but cheerful rooms are decorated with black-and-white movie stills. The convenience of this downtown location is offset by the proximity to the Tenderloin. **Pros:** near downtown, free nightly movies. **Cons:** close to the Tenderloin, small rooms. ⊠ *111 Mason St., at Eddy St., Union Square* ☎ *415/771–1200 or 800/771–1022* ⊕ *www.hotelbijou. com* ↘ *65 rooms* ᗘ *In-room: no a/c, Wi-Fi. In-hotel: laundry service, concierge, public Internet, public Wi-Fi, parking (fee), no-smoking rooms* ⊟ *AE, D, DC, MC, V* ⦿ *CP* ✢ *4:E5.*

$–$$ **Hotel des Arts.** You'll need to climb a narrow, nondescript staircase to discover this hotel, which doubles as an art gallery. The hallways and rooms of this small, funky property have been transformed by international artists, who painted the walls and installed site-specific small sculptures. Check the Web site to scope out the painted rooms; specific ones can be reserved by phone. The exhibited art is constantly rotating, so you can also let serendipity be your guide. If you're looking for a cool souvenir of your stay, select small paintings in the hallways are available for purchase. **Pros:** art-gallery atmosphere, good location. **Cons:** only about half of the rooms have private baths. ⊠ *447 Bush St., Union Square* ☎ *415/956–3232 or 800/956–4322* ⊕ *sfhoteldesarts.com* ↘ *43 rooms* ᗘ *In-room: refrigerator (some), Wi-Fi. In-hotel: parking (fee)* ⊟ *AE, D, DC, MC, V* ⦿ *CP* ✢ *4:H2.*

$$$–$$$$ **Hotel Diva.** Entering this hotel requires stepping over footprints, handprints, and autographs embedded into the sidewalk by visiting stars. With two major theaters, the Curran and Geary (home of the acclaimed

American Conservatory Theater company), just across the street, this hotel has long been a magnet for actors, musicians, writers, and artists. It's definitely a hip place, and the updated rooms, especially the suites, feel urban and modern. A new digital movie system plays on flat-screen TVs. Cobalt-blue carpets and brushed-steel headboards echoing the shape of ocean waves lend a nautical touch to the white-wall rooms, which have silver bedspreads and sleek steel light fixtures. Bathrooms are tiny but well equipped. A Starbucks and Colibri Mexican Bistro are in the lobby. **Pros:** clean, safe, in the heart of the theater district, accommodating service. **Cons:** no frills, tiny bathrooms. ⊠ *440 Geary St., Union Square* ☎ *415/885–0200 or 800/553–1900* ⊕ *www.hoteldiva. com* ⇱ *115 rooms, 1 suite* △ *In-room: safe, refrigerator (some), DVD (some), Wi-Fi. In-hotel: gym, laundry service, concierge, public Internet, public Wi-Fi, parking (fee), some pets allowed (fee), no-smoking rooms* ⊟ *AE, D, DC, MC, V* ⊠ *CP* ✛ *4:D4.*

14

$$$$ **Hotel Monaco.** A cheery 1910 Beaux Arts facade and snappily dressed
Fodor's Choice   doormen welcome you into a plush lobby dominated by a French ingle-
★   nook fireplace, vaulted ceilings painted with whimsical murals of hot-air balloons, a marble staircase, and a large metal baobab tree dedicated to hotelier Bill Kimpton. Rooms are strikingly decorated with vivid stripes and colors, Chinese-inspired armoires, canopy beds, and high-back upholstered chairs. Outer rooms feature bay-window seats overlooking the bustling theater district. If you didn't bring a pet, request a "companion goldfish." Guests have cheered the hotel's staff for its "amazing service" and "attention to detail" and praised the ornate Grand Café and Bar, which serves French/California cuisine. Take advantage of complimentary access to the recently redone Spa, where you can soak, steam, or bake to your heart's content from 6 AM to 10 PM. **Pros:** amazing service, stylish, full of character, near theater district, you're never alone when you have a goldfish to keep you company. **Cons:** close to the Tenderloin, some discount-rate rooms are small. ⊠ *501 Geary St., Union Square* ☎ *415/292–0100 or 800/214–4220* ⊕ *www.monaco-sf. com* ⇱ *181 rooms, 20 suites* △ *In-room: safe, DVD, Wi-Fi. In-hotel: restaurant, room service, bar, gym, spa, laundry service, concierge, public Internet, parking (fee), some pets allowed, no-smoking rooms* ⊟ *AE, D, DC, MC, V* ✛ *4:D4.*

$$$$ **Hotel Nikko.** The vast gray-flecked white marble and gurgling foun-
Fodor's Choice   tains in the neoclassical lobby of this business traveler hotel have the
★   sterility of an airport. Crisply designed rooms in muted tones have flat-screen TVs, modern bathrooms with sinks that sit on top of black vanities, and "in-vogue" separate showers and tubs. Some higher-end rooms come with complimentary breakfast. The excellent, 10,000-square-foot Club Nikko fitness facility has traditional *ofuros* (Japanese soaking tubs), his-and-her *kamaburso* (Japanese meditation rooms), and a glass-enclosed 16-meter rooftop pool and a whirlpool. The Rrazz Room, San Francisco's only cabaret theater, located on the lobby level, is a venue for national talent and nostalgia acts most evenings. **Pros:** friendly multilingual staff, some rooms have ultramodern baths, very clean. **Cons:** rooms and antiseptic lobby lack color, some may find the atmosphere cold, expensive parking. ⊠ *222 Mason St., Union Square*

☎ *415/394–1111 or 800/248–3308* ⊕ *www.hotelnikkosf.com* ↩ *510 rooms, 22 suites* ♿ *In-room: refrigerator, Internet, Wi-Fi. In-hotel: restaurant, room service, bar, pool, gym, laundry service, concierge, public Internet, public Wi-Fi, parking (fee), some pets allowed (fee), no-smoking rooms* ☐ *AE, D, DC, MC, V* ✛ *4:E5.*

$$$ ▣ **Hotel Rex.** If this stylish literary-theme hotel—named after San Francisco Renaissance poet, translator, and essayist Kenneth Rexroth and frequented by artists and writers—

WORD OF MOUTH

"From the moment the valet greets you as you pull up to the moment he hands you back the keys after you check out, Hotel Triton is top notch. Service is accommodating, attentive and personalized. I have stayed here over 30 times, each stay lasting one week. Each time, I feel like royalty."

—KWL

had a kindred spirit, it would The New Yorker magazine. Paintings and shelves of antiquarian books line the "library," a homey lobby lounge where book readings and roundtable discussions take place. Although the small, somewhat dark, cramped rooms with restored period furnishings and striped carpeting evoke the spirit of salon society—excerpts from historic San Francisco social registers paper the elevator—they also have modern touches like a study decorated with a collection of vintage typewriters (and two high-tech workstations). California seasonal cuisine is served in the hotel's petite bistro, Andrée. **Pros:** convenient location, literary pedigree. **Cons:** cramped airless rooms, tiny baths and closets, musty hallways. ✉ *562 Sutter St., Union Square* ☎ *415/433–4434 or 800/433–4434* ⊕ *www.thehotelrex.com* ↩ *92 rooms, 2 suites* ♿ *In-room: refrigerator, Wi-Fi. In-hotel: restaurant, room service, bar, laundry service, concierge, public Internet, parking (fee), some pets allowed, no-smoking rooms* ☐ *AE, D, DC, MC, V* ✛ *4:E3.*

$$–$$$$ ▣ **Hotel Triton.** The spirit of fun has taken up full-time residence in this Kimpton property, which has a youngish, super-friendly staff; pink and blue neon elevators; and a colorful psychedelic lobby mural depicting the San Francisco art and music scene—think flower power mixed with Andy Warhol. Playful furniture includes a green-and-gold metallic couch and striped carpeting, a whimsical and far-out setting for free morning coffee and tea, fresh afternoon cookies, evening wine events, and the on-call tarot reader. Smallish rooms are painted silver-gray and tomato-soup red and come with ergonomic desk chairs, flat-screen TVs, and oddball light fixtures; sinks are positioned outside the bathrooms, European style. Twenty-four "environmentally sensitive" rooms have water- and air-filtration systems and biodegradable soap. A 24-hour yoga channel will help you find that elusive path to inner peace. **Pros:** attentive service, refreshingly funky atmosphere, hip arty environs, good location. **Cons:** rooms and baths are on the small side. ✉ *342 Grant Ave., Union Square* ☎ *415/394–0500 or 800/433–6611* ⊕ *www.hoteltriton.com* ↩ *133 rooms, 7 suites* ♿ *In-room: refrigerator, Wi-Fi. In-hotel: gym, laundry service, parking (fee), some pets allowed, no-smoking rooms* ☐ *AE, D, DC, MC, V* ✛ *4:H2.*

$–$$$ ⚑ **Hotel Vertigo.** Hitchcock's classic thriller *Vertigo* was set and partially shot in this ornate hotel, which was a speakeasy during Prohibition. Kim Novak, who played the elusive Judy Barton in the film, actually stayed in Room 301 (though filming took place two floors up). Undergoing a major remodel that extends to guest rooms, meeting rooms, corridors, lounge, and lobby, the hotel's exterior and interior have been redesigned and built around the film. Although the block includes several apartment buildings, a fancy salon, and cafés, the neighborhood is a bit dicey, so exercise caution when walking here at night. **Pros:** tons of personality. **Cons:** borderline neighborhood, no a/c. ⊠ *940 Sutter St., between Leavenworth and Hyde Sts., Tenderloin* ☎ *415/885–6800 or 800/553–1900* ⊕ *www.hotelvertigosf.coml.com* ⌑ *102 rooms, 8 suites* ♿ *In-room: no a/c, safe, refrigerator, Internet, Wi-Fi. In-hotel: restaurant, laundry service, concierge, public Internet, parking (fee), no-smoking rooms* ▭ *AE, D, DC, MC, V* ✛ *4:B3.*

$$$–$$$$ ⚑ **JW Marriott San Francisco.** Guests here are whisked skyward in bullet elevators from the rose-and-gray-marble foyer into this John Portman–designed, former Pan Pacific hotel. A graceful Matisse-inspired bronze sculpture encircles the fountain in the dramatically reconfigured 21-story lobby atrium. Guest rooms have new gold, olive, and maroon bedding, flat-screen TVs, versatile desks for dining or working. Elegant bathrooms boast new vanities and deep soaking tubs, which many guests rave about. **Pros:** recently renovated, convenient location, large rooms, luxurious bathrooms. **Cons:** comfortable but lacking character. ⊠ *500 Post St., Union Square* ☎ *415/771–8600* ⊕ *jwmarriottunion-square.com* ⌑ *329 rooms, 8 suites* ♿ *In-room: safe, Internet (fee). In-hotel: restaurant, room service, bar, gym, laundry service, concierge, public Wi-Fi, parking (fee), some pets allowed (fee), no-smoking rooms* ▭ *AE, D, DC, MC, V* ✛ *4:E3.*

$$–$$$ ⚑ **Kensington Park Hotel.** Built in the1920s in a Moorish/Gothic style, this intimate boutique hotel, originally designed to house the city's Elks Club, has retained its distinctive period feel and features. The lobby is classically refined, with rich marble and dark-wood accents, crystal chandeliers, vaulted ceilings, and antique furnishings. Although the hotel completed a major renovation of its guest rooms in 2008, the upgrade didn't include the bathrooms, which are sparkling, but on the small side. All rooms have flat-screen TVs, lacquer desks, and art deco touches. Complimentary morning coffee and evening tea and sherry are served daily in the lobby. The upper floors, whose rooms are equipped with telescopes to take in the city views, are the quietest, as are accommodations facing away from the busy downtown street. What the hotel lacks in amenities, it more than makes up for in convenience and service. Some guests have commented that staying here is more like visiting a friend than being at a hotel. Plus, the location can't be beat: Union Square is right outside the door. **Pros:** friendly personal service; guests rave about great location. **Cons:** some rooms have street noise; standard rooms are on the smallish side. ⊠ *450 Post St., Union Square* ☎ *415/788–6400 or 800/553–1900* ⊕ *www.kensingtonparkhotel.com* ⌑ *92 rooms, 1 suite* ♿ *In-room: no a/c, Wi-Fi. In-hotel: 1 restaurant,*

14

Hotel Nikko

Orchard Hotel

Hotel Monaco

room service, bar, laundry service, public Internet, public Wi-Fi, parking (fee), some pets allowed ⊟*AE, D, DC, MC, V* ✛*4:E3.*

$$–$$$ 🖾 **Larkspur Union Square.** This compact boutique hotel, housed in a 1913 Edwardian building near Union Square, is now managed by the Larkspur Hotels and Restaurants. The newly refurbished lobby entry area and Bar 1915 update the premises while retaining the period feel. Rooms come with new FeatherBorne beds, Lather natural bath and body products, and flat-screen TVs. A computer and printer are available in the library. Guests receive a complimentary morning paper and are invited to a nightly wine reception in the lobby. A recent remodeling project updated all the rooms and suites, adding air conditioners and ADA rooms. Note that as this is a historic building, some rooms, especially double rooms, and baths can feel cramped and claustrophobic—but for travelers who want to be near Union Square, it's a relatively inexpensive option. **Pros:** good location, moderately priced, spacious closets, clean. **Cons:** airless rooms and hallways, small baths. ⊠ *524 Sutter St., Union Square* ☎ *415/421–2865 or 866/823–4669* ⊕ *www.larkspurhotels.com* ⬎ *109 rooms, 5 suites* ♿ *In-room: Wi-Fi. In-hotel: laundry service, concierge, public Wi-Fi, parking (fee), some pets allowed, no-smoking rooms* ⊟*AE, D, DC, MC, V* 🍽⊪*BP* ✛ *4:F3.*

$$$–$$$$ 🖾 **Orchard Garden Hotel.** Feel virtuous and environmentally sensitive at the first San Francisco hotel built to environmentally stringent LEED specifications, exacting standards which mandate the use of eco-friendly features such as chemical-free cleaning agents, recycling bins, and a custom guest-room key card energy-control system. Local artist Archie Held's glass water sculpture in the lobby sets the stage for the hotel's high aesthetics. Highlights of the hotel include junior terrace rooms with private outdoor space and views of downtown, and a rooftop deck open to all guests, who are invited to bring their own refreshments and take in the sweeping views of the city. The owner's collection of original artwork is scattered throughout the hotel and rooftop garden. Amenities include complimentary car service to the Financial District. Buffet breakfast, as well as lunch and dinner, can be enjoyed at Roots restaurant, which is supplied by organic and local purveyors. The simply styled rooms offer low-flow toilets, textiles in soothing hues of green and gold, and natural woods. **Pros:** environmentally sensitive. **Cons:** a bit of a hike from Union Square. ⊠ *446 Bush St., Union Square* ☎ *415/399–9807 or 888/717–2881* ⊕ *www.theorchardgardenhotel.com* ⬎ *86 rooms* ♿ *In-room: safe, refrigerator, DVD, Wi-Fi. In-hotel: restaurant, concierge, parking (fee)* ⊟*AE, D, DC, V, MC* 🍽⊪*BP* ✛ *4:H2.*

$$$–$$$$ 🖾 **Orchard Hotel.** Unlike most other boutique hotels in the area, which
Fodor's Choice ★ sometimes occupy century-old buildings, the strictly-21st-century Orchard was built in 2000. The 104-room hotel embraces state-of-the-art technology—from CD and DVD players in each room to Wi-Fi access throughout the building—mixing cutting-edge Silicon Valley chic with classic European touches. The hotel's marble lobby, where the bronze statue *Spring Awakening* greets visitors, previews the dramatic architectural embellishments, like arched openings, vaulted ceilings, and stone floors that are found throughout the hotel. With just 12 rooms per floor, the hotel feels quite intimate; some guests have compared it

14

to a cozy (decidedly upscale) mountain inn. Rooms, sizable by boutique hotel standards, are done in a soft palette of relaxing colors, a balm for harried shoppers returning from a busy day of retail therapy in Union Square. The hotel's restaurant, Daffodil, serves seasonal California fare for breakfast and dinner. Like its "green sister," the Orchard Garden, this hotel has also received LEED certification (the only one in SF) giving SF visitors yet another eco-friendly option. **Pros:** cutting-edge technology. **Cons:** can be a bit pricey. ⊠ *665 Bush St., Union Square* ☏ *415/362–8878 or 888/717–2881* ⊕ *www.theorchardhotel. com* ⪥ *104 rooms, 9 suites* ⚭ *In-room: safe, DVD, Wi-Fi. In-hotel: restaurant, room service, laundry service, parking (fee), some pets allowed, no-smoking rooms* ⊟ *AE, D, DC, MC, V* ⊹ *4:F2.*

$$$ 🔅 **Phoenix Hotel.** From the piped-in, poolside jungle beat to the trendy Bambuddha restaurant-lounge's bamboo furnishings and Southeast Asian menu, the Phoenix (a riff on a classic 1950s Miami Beach motel) evokes a kitschy dream of the tropics. It's a magnet for the hip at heart and ultracool—Little Richard, Elijah Wood, Sean Lennon, and members of R.E.M. and Pearl Jam have stayed here—so it's not the best choice for those seeking peace and quiet (or anyone put off by the hotel's location, on the fringes of the sketchy Tenderloin District). All suites, deluxe, and superior rooms and baths have been completely redone; the simple accommodations—decorated with bamboo furniture, batik-print bedspreads, and original pieces by local artists—face the courtyard, an azure blue–tile pool, and a sculpture garden, where a free continental breakfast is served. The friendly staff is as groovy and hip as you'd expect. **Pros:** Boho atmosphere, popular with musicians. **Cons:** somewhat seedy location, no elevators. ⊠ *601 Eddy St., Tenderloin* ☏ *415/776–1380 or 800/248–9466* ⊕ *www.thephoenixhotel.com* ⪥ *41 rooms, 3 suites* ⚭ *In-room: no a/c, refrigerator (some), DVD (some), Wi-Fi. In-hotel: restaurant, bar, pool, no elevator, laundry service, concierge, public Wi-Fi, parking (no fee), no-smoking rooms* ⊟ *AE, D, DC, MC, V* ⍐ *CP* ⊹ *4:A6.*

$$$–$$$$ 🔅 **Prescott Hotel.** This relatively small establishment providing extremely personalized service prides itself on offering "good taste on Union Square." One guest described the hotel as making "you feel welcomed at every point of your stay." The casual Postrio café-bar offers three-cheese pizza, delectable sandwiches, and soups. The rooms, which were renovated in 2001, are filled with cherry furniture and are handsomely decorated in dark autumn colors; the bathrooms have marble-top sinks. Free coffee in the morning and wine in the evening are offered every day by a flickering fireplace in the living room. Executive Club Level rooms include a free continental breakfast and afternoon cocktails with Puck's pizza in the private Executive Club Level lounge. **Pros:** good location; excellent café and bar, and restaurant is top-notch, too. **Cons:** off-site valet service can be slow, some guests complain of street noise. ⊠ *545 Post St., Union Square* ☏ *415/563–0303 or 866/271–3632* ⊕ *www. prescotthotel.com* ⪥ *132 rooms, 32 suites* ⚭ *In-room: safe, Wi-Fi. In-hotel: restaurant, room service, bar, gym, concierge, public Internet, public Wi-Fi, parking (fee), some pets allowed, no-smoking rooms* ⊟ *AE, D, DC, MC, V* ⊹ *4:D4.*

$$–$$$ **Sir Francis Drake Hotel.** Beefeater-costumed doormen welcome you into the regal, dimly lighted and slightly run-down lobby of this 1928 landmark property, decked out with boldly striped banners, wrought-iron balustrades, chandeliers, Italian marble, and leather and velvet furnishings that are a little on the tired side. The cumulative effect is of a Scottish castle that's seen better days. The guest rooms, bathrooms, public spaces, gym, and meeting rooms are somewhat shopworn or downright shabby despite a $27-million renovation that added new carpeting, bedding, bathroom tiles, and the Bar Drake in the lobby. Be advised: service can be unresponsive. The trade-off is a first-rate location and an establishment steeped in history, including Harry Denton's Starlight Room, on the hotel's top floor. A tribute to faded 1920s glory, it's one of the city's best-known skyline bars. The hotel's surprisingly affordable restaurant, Scala's Bistro, serves better-than-average food in its somewhat noisy bi-level dining room. **Pros:** can't beat the location, free in-room Wi-Fi, on-site restaurant and bar are moderately priced. **Cons:** small baths and dated rooms, lobby furniture looks a bit tired, some complaints about unresponsive service and cleanliness. ⌂ *450 Powell St., Union Square* ☎ *415/392–7755 or 800/795–7129* ⊕ *www.sirfrancisdrake.com* ⬐ *390 rooms, 20 suites* ⌂ *In-room: DVD, Wi-Fi. In-hotel: restaurant, room service, bar, gym, laundry service, concierge, public Internet, parking (fee), some pets allowed, no-smoking rooms* ▭ *AE, D, DC, MC, V* ✛ *4:F3.*

14

$$$$ **Villa Florence.** This newly remodeled, mid-size hotel recently taken over and upgraded by the Larkspur Collection hotel group is indeed a little bit of Italy on Powell Street. Bar Norcini, an Italian café-bar with marble surfaces, is just off the street, and a glass wall separates a wide lobby with high ceilings, comfy furnishings, and Italianate chandeliers from Kuleto's, a boisterous, trendy restaurant often packed with locals. Guests can enter the restaurant directly from inside the hotel and eat or simply sit at the bar. The hotel's freshly painted, colorful hallways have plush orange-print carpets, and the traditional rooms, though not large, feel comfortable, upbeat, and expansive with inviting FeatherBorne beds and work desks. Bathrooms are clean and closets are spacious. Offering contemporary surroundings with Tuscan character and personalized service, it's an attractive alternative to the sterility of larger, chain hotels in the area. **Pros:** great location for those who want to be in the center of things; easy access to shopping, theater, and public transport. **Cons:** noise from cable cars; crowded street. ⌂ *225 Powell St., Union Square* ☎ *415/397–7700* ⊕ *www.villaflorence.com* ⬐ *154 rooms, 28 suites* ⌂ *In-room: refrigerator, DVD, Wi-Fi. In-hotel: restaurant, bars, gym, laundry service, some pets allowed, no-smoking rooms* ▭ *AE, D, DC, MC, V* ✛ *4:F5.*

$$$–$$$$ **Westin St. Francis.** The site of sensational, banner headline scandals, this hotel's past is shrouded in as much infamy as stardust. This is the place where Sara Jane Moore tried to assassinate Gerald Ford, where Al Jolson died playing poker; Suite 1219–1221 was the scene of a massive scandal, which erupted when a 30-year-old aspiring actress died after a night of heavy boozing in the close company of silent film comedian Fatty Arbuckle. The hotel is comprised of the original building

(Empire-style furnishings, Victorian moldings) and a modern 32-story tower (Asian-inspired lacquered furniture, glass elevators); guests are divided when it comes to the virtues of the modern addition vs. the historic building. In 2009, the hotel completed a $40-million renovation—the most extensive in its history—of all guest rooms and common areas. Now Wi-Fi is available throughout the hotel. Adding to the air of upscale sophistication is the cool chic of Michael Mina's classy restaurant and his new cocktail lounge, the Clock Bar, as well as the venerable Oak Room Restaurant and Lounge. **Pros:** fantastic beds, prime location, spacious rooms, some with great views. **Cons:** some guests comment on the long wait at check-in, rooms in original building can be small, glass elevators are not for the faint of heart. ⊠ *335 Powell St., Union Square* ☎ *415/397–7000 or 800/917–7458* ⊕ *www.westinstfrancis.com* ↻ *1,157 rooms, 38 suites* ♿ *In-room: safe, refrigerator (some), Internet, Wi-Fi. In-hotel: 3 restaurants, room service, bars, spa, laundry service, concierge, public Internet, public Wi-Fi, parking (fee), some pets allowed, no-smoking rooms* ☐ *AE, D, DC, MC, V* ✛ *4:F4.*

$$$–$$$$ ⬚ **White Swan Inn.** A cozy library with a crackling fireplace is the heart of this inviting, English-style B&B. Comfortable chairs and sofas encourage lingering in the lounge, where wine, cheese, and tea are served in the afternoon. Sizable rooms with plaid bedspreads, floral carpeting and wallpaper, and reproduction Edwardian furniture each have a gas fireplace topped by a book-lined mantel. Some guests, however, have complained of the rooms' "thin walls," meaning you can "hear your neighbor's hair dryer." The popular gourmet breakfast buffet and evening turndown with chocolates extend the personal touch. **Pros:** cozy B&B antidote to sterile chain hotels, nice lounge and patio area. **Cons:** thin walls make for noisy rooms, nearby streets can be a bit rough at night, Union Square is a bit of a hike (about three blocks). ⊠ *845 Bush St., Union Square* ☎ *415/775–1755 or 800/999–9570* ⊕ *www.jdvhotels. com* ↻ *25 rooms, 1 suite* ♿ *In-room: no a/c, refrigerator, Wi-Fi. In-hotel: gym, laundry service, concierge, parking (fee), no-smoking rooms* ☐ *AE, D, MC, V* ❙◯❙ *BP* ✛ *4:E2.*

Nightlife and the Arts

WORD OF MOUTH

"When I have to take a visitor out for a really fun night eating and drinking in the city, I always start at 16th Street and Valencia in the Mission every time. This is even true for when my parents come to town."

—KeithG

Updated by Sura Wood

Sophisticated, trendy, relaxed, quirky, and downright outrageous could all be used to describe San Francisco's diverse and vibrant collection of bars, clubs, and performance venues. It can be overwhelming to decide where to go in your short time here, but some neighborhood generalizations can help you find the kind of entertainment you want.

NIGHTLIFE

Nob Hill is noted for its old-money mansions; today's plush hotel bars and panoramic skyline lounges, the most famous being Top of the Mark, fit right in here. North Beach's historic bars invoke the city's beatnik past, and its sleek lounges catch diners leaving mom-and-pop Italian restaurants. Fisherman's Wharf is probably the most touristy part of the city, with many of the city's hotels; you could also find yourself here after a trip to the Exploratorium or a ferry ride back from Alcatraz, Angel Island, or Sausalito. Singles bars in tony Union Street and the nearby Marina attract well-dressed and well-to-do crowds in their 20s and 30s. (Be sure to break out your snazziest threads for the Marina.) South of Market—or SoMa—is a nightlife hub, with a bevy of popular dance clubs, bars, and supper clubs, as well as a few excellent live-music venues. The gay and lesbian scenes center on the Castro District and along Polk Street. Twentysomethings and alternative types should check out the ever-funky Mission District and Haight Street, although even these two neighborhoods have more upscale cocktail lounges and fewer dive bars every year. An up-and-coming area for a range of sleek clubs and lounges is Union Square and farther up Geary, where several new establishments have opened their doors, drawing well-heeled tourists, hip professionals, and Gen-Exers.

THE 4-1-1

Entertainment information is printed in the pink Sunday "Datebook" section (⊕ *www.sfgate.com/datebook*) and the more calendar-based Thursday "96 Hours" section (⊕ *www.sfgate.com/96hours*) in the *San*

TOP 5 BARS

■ **Cliff House:** Granted, it's pricey and the interior is ho-hum, but huge picture windows with views of the rolling Pacific create an ambience that's pure Zen.

■ **El Rio:** The perfect dive, with $2.50 drink specials, a stellar patio, and an ever-changing calendar of events (free oysters on Friday, salsa Sunday...).

■ **Hôtel Biron:** Everything a small wine bar should be: intimate, stylish, and slightly hard to find, with an eclectic wine list and good small plates.

■ **Martuni's:** Expertly mixed martinis, a relaxed and friendly clientele, and the off-chance that your traveling companion might belt out a Liza Minelli tune after a few drinks. What more could you ask for?

■ **Vesuvio Café:** One of those rare bars that everyone knows about. It's in one of the most touristy parts of town, but still manages to be cool.

15

Francisco Chronicle. Also consult any of the free alternative weeklies, notably the *SF Weekly* (⊕ *www.sfweekly.com*), which blurbs nightclubs and music, and the *San Francisco Bay Guardian* (⊕ *www.sfbg.com*), which lists neighborhood, avant-garde, and budget events. SF Station (⊕ *www.sfstation.com*; online only) has an up-to-date calendar of entertainment goings-on.

HOURS

Sports bars and hotel bars tend to be open Sunday, but others may be closed. A few establishments—especially wine bars and restaurant bars—also close Monday. Last call is typically 1:30 AM; Financial District bars catering to the after-work crowd, however, may stop serving as early as 9 or 10 PM, and generally close by midnight at the latest. Bands and performers usually take the stage between 8 and 11 PM. A handful of after-hours clubs are open until 4 AM or all night.

TICKETS AND COVERS

The cover charge at smaller, less popular clubs ranges from $5 to $10, and credit cards are rarely accepted for this. Covers at larger venues may spike to $30, and tickets usually can be purchased through Tickets.com or Ticketweb.com. Bars often have covers for live music—usually $5 to $15.

LATE-NIGHT TRANSPORTATION

You're better off taking public transportation or taxis on weekend nights, unless you're heading downtown (Financial District or Union Square) and are willing to park in a lot. There's only street parking in North Beach, the Mission, Castro, and the Haight, and finding a spot can be practically impossible. Muni stops running between 1 AM and 5 AM but has its limited Owl Service on 9 lines—including the N, L, 90, 91, 14, and 22—every 30 minutes; check ⊕ *www.sfmuni.com* for details. You can sometimes hail a taxi on the street in well-trod nightlife locations (like North Beach or the Mission), but you can also call for one (☎ *415/626–2345 Yellow Cab, 415/648–3181 Arrow*). ■TIP→ Be aware that cabs in SF are more expensive than in other areas in the United States; expect to pay at least $10 to get anywhere within the city.

WHAT TO WEAR

Except for a few skyline lounges, you're not expected to dress up. Still, San Franciscans are a stylish bunch. For women, dressed-up jeans with heels and cute tops are one popular uniform; for guys it's button-up shirts or designer tees and well-tailored jeans. Of course, stylish means a black designer outfit at one place and funky thrift-store togs at another, so you have to use your judgment.

SMOKING

By law, bars and clubs are smoke-free, except for the very few that are staffed entirely by the owners.

BARS AND LOUNGES

Balboa Cafe. Here you'll spy young (thirtysomething) and upwardly mobile former frat boys and sorority girls munching on tasty burgers (considered by some to be the best in town) while trying to add a few new names to their Blackberrys. ⊠ *3199 Fillmore St., at Greenwich St., Marina* 🕾 *415/921–3944* ⊕ *www.balboacafe.com.*

Bix. The retro-chic martini-bar craze keeps going strong at glam, gorgeous Bix. Jazz combos provide the backbeat for the cocktail-swilling gadabouts and nattily dressed diners who pack the small bar area of this spirited yet refined supper club. Plenty of regulars stop in just to sip the well-crafted cocktails, so you won't feel out of place if you're not eating—but you will if you're not wearing something chic. ⊠ *56 Gold St., off Montgomery St., North Beach* 🕾 *415/433–6300* ⊕ *www. bixrestaurant.com.*

Bourbon & Branch. The address and phone are unlisted, the black outer door unmarked, and when you make your reservation (required), you get a password for entry. In short, Bourbon & Branch reeks of Prohibition-era speakeasy cool. It's not exclusive, though: everyone is granted a password. The place has sex appeal, with tin ceilings, bordello-red silk wallpaper, intimate booths, and low lighting; loud conversations and cell phones are not allowed. The menu of expertly mixed cocktails and quality bourbon and whiskey is substantial, but the servers aren't always authorities. ■TIP➔ This place is small, so couples or groups of four or less are ideal. Your reservation dictates your exit time, which is strictly enforced. ⊠ *501 Jones St., Tenderloin* 🕾 *No phone* ⊕ *www. bourbonandbranch.com.*

★ **Buena Vista Café.** Smack-dab at the end of the Hyde Street cable-car line, the Buena Vista packs 'em in for its famous Irish coffee—which, according to owners, was the first served stateside (in 1952). The place oozes nostalgia, drawing devoted locals as well as out-of-towners relaxing after a day of sightseeing. It's narrow and can get crowded, but this spot is a welcome respite from the overpriced, generic tourist joints nearby. ⊠ *2765 Hyde St., at Beach St., Fisherman's Wharf* 🕾 *415/474–5044* ⊕ *www.thebuenavista.com.*

Circa. This classy lounge with shimmering chandeliers is dimly lighted, but fellow patrons will still notice the logo on your purse; dress

SAFETY AFTER DARK

San Franciscans sometimes seem to get a perverse thrill out of the grittiness of their city. Some of the best nightlife options are in slightly sketchy locations; in the areas we've listed below you're better off cabbing it. Bartenders can call you a ride when you're ready to leave.

■ **Civic Center:** After the symphony, ballet, or opera, don't wander north, east, or south. The one safe corridor is west to Gough, which will bring you to Hayes Valley. Especially avoid Market Street between 6th and 10th streets.

■ **SoMa:** More than five blocks or so south of Market is a sort of industrial no-man's land, though this area becomes more developed and inhabited by flashy residential skyscrapers with each passing year.

■ **The Tenderloin:** Plenty of locals walk to bars in the Tenderloin, but if crack addicts and sketchy dudes hanging out in front of hourly-rate motels make you uncomfortable (and really, can't imagine why they wouldn't), you should take a cab. The edges of the Tenderloin, closer to Jones (east) or Sutter (north), aren't too bad, however.

■ **The Outer Mission (below 24th Street):** If you're feeling out of sorts on Mission Street between 16th and 24th streets, cut over to Valencia.

It's safe to walk around the Financial District, Union Square, Haight Street and Cole Valley, Nob Hill, the Mission (above 24th Street), and SoMa north of Howard.

15

appropriately (par for the course in the Marina). At the central, square bar, attractive yuppies sip cosmos and nibble pan-seared scallops, while skilled DJs spin downtempo electronica. This place takes tongue-in-cheek chic seriously, down to the lobster-and-truffle mac-and-cheese. As expected, there's a strong list of specialty cocktails. ⊠ *2001 Chestnut St., at Fillmore St., Marina* ☎ *415/351–0175* ⊕ *www.circasf.com.*

Edinburgh Castle. Work off your fish-and-chips and Scottish brew with a turn at the dartboard or pool table at this cavernous pub. It's popular with locals and Brits who congregate at the long bar or in the scattered seating areas, downing single-malt scotch or pints of Fuller's. Live music alternates with spoken-word sessions, weekly trivia nights, and even Scottish cultural events (January's Robert Burns celebration is a favorite). Be aware that the area around the bar is gritty. ⊠ *950 Geary St., between Larkin and Polk Sts., Tenderloin* ☎ *415/885–4074* ⊕ *www.castlenews.com.*

Gordon Biersch Brewery and Restaurant. This giant microbrewery has outlasted the boutique-beer trend and continues to draw big after-work crowds. Part of a nationwide empire that got its start in nearby Palo Alto, Gordon Biersch is known for its German-style pilsners and brews—as well as what some have called the greatest garlic fries in creation (though regulars give the burgers at this location low marks). ■ TIP→ The outdoor seating area has killer views of the Bay Bridge, making this an ideal spot for an afternoon drink. ⊠ *2 Harrison St., at the Embarcadero, SoMa* ☎ *415/243–8246* ⊕ *www.gordonbiersch.com.*

Nightlife and the Arts In and Around Downtown

Harrington's. The epicenter for downtown festivities on St. Patrick's Day, this family-owned Irish saloon (closed Sunday) is an attitude-free place for the well-tailored-suit set to have an after-work drink the rest of the year. The restaurant serves American fare, with the occasional Irish special. It has a good selection

WORD OF MOUTH

"Try MatrixFillmore or 111 Minna.... [These] are considered "see-and-be-seen" type of places and you can definitely get your party on at any of them." —haydencat

of imported beers and a patio out back. Another local favorite, the Royal Exchange, is next door and eerily similar. ✉ *245 Front St., near Sacramento St., Financial District* ☎ *415/392–7595.*

Laszlo. Attached to the Foreign Cinema restaurant, Laszlo is a cavernous, classy space with an open, bi-level design; movies are projected onto the walls. Dim lighting, candles, and an upscale selection of cocktails and single-malts make it suitable for romance, but the loud music and cacophonic levels of conversation keep it lively. DJs spin most nights after 9. ✉ *2532 Mission St., between 21st and 22nd Sts., Mission* ☎ *415/401–0810* ⊕ *www.laszlobar.com.*

Le Colonial. Down an easy-to-miss alley off Taylor Street is what appears to be a two-story colonial plantation house in the center of the city. Without being kitschy, the top-floor bar successfully evokes French-colonial Vietnam, thanks to creaky wooden floors, Victorian sofas, a patio with potted palms, and tasty French-Vietnamese food and tropical cocktails. When you arrive, sweep right past the café tables downstairs, past the hostess, and up the stairs to your left (dining is downstairs). The bar occasionally has live, low-key music. ✉ *20 Cosmo Pl., Union Square* ☎ *415/931–3600* ⊕ *www.lecolonialsf.com.*

★ **MatrixFillmore.** Don a pair of Diesel jeans and a Michael Kors sweater and sip cosmos or Cabernet with the Marina's bon vivants. This is the premier spot in the "Triangle" (short for Bermuda Triangle, named for all of the singles who disappear in the bars clustered at Greenwich and Fillmore streets). Although there's a small dance floor where some folks bump and grind to high-energy DJ-spun dance tracks, the majority of the clientele usually vies for the plush seats near the central open fireplace, flirts at the bar, or huddles for romantic tête-à-têtes in the back. The singles scene can be overwhelming on weekends. ✉ *3138 Fillmore St., between Greenwich and Filbert Sts., Marina* ☎ *415/563–4180* ⊕ *www.matrixfillmore.com.*

Nihon. Whiskey-lovers *need* to check this place out, if only to drool over the 150 or so bottles behind the bar. This place has a super-swank, youngish scene. The pricey Japanese tapas are pretty good, and whiskey pairs with sushi surprisingly well. The dramatic lighting, close quarters, and blood-red tuffets make Nihon more suitable for romance than business. ✉ *1779 Folsom St., between Eire and 14th Sts., SoMa* ☎ *415/552–4400* ⊕ *www.nihon-sf.com.*

Otis. The brainchild of a transplanted New Yorker, this tiny, two-level, art-deco-tinged watering hole that seats 49 is an ideal environment for upscale city denizens, hipsters, and corporate jockeys who have made this their hangout and, for the most part, kept the place a secret. And why shouldn't they? Happy hour (weekdays 5–8 PM) offers light fare and a number of excellent specialty cocktails; the place doesn't get jumping until around 10 PM, especially on weekends. Red lacquered walls, white leather couches optimal for people-watching, and the pièce de résistance—a stuffed peacock above the bar—add a touch

WORD OF MOUTH

"In North Beach, you may get lucky and see Sean Penn hanging out in the Tosca bar. There are lots of good bars in the area, Specs [Twelve] Adler being one of my favorite 'dive' bars." —Wellvis

of class and sass. Retreat to the cozy upstairs if you need to escape the clamor. ⊠ *25 Maiden Lane, Union Square* ☎ *No phone* ⊕ *www. otissf.com.*

Perry's. It may be one of San Francisco's oldest singles bars, but Perry's still packs 'em in. You can dine on great hamburgers as well as more substantial fare while gabbing about the game with the well-scrubbed, khaki-clad, baseball-cap-wearing crowd. ⊠ *1944 Union St., at Laguna St., Cow Hollow* ☎ *415/922–9022* ⊕ *www.perryssf.com.*

The Rrazz Room. Tucked away in the marble lobby of Hotel Nikko, the newly opened Rrazz Room caters primarily to middle-aged business clientele staying at the hotel, though the crowd varies with the entertainment, which ranges from the sweet soulful sounds of local Paula Weston to nostalgia acts like the overripe Keely Smith. Shows are on tap most nights; 7 PM on Sunday, Tuesday through Saturday showtimes vary, with occasional late shows at 10:30. Light cuisine is offered for cabaret seats. A full bar, which serves a raft of specialty cocktails, wines, and coffee, is open daily beginning at 2 PM. Check the Web site for schedules and ticketing info. ⊠ *222 Mason St., Union Square* ☎ *415/394–1189* ⊕ *www.therrazzroom.com.*

Rite Spot Cafe. A Mission tradition for more than 50 years, this classy and casual charmer is like a cabaret club in an aging mobster's garage. Quirky lounge singers and other musicians entertain most nights. A small menu of affordable sandwiches and Italian food beats your average bar fare. Rite Spot is in a mostly residential and somewhat desolate part of the Mission, so you may feel like you're entering a no-man's land. ⊠ *2099 Folsom St., at 17th St., Mission* ☎ *415/552–6066* ⊕ *www. ritespotcafe.net.*

Royal Oak. Tiffany-style lamps and cascading ferns contribute to the clubby feel of this comfortable spot, walkable from other nearby neighborhood bars. Arrive early to snag a seat on one of the antique, swoopback tufted-velvet couches. ⊠ *2201 Polk St., at Vallejo St., Russian Hill* ☎ *415/928–2303.*

Specs Twelve Adler Museum Cafe. If you're bohemian at heart, you can groove on this hidden hangout for artists, poets, and heavy-drinking lefties. It's one of the few remaining old-fashioned watering holes in North Beach that still smacks of the Beat years and the 1960s. Though it's just off a busy street, Specs is strangely immune to the hustle and bustle outside. ⊠ *12 William Saroyan Pl., off Columbus Ave., between Pacific Ave. and Broadway, North Beach* ☎ *415/421–4112.*

15

Sugar. Just trendy enough, but never pretentious, Sugar has fun cocktails (lemon drops, grape 'o' tinis), good drink specials, and a low-key vibe. DJs spin world and house music in this small, narrow neighborhood favorite. ⊠ *377 Hayes St., Hayes Valley* ☎ *415/255–7144* ⊕ *www.sugarloungesf.com.*

★ **Tosca Café.** Like Specs and Vesuvio nearby, this historic charmer holds a special place in San Francisco lore. It has an Italian flavor, with opera, big-band, and Italian standards on the jukebox, an antique espresso machine that's nothing less than a work of art, and lived-in red leather booths. With Francis Ford Coppola's Zoetrope just across the street, celebrities and hip film industry types often stop by when they're in town; locals, like Sean Penn, have been known to shoot pool in the back room. ⊠ *242 Columbus Ave., near Broadway, North Beach* ☎ *415/391–1244.*

21st Amendment. Possibly the best brewpub in SF, 21st Amendment has a good range of beer types (unlike some other spots in town). The watermelon wheat gets rave reviews. The space has an upmarket warehouse feel, though exposed wooden ceiling beams, framed photos, whitewashed brick walls, and hardwood floors make it feel cozy. ⊠ *563 2nd St., between Federal and Brannan Sts., SoMa* ☎ *415/369–0900* ⊕ *www.21st-amendment.com.*

Vessel. A newly opened club/lounge that's warm, romantic, and ultrahip in one package, Vessel's cavalier glamour welcomes you as you descend the staircase into its sleekly designed 5,000-square-foot industrial space made intimate with glowing amber lighting and low-slung benches that line exposed brick walls. New York in attitude and decor, but quintessential San Francisco in its egalitarian mix of casual Gen-Xers, fortysomething professionals, and tourists, Vessel's classy, sexy vibe coos "this is the place to be" without snobbishness. Light food and signature cocktails are served in the lounge weekday evenings, 5 to 9. Action picks up after 11 PM, when DJs and live acts take the stage pumping through a multimillion-dollar sound system. You can escape to strategically placed cognac leather love seats or dance on top of the long plank tables spot-lighted from below. ⊠ *85 Campton Pl., at Stockton St. Union Square* ☎ *415/433–8585* ⊕ *www.vesselsf.com* 🖃 *No cover weeknights; weekends $10–$20; reserved seating $250–$500* ☉ *Wed. and Sat. 10 PM–2 AM, Thurs. 9:30 PM–2 AM; Fri. 4 PM–2 AM.*

★ **Vesuvio Café.** If you're only hitting one bar in North Beach, it should be this one. The low-ceiling second floor of this raucous boho hangout, little altered since its 1960s heyday (when Jack Kerouac frequented the place), is a fine vantage point for watching the colorful Broadway and Columbus Avenue intersection. Another part of Vesuvio's appeal is its diverse, always-mixed clientele (20s to 60s), from neighborhood regulars and young couples to Bacchanalian posses of friends. ⊠ *255 Columbus Ave., at Broadway, North Beach* ☎ *415/362–3370* ⊕ *www.vesuvio.com.*

BARS WITH LIVE MUSIC

Although they're not dedicated music venues, these bars often host up-and-coming bands. Drop in, and you might discover the next Pedro the Lion or Death Cab for Cutie.

Rock music one day and salsa the next keeps a diverse crowd coming to El Rio.

Fodor's Choice
★
El Rio. A dive bar in the best sense, El Rio has a calendar chock-full of events, from free bands and films to Salsa Sunday (seasonal), all of which keep Mission kids coming back. Bands play several nights a week—Tuesday is generally free, Saturday brings the "big acts" ($8 cover), which are still relatively unknown local bands. No matter what day you attend, expect to find a diverse gay–straight crowd. The large patio out back is especially popular when the weather's warm. ⊠ *3158 Mission St., between César Chavez and Valencia Sts., Mission* ☎ *415/282–3325* ⊕ *www.elriosf.com.*

The Hotel Utah Saloon. This funky hipster spot offers a mix of local bands and young national touring acts performing rock, indie pop, alt-country, and everything in between. The low-ceiling performance space is small, with a few tables grouped around the stage. (Be sure to grab a Cuban sandwich from the bar before the show.) The bar area takes up about half of this joint and is just as popular as the music. Monday is open-mike night. ⊠ *500 4th St., at Bryant St., SoMa* ☎ *415/546–6300* ⊕ *www.thehotelutahsaloon.com.*

The Knockout. In a grungy but hip section of the Mission, the king of dive bars (with requisite cheap bottled beer and photo booth) is popular with the discerning hipsters who dare to venture south of César Chavez St. There's usually a cover for bands or DJs on weekends, but it's never more than $10. Gong Show Karaoke on Sunday and Bingo on Thursday keep it real. An added bonus for trekking out to the southern edge of the Mission: some of the city's best taquerías are nearby. ⊠ *3223 Mission St., at Valencia, Mission* ☎ *415/550–6994* ⊕ *www.theknockoutsf.com.*

OUTDOOR BARS

You're on vacation, so there's no reason to wait until 5 to relax with a local brew—or even indulge in Champagne and oysters. These places are perfect for having a nip while the sun's still out (some of them turn lame after dark), so get going and get your afternoon drink on!

Hog Island Oyster Bar. On a sunny day, is there anything better than sipping wine and eating oysters? Only if it's here, on a waterside patio, with the looming Bay Bridge and the Oakland and Berkeley hills as a backdrop. The oysters are from Marin County, and many of the wines are from Sonoma or Napa. ⊠ *Ferry Bldg., 1 Embarcadero Plaza, Financial District* ☎ *415/391–7117* ⊕ *www.hogislandoysters.com.*

> ### TAKE ME OUT AFTER THE BALLGAME
>
> Two bars near the Giants' AT&T Park are especially popular on game day.
>
> Stylish American restaurant and trendy bar **MoMo's** (⊠ *760 2nd St., at King St., SoMa* ☎ *415/227–8660* ⊕ *www.sfmomos.com*) has an outdoor patio perfect for sunny days; it's the most popular pre- and postgame bar.
>
> **Nova** (⊠ *555 2nd St., near Bryant St., SoMa* ☎ *415/543–2282* ⊕ *www.novabar.com*) fills up before and after Giants games with fans thirsty for infused-vodka drinks and other chic cocktails.

Park Chalet. You'll feel like you're in a cabin in the woods as you relax in an Adirondack chair under a heat lamp, enclosed by the greenery of Golden Gate Park. In addition to serving pub food such as burgers, salads, steaks, and fish-and-chips, the brewery churns out its own beer. The Park Chalet shares a building with the Beach Chalet *(see below)*—but it isn't waterside, so you won't freeze if it's overcast. ⊠ *1000 Great Hwy., near Martin Luther King Jr. Dr., Golden Gate Park* ☎ *415/386–8439* ⊕ *www.beachchalet.com.*

Pier 23 Cafe. Beer arrives at your table in buckets at this waterfront bar, which has ample seating at plastic tables on a wooden deck. Although you'd expect to sit elbow-to-elbow with fishermen, you're more likely to share the space with twenty- and thirtysomethings drawn by the beer and food specials. ⊠ *Pier 23, Embarcadero* ☎ *415/362–5125* ⊕ *www.pier23cafe.com.*

Zeitgeist. It's a bit divey, a bit rock and roll, and the port-a-potties are arguably cleaner than the rest room, but Zeitgeist is a good place to relax with a cold one or an ever-popular (and ever-strong) bloody Mary in the large beer "garden" (there's not much greenery) on a sunny day. Grill food of the burger-and-hot-dog variety is available. If you own a trucker hat, a pair of Vans, and a Pabst Blue Ribbon T-shirt, you'll fit right in. ⊠ *199 Valencia St., at Duboce Ave., Mission* ☎ *415/255–7505.*

SKYLINE AND OCEAN-VIEW BARS

San Francisco is a city of spectacular vistas. Enjoy drinks, music, and sometimes dinner with views of the city or the Pacific Ocean at any of the places below. ■ TIP→ Don't bother going to these bars when it's foggy.

Beach Chalet. This restaurant-microbrewery, on the second floor of a historic building filled with 1930s Works Project Administration murals, has a stunning view of the Pacific Ocean, so you may want to time your visit to coincide with the sunset. ■TIP→ Get there at least 30 minutes before sunset to beat the dinner reservations. If you come right at dinnertime or even at lunch on weekends, diners with reservations will be given first dibs on the window seats (and on tables in general). The bar is toward the back, with a so-so view of the action. The American bistro food—which, for appetizers, includes ahi tuna tartare and fried calamari—is decent, the house brews are rich and flavorful, and there's a good selection of California wines by the glass. The seasonal Oktoberfest brew is a highlight of the beer menu. The cheaper **Park Chalet** (see above) on the ground floor has park, rather than ocean, views. ✉ 1000 Great Hwy., near Martin Luther King Jr. Dr., Golden Gate Park ☎ 415/386–8439 ⊕ www.beachchalet.com.

Carnelian Room. Only the birds get a better view of the San Francisco skyline than you will from the 52nd floor of the Bank of America Building—at least when the fog's not billowing. There's no official dress code for the bar, but the adjoining restaurant, popular with jacket-and-tie-clad bankers, doesn't allow jeans. This place is sometimes closed for private events, so call ahead. ✉ 555 California St., at Kearny St., Financial District ☎ 415/433–7500 ⊕ www.carnelianroom.com.

15

★ **Cliff House.** A bit classier than the Beach Chalet, with a more impressive, sweeping view of Ocean Beach, the Cliff House is our pick if you must choose just one oceanfront restaurant/bar. Sure, it's the site of many high-school prom dates, and you could argue that the food and drinks are overpriced, and some say the sleek facade looks like a mausoleum—but the views are terrific. The best window seats are reserved for diners, but there's a small upstairs lounge where you can watch gulls sail high above the vast blue Pacific. Come before sunset. ✉ 1090 Point Lobos, at Great Hwy., Lincoln Park ☎ 415/386–3330 ⊕ www.cliffhouse.com.

★ **Harry Denton's Starlight Room.** Forget low-key drinks—the only way to experience Harry Denton's is to go for a show. Cough up the cover charge and enjoy the opulent, over-the-top decor and entertainment (some of the best cover bands in the business, usually playing Top 40 hits from the '60s, '70s, and '80s). Velvet booths and romantic lighting help re-create the 1950s high life on the 21st floor of the Sir Francis Drake Hotel, and the small dance floor is packed on Friday and Saturday nights. Jackets are preferred for men. Call ahead—it's sometimes closed for private events on weekdays. ✉ Sir Francis Drake Hotel, 450 Powell St., between Post and Sutter Sts., Union Square ☎ 415/395–8595 ⊕ www.harrydenton.com.

Top of the Mark. A famous magazine photograph immortalized this place, on the 19th floor of the Mark Hopkins InterContinental, as a hot spot for World War II servicemen on leave or about to ship out. Entertainment ranges from solo jazz piano to six-piece jazz ensembles. Cover charges and schedules vary, but tend to be around $10 beginning at 7 PM weekdays and 9 PM weekends. ✉ Mark Hopkins InterContinental, 999 California St., at Mason St., Nob Hill ☎ 415/616–6916 ⊕ www. topofthemark.com.

View Lounge. Art-deco-influenced floor-to-ceiling windows frame superb views on the 39th floor of the San Francisco Marriott, and a jazz trio with vocalist performs Friday and Saturday evenings. You won't feel out of place here just getting a drink or two rather than dinner. It can get quite crowded on weekends. ⊠ *San Francisco Marriott, 55 4th St., between Mission and Market Sts., SoMa* ☎ *415/896–1600.*

SPORTS BARS

Bus Stop. Popular with frat boys and stockbrokers alike, this Marina/ Cow Hollow favorite has 20 screens and two pool tables. If you want to meet the local diehards, this is the place. It's also one of the few spots in this neighborhood where you'll feel comfortable dressed down. Order food from neighboring restaurants; the bar provides menus. ⊠ *1901 Union St., at Laguna St., Cow Hollow* ☎ *415/567–6905.*

Fourth Street Bar and Deli. San Francisco may not be the best sports town in the country, but you'd never guess it by the buzzing scene at this huge, modern sports wonderland on the ground floor of the Marriott Hotel. The bar has 44 beers, 23 televisions, and all the salty, fried snacks you'll need to enjoy the game properly. ⊠ *55 4th St., at Mission St., SoMa* ☎ *415/442–6734.*

Greens Sports Bar. Cramped and packed to the gills with sports memorabilia, Greens is the quintessential old-school neighborhood sports bar, with 18 screens and 18 beers on tap. Seating is on stools at high bar tables, and the TVs are positioned just right for optimal viewing. Food is not served here, but the bar has delivery menus. ⊠ *2239 Polk St., at Green St., Van Ness/Polk* ☎ *415/775–4287.*

Knuckles Historical Sports Bar and Grill. The marble bar tops are evidence of Knuckles' historic location, in the early-20th-century Joseph Musto Marble Works building. The original exposed beams and brick remain part of the decor. Because it's in Fisherman's Wharf, this lively spot draws a healthy stream of sports-crazed tourists. The venue has 28 TVs, including a jumbo screen, and some local sports memorabilia, like a San Francisco Giants pennant from the team's Candlestick Park days. If you're hungry for more than a game, be sure to try the famous Vida Blue burger, named after the great pitcher who won three World Series championships across the bay with the Oakland Athletics in the early '70s. Knuckles also has two pool tables and a vintage shuffleboard table in the back. ⊠ *555 N. Point St., Fisherman's Wharf* ☎ *415/486–4346* ⊕ *www.knucklessportsbar.com.*

WINE BARS

As you might expect, San Francisco has quite a few wine bars and wine connoisseurs. But the wine-bar scene is far from snobby. We've never encountered anything but helpful advice from wine-bar staff, even when making small-budget selections. Most of these spots offer tasting "flights," wines grouped together by type for contrast and comparison.

Bubble Lounge. Champagne is the specialty at this dark, upscale spot; the selection of bubbly is excellent, with more than 300 types to choose from. Upstairs, young executives nestle into wing chairs and overstuffed couches, and downstairs there's a re-created Champagne cellar. A full bar is available, as are sushi, caviar, desserts, and other delicate nibbles. You won't feel out of place in a suit or slinky dress and heels here. Make table reservations ($30 minimum) on weekends, or you'll be relegated to the tiny bar area. ⊠ *714 Montgomery St., at Washington St., North Beach* ☎ *415/434–4204* ⊕ *www.bubblelounge.com.*

CAV Wine Bar & Kitchen. Pair your Napa or French wines with a salumi platter or gratinée fondue at this sleek, contemporary space. CAV has an impressive selection of wines by the glass, a better-than-average food menu, and frequent wine classes—a great way to learn the lingo before you head up to Sonoma or Napa. ⊠ *1666 Market St., at Gough St., Hayes Valley* ☎ *415/437–1770* ⊕ *www.cavwinebar.com.*

★ **Eos Restaurant and Wine Bar.** Though it's just a few blocks away, Cole Valley is a world apart from funky, grungy Haight Street. Eos, along with the handful of restaurants and bars that line this part of Cole Street, manages to be both sophisticated and unpretentious—and truly fantastic. This narrow and romantically lighted space, with more than 400 wines by the bottle and 40-plus by the glass, offers two different wine flights—one red and one white—every month. The adjoining restaurant's excellent East-meets-West cuisine is available at the bar. ⊠ *901 Cole St., at Carl St., Haight* ☎ *415/566–3063* ⊕ *www.eossf.com.*

The Hidden Vine. True to its name, this tiny wine bar is in a little alley (just north of Market Street) and down a set of stairs. The location is part of the appeal, but the wines and amuse-bouches make it truly worthwhile. A jumble of velvet chairs and love seats fills the carpeted space, and the owner, who serves most nights, acts as your sommelier. Another hidden find, Le Colonial *(see* Bars and Lounges, *above)* is just across the alley. ⊠ *½ Cosmo Pl., at Taylor St., Union Square* ☎ *415/674–3567* ⊕ *www. thehiddenvine.com.*

★ **Hôtel Biron.** Sharing an alleylike block with the backs of Market Street restaurants, this tiny, cavelike (in a good way) spot displays rotating artwork of the Mission School aesthetic on its brick walls. The clientele is well-behaved twenty- to thirtysomethings who enjoy the cramped quarters, good range of wines and prices, off-the-beaten path location, soft lighting, and hip music. If it's too crowded, CAV is just around the corner. ⊠ *45 Rose St., off Market St., Hayes Valley* ☎ *415/703–0403* ⊕ *www.hotelbiron.com.*

Nectar. Classy Nectar has reasonable tasting flights (around $20) and decent food that looks more impressive than it tastes. No complaints about the wine choices, though, which are consistently excellent. The small storefront lounge is warmly lighted, with modern furnishings, including a signature beehive-shape wine display. On weekends the decibel level rises considerably and space is at a premium. ⊠ *3330 Steiner St., Marina* ☎ *415/345–1377* ⊕ *www.nectarwinelounge.com.*

CABARET

San Francisco's modest cabaret scene tends toward the outlandish—case in point, the cross-dressing, lip-synching waitresses at asiaSF. The only traditional cabaret is at the Plush Room, where old standards and new talent alike draw appreciative crowds.

asiaSF. Saucy, sexy, and fun, this is one of the hottest places in town for a drag-show virgin. (Veterans might try something more specialized, like the Stud's "Trannyshack.") The entertainment, as well as gracious food service, is provided by some of the city's most gorgeous "gender illusionists," who strut in impossibly high heels on top of the catwalk bar, vamping to tunes like "Cabaret" and "Big Spender." The creative Asian-influenced cuisine is surprisingly good. ■ TIP➔ Go on a weekday to avoid a deluge of bachelorette parties. Make reservations, or risk being turned away. Oh, and bring a camera. ✉ *201 9th St., at Howard St., SoMa* ☎ *415/255–2742* ⊕ *www.asiasf.com.*

WORD OF MOUTH

"[We caught] the early show of Beach Blanket Babylon at Club Fugazi…a few weeks before our trip we bought tickets online for the show. it was great!!!! This is a really outrageous, fun musical. lots of topical and political humor, with constant costume changes (giant hats and wigs), and we laughed the entire time. Really worth it." —CarolM

Fodor's Choice ★ **Club Fugazi.** Club Fugazi's claim to fame is *Beach Blanket Babylon,* a wacky musical send-up of San Francisco moods and mores that has been going strong since 1974, making it the longest-running musical revue anywhere. Although the choreography is colorful, the singers brassy, and the satirical songs witty, the real stars are the comically exotic costumes and famous ceiling-high "hats"—which are worth the price of admission alone. The revue sells out as early as a month in advance, so order tickets as far ahead as possible. Those under 21 are admitted only to the Sunday matinee. ■ TIP➔ If you don't shell out the extra $15–$20 for reserved seating, you won't have an assigned seat—so get your cannoli to go and arrive at least 30 minutes prior to showtime to get in line. ✉ *678 Green St., at Powell St., North Beach* ☎ *415/421–4222* ⊕ *www.beachblanketbabylon.com.*

COMEDY

Despite San Francisco's diverse arts-and-entertainment landscape, its comedy scene is rather limp. Big-name acts, however, often perform at its two main comedy clubs, Cobb's and Punch Line.

Cobb's Comedy Club. Stand-up comics such as Bill Maher, Paula Poundstone, and Sarah Silverman have appeared at this club. You can also see sketch comedy and comic singer-songwriters here. No one under 18 is admitted. ✉ *915 Columbus Ave., at Lombard St., North Beach* ☎ *415/928–4320* ⊕ *www.cobbscomedyclub.com.*

Punch Line. A launch pad for the likes of Jay Leno and Whoopi Goldberg, this place books some of the nation's top talents. Headliners have included Dave Chappelle, Margaret Cho, and Jay Mohr. No one under 18 is admitted. ✉ *444 Battery St., between Clay and Washington Sts., Financial District* ☎ *415/397–7573* ⊕ *www.punchlinecomedyclub.com.*

Purple Onion. This intimate nightspot ranks right up there with Bimbo's and the Fillmore on the list of San Francisco's most famous clubs; the Onion provided an early platform for both folk-music troubadours such as the Kingston Trio and comedic acts like the Smothers Brothers. In addition to stand-up, you can catch sketch comedies, open mikes, and improv shows. ✉ *140 Columbus Ave., at Broadway, North Beach* ☎ *415/956–1653* ⊕ *www.purpleonioncomedy.com.*

DANCE CLUBS

Compared to other big cities, San Francisco doesn't have many dedicated dance clubs. Lots of places are hit or miss—out of control one night, crickets the next. ■TIP→ Go on popular theme nights to avoid feeling like a private dancer. You will rarely be denied entry based on the bouncer's whims (though we've heard of "sliding" cover scales at some clubs). Dress nicely, act nicely, and you shouldn't have any problems. Many rock, blues, and jazz clubs (*see below*) also have active dance floors; some have DJ-spun music when live acts aren't performing. For dance party news, check out the San Francisco edition of ⊕ *www.nitevibe.com*.

> **SHOOK ME ALL NIGHT LONG**
>
> The EndUp is San Francisco's only serious after-hours place. It's open nonstop from 10 PM Friday until 4 AM Monday, and generally 10 PM–4 AM weekdays. People from all walks of life end up here.

15

Annie's Social Club. Anglophiles, unite! You can work on your karaoke rendition of "God Save the Queen" in the back room. Good fun! ⊠ *917 Folsom St., at 5th St., SoMa* ☎ *415/974–1585* ⊕ *www. anniessocialclub.com.*

★ **DNA Lounge.** The sounds change nightly at the venerable DNA Lounge, but this club gets a star solely for **Bootie.** Held the second Saturday of each month, this popular mashup unites hardcore and indie rockers, hip-hop devotees, and emo fans. If a DJ mix of Gorillaz, Donna Summer, and Joy Division sounds like your bag, you're in for a treat. **Remedy,** which brings deep-house and hip-hop DJs most Friday nights, is also popular. On other nights, the place can be dead. Three bars and dance floors on two levels mean it's rarely uncomfortably crowded. ⊠ *375 11th St., between Harrison and Folsom Sts., SoMa* ☎ *415/626–1409.*

The EndUp. Sometimes 2 AM is just too early. The EndUp is by far SF's most popular after-hours place, with possibly the best sound system in the city. ■TIP→ Said system is cranked. Even the cool kids wear earplugs. It can be a bit of a meat market (which ladies can avoid on Fag Fridays), but this San Francisco institution doesn't adhere to any particular scene. ⊠ *401 6th St., at Harrison St., SoMa* ☎ *415/646–0999* ⊕ *www. theendup.com.*

Mezzanine. If you like megaclubs, then you'll dig this industrial-chic two-story club, which doubles as a gallery and performance venue. Live acts have included Mos Def, the Dandy Warhols, and Def Jux artists. The crowd is generally mixed, straight and gay. If the jam-packed dance floor (which can accommodate nearly 1,000 people) overwhelms you, head upstairs to the quietish mezzanine lounges to converse or to ogle the sexy crowd. ⊠ *444 Jessie St., at 5th St., SoMa* ☎ *415/625–8880* ⊕ *www.mezzaninesf.com.*

★ **111 Minna Gallery.** Gallery by day, bar–dance club by night, this unpretentious warehouse space is often full of artsy young San Franciscans who prefer it to glitzier spots. The door is unmarked, and it's on a small side street just south of Mission. Dance events typically take place Wednesday through Saturday 9 PM–2 AM (though the bar opens at 5), but the dance party starts earlier on Wednesday for popular **Qoöl**

The Mission/Castro
Nightlife and the Arts

KEY

M Muni stops

b BART stations

Badlands **2**
Bottom of the Hill **16**
The Café **4**
Café du Nord **8**
Castro Theatre **3**
El Rio **23**

Eos Restaurant and
Wine Bar **1**
The Knockout **21**
Laszlo **18**
Lime **6**
Lexington Club **13**
The Marsh **17**

Martuni's **9**
The Mint **7**
Moby Dick **5**
Pilsner Inn **10**
Rite Spot Cafe **15**
Roccapulco **22**
Roxie Cinema **11**

Savanna Jazz **19**
Theatre Rhinoceros **14**
Wild Side West **20**
Zeitgeist **12**

(5 PM–10 PM). It's closed for private events on Monday. ✉ *111 Minna St., between 2nd and New Montgomery Sts., SoMa* ☎ *415/974–1719* ⊕ *www.111minnagallery.com.*

Roccapulco. Salsa, salsa, salsa. With dancing and live music from big-name salsa bands on Friday and Saturday, this cavernous dance hall and restaurant knows how to pack 'em in. Pick up some moves at the Wednesday, Friday, and Saturday evening salsa lessons. The club enforces a dress code, so don't wear jeans or sneakers. This place is also a supper club serving Latin-nouveau cuisine. ✉ *3140 Mission St., between Precita and César Chavez Sts., Mission* ☎ *415/648–6611* ⊕ *www.roccapulco.com.*

330 Ritch Street. One of the city's best parties, the long-running **Popscene** features Brit pop, '60s soul, and New Wave every Thursday. Live acts—such as the Killers, Hot Hot Heat, and Lily Allen—are thrown into the mix. The stylish, modern space also serves pizza and has 16 beers on tap. ✉ *330 Ritch St., between 3rd and 4th Sts., SoMa* ☎ *415/541–9574* ⊕ *www.330ritch.com.*

15

GAY AND LESBIAN NIGHTLIFE

In the days before the gay liberation movement, bars were more than mere watering holes—they also served as community centers where members of a mostly undercover minority could network and socialize. In the 1960s the bars became hotbeds of political activity; by the 1970s other social opportunities had become available to gay men and lesbians, and the bars' importance as centers of activity decreased.

Old-timers may wax nostalgic about the vibrancy of pre-AIDS, 1970s bar life, but you can still have plenty of fun. The one difference is the one-night-a-week operation of some of the best clubs, which may cater to a different (sometimes straight) clientele on other nights. This type of club tends to come and go, so it's best to pick up one of the two main gay papers to check the latest happenings. The *Bay Area Reporter* (☎ *415/861–5019* ⊕ *www.ebar.com*), a biweekly newspaper, lists gay and lesbian events in its calendar. The biweekly *San Francisco Bay Times* (☎ *415/626–0260* ⊕ *www.sfbaytimes.com*) is aimed at gay and lesbian readers.

GAY MALE BARS

"A bar for every taste, that's the ticket" was how the curious film *Gay San Francisco* described late-1960s nightlife here. Leather bars, drag-queen hangouts, piano bars, and bohemian cafés were among the many options for gay men back then. The scene remains just as versatile today. Unless otherwise noted, there is no cover charge at the following establishments.

Badlands. Shirts off! If a sweaty muscle sandwich sounds like your idea of a good time, head to Badlands, where serious party boys come to grind to throbbing music on a packed dance floor. The lines can be ridiculous on weekends; those in the know go on Wednesday or Thursday. Tight-teed patrons range from 20s to 40s. ✉ *4121 18th St., between Castro and Collingwood Sts., Castro* ☎ *415/626–9320* ⊕ *www.sfbadlands.com.*

The Café. Always comfortable and often packed with a mixed gay, lesbian, and straight crowd, this is a place where you can dance to house or disco music, shoot pool, or meet guys in their 20s at the bar. The outdoor deck—a rarity—makes it a favorite destination for smokers. Weekend cover is $3; expect a line to get in. ⊠ *2369 Market St., at 17th St., Castro* ☎ *415/834–5840* ⊕ *www.cafesf.com.*

The Cinch. This Wild West–theme neighborhood bar has pinball machines, pool tables, and a smoking patio. It's not the least bit trendy, which is part of the charm for regulars. ⊠ *1723 Polk St., between Washington and Clay Sts., Van Ness/Polk* ☎ *415/776–4162* ⊕ *www.thecinch.com.*

Divas. In the rough-and-tumble Tenderloin, around the corner from the Polk Street bars, trannies (transvestites and transsexuals) and their admirers come here for the racy entertainment. (Naughty Schoolgirls night is a fave.) This multilevel space has separate areas for stage performances, dancing, and quiet chats. It's not a drag bar, as there is no sense of irony or camp about the place; the girls here are charming, and the fun is in the titillation. ⊠ *1081 Post St., between Larkin and Polk Sts., Tenderloin* ☎ *415/474–3482* ⊕ *www.divassf.com.*

★ **Eagle Tavern.** Bikers are courted with endless drink specials and, increasingly, live rock music at this humongous indoor-outdoor leather bar, one of the few SoMa bars remaining from the days before AIDS and gentrification. The Sunday-afternoon "Beer Busts" (3–6 PM) are a social high point and benefit charitable organizations. It's a surprisingly welcoming place for people from all walks of life. ⊠ *398 12th St., at Harrison St., SoMa* ☎ *415/626–0880* ⊕ *www.sfeagle.com.*

★ **Lime.** The 1960s mod design of this chic cocktail lounge and restaurant (with rainbow-color Plexiglas at every turn) evokes L.A. more than SF, but it's the top choice for Abercrombie-wearing A-gays who swill mojitos by the bucket. There's also a diverse and delicious menu of small plates, good for sharing. ⊠ *2247 Market St., between Noe and Sanchez Sts., Castro* ☎ *415/621–5256.*

Lion Pub. With big comfy chairs, cascades of potted plants, and a small fireplace, this bar is so welcoming that—even though it's one of the oldest gay bars in the city—it tends to draw every sort of San Franciscan, young and old, gay and straight. Specialty drinks made with fresh-squeezed fruit juices attract cocktail connoisseurs. ⊠ *2062 Divisadero St., at Sacramento St., Pacific Heights* ☎ *415/567–6565.*

★ **Martuni's.** A mixed crowd enjoys cocktails in the semi-refined environment of this elegant bar at the intersection of the Castro, the Mission, and Hayes Valley; variations on the martini are a specialty. In the intimate back room, a pianist plays nightly and patrons take turns singing show tunes. It's a favorite post-theater spot—especially after the symphony or opera, which are within walking distance. ⊠ *4 Valencia St., at Market St., Mission* ☎ *415/241–0205.*

Moby Dick. The quintessential neighborhood watering hole, this unpretentious spot has a pool table, pinball machines, and a live "DVJ" mixing pop videos and music. A giant fish tank sits over the bar, giving shy types something to look at other than their shoes. An eclectic (in style and age) mix of casually dressed couples and guys with nothing to prove frequent this place, but there's some pick-up potential, too.

✉ *4049 18th St., at Hartford St., Castro* ☎ *415/861–1199* ⊕ *www. mobydicksf.com.*

Pilsner Inn. Casual and comfortable—yet still hip and cruise-y—Pilsner is the type of neighborhood joint you quickly claim as your own. Kick back with a pint on the fantastic year-round patio (it's covered), and enjoy eye candy of the thirtysomething variety (ranging from conservative yuppie guys to Mission emo boys). Pilsner Inn is technically a sports bar, which means it has a pool table and sponsors some local amateur teams. ✉ *225 Church St., at Market St., Castro* ☎ *415/621–7058* ⊕ *www. pilsnerinn.com.*

BEYOND THE BARS

Of course, there's more to gay nightlife than the bars. Most nights **Theatre Rhinoceros** (✉ *1360 Mission St., Suite 200, Mission* ☎ *800/838–3006* ⊕ *www. therhino.org*) has plays and solo shows on two stages. The **San Francisco Lesbian, Gay, Bisexual, and Transgender Community Center** (✉ *1800 Market St., Hayes Valley* ☎ *415/865–5555* ⊕ *www.sfcenter.org*) is home to many social activities, from writers' groups to yoga.

★ **The Stud.** Mingle with glam trannies, tight-teed pretty boys, ladies and their ladies, and a handful of straight onlookers who dance to the live DJ and watch world-class drag performers on the small stage. The entertainment is often campy, pee-your-pants funny, and downright talented. Each night's music is different—from funk, soul, and hip-hop to '80s tunes and disco favorites. The club is sometimes closed Sunday. ✉ *399 9th St., at Harrison St., SoMa* ☎ *415/863–6623* ⊕ *www.studsf.com.*

Trax. "Laid back" would be an understatement. Once inside, you won't feel like you're in a gay bar—or in San Francisco. And that's the way the regulars like it. Cheap beer specials draw people from every ilk. And though you don't have to don your cruise wear for this place, it's still social. ✉ *1437 Haight St., Haight* ☎ *415/864–4213.*

KARAOKE BARS

Bow Bow Cocktail Lounge. An inclusive quirky, divey karaoke bar where you can get your kicks performing in front of a sometimes rowdy—but almost always supportive—audience of hip young things and Asian business men. Plus, where else can you get boiled eggs and hot sauce after midnight? ✉ *1155 Grant Ave., near Broadway, Chinatown* ☎ *415/421–6730.*

★ **The Mint.** A mixed gay-straight crowd that's drop-dead serious about its karaoke (to the point where you'd think an *American Idol* casting agent was in the crowd) comes here seven nights a week. Regulars sing everything from Simon and Garfunkel songs to disco classics in front of an attentive audience. Do *not* go here unprepared! Check out the songbook online to perfect your debut before you attempt to take the mike. ✉ *1942 Market St., between Duboce and Laguna Sts., Hayes Valley* ☎ *415/626–4726* ⊕ *www.themint.net.*

LESBIAN BARS

For a place known as a gay mecca, San Francisco has always suffered from a surprising drought of women's bars. The Lexington Club, in the nightlife-filled Mission District, is the best-known bar. The Café *(see above) is* probably the most lesbian-friendly Castro bar, though you'll find queer gals (and many more queer guys) at the Mint and the Stud, too.

The calendar at ⊕ *www.hillgirlz.com*, one of the best places for detailed information about the city's lesbian scene, covers everything from dance events to social and political gatherings.

★ **Lexington Club.** According to its slogan, "every night is ladies' night" at this all-girl club geared to urban alterna-dykes in their 20s and 30s (think piercings and tattoos, not lipstick). Catfights are not uncommon. ■ TIP→ The women's room has awesome graffiti. ⊠ *3464 19th St., at Lexington St., Mission* ☎ *415/863–2052* ⊕ *www.lexingtonclub.com.*

Wild Side West. A friendly pool game is always going on at this mellow, slightly out-of-the-way neighborhood hangout, where all are welcome. Outside is a large deck and one of San Francisco's best bar gardens, where acoustic-guitar sing-alongs are not uncommon. ⊠ *424 Cortland Ave., Bernal Heights* ☎ *415/647–3099.*

JAZZ CLUBS

Traditionally, San Francisco hasn't had world-renowned jazz clubs like, say, New York and Paris—but that began to change with the arrival of Yoshi's. The fabled Oakland-based jazz club opened a hot new outpost in San Francisco's Fillmore District at the end of 2007. Jazz fans can also get their kicks at venues ranging from mellow restaurant cocktail lounges to hip Mission District venues. Be sure to check rock, pop, folk, and blues venues for special jazz events. Most clubs charge a cover that varies with the act; call for specific details.

★ **Savanna Jazz.** Deep in the Outer Mission, this is one of the best jazz joints in SF, an unexpected find in a neighborhood filled with hipster bars. Loungey booths and low lighting set the scene for consistently good old-school Latin and Brazilian jazz acts. Cover is generally $5–$8. ⊠ *2937 Mission St., between 25th and 26th Sts., Mission* ☎ *415/285–3369* ⊕ *www.savannajazz.com.*

★ **Yoshi's.** The legendary Oakland club that has pulled in some of the world's best jazz musicians—Pat Martino, Branford Marsalis, Betty Carter, and Dizzy Gillespie, to name just a few—opened a San Francisco location in late 2007. The new club has terrific acoustics, a 9-foot Steinway grand piano (broken in by Chick Corea), and seating for 411; it's been hailed as "simply the best jazz club in the city." Yoshi's also serves Japanese food in an adjoining restaurant set in a soaring two-story space, decorated with blond wood and hanging paper lanterns (you can also order food at café tables in the club). And yes, the coupling of sushi and jazz *is* as elegant as it sounds. Sightlines are good from just about any vantage point, including the back balcony. Yoshi's is located in the Fillmore District, which was known as the "Harlem of the West" in its heyday during the 1940s and '50s. Be advised, the strip where the club is located is part of a new city redevelopment project—it's on a tough block in an even tougher neighborhood; so, take advantage of the valet parking. ⊠ *1330 Fillmore St., at Eddy St., Japantown* ☎ *415/655–5600* ⊕ *www.yoshis.com.*

ROCK, POP, HIP-HOP, FOLK, AND BLUES CLUBS

★ **Bimbo's 365 Club.** The plush main room and adjacent lounge of this club, here since 1951, retain a retro vibe perfect for the "Cocktail Nation" programming that keeps the crowds entertained. For a taste of the old-school San Francisco nightclub scene, you can't beat this place. Indie low-fi and pop bands like Stephen Malkmus and the Jicks and Camera Obscura fill the bill. ✉ *1025 Columbus Ave., at Chestnut St., North Beach* ☎ *415/474–0365* ⊕ *www.bimbos365club.com.*

Fodor's Choice **BooM BooM RooM.** John Lee Hooker's old haunt has been an old-school
★ blues haven for years, attracting top-notch acts from all around the country. Luck out with legendary masters like James "Super Chikan" Johnson, or discover new blues and funk artists. ✉ *1601 Fillmore St., at Geary Blvd., Japantown* ☎ *415/673–8000* ⊕ *www.boomboomblues. com.*

★ **Bottom of the Hill.** This is a great live-music dive—in the best sense of the word—and truly the epicenter for independent rock in the Bay Area. The club has hosted some great acts over the years, including the Strokes and the Throwing Muses. Rap and hip-hop acts occasionally make it to the stage. ✉ *1233 17th St., at Texas St., Potrero Hill* ☎ *415/621–4455* ⊕ *www.bottomofthehill.com.*

Café du Nord. You can hear some of the coolest jazz, blues, rock, and alternative sounds in town at this basement bar. Built in 1907, it has retained some of its original Victorian features, which contribute to the hip, vaguely illicit feel—reminiscent of its days as a speakeasy. The music, a mix of local talent and indie headliners like Kristin Hersh and Bettie Serveert, is strictly top-notch. ✉ *2170 Market St., between Church and Sanchez Sts., Castro* ☎ *415/861–5016* ⊕ *www.cafedunord. com.*

The Fillmore. This is *the* club that all the big names, from Coldplay to Clapton, want to play. San Francisco's most famous rock-music hall serves up a varied menu of national and local acts: rock, reggae, grunge, jazz, folk, acid house, and more. Most tickets cost $20–$30, and some shows are open to all ages. ■ TIP➔ Avoid steep service charges by buying tickets at the Fillmore box office on Sunday (10–4). ✉ *1805 Geary Blvd., at Fillmore St., Western Addition* ☎ *415/346–6000* ⊕ *www.thefillmore. com.*

Fodor's Choice **Great American Music Hall.** You can find top-drawer entertainment at this
★ great, eclectic nightclub. Acts range from the best in blues, folk, and jazz to up-and-coming college-radio and American-roots artists to of-the-moment indie rock stars (OK Go, Mates of State) and the establishment (Cowboy Junkies). The colorful marble-pillared emporium (built in 1907 as a bordello) also accommodates dancing at some shows. Pub grub is available most nights. ✉ *859 O'Farrell St., between Polk and Larkin Sts., Tenderloin* ☎ *415/885–0750* ⊕ *www.gamh.com.*

The Independent. Originally called the Box for its giant cube-shape interior, this off-the-beaten-path music venue showcases an eclectic mix of rock, heavy metal, folk, soul, reggae, hip-hop, and DJ acts. There's a big dance floor. Recent shows include Lyrics Born, Sonya Kitchell and The Slip, Testament, and the Dears. ✉ *628 Divisadero St., at Hayes St., Western Addition* ☎ *415/771–1421* ⊕ *www.theindependentsf.com.*

15

Lou's Pier 47. Nightly blues accompany the hot Cajun seafood at this waterfront spot. Bands typically start playing in the late afternoon and continue until midnight. If you're staying near the Wharf, this is your best bet for live music without having to take a taxi. ⊠ *300 Jefferson St., at Jones St., Fisherman's Wharf* ☎ *415/771–5687* ⊕ *www.louspier47.com.*

The Plough and Stars. This decidedly unglamorous pub, where crusty old-timers swap stories over pints of Guinness, is the city's best bet for traditional Irish music. Bay Area musicians (and, once in a while, big-name bands) perform Thursday through Saturday. Talented locals gather to play on Tuesday and Sunday *seisiúns,* informal "sessions" where musicians sit around a table and drink and eat while chiming in; anyone skilled at Irish traditional music can join in. ⊠ *116 Clement St., at 2nd Ave., Richmond* ☎ *415/751–1122* ⊕ *www.theploughandstars.com.*

Red Devil Lounge. Local and up-and-coming hip-hop, rap, funk, indie rock, and jazz acts perform at this plush, dimly lighted lounge. Intimate (read: tightly spaced) tables line the narrow balcony overlooking the dance floor. Call ahead for schedules. ⊠ *1695 Polk St., at Clay St., Van Ness/Polk* ☎ *415/921–1695* ⊕ *www.reddevillounge.com.*

The Saloon. Hard-drinkin' in-the-know North Beach locals favor this raucous spot, known for great blues. Get the schedule at ⊕ *www.sfblues.net/Saloon.html.* Built in the 1860s, the one-time bordello is purported to be the oldest bar in the city. This is not the place to order a mixed drink. You've been warned. ⊠ *1232 Grant Ave., near Columbus Ave., North Beach* ☎ *415/989–7666.*

Slim's. National touring acts—mostly along the pop-punk and hard- and alt-rock lines—are the main event at this venue, one of SoMa's most popular nightclubs. Co-owner Boz Scaggs helps bring in the crowds and famous headliners like Dressy Bessy and Dead Meadow. ⊠ *333 11th St., between Harrison and Folsom Sts., SoMa* ☎ *415/255–0333* ⊕ *www.slims-sf.com.*

Warfield. This former movie palace—a "palace" in every sense of the word—is now one of the city's largest rock-and-roll venues, with tables and chairs downstairs and theater seating upstairs. The historic venue has booked everyone from Phish and the Grateful Dead to the Pretenders and Green Day. Check schedules and buy tickets at Ticketmaster. com. ⊠ *982 Market St., at 6th St., Civic Center* ☎ *415/345–0900.*

TOP LIVE SHOW VENUES
■ BooM BooM RooM
■ City Arts & Lectures
■ Club Fugazi
■ Great American Music Hall
■ Stern Grove Festival
■ Teatro ZinZanni

THE ARTS

San Francisco's symphony, opera, and ballet all perform in the Civic Center area, also home to the 928-seat Herbst Theatre, which hosts many fine soloists and ensembles. **San Francisco Performances** (⊠ *500*

Built as a bordello in 1907, the Great American Music Hall now pulls in top-tier performers.

Sutter St., Suite 710 ☎ *415/398–6449* ⊕ *www.performances.org*) brings an eclectic array of topflight global music and dance talents to various venues—mostly the Yerba Buena Center for the Arts, Davies Symphony Hall, and Herbst Theatre. Artists have included the Los Angeles Guitar Quartet, Edgar Meyer, the Paul Taylor Dance Company, and Midori.

TICKETS

The opera, symphony, the San Francisco Ballet's *Nutcracker,* and touring hit musicals are often sold out in advance. Tickets are usually available for other shows within a day of the performance.

City Box Office (⊠ *180 Redwood St., Suite 100, off Van Ness Ave. between Golden Gate Ave. and McAllister St., Civic Center* ☎ *415/392–4400* ⊕ *www.cityboxoffice.com*), a charge-by-phone service, offers tickets for many performances and lectures. You can buy tickets in person at its downtown location weekdays 9:30–5:30. You can charge tickets for everything from jazz concerts to Giants games by phone or online through **Tickets.com** (☎ *800/955–5566* ⊕ *www.tickets.com*). Half-price, same-day tickets for many local and touring stage shows go on sale (cash only) at 11 AM Tuesday through Saturday at the **TIX Bay Area** (⊠ *Powell St. between Geary and Post Sts., Union Square* ☎ *415/433–7827* ⊕ *www.tixbayarea.com*) booth on Union Square. TIX is also a full-service ticket agency for theater and music events around the Bay Area, open Tuesday through Friday 11 to 6, Saturday 10 to 6, and Sunday 10 to 3.

LATE-NIGHT TRANSPORTATION

For information on getting around after dark, see Late-Night Transportation in Nightlife.

Nightlife: Japantown, Pacific Heights and the Marina

THE 4-1-1

The best guide to the arts is the Sunday "Datebook" section (⊕ *www.sfgate.com/datebook*), printed on pink paper, in the *San Francisco Chronicle*. The four-day entertainment supplement "96 Hours" (⊕ *www.sfgate.com/96hours*) is in the Thursday *Chronicle*. Also be sure to check out the city's free alternative weeklies, including *SF Weekly* (⊕ *www.sfweekly.com*) and the more avant-garde *San Francisco Bay Guardian* (⊕ *www.sfbg.com*).

Online, SF Station (⊕ *www.sfstation.com*) has a frequently updated arts and nightlife calendar. San Francisco Arts Monthly (⊕ *www.sfarts.org*), which is published at the end of the month, has arts features and events, plus a helpful "Visiting San Francisco?" section. For offbeat, emerging artist performances, consult CounterPULSE (⊕ *www.counterpulse.org*).

TOP ARTS PICKS

Berkeley Repertory Theatre. The Bay Area's most satisfying theatrical performances are just a quick BART trip away.

Castro Theatre. This dramatic art-deco palace is the perfect spot for munching buttery popcorn and watching a Judy Garland or Jimmy Stewart flick.

Yoshi's. Amazing jazz and great Japanese food in a stylish theater.

Stern Grove Festival. While away a Sunday afternoon listening to opera, jazz, rock, and other musical genres in a gorgeous eucalyptus-enclosed amphitheater.

15

DANCE

San Francisco has long been a hub for dancers. Isadora Duncan danced in the courtyard of the Palace of the Legion of Honor, and the San Francisco Ballet presented the American debut of the *Nutcracker* in 1944. The dot-com real-estate boom displaced many troupes and forced them to disband, but dance is still a major part the city's cultural life. Today San Francisco is gaining recognition for its exciting modern and experimental dance companies. Local groups such as Alonzo King's Lines Ballet and ODC/San Francisco tour extensively and are well regarded by national dance critics. The San Francisco Ballet excels at both traditional and contemporary repertoires.

Dancers' Group (⊕ *www.dancersgroup.org*) is a Web site with events and resource listings for dancers and dance aficionados. **Voice of Dance** (⊕ *www.voiceofdance.org*) is a national publication with local calendars. Web-only **DanceView Times** (⊕ *www.danceviewtimes.com*) reviews productions and events.

★ **Alonzo King's Lines Ballet.** Since 1982 this company has been staging the fluid and gorgeous ballets of choreographer and founder Alonzo King, sometimes in collaboration with top-notch world musicians such as Zakir Hussain and Hamza El Din. Ballets incorporate both classical and modern techniques, with experimental set design, costumes, and music. The San Francisco season is in the spring. ☎ *415/863–3040* ⊕ *www.linesballet.org*.

★ **ODC/San Francisco.** Popular with kids, this 10-member group's annual
☾ Yuletide version of *The Velveteen Rabbit* (mid-November–mid-

December), at the Yerba Buena Center for the Arts, ranks among the city's best holiday-season performances. The group's main repertory season generally runs intermittently between January and June. ☎ *415/863–6606* ⊕ *www.odcdance.org.*

★ **San Francisco Ballet.** Under artistic director Helgi Tomasson, the San Francisco Ballet's works—both classical and contemporary—have won admiring reviews. The primary season runs from February through May. Its repertoire includes full-length ballets such as *Don Quixote* and *Sleeping Beauty*; the December presentation of the *Nutcracker* is one of the most spectacular in the nation. The company also performs bold new dances from star choreographers such as William Forsythe and Mark Morris, alongside modern classics by George Balanchine and Jerome Robbins. Tickets and information are available at the **War Memorial Opera House.** ⊠ *War Memorial Opera House, 301 Van Ness Ave., Civic Center* ☎ *415/865–2000* ⊕ *www.sfballet.org* ☉ *Weekdays 10–4.*

FILM

The San Francisco Bay Area, including Berkeley and Marin County, is considered one of the nation's most savvy movie markets. Films of all sorts find an audience here. The area is also a filmmaking center, where documentaries and experimental works are produced on modest budgets and feature films and television programs are shot on location. In San Francisco about a third of the theaters regularly show foreign and independent films.

San Francisco Cinematheque (☎ *415/552–1990* ⊕ *www.sfcinematheque. org*) showcases experimental film and digital media, with most screenings at the Yerba Buena Center for the Arts or at Artists' Television Access.

MOVIE THEATERS

Many of these theaters screen high-quality independent and foreign-language films (Friday and Saturday evening shows often sell out, so consider buying tickets in advance via ⊕ *www.moviefone.com* or ☎ *777–FILM[preceded by the local area code]*).

The Bridge. This theater, built in 1939, has been showing films on its single screen since the 1950s. ⊠ *3010 Geary Blvd., at Blake St., Western Addition* ☎ *415/267–4893.*

Fodor's Choice ★   **Castro Theatre.** Designed by art-deco master Timothy Pfleuger and opened in 1922, the most dramatic movie theater in the city hosts revivals as well as foreign and independent engagements and the occasional sing-along movie musical. Parking is limited in the Castro District, so taking public transportation is advised. ⊠ *429 Castro St., near Market St., Castro* ☎ *415/621–6120* ⊕ *www.castrotheatre.com.*

The Clay. This small but comfortable and well-kept single-screen theater dates to 1910 and has first-run art-house films. ⊠ *2261 Fillmore St., at Clay St., Pacific Heights* ☎ *415/267–4893.*

Embarcadero Center Cinemas. Shows often sell out at this modern, extremely popular five-screen theater, which has the best in first-run independent and foreign films. ⊠ *1 Embarcadero Center, Promenade level, Embarcadero* ☎ *415/267–4893.*

Lumière. This three-screen theater tends toward experimental and foreign films, as well as documentaries. ⊠ *1572 California St., between Polk and Larkin Sts., Van Ness/Polk* ☎ *415/267–4893.*

Opera Plaza Cinemas. The four theaters and their screens are small, but this is often the last place you can see an independent or foreign film before it ends its run in the city. It's great for indie-film-loving procrastinators, but if you arrive late for the show, you may have to sit in the front row of the tiny screening room. ⊠ *601 Van Ness Ave., between Turk St. and Golden Gate Ave., Civic Center* ☎ *415/267–4893.*

Red Vic Movie House. An adventurous lineup of hard-to-find contemporary and classic American and foreign indies and documentaries is screened in a funky setting, which is California's only worker-owned and -operated movie house. ⊠ *1727 Haight St., between Cole and Shrader Sts., Haight* ☎ *415/668–3994* ⊕ *www.redvicmoviehouse.com.*

Roxie Cinema. Film noir and indie features and documentaries, as well as first-run movies and classic foreign cinema, are the specialties here. ⊠ *3117 16th St., between Valencia and Guerrero Sts., Mission* ☎ *415/863–1087* ⊕ *www.roxie.com.*

15

MUSIC

San Francisco's symphony and opera perform in the Civic Center area, but musical ensembles can be found all over the city: in churches, museums, restaurants, and parks—not to mention in Berkeley and on the Peninsula.

★ **Chanticleer.** A Bay Area treasure, this all-male a-cappella ensemble stages lively and technically flawless performances that show off a repertoire ranging from sacred medieval music to show tunes to contemporary avant-garde works. ☎ *415/252–8589* ⊕ *www.chanticleer.org.*

42nd Street Moon. This group produces delightful "semistaged" concert performances of rare chestnuts from Broadway's golden age of musical theater, such as *L'il Abner* and *The Boys From Syracuse*. The **Eureka Theatre** (⊠ *215 Jackson St., between Front and Battery Sts., Financial District*) hosts most 42nd Street Moon shows. ☎ *415/255–8207* ⊕ *www.42ndstmoon.com.*

★ **Kronos Quartet.** Twentieth-century works and a number of premieres make up the programs for this always entertaining, Grammy Award–winning string ensemble, which spends much of the year traveling throughout the United States and abroad. ⊕ *www.kronosquartet.org.*

Noontime Concerts at Old St. Mary's Cathedral. This Gothic Revival church, completed in 1872 and rebuilt after the 1906 earthquake, hosts a notable chamber-music series on Tuesday at 12:30; suggested donation is $5. ⊠ *660 California St., Financial District* ☎ *415/777–3211* ⊕ *www. noontimeconcerts.org.*

Old First Concerts. The well-respected Friday-evening and Sunday-afternoon series includes chamber music, choral works, vocal soloists, new music, and jazz. Tickets are $15. ⊠ *Old First Presbyterian Church, 1751 Sacramento St., at Van Ness Ave., Van Ness/Polk* ☎ *415/474–1608* ⊕ *www.oldfirstconcerts.org.*

CLOSE UP

Arts and Culture Beyond the City

Although most folks from outlying areas drive *into* San Francisco to enjoy the nightlife, there are plenty of reasons to head *out* of the city.

FILM

The **Pacific Film Archive** (⊠ 2575 Bancroft Way, near Bowditch St., Berkeley ☎ 510/642-0808 ⊕ www.bampfa.berkeley.edu), affiliated with the University of California, screens a comprehensive mix of old and first-run American and foreign films. The spectacular art-deco **Paramount Theatre** (⊠ 2025 Broadway, near 19th St. BART station, Oakland ☎ 510/465-6400 ⊕ www.paramounttheatre.com) screens a few vintage flicks (*The Sting, Casablanca*) every month.

PERFORMING ARTS AND MUSIC

Some of the most talented practitioners of folk, blues, Cajun, and bluegrass perform at the alcohol-free **Freight & Salvage Coffee House** (⊠ 1111 Addison St., Berkeley ☎ 510/548-1761 ⊕ www.freightandsalvage.org). Oakland is home to **Yoshi's** (⊠ 510 Embarcadero St., between Washington and Clay Sts., Oakland ☎ 510/238-9200 ⊕ www.yoshis.com), one of the nation's best jazz venues.

The East Bay's **Berkeley Symphony Orchestra** (☎ 510/841-2800 ⊕ www.berkeleysymphony.org) has risen to considerable prominence under artistic director Kent Nagano's baton. The emphasis is on 20th-century composers. The orchestra plays a handful of concerts each year, in the University of California–Berkeley's Zellerbach Hall and in other locations around Berkeley. ■ TIP→ The acoustics in Zellerbach Hall are notoriously dead; sit in the front or middle orchestra for the best sound. The **Cal Performances** (☎ 510/642-9988 ⊕ www.calperformances.org) series, held at various venues on the University of California–Berkeley campus from September through May, offers the Bay Area's most varied bill of internationally acclaimed artists in all disciplines. The Tony Award–winning **Berkeley Repertory Theatre** (⊠ 2025 Addison St., Berkeley ☎ 510/647-2949 ⊕ www.berkeleyrep.org) is the American Conservatory Theatre's major rival for leadership among the region's resident professional companies. It performs an adventurous mix of classics and new plays from fall to spring in its theater complex, near BART's Downtown Berkeley Station. Parking is at a premium, so plan to arrive early if you're coming by car.

★ **San Francisco Symphony.** One of America's top orchestras, the San Francisco Symphony performs from September through May, with additional summer performances of light classical music and show tunes; visiting artists perform here the rest of the year. Michael Tilson Thomas, who is known for his innovative programming of 20th-century American works (most notably his Grammy Award–winning Mahler cycle), is the music director, and he and his orchestra often perform with soloists of the caliber of Andre Watts, Gil Shaham, and Renée Fleming. Just to illustrate the more adventuresome side of the organization, this symphony once collaborated with the heavy-metal group Metallica. David Byrne has performed here, as well. Tickets run about $15–$100.

Many members of the San Francisco Symphony perform in the **Summer in the City** (☎ *415/864–6000* ⊕ *www.sfsymphony.org*) concert series, held in the 2,400-seat Davies Symphony Hall. The schedule includes light classics and Broadway, country, and movie music. ⊠ *Davies Symphony Hall, 201 Van Ness Ave., at Grove St., Civic Center* ☎ *415/864–6000* ⊕ *www.sfsymphony.org.*

MUSIC FESTIVALS

Hardly Strictly Bluegrass Festival. The city's top free music event, as well as one of the greatest gatherings for bluegrass, country, and roots music in the country, takes place from late September to early October. Roughly 50,000 folks turn out to see the likes of Willie Nelson, Emmylou Harris, Jimmie Dale Gilmore, and Del McCoury at Speedway Meadows in Golden Gate Park. ☎ *No phone* ⊕ *www.strictlybluegrass.com.*

Noise Pop Festival. Widely considered to be one of the country's top showcases for what's new in indie-pop and alt-rock, Noise Pop is a weeklong festival in February or March held at Slim's, the Great American Music Hall, and other cool clubs. Founded in 1993, the low-key festival has helped local fans discover such talented acts as Modest Mouse, Kristin Hersh, and Bettie Serveert. (Phone info on the event is best obtained by calling the individual venues.) ☎ *415/375–3370* ⊕ *www.noisepop.com.*

San Francisco Bluegrass Festival. While the Hardly Strictly Bluegrass Festival attracts both die-hard fans and casual listeners, this event targets those who can name all the players in Ralph Stanley's band. The festival takes place each February at various small venues both in and around San Francisco. Past participants have included Kenny Hall, Laurie Lewis, Jackstraw, and, yes, Ralph Stanley. ☎ *No phone* ⊕ *www.sfbluegrass.org.*

San Francisco Blues Festival. Billed as the country's oldest ongoing blues festival, SFBF has hosted a hall of fame's worth of blues legends over the years, including John Lee Hooker, B.B. King, Buddy Guy, and James Cotton. It's also a great place to catch rising Bay Area blues stars like J.C. Smith and Tommy Castro. The festival, which was founded by local blues historian Tom Mazzolini in 1973, is held each September at Fort Mason's Great Meadow, which has stunning views of the Golden Gate Bridge and the bay. ☎ *415/979–5588* ⊕ *www.sfblues.com.*

San Francisco Jazz Festival. Every year starting in October, concert halls, clubs, and churches throughout the city host this acclaimed two-week festival. The popular event, which got its start in 1983, has featured such big-name acts as Ornette Coleman, Sonny Rollins, and McCoy Tyner, as well as talked-about up-and-comers like Brad Mehldau and Chris Botti. ☎ *415/398–5655* ⊕ *www.sfjazz.org.*

San Francisco World Music Festival. Founded in 2000, this respected festival draws musicians from around the world to various venues in the city. Unlike some so-called world music festivals, this event truly *is* a global affair, offering more than just the standard assortment of Celtic acts and Latin jazz players. The event takes place each fall, usually starting in September. ☎ *415/561–6571* ⊕ *www.sfworldmusicfestival.org.*

SFJAZZ Spring Season. The increasingly popular counterpart to the fall festival, the Spring Season is programmed by artistic director Joshua

Redman, a saxophone colossus who grew up across the Bay in Berkeley. Founded in 2000, the lengthy festival runs roughly from mid-March to early June and features an array of top-notch headliners. ☎ *415/398–5655* ⊕ *www.sfjazz.org.*

Fodor'sChoice **Stern Grove Festival.** The nation's oldest continual free summer music
★ festival hosts Sunday-afternoon performances of symphony, opera, jazz,
☼ pop music, and dance. The amphitheater is in a beautiful eucalyptus grove below street level, perfect for picnicking before the show. (Dress for cool weather.) ⊠ *Sloat Blvd. at 19th Ave., Sunset* ☎ *415/252–6252* ⊕ *www.sterngrove.org.*

OPERA

★ **San Francisco Opera.** Founded in 1923, this world-renowned company has resided in the Civic Center's War Memorial Opera House since the building's completion in 1932. Over its split season—September through January and June through July—the opera presents about 70 performances of 10 to 12 operas. Translations are projected above the stage during almost all non-English operas. Long considered a major international company and the most important operatic organization in the United States outside New York, the opera frequently embarks on productions with European opera companies. Ticket prices can range from $25 to $195. The full-time box office (Monday 10–5, Tuesday–Friday 10–6) is at 199 Grove Street, at Van Ness Avenue. ⊠ *War Memorial Opera House, 301 Van Ness Ave., at Grove St., Civic Center* ☎ *415/864–3330 tickets* ⊕ *www.sfopera.com.*

SPOKEN WORD

Nearly every night of the week, aspiring and established writers, poets, and performers step up to the mike and put their words and egos on the line. Check "Listings" in the free alternative weekly papers and the *San Francisco Sunday Chronicle* "Book Review" section for other options.

Cafe International. An open-mike session follows one or more featured readers here every Friday night at 8. Spoken-word performances are interspersed with acoustic musical acts. ⊠ *508 Haight St., at Fillmore St., Lower Haight* ☎ *415/552–7390.*

Fodor'sChoice **City Arts & Lectures.** Each year this program includes more than 20 fasci-
★ nating conversations with writers, composers, actors, politicians, scientists, and others. The Herbst Theatre, in the Civic Center area, is usually the venue. Past speakers include Nora Ephron, Salman Rushdie, Ken Burns, and Linda Ronstadt. ☎ *415/392–4400* ⊕ *www.cityarts.net.*

★ **Commonwealth Club of California.** The nation's oldest public-affairs forum hosts speakers as diverse as Erin Brockovich and Bill Gates; every president since Teddy Roosevelt has addressed the club. Topics range from culture and politics to economics and foreign policy. Events are open to nonmembers; contact the club for the current schedule of events. Venues vary by speaker. Lectures are broadcast on NPR. ⊠ *595 Market St., at 2nd St., Financial District* ☎ *415/597–6700* ⊕ *www.commonwealthclub.org.*

★ **West Coast Live.** Billed as "San Francisco's Live Radio Show to the World," the program invites an audience to its weekly broadcasts, many at Fort Mason's Magic Theater, the Empire Plush Room, and the Freight & Salvage Coffee House in Berkeley. The ever-changing guest list includes authors, musicians, comedians, and pundits. Recent guests include Dave Barry, Charlie Owen, and Jamaica Kincaid. ☏ *415/664–9500* ⊕ *www.wcl.org.*

THEATER

San Francisco's theaters are concentrated on Geary Street west of Union Square, but a number of additional commercial theaters, as well as resident companies that enrich the city's theatrical scene, are within walking distance of this theater row. The three major commercial theaters—Curran, Golden Gate, and Orpheum—are operated by the Shorenstein-Nederlander organization, which books touring plays and musicals, some before they open on Broadway. Theatre Bay Area (⊕ *www.theatrebayarea.org*) lists most Bay Area performances online.

15

★ **American Conservatory Theater.** Not long after its founding in the mid-1960s, the city's major nonprofit theater company became one of the nation's leading regional theaters. During its season, which runs from early fall to late spring, ACT presents approximately eight plays, from classics to contemporary works, often in rotating repertory. In December ACT stages a much-loved version of Charles Dickens's *A Christmas Carol.* The **ACT ticket office** (✉ *405 Geary St., Union Square* ☏ *415/749–2228*) is next door to **Geary Theater,** the company's home. ✉ *Geary Theater, 425 Geary St., Union Square* ⊕ *www.act-sf.org.*

Curran Theater. Some of the biggest touring shows mount productions at this theater, which has hosted classical music, dance, and stage performances since its 1925 opening. Shows are of the long-running Broadway musical variety, such as *Stomp* and *Jersey Boys,* and the seasonal *A Christmas Carol.* ✉ *445 Geary St., at Mason St., Union Square* ☏ *415/551–2000* ⊕ *www.shnsf.com.*

Exit Theatre. *The* place for absurdist and experimental theater, this three-stage venue also presents the annual **Fringe Festival** in September. ✉ *156 Eddy St., between Mason and Taylor Sts., Union Square* ☏ *415/931–1094* ⊕ *www.sffringe.org.*

Golden Gate Theater. This stylishly refurbished movie theater is now primarily a musical house. Touring productions of popular Broadway shows and revivals are its mainstay. ✉ *Golden Gate Ave. at Taylor St., Tenderloin* ☏ *415/551–2000* ⊕ *www.shnsf.com.*

Lorraine Hansberry Theatre. The performance of plays by black writers such as August Wilson and Langston Hughes is the raison d'être of this company. The 300-seat space is intimate. ✉ *777 Jones St., at Sutter St., Union Square* ☏ *415/345–3980* ⊕ *www.lorrainehansberrytheatre.com.*

Magic Theatre. Once Sam Shepard's favorite showcase, the pint-size Magic presents works by rising American playwrights, such as Matthew Wells, Karen Hartman, and Claire Chafee. ✉ *Fort Mason, Bldg. D, Laguna St. at Marina Blvd., Marina* ☏ *415/441–8822* ⊕ *www.magictheatre.org.*

The Marsh. Experimental works, including one-man and one-woman shows, works in progress, and new vaudeville shows, can be seen here. ✉ *1062 Valencia St., at 22nd St., Mission* ☎ *800/838–3006 tickets, 415/826–5750 information* ⊕ *www.themarsh.org.*

New Conservatory Theatre Center. This three-stage complex hosts the annual **Pride Season,** focusing on contemporary gay- and lesbian-themed works, as well as other events, including educational plays for young people. ✉ *25 Van Ness Ave., between Fell and Oak Sts., Hayes Valley* ☎ *415/861–8972* ⊕ *www.nctcsf.org.*

Orpheum Theater. The biggest touring shows, such as *Hairspray* and *The Lion King,* are performed at this gorgeously restored 2,500-seat venue. The theater, opened in 1926 as a vaudeville stage, is as much an attraction as the shows. It was modeled after the Spanish baroque palaces and is considered one of the most beautiful theaters in the world; the interior walls have ornate cathedral-like stonework, and the gilded plaster ceiling is perforated with tiny lights. ✉ *1192 Market St., at Hyde St., Tenderloin* ☎ *415/551–2000* ⊕ *www.shnsf.com.*

★
⟲ **San Francisco Mime Troupe.** The politically leftist, barbed satires of this Tony Award–winning troupe are hardly mime in the Marcel Marceau sense. The group performs afternoon musicals at area parks from the July 4 weekend through September, and taking one in is a perfect way to spend a sunny summer day. ☎ *415/285–1717* ⊕ *www.sfmt.org.*

Fodor's Choice
★ **Teatro ZinZanni.** Contortionists, chanteuses, jugglers, illusionists, and circus performers ply the audience as you're served a surprisingly good five-course dinner in a fabulous antique Belgian traveling-dance-hall tent. Be ready to laugh, and arrive early for a front-and-center table. Reservations are essential; tickets are $125 to $150. Dress fancy. ✉ *Pier 29, Embarcadero at Battery St., Embarcadero* ☎ *415/438–2668* ⊕ *www.zinzanni.org.*

Theatre Rhinoceros. Gay and lesbian performers and playwrights are showcased in this small Mission theater. ✉ *1360 Mission St., Suite 200, Mission* ☎ *800/838–3006 tickets, 415/552–4100 offices* ⊕ *www.therhino.org.*

★ **Yerba Buena Center for the Arts.** Across the street from the Museum of Modern Art and abutting a lovely urban garden, this performing arts complex schedules interdisciplinary art exhibitions, dance, music, film programs, and contemporary theater events. You can depend on the quality of the productions at Yerba Buena. ✉ *3rd and Howard Sts., SoMa* ☎ *415/978–2787* ⊕ *www.ybca.org.*

Sports and the Outdoors

WORD OF MOUTH

"Too cold for walking? Never. But too wet, that's another thing . . . so keep your plans flexible. . . . Muir Woods can be lovely but slippery during the winter. Even if it rains, there are days in between the storms where the weather is clear, bright and brisk—ideal conditions for a drive."

—dovima

Updated by
Fiona G.
Parrott

San Francisco's surroundings—the bay, ocean, mountains, and forests—make getting outdoors outside the city a no-brainer. Muir Woods, Point Reyes, and Stinson Beach in Marin County (⇨ *see Chapter 18*) offer dozens of opportunities for exploring the natural beauty of the Bay Area. But the peninsular city—with its many green spaces, steep inclines, and breathtaking views—has plenty to offer itself.

Bikers and hikers traverse the majestic Golden Gate Bridge, bound for the Marin Headlands or the winding trails of the Presidio. Runners, strollers, in-line skaters, and cyclists head for Golden Gate Park's wooded paths, and water lovers satisfy their addictions by kayaking, sailing, or kite-surfing in the Bay and along the rugged Pacific coast. The monthly *Competitor Nor Cal Magazine* (⊕ *www.competitornorcal. com*), available for free at sporting-goods stores, tennis centers, and other recreational sites, lists running and bicycle races, and other participant sports events, in Northern California.

Prefer to watch from the sidelines? The Giants (baseball) and the '49ers (football) are San Francisco's professional sports teams; the Athletics (baseball) and the Golden State Warriors (basketball) play in Oakland. But the city has plenty of other periodic sporting events to watch (including the roving costume party–like Bay to Breakers race). For events listings and local perspectives on Bay Area sports, pick up a copy of the *San Francisco Chronicle* (⊕ *www.sfgate.com*) or the *Examiner* (⊕ *www.examiner.com*), both of which list schedules and scores.

BASEBALL

Ⓒ
Fodor'sChoice
★

The National League's New York Giants became the **San Francisco Giants** (⊠ *AT&T Park, 24 Willie Mays Plaza, between 2nd and 3rd Sts., SoMa* 🕾 *415/972–2000 or 800/734–4268* ⊕ *sanfrancisco.giants.mlb.com*) when they moved to California in 1958, the same year that the Brooklyn Dodgers moved to Los Angeles. Today the beautiful, classic design of the Giants' AT&T Park has created a new legion of fans—some more interested in the baseball experience than the Giants, per se. Still, buy your tickets in advance—nearly every game sells out.

GETTING TICKETS

The park is small and there are 30,000 season-ticket holders (for 43,000 seats), so Giants tickets for popular games routinely sell out the day they go on sale, and other games

> **TOP OUTDOOR ACTIVITIES**
>
> ■ Ride a bike over the Golden Gate Bridge to Sausalito, then take the ferry back.
>
> ■ Hike to the top of Angel Island.
>
> ■ Catch a Giants game at AT&T Park.

sell out quickly. If tickets aren't available at Tickets.com, try the Double Play Ticket Window Web site, or even try showing up on game day—there are usually plenty of scalpers, some selling at reasonable prices.

Tickets.com (☏ 877/473–4849 ⊕ *www.tickets.com*) sells game tickets over the phone and charges a per-ticket fee of $2–$10, plus a per-call processing fee of up to $5. The **Giants Dugout** (✉ *AT&T Park, 24 Willie Mays Plaza, SoMa* ☏ *415/972–2000 or 800/734–4268* ✉ *4 Embarcadero Center, Embarcadero* ☏ *415/951–8888*) sells tickets in any of its stores (check the Web site, ⊕ *sanfrancisco.giants.mlb.com/sf/ballpark/ dugout_stores.jsp*, for all locations); a surcharge is added at all but the ballpark store.

The Giants' Web-only **Double Play Ticket Window** (⊕ *sanfrancisco.giants. mlb.com*) allows season-ticket holders to resell their unused tickets. You won't always find a deal, but you might get a seat at an otherwise sold-out game. Click the "Tickets" link on the home page.

BICYCLING

San Francisco is known for its treacherously steep hills, so it may be surprising to see so many cyclists. This is actually a great city for biking—there are ample bike lanes, it's not hard to find level ground with great scenery (along the water), and if you're willing to tackle a challenging uphill climb, you're often rewarded with a fabulous view—and a quick trip back down.

The **San Francisco Bicycle Coalition** (☏ *415/431–2453* ⊕ *www.sfbike.org*) has extensive information about the policies and politics of riding a bicycle in the city and lists local events for cyclists on its Web site. You can also download (but not print) a PDF version of the *San Francisco Bike Map and Walking Guide*.

WHERE TO RENT

Bike and Roll. You can rent bikes here for $7 per hour or $28 per day; discounted weekly rates are available. They have three locations and also have complimentary maps. ✉ *899 Columbus Ave., North Beach* ✉ *353 Jefferson St. between Jones and Leavenworth Sts., Fisherman's Wharf* ✉ *Leavenworth St. between Jefferson and Beach Sts., Fisherman's Wharf* ☏ *415/229–2000 or 888/245–3929* ⊕ *www.bicyclerental.com*.

CLOSE UP

Where Giants Tread

The size of AT&T Park hits you immediately—the field, McCovey Cove, and the Lefty O'Doul drawbridge all look like miniature models. At only 13 acres, the San Francisco Giants' ballpark is one of the country's smallest. After Boston's Fenway, AT&T Park has the shortest distance to the wall; from home plate it's just 309 feet to the right field. But there's something endearing about its petite stature—not to mention its location, with yacht masts poking up over the outfield and the blue bay sparkling beyond.

From 1960 to 2000 the Giants played at Candlestick Park (now Monster Park, the home of the NFL's '49ers). The huge, modern stadium has nice views, but it's also in one of the coldest, windiest parts of the city. (Giants' pitcher Stu Miller was famously "blown off the mound" here in 1961.)

In 2000, the Giants played their first game at AT&T Park (then Pacific Bell Park, later SBC Park—in fact, some locals jokingly call it the Phone Company Park). All told, $357 million was spent on the privately funded park, and it shows in the retro red-brick exterior, the quaint clock tower, handsome bronze statues and murals, above-average food (pad Thai, anyone?), and tiny details like baseball-style lettering on no smoking signs. There isn't a bad seat in the house, and the park has an unusual level of intimacy and access. Concourses circle the field on two levels—on the field level you can stand inches from players as they exit the locker rooms. On the street level non-ticket-holders can get up close, too, outside a gate behind the visiting team's dugout.

Diehards may miss the grittiness of Candlestick, but it's hard not to love this park. It's a new stadium with an old-time aura, already a San Francisco institution.

THE FAMOUS "SPLASH HIT"
Locals show up in motorboats and inflatable rafts, with fishing nets ready to scoop up home-run balls that clear the right field wall and land in McCovey Cove. Hitting one into the water isn't easy: the ball has to clear a 26-foot wall, the elevated walkway, and the promenade outside. Barry Bonds had the first splash hit on May 1, 2000.

GETTING THERE
Parking is pricey ($25 and up), and 5,000 spaces for 43,000 seats doesn't add up. Take public transportation. Muni line N (to CalTrain/Mission Bay) stops right in front of the park, and Muni bus lines 10, 15, 30, 42, 45, and 47 stop a block away. Or you can arrive in style—take the ferry from Jack London Square in Oakland (⊕ www.eastbayferry.com).

AT&T Park (⊠ 24 Willie Mays Plaza, SoMa ☎ 415/972–2000 or 800/734–4268 ⊕ www.attpark.com).

Park Tours (🎟 $12.50 ⏲ Daily at 10:30 and 12:30).

🕘 The giant Coca-Cola bottle and mitt you see beyond the outfield are part of a **playground**. The bottle is a slide and the mitt actually has decent views of the field. It also alongside a mini-version of the park used for minor league tryouts and pee-wee baseball.

—Shannon Kelly

Bike Hut. Known for its mom-and-pop–style service, the Hut is a small rental, repair, and used-bike shop. Hourly rentals go for $6, daily rentals for $22. ⊠ *Pier 40, SoMa* ☎ *415/543–4335* ⊕ *www.thebikehut.com* ⊗ *Closed Mon. and Tues.*

Blazing Saddles. This outfitter rents bikes for $7 to $11 an hour, depending on the type of bike, or $28 to $68 a day, and shares tips on sights to see along the paths. ⊠ *2715 Hyde St., Fisherman's Wharf* ⊠ *465 Jefferson St., at Hyde St., Fisherman's Wharf* ⊠ *Pier 43½ near Taylor St., Fisherman's Wharf* ⊠ *Pier 41 at Powell St., Fisherman's Wharf* ⊠ *1095 Columbus, North Beach* ☎ *415/202–8888* ⊕ *www.blazingsaddles.com.*

WORD OF MOUTH

"For something a little different, rent bikes from Blazing Saddles and ride along the shore and over the Golden Gate to Sausalito. Have lunch at Baja Tacos outside on their little porch and then take the ferry back to San Francisco. Unforgettable views of everything and not too strenuous."   —cindyj

San Francisco Cyclery. Rent a bike for $15 for one to two hours, $20 for two to four hours, or $30 for eight hours. ⊠ *672 Stanyan St., between Page and Haight Sts., Haight* ☎ *415/379–3870* ⊕ *www.sanfranciscocyclery.com* ⊗ *Wed.–Mon. 10–6.*

From April through October you can rent mountain bikes on **Angel Island** (☎ *415/435–1915* ⊕ *www.angelisland.org*) for $15 an hour or $50 a day.

16

THE EMBARCADERO

A completely flat, sea-level route, the Embarcadero hugs the eastern and northern bay and gives a clear view of open waters, the Bay Bridge, and sleek high-rises. The route from Pier 40 to Aquatic Park takes about 30 minutes, and there are designated bike lanes the entire way. Along the way you can see—from east to west—the Ferry Building, the Bay Bridge, a view of Coit Tower near Pier 19 (look inland), and various ferries and historic ships. At Aquatic Park there's a nice view of Golden Gate Bridge. If you're not tired yet, continue along the Marina and through the Presidio's Crissy Field. You may want to time your ride so you end up at the Ferry Building, where you can refuel with a sandwich, a gelato, or—why not?—fresh oysters.

■ TIP → Be sure to keep your eyes open along this route—cars move quickly here, and streetcars and tourist traffic can cause congestion. Near Fisherman's Wharf you can bike on the promenade, but take it slow—we've seen more than one near miss between bicyclist and pedestrian.

CAUTION Streetcar tracks can wreak havoc on skinny bike tires—and the bicyclist perched above them. Watch the ground and cross the tracks perpendicularly.

GOLDEN GATE PARK

A beautiful maze of roads and hidden bike paths crisscrosses San Francisco's most famous park, winding past rose gardens, lakes, waterfalls, museums, horse stables, bison, and, at the park's western edge, spectacular views of the Pacific Ocean. John F. Kennedy Drive is closed to motor vehicles on Sunday (and sometimes Saturday), when it's crowded with people-powered wheels.

■TIP→ Get a map of the park before you go—it's huge.

From the eastern entrance of the park between Oak and Fell streets, veer right to begin a 30- to 45-minute, 3-mi ride down John F. Kennedy Drive through the park to the Great Highway, where land meets ocean. Take a break and watch the waves roll in at Ocean Beach, or cross the street for a drink or a bite to eat at the casual, tree-shrouded Park Chalet (behind the Beach Chalet). Extend your ride a few more miles by turning left, riding a few blocks, and connecting with a raised bike path that runs parallel to the Pacific, winds through fields of emerald-green ice plant, and, after 2 mi, leads to Sloat Boulevard and the San Francisco Zoo. ■TIP→ On exceptionally windy days, expect to encounter blowing sand along this route.

THE MARINA GREEN AND GOLDEN GATE BRIDGE

★ The Marina Green, a vast lawn at the edge of the northern bay front, stretches along Marina Boulevard, adjacent to Fort Mason. It's the starting point of a well-trod, paved bike path that runs through the Presidio along Crissy Field's waterfront wetlands, then heads for the Golden Gate Bridge and beyond. To do this ride, first take the path from Aquatic Park through Fort Mason to the Marina Green. Continue into the Presidio, and you'll eventually reach the base of the bridge, a 60-minute ride round-trip. To view the bridge from underneath, stay at water level and ride to Fort Point (where Kim Novak leaped into the drink in the film *Vertigo*).

If you want to cross the bridge, take Lincoln Boulevard to reach the road-level viewing area and continue across the bridge (signs indicate which side you must use). Once you're across, turn right on the first road leading northeast, Alexander Avenue. After a 10-minute all-downhill ride, you'll arrive on Bridgeway in downtown Sausalito, where you can rest in a café. After a little shopping, board the

---

NO UPHILL BATTLE

Don't want to get stuck slogging up 30-degree inclines? Then be sure to pick up a copy of the foldout *San Francisco Bike Map and Walking Guide* ($3), which indicates street grades by color and delineates bike routes that avoid major hills and heavy traffic. You can pick up a copy in bicycle shops, select bookstores, or at the San Francisco Bicycle Coalition's Web site (⊕ *www.bikesf.org*).

LEGS OF STEEL

After crossing the Golden Gate, the superfit can ride alongside triathletes and hardcore cyclists in the Marin Headlands. Take the Alexander Avenue exit off the bridge as if you were going to Sausalito, but turn left instead and double back under the freeway. Just before the road merges with San Francisco–bound traffic, bear right and ascend the steep, rolling hills of the Marin Headlands. Follow the road to the top, where it becomes one-way and drops toward the ocean. Loop around the backside of the hills and through the tunnel, back to the bridge. On a clear day the views along this route are stunning.

Blue & Gold Fleet's ferry (the ferry terminal is at the end of Bridgeway) with your bike for the half-hour ride back to Fisherman's Wharf. ■TIP→ If it's overcast, foggy, or windy, don't bother doing the Golden Gate Bridge bike ride—the wind can feel downright dangerous on the bridge, and the trip is only awe-inspiring when you can take in the view.

ANGEL ISLAND STATE PARK

★ A former military garrison and a beautiful wildlife preserve, Angel Island has some steep roads and great views of the city and the bay. Bicycles must stay on roadways; there are no single-track trails on the island. A ferry operated by **Blue & Gold Fleet** (☎415/705–8200 ⊕ *www.blueandgoldfleet.com*) runs to the island from Pier 41 at Fisherman's Wharf and takes about 20 minutes one way; the fare is $18 round-trip, which includes park admission. Ferries leave once a day at 10 AM weekdays and 10:30 AM weekends, returning at around 3:30 PM; schedules change, so call for up-to-date info. Twenty-five bicycles are permitted on board on a first-come, first-served basis. The café is closed mid-November through February, so bring your own grub. ☎415/435–1915 ⊕ *www.angelisland.org.*

BOATING AND SAILING

16

San Francisco Bay has year-round sailing, but tricky currents and strong winds make the bay hazardous for inexperienced navigators. Boat rentals and charters are available throughout the Bay Area and are listed under "Boat Renting" in the Yellow Pages.

☺ Near Fisherman's Wharf, from spring through fall, **Adventure Cat Sailing** (⊠ *Pier 39, Fisherman's Wharf* ☎ 800/498–4228 or 800/979–3370 ⊕ *www.adventurecat.com*) takes passengers aboard a 55-foot-long catamaran. The kids can play on the trampoline-like net between the two hulls while you sip drinks on the wind-protected sundeck. A 90-minute bay cruise costs $30; sunset sails with drinks and hors d'oeuvres are $45. **Rendezvous Charters** (⊠ *Pier 40, South Beach Harbor* ☎ 415/543–7333 ⊕ *www.rendezvouscharters.com*) offers individually ticketed trips on large sailing yachts, including sunset sails ($30) and Sunday brunch cruises on a schooner ($45). **Spinnaker Sailing** (⊠ *Pier 40, South Beach Harbor* ☎415/543–7333 ⊕ *www.spinnaker-sailing.com*) offers sailing instruction and charters private sailboats with or without a skipper (bring your logbook if you want to captain a boat yourself). Both Rendezvous and Spinnaker are south of the Ferry Building on the eastern waterfront, right next to AT&T Park, *not* next to Pier 39.

☺ If you prefer calm freshwater, you can rent rowboats ($20 per hour), pedal boats ($25 per hour), and electric motorboats ($35 per hour) at **Stow Lake** (⊠ *Off John F. Kennedy Dr., ½ mi west of 10th Ave., Golden Gate Park* ☎415/752–0347), in Golden Gate Park. They take both cash and credit cards; also remember to bring bread for the ducks. The lake is open daily 10 AM-4 PM for boating, weather permitting, but call for seasonal hours.

FISHING

Fishing boats angle for salmon and halibut outside the bay or striped bass and giant sturgeon within. On land, you can cast your line at the Municipal Pier, Fisherman's Wharf, Baker Beach, or Aquatic Park. Fishing licenses are not necessary when casting from public piers. (The exception is sturgeon fishing, for which you need a Sturgeon Fishing Report Card.) Licenses are required for all other types of fishing, and can be purchased from the **California Department of Fish and Game** (⊕ www.dfg.ca.gov). Non-California residents can purchase one-, two-, or 10-day licenses for $14, $21, and $42, respectively. Sportfishing charters depart daily from Fisherman's Wharf during the salmon-fishing season (March or April through October), and cost about $95.

Lovely Martha's Sportfishing (⊠ *Fisherman's Wharf, Berth 3, Fisherman's Wharf* ☎ *650/871–1691* ⊕ *www.lovelymartha.com*) has salmon-fishing excursions and bay cruises. **Wacky Jacky** (⊠ *Foot of Jones St. at Jefferson St., Fisherman's Wharf* ☎ *415/586–9800* ⊕ *www.wackyjackysportfishing.com*), skippered by a straight-shootin' woman named Jacky, takes you salmon fishing in a sleek, fast, and comfortable 50-foot boat.

FOOTBALL

The **San Francisco '49ers** (⊠ *Candlestick Park, 490 Jamestown Ave., Bayview Heights* ☎ *415/656–4900* ⊕ *www.sf49ers.com*) play at **Candlestick Park** near the San Mateo County border, just north of the airport. Single-game tickets, available via **Ticketmaster** (☎ *415/421–8497* ⊕ *www.ticketmaster.com*), almost always sell out far in advance.

> **DID YOU KNOW?**
>
> The Beatles played their last concert together at Candlestick Park on August 29, 1966.

■TIP→ The park has gone through several names in recent years, due to various sponsors and naming rights deals—from 3Com Park at Candlestick Point to Monster Park to the San Francisco Stadium at Candlestick Point. Today it has reverted back to its original name: Candlestick Park, but in 2007 the city named the field part of the stadium after Bill Walsh, the late and popular '49ers coach. The entire area is now referred to as the Bill Walsh Field/Candlestick Park.

GOLF

You can get detailed directions to the city's public golf courses or reserve a tee time ($1 reservation fee per player) up to six days in advance through San Francisco's automated **municipal tee times reservation line** (☎ *415/750–4653* ⊕ *www.parks.sfgov.org*) and online site (click on the link for "Golf Courses").

Expect to use every club in your bag to tackle the fast, sloping greens and unpredictable winds at the challenging **Gleneagles International Golf Course** (⊠ *McLaren Park, 2100 Sunnydale Ave., Excelsior/Visitacion*

Valley ☎ *415/587–2425* ⊕ *www. gleneaglesgolfsf.com*). The 9-hole, par-36 course is a little worse for wear.

Golden Gate Park Golf Course (✉ *970 47th Ave. Golden Gate Park* ☎ *415/751–8987* ⊕ *www. goldengateparkgolf.com*) is a 9-hole, par-27 course in lovely Golden Gate Park, just above Ocean Beach. It's a beginner's paradise, but more seasoned players might be put off by the lax play and wayward balls. There's first-come, first-served play only (no reservations).

> ### TAKE IT TO THE BRIDGE
>
> We prefer biking across the bridge rather than walking, but you can get the same spectacular views either way. Be sure to wear a jacket, and save this for fair-weather days. Set aside four hours if you plan to walk all the way across and back.

★ **Harding Park Golf Course** (✉ *99 Harding Rd., at Skyline Blvd., Lake Merced* ☎ *415/664–4690* ⊕ *www.harding-park.com*) has an 18-hole, par-72 course and a 9-hole, par-32 Jack Fleming–designed course. The 9-hole course has all the characteristics of a championship course, but is less difficult. Both have fantastic views. About $15 million has been invested into the place over the past few years, and it shows. Book tee times as far in advance as possible. The 18-hole, par-68 **Lincoln Park Golf Course** (✉ *300 34th Ave., at Clement St., Richmond* ☎ *415/221–9911* ⊕ *www.lincolnparkgc.com*) offers magnificent views of the Golden Gate Bridge, but the somewhat scraggly greens don't hold up well in damp weather. Arnold Palmer Golf Management runs the challenging and well-maintained 18-hole, par-72 **Presidio Golf Course** (✉ *300 Finley Rd., at Arguello Blvd., Presidio* ☎ *415/561–4661* ⊕ *www.presidiogolf.com*). You can book tee times online for an additional $8–$12 fee.

16

HIKING

Hills and mountains—including Mt. Tamalpais in Marin County and Mt. Diablo in the East Bay, which has the second-longest sight lines anywhere in the world after Mt. Kilimanjaro—form a ring around the Bay Area. The **Bay Area Ridge Trail** (⊕ *ridgetrail.org*) is an ongoing project to connect all of the region's ridgelines. The trail is currently 300 mi long, but when finished it will extend 500 mi, stretching from San Jose to Napa and encompassing all nine Bay Area counties.

One of the most impressive ridgelines of the Bay Area Ridge Trail can be found on Mt. Tamalpais, in Marin County. The **Rock Spring Trail** starts at the Mountain Theater and gently climbs about 1¾ mi to the **West Point Inn,** once a stop on the Mt. Tam railroad route. Relax at a picnic table and stock up on water before forging ahead, via Old Railroad Grade Fire Road and the Miller Trail, to Mt. Tam's Middle Peak, about 2 mi uphill.

Starting at the Pan Toll Ranger Station, the precipitous **Steep Ravine Trail** brings you past stands of coastal redwoods and, in the springtime, numerous small waterfalls. Take the connecting **Dipsea Trail** to reach the town of Stinson Beach and its swath of golden sand. If you're too

CLOSE UP

Spa Day

Traditional sit-down Japanese showers and communal bathing are two out-of-the-ordinary features of **Kabuki Springs & Spa** (✉ *1750 Geary Blvd., Japantown* ☎ *415/922–6000* ⊕ *www. kabukisprings.com*). The renowned $155 Javanese Lulur Treatment includes a combination massage with jasmine oil, exfoliation with turmeric and ground rice, yogurt application, and a candlelight soak with rose petals. Men and women are welcome every day for private treatments, but call ahead regarding communal bathing schedules; the baths are coed only on Tuesday. Note that clothing is optional, except on coed days.

The futuristic **Tru Spa** (✉ *750 Kearney St., Financial District* ☎ *415/339–9700* ⊕ *www.truspa.com*) is a local favorite, and for good reason. Its uncluttered space radiates calm. They offer face, body, and nail treatments, all excellent. Try the Trutherapy75, a beautiful 75-minute, personally tailored full-body massage enhanced with aromatherapy and colored light therapy, bringing the treatment to a whole new level of indulgence. Prices range from $70 to $230 for body treatments.

Warning: after experiencing the serene and luxurious **Nob Hill Spa** (✉ *1075 California St., Nob Hill* ☎ *415/345– 2888* ⊕ *www.huntingtonhotel.com*) at the Huntington Hotel, you'll start to *expect* Champagne with your massage. Unique features include the eucalyptus steam bath and a gorgeous infinity pool that overlooks the city through a glass wall. After your treatments, you can hang here all day: take a yoga or Pilates class, get a green-tea body scrub, or just read on the sundeck.

All treatments at the St. Regis Hotel's très chic **Remède Spa** (✉ *125 3rd St., at Mission St., SoMa* ☎ *415/284–4060* ⊕ *www.remede.com*) incorporate a line of high-end French skin-care products. Offerings include custom skin therapy, massage, body scrubs, seaweed wraps, and a variety of mani–pedi, facial, and waxing options. Prices range from $40 for a manicure to $240 for a massage.

Elegant but casual **Spa Radiance** (✉ *3011 Fillmore St., between Union and Filbert Sts., Cow Hollow* ☎ *415/346–6281* ⊕ *www.sparadiance. com*) specializes in facials and draws the occasional celebrity. Try a vitamin-and-oxygen treatment, or the "super-duper" series—a deep-pore cleaning followed by dermabrasion.

---

weary to make the 3½-mi trek back up, Golden Gate Transit Bus 63 (Saturday, Sunday, and holidays from mid-March through early December) takes you from Stinson Beach back to the ranger station.

But you don't have to leave the city for a nice hike. In the middle of San Francisco you can climb to the top of Mt. Davidson, Bernal Heights, Corona Heights, or Buena Vista Park. Little more than undeveloped hilltops, they offer spectacular views of the city and beautiful shows of wildflowers in spring.

In the Presidio, hiking and biking trails wind through nearly 1,500 acres of woods and hills, past old redbrick military buildings and jaw-dropping scenic overlooks with bay and ocean views. Rangers and docents lead guided hikes and nature walks throughout the year. For a current schedule, pick up a copy of the quarterly *Park News* at the **Presidio Visitor Center** (⊠ *Presidio Officers' Club, Bldg. 50, Moraga Ave., in Main Post area* ☎ *415/561–4323* ⊕ *www.nps.gov/prsf*) or go online.

☺ Stop by the **Warming Hut** (⊠ *Bldg. 983 off Old Mason Rd., facing water just east of Fort Point* ☎ *415/561–3040*) to refuel on snacks and to browse through the extensive selection of books (including good ones for kids) and the many ingenious gifts made from recycled materials.

WORD OF MOUTH

"We headed to Crissy Field and oh what a great place that is. Loved seeing all the people with their dogs, Frisbees, kites and bikes. We stayed there a long time, walking along the shoreline and just hanging out. By now our girls are both plotting to find colleges in San Francisco because they have fallen in love with the city."

—mwessel

Fodor's Choice

★ The Presidio is part of **Golden Gate National Recreation Area (GGNRA)** (☎ *415/561–4700* ⊕ *www.nps.gov/goga*), which also encompasses the San Francisco coastline, the Marin Headlands, and Point Reyes National Seashore. It's veined with hiking trails, and guided walks are available. You can find current schedules at GGNRA visitor centers in the Presidio and Marin Headlands; they're also online at ⊕ *www.nps.gov/goga/parknews*. For descriptions of each location within the recreation area—along with rich color photographs, hiking information, and maps—pick up a copy of *Guide to the Parks*, available in local bookstores or online from the **Golden Gate National Parks Conservancy** (☎ *415/561–3000* ⊕ *www.parksconservancy.org*).

☺ The **Golden Gate Promenade** is another great walk; it passes through Crissy Field, taking in marshlands, kite-flyers, beachfront, and windsurfers, with the Golden Gate Bridge as a backdrop. The 3.3-mi walk is flat and easy—it should take about two hours round-trip. If you begin at Aquatic Park, you'll end up practically underneath the bridge at Fort Point Pier. ■ TIP→ **If you're driving, park at Fort Point and do the walk from west to east.** It can get blustery, even when it's sunny, so be sure to layer.

KAYAKING

Surrounded by water on three sides, San Francisco has plenty of opportunities for kayaking enthusiasts of all levels. **City Kayak** (⊠ *Pier 39, Embarcadero at Stockton St., Fisherman's Wharf* ⊠ *Pier 40, South Beach Harbor, SoMa* ☎ *415/357–1010* ⊕ *www.citykayak.com*), the only kayak-rental outfit in the city, operates bay tours along the waterfront and beneath the Bay Bridge starting from $50; they also run fullmoon night paddles and trips to Alcatraz. Rentals are $15 per hour for a single; $28 for a double; and $50 for a four-person kayak. Half-day trips depart at 10 AM daily. No prior experience is necessary, but you must watch an instructional video. ■ TIP→ **The Pier 39 location is for tours only, not rentals.** Trips run by **Outdoor Programs** (⊠ *500 Parnassus Ave., at 3rd Ave., Inner Sunset* ☎ *415/476–2078* ⊕ *www.outdoors.ucsf. edu*) originate in either Sausalito or Mission Bay in San Francisco and range from moonlight paddles from Sausalito (with views of the San Francisco skyline) to daytime sea-kayaking classes for all levels.

Sea Trek Kayaking (☎ *415/488–1000* ⊕ *www.seatrekkayak.com*) offers trips around Angel Island and the Golden Gate Bridge, moonlight paddles, and many trips in Marin County. Three-hour trips are $65 to $75 and full-day trips are $85 to $130. Most excursions leave from Sausalito (*see Chapter 18*), but Angel Island tours leave from the island.

RUNNING

PLACES TO RUN

The *San Francisco Bike Map and Walking Guide (see Bicycling, above)*, which indicates hill grades on city streets by color, is a great resource. Online, check the **San Francisco Road Runners Club** site (⊕ *www.sfrrc.org*) for some recommended routes and links to several local running clubs.

★ The city is spectacular for running—*Runner's World* magazine named San Francisco number one in its list of the top 25 running cities in 2005. There are more than 7 mi of paved trails in and around **Golden Gate Park**; circling **Stow Lake** and then crossing the bridge and running up the path to the top of Strawberry Hill is a total of 2½ mi. An enormously popular route is the 2-mi raised bike path that runs from Lincoln Way along the ocean, at the southern border of Golden Gate Park, to Sloat Boulevard, which is the northern border of the San Francisco Zoo. (Stick to the park's interior when it's windy, as ocean gusts can kick up sand.) From Sloat Boulevard you can pick up the **Lake Merced** bike path, which loops around the lake and the golf course, to extend your run another 5 mi. The paved path along the **Marina** runs 1½ mi (round-trip) along a flat, well-paved surface and has great bay views. You can extend your run by jogging the paths through the restored wetlands of Crissy Field (just past the yacht harbor), then up the hill to the Golden Gate Bridge: its walkway is 1.7 mi long.

EVENTS

First run in 1912, the 12K **Bay to Breakers race** (☎ *415/359–2800* ⊕ *www.baytobreakers.com*), held the third Sunday in May, is one of the world's oldest footraces—but in true San Francisco fashion there's nothing typical about it. About a third of the 50,000 to 100,000 runners are serious athletes; the rest are "fun runners" who wear famously wacky costumes—or no costumes at all (there's a faithful nude contingency). The race makes its way from the Embarcadero at the bay to the Pacific Ocean, passing through Golden Gate Park.

The **San Francisco Marathon** (☎ *888/958–6668* ⊕ *www.runsfm.com*), held annually on a Sunday in late July or early August, starts and finishes at the Embarcadero. Up to 7,000 runners pass through downtown, the Marina, the Presidio, and Golden Gate Park, and cross the Golden Gate Bridge, tackling some of the city's milder hills along the way.

CLOSE UP

A Shore Thing

Taking in a beachside sunset is the perfect way to end a busy day in the city (assuming the fog hasn't blown in for the afternoon). Always bring a sweater—even the sunniest of days can become cold and foggy without warning. Icy temperatures and treacherous currents make most waters too dangerous for swimming without a wet suit, but with a Frisbee, picnic, or some good walking shoes, you can have a fantastic day at the beach without leaving the city.

An urban beach, surrounded by Fort Mason, Ghirardelli Square, and Fisherman's Wharf, ☾ **Aquatic Park Beach** (⊕ www.nps.gov/safr) is a tiny, ¼-mi-long strip of sand with gentle water, bordered by docks and piers. The waters near shore are shallow, safe for kids to swim or wade, and fairly clean (admirably so, for a city). Locals—including the seemingly ubiquitous older-man-in-Speedo—come out for quick dips in the frigid water. The Golden Gate Promenade, with dog-walkers, inline-skaters, and cyclists, passes just behind the beach, so this isn't a secluded spot. Facilities include restrooms and showers.

Members of the Dolphin Club come every morning for a dip in the ice-cold waters of Aquatic Park; an especially large and raucous crowd braves the cold on New Year's Day.

Baker Beach (✉ Gibson Rd., off Bowley St., southwest corner of Presidio), with gorgeous views of the Golden Gate Bridge and the Marin Headlands, is a local favorite and an established nudist spot. (Never seen nude Frisbee? This is the place.) The pounding surf and strong currents make swimming a dangerous prospect, but the mile-long shoreline is ideal for fishing,

building sand castles, or watching sea lions at play. On warm days the entire beach is packed with bodies—including those nudists, who hang out at the north end. Picnic tables, grills, restrooms, and drinking water are available. Rangers give tours of the 95,000-pound cannon at Battery Chamberlin, overlooking the beach, the first weekend of every month.

Sheltered **China Beach,** one of the city's safest swimming beaches, was named for the impoverished Chinese fishermen who once camped here. (Some maps label it James D. Phelan Beach.) This 600-foot strip of sand, south of the Presidio and Baker Beach, has gentle waters as well as changing rooms, restrooms, showers, grills, drinking water, and picnic tables. Despite its humble beginnings, China Beach today is bordered by the multimillion-dollar homes of the Seacliff neighborhood. The hike down to the beach is steep.

☾ The largest—and probably best—of San Francisco's city beaches, **Ocean Beach** stretches for more than 3 mi along the Great Highway south of the Cliff House, making it ideal for long walks and runs. It isn't the cleanest shore, but it's an easy-to-reach place to chill; spot sea lions sunning themselves atop Seal Rock, at the north end of the beach; or watch daredevil surfers riding the roiling waves. Because of extremely dangerous currents, swimming isn't recommended. After the sun sets, bonfires form a string of lights along the beach in summer. (Fires are prohibited north of Fulton Street or south of Lincoln Way, the northern and southern edges of Golden Gate Park.) Restrooms are at the north end.

16

TENNIS

The **San Francisco Recreation and Park Department** (☎ *415/831–2700* ⊕ *www.parks.sfgov.org*) maintains 132 public tennis courts throughout the city. All courts listed here are free except for those in Golden Gate Park. **Golden Gate Park** (⊠ *John F. Kennedy Dr. near 3rd Ave.* ☎ *415/753–7131 reservations, 415/753–7001 information*) has 21 tennis courts. Court fees are $5 to $10. Call for weekend reservations. Weekdays are first come, first served; avoid times after 4 PM on weekdays, when school teams show up for practice. In the southeast corner of the beautiful Presidio, **Julius Kahn Park** (⊠ *W. Pacific Ave. between Spruce and Locust Sts., Presidio*) has four courts; the park and fantastic playground are great distractions for kids if the courts are full when you arrive. **Mission Dolores Park** (⊠ *18th and Dolores Sts., Castro*) has six lighted courts, available on a first-come, first-served basis. **Mountain Lake Park** (⊠ *Lake St. and 8th Ave., Richmond*), on the southern edge of the Presidio, has nice courts; it's an in-the-know tennis spot.

WHALE-WATCHING

Between January and April, hundreds of gray whales migrate along the coast; the rest of the year humpback and blue whales feed offshore at the Farallon Islands. The best place to watch them from shore is Point Reyes, in Marin County (*see Chapter 18*).

California Whale Adventures (☎ *415/760–8613 or 650/579–7777* ⊕ *www.californiawhaleadventures.com*) has year-round whale-watching trips ($95) Friday through Sunday. In October you can take a great white shark tour, and seabird tours run July through October; these tours cost $150 per person and are operated on weekends only. All trips leave from Fisherman's Wharf.

★ **The Oceanic Society** (☎ *415/441–1106 or 800/326–7491* ⊕ *www.oceanicsociety.org*) operates year-round full- and half-day whale-watching excursions ($90 Friday, $95 weekends) with top-notch guides. In winter they also run half-day trips ($50 Friday, $55 weekends) from Bodega Bay and Half Moon Bay. The society also has a whale-watching hotline (☎ *415/474–3385*) and publishes the excellent *Oceanic Society Field Guide to the Gray Whale*. Most trips leave from the San Francisco Yacht Harbor, outside the harbormaster's office in the Marina District.

Shopping

WORD OF MOUTH

"Shop 'Til We Drop was the order of my daughter's day. We checked out shopping downtown at Union Square, Hayes Valley (boutique big bucks), Haight-Ashbury (of course my old hippie soul loved this very reasonable shopping mecca), [and] Chinatown (absolutely great souvenirs)."

—joan

Updated by Natasha Sarkisian and Fiona G. Parrott

From its swank boutiques to its funky thrift stores, San Francisco is simply one of the best shopping destinations in the United States. Deep-pocketed buyers as well as window-shoppers mob the dozens of pricey shops packed into the blocks bordering Union Square, while bargain hunters dig through record shops and thrift stores in the Mission District and the Haight. From the anarchist bookstore to the mouthwatering specialty food purveyors at the gleaming Ferry Building, the local shopping opportunities reflect the city's personality.

Visitors with limited time often focus their energies on the high-density Union Square area, where several major department stores tower over exclusive boutiques. But if you're keen to find unique local shops, you should definitely move beyond the Union Square radius. Each neighborhood has its own distinctive finds.

If shopping in San Francisco has a downside, it's that real bargains can be few and far between. Sure, neighborhoods such as the Lower Haight and the Mission have thrift shops and other inexpensive stores, but you won't find many discount outlets in the city, where rents are sky-high and space is at a premium. And the 9.5% sales tax adds up for serious shoppers, though tax is waived if you arrange to have your purchases shipped to an out-of-state address.

Seasonal sales, usually in late January and late July or August, are good opportunities for finding deep discounts on fashionable clothing. The *San Francisco Chronicle* and *San Francisco Examiner* advertise sales. For smaller shops check the two free weeklies the *San Francisco Bay Guardian* and *SF Weekly,* which can be found on street corners every Wednesday. Sample sales are usually held by individual manufacturers, so check your favorite company's site before visiting. Splendora

(⊕ *www.splendora.com/cityguide/san_francisco*) is a good site to check for upcoming sales and promotions around the city.

MAJOR SHOPPING DISTRICTS

Many San Francisco neighborhoods keep their own hours, and the shops in those neighborhoods follow suit. In the Castro, for example, which is filled with restaurants and nightspots, many of the shops are open until 8 PM or later to take advantage of the evening foot traffic. The same is generally true of the nightlife mecca of the Mission. More sedate residential neighborhoods like Noe Valley, Pacific Heights, and Union Street tend to close up earlier, though, often by 6 PM and rarely past 7. (In these quieter neighborhoods, stores also tend to be closed Sunday, Monday, and sometimes even Tuesday.) Many Chinatown shops keep long hours, opening by 8 or 9 AM and staying open into the evening. Little boutiques in fashionable Hayes Valley and Jackson Square, on the other hand, usually keep shorter hours, often 10 or 11 AM to around 6 PM. And though the Union Square area attracts serious shoppers, you won't find anything to buy until around 10 AM, when most of the stores open. The neighborhoods below are profiled in alphabetical order.

THE CASTRO AND NOE VALLEY

The Castro, often called the gay capital of the world, is also a major shopping destination for all travelers. It's filled with men's clothing boutiques and home-accessories stores geared to the neighborhood's fairly wealthy demographic. Of course, there are plenty of places hawking kitsch, too, and if you're looking for something to shock your Aunt Martha back home, you've come to the right place. Just south of the Castro on 24th Street, largely residential Noe Valley is an enclave of fancy-food stores, bookshops, women's clothing boutiques, and specialty gift stores.

CHINATOWN

The intersection of Grant Avenue and Bush Street marks the gateway to Chinatown. The area's 24 blocks of shops, restaurants, and markets are a nonstop tide of activity. Dominating the exotic cityscape are the sights and smells of food: crates of bok choy, tanks of live crabs, cages of live partridges, and hanging whole chickens. Racks of Chinese silks, colorful pottery, baskets, and carved figurines are displayed chockablock on the sidewalks, alongside fragrant herb shops where your bill might be tallied on an abacus. And if you need to knock off souvenir shopping for the kids and office-mates in your life, the dense and multiple selections of toys, T-shirts, mugs, magnets, decorative boxes, and countless other trinkets make it a quick, easy, and inexpensive proposition.

EMBARCADERO CENTER

Four sprawling buildings of shops, restaurants, offices, and a popular independent movie theater—plus the Hyatt Regency hotel—make up the Embarcadero Center, downtown at the end of Market Street. Most of the stores are branches of upscale national chains, such as Ann Taylor, Banana Republic, and Crane & Co. It's one of the few major shopping centers with an underground parking garage and is a

17

Shopping
In and Around
Downtown

Marina Blvd.

The Embarcadero

Jefferson St.
Beach St.
North Point St.

Bay St.

1
2

3

Francisco St.
Chestnut St.

Francisco St.
Chestnut St.
Lombard St.

Lombard St.

Lombard St.

Columbus Ave.

Steiner St.
Fillmore St.
Webster St.
Laguna St.
Octavia St.
Gough St.
Franklin St.
Van Ness Ave.
Polk St.
Larkin St.
Hyde St.
Leavenworth St.

Greenwich St.
Filbert St.
Union St.

59

58

60
5

4

**RUSSIAN
HILL**

**NORTH
BEACH**

55
56 **54**
53

**PACIFIC
HEIGHTS**

Broadway

5
7
6

Green St.
Vallejo St.

51
52

8

Broadway Tunnel
Pacific St.
Jackson St.

50

Jackson St.
Washington St.
Clay St.
Sacramento St.
California St.

Taylor St.
Mason St.
Powell St.
Stockton St.
Grant Ave.

34

**NOB
HILL**

35 **36**

**See Pacific Heights
Shopping detail map**

Polk St.
Larkin St.
Hyde St.
Leavenworth St.
Jones St.

9

California St.

CHINATOWN

Pine St.
Bush St.
Sutter St.
Post St.

12
11

**UNION
SQUARE**

10

Geary St.

**See Pacific Heights
Shopping detail map**

Grove St. **13**
Ivy St. **14**
15 **16**

21

Hayes St.
20

22 **23**

O'Farrell St.
Ellis St.

**See Union Square
Shopping detail map**

17 **19**
18

24 **25** **26**

Linden St.

Franklin St.
Gough St.

Laguna St.
Octavia St.

Fell St.

Hickory St.

Eddy St.
Turk St.
Golden Gate Ave.
McAllister St.

37

4th St.
5th St.
6th St.
Howard St.

**CIVIC
CENTER**

Fulton St.

Grove St.
Hayes St.

**HAYES
VALLEY**

See Inset

United Nations Plaza;
Heart of the City
Farmers' Market

Mission St.
7th St.
8th St.
9th St.

Oak St.
Page St.
Haight St.

Buchanan St.
Laguna St.

10th St.
11th St.
12th St.

Market St.

27

28

29

30

Folsom St.
Harrison St.

31

32

popular spot for Financial District workers running errands on their lunch breaks.

FISHERMAN'S WHARF

A constant throng of sightseers crowds Fisherman's Wharf, and with good reason: Pier 39, the Anchorage, Ghirardelli Square, and the Cannery are all here, each with shops and restaurants, as well as outdoor entertainment—musicians, mimes, and magicians. Best of all are the Wharf's view of the bay and its proximity to cable-car lines, which can shuttle shoppers directly to Union Square. Many of the tourist-oriented shops border on tacky, peddling the requisite Golden Gate tees, taffy, and baskets of shells, but tucked into the mix are a few fine galleries, clothing shops, and groceries that even locals will deign to visit.

> ### TOP LOCAL SHOPS
>
> ■ **Cookin': Recycled Gourmet Appurtenances.** Terrific browsing through all sorts of vintage cookware.
>
> ■ **Great China Herb Co.** Like an insta-trip across the Pacific; hundreds of herbs and surprises like dried sea horses.
>
> ■ **Lululemon.** Comfy, cool loungewear, especially the perfect-fit pants.
>
> ■ **Margaret O'Leary.** Knitwear like no other; it'll last for decades.
>
> ■ **Metier.** Outstanding selection for women; a one-stop for shoes, dresses, jewelry.

THE HAIGHT

Haight Street is a perennial attraction for visitors, if only to see the sign at Haight and Ashbury streets—the geographic center of the Flower Power movement during the 1960s, so it can be a bummer to find this famous intersection is now the turf for Gap and Ben & Jerry's. Don't be discouraged; it's still possible to find high-quality vintage clothing, funky shoes, folk art from around the world, and used records and CDs galore in this always-busy neighborhood.

HAYES VALLEY

A community park called Hayes Green breaks up a crowd of cool shops just west of the Civic Center. Here you can find everything from hip housewares to art galleries to handcrafted jewelry. The density of unique stores—as well as the lack of chains anywhere in sight—makes it a favorite destination for many San Francisco shoppers.

JACKSON SQUARE

Clustered in the shadow of the Transamerica building, the city's finest retail antiques dealers, along with law firms and cafés, occupy three-story brick buildings, some of which date to the city's gold-rush days. A few boutiques and modern design houses have joined the mix of intimate showrooms targeting serious collectors of tribal rugs, botanical prints, and antique silver.

JAPANTOWN

Unlike the ethnic enclaves of Chinatown, North Beach, and the Mission, the 5-acre **Japan Center** (⊠ *Bordered by Laguna, Fillmore, and Post Sts. and Geary Blvd.* ☎ *No phone*) is under one roof. The three-block complex includes a reasonably priced public garage and three shop-filled buildings. Especially worthwhile are the Kintetsu and Kinokuniya buildings, where shops sell things like bonsai trees, tapes and records, jewelry, antique kimonos, *tansu* (Japanese chests), electronics, and colorful glazed dinnerware and teapots.

THE MARINA DISTRICT

With the city's highest density of (mostly) non-chain stores, the

SALE KICKOFF

The week after Black Friday kicks off sample-sale season with the **Annual Third Street Warehouse Sale** (☎ 415/561–9703 ⊕ www.3rdstreetsale.com). This event pulls together small local merchants selling everything from punky jewelry to yoga mats to olive oil, all at 30% to 60% off.

Marina is an outstanding shopping nexus. But it's nobody's secret—those with plenty of cash and style to burn flood the boutiques to snap up luxe accessories and housewares. Union Street and Chestnut Street in particular cater to the shopping whims of the grown-up sorority sisters and frat boys who live in the surrounding pastel Victorians.

THE MISSION

The aesthetic of the resident Pabst Blue Ribbon–downing hipsters and starving-artist types contributes to the affordability and individuality of shopping here. These night owls keep the city's best thrift stores, vintage-furniture shops, alternative bookstores, and, increasingly, small clothing boutiques afloat. As the Mission gentrifies, though, bargain hunters find themselves trekking the long blocks in search of truly local flavor. Thankfully, many of the city's best bakeries and cafés are sprinkled throughout the area.

NORTH BEACH

Although it's sometimes compared to New York City's Greenwich Village, North Beach is only a fraction of the size, clustered tightly around Washington Square and Columbus Avenue. Most of its businesses are small eateries, cafés, and shops selling clothing, antiques, and vintage wares. Once the center of the Beat movement, North Beach still has a bohemian spirit that's especially apparent at the rambling City Lights Bookstore, where Beat poetry lives on.

PACIFIC HEIGHTS

The rest of the city likes to deprecate its wealthiest neighborhood, but no one has any qualms about weaving through the mansions to come to Fillmore and Sacramento streets to shop. With grocery and hardware stores sitting alongside local clothing ateliers and international designer outposts, these streets manage to mix small-town America with big-city glitz. After you've splurged on a cashmere sweater or a handblown glass vase, snag an outdoor seat at Peet's or Coffee Bean; it's the perfect way to pass an afternoon watching the parade of Old Money, dogs, and strollers.

17

SOMA

High San Francisco rents mean there aren't many discount outlets in the city, but a few do exist in the renovated warehouses south of Market Street, called SoMa. Most outlets are along the streets and alleyways bordered by 2nd, Townsend, Howard, and 10th streets. At the other end of the spectrum is the gift shop of the San Francisco Museum of Modern Art, which sells handmade jewelry, upscale and offbeat housewares, and other great gift items.

UNION SQUARE

Serious shoppers head straight to Union Square, San Francisco's main shopping area and the site of most of its department stores, including Macy's, Neiman Marcus, Barneys, and Saks Fifth Avenue along with Borders Books, Music & Cafe. Nearby are such platinum-card international boutiques as Yves Saint Laurent, Cartier, Emporio Armani, Gucci, Hermès of Paris, Louis Vuitton, and Gianni Versace.

The latest major arrival is the **Westfield San Francisco Shopping Centre** (⊠ *865 Market St., between 4th and 5th Sts., Union Square* ☎ *415/495–5656*), anchored by Bloomingdale's and Nordstrom. Besides the sheer scale of this mammoth mall, it's notable for its gorgeous atriums and its top-notch dining options (no typical food courts here—instead you'll find branches of a few top local restaurants). The area is also home to the new Barneys CO-OP; the New York institution's SF outpost has high, urban fashion on seven exquisitely appointed floors.

■ TIP→ Although the department stores and some boutiques may remain open until 9 PM and beyond, most retailers in the square don't open until 10 AM or later, so there isn't much advantage to docking in the neighborhood before then unless you're grabbing an early breakfast nearby.

ANTIQUES

The most obvious place to look for antiques is Jackson Square. Another option is the San Francisco Design Center, where three buildings and more than 100 showrooms display furnishings and other home-design items. Although the showrooms are open to the public, many sell only to design professionals.

Antonio's Antiques. The two busily packed stories of furniture and objets d'art might include an 18th-century French harp or delicate tortoiseshell miniatures. If you like the shop's pieces, which lean toward items from the 17th and 18th centuries, you may also want to visit its larger store in SoMa, a maze of museum-quality English and French antiques. Italian pieces are housed across the street. ⊠ *701 Sansome St., at Jackson St., Financial District* ☎ *415/781–1737* ⊠ *Warehouse, 701 Bryant St., at 5th St., SoMa* ☎ *415/781–1737*.

Evelyn's Antique Chinese Furniture. The precious pieces of Han dynasty pottery and 19th-century bamboo bookcases artfully arranged in the front room are only a small portion of the restored and unrestored items sold at this store, which they claim has the largest selection of antique Chinese furniture in the United States. In the spacious back room items both large (cabinets) and small (steel tea stoves) are stacked high. ✉ *381 Hayes St., between Franklin and Gough Sts., Hayes Valley* ☎ *415/255–1815.*

★ **Forgotten Shanghai.** The Asian antiques for sale here are both beautiful and practical, with camphor-wood trunks and beautifully aged leather boxes among the treasures. ✉ *245 Kansas St., near 16th St., Potrero Hill* ☎ *415/701–7707.*

Grand Central Station Antiques. This large, three-story space stocks mostly 19th- and early-20th-century European and American storage pieces—armoires, highboys, buffets, and the occasional barrister bookcase—with an emphasis on the small and practical. Service is affable. ✉ *333 9th St., between Folsom and Ringold Sts., SoMa* ☎ *415/252–8155.*

Hunt Antiques. Full of fine 17th- to 19th-century period English furniture, porcelains, Staffordshire pottery, paintings, and grandfather clocks, this Jackson Square shop feels like an English town house. ✉ *478 Jackson St., between Montgomery and Sansome Sts., Financial District* ☎ *415/989–9531.*

Interior Visions. The welcoming proprietor is happy to tell you about her collection of mostly 19th- and early-20th-century pieces. Among the treasures might be a French gold-velvet chaise longue from the 1930s or a turn-of-the-20th-century Belgian oak highboy. ✉ *2206 Polk St., between Vallejo and Green Sts., Russian Hill* ☎ *415/771–0656.*

Lotus Collection. The handmade pillows, tapestries depicting iconic events in Europe, and Japanese brocades make this one of the finest collections of decorative antique textiles in the States. It's also a secret source for the city's interior designers outfitting Pac Heights mansions. ✉ *445 Jackson St., between Montgomery and Sansome Sts., Financial District* ☎ *415/398–8115.*

Schein & Schein. This tiny, sunny spot houses thousands of antique maps and engraved prints, many with a local focus. Whether you're looking for a chart of the world from the 13th century or a map of the Barbary Coast—they have it all, from very inexpensive small prints to genuine collector pieces. Even if you're no cartographer, the helpful owners will enthrall you with their historical anecdotes and educate you with their vast knowledge. ✉ *1435 Grant Ave., between Green and Union Sts., North Beach* ☎ *415/399–8882.*

ART GALLERIES

Art galleries are ubiquitous in San Francisco. Although most surround Union Square, Hayes Valley, near the Civic Center, has become another gallery enclave, and the Mission District and SoMa are the spots for less expensive works by local emerging artists. The free *San Francisco Bay Area Gallery Guide*, available at most galleries, includes a handy map and addresses of galleries all over the city. For a quick overview, stop by 49 Geary Street by Union Square, which houses several of the city's best galleries. Most galleries are closed on Sunday and Monday.

Catharine Clark Gallery. Although nationally known artists—like Masami Teraoka and Nina Katchadourian—display their sculpture, paintings,

Union Square Shopping

Pine St.

Powell St.

Bush St.

Stockton St.

Grant Ave.

Sutter St.

Kearny St.

Post St.

UNION SQUARE

Maiden Lane

Mason St.

Geary St.

O'Farrell St.

Market St.

3rd St.

Mission St.

Ellis St.

4th St.

0   1/8 mi

0   1/8 km

Eddy St.

Westfield San Francisco
Shopping Centre

photographs, and installation artwork here, emerging artists with a Bay Area connection get the spotlight, like Chester Arnold and Josephine Taylor. ⊠ *150 Minna St., between 3rd and New Montgomery Sts., SoMa* 🕾 *415/399–1439.*

★ **Fraenkel Gallery.** One of the world's preeminent photography galleries, Fraenkel has represented museum-caliber photographers like Richard Avedon, Garry Winogrand, and Idris Khan since 1979. They usually exhibit one or two of their artists at a time, but each July at their annual exhibit titled "Several Exceptionally Good Recently Acquired Pictures" you can see a full range of their work. ⊠ *49 Geary St., between Kearny St. and Grant Ave., Union Square* 🕾 *415/981–2661.*

Hackett-Freedman Gallery. The gallery prides itself on its friendly staff, who will educate you about the art or leave you alone—whichever you prefer. Contemporary realist works, including still lifes, landscapes, and figurative paintings, compose the core of its collection. ⊠ *250 Sutter St., Suite 400, between Grant Ave. and Kearny St., Union Square* 🕾 *415/362–7152.*

Fodor's Choice **Hang Art.** A spirit of fun imbues this industrial-chic space, where emerg-
★ ing artists display their works. Prices range from a few hundred dollars to several thousand, making it an ideal place for novice art collectors to get their feet wet. A rental program lets you take a piece home before buying it. ⊠ *567 Sutter St., between Mason and Powell Sts., Union Square* 🕾 *415/434–4264.*

Hespe Gallery. Priced between three and 50 grand, the paintings and sculptures here by mid-career artists, like Eric Zener and Kim Cogan, especially Californians, are primarily done in an abstract style. Owner Charles Hespe is an instantly likable art enthusiast who equally delights buyers and browsers. ⊠ *251 Post St., Suite 420, between Stockton and Grant Sts., Union Square* 🕾 *415/776–5918.*

John Berggruen Gallery. Twentieth-century American and European paintings are displayed throughout three airy floors here. Works by Bay Area figurative artists such as Richard Diebenkorn are a specialty. ⊠ *228 Grant Ave., at Post St., Union Square* 🕾 *415/781–4629.*

John Pence Gallery. The 8,000-square-foot facility, San Francisco's largest gallery, can display more than 100 works. Drawings, paintings, and sculpture are all represented, with many of the works by important contemporary academic realists. ⊠ *750 Post St., between Leavenworth and Jones Sts., Tenderloin* 🕾 *415/441–1138.*

Meyerovich Gallery. Sculpture and works on paper by masters such as Pablo Picasso, Marc Chagall, Robert Motherwell, and Henry Moore are the attraction. Colorful, whimsical sculptures by contemporary artist Ron Tatro draw the eye from across the room. ⊠ *251 Post St., 4th fl., between Stockton St. and Grant Ave., Union Square* 🕾 *415/421–7171.*

San Francisco Camerawork. This nonprofit artists' organization holds frequently changing thematic exhibits. It's also an excellent photography resource center with a well-stocked bookstore and a reference library. The lecture program includes noted photographers and critics. ⊠ *657 Mission St., 2nd fl., between 2nd and New Montgomery Sts., SoMa* 🕾 *415/512–2020.*

17

Southern Exposure. One of the city's most established venues for cutting-edge art is this artist-run, nonprofit gallery. Juried shows and accompanying lectures and films change frequently in the custom-designed galleries. ⊠ *3030 20th St., at Alabama St., Mission* ☎ *415/863–2141.*

Varnish Fine Art. The cast-metal sculptures that are a specialty here look right at home in the artsy-industrial gallery with high corrugated metal ceilings. A wine bar on the ground floor encourages visitors to linger and look at the artwork, and if you settle into one of the couches upstairs to peruse their small library of art books you could end up pleasantly whiling away the afternoon. ⊠ *77 Natoma St., between 1st and 2nd Sts., SoMa* ☎ *415/222–6131.*

BEAUTY

★ **BeneFit.** You can find the locally based BeneFit line of cosmetics and skin-care products at Macy's and Sephora, but it's much more fun to come to one of the eponymous boutiques. No-pressure salespeople dab you with whimsical makeup such as Ooh La Lift concealer and Tinted Love, a stain for lips and cheeks. ⊠ *2117 Fillmore St., between California and Sacramento Sts., Pacific Heights* ☎ *415/567–0242* ⊠ *2219 Chestnut St., between Scott and Pierce Sts., Marina* ☎ *415/567–1173.*

Kiehl's. Perhaps because it started out in 1851, Kiehl's has a no-nonsense appeal. Fans swear by its high-quality, simply packaged skin- and hair-care products. This spacious store stocks a wide variety of its lotions, potions, and soaps. Not sure whether the Formula 133 Hair Conditioner and Grooming Aid is right for you? Ask for a sample. ⊠ *2360 Fillmore St., between Washington and Clay Sts., Pacific Heights* ☎ *415/359–9260* ⊠ *865 Market St., between 4th and 5th Sts., Union Square* ☎ *415/644–0112.*

★ **Lush.** Towers of bulk soap, which can be cut to order, and mountains of baseball-size fizzing "bath bombs" are some of the first items you'll see in this tightly packed and extremely fragrant little shop. They pride themselves on using the highest-quality ingredients, and some potions are so fresh (and perishable) they're stored in a refrigerator and come with an expiration date. ⊠ *240 Powell St., between O'Farrell and Geary Sts., Union Square* ☎ *415/693–9633* ⊠ *2116 Union St., at Webster St., Cow Hollow* ☎ *415/921–5874.*

Nancy Boy. This sparse white-on-white locally owned store, sells indulgent skin- and hair-care products for men, as well as a small selection of aromatherapy items, such as soy travel candles scented with essential oils. ⊠ *347 Hayes St., between Franklin and Gough Sts., Hayes Valley* ☎ *415/552–3802.*

BOOKS

Book Passage. Windows at this modest-size bookstore frame close-up views of the Ferry Building docks and San Francisco Bay. Commuters snatch up magazines by the front door as they speed off to catch their ferries, while leisurely shoppers thumb through the thorough selection of cooking and travel titles. Author events typically take place several

The Mission/Noe Valley Shopping

KEY
M Muni stops
b BART stations

CLOSE UP

Cool Local Souvenirs

■ Something from McEvoy Ranch's body-care line, like their olive mud soap or their gardener's hand salve, all made with locally produced, organic olive oil.

■ A book published by City Lights, like one of their new political dynamos or something old-school like Allen Ginsberg's evergreen *Howl.*

■ A Phthalates-free EarthLust stainless-steel water bottle overlaid with intricate graphics, of, say, an owl, that you can stylishly sip from while climbing the hills, available at Spring.

■ A cashmere weekender cardigan from Margaret O'Leary—something to live in every Saturday.

■ A collectible bottle of California wine from K&L Wine Merchants or a rare Armagnac from D&M Wines and Liquors.

■ A vintage 1960s sundress from American Rag for something retro but not too costumey.

■ A striking porcelain tea and coffee service designed by the renowned chef Thomas Keller, found at Gump's.

—Natasha Sarkisian

times a month. ⊠ *1 Ferry Bldg., #42, Embarcadero at foot of Market St., Embarcadero* ☎ *415/835–1020.*

Booksmith. Founded in 1976, this fine bookshop sells current releases, children's titles, and offbeat periodicals. Authors passing through town often make a stop at this neighborhood institution. ⊠ *1644 Haight St., between Cole and Clayton Sts., Haight* ☎ *415/863–8688.*

Bound Together Anarchist Book Collective. This old-school collective, in operation since 1976, stocks books on anarchist theory and practice, as well as an array of books on other forms of radicalism, gender issues, and other left-leaning topics. A portion of the revenue goes to the support of anarchist projects and the Prisoners' Literature Project. ⊠ *1369 Haight St., at Masonic Ave., Haight* ☎ *415/431–8355.*

Fodor'sChoice **City Lights Bookstore.** The city's most famous bookstore is where the Beat
★ movement of the 1950s was born. Neal Cassady and Jack Kerouac hung out in the basement and now regulars and tourists while hours away in this well-worn space. The upstairs room highlights impressive poetry and Beat literature collections. Poet Lawrence Ferlinghetti, the owner, remains active in the workings of this three-story place. Since publishing Allen Ginsberg's *Howl* in 1956, City Lights' press continues to publish a dozen new titles each year. ⊠ *261 Columbus Ave., at Broadway, North Beach* ☎ *415/362–8193.*

★ **A Different Light.** San Francisco's most extensive gay and lesbian bookstore has books by, for, and about lesbians, gay men, bisexuals, and transgendered people. Subjects run the gamut from sci-fi and fantasy to religion and film criticism. The magazine section is large. A rack in front is chock-full of flyers for local events. ⊠ *489 Castro St., between Market and 18th Sts., Castro* ☎ *415/431–0891.*

Dog Eared Books. An eclectic group of shoppers—gay and straight, fashionable and practical—wanders the aisles of this pleasantly ramshackle bookstore. The diverse selection of publications, about 85% of them used, includes quirky selections like vintage children's books, remaindered art books, and local 'zines. A bin of free books just outside the front door is fun to browse, if only to see the odd assortment of out-of-date titles. ⊠ *900 Valencia St., at 20th St., Mission* ☎ *415/282–1901.*

Get Lost Travel Books, Maps & Gear. Here travel literature is mixed in for inspiration amid the guidebooks—totaling more than 9,000 titles. You can also find language-instruction materials, luggage, and other travel accessories. ⊠ *1825 Market St., at Guerrero St., Mission* ☎ *415/437–0529.*

Kinokuniya Bookstore. The selection of English-language books about Japanese culture—everything from medieval history to origami instructions—is one of the finest in the country. Kinokuniya is the city's biggest seller of Japanese-language books. Dozens of glossy Asian fashion magazines attract the young and trendy, and books and DVDs related to the Japanese anime director Hayao Miyazaki are the latest trend. ⊠ *Kinokuniya Bldg., 1581 Webster St., 2nd fl., Japantown* ☎ *415/567–7625.*

Modern Times Bookstore. Named after Charlie Chaplin's politically subversive film, the store stocks high-quality literary fiction and nonfiction, much of it with a political bent. There are also sections for children's books, Spanish-language titles, and magazines and local subversive 'zines. Author readings and public forums are held regularly. ■ TIP→ If you're looking to kill a little time in the Mission before hooking up with dinner companions, this is a low-key and inviting place to hide out in the stacks. ⊠ *888 Valencia St., between 19th and 20th Sts., Mission* ☎ *415/282–9246.*

★ **William Stout Architectural Books.** Architect William Stout began selling books out of his apartment 25 years ago. Today the store sources libraries from around the world and Bay Area professionals with serious-minded tomes on architecture and design. Head down into the crumbling whitewashed basement for beautifully illustrated coffee-table books. Stout is also the sole distributor of the über-popular IDEO method cards, which offer and inspire design solutions. ⊠ *804 Montgomery St., at Jackson St., Financial District* ☎ *415/391–6757.*

CHILDREN'S CLOTHING

Dottie Doolittle. Pacific Heights mothers shop here for charming silk dresses and other special-occasion outfits for their little ones. Less pricey togs for infants, boys to size 12, and girls to size 16, are also on hand. ⊠ *3680 Sacramento St., at Spruce St., Pacific Heights* ☎ *415/563–3244.*

Murik. Those with fashion-forward five-year-olds will be grateful to discover this tiny shop. From Petit Bateau jumpers for infants to linen pants and ruffled shirts for your grade-schooler, the pricey garments are so adorable you might wish you could wear them yourself. ⊠ *73 Geary St., between Grant Ave. and Kearny St., Union Square* ☎ *415/395–9200.*

17

Small Frys. The colorful cottons carried here are mainly for infants, with some articles for older children. The mix includes OshKosh and many Californian and French labels. A few shelves of toys and whimsical finger puppets round out the store's selection. ☒ *4066 24th St., between Castro and Noe Sts., Noe Valley* ☎ *415/648–3954.*

CLOTHING: MEN AND WOMEN

COOL AND CASUAL

AB fits. The friendly staff can help guys and gals sort through the jeans selection, one of the hippest in the city (check out the Del Forte organic denim). The salespeople pride themselves on being able to match the pants to the person. Though many of the same designers are stocked at both locations, the Union Square branch leans toward slightly dressier fashions. ☒ *1519 Grant Ave., between Filbert and Union Sts., North Beach* ☎ *415/982–5726.*

Behind the Post Office. There's no "return to sender" here, as covetable women's clothes fill this little shop. In spite of its limited size, this store attracts a devoted clientele for its casual clothing, including slinky knits by Ella Moss and jeans by Citizens of Humanity. ☒ *1510 Haight St., at Ashbury St., Haight* ☎ *415/861–2507.*

★ **Blues Jean Bar.** With more than a dozen different brands of jeans on tap, this Western-theme shop takes the pain out of finding the perfect pair of denims. Simply tell the "bartender" the size and style you're looking for and he or she will load you up with several trendy pairs by designers such as Carpe Denim and True Religion to try on in either the "Him," "Her," or "Them" dressing rooms. ☒ *1827 Union St., between Octavia and Laguna Sts., Cow Hollow* ☎ *415/346–4280.*

Eco Citizen. The men's and women's clothes here are not just green, they're also fair-trade, organic, sustainable, and trendy—yet still basic enough to wear for more than one season (so you won't have to throw them out after two months, which makes them truly green). ☒ *1488 Vallejo St., between Polk and Larkin Sts., Russian Hill* ☎ *415/614–0100.*

Loyal Army. This locally based graphic design company creates hilarious graphic tees inspired by Japanese kawaii or cutesy comics. Think a stack of pancakes with the inscription "I'm a hot mess." Their designs embellish super-soft tees, hoodies, and totes. ☒ *1728 Haight St., between Cole and Shrader Sts., Haight* ☎ *415/221–6200.*

RAG. To really get your pulse on the local fashion scene, seek out the Residents Apparel Gallery. Bay Area designers rent racks to showcase their deconstructed tees and socially responsible designs. Above each rack hangs a photo and a bio of the aspiring designer. ☒ *541 Octavia St., between Hayes and Grove Sts., Hayes Valley* ☎ *415/621–7718.*

Self Edge. Hanging from metal rods on perfectly separated wooden hangers are dozens of pairs of Japanese selvage denim. The industrial-weight fabric that makes up these jeans will run you between $160 and $450, but they'll hem them for free with their vintage chain-stitching machine. ☒ *714 Valencia St., at 18th St., Mission* ☎ *415/558–0658.*

San Francisco shoppers are spoiled for choice on Haight Street.

Three Bags Full. Everything here is hand-knit—whether it be a feather-weight cashmere shrug or a chunky wool cable sweater. Local business-women come here to replace their stuffy suit jackets with a cozy but sleek wool or cotton blazer. ✉ *2181 Union St., at Fillmore St., Cow Hollow* ☎ *415/567–5753* ✉ *500 Sutter St., at Powell St., Union Square* ☎ *415/398–7987* ✉ *3314 Sacramento St., near Fillmore St., Pacific Heights* ☎ *415/923–1454.*

FLIRTY

Dema. Dema Grim's classically cut clothes in ethnic and vintage fabrics that really pop truly capture the spirit of the Mission. ✉ *1038 Valencia St., between 21st and 22nd Sts., Mission* ☎ *415/206–0500.*

Dish. Many of the women's clothes displayed within this spare, concrete-floor space are romantic, minus the frills. Look for the flowing dresses of local designer Erica Tanov, as well as clothes and accessories by more widely known designers like BCBG and Theory. ✉ *541 Hayes St., between Laguna and Octavia Sts., Hayes Valley* ☎ *415/252–5997.*

Elizabeth Charles. Parlaying the city's current obsession with the land down under, this intimate boutique stocks only Australian and New Zealand designers, with an emphasis on flowing frocks in the very finest fabrics. ✉ *2056 Fillmore St., between California and Pine Sts., Pacific Heights* ☎ *415/440–2100.*

HeidiSays. Fanciful windows brimming with bright and festive prints draw passersby into this store. Perky salespeople help you choose between Catherine Malandrino, Trina Turk, and Rebecca Taylor frocks. To complete your emblematic San Fran chic outfit, head down the street, where the Heidi empire continues with HeidiSays Casual and HeidiSays Shoes, where you can pick up lingerie, loungewear, bags, and pumps. ✉ *2426, 2416, and 2105 Fillmore St., Pacific Heights* ☎ *415/749–0655.*

WORD OF MOUTH

"For funky, one-of-a-kind shops, my favorite area is Valencia Street, roughly between 16th and 22nd or so. Little artisanal boutiques selling cool clothing, objets d'art, etc. Plus you are in the 'hot belt' of some of San Francisco's most forward-thinking restaurants."
—dovima

Lemon Twist. A fashionable family affair: Dannette Scheib is known for her inspired details, such as her signature tulle petticoats that go underneath her A-line skirts. Her husband Eric's T-shirts capture an urban essence in a simply stenciled telephone pole design. Their Lemon Drop baby line is both sweet and tart. ■ TIP→ If you see a print you like on the workshop table in back, she's happy to make you a custom piece at no additional charge and ship it to you back home. ✉ *537 Octavia Blvd., between Hayes and Grove Sts., Hayes Valley* ☎ *415/558–9699.*

Ooma. The delicious fashions, many made by local designers, tend toward the feminine and flirty (no men's stuff here). A wide range of jewelry and accessories complements the colorful clothes. ✉ *1422 Grant Ave., between Green and Union Sts., North Beach* ☎ *415/627–6963.*

Sarah Shaw. Specializing in cocktail and party dresses, this boutique racks up American designers like Wendy Hil, Trina Turk, and Robert Rodriguez. Businesswomen looking to give their corporate suits a feminine spin take their cues from her inspired outfits. ✉ *3095 Sacramento St., at Baker St., Presidio Heights* ☎ *415/929–2990.*

HIGH DESIGN

Anica. This avant-garde women's clothing boutique—whose name means "charismatic" in Hindi—specializes in low-maintenance high-fashion. The designs here, from serious up-and-coming designers, actually look good off the hanger. ✉ *2418 Polk St., between Filbert and Union Sts., Russian Hill* ☎ *415/447–2878.*

The Archive. The closest thing you'll get to Savile Row in San Francisco, this small and narrow cutting-edge men-only fashion boutique has everything from handmade suits to large handmade silver belt buckles from top-shelf Japanese and Italian designers. ✉ *317 Sutter St., between Grant Ave. and Stockton St., Union Square* ☎ *415/391–5550.*

Carrots. The former location of Ernie's (the historic restaurant made famous in Hitchcock's Vertigo) was transformed by Melissa Grimm and her sister Catie. The name points to the sisters' background as members of the Grimm family of Grimmway Farms fame (the world's largest grower of carrots). Their spacious emporium showcases Bay Area superstar designers Alexander Wang and Peter Som alongside Narciso Rodriguez and Stella McCartney. The icing on the cake (literally!) is a bar that serves mini carrot cupcakes. ✉ *843 Montgomery St., between Gold and Jackson Sts., Jackson Square* ☎ *415/834–9040.*

Erica Tanov. The designer's background in lingerie and bedding guides the delicate designs here: wispy cashmere, silk organza and charmeuse, and linen. Sweaters tend to drape and wrap; skirts and pajama-wide pants are often brightened with florals or stripes. ⊠ *2408 Fillmore St., between Jackson and Washington Sts., Pacific Heights* ☎ *415/674–1228.*

Gucci. The gold-label designer upped the ante with its palatial, brand-new, 11,000 square feet of black lacquer, bronze, and marble.

WORD OF MOUTH

"Union Street has good shopping, but it's not what I'd consider funky. Hayes Valley, the Mission, and that old standby the Haight are all funkier."   —Leely

The first floor is dominated by fine jewelry, handbags, and luggage. Shoes run the show on the second floor, and if you make it to the third floor without maxing out your credit card you'll be rewarded for trying on an evening gown or dinner coat with a flute of champagne. ⊠ *240 Stockton St., at Post St., Union Square* ☎ *415/392–2808.*

Fodor's Choice ★ **Margaret O'Leary.** If you can only buy one piece of clothing in San Francisco, make it a hand-loomed, locally made cashmere sweater by this Irish-born local legend. The perfect antidote to the city's wind and fog, the sweaters are so beloved by San Franciscans that some people literally never wear anything else. The Fillmore location, the larger of the two, is rounded out with a nice selection of Margaret's other favorite designers like jeans by AG Denim. Pick up an airplane wrap for your trip home and a media cozy to keep your iPod toasty, too. ⊠ *1 Claude La., at Sutter St., Union Square* ☎ *415/391–1010* ⊠ *2400 Fillmore St., at Washington St., Pacific Heights* ☎ *415/771–9982.*

17

Metier. For boutique shopping that's anything but hit or miss, browse through this unusual selection of clothes by brands like Blumarine and See by Chloe. An even more impressive selection of jewelry by artists like Cathy Waterman and Philip Crangi has won this boutique an obsessively loyal following. ⊠ *355 Sutter St., between Stockton and Grant Sts., Union Square* ☎ *415/989–5395.*

Rolo. The store sells hard-to-find men's and women's denim, sportswear, shoes, and accessories with a distinct European influence, including clothes designed by Comme des Garçons, Corpus Denim, and Fred Perry. The Market Street location carries menswear only. ■ TIP→ The branch at 1301 Howard St. sells past-season items at a discount of up to 50%. ⊠ *2351 Market St., at Castro St., Castro* ☎ *415/431–4545* ⊠ *1301 Howard St., at 9th St., SoMa* ☎ *415/861–2097.*

Tory Burch. The East Coast socialite–turned–CFDA Accessories Designer of the Year brightened the notoriously staid Maiden Lane with her new outpost for Bergdorf Blondes. Inspired by designs from the sixties and seventies, the carpet is a rich avocado, walls are magenta among other colors, and velvet curtains frame floor-to-ceiling mirrors in other candy colors. In addition to her ubiquitous ballet flats (even available in toddler sizes), her signature tunics, silk blouses, and suits are on offer. ⊠ *50 Maiden La., between Kearney and Grant Sts., Union Square* ☎ *415/398–1525.*

OUTLET AND DISCOUNT CLOTHING

Christine Foley. Discounts of up to 50% apply to the hand-loomed cotton sweaters with fanciful, intricate designs. There's a particularly large selection of colorful sweaters for children. Pillows, stuffed animals, and assorted knickknacks sell at retail prices in the small storefront showroom. ⊠ *950 Mason St., between Sacramento and California Sts., Union Square* ☎ *415/399–9938.*

★ **Jeremy's.** A discount store for people who usually wouldn't be caught dead discount shopping, this store offers steep discounts (generally 20% to 50%, with occasional clearance items even more deeply discounted) on top-notch men's and women's apparel by designers such as Prada and Jil Sander. The space is cleanly organized, so you won't need to rack-rake. ⊠ *2 S. Park Rd., at 2nd St., SoMa* ☎ *415/882–4929.*

Fodor's Choice **Loehmann's.** Renovations have tamed the chaos that used to reign among
★ these drastically reduced designer labels, resulting in more orderly racks and more spacious changing rooms. Credit is due to their massive inventory, from gym clothes to business wear. The racks for in-season overruns are tidier; the sections of past seasons' clothes are messier but have even deeper discounts. The shoe department is across the street from the main store. ⊠ *222 Sutter St., at Kearny St., Union Square* ☎ *415/982–3215.*

My Roommate's Closet. Fed by more than 25 boutiques in San Francisco, New York, and Los Angeles, the Closet carries clothing and accessories by designers like Vera Wang, Chaiken, and Theory, all at less than 50% of their retail price. ⊠ *3044 Fillmore St., at Union St., Marina* ☎ *415/447–7703.*

TAILORED

★ **Cable Car Clothiers.** This classic British menswear store, open since 1939, is so chock-full of inventory that a whole room is dedicated to hats, pants are cataloged like papers in file cabinets, and entire displays showcase badger-bristle shaving brushes. ■TIP→ Their cable-car logo gear, from silk ties to pewter banks, makes for dashing souvenirs. ⊠ *200 Bush St., at Sansome St., Union Square* ☎ *415/397–4740.*

Mrs. Dewson's Hats. Although this shop was the famous purveyor of hats to nattily dressed former San Francisco mayor Willie Brown, Ruth Garland Dewson has been selling chapeaus—some of her own design—since 1978. The popular "Willie Brim" is a fur felt fedora; the brim comes in three sizes. ⊠ *2050 Fillmore St., at California St., Pacific Heights* ☎ *415/346–1600.*

Red Lantern. Chinese fashions of centuries past get a modern updating at this pretty little boutique where luxe fabrics—silk, brocade, and faux fur—give each item a sumptuous feel. If none of the mandarin-style jackets or *cheongsams* (traditional formfitting Chinese dresses) suits you, owner Fong Chong can make clothing to order. ⊠ *2030-A Union St., between Webster and Buchanan Sts., Cow Hollow* ☎ *415/776–8876.*

VINTAGE AND RESALE CLOTHING

American Rag. This might be the only place in the city where a $500 Marc Jacobs frock is sold alongside a $15 vintage dress, but it certainly mirrors San Francisco's style. The large vintage section in back carries an impressive selection of furs, sailor outfits, and Army jumpsuits. You can also rummage through shoes, sunglasses, and other accessories. ⊠ *1305 Van Ness Ave., between Sutter and Bush Sts., Russian Hill* ☎ *415/474–5214.*

Buffalo Exchange. Both men and women can find fashionable, high-quality used clothing at this national chain. Among the items: a wide selection of Levi's, leather jackets, sunglasses, and vintage lunch boxes. Some new clothes are available, too. ⊠ *1555 Haight St., between Clayton and Ashbury Sts., Haight* ☎ *415/431–7733* ⊠ *1210 Valencia St., at 23rd St., Mission* ☎ *415/647–8332.*

Held Over. The extensive collection of clothing from the 1920s through 1980s is organized by decade, saving those looking for flapper dresses from having to wade through lime-green polyester sundresses of the '70s. Shoes, hats, handbags, and jewelry complete the different looks. ⊠ *1543 Haight St., between Ashbury and Clayton Sts., Haight* ☎ *415/864–0818.*

Helpers' Bazaar. Arguably the city's best-dressed philanthropist, Joy Bianchi, along with other volunteers, runs this store to benefit the mentally disabled. A red Bill Blass cocktail dress, a Chanel suit, or a Schiaparelli hat are among the vintage masterpieces you might expect to find here—to see the good stuff, all you have to do is ask nicely. Don't miss a look at Bianchi's "mouse couture," a clever fund-raiser display in which designers like Armani and Carolina Herrera dress up 4-inch stuffed mice. ⊠ *900 N. Point St., Ghirardelli Square, Fisherman's Wharf* ☎ *415/441–0779.*

Schauplatz. Vintage clothing from the 1920s to the 1980s can be unearthed on the racks of this narrow little store on a hip block in the Mission. Some of the dramatic women's wear—go-go boots, pillbox hats, faux Chanel suits—is suitable for street wear or dress-up, depending on your style, while the menswear tends more toward fashionably retro jackets and button-up shirts from the classic to the gaudy. ⊠ *791 Valencia St., between 18th and 19th Sts., Mission* ☎ *415/864–5665.*

Shige Nishiguchi Kimonos. Though cotton *yukatas* (casual, lightweight kimonos) are the biggest sellers, vintage silk kimonos—some of them hand-painted—and vintage *obis* (kimono sashes) are the reason this tiny shop in the Japan Center is a destination for aficionados of Japanese dress. ⊠ *1730 Geary Blvd., Suite 203, Japantown* ☎ *415/346–5567.*

★ **Ver Unica.** Though you can find a few items from the psychedelic '60s, beautifully preserved fashions from the '40s and '50s are the best reason for visiting. You can even find purses and several pairs of hard-to-find vintage shoes to go along with that faux-fur-trimmed jacket. ⊠ *437B Hayes St., between Gough and Octavia Sts., Hayes Valley* ☎ *415/431–0688.*

DEPARTMENT STORES

Because most of San Francisco's department stores cluster around Union Square and the recently expanded Westfield San Francisco Shopping Centre, you don't need to drive or walk from one end of town to the other to hit all the major players.

Barneys New York. Barneys sets itself apart by identifying up-and-coming designers first. Fashion is taken seriously here—a pair of distressed shoes that look like they've been mowed down on the highway can cost you over a grand—but, it's always done with a wink and a smile. Check out the witty touches from their infamous store windows to the details of design (on the third floor copper pennies create a rack for designer ready-to-wear). As you enter Barneys' six-story corner locale, a flight of stairs extends to the mezzanine, where 20,000 shoes make up their infamous shoe salon. Below street level, cosmetics and fragrances reign: there are even state-of-the-art cylindrical sniffing chambers where you can sample new scents. ⊠ *77 O'Farrell St., at Stockton St., Union Square* ☎ *415/268–3500.*

Bloomingdales. The shiny newness (the store opened in late 2006), the black-and-white checkerboard theme, the abundance of glass, and the sheer size might remind you of Vegas. The store emphasizes American labels like Diane von Furstenberg and Jack Spade. Its well-planned layout defines individual departments without losing the grand and open feel. ⊠ *845 Market St., between Grant Ave. and Kearny St., Union Square* ☎ *415/856–5300.*

★ **Gump's.** It's a San Francisco institution, dating to the 19th century, and it's a strikingly luxurious one. The airy store exudes a museumlike air, with its large decorative vases, sumptuous housewares, and a gob-smacking Tahitian pearl display. Locals line up to register for weddings. But it's also a great place to pick up gifts, such as their Golden Gate Bridge note cards or their silver-plated butter spreaders in a signature Gump's box. ⊠ *135 Post St., between Grant Ave. and Kearny St., Union Square* ☎ *415/982–1616.*

Macy's. Downtown has two behemoth branches of this retailer, where you can find almost anything you could want, if only you have the patience to find it. One—with entrances on Geary, Stockton, and O'Farrell streets—houses the women's, children's, furniture, and housewares departments. With its large selection and its emphasis on American designers like DKNY and Marc Jacobs, the department for young women stands out. The men's department occupies its own building across Stockton Street. During the holidays, pups up for adoption bark in the ground-level windows. ⊠ *170 O'Farrell St., at Stockton St., Union Square* ☎ *415/397–3333 Men's branch:* ⊠ *50 O'Farrell St., entrance on Stockton St., Union Square* ☎ *415/397–3333.*

Neiman Marcus. The surroundings, which include a Philip Johnson–designed checkerboard facade, gilded atrium, and stained-glass skylight, are as ritzy as the goods showcased in them. The mix includes designer men's and women's clothing and accessories as well as posh household wares. ■ TIP→ Although the prices may raise an eyebrow or two, Neiman's biannual Last Call sales—in January and July—draw a crowd. After hitting the vast handbag salon, ladies who lunch daintily order consommé and bread laden with strawberry butter in the Rotunda Restaurant. ⊠ *150 Stockton St., at Geary Blvd., Union Square* ☎ *415/362–3900.*

★ **Nordstrom.** Somehow Nordstrom manages to be all things to all people, and this location, with spiral escalators circling a four-story atrium, is no exception. Whether you're an elegant lady of a certain age shopping for a new mink coat or a teen on the hunt for a Roxy hoodie, the salespeople are known for being happy to help. While still carrying the best selections in town of new designers like Tory Burch, their own Nordstrom brands have loyal followings. The latest addition is a Nordstrom Spa. ⊠ *San Francisco Shopping Centre, 865 Market St., between 4th and 5th Sts., Union Square* ☎ *415/243–8500.*

Saks Fifth Avenue. As the West Coast counterpart to the New York flagship, this branch claims a prime chunk of Union Square territory and it's chockablock with women swinging the latest "it" handbag. Where the store really outshines the competition is in the incredibly well-stocked Men's Store. The impeccable service will get any casual guy into a suit and tie—and the staff can convince almost anyone to enjoy dressing up. ⊠ *384 Post St., at Powell St., Union Square* ☎ *415/986–4300* ⊠ *Men's Store, 220 Post St., at Grant St., Union Square* ☎ *415/986–4300.*

WORD OF MOUTH

"Saturday was the [Ferry Plaza] Farmers' Market. We knew it would be a happenin' place but were surprised when we looked out our window at 8 AM to see how busy it really was!"
                    —BeachGirl247

FARMERS' MARKETS

Fodor's Choice ★ **Ferry Plaza Farmers' Market.** The most upscale and expensive of the city's farmers' markets, in front of the restored Ferry Building, places baked goods and fancy pots of jam alongside organic basil and heirloom tomatoes. The Saturday market is the grandest, with about 100 vendors packed both in front of and behind the building. The Tuesday and Thursday markets are smaller. At the Sunday garden market, vegetable and ornamental plants crop up next to a small selection of food items. (The Thursday and Sunday markets don't operate in winter, generally December or January through March.) ■TIP➔ On Saturday, don't miss the coffee at Blue Bottle—and yes, the line is worth it. ⊠ *Ferry Plaza, Embarcadero at north end of Market St., Financial District* ☎ *415/291–3276* ⊕ *www.ferryplazafarmersmarket.com* ⊙ *Tues. and Sun. 10–2, Thurs. 4–8, Sat. 8–2.*

Heart of the City Farmers' Market. Held every Sunday and Wednesday near the Civic Center, this market sells heaps of cheap produce, along with occasional baked goods, potted herbs, and even live chickens. ⊠ *United Nations Plaza, between 7th and 8th Sts., Civic Center* ☎ *415/558–9455* ⊙ *Wed. 7–5:30, Sun. 7–5.*

FOOD AND DRINK

Blue Bottle Cafe. After operating from a booth at the farmers' outfit for years and more recently out of a back-alley garage, the highly sought-after Berkeley microroaster has finally quelled its long lines with a roomy and permanent locale. Here they brew their sacred beans in a $20,000 siphon bar from Japan (it's the only one in the U.S.) with halogen-lighted glass globes that resemble a science experiment. Just a stone's throw from the mall, it's the perfect shopping reprieve. Don't forget to take a bag of java home with you. ⊠ *66 Mint St, at Jesse St., SoMa* ☎ *415/495–3394.*

17

A San Francisco institution, the farmers' market delivers sensory overload.

Cowgirl Creamery Artisan Cheese. Fantastic organic-milk cheeses—such as the mellow, triple-cream Mt. Tam and *bocconcini* (small balls of fresh mozzarella)—are produced at a creamery an hour north of the city. These and other carefully chosen artisanal cheeses and dairy products, including a luscious, freshly made crème fraîche, round out the selection at the in-town store. ✉ *1 Ferry Bldg., #17, Embarcadero at foot of Market St., Embarcadero* ☎ *415/362–9354.*

Graffeo Coffee Roasting Company. Forget those fancy flavored coffees if you're ordering from this North Beach emporium, open since 1935. This shop, one of the best-loved coffee stores in a city that's truly devoted to its java, sells dark roast, light roast, and dark roast decaf beans only. ✉ *735 Columbus Ave., at Filbert St., North Beach* ☎ *415/986–2420.*

Great China Herb Co. Since 1922, this aromatic shop has been treating the city with its wide selection of ginseng, tea, and other herbs. You might even hear the click of an abacus as a purchase is tallied up. A Chinese (but English-speaking) doctor is always on hand to recommend the perfect remedy. ✉ *857 Washington St., between Grant Ave. and Stockton St., Chinatown* ☎ *415/982–2195.*

Lucca Delicatessen. At this bit of old Italy in the upscale Marina District, take a number and wait your turn to choose from a wide selection of homemade pastas, Italian sausages, prepared salads, and imported cheeses and olive oils. ✉ *2120 Chestnut St., at Steiner St., Marina* ☎ *415/921–7873.*

McEvoy Ranch. The only retail outpost of this Petaluma ranch, a producer of outstanding organic, extra-virgin olive oil. Depending on seasonal availability, the store also gets olive trees, plants, and flowers in from the ranch. ■TIP→ If you stop by in fall or winter, don't miss the Olio Nuovo, the days-old green oil produced during the harvest. ✉ *1 Ferry Bldg., #30, Embarcadero at foot of Market St., Embarcadero* ☎ *415/291–7224.*

★ **Miette Confiserie.** There is truly nothing sweeter than a cellophane bag tied with blue-and-white twine and filled with malt balls or chocolate

WORD OF MOUTH

"San Francisco sourdough is special. It's the recipe, the particular humidity in the air, the ovens. As one who left the Bay Area 30 years ago, I know, there's nothing like it." —crefloors

sardines from this European-style apothecary. The lovely pastel-color cake stands make even window-shopping a treat. ✉ *449 Octavia Blvd., between Hayes and Linden Sts., Hayes Valley* ☎ *415/626–6221.*

Fodor's Choice **Molinari Delicatessen.** Billing itself as the oldest delicatessen west of the
★ Rockies, the store has been making its own salami, sausages, and cold cuts since 1896. Other homemade specialties include meat and cheese ravioli, tomato sauces, and fresh pastas. ■TIP→ In-the-know locals grab a made-to-order sandwich for lunch and eat it at one of the sidewalk tables. ✉ *373 Columbus Ave., at Vallejo St., North Beach* ☎ *415/421–2337.*

Victoria Pastry Co. In business since the early 1900s, and a throwback to the North Beach of old, this bakery has display cases full of Italian pastries, cookies, and St. Honoré cakes. ✉ *1362 Stockton St., at Vallejo St., North Beach* ☎ *415/781–2015.*

WINES AND SPIRITS

Arlequin Wine Merchant. If you like the wine list at Absinthe Brasserie, you can walk next door and pick up a few bottles from its highly regarded sister establishment. This small, unintimidating shop carries hard-to-find wines from small producers. Why wait to taste? Crack a bottle in the patio out back. ✉ *384 Hayes St., at Gough St., Hayes Valley* ☎ *415/863–1104.*

Cellar 360. If you can't make it to Napa, come here to browse through 6,000 square feet of wine retail space in the historic Woolen Mill building. During happy hour, tourists and locals alike pack the longest bar in the city to taste the 250 wines available. After a few glasses you might be sold on a case . . . and if you're not: a Copia education class in their fully equipped classroom will probably do the trick. ✉ *900 Northpoint St., Suite F301, Ghirardelli Square, Fisherman's Wharf* ☎ *415/440–0772.*

City Beer. Think beer isn't as sophisticated as wine? Think again. At City Beer more than 300 beers are for sale (many refrigerated)—and with six on tap you can imbibe while you shop. You'll get 10% off when you mix and match your six-pack with everything from Allagash Curieux, a dark beer aged in Jim Beam barrels, to Zatec, an authentic Czech beer. ✉ *1168 Folsom St., Suite 100, between 7th and 8th Sts., SoMa* ☎ *415/503–1033.*

D&M Wines and Liquors. This family-owned liquor store appears to be like any neighborhood liquor store at first glance, but it's actually a rare and wonderful specialist. In a city obsessed with wine, these spirit devotees distinguished themselves by focusing on rare, small-production Armagnac, Calvados, and Champagne. ✉ *2200 Fillmore St., at Sacramento St., Pacific Heights* ☎ *415/346–1325.*

17

★ **K&L Wine Merchants.** More than any other wine store, the Merchants has an ardent cult following around town. The friendly staffers promise not to sell what they don't taste themselves, and weekly events open the tastings to customers. Their best-seller list for varietals and regions for both the under- and over-$30 categories appeal to the wine dork in everyone. ⊠ *638 4th St., between Brannan and Townsend Sts., SoMa* ☎ *415/896–1734.*

PlumpJack Wines. A small selection of imported wines complements the well-priced, well-stocked collection of hard-to-find California wines here. Gift baskets—such as the Italian market basket, containing wine, Italian foods, and a cookbook—are popular hostess gifts. ⊠ *3201 Fillmore St., at Greenwich St., Cow Hollow* ☎ *415/346–9870* ⊠ *4011 24th St., between Castro and Noe Sts., Noe Valley* ☎ *415/282–3841.*

San Francisco Wine Trading Company. Owner and noted wine expert Gary Marcaletti provides the only place in the city with well-known Bay Area importer Kermit Lynch's line of wines. It also has Saturday-afternoon tastings. ⊠ *250 Taraval St., between Funston and 12th Aves., Ingleside* ☎ *415/731–6222.*

True Sake. Though it would be reasonable to expect a Japanese aesthetic at the United States' first store dedicated entirely to sake, you might instead hear dance music thumping quietly in the background while you browse. Each of the many sakes is displayed with a label describing the drink's qualities and food pairing suggestions. Should these prove insufficient, simply pick up a copy of *The Sake Handbook* or another of the sake-related publications. ⊠ *560 Hayes St., between Laguna and Octavia Sts., Hayes Valley* ☎ *415/355–9555.*

William Glen. The more than 400 whiskies arranged along the back wall—mostly single-malt scotches—are organized by their region of origin, so you can easily distinguish those made in Islay from those from Speyside or Lowland. The charming Scottish proprietor can tell you about his favorites, help you with the selection of tartan scarves or cashmere sweaters, or even equip you with a kilt. ⊠ *360 Sutter St., Union Square* ☎ *415/989–1030.*

Wine Club. The large selection of wines at some of the best prices in the city makes up for the bare-bones feel of this place. A self-serve wine bar tucked in the back allows you to taste a wide variety of wines for a modest fee, a great boon to those who'd like to try before they buy. A small collection of caviar and wine paraphernalia, including Riedel wineglasses, books, openers, and decanters, is also available. ⊠ *953 Harrison St., between 5th and 6th Sts., SoMa* ☎ *415/512–9086.*

FURNITURE, HOUSEWARES, AND GIFTS

Aldea. A visit to this shop is like being in someone's home and being able to buy everything you see, from the sheets to the chairs to the shampoo in the shower. The aesthetic is modern, with bright references to Mexico, India, Turkey, and Japan. It's the perfect place to find a hostess gift or for that corner missing something special. ⊠ *3338 17th St., Suite 100B, between Valencia and Mission Sts., Mission* ☎ *415/865–9807.*

Biordi Art Imports. Hand-painted Italian pottery, mainly imported from Tuscany and Umbria, has been shipped worldwide by this family-run business since 1946. Dishware sets can be ordered in any combination. ⊠ *412 Columbus Ave., at Vallejo St., North Beach* ☎ *415/392–8096.*

Candelier. This fragrant little shop on tony Maiden Lane sells every sort of candle you can imagine. Tapers, votives, and pillars are popular purchases, as are the luxury bath products and small decorative baubles. ⊠ *33 Maiden La., between Grant Ave. and Kearny St., Union Square* ☎ *415/989–8600.*

WORD OF MOUTH

"Both Union Street and Polk were filled with cute little upscale boutiques. I don't think there were any chains. Coming from NYC this is truly the kind of unique shopping you hope for! It was by far my favorite day of shopping."
—Rael81

Fodor's Choice ★ **Diptyque.** The original Diptyque boutique in Paris has long attracted a following of celebrities. You can find the full line of scented candles and fragrances in this chic shop that would be at home on the boulevard St-Germain. Trademark black-and-white labels adorn the popular L'eau toilet water, scented with geranium and sandalwood. Candles come in both traditional and esoteric scents, including lavender, basil, leather, and fig tree. Also available is a collection of French Mariage Frères teas. ⊠ *171 Maiden La., between Grant and Stockton Sts., Union Square* ☎ *415/402–0600.*

Ferrari Store. Even if you can't afford a new Spyder, there's something for everyone at the new 4,000-square-foot Ferrari Store. You can pick up a show-stopping, fire engine–red racing jacket, or an actual key for the ultimate aspirational shopper (or practical joker). Something for the Mrs.? Purchase signature Ferrari china cups or a pastel argyle sweater—all complete with the signature prancing stallion. To add to the fun: A racecar is parked by the front door and the salespeople wear head-to-toe racing suits. ⊠ *2 Stockton St., at Market St., Union Square* ☎ *415/834-9200.*

★ **Flight 001.** Über-stylish travel accessories—retro-looking flight bags, supersoft leather passport wallets, and tiny Swiss travel alarm clocks—line the shelves of this brightly lighted shop, which vaguely resembles an airplane interior. High-tech travel gear and a small collection of guidebooks speed you on your way. ⊠ *525 Hayes St., between Laguna and Octavia Sts., Hayes Valley* ☎ *415/487–1001.*

JAK home. Against their Golden Delicious–green backdrop, an eclectic assortment of one-of-a-kind home furnishings leaps off the shelves: Cake pedestals, a globe collection, and candles are completely irresistible. It's so cozy and inviting you'll want to take a seat in one of their brightly reupholstered armchairs and ponder how to re-create the look. ⊠ *2423 Polk St., between Union and Filbert Sts., Russian Hill* ☎ *415/839–8264.*

Modern Artifacts. From Eames chairs and a Hans Wegner sofa covered in nubby fabric to a sensuous lamp designed by Italian architect Gae Aulenti, this store has all the accoutrements for a stylish modernist

17

apartment. ⊠ *1639 Market St., between Franklin and Gough Sts., Hayes Valley* ☎ *415/255–9000*.

Nest. A mix between a Parisian antiques show and a Jamaican flea market, this cozy store could get even the most monochrome New Yorker excited about color. You can turn up the volume on your SF souvenirs with vibrant handmade quilts, Chan Luu jewelry, Les Indiennes hand-blocked cotton fabrics, and M. Sasek's cheerfully illustrated book *This Is San Francisco.* ⊠ *2300 Fillmore St., at Clay St., Pacific Heights* ☎ *415/292–6199*.

★ **Paxton Gate.** Elevating gardening to an art, this serene shop offers beautiful earthenware pots, amaryllis and narcissus bulbs, decorative garden items, and coffee-table books such as *An Inordinate Fondness for Beetles.* The collection of taxidermy and preserved bugs presents more unusual gift ideas. ⊠ *824 Valencia St., between 19th and 20th Sts., Mission* ☎ *415/824–1872*.

★ **Scheuer Linens.** Designers and other fans make their way to this store, a Union Square fixture since 1953, for luxurious bed and bath items and linens. The pretty tablecloths, runners, and napkins, fragrant candles, and luxurious bath accessories are popular gifts to indulge loved ones. ⊠ *340 Sutter St., at Stockton St., Union Square* ☎ *415/392–2813*.

★ **Spring.** Under the exposed beams of this loftlike space and fittingly surrounded by plants are hundreds of products for an environmentally friendly home. In true SF style, residents with sustainability concerns buy up everything from hemp dishcloths to nontoxic home-care products to organic bedding. A visit is an education on what it really means to be green. ⊠ *2162 Polk St., at Vallejo St., Russian Hill* ☎ *415/673–2065*.

Sue Fisher King Company. When Martha Stewart or the buyers at Williams-Sonoma need some inspiration they come to see how Sue has set her sprawling table or dressed her stately bed. (Her specialty is opulent linens for every room.) When Pacific Heights residents are looking for an impeccable hostess or bridal gift, they come by for a hand-embroidered velvet pillow or a piece of Astier de Villatte white pottery. Out back is a tiny, charming garden area overflowing with plants. ⊠ *3067 Sacramento St., between Baker and Broderick Sts., Pacific Heights* ☎ *415/922–7276*.

Therapy. Housewares range from ever-practical refrigerator magnets to downright silly items such as a soap-on-a-rope tribute to the cartoon character Strawberry Shortcake. A retro theme runs to stationery and other reasonably priced items, and the adjacent annex sells retro-style furniture. ⊠ *545 Valencia St., between 16th and 17th Sts., Mission* ☎ *415/865–0981*.

Under One Roof. Profits from its home and garden necessities, gourmet foods, bath products, books, frames, cards, and silly gift items go to Northern California AIDS organizations, which makes it easy to justify buying such playful objects as an Oscar Wilde action figure or a bath mat shaped like a T-bone steak. ⊠ *518A Castro St., between 18th and 19th Sts., Castro* ☎ *415/503–2300*.

The Castro and the Haight Shopping

17

COOKWARE

City Discounts. This small restaurant-supply store sells commercial-grade pans, knives, and microplanes at a fraction of the price you'd pay at a national kitchenware chain store. There's a nice selection of imported Italian food, and the Italian proprietress is a great help in making selections. ⊠ *1542 Polk St., between Sacramento and California Sts., Russian Hill* ☎ *415/771–4649.*

Fodor's Choice
★

Cookin': Recycled Gourmet Appurtenances. People trek here from all over the world for the impressive collection of indestructible vintage Le Creuset in discontinued colors. If you can't make sense of this store's jumble of used cookware—stacked ceiling high in some places—ask the helpful owner, who will likely interrogate you about what you're preparing to cook before leading you to the right section, whether that be the corner with hundreds of ramekins or the bewildering selection of garlic presses. ⊠ *339 Divisadero St., between Oak and Page Sts., Western Addition* ☎ *415/861–1854.*

Sur la Table. Everything the home chef could need is here, along with some things many cooks have never heard of—such as round aspic cutters and larding needles. Cooking classes and demonstrations are often held downstairs at the Maiden Lane location. ⊠ *77 Maiden La., between Grant Ave. and Kearny St., Union Square* ☎ *415/732–7900*

✉ *1 Ferry Bldg., Embarcadero at foot of Market St., Financial District* ☎ *415/262–9970.*

Williams-Sonoma. Behind the striped awnings and historic facade is the massive mother ship of the Sonoma-founded kitchen-store empire. La Cornue custom stoves beckon you inward, and two grand staircases draw you upward to the world of dinnerware, linens, and chefs' tools. Antique tart tins, eggbeaters, and pastry cutters from the personal collection of founder Chuck Williams line the walls. ✉ *340 Post St., in between Powell and Stockton Sts., Union Square* ☎ *415/362–9450.*

The Wok Shop. The store carries woks, of course, but also anything else you could need for Chinese cooking—bamboo steamers, ginger graters, wicked-looking cleavers—as well as accessories for Japanese cooking, including sushi paraphernalia and tempura racks. ✉ *718 Grant Ave., at Sacramento St., Chinatown* ☎ *415/989–3797.*

VINTAGE HOUSEWARES

Zonal. Most of the refurbished vintage steel filing cabinets, dining-room tables, desks, and even barrister bookcases were built in the 1930s and '40s. Upholstered pieces, such as a generously sized slipper chair, are contemporary but have a sleek retro look. ✉ *568 Hayes St., at Laguna St., Hayes Valley* ☎ *415/255–9307.*

HANDBAGS, LUGGAGE, AND LEATHER GOODS

Goyard. After more than a century of selling trunks, handbags, and pet leashes on the rue St-Honoré in Paris, Goyard opened their second store here to offer San Franciscans a relatively discreet alternative to Louis Vuitton. Rather than splashing their name everywhere, they signal luxury with a signature chevron pattern. Even if you walk away empty-handed, you'll be reminded of what travel used to mean. ✉ *345 Powell St., between Post and Geary Sts., Union Square* ☎ *415/398–1110.*

Kate Spade. Slightly retro, a bit tongue in cheek, and well made—the formula has made these purses wildly popular among ladies of all ages. Case in point: the boxy Tarrytown Quinn bag that comes in saturated colors and features a little price tag that reminds you to "call your mom." The shop also stocks a few shoes as well as cosmetics cases, date books, and note cards. ✉ *227 Grant Ave., between Post and Sutter Sts., Union Square* ☎ *415/216–0880.*

HANDICRAFTS AND FOLK ART

F. Dorian. In addition to cards, jewelry, and other crafts from Central and South America, Africa, Asia, and the Middle East—a carved wooden candleholder from the Ivory Coast is one example—this store carries brightly colored glass and ceramic works by local artisans and whimsical mobiles. ✉ *370 Hayes St., between Franklin and Gough Sts., Hayes Valley* ☎ *415/861–3191.*

Global Exchange. A branch of the well-known nonprofit organization, the store carries handcrafted items from more than 40 countries. The staff works directly with village cooperatives and workshops. Whether you buy a Nepalese sweater, a South African wood carving, or Balinese textiles, employees can explain the origin of your purchase. ⊠ *4018 24th St., between Noe and Castro Sts., Noe Valley* ☎ *415/648–8068.*

Ma-Shi'-Ko Folk Craft. Beautiful Mashiko pottery, rustic pieces fired in a wood kiln and coated with a natural glaze, are the specialty here. The wealth of unique pottery and antiques, including many ceramic vases and wooden chests, makes a visit here worth the somewhat chilly reception from the proprietor. ⊠ *Kinokuniya Bldg., 1581 Webster St., 2nd fl., Japantown* ☎ *415/346–0748.*

Polanco. Devoted to showcasing the arts of Mexico, this gallery sells everything from antiques and traditional folk crafts to fine contemporary paintings. Brightly painted animal figures and a virtual village of Day of the Dead figures share space with religious statues and modern linocuts and paintings. ⊠ *393 Hayes St., between Franklin and Gough Sts., Hayes Valley* ☎ *415/252–5753.*

Ruby Gallery. A pooch named Ruby presides over this small artists' cooperative where the jewelry, clothing, handbags, candleholders, intricately crafted cards, and other gift items are made by local artists. Hair accessories—from elegant clips studded with vintage Czech glass to barrettes fashioned out of buttons—are especially charming. ⊠ *3602 20th St., at Valencia St., Mission* ☎ *415/550–8052* ⊠ *1431 Haight St., between Masonic Ave. and Ashbury St., Haight* ☎ *415/554–0555.*

Soko Hardware. Run in Japantown by the Ashizawa family since 1925, this shop specializes in beautifully crafted Japanese tools for gardening and woodworking. In addition to the usual hardware-store items, you can find seeds for Japanese plants and books about topics such as making shoji screens. ⊠ *1698 Post St., at Buchanan St., Japantown* ☎ *415/931–5510.*

Studio 24. The gift shop of the acclaimed Galería de la Raza sells crafts from Mexico and Central and South America. Prints and calendars by Latino artists, Day of the Dead folk art, and masks and wood carvings from Latin America are a few of the objects for sale. ⊠ *2857 24th St., at Bryant St., Mission* ☎ *415/826–8009.*

Fodor'sChoice **Xanadu Gallery San Francisco.** The spectacular collection of international
★ art and antiquities here includes such treasures as Latin American folk art and masks, sculptures, woven baskets, tapestries, and textiles from Africa, Oceania, and Indonesia. Museum-quality pieces such as a gilt bronze figure of a lama (Tibetan Buddhist holy man) can go for nearly $100,000, but beautiful books on subjects such as Tibetan art make more affordable souvenirs. ■ TIP→ If nothing else, the shop is worth a visit to see its Frank Lloyd Wright–designed home, where a spiral ramp recalls New York City's Guggenheim Museum. ⊠ *140 Maiden La., between Stockton St. and Grant Ave., Union Square* ☎ *415/392–9999.*

Xela Imports. Africa, Southeast Asia, and Central America are the sources for the merchandise, which includes jewelry, religious masks, fertility statuary, and decorative wall hangings. The name of the store is pronounced *shay*-la. ⊠ *3925 24th St., between Sanchez and Noe Sts., Noe Valley* ☎ *415/695–1323.*

JEWELRY AND COLLECTIBLES

De Beers. From one of the world's original diamond miners comes a surprisingly sparse, modern showroom: ebony counters with square glass cases and sheets of etched glass over dark hardwood. Even more surprising: the price is displayed next to each sparkler, a rarity for upscale jewelers. ✉ *185 Post St., between Grant Ave. and Robert Kirk Ln., Union Square* ☎ *415/391–1400.*

De Vera. Nature inspires these beautiful, curious objets d'art and jewelry, such as an oversize gold rose thorn, life-size handblown glass ants, and branching coral jewelry. Some, like the cameos, are antiques to boot. ✉ *29 Maiden La., at Kearney St., Union Square* ☎ *415/788–0828.*

Goldberry Jewelers. The former long-time girlfriend of Bob Dylan, Margie Rogerson opened this store to showcase her platinum-only designs. While she carries a large selection of engagement rings, her specialty is colored stones: rubies, sapphires, and emeralds. Their colors really sparkle against the background of this all white and Lucite space. ✉ *3516 Sacramento St., between Laurel and Locust Sts., Presidio Heights* ☎ *415/921–4389.*

★ **San Francisco Museum of Modern Art Museum Store.** The shop is known for its exclusive line of watches and jewelry, as well as artists' monographs and artful housewares. Posters, calendars, children's art sets and books, and art books for adults round out the merchandise. Larger items include sleek, modernist furniture. ✉ *151 3rd St., between Mission and Howard Sts., SoMa* ☎ *415/357–4035.*

Shreve & Co. Along with gems in dazzling settings, San Francisco's oldest retail store—it's been at this location since 1852—carries lovely watches by Jaeger-LeCoultre and others. On weekends well-heeled couples crowd around the glass cases scoping out hefty diamond engagement rings. ✉ *200 Post St., at Grant Ave., Union Square* ☎ *415/421–2600.*

Tiffany & Co. This gray marble beauty towers over Union Square with almost as much leverage as its signature blue box. The company that all but invented the modern engagement ring makes more than just brides swoon with Elsa Peretti's sinuous silver and architect Frank Gehry's collection using materials like Pernambuco wood and black gold. ✉ *350 Post St., between Powell and Stockton Sts., Union Square* ☎ *415/781–7000.*

Union Street Goldsmith. Open since 1976, this local favorite prides itself on its wide selection of rare gemstones, such as golden sapphires and violet tanzanite. Custom work is a specialty, and a number of no-pressure design consultants are happy to talk with you about how to make the jewelry you're dreaming of a reality. ✉ *1909 Union St., at Laguna St., Cow Hollow* ☎ *415/776–8048.*

Velvet da Vinci. Each contemporary art piece here is one-of-a-kind or limited edition. The beautiful, unusual items might be sculpted out of resin, hammered from copper, or woven with silver wires. ✉ *2015 Polk St., between Broadway and Pacific Ave., Russian Hill* ☎ *415/441–0109.*

ANTIQUE JEWELRY

Brand X Antiques. The vintage jewelry, mostly from the early part of the 20th century, includes a wide selection of estate pieces and objets d'art. With rings that range from $5 to $50,000, there's something for everyone. ✉ *570 Castro St., at 18th St., Castro* ☎ *415/626–8908.*

Fodor's Choice **Lang Antiques and Estate Jewelry.**
★ Dozens of diamond bracelets in the window attract shoppers to one of the city's best vintage jewelry shops, where rings, brooches, and other glittering items represent a wide spread of eras, from Victorian and Edwardian to art nouveau and Arts and Crafts. The shop has been selling fine jewelry, including engagement rings and a small number of vintage watches, since 1969. ✉ *323 Sutter St., at Grant Ave., Union Square* ☎ *415/982–2213.*

BEADS

Bead Store. More than a thousand kinds of strung and unstrung pieces include such stones as lapis and carnelian, Czech and Venetian glass, African trade beads, Buddhist and Muslim prayer beads, and Catholic rosaries. Silver jewelry is another specialty. ✉ *417 Castro St., between 17th and 18th Sts., Castro* ☎ *415/861–7332.*

Yone. In business since 1965, the store carries so many types of beads that the owner has lost track (though it's probably somewhere between 5,000 and 10,000). Individual beads, made of glass, wood, plastic, bone, sterling silver, and countless other materials, can cost up to $100. ✉ *478 Union St., at Grant Ave., North Beach* ☎ *415/986–1424.*

> ### WORD OF MOUTH
>
> "On our last visit my fiancé managed to spend 3 hours in Amoeba and only left when he physically couldn't carry any more stuff. We unearthed some real gems, especially in the $1 singles." —joxxxxx

MUSIC

Fodor's Choice **Amoeba Music.** With more than 2.5 million new and used CDs, DVDs,
★ and records, this warehouselike store (and the original Berkeley location) carries titles you can't find on Amazon at bargain prices. No niche is ignored—from electronica and hip-hop to jazz and classical—and the stock changes daily. Weekly in-store performances attract large crowds. ✉ *1855 Haight St., between Stanyan and Shrader Sts., Haight* ☎ *415/831–1200.*

Aquarius Records. Owner Windy Chien carries on the tradition in this space, which was *the* punk-rock store in the 1970s. These days it carries a variety of music, including a large selection of experimental electronica, all of it handpicked by staffers, so you can be sure you're getting the latest and hippest. ✉ *1055 Valencia St., between 21st and 22nd Sts., Mission* ☎ *415/647–2272.*

Recycled Records. A Haight Street landmark, the store buys, sells, and trades a vast selection of used records, including hard-to-find imports and sides by obscure alternative bands. The CD collection is large, but the vinyl is the real draw. ✉ *1377 Haight St., between Masonic and Central Aves., Haight* ☎ *415/626–4075.*

17

Japantown, Pacific Heights and Cow Hollow Shopping

Streetlight Records. Thousands of used CDs, with an emphasis on rock, jazz, soul, and R&B, are bought and sold here. But there's plenty of vinyl for purists. The Noe Valley branch has been a neighborhood staple since 1973. ✉ *2350 Market St., at Castro St., Castro* ☎ *415/282–8000.*

MEMORABILIA

San Francisco Rock Posters and Collectibles. The huge selection of rock-and-roll memorabilia, including posters, handbills, and original art, takes you back to the 1960s. Also available are posters from more recent shows—many at the legendary Fillmore Auditorium—with such musicians as George Clinton, Porno for Pyros, and the late Johnny Cash. ✉ *1851 Powell St., between Filbert and Greenwich Sts., North Beach* ☎ *415/956–6749.*

PAPER AND STATIONERY

★ **Flax.** In addition to paints, brushes, and various art supplies, this sprawling creator's playground sells beautifully made photo albums and journals, fine pens and pencils, crafts kits, scads of stationery, and inspiring doodads for kids. ✉ *1699 Market St., near Valencia St., Mission* ☎ *415/552–2355.*

Kozo Arts. The art of papermaking rises to new levels here. The store's specialty is silk-screened Chiyogami papers from Japan. The papers are also made into hand-bound photo albums, cards, and journals. ✉ *1969-A Union St., between Buchanan and Laguna Sts., Cow Hollow* ☎ *415/351–2114.*

Lola of North Beach. For a card that is anything but Hallmark, snap up something from local letterpresses; many have San Francisco themes. A section of the intimate North Beach store is devoted to the various stages of a relationship: friendship, I like you, I love you, I miss you, I'm sorry, and I'm here for you. It also carries an impressive collection of baby clothes, including some adorable tees. ■ TIP→ The Ghirardelli Square branch flutters with more tourist-geared, SF-centric cards. ✉ *1415 Grant Ave., at Green St., North Beach* ☎ *415/781–1817* ✉ *900 N. Point St., in Ghirardelli Square, Fisherman's Wharf* ☎ *415/567–7760.*

Paper Source. Beautiful handmade papers, cards, envelopes, ribbons, and bookbinding materials line the walls of this shop, which embodies the Bay Area's do-it-yourself spirit. Assembly is required here and that's the fun of it. ✉ *1925 Fillmore St., at Pine St., Pacific Heights* ☎ *415/409–7710* ✉ *2061 Chestnut St., between Fillmore and Steiner Sts., Marina* ☎ *415/614–1585.*

SHOES

Gimme Shoes. From the chunky to the sleek, the shoes carried here—including those by Robert Clergerie, Helmut Lang, Prada, and John Varvatos—are top-notch. And if $600 seems steep for pale-green pumps, perhaps you haven't seen the perfect pair by Dries Van Noten. ✉ *416 Hayes St., at Gough St., Hayes Valley* ☎ *415/864–0691* ✉ *2358 Fillmore St., at Washington St., Pacific Heights* ☎ *415/441–3040.*

17

★ **John Fluevog.** The selection of trendy but sturdily made footwear for men and women is one of the best in the city. Club kids go for the Canadian brand's shoes and especially their boots, handing over a pretty penny for dramatic styles such as the popular 5-inch-heel knee-high boots made out of red pony fur. ⊠ *1697 Haight St., at Cole St., Haight* ☎ *415/436–9784.*

SPORTING GOODS

★ **Lululemon Athletica.** This yoga-inspired company makes all kinds of athletic gear with their Luon fabric—it's non-chafing, moisture wicking, preshrunk, and best of all it can be washed in warm water. Their pants are known for being the best thing in town for your derriere. ⊠ *1981 Union St., between Laguna and Buchanan Sts., Marina* ☎ *415/776–5858* ⊠ *327 Grant Ave., between Bush and Sutter Sts., Union Square* ☎ *415/402–0914.*

Niketown. More glitzy multimedia extravaganza than true sporting-goods store, this emporium is nevertheless the best place in town to find anything and everything with the famous swoosh. ⊠ *278 Post St., at Stockton St., Union Square* ☎ *415/392–6453.*

The North Face. The Bay Area–based national retailer is famous for its top-of-the-line tents, sleeping bags, backpacks, and outdoor apparel, including rugged Gore-Tex jackets and pants. ⊠ *180 Post St., between Kearny St. and Grant Ave., Union Square* ☎ *415/433–3223.*

Patagonia. Technical wear for serious outdoors enthusiasts is the specialty. Along with sportswear and casual clothing, it carries activewear for backpacking, fly-fishing, kayaking, and the like. ⊠ *770 N. Point St., at Hyde St., Fisherman's Wharf* ☎ *415/771–2050.*

★ **REI.** The beloved Seattle-based co-op was founded by a group of mountain climbers in 1938. In addition to carrying a vast selection of clothing and outdoor gear, the store rents camping equipment and repairs snowboards and bikes. ⊠ *840 Brannan St., between 7th and 8th Sts., SoMa* ☎ *415/934–1938.*

Sports Basement. These sprawling places reward intrepid shoppers with significant discounts on name-brand sportswear, accessories, and camping and outdoor gear. Helpful salespeople, more knowledgeable than you would expect at a discount warehouse, will help you find just the right running shoes, biking shorts, or yoga tights. ⊠ *1590 Bryant St., between 15th and 16th Sts., Potrero Hill* ☎ *415/437–0100* ⊠ *610 Old Mason St., across from Crissy Field, Marina* ☎ *415/437–0100.*

TOYS AND GADGETS

★ **Apple Store San Francisco.** A shiny, stainless-steel box is the setting for San Francisco's flagship Apple store, a high-tech temple to Macs and the people who use them. Play around with iPods, laptops, and hundreds of geeky accessories; then watch a theater presentation or attend an educational workshop. ⊠ *1 Stockton St., at Market St., Union Square* ☎ *415/392–0202.*

Giant Robot features toys for tots and too-cool-for-school hipsters.

Ark Toys, Books & Crafts. The store emphasizes high-quality toys, many of which have an educational bent (books, science kits) or encourage imaginative play (dress-up costumes, paper dolls). The stock includes numerous toys manufactured in Europe. Most are for toddlers through 12-year-olds. ✉ *3845 24th St., between Church and Sanchez Sts., Noe Valley* ☎ *415/821–1257.*

ATYS. Gadgets for the home and office with a sleek modern design are imported from Scandinavia, Italy, Germany, and Japan. Among the eye-catching items are a digital watch designed by Philippe Starck and Japanese knives that could be displayed as sculptures. ✉ *2149-B Union St., between Fillmore and Webster Sts., Cow Hollow* ☎ *415/441–9220.*

Chinatown Kite Shop. Kites at this family-owned business (operating since 1969) range from basic diamond shapes to box- and animal-shape configurations. Colorful dragon kites make great Chinatown souvenirs. ✉ *717 Grant Ave., between Clay and Sacramento Sts., Chinatown* ☎ *415/989–5182.*

★ **826 Valencia.** The brainchild of author Dave Eggers is primarily a center established to help kids with their writing skills via tutoring and storytelling events. But the storefront is also "San Francisco's only independent pirate supply store," a quirky space filled with eye patches, spyglasses, and other pirate-theme paraphernalia. Eggers's quarterly journal, *McSweeney's,* and other publications are available here. Proceeds benefit the writing center. ✉ *826 Valencia St., between 18th and 19th Sts., Mission* ☎ *415/642–5905.*

Exploratorium. The educational gadgets and gizmos sold here are so much fun that your kids—whether they're in grade school or junior high—might not realize they're learning while they're playing with them. Space- and dinosaur-related games are popular, as are science videos and CD-ROMs. ✉ *3601 Lyon St., at Marina Blvd., Marina* ☎ *415/561–0360.*

Giant Robot. This superhip spot feeds San Franciscans' passion for Asian pop-cultural fluff, from Gama-Go Ninja Kitty bike messenger bags and Uglydoll keychains and figurines to Astro Boy stationery sets. Of course, the store also carries *Giant Robot* magazine, as well as a large selection of T-shirts. ✉ *618 Shrader St., at Haight St., Haight* ☎ *415/876–4773.*

Marin County, Berkeley, and Oakland

WORD OF MOUTH

"It was quite easy to get to Muir Woods. You have to go over the Golden Gate Bridge. After you get over the bridge, there are signs. I would suggest getting there as soon as it opens—it is so peaceful!"

—Kerry392

WELCOME TO MARIN COUNTY, BERKELEY, AND OAKLAND

TOP REASONS TO GO

★ **Walk among giants:** Walking into Muir Woods, a mere 12 mi north of the Golden Gate Bridge, is like entering a cathedral built by God.

★ **Attend a reading:** Chances are, an author you admire will be reading somewhere in the Bay Area during your trip. Berkeley draws an especially erudite crowd; Q&A sessions can feel like a grad-school discussion.

★ **Bite into the "Gourmet Ghetto":** Eat your way through this area of Berkeley, starting with a slice of pizza from the Cheeseboard.

★ **Sit on a dock by the bay:** Admire the beauty and tranquillity of the Bay Area from the rocky, picturesque shores of Sausalito.

★ **Find solitude at Point Reyes National Seashore:** Head here to hike beautifully rugged— and deserted—beaches.

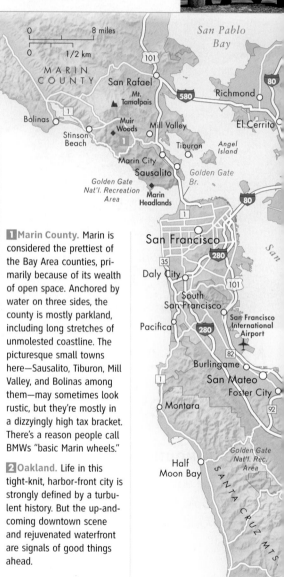

1 Marin County. Marin is considered the prettiest of the Bay Area counties, primarily because of its wealth of open space. Anchored by water on three sides, the county is mostly parkland, including long stretches of unmolested coastline. The picturesque small towns here—Sausalito, Tiburon, Mill Valley, and Bolinas among them—may sometimes look rustic, but they're mostly in a dizzyingly high tax bracket. There's a reason people call BMWs "basic Marin wheels."

2 Oakland. Life in this tight-knit, harbor-front city is strongly defined by a turbulent history. But the up-and-coming downtown scene and rejuvenated waterfront are signals of good things ahead.

GETTING ORIENTED

3 Berkeley. This college town has long been known for its liberal ethos, stimulating university community (and perhaps even more stimulating coffee shops), and activist streak. But these days the booming restaurant and arts scenes are luring even those who wouldn't be caught dead in Birkenstocks.

Cross the Golden Gate Bridge and head north to reach Marin County's rolling hills and green expanses, where residents enjoy an haute-suburban lifestyle. Farther afield, the wild landscapes of the Marin Headlands, Muir Woods, Mt. Tamalpais, Stinson Beach, and Point Reyes National Seashore await.

East of the city, across the San Francisco Bay, are Berkeley and Oakland, which most Bay Area residents refer to as the East Bay. These two towns have distinct personalities, but life here feels more relaxed than in the city—though every bit as vibrant.

18

MARIN COUNTY, BERKELEY, AND OAKLAND PLANNER

Making the Most of Your Time

Berkeley is a university town, and the rhythm of the school year might affect your visit. It's easier to navigate the streets and find parking near the university between semesters, but there's also less buzz around town. Surprisingly, summer is chock-full of students attending the many summer sessions on campus. Moving-in weeks before the fall semester bring a massive influx of students *and* parents and other family members—definitely not the best time to take a campus tour.

BART trains can be packed during traditional morning and evening rush hours, but things are much less congested at other times. BART can get you from downtown San Francisco to a coffee shop in Rockridge in about 25 minutes. (It's closer to 30 minutes for farther points in Berkeley.)

It'll take about the same amount of time to reach Tiburon if traffic is clear on the Golden Gate Bridge (also depending, of course, on what part of the city you're departing from).

About the Restaurants and Hotels

The Bay Area is home to some of the most popular and innovative restaurants in the country, including Chez Panisse Café & Restaurant, in Berkeley, and Lark Creek Inn, in Larkspur—for which reservations must be made well in advance. Expect an emphasis on locally grown produce, hormone-free meats, and California wine. The coast provides a spectacular waterfront setting for dining as well as lodging; in many instances the views are the most important part of the experience. Keep in mind that many Marin cafés don't serve dinner, and that dinner service ends on the early side. (No 10 PM reservations in this neck of the woods.)

There aren't many hotels in Berkeley or Oakland, but Marin is a destination where hotels package themselves as cozy retreats. Summer is often booked well in advance, despite weather that is often mercurial and sometimes downright chilly. Check for special packages during this season.

Getting Around

If you don't want to worry about finding a parking space, using public transportation to reach Berkeley or Oakland is ideal; BART has several central stops in both towns. For sheer romance, nothing beats the ferry; there's service from San Francisco to Sausalito and Tiburon in Marin County, and to Alameda and Oakland in the East Bay. To visit the outer reaches of Marin, a car is essential (unless you want to spend all day on the bus).

DINING AND LODGING PRICE CATEGORIES

	¢	$	$$	$$$	$$$$
Restaurants	under $10	$10–$14	$15–$22	$23–$30	over $30
Hotels	under $90	$90–$149	$150–$199	$200–$250	over $250

Restaurant prices are per person for a main course at dinner, or the equivalent. Hotel prices are for two people in a standard double room in high season.

Updated by
Fiona G.
Parrott

It's rare for a metropolis to compete with its suburbs for visitors, but the view from any of San Francisco's hilltops shows that the Bay Area's temptations extend far beyond the city limits. To the north is Marin County, the beauty queen, with small but chic villages like Tiburon and Mill Valley, plus dramatic coastal scenery. East of town are two energetic urban centers, Berkeley and Oakland. Formerly radical Berkeley is getting more glam, while Oakland is shaking off its image as San Francisco's ugly stepsister.

18

Up in Marin, the birthplace of mountain biking, trail-veined Mt. Tamalpais and the woods below draw hikers and cyclists. Beaches lure families and thrill seekers, while little towns offer urbanites respite from busy city streets. In the mid-1960s and '70s alternative-lifestyle seekers established Marin's reputation as ground zero for gurus, granola, and redwood hot tubs. Despite the influx of stock-market millionaires and chic boutiques, the counterculture identity still sticks. Immediately after crossing the Golden Gate Bridge on Highway 101 northbound, you'll pass through a tunnel whose archway is painted with a rainbow that welcomes you to magical Marin, "Land of Oz."

Meanwhile, the town often referred to as the People's Republic of Berkeley retains its liberal image, though it's drastically tamer than it was in the late 1960s. It's now as famous for chef and food activist Alice Waters (and her pricey restaurant Chez Panisse) as it is for its role as the birthplace of the Free Speech movement. Oakland is polishing some of its rough edges, too, with a successful port and a revitalized downtown, an alternative arts scene, and hipster cafés and boutiques.

MARIN COUNTY

Marin is quite simply a knock-out—some go so far as to call it spectacular and wild. This isn't an extravagant claim, since more than 40% of the county (180,000 acres), including the majority of the coastline, is parkland. The territory ranges from chaparral, grassland, and coastal scrub to broadleaf and evergreen forest, redwood, salt marsh, and rocky shoreline.

WORD OF MOUTH

"Be sure to get out onto the water. A ferry ride to Sausalito, Tiburon, or Larkspur will reward you with wonderful views and there are things to be seen in each of those places."
—Grasshopper

Regardless of its natural beauty, what gave the county its reputation was Cyra McFadden's 1977 book *The Serial*, a literary soap opera that depicted the county as a bastion of hot-tubbing and "open" marriages. Indeed old-time bohemian, but also increasingly jet-set, Marinites still spend a lot of time outdoors, and surfing, cycling, and hiking are common after-work and weekend activities. Adrenaline junkies mountain bike down Mt. Tamalpais, and those who want solitude take a walk on one of Point Reyes's many empty beaches. The hot tub remains a popular destination after hours, but things have changed since the boho days. Artists and musicians who arrived in the 1960s have set the tone for mellow country towns, but Marin is now undeniably chic, with BMWs supplanting VW buses as the car of choice.

Most cosmopolitan is Sausalito, the town just over the Golden Gate Bridge from San Francisco. Across the inlet from Sausalito, Tiburon and Belvedere are lined with grand homes that regularly appear on fund-raising circuits, and to the north, landlocked Mill Valley is a hub of wining and dining and tony boutiques.

In general, the farther you get from the Golden Gate Bridge, the more country things become, and West Marin is about as far as you can get from the big city, both physically and ideologically. Separated from the inland county by the slopes and ridges of giant Mt. Tamalpais, this territory beckons to mavericks, artists, ocean lovers, and other free spirits. Stinson Beach has tempered its isolationist attitude to accommodate out-of-towners, as have Inverness and Point Reyes Station. Bolinas, on the other hand, would prefer you not know its location.

PLANNING

GETTING HERE AND AROUND
BOAT AND FERRY TRAVEL
The Golden Gate Ferry crosses the bay to Sausalito from the south wing of San Francisco's Ferry Building (at Market Street and the Embarcadero). Blue & Gold Fleet ferries depart daily for Sausalito and Tiburon from Pier 41 at Fisherman's Wharf; weekday commuter ferries leave from the Ferry Building for Tiburon. The trip to Sausalito takes 30 minutes; to Tiburon, it takes 20 minutes. Seas can be choppy, but the

ride is not long. Expect more crowds on weekends and during peak commute times.

The Angel Island–Tiburon Ferry sails across the strait to the island daily April through September and weekends the rest of the year.

Boat and Ferry Lines Angel Island–Tiburon Ferry (☎ *415/435–2131* ⊕ *www.angelislandferry.com*). **Blue & Gold Fleet** (☎ *415/705–8200* ⊕ *www. blueandgoldfleet.com*). **Golden Gate Ferry** (☎ *415/455–2000* ⊕ *www. goldengateferry.org*).

BUS TRAVEL

Golden Gate Transit buses travel to Sausalito, Tiburon, and Mill Valley from 1st and Mission streets as well as from other points in San Francisco. For Mt. Tamalpais State Park, take Bus 10, 70, or 80 to Marin City; in Marin City transfer to Golden Gate Transit Bus 63 (weekends and holidays, mid-March through early December only). To reach points in West Marin (e.g., Bolinas, Point Reyes Station, and the edge of Mt. Tamalpais State Park) on weekdays only, take West Marin Stagecoach vans from Marin City; call for routes and schedules. San Francisco MuniBus 76 runs hourly from 4th and Townsend streets to the Marin Headlands Visitor Center on Sunday and major holidays only. The trip takes roughly 45 minutes.

Bus Lines Golden Gate Transit (☎ *415/455–2000* ⊕ *www.goldengate.org*). **San Francisco Muni** (☎ *415/701–2311* ⊕ *www.sfmuni.com*). **West Marin Stagecoach** (☎ *415/526–3239* ⊕ *www.marin-stagecoach.org*).

SIGHTSEEING GUIDES

Blue & Gold Fleet has a one-hour narrated tour of the San Francisco Bay, for $24, with frequent daily departures from Pier 39 in San Francisco. Super Sightseeing offers a four-hour bus tour of Muir Woods. The tour, which stops in Sausalito en route, leaves at 9 AM and 2 PM daily from North Point and Taylor Street at Fisherman's Wharf and costs $46 ($45 senior citizens, $24 ages 5–11); 24-hour advance reservations are recommended. Great Pacific Tour Co. runs four-hour morning and afternoon tours of Muir Woods and Sausalito for $49 ($47 senior citizens, $39 ages 5–11), with hotel pickup in 14-passenger vans with excellent interpretation.

By Bus and Van Blue & Gold Fleet (☎ *415/705–8200* ⊕ *www. blueandgoldfleet.com*). **Great Pacific Tour Co.** (☎ *415/626–4499* ⊕ *www. greatpacifictour.com*). **Super Sightseeing** (☎ *415/777–2288* ⊕ *www. supersightseeing.com*).

VISITOR INFORMATION

Contact Marin County Visitors Bureau (✉ *1013 Larkspur Landing Circle, Larkspur* ☎ *866/925–2060* ⊕ *www.visitmarin.org*).

SAUSALITO

2 mi north of Golden Gate Bridge.

Bougainvillea-covered hillsides and an expansive yacht harbor give Sausalito the feel of an Adriatic resort. The town sits on the northwestern

The crowded piers and rolling hillside of the Sausalito waterfront.

edge of San Francisco Bay, where it's sheltered from the ocean by the Marin Headlands; the mostly mild weather here is perfect for strolling and outdoor dining. Nevertheless, morning fog and afternoon winds can roll over the hills without warning, funneling through the central part of Sausalito once known as Hurricane Gulch.

South on **Bridgeway** (toward San Francisco), which snakes between the bay and the hills, a waterside esplanade is lined with restaurants on piers that lure diners with good seafood and even better views. Stairs along the west side of Bridgeway climb the hill to wooded neighborhoods filled with both rustic and opulent homes. As you amble along Bridgeway past boutiques, gift shops, and galleries, you'll notice the absence of basic services. If you need an aspirin or some groceries (or if you want to see the locals), you'll have to head to Caledonia Street, which runs parallel to Bridgeway, north of the ferry terminus and inland a couple of blocks. The streets closest to the ferry landing flaunt their fair share of shops selling T-shirts and kitschy souvenirs. Venture into some of the side streets or narrow alleyways to catch a bit more of the town's taste for eccentric jewelry and handmade crafts.

■ TIP → The ferry is the best way to get to Sausalito from San Francisco; you get more romance (and less traffic) and disembark in the heart of downtown.

Like much of San Francisco, Sausalito had a raffish reputation before it went upscale. Discovered in 1775 by Spanish explorers and named Sausalito (Little Willow) for the trees growing around its springs, the town served as a port for whaling ships during the 19th century. By the mid-1800s wealthy San Franciscans were making Sausalito their getaway across the bay. They built lavish Victorian summer homes in the hills, many of which still stand. In 1875 the railroad from the north connected with ferryboats to San Francisco, bringing the merchant and working classes with it. This influx of hardworking, fun-loving folk polarized the town into "wharf rats" and "hill snobs," and the waterfront area grew thick with saloons, gambling dens, and bordellos. Bootleggers flourished during Prohibition, and shipyard workers swelled the town's population in the 1940s.

Sausalito developed its bohemian flair in the 1950s and '60s, when a group of artists, led by a charismatic Greek portraitist named Varda, established an artists' colony and a houseboat community here. Today more than 450 houseboats are docked in Sausalito, which has since also become a major yachting center. Some of the houseboats are ragged, others deluxe, but all are quirky (one, a miniature replica of a Persian castle, even has an elevator inside). For a close-up view of the community, head north on Bridgeway—Sausalito's main thoroughfare—from downtown, turn right on Gate Six Road, and park where it dead-ends at the public shore. Keep a respectful distance; these are homes, after all, and the residents become a bit prickly from too much ogling.

ESSENTIALS

Visitor Information Sausalito Chamber of Commerce (⊠ *780 Bridgeway* ☎ *415/332–0505 or 415/331–7262* ⊕ *www.sausalito.org*).

Get your bearings and find out what's happening in town at the **Sausalito Visitors Center and Historical Exhibit** (⊠ *780 Bridgeway* ☎ *415/332–0505*), operated by the town's historical society. It's closed Monday.

The landmark **Plaza Viña del Mar** (⊠ *Bridgeway and Park St.*), named for Sausalito's sister city in Chile, marks the center of town. Flanked by two 14-foot-tall elephant statues (created in 1915 for the Panama-Pacific International Exposition), the fountain is a great setting for snapshots and people-watching.

On the waterfront between the Hotel Sausalito and the Sausalito Yacht Club is an unusual historic landmark—a **drinking fountain.** It's inscribed with HAVE A DRINK ON SALLY in remembrance of Sally Stanford, the former San Francisco madam who later became the town's mayor in the 1970s. Sassy Sally, as they called her, would have appreciated the fountain's eccentric custom attachment: a knee-level basin that reads HAVE A DRINK ON LELAND, in memory of her beloved dog.

NEED A BREAK?

Judging by the crowds gathered outside Hamburgers (⊠ *737 Bridgeway* ☎ *415/332–9471*), you'd think someone was juggling flaming torches out front. They're really gaping at the juicy hand-formed beef patties sizzling on a rotating grill. Brave the line (it moves fast), get your food to go, and head for the esplanade to enjoy the sweeping views. Hours are 11 AM to 5 PM.

An anonymous-looking World War II shipyard building holds one of Sausalito's great treasures: the sprawling (more than 1½ acres) **Bay Model** of the entire San Francisco Bay and the San Joaquin–Sacramento River delta, complete with flowing water. The U.S. Army Corps of Engineers uses the model to reproduce the rise and fall of tides, the

Marin County

flow of currents, and the other physical forces at work on the bay. *2100 Bridgeway, at Marinship Way ☎ 415/332–3870 recorded information, 415/332–3871 operator assistance ⊕ www.spn.usace.army.mil/bmvc ☑ Free ⊙ Memorial Day–Labor Day, Tues.–Fri. 9–4, weekends 10–5; Labor Day–Memorial Day, Tues.–Sat. 9–4.*

The **Bay Area Discovery Museum** fills five former military buildings with entertaining and enlightening hands-on exhibits related to science and the arts. Kids and their families can fish from a boat at the indoor wharf, imagine themselves as marine biologists in the Wave Workshop, and play outdoors at Lookout Cove, a 2½-acre bay-in-miniature made up of scaled-down sea caves, tidal pools, and even a re-created shipwreck. At Tot Zone, toddlers and preschoolers can play in an indoor-outdoor interactive area. From San Francisco, take the Alexander Avenue exit from U.S. 101 and follow signs to East Fort Baker. ⊠ *557 McReynolds Rd., at East Fort Baker ☎ 415/339–3900 ⊕ www.baykidsmuseum.org ☑ $10; children under 1 free ⊙ Tues.–Fri. 9–4, weekends 10–5.*

WHERE TO EAT AND STAY

¢ ✕ **Bridgeway Cafe.** For a straight-shooting American menu, head to this CAFÉ little diner-café right on the main drag across the road from the bay. People line up on weekends for great breakfasts of pancakes and eggs and lunches of hot and cold sandwiches. Take in a view of the water while enjoying a morning croissant, well-crafted BLT, or their excellent fries. The Mediterranean dishes are also a hit—try the mixed appetizer platter or a hearty Greek salad. The café serves continuously until 5 PM. ✉ *633 Bridgeway* ☎ *415/332–3426* ▭ *AE, D, MC, V* ☻ *No dinner.*

$–$$
SEAFOOD
☺
Fodor's Choice
★

✕ **Fish.** If you're wondering where the locals go, this is the place. For fresh seafood you can't beat this gleaming dockside fish house a mile north of downtown. Order at the counter, and then grab a seat by the floor-to-ceiling windows or at a picnic table on the pier, overlooking the yachts and fishing boats. Most of the sustainably caught fish is hauled in from the owner's boats, right at the dock outside. Try the ceviche, crab Louis, cioppino, barbecue oysters, or anything fresh that day that's being grilled over the oak-wood fire. Outside, kids can doodle with sidewalk chalk on the pier. ✉ *350 Harbor Dr.* ☎ *415/331–3474* ⚲ *Reservations not accepted* ▭ *No credit cards.*

$$
FRENCH BISTRO

✕ **Le Garage.** When Sausalito executives and entrepreneurs want a stylish lunch with a bayside setting, they head to Chef Olivier Souvestre's local lunch hot spot. Brittany born Souvestre serves traditional French bistro fare in a relaxed, sidewalk café–style setting. The menu is small, but the dishes are substantial in flavor and presentation. Standouts include frisée salad with poached egg, bacon, croutons, and pancetta vinaigrette; steak frites with a shallot confit and crispy fries; and a chef's selection of cheese or charcuterie with soup and mixed greens. The restaurant only seats 35 inside and 15 outside, so to avoid a long wait for lunch, arrive before 11:30 or after 1:30 PM. ✉ *85 Liberty Ship Way, Suite #109, Sausalito* ☎ *415/332–5625* ▭ *MC, V.*

$$–$$$
AMERICAN

✕ **Paradise Bay.** The views from this gem of a restaurant—which is a five-minute walk north of the tourist hub—will make you feel like you're in a secluded paradise; boats, sea kayaks, and the beautiful bay stretch before you. Outdoor seating in the Bay Area doesn't get much better than this, and the inventive, well-balanced, local- and organic-based menu won't disappoint either. Try the Paradise Bay cioppino in a rich tomato-fennel broth or the grilled organic lamb sirloin with goat cheese and garlic flan. The trio crème brûlée—espresso, mango, and coconut— is divine, as is the extensive cocktail list. This is also the perfect place for weekend brunch—the buttermilk ginger pancakes topped with banana and mango are out of this world. ✉ *1200 Bridgeway* ☎ *415/331–3226* ▭ *AE, D, MC, V.*

$$–$$$
ITALIAN
★

✕ **Poggio.** One of the few restaurants in Sausalito to attract both food-savvy locals and tourists, Poggio serves modern Tuscan cuisine in a handsome, open-wall space that spills onto the street. Expect dishes such as grilled lamb chops with roasted eggplant, braised artichokes with polenta, feather-light gnocchi, and pizzas from the open kitchen's wood-fired oven. ✉ *777 Bridgeway* ☎ *415/332–7771* ⚲ *Reservations essential* ▭ *AE, D, MC, V.*

$$–$$$
SEAFOOD

✕ **Spinnaker.** Okay, let's not mince words: you go to Spinnaker for the view, not the food. Sure, the plain-Jane menu of seafood, steaks, and pastas is solid, but it can't compare to the spectacular waterfront setting of its contemporary glass-wall building, on a point beyond the harbor near the yacht club. If you're lucky, you can spot pelicans diving and harbor seals frolicking just outside the windows. Just don't expect to

18

see any locals. ⊠ *100 Spinnaker Dr.* ☎ *415/332–1500* ☰ *AE, D, DC, MC, V.*

$$–$$$ ✕ **Sushi Ran.** Sushi aficionados swear this is the Bay Area's best for
JAPANESE raw fish, but don't overlook the excellent Pacific Rim fusions, a result
★ of Japanese ingredients and French cooking techniques, served in
unusual presentations. Because Sushi Ran is so highly ranked among
area foodies, book two to seven days in advance for dinner. Otherwise,
expect a long wait, which you can soften by sipping one of the 45 by-
the-glass sakes from the outstanding wine-and-sake bar. ■**TIP→ If you
wander in after a day of sightseeing and can't get a table, you can sup in
the noisy bar.** ⊠ *107 Caledonia St.* ☎ *415/332–3620* ☰ *AE, D, MC, V*
⊗ *No lunch weekends.*

$$$$ 🏨 **Casa Madrona.** What began as a small inn in a 19th-century landmark
house has expanded over the decades to incorporate a variety of lodgings and a full-service spa, all tiered down the hill in the center of town.
The design in the original rooms and suites ranges from the cutesiness
of what's called the Artist's Loft to elegant Mediterranean motifs. An
adjacent three-story building contains newer rooms that are uniformly
contemporary, with wet bars, sunken tubs, and bay windows; some
have balconies overlooking Richardson Bay. Bay-view rooms are pricey,
but the vistas are spectacular. **Pros:** free Wi-Fi, spacious rooms, the bay
is a 5-minute walk away. **Cons:** rooms in older section don't have a/c or
elevator access, parking is pricey. ⊠ *801 Bridgeway* ☎ *415/332–0502 or
800/567–9524* ⊕ *www.casamadrona.com* ➭ *59 rooms, 2 suites* ⚒ *In-
room: DVD (some), Wi-Fi. In-hotel: restaurant, spa, laundry service,
concierge* ☰ *AE, D, DC, MC, V.*

$$$$ 🏨 **Cavallo Point.** Set in Golden Gate National Park, this luxury hotel
and resort's location is truly one of a kind. A former Army post, it features turn-of-the-century buildings converted into well-appointed yet
eco-friendly rooms. Both historic and contemporary guest rooms are
scattered around the property, most overlooking a massive lawn with
stunning views of the Golden Gate Bridge and San Francisco Bay. The
staff is accommodating and helpful. Murray Circle, the notable on-site
restaurant with a Michelin-starred chef, serves top-notch California
ingredients and features an impressive wine cellar. The neighboring
casual bar offers food and drink on a large porch. **Pros:** numerous activities: a cooking school, yoga classes, and nature walks; spa with a tea
bar; art gallery. **Cons:** landscaping feels incomplete, some staff act a bit
informal. ⊠ *601 Murray Circle, Fort Baker, Sausalito* ☎ *415/339–4700*
⊕ *www.cavallopoint.com* ➭ *68 historic and 74 contemporary guest
rooms* ⚒ *In-room: no a/c (some), safe, refrigerator, Internet, Wi-Fi. In
hotel: 2 restaurants, room service, bar, pool, gym, spa, water sports,
laundry service, parking (fee), some pets allowed (fee), no-smoking
rooms* ☰ *AE, D, DC, MC, V.*

$$ 🏨 **Hotel Sausalito.** Handmade furniture and tasteful original art and
reproductions give this well-run inn the feel of a small European hotel.
The Mediterranean-like glow comes from the soft yellow, green, and
orange tones bathing the rooms, some of which have harbor or park
views. Space ranges from small quarters for budget-minded travelers (a
rarity in pricey Marin) to commodious suites. Best of all, it's smack-dab

downtown, right next to the ferry landing and above a row of shops. **Pros:** great staff, excellent central location, feels like home away from home. **Cons:** no room service, some rooms feel cramped. ⊠ *16 El Portal* ☎ *415/332–0700 or 888/442–0700* ⊕ *www.hotelsausalito.com* ⤵ *14 rooms, 2 suites* ⚬ *In-room: DVD, Wi-Fi. In-hotel: concierge* ⊟ *AE, DC, MC, V* ⎮⊙⎮ *CP.*

WORD OF MOUTH

"I would go with the Inn above the Tide in Sausalito, make sure you get a corner room with a sea view." —andrew8

$$$$ ⌂ **The Inn Above Tide.** This is the only hotel in the Bay Area with balconies literally hanging over the water, and each of its rooms has a perfect-10 view that takes in wild Angel Island as well as the city lights across the bay. In the corner Vista Suite (the most expensive room here, at nearly triple the standard-room rate), you can even watch San Francisco twinkle from the king-size bed. Lovely touches—gardenias by the sink, large tubs, binoculars in every room, complimentary California wine and imported cheese—abound, and most rooms have wood-burning or gas fireplaces. Although it's set in the middle of town, this place is tranquil. **Pros:** great complimentary breakfast, minutes from restaurants/ attractions, free in-room binoculars let you indulge in the incredible views. **Cons:** costly parking, some rooms are on the small side, no room service. ⊠ *30 El Portal* ☎ *415/332–9535 or 800/893–8433* ⊕ *www. innabovetide.com* ⤵ *29 rooms, 2 suites* ⚬ *In-room: DVD, Wi-Fi. In-hotel: laundry service, concierge* ⊟ *AE, DC, MC, V* ⎮⊙⎮ *CP.*

SPORTS AND THE OUTDOORS

Specializing in sea kayaking, **Sea Trek Ocean Kayaking Center** (⊠ *Schoon-maker Point Marina, off Libertyship Way* ☎ *415/488–1000* ⊕ *www. seatrekkayak.com*) offers guided half-day trips underneath the Golden Gate Bridge and full- and half-day trips to Angel Island, both for beginners. Starlight and full-moon paddles are particularly popular. Trips for experienced kayakers, classes, and rentals also are available. Prices start at $20 per hour for rentals; $65 for a three-hour guided trip.

THE ARTS

The annual **Sausalito Art Festival** (☎ *415/332–3555 or 415/331–3757* ⊕ *www.sausalitoartfestival.org*), held over Labor Day weekend, attracts more than 50,000 people to the northern waterfront area; Blue & Gold Fleet ferries from San Francisco dock at the pier adjacent to the festival. Tickets are $20.

SHOPPING

Something/Anything Gallery. Tucked away where Broadway ends and curves toward the dock, this gallery has a huge array of jewelry and gifts, from unique watches to humorous pendants. With friendly service and carefully crafted mementos of Sausalito, it's easy to find an inexpensive souvenir. ⊠ *20 Princess St., Sausalito* ☎ *415/339–8831.*

18

TIBURON

2 mi north of Sausalito, 7 mi north of Golden Gate Bridge.

On a peninsula that was called Punta de Tiburon (Shark Point) by the Spanish explorers, this beautiful Marin County community retains the feel of a village, despite the encroachment of commercial establishments from the downtown area. The harbor faces Angel Island across Raccoon Strait, and San Francisco is directly south across the bay—which makes the views from the decks of harbor restaurants a major attraction. Tiburon is slightly more low-key than Sausalito, and the community favors Sunday brunch and cocktail hour. Since its incarnation, in 1884, when ferries from San Francisco connected the point with a railroad to San Rafael, the town has centered on the waterfront. ■TIP→ The ferry is the most relaxing (and fastest) way to get here whenever the weather is pleasant, particularly in summer, allowing you to skip traffic and parking problems. Think about avoiding a midweek visit to Tiburon. Although there will be fewer strollers on the street, most shops close either Tuesday or Wednesday, or both.

ESSENTIALS

Visitor Information Tiburon Peninsula Chamber of Commerce (⊠ 96-B Main St. ☎ 415/435–5633 ⊕ www.tiburonchamber.org).

Tiburon's narrow **Main Street** is on the bay side; you can browse the shops and galleries or relax on a restaurant's deck jutting out over the harbor.

Past the pink-brick bank building, Main Street is known as **Ark Row** (⊕ www.landmarks-society.org) and has a tree-shaded walk lined with antiques and specialty stores. Look closely and you can see that some of the buildings are actually old houseboats. They floated in Belvedere Cove before being beached and transformed into stores. If you're curious about architectural history, the Tiburon Heritage & Arts Commission prints a self-guided walking-tour map, which you can pick up at local businesses.

The stark-white **Old St. Hilary's Landmark and Wildflower Preserve,** an 1886 Carpenter Gothic church barged over from Strawberry Point in 1957, overlooks the town and the bay from its hillside perch. ■TIP→ The church is surrounded by a wildflower preserve that is spectacular in May and June, when the rare black jewel flower blooms. Expect a steep walk uphill to reach the preserve. ⊠ 201 Esperanza St., off Mar West St. ☎ 415/435–1853 ⊕ www.landmarks-society.org ☞ $2 suggested donation ☉ Apr.–Oct., Wed. and Sun. 1–4 and by appointment.

WHERE TO EAT AND STAY

$–$$ ✕ **Guaymas.** The festive Mexican restaurant at the ferry terminal claims

MEXICAN a knockout view of the bay, handsome whitewashed adobe walls, tile floors, and a heated terrace bar—and it serves a top-notch margarita. The large open kitchen churns out a long list of fairly authentic Mexican dishes such as ceviche, *carnitas uruapan* (slow-roasted pork with salsa and black beans), mesquite-grilled fish, and tamales. ■TIP→ Sunday brunch is popular, so make a reservation. ⊠ 5 Main St. ☎ 415/435–6300 ⚘ Reservations essential ▤ AE, D, DC, MC, V.

¢–$
AMERICAN
✕**New Morning Cafe.** If you ran straight for the morning ferry and didn't have time to eat, break your fast at this homey café with cozy booths and bright tablecloths. Omelets and scrambles are served all day long alongside more innovative egg dishes such as the "Scrumptious," which mixes in vegetables. If you're past morning treats, choose from the many soups, salads, and sandwiches. It's open 6:30 AM–2:30 PM weekdays and 6:30 AM–4 PM weekends. ⊠ *1696 Tiburon Blvd.* ☎ *415/435–4315* ▤ *MC, V* ⊗ *No dinner.*

WORD OF MOUTH

"San Francisco's Marin Headlands is part of the National Park Service, and is a wonderful place for hiking, biking, and walking on the beach. It is also home to the most breath-taking view of the Golden Gate Bridge and the city skyline."
—DoreenD

$–$$
AMERICAN
✕**Rooney's.** Beloved by locals, this is a Tiburon favorite. A friendly greeting will make you feel as if you're at home, as will the lanterns and polished wood floors (head inside over dining dockside). Comfort food anchors the lunch menu with choices like "New York–style" sandwiches, salads, and a few surprises such as African chicken. For dinner, choose from fresh Dungeness crab, rib-eye steak, or seasonal specials. Last orders are taken at 9 PM except on Friday and Saturday, when you have an extra half-hour. ⊠ *38 Main St.* ☎ *415/435–1911* ▤ *MC, V* ⊗ *No dinner Mon. or Tues.*

$$–$$$
AMERICAN
✕**Sam's Anchor Cafe.** Open since 1921, this casual dockside restaurant with mahogany wainscoting is the town's most famous eatery. Today most people flock here for the deck, where out-of-towners and old salts sit shoulder to shoulder for bay views, beer, seafood, and Ramos fizzes. The lunch menu is nothing special—burgers, sandwiches, salads, fried fish with tartar sauce—and you'll sit on plastic chairs at tables covered with blue-and-white-checked oilcloths. At night you can find standard seafood dishes with vegetarian and meat options. Expect a wait for outside tables on weekends (there are no reservations for deck seating or weekend lunch). Mind the seagulls; they know no restraint. ⊠ *27 Main St.* ☎ *415/435–4527* ▤ *AE, D, DC, MC, V.*

$–$$
PIZZA
✕**Waypoint Pizza.** A nautical decor theme and a tasty "between the sheets" pizza-style sandwich are signatures of this creative pizzeria that also serves slices and whole gourmet pies. Booths are brightened with blue-checked tablecloths, and a playful air is added by indoor deck chairs, a picnic table complete with umbrella, and lighthouse salt-and-pepper shakers. If you're dining alone, peruse the aluminum rack for an excellent selection of magazines and newspapers. ⊠ *15 Main St.* ☎ *415/435–3440.*

$$–$$$
★
🛏 **Waters Edge Hotel.** Checking into this spacious and elegant hotel feels like tucking away into a cozy retreat by the water. The views are stunning, the lighting perfect. Most rooms have a gas fireplace, and many have balconies with bay views at this stylish small hotel in downtown Tiburon. Furnishings are chic and modern in cocoa and cream colors; down comforters and high-thread-count linens make the beds deliciously comfortable. High-vaulted ceilings show off the carefully placed, Asian-influenced objects, which line the hallways and

18

front living room area. ■TIP➜ In the morning, breakfast is delivered to your door, but take your coffee outside to the giant communal sundeck over the water; the south-facing views of San Francisco Bay are incredible. **Pros:** complimentary wine and cheese for guests every evening, restaurants/sights are minutes away. **Cons:** no room service, extra charge for Wi-Fi access, not a great place to bring small children. ⊠ *25 Main St.* ☎ *415/789–5999 or 877/789–5999* ⊕ *www.marinhotels.com* ⤻ *23 rooms* ♿ *In-room: DVD, Wi-Fi. In-hotel: laundry service, concierge* ⊟ *AE, D, DC, MC, V* ⑩ *CP.*

SHOPPING

♻ **The Candy Store on Main Street.** If you long for sheets of candy dots or to bite the tops off wax bottles, come here to score the retro candy of your childhood. There's also ice cream, freshly made fudge, and a space-age-looking dispenser for pucker powder. ⊠ *7 Main St., Tiburon* ☎ *415/435–0434.*

MILL VALLEY

2 mi north of Sausalito, 4 mi north of Golden Gate Bridge.

One of just a few towns that are simultaneously woodsy and chic, Mill Valley has a dual personality. Here, as elsewhere in the county, the foundation is a superb natural setting. Virtually surrounded by parkland, the town lies at the base of Mt. Tamalpais, the Bay Area's tallest mountain, and includes dense redwood groves traversed by countless creeks. But this is no lumber camp. Smart restaurants and chichi boutiques line the streets, and more rock stars than one might suspect make their homes here.

The small downtown area, no more than five blocks square, has the constant bustle of a leisure community; even at noon on a Tuesday, people are out shopping for fancy cookware and lacy pajamas.

ESSENTIALS

Visitor Information Mill Valley Chamber of Commerce (⊠ *85 Throckmorton Ave.* ☎ *415/388–9700* ⊕ *www.millvalley.org).*

In the center of it all is **Lytton Square**, at the corner of Miller and Throckmorton avenues, where locals and visitors congregate on weekends to socialize in the many coffeehouses.

♻ To see one of the numerous outdoor oases that make Mill Valley so appealing, follow Throckmorton Avenue ¼ mi south from Lytton Square to **Old Mill Park**, a shady patch of redwoods that shelters a playground and reconstructed sawmill. From the park, Cascade Drive winds its way past creek-side homes to the trailheads of several forest paths.

WHERE TO EAT AND STAY

$$$

AMERICAN

✕ **The Balboa Café.** Mill Valley's newest eatery (opened in September 2008) is where the trendy locals come to eat, drink, and be seen seven days a week. One of four restaurants in the celebrated Plumpjack franchise, Balboa offers an upscale dining experience with intimate lighting, rich wood accents, and fresh-pressed white linens. Hanging on the walls are old black-and-white photos depicting Mill Valley in its lumber years.

The bar is so busy that you'll be lucky if your elbow gets anywhere near it. Although the cocktails are not as stiff as their price tags, the food is creative, local, and beautifully presented. Try the Black Angus rib eye, wild mushroom risotto, or seared sea scallops—and be sure to save room for the blueberry brioche bread pudding. The wine list is extensive and even offers wines from Marin County. If you prefer something on the lighter side, they purify and carbonate their own water. ⊠ *38 Miller Ave.* ☎ *415/381–7321* ⌖ *Reservations essential* ▤ *AE, DC, MC, V.*

\$\$–\$\$\$
AMERICAN

✕ **Buckeye Roadhouse.** This is Mill Valley's secret den of decadence, where house-smoked meats and fish, grilled steaks, and old-fashioned dishes such as brisket bring the locals coming back for more. They also serve beautiful organic, locally grown salads and desserts so heavenly—like their rich but light crème brûlée—you'll just about melt into the floor. The look of the 1937 roadhouse is decidedly hunting-lodge chic, with trophy heads and a river-rock fireplace dominating one wall. Marin County's Jaguar-driving bon vivants pack the place every night. The busy but cozy bar with elegant mahogany paneling and soft lighting is a good place to quench your thirst for a Marin martini or Californian merlot. ⊠ *15 Shoreline Hwy.* ☎ *415/331–2600* ⌖ *Reservations essential* ▤ *D, DC, MC, V.*

\$
FRENCH/
AMERICAN

✕ **Champagne.** This adorable little bakery/café on Mill Valley's main shopping street is a nice place to pop into for breakfast, a light lunch, dinner, or afternoon pick-me-up. Filled with light, authentic French decor and only a dozen tables, Champagne serves amazing crepes with roasted chicken, creamed spinach, and Swiss cheese, as well as an assortment of savory flatbreads—try the pesto and tomato version. It's a popular place for breakfast, too, with a wide selection of omelets, as well as a perennial favorite: brioche French toast with bacon. The afternoon crowd keeps the tables busy as they chat over cappuccinos, raspberry-almond croissants, and meringue cookies. There's also a tempting assortment of baked goods to take home with you. ⊠ *41 Throckmorton Ave.* ☎ *415/380–0410* ▤ *AE, MC, V.*

\$\$
AMERICAN

✕ **The Dipsea Cafe.** There is no better place for breakfast than the Dipsea, which is named after the gorgeous trail that stretches from Mill Valley to Stinson Beach. Locals crowd its cozy interior most mornings, but weekends are especially popular. Choose from huge plates of French toast, eggs Benedict, and huevos rancheros; the homemade fries and jam that accompany the breakfast entrées are to die for. The café also serves hearty lunches, like Chinese salad with seared salmon and enormous BLTs. This is a great spot to duck into on your way to Muir Woods or Stinson Beach. ⊠ *200 Shoreline Hwy.* ☎ *415/381–0298* ▤ *AE, MC, V* ⊘ *No dinner Sun.–Thurs.*

\$
MEXICAN

✕ **Joe's Taco Lounge.** This funky, bright lounge (and it really does feel like someone's lounge) is a fun place to go for a casual, cheap, and delicious Mexican meal. There are all sorts of colorful relics on the walls and chili-pepper lights adorn the windows. The signature dishes are fish tacos and snapper burritos—which are generous in both size and flavor. The organic burger with spicy fries and the fire-grilled corn on the cob are also yummy. Choose from a wide selection of Mexican beers or go for a wine-based margarita, which is refreshingly tasty. This

18

is a popular place for families between 5 and 7 PM. ⊠ *382 Miller Ave.* ☎ *415/383–8164* ▭ *AE, MC, V.*

$$$–$$$$
NEW AMERICAN
★

✕ **Lark Creek Inn.** Occupying a refurbished 100-year-old house surrounded by lush, mature gardens and towering redwoods, this is one of Marin's prettiest—and best—restaurants, especially for Sunday brunch. The menu, which changes daily, is New American and highlights top-notch meats and organic produce from local farmers. The Caesar salad boasts a secret ingredient and is succulently presented with whole leaf spears. The signature dessert, butterscotch pudding, sounds humble but has a sumptuous flavor. Sit outside on the patio or inside the country-elegant dining room beneath a dramatic greenhouse ceiling. Be mindful that all this beauty of place and plate comes at a price. ⊠ *234 Magnolia Ave., Larkspur* ☎ *415/924–7766* ⌂ *Reservations essential* ▭ *AE, MC, V* ☾ *No lunch Mon.–Sat.*

$$–$$$
ITALIAN

✕ **Piazza D'Angelo.** In the heart of downtown, busy D'Angelo's is known for its osso buco and veal saltimbocca, as well as pastas and delicious crème brûlée. The food is authentic and fresh; another draw is the scene, especially in the lounge area, which hosts a lively cocktail hour packed with beautiful people and serves food until 10 or 11 PM—late for Mill Valley. The sprawling space encompasses a bright front room, romantic booths, and a warm patio. ⊠ *22 Miller Ave.* ☎ *415/388–2000* ▭ *AE, MC, V.*

$$$–$$$$

⛺ **Mill Valley Inn.** The only hotel in downtown Mill Valley has smart-looking rooms done up in Tuscan colors of ocher and olive, with hand-crafted beds, armoires, and lamps by local artisans. Beds are made with crisp white linens, starkly contrasting the deep browns and greens of the towering redwoods just outside the windows. There's a nice complimentary wine reception every evening on the sun terrace. The cottages in the back of the hotel are something special. **Pros:** minutes from local shops and restaurants, great complimentary continental breakfast. **Cons:** dark in the winter months because of surrounding trees, some rooms are not accessible via elevator. ⊠ *165 Throckmorton Ave.* ☎ *415/389–6608 or 800/595–2100* ⊕ *www.marinhotels.com* ⇌ *25 rooms, 1 suite, 2 cottages* ⌂ *In-room: Wi-Fi. In-hotel: no elevator (some), laundry service* ▭ *AE, D, DC, MC, V* ☉ *CP.*

$$–$$$
★

⛺ **Mountain Home Inn.** Abutting 40,000 acres of state and national parks, the inn sits on the skirt of Mt. Tamalpais, where you can follow hiking trails all the way to Stinson Beach. The inn's multilevel, airy wooden building has pristine wilderness on one side and an unparalleled view of the bay on the other. Rooms are built for romance, each mixing huge views with some combination of balcony, fireplace, and whirl-pool tub. ■TIP→ **For full-moon nights, book far in advance.** The on-site wine bar and dining room (closed Monday and Tuesday) serves lunch on the deck (May to October) and a terrific $38 prix-fixe dinner of American regional cuisine inside by the fire. The restaurant (reservations recommended) serves sumptuous meals with spectacular views. Top your Niman Ranch beef burger with caramelized onions, roasted red peppers, local blue cheese, or a range of other options. There's a late-afternoon American cheese–tasting course, as well as an après-trek menu of small plates for hungry hikers. Dinner features modern riffs on classic American fare. **Pros:** amazing deck and views, peaceful, remote setting. **Cons:** nearest town is a 20-minute drive away, Wi-Fi connection is spotty. ✉ *810 Panoramic Hwy.* ☎ *415/381–9000* ⊕ *www.mtnhomeinn.com* ⤴ *10 rooms* ⚿ *In-room: no a/c, no TV, Wi-Fi (some). In-hotel: restaurant, bar* ⊟ *AE, MC, V* ⦆⦆ *BP.*

WORD OF MOUTH

"Mountain Home Inn is perfect [since] it is just above Muir Woods, in fact there is a trail down to Muir Woods just across the street from Mountain Home. It's 1,000 feet down, over a mile, steep but the trail is good, with wooden steps…."   —sequoia370

NIGHTLIFE AND THE ARTS

The **Mill Valley Fall Arts Festival** (☎ *415/383–5256* ⊕ *www.mvfaf.org*) takes place in mid-September in Old Mill Park, with live music, a kids' stage, and artisans selling crafts, jewelry, and art.

SHOPPING

The area around Throckmorton Avenue in downtown Mill Valley brims with stylish and quirky stores—indies as well as chains. One of the chains, Banana Republic, actually began life here as a small safari-focused retailer.

Book Passage. This sprawling independent bookstore in nearby Corte Madera is a magnet for book lovers. The calendar of author events is packed with readings by such big names as Alice Walker, Calvin Trillin, Michael Connelly, and Peter Mayle. Pick-me-up snacks are available at the in-store café. ✉ *The Marketplace, 51 Tamal Vista Blvd., Corte Madera* ☎ *415/927–0960 or 800/999–7909.*

Maison Rêve. French farmhouse meets contemporary style here. Clusters of interesting objects, such as vintage glass bottles, gather gracefully in vignettes. The price range is admirable, with unique finds possible at a reasonable cost. They also have charming children's gifts. ✉ *108 Throckmorton Ave., Mill Valley* ☎ *415/383–9700.*

THE MARIN HEADLANDS

★ The term "Golden Gate" may now be synonymous with the world-famous bridge, but it originally referred to the grassy, poppy-strewn hills flanking the passageway into San Francisco Bay. To the north of the gate lie the **Marin Headlands,** part of the Golden Gate National Recreation Area (GGNRA) and the most dramatic scenery in these parts. The raw beauty of the headlands, which consist of several small but steep bluffs, is particularly striking if you've just come from the enclosed silence of the nearby redwood groves. Windswept hills plunge down to the ocean, and creek-fed thickets shelter swaying wildflowers.

The headlands stretch from the Golden Gate Bridge to Muir Beach. Photographers flock to the southern headlands for shots of the city, with the Golden Gate Bridge in the foreground and the skyline on the horizon. Equally remarkable are the views north along the coast and out to sea, where the Farallon Islands are visible on clear days. ■ TIP➔ Almost any of the roads, all very windy, offer great coast views, especially as you drive at higher elevations. You'll see copious markers for scenic spots.

The headlands' strategic position at the mouth of San Francisco Bay made them a logical site for World War II military installations. Today you can explore the crumbling concrete batteries where naval guns protected the approaches from the sea; kids especially love climbing on these structures. The headlands' main attractions are centered on Forts Barry and Cronkhite, which lie just across Rodeo Lagoon from each other. Fronting the lagoon is Rodeo Beach, a dark stretch of sand that attracts sand-castle builders and dog owners.

⚠ Note: The beaches at the Marin Headlands are not safe for swimming. The giant cliffs are steep and unstable, so hiking down them can be dangerous. Stay on trails. Head farther north, to Muir Beach and beyond, for better ocean access.

The **Marin Headlands Visitor Center** (⊠ *Fort Barry, Field and Bunker Rds., Bldg. 948* ☎ *415/331–1540* ⊕ *www.nps.gov/goga/marin-headlands. htm*), open daily 9:30–4:30, sells a useful guide to historic sites and wildlife and has exhibits on the area's history and ecology. Pick up the park newspaper, which lists a calendar of events, including a schedule of guided walks. Kids will enjoy the "please touch" educational sites and small play area inside.

☾ ★ At the end of Conzelman Road, in the southern headlands, is the **Point Bonita Lighthouse,** a restored beauty that still guides ships to safety with its original 1855 refractory lens. Half the fun of a visit is the steep ½-mi walk from the parking area down to the lighthouse, which takes you through a rock tunnel and across a suspension bridge. Signposts along the way detail the bravado of surfmen, as the early lifeguards were called, and the tenacity of the "wickies," the first keepers of the light. ⊠ *End of Conzelman Rd.* ▨ *Free* ☾ *Sat.–Mon. 12:30–3:30.*

If you're an art lover, stop by the **Headlands Center for the Arts** (⊠ *944 Fort Barry* ☎ *415/331–2787* ⊕ *www.headlands.org* ☾ *Weekdays 10–5, Sun. noon–5*), where you can see contemporary art in a rustic natural setting. All but one of the center's nine converted military buildings are usually closed to the public, but you can visit the main building (the former barracks) to see several changing installations. The downstairs "archive room" features an odd assortment of objects found and created by residents, such as natural rocks, interesting glass bottles filled with collected items, and unusual masks. Stop by the industrial gallery space, two flights up, to see what the resident visual artists are up to—most of the work is quite contemporary. The center also hosts biweekly public programs, from artist talks to open studios. Call for current schedules.

☾ Small but scenic, **Muir Beach,** a rocky patch of shoreline off Route 1 in the northern headlands, is a good place to stretch your legs and gaze out at the Pacific. Locals often walk their dogs here, and anglers and boogie boarders share the gentle surf. Families and cuddling couples come for picnicking and sunbathing. At one end of the sand is a cluster of waterfront homes, and at the other are the bluffs of Golden Gate National Recreation Area.

Shutterbugs rejoice in catching a scenic Muir Beach sunset.

WHERE TO STAY

¢ 🏠 **Marin Headlands Hostel.** As hostels go, it's hard to beat this beautifully located, well-maintained property in a valley on the north side of the headlands. This is also the only lodging in the GGNRA that isn't a campsite. Accommodations, inside the old military infirmary, consist of private rooms with space for up to five, or shared dorm-style rooms that sleep six to 22 people in bunk beds. Cook your own food in the communal kitchen and eat at a table in the giant common area near the woodstove; big windows look out onto stands of pine and eucalyptus. Couples can share rooms in a separate two-story house made cozy with couches in some rooms, comfortable wooden tables, and forest views. Don't miss the map of the world, which reaches over a corner and across two walls in the main house. **Pros:** plenty of peace and quiet, great prices, lovely setting. **Cons:** no Wi-Fi, difficult to get to without a car or bike, far from restaurants and shops. ✉ *941 Fort Barry* ☎ *415/331–2777* ⊕ *www.norcalhostels.org/marin* 🛏 *7 private rooms, 8 dormitory rooms; all with shared bath* ⚒ *In-room: no a/c, no phone, no TV. In-hotel: no elevator, laundry facilities* ▤ *D, MC, V.*

$$$–$$$$ 🏠 **Pelican Inn.** From its slate roof to its whitewashed plaster walls, this
★ inn looks so Tudor that it's hard to believe it was built in the 1970s. The Pelican is English to the core, with its smallish guest rooms upstairs (no elevator), high half-tester beds draped in heavy fabrics, and bangers and grilled tomatoes for breakfast. Downstairs, the little pub pours ales and ports, and "the snug" is a private fireplace lounge for overnight guests. At dinner in the tavernlike or solarium dining rooms ($$–$$$), keep it simple with fish-and-chips, roasted hen, or prime rib and focus on the well-crafted wine list. Lunch is served, too . . . a good thing,

since your nearest alternatives are miles away via slow, winding roads. **Pros:** 5-minute walk to beach, great bar and restaurant, peaceful setting. **Cons:** 20-minute drive to nearby attractions, no Wi-Fi or wheelchair access to bedrooms. ⊠ *10 Pacific Way, off Rte. 1, Muir Beach* 🕾 *415/383–6000* ⊕ *www.pelicaninn.com* ↙*7 rooms* ♿ *In-room: no a/c, no phone, no TV. In-hotel: restaurant, bar, no elevator* ⊟ *MC, V* ⫼ *BP.*

MUIR WOODS NATIONAL MONUMENT

�८ *12 mi northwest of the Golden Gate Bridge.*

Fodor'sChoice
★

One hundred fifty million years ago, ancestors of redwood and sequoia trees grew throughout the United States. Today the *Sequoia sempervirens* can be found only in a narrow, cool coastal belt from Monterey to Oregon. The 550 acres of Muir Woods National Monument contain some of the most majestic redwoods in the world—some nearly 250 feet tall and 1,000 years old. The stand was saved from destruction in 1905, when it was purchased by a couple who donated it to the federal government. Three years later it was named after naturalist John Muir, whose environmental campaigns helped to establish the national park system. His response: "This is the best tree lover's monument that could be found in all of the forests of the world. Saving these woods from the ax and saw is in many ways the most notable service to God and man I have heard of since my forest wandering began."

Muir Woods, part of the Golden Gate National Recreation Area, is a pedestrian's park. The trails vary in difficulty and distance. Beginning from the park headquarters, a 2-mi, wheelchair-accessible **loop trail** crosses streams and passes ferns and azaleas, as well as magnificent redwood groves. Among the most famous are **Bohemian Grove** and the circular formation called **Cathedral Grove.** On summer weekends visitors oohing and aahing in a dozen languages line the trail. If you prefer a little more serenity, consider the challenging **Dipsea Trail,** which climbs west from the forest floor to soothing views of the ocean and the Golden Gate Bridge. For a complete list of trails, check with rangers, who can also help you pick the best one for your ability level.

■ TIP→ The weather in Muir Woods is usually cool and often wet, so wear warm clothes and shoes appropriate for damp trails. Picnicking and camping aren't allowed, and pets aren't permitted. Parking can be difficult here—the lots are small and the crowds are large—so try to come early in the morning or late in the afternoon. The **Muir Woods Visitor Center** has a wide selection of books and exhibits on redwood trees and the history of Muir Woods.

To get here from San Francisco, take U.S. 101 north across the Golden Gate Bridge to the Mill Valley/Stinson Beach exit and then follow signs to Highway 1 north. On weekends, Memorial Day through Labor Day, Golden Gate Transit operates a free shuttle from Mill Valley every half hour. Park in Marin City at the Gateway Shopping Center (look for lighted signs directing you from U.S. 101) or at the Manzanita Park-and-Ride, at the Highway 1 exit off U.S. 101 (look for the lot under the elevated freeway), or take connecting bus service from San

DID YOU KNOW?

The gorgeous old-growth redwood trees in Muir Woods are often enveloped in fog, a useful dampness for the trees, especially to counteract the dry summers.

Francisco with Golden Gate Transit. At this writing, there were plans to expand the service to year-round operation; call ahead. ⊠ *Panoramic Hwy. off Hwy. 1, approximately 12 mi north of Golden Gate Bridge,* 🕾 *415/388–2595 park information, 415/925–4501 shuttle information* ⊕ *www.nps.gov/muwo* 🎟 *$5* ⊙ *Daily 8 AM–sunset.*

> **WORD OF MOUTH**
>
> "We spent one day hiking in Muir Woods. Beautiful was an understatement. It was peaceful and we saw lots of deer. You can really feel one with nature here." —SAO

MT. TAMALPAIS STATE PARK

16 mi northwest of Golden Gate Bridge.

Although the summit of Mt. Tamalpais is only 2,571 feet high, the mountain rises practically from sea level, dominating the topography of Marin County. Adjacent to Muir Woods National Monument, Mt. Tamalpais State Park affords views of the entire Bay Area and the Pacific Ocean to the west. The mountain was sacred to Native Americans, who saw in its profile—as you can see today—the silhouette of a sleeping Indian maiden. Locals fondly refer to it as the "Sleeping Lady." For years the 6,300-acre park has been a favorite destination for hikers. There are more than 200 mi of trails, some rugged but many developed for easy walking through meadows, grasslands, and forests and along creeks. Mt. Tam, as it's called by locals, is also the birthplace (in the 1970s) of mountain biking, and today many spandex-clad bikers whiz down the park's winding roads.

The park's major thoroughfare, the Panoramic Highway, snakes its way up from U.S. 101 to the **Pantoll Ranger Station** (⊠ *3801 Panoramic Hwy., at Pantoll Rd.* 🕾 *415/388–2070* ⊕ *www.parks.ca.gov*). The office is staffed sporadically, depending on funding, but if you leave a phone message, a ranger will call you back (within several days) during business hours. From the ranger station, the Panoramic Highway drops down to the town of Stinson Beach. Pantoll Road branches off the highway at the station, connecting up with Ridgecrest Boulevard. Along these roads are numerous parking areas, picnic spots, scenic overlooks, and trailheads. Parking is free along the roadside, but there's a fee at the ranger station and at some of the other parking lots.

STINSON BEACH

20 mi northwest of Golden Gate Bridge.

Stinson Beach is the most expansive stretch of sand in Marin County. It's as close (when the fog hasn't rolled in) as you can get to the stereotypical feel of a Southern California beach. ⚠ Swimming here is recommended only from early May through September, when lifeguards are on duty, because the undertow can be strong and shark sightings, although infrequent, aren't unusual. There are several clothing-optional areas (such as Red Rock Beach). On any hot summer weekend every road to Stinson Beach is jam-packed, so factor this into your plans. The town itself is very down to earth—like tonier Mill Valley, but more relaxed.

WHERE TO EAT AND STAY

$$–$$$
AMERICAN
✕ **Parkside Cafe.** Most people know the Parkside for its beachfront snack bar (cash only), but inside is the best restaurant in Stinson Beach. The food is classic Cal cuisine, with appetizers such as day-boat scallops, ceviche, and mains such as lamb with goat-cheese-stuffed red peppers. Breakfast, a favorite among locals, is served until 2 PM. Eat on the sunny patio, which is sheltered from the wind by creeping vines, or by the fire in the contemporary dining room. ⊠ *43 Arenal Ave.* ☎ *415/868–1272* ▤ *MC, V.*

WORD OF MOUTH

"The Redwoods at Muir Woods National Monument may be smaller than some you can find at Redwood or Sequoia National Park, but they are still gigantic… and are impressive even on a rainy February day!"
—dansnktwom

$–$$
AMERICAN
✕ **Sand Dollar.** The town's oldest restaurant still attracts all the old salts from Muir Beach to Bolinas, but these days they sip whiskey over an up-to-date bar or beneath market umbrellas on the spiffy deck. The food is good—try the panfried sand dabs (small flatfish) and pear salad with blue cheese—but the big draw is the lively atmosphere. Musicians play weekends in summer, and on sunny afternoons the deck gets so packed that people sit on the fence rails, sipping beer. ⊠ *3458 Rte. 1* ☎ *415/868–0434* ▤ *AE, MC, V* ☉ *No lunch Tues. Nov.–Mar.*

$–$$
▥ **Stinson Beach Motel.** Built in the 1930s, this motel surrounds three courtyards that burst with flowering greenery. Rooms are immaculate, simple, and summery, with freshly painted walls, good mattresses, and some kitchenettes. The motel is on the main drag, so it's convenient to everything in town, but it can get loud on busy summer weekend days. ■TIP➔ Room 3 has the most privacy, though all rooms face a central courtyard, not the street. Weekday room rates ($90–$150) are a bargain for the north coast. **Pros:** minutes from the beach, cozy, unpretentious rooms. **Cons:** no Wi-Fi, not much to do once the sun sets. ⊠ *3416 Hwy. 1* ☎ *415/868–1712* ⊕ *www.stinsonbeachmotel.com* ⇄ *7 rooms* ⌂ *In-room: no a/c, no phone, kitchen (some). In-hotel: no elevator* ▤ *D, MC, V.*

18

BOLINAS

7 mi north of Stinson Beach.

The tiny town of Bolinas wears its 1960s idealism on its sleeve, attracting potters, poets, and peace lovers to its quiet streets. With a funky gallery, a general store selling organic produce, a café, and an offbeat saloon, the main thoroughfare, Wharf Road, looks like a hippie-fied version of Main Street USA. Although privacy-seeking locals openly dislike tourism and have torn down signs to the town, Bolinas isn't difficult to find: heading north from Stinson Beach on Route 1, make a left at the first road just past the Bolinas Lagoon (Bolinas-Olema Road), and then turn left at the stop sign. ■TIP➔ The road dead-ends smack-dab in the middle of the tiny town, so drive slowly lest you find yourself in a confrontation with an angry local.

WHERE TO EAT

$–$$ ✕ **Coast Cafe.** Decked out in a nautical theme with surfboards and buoys,
AMERICAN   the dining room at the Coast serves dependably good American fare,
including specials such as shepherd's pie, pot roast, local fresh fish,
grass-fed steaks, and gorgeous salads. It's also open for breakfast on
weekends. ⊠ *46 Wharf Rd.* ☎ *415/868–2298* ▭ *AE, D, DC, MC, V.*

POINT REYES NATIONAL SEASHORE

Fodor'sChoice   *Bear Valley Visitor Center is 12 mi north of Bolinas.*
★   One of the Bay Area's most spectacular treasures and the only national
seashore on the West Coast, the 66,500-acre **Point Reyes National Seashore**
(⊕ *www.nps.gov/pore*) encompasses hiking trails, secluded beaches, and
rugged grasslands as well as **Point Reyes,** a triangular peninsula that juts
into the Pacific. The town itself is a quaint, one-main-drag affair, with a
charming bakery, some good gift shops with imported goods, and a few
places to eat. It's nothing fancy, but that's part of its relaxed charm.

In the southernmost part of Point Reyes National Seashore, accessed
through Bolinas, is the free **Point Reyes Bird Observatory** (*[PRBO]* ⊠ *Mesa
Rd.* ☎ *415/868–0655* ⊕ *www.prbo.org*). Those not interested in birds
might find it ho-hum, but birders adore it. The compact visitor center,
open daily 9–5, is small yet has excellent interpretive exhibits, including a comparative display of real birds' talons. What really warrant
a visit, though, are the surrounding woods, which harbor nearly 225
bird species. As you hike the quiet trails through forest and along ocean
cliffs, you're likely to see biologists banding birds to aid in the study
of their life cycles.

Mile-long **Duxbury Reef** is the largest shale intertidal reef in North America. Look for starfish, barnacles, sea anemones, purple urchins, limpets,
sea mussels, and the occasional abalone. But check a tide table (⊕ www.
wrh.noaa.gov/mtr/marine.php) or the local papers if you plan to explore
the reef—it's accessible only at low tide. To get here, take Mesa Road
and turn left onto Overlook Drive and then right on Elm Avenue.

The **Bear Valley Visitor Center** (⊠ *Bear Valley Rd. west of Rte. 1* ☎ *415/
464–5100*), open weekdays 9–5 and weekends 8–5, has informative
exhibits about the park wildlife. Rangers here dispense information
about beaches, whale-watching, hiking trails, and camping. The infamous San Andreas Fault runs along the eastern edge of the park and up
the center of Tomales Bay; take the short **Earthquake Trail** from the visitor center to see the impact near the epicenter of the 1906 earthquake
that devastated San Francisco. A ½-mi path from the visitor center leads
to **Kule Loklo,** a brilliantly reconstructed Miwok village that sheds light
on the daily lives of the region's first inhabitants. From here trails also
lead to the park's free campgrounds (camping permits are required).

★   The **Point Reyes Lighthouse** (⊠ *Western end of Sir Francis Drake Blvd.*
☽   ☎ *415/669–1534* ☉ *Thurs.–Mon. 10–4:30; weather lens room 2:30–4,
except during very windy weather*), in operation since December 1,
1870, is one of the premier attractions of the Point Reyes National

Seashore. It occupies the tip of Point Reyes, 22 mi from the Bear Valley Visitor Center, a scenic 45-minute drive over hills scattered with old cattle ranches. The lighthouse originally cast a rotating beam lighted by four wicks that burned lard oil. Keeping the wicks lighted and the lens soot-free in Point Reyes's perpetually foggy climate was a constant struggle that reputedly drove the early attendants to alcoholism and insanity. On busy whale-watching weekends (late December through mid-April), parking at the forged-iron-plate lighthouse may be restricted by park staff; on these days buses shuttle visitors from the Drakes' Beach lot to the top of the stairs leading down to the lighthouse (bus $5, admission free). Once there, consider whether you have it in you to walk down—and up—the 308 steps to the lighthouse. The view from the bottom is worth the effort, but the whales are visible from the cliffs above the lighthouse. ■TIP➜ **In late winter and spring, wildlife enthusiasts should make a stop at Chimney Rock, just before the lighthouse, and take the short walk to the Elephant Seal Overlook.** Even from up on the cliff, the males look enormous as they spar for the resident females.

WHERE TO EAT AND STAY

¢–$
AMERICAN

✕ **Pine Cone Diner.** For California country-kitchen cooking, you can't beat the Pine Cone. A block off the main drag, this oh-so-cute diner serves great traditional breakfasts as well as Mexican specialties such as huevos rancheros. At lunch expect hearty homemade soups, fresh salads, and thick sandwiches, all made with local, organic ingredients. The dinner menu has a good selection of comfort food. ■TIP➜ **Kids love the outdoor picnic tables.** ✉ 60 4th St., Point Reyes Station ☎ 415/663–1536 ▭ No credit cards ☾ No dinner.

$$
AMERICAN

✕ **Station House Cafe.** In good weather hikers fresh from the park fill the garden to enjoy alfresco dining, and on weekends there's not a spare seat on the banquettes in the wide-open dining room. The focus is on traditional American food—fresh popovers hit the table as soon as you arrive—and there's a little of everything on the menu. Grilled salmon, barbecued oysters, and burgers are all predictable hits. The place is also open for breakfast, and there's a full bar, too. ✉ 11180 Rte. 1, Point Reyes Station ☎ 415/663–1515 ▭ AE, D, MC, V ☾ Closed Wed.

¢–$
AMERICAN
★

✕ **Tomales Bay Foods.** A renovated hay barn off the main drag houses this collection of food shops, a favorite stopover among Bay Area foodies. Watch workers making Cowgirl Creamery cheese; then buy some at a counter that sells exquisite artisanal cheeses from around the world. Tomales Bay Foods showcases local organic fruits and vegetables and premium packaged foods, and the kitchen turns the best ingredients into creative sandwiches, salads, and soups. You can eat at a small café table or on the lawn, or take it away for a picnic. The shops are open until 6 PM. ✉ 80 4th St., Point Reyes Station ☎ 415/663–9335 cheese shop, 415/663–8478 deli ▭ MC, V ☾ Closed Mon. and Tues.

$$$–$$$$

⌂ **Blackthorne Inn.** There's no other inn quite like the Blackthorne, a combination of whimsy and sophistication tucked on a hill in the woods. The giant tree-house-like structure has spiral staircases, a 3,500-square-foot deck, and a fireman's pole. The solarium was made with timbers from San Francisco wharves, and the outer walls are salvaged doors from a railway station. The best room is aptly named the Eagle's Nest,

18

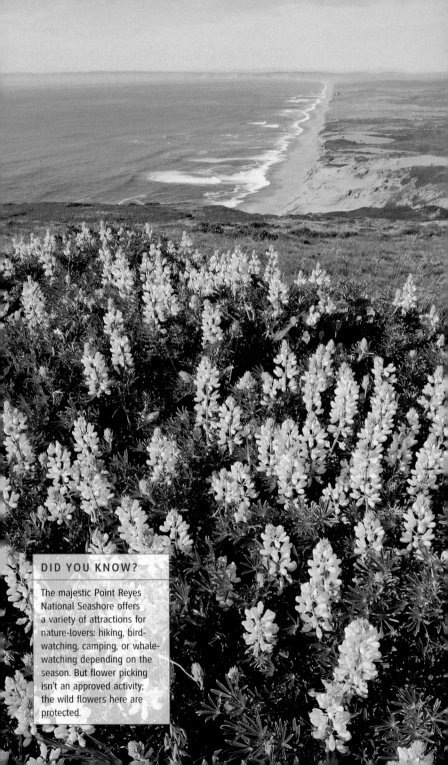

DID YOU KNOW?

The majestic Point Reyes National Seashore offers a variety of attractions for nature-lovers: hiking, bird-watching, camping, or whale-watching depending on the season. But flower picking isn't an approved activity; the wild flowers here are protected.

perched as it is in the glass-sheathed octagonal tower that crowns the inn. **Pros:** great views, quiet atmosphere. **Cons:** not a good place for kids, steep spaces. ⊠ *266 Vallejo Ave., Inverness Park* ☎ *415/663–8621* ⊕ *www.blackthorneinn.com* ➟ *3 rooms, 1 suite* ♿ *In-room: no a/c, no phone, no TV. In-hotel: restaurant, no elevator, no kids under 14* ☰ *MC, V* ⦿ *BP.*

$$ 🏨 **Inverness Valley Inn.** Nestled within a 15-acre valley on the north end of town, this secluded getaway offers private cabins with plenty of room and peace and quiet. All cabins have their own entrances with patios that are perfect for sunset barbecues and leisurely breakfasts. The cabins are modern and well lighted, with large windows and impressive skylights. They're ideal for families who want extra space and a kitchen (or kitchenette) for cooking. In the back of the property there are chickens, sheep, and goats for those in need of a taste of farm life. **Pros:** spacious accommodations, great place to bring kids. **Cons:** over 3 mi from downtown Inverness. ⊠ *13275 Sir Francis Drake Blvd., Inverness* ☎ *415/669–7250* ⊕ *www.invernessvalleyinn.com* ➟ *20 cabins* ♿ *In-room: kitchen, Wi-Fi. In-hotel: tennis courts, pool, spa, no elevator, some pets allowed* ☰ *AE, MC, V.*

$–$$ 🏨 **Motel Inverness.** This roadside row of rooms has everything a small-town motel should offer: friendly management; spotless, thoughtfully maintained accommodations (some quite small); and extras that add real value. Some rooms have a small kitchen with cooking utensils. The lodge, a window-lined common room with skylighted cathedral ceiling, has a fireplace, big-screen TV, billiards table, kitchenette, and well-maintained fish tank. Sliding glass doors open to a deck overlooking Tomales Bay. For $400 you can have the two-story suite (sleeps four) and its two decks, full kitchen, fireplace, and jetted tub; $500 rents you the ornate Dacha, a three-bedroom Russian-style house on stilts over the bay. **Pros:** great views of Tomales Bay, comfy communal lodge with fireplace and pool table. **Cons:** some of the rooms are on the small side, the closest restaurant is over 3 mi away. ⊠ *12718 Sir Francis Drake Blvd., Inverness* ☎ *415/669–1081 or 888/669–6909* ⊕ *www.motelinverness.com* ➟ *7 rooms, 2 suites, 1 house* ♿ *In-room: no a/c, no phone, kitchen (some). In-hotel: no elevator* ☰ *MC, V.*

$$ 🏨 **Olema Inn & Restaurant.** Built in 1876, the inn retains all its 19th-century architectural charm but has been decorated in a sophisticated, uncluttered style. The spartan, understated rooms have antique armoires and sumptuous beds with crisp linens; the white-tile baths have gleaming fixtures. But the main attraction is the top-notch Northern California cooking served in the restaurant ($$$, reservations essential). The preparations of organic, local, and free-range ingredients include fresh oysters, pork chops with apple-cider glaze, and house-made ricotta gnocchi. ■ TIP➜ Come on Monday, locals' night, when the place hops with live music and you can browse through a delectable small-plates menu. **Pros:** great restaurant, magnificent scenery. **Cons:** extremely remote, sporadic Wi-Fi and cell phone reception. ⊠ *10000 Sir Francis Drake Blvd., Olema* ☎ *415/663–9559* ⊕ *www.theolemainn.com* ➟ *6 rooms* ♿ *In-room: no a/c, no phone. In-hotel: no elevator, some pets allowed* ☰ *AE, MC, V* ⊗ *Closed Tues. No lunch weekdays.*

18

$$ 🛏 **Ten Inverness Way.** This is the kind of down-to-earth place where you sit around after breakfast and share tips for hiking Point Reyes. The living room of this low-key inn has a stone fireplace and library. Some rooms have dormer ceilings with skylights; patchwork quilts, folksy murals, and well-worn antiques are among the homespun touches. Wine and cheese and fresh-baked cookies are nice extras. ■**TIP→** The innkeepers also lead guided hikes of the park. No children under 12, except in the suite. **Pros:** great base for exploring nearby wilderness, feels like you're staying with family. **Cons:** overly folksy decor, no Wi-Fi. ✉ *10 Inverness Way, Inverness* ☎ *415/669–1648* ⊕ *www.teninvernessway. com* ➷ *4 rooms, 1 suite* ⚴ *In-room: no a/c, no phone, no TV. In-hotel: restaurant, no elevator, no kids under 12* ▭ *D, MC, V* ❍❘ *BP.*

SPORTS AND THE OUTDOORS

Blue Waters Kayaking (✉ *12938 Sir Francis Drake Blvd., Inverness* ☎ *415/669–2600* ⊕ *www.bwkayak.com*) rents kayaks and offers tours and lessons. **Five Brooks Stable** (✉ *8001 Hwy. 1, Olema* ☎ *415/663–1570* ⊕ *www.fivebrooks.com*) rents horses and equipment. Trails from the stables wind through Point Reyes National Seashore and along the beaches. Rides run from one to six hours and cost $50–$240.

THE EAST BAY

When San Franciscans refer to it, the East Bay often means nothing more than what you can see across the bay from the city—mainly Oakland and Berkeley, both of which are in Alameda County. In fact, the East Bay stretches north and east of Alameda to Contra Costa County, which itself has emerged as a powerful business nexus. East Bay towns south of Alameda and Contra Costa counties have become bedroom communities for workers in the high-tech industry. These begin to run into one another, reaching critical mass on the edge of Silicon Valley.

PLANNING

GETTING HERE AND AROUND

BOAT AND FERRY TRAVEL

The Alameda/Oakland Ferry runs several times daily between San Francisco's Ferry Building or Pier 39, Alameda, and the Clay Street dock near Oakland's Jack London Square; one-way tickets are $6.25. The trip lasts 30 to 45 minutes, depending on your departure point, and leads to the heart of Oakland's gentrified shopping and restaurant district. Arriving in Oakland by boat conveys a historic sense of the city's heyday as a World War II–era shipbuilding center. Purchase tickets on board.

Contacts Alameda/Oakland Ferry (☎ *510/522–3300* ⊕ *www.eastbayferry.com*).

BUS TRAVEL

Although Bay Area Rapid Transit (BART) travel is often cheaper and more convenient, buses run frequently between San Francisco's Trans-Bay Terminal (at 1st and Mission streets) and the East Bay. AC Transit's F and FS lines stop near the university and 4th Street shopping in

Berkeley. Lines C and P travel to Piedmont in Oakland. The O bus stops at the edge of Chinatown near downtown Oakland.

Contacts AC Transit (☎ *817–1717 after any Bay Area area code* ⊕ *www. actransit.org*).

TRAIN TRAVEL

BART (Bay Area Rapid Transit, formally) trains make stops in downtown Berkeley and in several parts of Oakland, including Rockridge. Use the Lake Merritt Station

WORD OF MOUTH

"I believe the downtown/historic area of Oakland is undergoing/has undergone a bit of a renaissance—galleries, restaurants, etc. . . . I'm not referring to Jack London Square, which does have the dubious honor of being home to the oldest bar in California. Anyone know if that's true? That tiny old place that slants?" —Leely

for the Oakland Museum and southern Lake Merritt; the Oakland City Center–12th Street Station for downtown, Chinatown, and Old Oakland; and the 19th Street Station for the Paramount Theatre and the north side of Lake Merritt. From the Berkeley (not North Berkeley) Station, walk a block up Center Street to get to the western edge of campus. Both trips take 30 to 45 minutes one way from the center of San Francisco.

Contacts BART (☎ *510/465–2278* ⊕ *www.bart.gov*).

OAKLAND

Directly east of Bay Bridge.

Often overshadowed by San Francisco's beauty and Berkeley's offbeat antics, Oakland's allure lies in its amazing diversity. Here you can find a Nigerian clothing store, a beautifully renovated Victorian home, a Buddhist meditation center, and a lively salsa club, all within the same block. Oakland's multifaceted nature reflects its colorful and often tumultuous history. Once a cluster of Mediterranean-style homes and gardens that served as a bedroom community for San Francisco, the city became a hub of shipbuilding and industry almost overnight when the United States entered World War II. New jobs in the city's shipyards and factories attracted thousands of workers, including some of the first female welders, and the city's neighborhoods were imbued with a proud but gritty spirit. In the 1960s and '70s this intense community pride gave rise to such militant groups as the Black Panther Party and the Symbionese Liberation Army, but they were little match for the economic hardships and racial tensions that plagued Oakland. In many neighborhoods the reality was widespread poverty and gang violence—subjects that dominated the songs of such Oakland-bred rappers as the late Tupac Shakur.

Today Oakland is a mosaic of its past. The affluent have once again flocked to the city's hillside homes as a warmer, more spacious, and more affordable alternative to San Francisco, and a constant flow of newcomers—many from Central America and Asia—ensures continued diversity, vitality, and growing pains. Many neighborhoods to the west and south of downtown remain run-down and unsafe, but a renovated

18

downtown area—including one of the most vibrant arts scenes in the Bay Area—and the thriving though sterile Jack London Square have injected new life into the city. The national visibility from the 1998 election of former California governor Jerry Brown as Oakland mayor (his term ended in early 2007) further invigorated the city's rising spirits.

Everyday life here revolves around the neighborhood, with a main business strip attracting both shoppers and strollers. In some areas, such as high-end Piedmont and Rockridge, you'd swear you were in Berkeley or San Francisco's Noe Valley or Cow Hollow. These are perfect places for browsing, eating, or just relaxing between sightseeing trips to Oakland's architectural gems, rejuvenated waterfront, and numerous green spaces. Between Rockridge and Piedmont and to the west, you can find the Temescal District, along Telegraph Avenue just south of 51st Street, which is beginning to attract a small collection of eateries and shops.

ESSENTIALS

Visitor Information Oakland Convention and Visitors Bureau (⊠ *463 11th St.* ☎ *510/839–9000* ⊕ *www.oaklandcvb.com*).

❹ One of Oakland's top attractions, the **Oakland Museum of California** is an
ⓒ excellent introduction to a tour of California, and its detailed exhibits
★ on the state's art, history, and natural wonders can help fill the gaps on a brief visit. You can travel through the state's myriad ecosystems in the Natural Sciences Gallery, from the sand dunes of the Pacific to the coyotes and brush of the Nevada border. Kids love the lifelike wild-animal exhibits, especially the snarling wolverine, big-eyed harbor seal, and trove of hidden creatures. The rambling Cowell Hall of California History includes everything from Spanish-era armor to a small but impressive collection of vintage vehicles, including a gorgeous, candy-apple-red "Mystery" car from the 1960s and a gleaming red, gold, and silver fire engine that battled the flames in San Francisco in 1906. The Gallery of California Art holds an eclectic collection of modern works and early landscapes. Of particular interest are paintings by Richard Diebenkorn, Joan Brown, Elmer Bischoff, and David Park, all members of the Bay Area Figurative School, which flourished here after World War II. Fans of Dorothea Lange won't want to miss the gallery's comprehensive collection of her work. The museum also has a sculpture garden with a view of the Oakland and Berkeley hills in the distance. ⊠ *1000 Oak St., at 10th St.* ☎ *510/238–2200* ⊕ *www. museumca.org* ⌁ *$8, free 2nd Sun. of month* ⊙ *Wed.–Sat. 10–5, until 9 1st Fri. of month, Sun. noon–5.*

❸ The 155-acre **Lake Merritt** (⊠ *Bordered by Lakeshore Ave. on the south, Lakeside Dr. on the west, Harrison St. on the north, and Bellevue Ave. on the east*), a natural saltwater lake, sits in the middle of downtown Oakland. Joggers and power-walkers charge along the 3-mi path that encircles the lake, crew teams often glide across the water, and boatmen guide snuggling couples in authentic Venetian gondolas. **California gondoliers** (⊠ *568 Bellevue Ave., Lake Merritt* ☎ *866/737–8494* ⊕ *www. gondolaservizio.com*) is by the sign that says "Sailboat House, Gondola Servizio." Fares start at $45 per couple for 30 minutes.

KEY

🅱️ *BART station*

18

Lakeside Park, which surrounds the north side of Lake Merritt, has several outdoor attractions, including a children's park. The **Rotary Nature Center and Waterfowl Refuge** is the nesting site of herons, egrets, geese, and ducks in spring and summer. Migrating birds pass through from September through February, and you can watch the birds being fed daily at 3:30 (year-round). ⊠ *600 Bellevue Ave.* ☎ *510/238–7275* ⊕ *www.oaklandnet.com/parks/Facilities/points_lakeside_park.asp* ⊑ *Free* ⊙ *Daily 10–5.*

Given Oakland's reputation for Victorian and Craftsman homes, new-comers are generally surprised by the profusion of art-deco architecture in the downtown neighborhood around the 19th Street BART station. Some of these buildings have fallen into disrepair, but the **Paramount Theatre,** perhaps the most glorious example of art-deco architecture in the city, if not the entire Bay Area, still operates as a venue for concerts and performances of all kinds, from the Oakland Ballet to Tom Waits and Elvis Costello. You can take a two-hour tour of the building, which starts near the box office on 21st Street at 10 AM on the first and third Saturday of each month. Just behind the Paramount on Telegraph Avenue, the Fox Theater, another art-deco landmark, was saved from the wrecking ball and is being lovingly restored. ⊠ *2025 Broadway* ☎ *510/465–6400* ⊕ *www.paramounttheatre.com* ⊑ *Tour $5.*

⑤ Shops, restaurants, small museums, and historic sites line **Jack London Square,** which is named after one of California's best-known authors; London wrote *The Call of the Wild and The Sea Wolf,* among many other books. When he lived in Oakland, he spent many a day boozing and brawling in the waterfront area. The tiny, wonderful **Heinold's First and Last Chance Saloon** (✉ *48 Webster St.* ☎ *510/839–6761*) was one of London's old haunts. It has been serving since 1883, although it's a little worse for the wear since the 1906 earthquake. The Klondike cabin in which London spent a summer in the late 1890s was moved from Alaska and reassembled here, next door to Heinold's saloon, in 1970. The square also contains a bronze bust of London. ■ TIP→ Since it's on the waterfront, the square is an obvious spot for tourists to visit and is worth a peek if you take a ferry that docks here; to really get a feel for Oakland, though, you're better off browsing downtown, or at least in Rockridge. ✉ *Embarcadero at Broadway* ☎ *866/295–9853* ⊕ *www. jacklondonsquare.com.*

Bordered by 7th, 10th, Clay, and Washington streets in the shadow of the convention center and towering downtown hotels, **Old Oakland** was once a booming business district. Today the restored Victorian storefronts lining these four blocks house restaurants, cafés, shops, galleries, and a lively three-block farmers' market, which takes place Friday morning. Architectural consistency distinguishes the area from surrounding streets and lends it a distinct neighborhood feel. **Ratto's International Market** (✉ *827 Washington St.* ☎ *510/832–6503*), the Italian grocer that's been dishing up meat, cheese, imported sweets, and liquor to the neighborhood since 1897, has fresh deli sandwiches. **Pacific Coast Brewing Company** (✉ *906 Washington St.* ☎ *510/836–2739*) is a homey place for some pub grub and a microbrew. The block-long Swan's Marketplace houses shops and the **Housewives Market** (✉ *907 Washington St.*), an old-fashioned market with stalls for meat, seafood, and even a sausage maker.

Across Broadway from Old Oakland but worlds apart, **Chinatown** is a densely packed, bustling neighborhood. Unlike its San Francisco counterpart, Oakland's Chinatown makes no concessions to tourists; you won't find baskets of trinkets lining the sidewalk and souvenir displays in the shop windows. Supermarkets such as **Yuen Hop Noodle Company and Asian Food Products** (✉ *824 Webster St.*), open since 1931, overflow with goodies. The line for sweets, breads, and towering cakes snakes out the door of **Napoleon Super Bakery** (✉ *810 Franklin St.*).

The upscale neighborhood of **Rockridge** is one of Oakland's most desirable places to live. Explore the tree-lined streets that radiate out from College Avenue just north and south of the Rockridge BART station for a look at California bungalow architecture at its finest.

College Avenue is the main shopping drag in Rockridge. By day it's crowded with shoppers buying fresh flowers, used books, and clothing; by night the same folks are back for dinner and locally brewed ales in the numerous restaurants and pubs. The hub of College Avenue life in Rockridge is **Market Hall** (✉ *5655 College Ave.* ☎ *510/250–6000* ⊕ *www.rockridgemarkethall.com*), an airy European-style marketplace

A fun place to wet your whistle, Heinold's First and Last Chance Saloon.

with pricey specialty-food shops. The avenue ends at the California College of the Arts campus.

WHERE TO EAT AND STAY

$ **À Côté.** This is the place for Mediterranean food in the East Bay. It's all
MEDITERRANEAN about small plates, cozy tables, and family-style eating here—and truly excellent food. The butternut-squash ravioli, Alsatian goose sausage, and pear-and-walnut flatbread are all lovely choices. And you won't find a better plate of pommes frites anywhere. The restaurant offers over 40 wines by the glass from an extensive, ever-changing wine list. Desserts here are tempting: try the warm crème-fraîche pound cake with apple confit, vanilla ice cream, and huckleberry sauce or a tangy pomegranate sorbet. The heavy wooden tables, cool tiles, and natural light make this a coveted destination for students, families, couples, and after-work crowds. ⊠ *5478 College Ave., Rockridge* ☎ *510/655–6469* ☖ *Reservations not accepted* ▭ *AE, MC, V* ☾ *No lunch.*

$$ **Camino.** This first solo venture from chef-owner Russell Moore (a
AMERICAN Chez Panisse alum of 21 years) and co-owner Allison Hopelain was quite the labor of love. Many of the menu's simple, seasonal, and straightforward dishes emerge from the enormous crackling camino (Italian for "fireplace"). Everything is made with top-notch ingredients, including local sardines; grilled lamb and sausage with shell beans; and grilled white sea bass with green beans and new potatoes. The menu of approximately eight dishes rotates nightly, with vegetarian options such as eggplant gratin available as well. The restaurant is decorated in a craftsman-meets-refectory style, with brick walls and two long redwood communal tables filled with East Bay couples and friends.

Seasonally inspired cocktails from the small bar are not to be missed; the gin-based drink with house-made cherry and hibiscus bitters is notably delicious. ✉ *3917 Grand Ave., Oakland* 🕾 *510/547–5035* ▱ *AE, MC, V* ⊗ *Closed Tues. No lunch.*

WORD OF MOUTH

"Oakland has one of the most beautiful urban drives in the USA: Skyline Drive/Boulevard. It's a winding drive, bordering the Oakland/Berkeley Hills. From it, you have absolutely stunning views of the entire Bay. One advantage of a view from Oakland is that you are looking at San Francisco's famous landmarks." —CaliNurse

$$
MEXICAN
✕ **Doña Tomás.** A neighborhood favorite, this spot in Oakland's up-and-coming Temescal District serves seasonal Mexican fare to a hip but low-key crowd. Mexican textiles and art adorn walls in two long rooms; there's also a vine-covered patio. Banish all images of taquería grub and tuck into starters such as quesadillas filled with butternut squash and goat cheese and entrées such as *albondigas en sopa de zanahoria* (pork-and-beef meatballs in carrot puree). A fine selection of tequilas rounds out the offerings. ✉ *5004 Telegraph Ave.* 🕾 *510/450–0522* ▱ *AE, MC, V* ⊗ *Closed Sun. and Mon. No lunch.*

¢–$
CAFÉ
✕ **L'Amyx Tea Bar.** Light through the large windows bathes the blond-wood tables, comfy chairs, and long bar, all filled with absorbed students, chatting friends, and tired shoppers in need of a boost. A small area in the back sells first-rate tea accoutrements, but sink into a couch or private nook to bask in much more than the usual cuppa. Try a tea smoothie or an herbal remedy such as Tealaxation. ✉ *4179 Piedmont Ave.* 🕾 *510/594–8322* ▱ *MC, V.*

$–$$
FRENCH
✕ **Luka's Taproom & Lounge.** Luka's is a real taste of downtown Oakland: hip and urban, with an unpretentious vibe. Diners nibble on *frites* any Belgian would be proud of and entrées like *choucroute garni* (sauerkraut with duck confit, ham hock, and pork shoulder). The brews draw 'em in, too—you'd be hard pressed to find a larger selection of Belgian beer this side of the pond—and the DJs in the adjacent lounge keep the scene going late. ✉ *2221 Broadway, at West Grand Ave.* 🕾 *510/451–4677* ▱ *AE, MC, V* ⊗ *No lunch Sat.*

$$–$$$
MEDITERRANEAN
✕ **Oliveto Cafe & Restaurant.** Respected chef Paul Bertolli is at the helm of this locally renowned eatery that anchors Market Hall in the Rockridge neighborhood. The first-class dining room ($$–$$$$) upstairs serves straightforward Italian cuisine; the menu changes daily but might include house-made duck prosciutto, pan-seared swordfish, or spit-roasted leg of lamb. Downstairs, in the terra-cotta-wall café ($–$$), everything from a morning espresso to pizza to a full-blown Italian meal (at half the upstairs price) can be enjoyed at one of the small tables or at the bar. ✉ *5655 College Ave.* 🕾 *510/547–5356* ▱ *AE, MC, V* ⊗ *No lunch weekends in restaurant.*

$–$$
🏨 **Executive Inn & Suites.** This two-building hotel is convenient to both the Oakland airport and downtown Oakland. To make up for its removed location, the property offers free shuttle service to the Oakland airport, BART stations, and Jack London Square. Rooms in the older building are renovated, but those in the newer one are generous

in size and have extra-large desks, kitchen areas, and large whirlpool tubs. Each room has either a patio or a balcony, and Wi-Fi access. **Pros:** west-facing rooms overlook the peaceful waters of the Oakland Estuary, all rooms have microwaves and fridges. **Cons:** east-fac-

WORD OF MOUTH

"The weather is nicer [in Oakland] than San Francisco, because we have the same breeze without so much fog."   —oaklander

ing rooms look out onto the freeway and can be noisy, the decor is overly bright and busy. ⊠ *1755 Embarcadero, off I–880 at 16th St. exit* ☎ *510/536–6633 or 800/346–6331* ⊕ *www.executiveinnoakland.com* ↗ *143 rooms, 81 suites* ♿ *In-room: safe (some), refrigerator, microwave, Internet, Wi-Fi. In-hotel: restaurant, bar, pool, gym, laundry facilities, laundry service, concierge, public Wi-Fi, airport shuttle, parking (no fee)* ⊟ *AE, D, DC, MC, V* ⏆ *CP.*

$–$$ ▥ **Washington Inn Hotel.** This stylish four-story brick hotel sits across the street from the convention center, in the heart of Old Oakland. In operation since 1905, the hotel has up-to-the-minute decor. Red couches brighten the spacious lobby, which has Wi-Fi access. Elegant touches include intricately molded ceiling tiles and a wrought-iron elevator, a relic of the building's early days. Guest rooms are chic but on the small side. Rooms overlooking the atrium lobby are the quietest (and smallest); corner rooms get the most sunlight. **Pros:** central location, good restaurant. **Cons:** rooms are small, parking is pricey. ⊠ *495 10th St., at Washington St.* ☎ *510/452–1776* ⊕ *www.thewashingtoninn.com* ↗ *47 rooms, 6 suites* ♿ *In-room: safe, DVD, Wi-Fi. In-hotel: restaurant, bar, gym, laundry service, public Wi-Fi, parking (fee)* ⊟ *AE, D, DC, MC, V* ⏆ *CP.*

$$–$$$ ▥ **Waterfront Plaza Hotel.** One of Oakland's more appealing neighborhoods is home to this thoroughly modern waterfront hotel. Rooms in the hotel's five-story section overlook Jack London Square and have shared balconies; those in the three-story building each have a private balcony facing the water. Some rooms have fireplaces. **Pros:** great location, dog friendly ($35 per day), newly remodeled rooms. **Cons:** pricey, service can be spotty. ⊠ *10 Washington St., Jack London Sq.* ☎ *510/836–3800 or 800/729–3638* ⊕ *www.waterfrontplaza.com* ↗ *143 rooms* ♿ *In-room: safe, Wi-Fi. In-hotel: restaurant, room service, bar, pool, gym, laundry service, concierge, public Wi-Fi, parking (fee)* ⊟ *AE, D, DC, MC, V.*

NIGHTLIFE AND THE ARTS

Oakland is where practicing artists have found cheaper rent and loft spaces. Oakland's underground arts scene—visual arts, indie music, spoken word, film—is definitely buzzing.

Fodor's Choice **Café van Kleef.** When Dutch artist Peter van Kleef first opened his gallery
★ in this downtown space, the booze flowed freely—and free, for lack of a liquor license. That gallery has morphed into this candle-strewn, funky café-bar that crackles with creative energy. Van Kleef has a lot to do with the convivial atmosphere; the garrulous owner loves sharing tales about his quirky, floor-to-ceiling collection of mementos, including what he claims are Cassius Clay's boxing gloves and Dorothy's ruby slippers.

18

The café also has a consistently solid calendar of live music, heavy on the jazz side. And the drinks may not be free anymore, but they're quite possibly the stiffest in town. ✉ *1621 Telegraph Ave., between 16th and 17th Sts.* ☎ *510/763–7711* ⊕ *www.cafevankleef.com.*

Mama Buzz Café. At this well-worn café-gallery, a kind of living room for the indie arts crowd, you can get the lowdown on one of the most diverse arts communities around. In addition to coffee and light fare, the calendar includes poetry readings, live-music events, art exhibits, and hard-to-categorize events such as Punk Rock Haircut Night (get a new 'do, cheap), the Knitty Gritty knitting circle, and the Left-Wing Letter Bee. The owners publish the 'zine *Kitchen Sink.* ✉ *2318 Telegraph Ave.* ☎ *510/465–4073* ⊕ *www.mamabuzzcafe.com.*

Fodor's Choice ★ **Yoshi's.** Oma Sosa and Charlie Hunter are among the musicians who play at Yoshi's, one of the area's best jazz venues. Monday through Saturday shows start at 8 PM and 10 PM; Sunday shows usually start at 2 PM and 8 PM. The cover runs from $10 to $30. ✉ *510 Embarcadero St., between Washington and Clay Sts.* ☎ *510/238–9200* ⊕ *www.yoshis.com.*

SPORTS AND THE OUTDOORS

BASEBALL The American League's **Oakland A's** (✉ *McAfee Coliseum, 7000 Coliseum Way, off I–880, north of Hegenberger Rd.* ☎ *510/638–4900* ⊕ *oakland.athletics.mlb.com*), formally the Oakland Athletics, play at the **McAfee Coliseum.** Same-day tickets usually can be purchased at the stadium box office (Gate D), but advance purchase is recommended. On Wednesday, entry is a bargain at $2, and you can buy a hot dog for a dollar. To get to the game, take a BART train to the Coliseum/Oakland Airport Station.

BASKETBALL The National Basketball Association's **Golden State Warriors** (✉ *Oakland Arena, 7000 Coliseum Way, off I–880, north of Hegenberger Rd.* ☎ *510/986–2200 or 888/479–4667* ⊕ *www.nba.com/warriors*) play at the **Oakland Arena** from November through April. Basketball tickets are available through **Ticketmaster** (☎ *415/421–8497* ⊕ *www. ticketmaster.com*). You can take a BART train to the game. Get off at the Coliseum/Oakland Airport Station.

FOOTBALL The National Football League's **Oakland Raiders** (✉ *McAfee Coliseum, 7000 Coliseum Way, off I–880, north of Hegenberger Rd., Oakland* ☎ *510/864–5000* ⊕ *www.raiders.com*) play at **McAfee Coliseum.** Tickets, sold through **Tickets.com** (☎ *510/762–2277* ⊕ *www.tickets.com*), are usually available, except for high-profile games.

SHOPPING

College Avenue is great for upscale strolling, shopping, and people-watching. The streets around Lake Merritt and the Grand Lake have more casual fare and smaller boutiques.

Diesel. Wandering bibliophiles collect armfuls of the latest fiction and nonfiction here. The loftlike space, with its high ceilings and spare design, encourages airy contemplation, and on chilly days (a rarity) there's a fire going in the hearth. Keep an eye out for their excellent reading series. ✉ *5433 College Ave., Oakland* ☎ *510/653–9965.*

Maison d'Etre. Close to the Rockridge BART station, this store crystallizes the funky-chic shopping scene of Rockridge. Look for impulse buys like whimsical watches, imported fruit tea blends, and a basket of funky slippers near the back. ✉ *5640 College Ave., Oakland* ☎ *510/658–2801*.

BERKELEY

2 mi northeast of Bay Bridge.

The birthplace of the Free Speech Movement, the radical hub of the 1960s, the home of arguably the nation's top public university, and the city whose government condemned the bombing of Afghanistan—Berkeley is all of those things. The city of 100,000 facing San Francisco across the bay is also culturally diverse, a breeding ground for social trends, a bastion of the counterculture, and an important center for Bay Area writers, artists, and musicians. Berkeley residents, students, and faculty spend hours nursing various coffee concoctions while they read, discuss, and debate at any of the dozens of cafés that surround the campus. Oakland may have Berkeley beat when it comes to cutting-edge arts, and the city may have forfeited some of its renegade 1960s spirit, as some residents say, but unless a guy in a hot-pink satin body suit, skull cap, and cape rides a unicycle around *your* town, you'll likely find that Berkeley remains plenty offbeat.

It's the quintessential university town, and many who graduated years ago still bask in daily intellectual conversation, great weather, and good food. Residents will walk out of their way to go to the perfect bread shop or consult with their favorite wine merchant. And every September, residents gently lampoon themselves during the annual "How Berkeley Can You Be?" parade and festival where they celebrate their tie-dyed past and consider its new incarnations.

18

ESSENTIALS

Visitor Information Berkeley Convention and Visitors Bureau (✉ *2015 Center St.* ☎ *510/549–7040* ⊕ *www.visitberkeley.com*).

The state legislature chartered the **University of California** (⊕ *www.berkeley.edu*) in 1868 as the founding campus of the state university system, and established it five years later on a rising plain of oak trees split by Strawberry Creek. Frederick Law Olmsted, who designed New York City's Central Park, proposed the first campus plan. University architects over the years have included Bernard Maybeck as well as Julia Morgan, who designed Hearst Castle at San Simeon. The central campus occupies 178 acres, bounded by Bancroft Way to the south, Hearst Avenue to the north, Oxford Street to the west, and Gayley Road to the east. With more than 30,000 students and a full-time faculty of 1,400, the university, known simply as "Cal," is one of the leading intellectual centers in the United States and a major site for scientific research.

❶ The **Berkeley Visitor Information Center** (✉ *University Hall, Room 101, 2200 University Ave., at Oxford St.* ☎ *510/642–5215* ☉ *Weekdays 8:30–4:30*) is the starting point for the free, student-guided tours of the campus, which last 1½ hours and start at 10 on weekdays. (Weekend tours depart from Sather Tower, *see below.*)

Berkeley in the 1960s

Those looking for traces of Berkeley's politically charged past need go no farther than Sather Gate. Both the Free Speech Movement and the fledgling political life of actor-turned-politician Ronald Reagan have their roots here. It was next to Sather Gate, on September 30, 1964, that a group of students defied the University of California–Berkeley chancellor's order that all organizations advocating "off-campus issues" (such as civil rights and nuclear disarmament) keep their information tables off campus. Citation of the tablers brought more than 400 sympathetic students into Sproul Hall that afternoon. They stayed until 3 AM, setting a precedent of protest that would be repeated in the coming months, with students jamming Sproul Hall in greater numbers each time.

Conservative U.C. president Clark Kerr eventually backed down and allowed student groups to pass out information on campus. By then, the Free Speech Movement had gathered momentum, and the conflict had made a national hero of student leader Mario Savio. Political newcomer Ronald Reagan played on Californians' unease about the unruly Berkeley students in his successful 1966 bid for governor, promising to rein in the "unwashed kooks."

By the end of the 1960s, the cohesion of the groups making up the Free Speech Movement had begun to fray. Some members began questioning the efficacy of sit-ins and other nonviolent tactics that had, until then, been the hallmark of Berkeley student protests. The Black Panthers, headquartered just over the border in Oakland, were ascending into the national spotlight, and their "take no prisoners" approach appealed to some Berkeley activists

who had seen little come of their efforts to affect national policy.

By 1969 both Robert Kennedy and Martin Luther King Jr. were dead, and the issue of the day—stopping the flow of troops heading to Vietnam—was not as easy as overpowering a school administration's resistance to free speech. But a more dramatic clash with the university came when it brought in police units to repossess People's Park, a university-owned plot of land at Telegraph Avenue and Haste Street that students and community members had adopted as a park. On the afternoon of May 15, 1969, nearly 6,000 students and residents moved to reclaim the park. In the ensuing riot, police and sheriff's deputies fired both tear gas and buckshot, blinding one observer and killing another. Governor Ronald Reagan ordered the National Guard into Berkeley. Despite a ban on public assembly, crowds continued to gather and march in the days after the first riot. The park changed hands several times in the following tear-gas-filled months, with the fence coming down for the last time in 1972.

A colorful mural on the side of Amoeba Records (Haste Street at Telegraph Avenue) offers the protestors' version of park history. Although the area around People's Park and Sather Gate may seem quiet now, issues such as affirmative action and tuition increases still bring protests to the steps of Sproul. Protests over civil rights, war, and other inequities march through the center of the campus, though students also gather to rally for sports events, social gatherings, and shows of school spirit.

—Chris Baty

2 Student-guided campus tours leave from **Sather Tower,** the campus land-mark popularly known as the Campanile, at 10 on Saturday and 1 on Sunday. The 307-foot structure, modeled on St. Mark's Tower in Venice and completed in 1914, can be seen for miles. The carillon is played daily at 7:50 AM, noon, and 6 PM and for an extended 45-minute concert Sunday at 2. Take the elevator up 175 feet; then walk another 38 steps to the observation deck for a view of the campus and a close-up look at the iron bells, each of which weighs up to 10,500 pounds. ⌂ *South of University Dr.* ⌂ *$2* ⊙ *Weekdays 10–4, Sat. 10–5, Sun. 10–1:30 and 3–5.*

3 **Sproul Plaza** (⌂ *Telegraph Ave. and Bancroft Way*), just inside the U.C. Berkeley campus border on Bancroft Way, was the site of several free-speech and civil-rights protests in the 1960s. Today a lively panorama of political and social activists, musicians, and students show off Berkeley's flair for the bizarre. Preachers orate atop milk crates, amateur enter-tainers bang on makeshift drum sets, and protesters distribute leaflets about everything from marijuana to the Middle East. No matter what the combination, on weekdays when school is in swing, it always feels like a carnival. ■ TIP→ Walk through at noon for the liveliest show of student spirit.

4 The collection of the **Phoebe A. Hearst Museum of Anthropology** counts almost 4 million artifacts, of which fewer than 1% are on display at any time. The Native Californian Cultures gallery showcases items related to the native peoples of California. Changing exhibits may cover the archaeology of ancient America or spotlight the museum's especially strong ancient Egyptian holdings. Mood music enhances the experience. ⌂ *Kroeber Hall, Bancroft Way, at end of College Ave.* ☎ *510/642–3682* ⊕ *hearstmuseum.berkeley.edu* ⌂ *Free; guided tour $5* ⊙ *Wed.–Sat. 10–4:30, Sun. noon–4.*

5 The **University of California, Berkeley Art Museum & Pacific Film Archive** has an interesting collection of works that spans five centuries. Changing exhib-its line the spiral ramps and balcony galleries. Look for the museum's enormous orange-red statue of a man hammering, which can be seen from the outside when strolling by its floor-to-ceiling windows. Don't miss the museum's series of vibrant paintings by abstract expressionist Hans Hofmann. On the ground floor, the Pacific Film Archive has a library and hosts programs about historic and contemporary films, but the exhibition theater is across the street at 2575 Bancroft Way, near Bowditch Street. The downstairs galleries, which house rotating exhibits, are always free. The museum's raw foods café is famous, and you can also find some cooked options, too. ⌂ *2626 Bancroft Way, entrance to theater at 2575 Bancroft Way, between College and Telegraph* ☎ *510/642–0808, 510/642–1124 film-program information* ⊕ *www. bampfa.berkeley.edu* ⌂ *$8* ⊙ *Wed. and Fri.–Sun. 11–5, Thurs. 11–7.*

6 At the fortresslike **Lawrence Hall of Science,** a dazzling hands-on science center, kids can look at insects under microscopes, solve crimes using chemical forensics, and explore the physics of baseball. On weekends there are special lectures, demonstrations, and planetarium shows. The museum runs a popular (and free) stargazing program, which is held on

18

the first and third Saturday of each month, weather permitting. (Call for times.) ⊠ *Centennial Dr. near Grizzly Peak Blvd.* ☎ *510/642–5132* ⊕ *www.lawrencehallofscience.org* ⊑ *$12* ⊙ *Daily 10–5.*

South of campus, along College Avenue between Ashby Avenue and Claremont, shops and cafés pack the area known as **Elmwood,** a local favorite for browsing. **Nabolom Bakery** (⊠ *2708 Russell St.* ☎ *510/845–2253*), which has been around since 1976, is a workers' collective where politics and delicious pastries collide. Shingled houses line tree-shaded streets nearby.

Telegraph Avenue is Berkeley's student-oriented thoroughfare and the best place to get a dose of the city's famed counterculture. On any given day you might encounter a troop of chanting Hare Krishnas or a drumming band of Rastafarians. First and foremost, however, Telegraph is a place for socializing and shopping, the only uniquely Berkeley shopping experience in town and a definite don't-miss. ■ TIP→ Take care when wandering the street at night, things can feel a bit edgy. Nearby People's Park, mostly harmless by day, is best avoided at night. Cafés, bookstores, poster shops, and street vendors line the avenue. T-shirt vendors and tarot-card readers come and go on a whim, but a few establishments— **Rasputin Music** (No. 2401), **Amoeba Music** (No. 2455), and **Moe's Books** (No. 2476)—are neighborhood landmarks. Allen Ginsberg wrote his acclaimed poem "Howl" at **Caffe Mediterraneum** (No. 2475), a relic of 1960s-era café culture.

An industrial area on **4th Street** north of University Avenue has been converted into a pleasant shopping stretch with popular eateries and shops selling handcrafted and eco-conscious goods. About six blocks long, this compact area is busiest on bright weekend afternoons. Popular destinations are the Stained Glass Garden, Hear Music, and the Crate and Barrel Outlet, along with a mini-slew of upscale boutiques and wonderful paper stores.

Northwest of the U.C. Berkeley campus, **Walnut Square**, at Walnut and Vine streets, has coffee shops and an eclectic assortment of boutiques proffering such goodies as holistic products for your pet, African masks, and French children's clothing. Around the corner on Shattuck Avenue is Chez Panisse Café & Restaurant, at the heart of what is locally known as the **Gourmet Ghetto,** a three-block stretch of specialty shops and eateries. Your senses will immediately perk up as you enter the upscale market **Epicurious Garden** (✉ *1509–1513 Shattuck Ave.*), which has everything from impeccable sushi to gelato. Outside, you can find a terraced garden—the only place to sit—that winds up four levels and ends at the Imperial Tea Court. The restaurant Taste anchors this zone; it offers a rechargeable wine-tasting card that guests use to help themselves to one-ounce automated pours from new wine selections.

NEED A BREAK?

With a jazz combo playing in the storefront and a long line snaking down the block, Cheeseboard Pizza (✉ *151 Shattuck Ave.* ☎ *510/549–3055* ⊙ *Tues.–Fri. 11:30–2 and 4:30–7, Sat. 11:30–3*) counts out the pulse of the Gourmet Ghetto. This cooperatively owned take-out spot draws devoted customers with the smell of just-baked garlic, fresh vegetables, and perfect sauces. Next door at the bakery–cheese shop, customers take a playing card instead of a number and are served in suites.

18

Vine Street is another culinary destination. In a historic building **Vintage Berkeley** (✉ *2113 Vine St.* ☎ *510/665–8600*) gathers locals in its large front garden for nightly wine-tastings of California wines from smaller vineyards. Take the stairs up to the top floor of Walnut Square to find **Love at First Bite** (✉ *1510 Walnut St., Suite G* ☎ *510/848–5727*) a cup-cakery showcasing scrumptious confections. **Twig & Fig** (✉ *210 Vine St., Suite B* ☎ *510/848–5599*) invites you in for a peek at its three rhythmically clacking letterpresses. Stop in for one-of-a-kind papery gifts and publications such as *Inside the Brambles*, a local's guide to Tilden Park. Of all the coffeehouses in caffeine-crazed Berkeley, the one that deserves a pilgrimage is **Peet's** (✉ *2124 Vine St.* ☎ *510/841–0564*). When this, the original, opened at Vine and Walnut streets in 1966, the unparalleled coffee was roasted in the store and brewed by the cup. Named after the Dutch last name of the founder, Peet's has since expanded, but this isn't a café where you can sit on sofas or order quiche. It's strictly coffee, tea, and sweets to go.

WHERE TO EAT AND STAY

Dining in Berkeley is a low-key affair; even in the finest restaurants—and some are quite fine—most folks dress casually. Late diners be forewarned: Berkeley is an "early to bed" kind of town. For inexpensive lodging, investigate University Avenue, west of campus. The area is noisy, congested, and somewhat dilapidated, but does include a few decent motels and chain properties. All Berkeley lodgings, except for the swanky Claremont, are strictly mid-range.

WORD OF MOUTH

"I am a BIG fan of the Cafe at Chez Panisse and still go there even after having started eating there in the '70s.... While in that area you might also check out The Cheeseboard Pizza.... This is unlike any pizza you have ever had. Pastries can (and should be) taken at Masse's just up Shattuck from The Cheeseboard." —PamSF

¢–$
AMERICAN

× **Bette's Oceanview Diner.** Buttermilk pancakes are just one of the specialties at this 1930s-inspired diner, complete with checkered floors and burgundy booths. Huevos rancheros and lox and eggs are other breakfast options; kosher franks, generous slices of pizza, and a slew of sandwiches are available for lunch. The wait for a seat can be quite long; thankfully, 4th Street was made for strolling. ■**TIP→** If you're starving, head to Bette's to Go, next door, for takeout. ⊠ *1807 4th St.* ☎ *510/644–3230* ⌕ *Reservations not accepted* ▭ *MC, V* ⊘ *No dinner.*

$$$–$$$$
AMERICAN

× **Café Rouge.** You can recover from 4th Street shopping in this spacious two-story bistro, complete with zinc bar, skylights, and festive lanterns. The short, seasonal menu ranges from the sophisticated, such as rack of lamb and juniper-berry-cured pork chops, to the homey, such as spit-roasted chicken or pork loin, or cheddar-topped burgers. If you visit by day, be certain to peek at the meat market in the back. ⊠ *1782 4th St.* ☎ *510/525–1440* ▭ *MC, V* ⊘ *No dinner Mon.*

$$–$$$
SPANISH

× **César.** Suitably keeping near-Spanish hours for the Spanish cuisine here, dinners are served late at César, whose kitchen closes at 11:30 PM on Friday and Saturday and at 11 PM the rest of the week. Couples spill out from its street-level windows on warm nights, or rub shoulders at the polished bar or center communal table. Founded by a trio of former Chez Panisse chefs, César is like a first cousin to Chez Panisse, each restaurant recommending the other if there's a long wait ahead. For tapas and perfectly grilled bocadillos (small sandwiches), there's no better choice. The bar also makes a mean martini and has an impressive wine list. ■**TIP→** Come early to get seated quickly and also to hear your tablemates; the room gets loud when the bar is in full swing. ⊠ *1515 Shattuck Ave.* ☎ *510/883–0222* ⌕ *Reservations not accepted* ▭ *MC, V.*

$$$–$$$$
AMERICAN
Fodor's Choice
★

× **Chez Panisse Café & Restaurant.** At Chez Panisse even humble pizza is reincarnated, with innovative toppings of the freshest local ingredients. The downstairs portion of Alice Waters's legendary eatery is noted for its formality and personal service. The daily-changing multicourse dinners are prix-fixe ($$$$), with the cost slightly lower on weekdays. Upstairs, in the informal café, the crowd is livelier, the prices are lower ($$–$$$$), and the ever-changing menu is à la carte. The food is simpler, too: penne with new potatoes, arugula, and sheep's-milk cheese;

The pioneer restaurant Chez Panisse focuses on seasonal local ingredients.

fresh figs with Parmigiano-Reggiano cheese and arugula; and grilled tuna with Savoy cabbage, for example. Legions of loyal fans insist Chez Panisse lives up to its reputation and delivers a dining experience well worth the price. Visiting foodies won't want to miss a meal here; be sure to make reservations a few weeks ahead of time. ⊠ *1517 Shattuck Ave., north of University Ave.* ☎ *510/548–5525 restaurant, 510/548–5049 café* ⚇ *Reservations essential* ⊟ *AE, D, DC, MC, V* ⊙ *Closed Sun. No lunch in restaurant.*

$$–$$$
MEDITERRANEAN
★

✕ **Lalime's.** The food served in this charming, flower-covered house reflects the entire Mediterranean region. The menu, constantly changing and unfailingly great, depends on the availability of fresh seasonal ingredients. Choices might include grilled ahi tuna or creamy Italian risotto. The light colors of the dining room, which has two levels, help to create a cheerful mood. A star in its own right, Lalime's is a good second choice if Chez Panisse is booked. ⊠ *1329 Gilman St.* ☎ *510/527–9838* ⚇ *Reservations essential* ⊟ *AE, DC, MC, V* ⊙ *No lunch.*

¢–$
MEXICAN

✕ **Picante Cocina Mexicana.** A barnlike space full of cheerful Mexican tiles and folk-art masks, Picante is a find for anyone seeking good Mexican food for a song. The *masa* (flour) is freshly ground for the tortillas and tamales, the salsas are complex, and the combinations are inventive. Try tamales filled with butternut squash and chilies or a simple taco of roasted poblanos and sautéed onions; we challenge you to finish a plate of super nachos. ⊠ *1328 6th St.* ☎ *510/525–3121* ⚇ *Reservations not accepted* ⊟ *MC, V.*

¢–$$
AMERICAN

✕ **Rick & Ann's.** Haute comfort food is the signature here. The brunches are legendary for quality and value, and customers line up outside the door before the restaurant opens on the weekend. If you come during prime brunch time, expect a long wait, but their soft-style eggs are worth it. Pancakes, waffles, and French toast are more flavorful than usual with variations such as potato-cheese and orange-rice pancakes. Lunch and dinner offer burgers, favorites such as Mom's macaroni and cheese, and chicken potpie, but always with a festive

WORD OF MOUTH

"Berkeley has always taken pride in being one of the most car-UNfriendly cities in the U.S. And this is in a metropolitan area for which a car is completely unnecessary."   —PaulRabe

twist. Reservations are accepted 48 hours in advance for dinner and for lunch parties of six or more, but you can't reserve a table for brunch. ⊠ *2922 Domingo Ave.* ☎ *510/649–8568* ▤ *MC, V* ⊘ *No dinner Mon.*

$$$$
Fodor'sChoice
★

🏨 **Claremont Resort and Spa.** Straddling the Oakland–Berkeley border, the hotel beckons like a gleaming white castle in the hills. Traveling executives come for the business amenities, including T-1 Internet connections, guest e-mail addresses, and oversize desks. The Claremont also draws honeymooners and leisure travelers with its luxurious suites, therapeutic massages, and personalized yoga workouts at the on-site spa. The rooms on the spa side of the hotel glow with new fixtures and furniture. Some offer spa tubs and, if you're high enough up, spectacular bay views. ■TIP➡ Another advantage: the scents wafting upward from the spa treatment rooms. **Pros:** amazing spa, supervised childcare, some rooms have great views of the bay. **Cons:** parking is pricey, the hotel can be busy with weddings, so-so lobby. ⊠ *41 Tunnel Rd., at Ashby and Domingo Aves.* ☎ *510/843–3000 or 800/551–7266* ⊕ *www. claremontresort.com* ⇗ *249 rooms, 30 suites* ⚏ *In-room: safe, refrigerator (some), Wi-Fi. In-hotel: 2 restaurants, bars, tennis courts, pools, gym, spa, children's programs (ages 6 wks–10 yrs), laundry service, concierge, public Wi-Fi, parking (fee)* ▤ *AE, D, DC, MC, V.*

$

🏨 **French Hotel.** The only hotel in north Berkeley, one of the best walking neighborhoods in town, this three-level brick structure has a certain *pensione* feel—guests check in at a counter at the back of the café, and the only public space in the hotel is the hallway to the elevator. Rooms have pastel or brick walls and cherrywood armoires and writing tables. Balconies make the rooms seem larger than their modest dimensions. The bedspreads and decor are '70s-chic, but you couldn't ask for a more central location. A ground-floor café, serving arguably the best latte in town, buzzes day and night with overflow from the Gourmet Ghetto (Chez Panisse is across the street). **Pros:** great location, affordable. **Cons:** don't expect a lot of peace and quiet, rear rooms are small and dark. ⊠ *1538 Shattuck Ave.* ☎ *510/548–9930* 🖷 *510/548–9930* ⇗ *18 rooms* ⚏ *In-room: no a/c. In-hotel: restaurant, concierge, public Wi-Fi, parking (no fee)* ▤ *AE, D, MC, V.*

$

🏨 **Holiday Inn Express.** Convenient to the freeway and 4th Street shopping, this inviting, peach-and-beige-hue hotel offers lots of bang for the buck. The two-story property is surprisingly elegant; high ceilings lend the lobby and rooms an airy quality. Each room has a small kitchen area with a refrigerator, microwave, sink, and cabinets. The hotel also offers a free breakfast bar, a small but well-equipped gym, and free access to a business center. **Pros:** spacious rooms, central location. **Cons:** gets packed during graduation season, area can get noisy and congested with traffic. ⊠ *1175 University Ave.* ☎ *510/548–1700 or 866/548–1700* ⊕ *www.hiexberkeley.com* ➯ *69 rooms, 3 suites with spas* ♿ *In-room: refrigerator, Wi-Fi. In-hotel: gym, laundry facilities, laundry service, parking (no fee)* ⊟ *AE, D, DC, MC, V* ⦶ *CP.*

$$ ⛨ **Hotel Durant.** This newly renovated boutique hotel has long been the mainstay of parents visiting their children at U.C. Berkeley; it's also a good option for those who want to be a short walk from Telegraph Avenue. The rooms, updated in 2006 with new bathrooms and dark wood set against deep jewel tones, are small without feeling cramped. The historic photos of Berkeley highlight the hotel's storied past, and the central location is perfect for the car-less. This hotel is also eco-conscious, using nonchemical, all-natural cleaning products. ■**TIP**➔ **Guests receive free passes to the extensive Cal Recreational Sports Facility, known as RSF.** **Pros:** blackout shades, organic bathrobes, fantastic attention to detail. **Cons:** downstairs bar can get a little noisy during Cal games, pricey parking. ⊠ *2600 Durant Ave.* ☎ *510/845–8981* ⊕ *www.hoteldurant. com* ➯ *139 rooms, 5 suites* ♿ *In-room: no a/c, safe, refrigerator. In-hotel: restaurant, room service, bar, laundry service, concierge, public Wi-Fi, parking (fee)* ⊟ *AE, D, DC, MC, V.*

NIGHTLIFE AND THE ARTS

Berkeley Repertory Theatre. One of the region's highly respected resident professional companies and a Tony Award winner for Outstanding Regional Theatre (in 1997), the theater performs classic and contemporary plays from autumn to spring. Well-known pieces such as *Mother Courage* and *Oliver Twist* mix with edgier fare. The theater's complex is near BART's Downtown Berkeley Station. ⊠ *2025 Addison St.* ☎ *510/845–4700* ⊕ *www.berkeleyrep.org.*

Berkeley Symphony Orchestra. The ensemble has risen to considerable prominence under artistic director Kent Nagano. The works of 20th-century composers are a focus, but traditional pieces are also performed. The orchestra plays a handful of concerts each year, in Zellerbach Hall and other locations. ⊠ *1942 University Ave.,Suite 207* ☎ *510/841–2800* ⊕ *www.berkeleysymphony.org.*

★ **Cal Performances.** The series, running from September through May at various U.C. Berkeley venues, offers the Bay Area's most varied bill of internationally acclaimed artists in all disciplines, from classical soloists to the latest jazz, world-music, theater, and dance ensembles. Look for frequent campus colloquia or preshow talks featuring Berkeley's professors. ⊠ *University of California, Zellerbach Hall, Telegraph Ave. and Bancroft Way* ☎ *510/642–9988* ⊕ *www.calperfs.berkeley.edu.*

Fodor'sChoice ★ **Freight & Salvage Coffee House.** Some of the most talented practitioners of folk, blues, Cajun, and bluegrass perform in this alcohol-free space, one of the finest folk houses in the country. Most tickets are less than $20. ⊠ *2020 Addison St.* ☎ *510/548–1761* ⊕ *www.thefreight.org.*

SHOPPING

Fodor'sChoice ★ **Amoeba Music.** Heaven for audiophiles, this legendary Berkeley favorite is *the* place to go for new and used CDs, records, cassettes, and DVDs. The dazzling stock includes thousands of titles for all music tastes—no

18

matter what you're looking for, you can probably find it here. The store even has its own record label. There are now branches in San Francisco and Hollywood, but this is the original. ⊠ *2455 Telegraph Ave., at Haste St.* ☎ *510/549–1125.*

Body Time. The local chain, founded in Berkeley in 1970, emphasizes the premium-quality ingredients it uses in its natural perfumes and skin-care and aromatherapy products. Sustainably harvested essential oils that you can combine and dilute to create your own personal fragrances are the specialty. Its distinct Citrus, Lavender-Mint, and China Rain scents are all popular. ⊠ *1942 Shattuck Ave.* ☎ *510/841–5818.*

Kermit Lynch Wine Merchant. Kermit Lynch's friendly salespeople can direct you to the latest French bargains. Lynch's newsletters describing his finds are legendary, as is his friendship with Alice Waters of Chez Panisse. Responsible for taking American appreciation of French wine to another level, the shop is a great place to peruse as you educate your palate. ⊠ *1605 San Pablo Ave., at Dwight Way* ☎ *510/524–1524.*

Moe's Books. The spirit of Moe—the cantankerous, cigar-smoking late proprietor—lives on in this four-story house of books. Students and professors come here for used books, including large sections of literary and cultural criticism, art books, and literature in foreign languages. ■ TIP→ Wear good shoes and eat lunch first; you won't want to come out for hours. ⊠ *2476 Telegraph Ave., near Haste St.* ☎ *510/849–2087.*

Rasputin Music. A huge selection of new music for every taste draws crowds. In any other town, its stock of used CDs and vinyl would certainly be unsurpassed. ⊠ *2401 Telegraph Ave., at Channing Way* ☎ *800/350–8700 or 510/848–9004.*

The Wine Country

WORD OF MOUTH

"We went to Cline Cellars . . . which makes some French style wines with Rhône varietals. The tasting was free, and we really enjoyed the wines—the best part, though, was that they had "wooly weeders" at work in the vineyards, which means sheep grazing between the vines. My wife thought this was endlessly cute."

—smetz

WELCOME TO WINE COUNTRY

TOP REASONS TO GO

★ **Biking:** Cycling is one of the best ways to see the Wine Country—the Russian River and Dry Creek valleys are particularly beautiful.

★ **Browsing the farmers' markets:** Almost every town in Napa and Sonoma has a seasonal farmers' market, each rounding up an amazing variety of local produce.

★ **Touring di Rosa:** Though this art and nature preserve is just off the busy Carneros Highway, it's a relatively unknown treasure. The galleries and gardens are filled with hundreds of artworks.

★ **Canoeing on the Russian River:** Trade in your car keys for a paddle and glide down the Russian River. May through October is the best time to be on the water.

★ **Cocktails at Cyrus:** At the bar of Healdsburg's well-loved restaurant, the bartenders mix superb, inventive drinks with house-made infused syrups and seasonal ingredients like local Meyer lemons.

1 Napa Valley. You'll find big names all around, from high-profile wineries to world-renowned chefs. Napa, the valley's oldest town, sweet-life St. Helena, and down-to-earth Calistoga all make good home bases here. (Calistoga has the extra draw of local thermal springs.) Yountville has become a culinary boomtown, while the tiny communities of Oakville and Rutherford are surrounded by major vintners like Robert Mondavi and Francis Ford Coppola. Rutherford in particular is the source for outstanding cabernet sauvignon.

2 Sonoma Valley. Historic attractions and an unpretentious attitude prevail here. The town of Sonoma, with its atmospheric central plaza, is rich with 19th-century buildings. Glen Ellen, meanwhile, has a special connection with author Jack London.

3 **Elsewhere in Sonoma.** The winding, rural roads here feel a world away from Napa's main drag. The lovely Russian River, Dry Creek, and Alexander valleys are all excellent places to seek out pinot noir, zinfandel, and chardonnay. The small town of Healdsburg gets lots of attention, thanks to its terrific restaurants, bed-and-breakfasts, and chic boutiques.

GETTING ORIENTED

The Napa and Sonoma valleys run roughly parallel, northwest to southeast, and are separated by the Mayacamas Mountains. Northwest of the Sonoma Valley are several more important viticultural areas in Sonoma County, including the Dry Creek, Alexander, and Russian River valleys. The Carneros region, which spans southern Sonoma and Napa counties, is just north of San Pablo Bay, and the closest of all these wine regions to San Francisco.

19

WINE COUNTRY PLANNER

Getting Around

Driving your own car is by far the best way to explore the Wine Country. Well-maintained roads zip through the centers of the Napa and Sonoma valleys, while scenic routes thread through the backcountry. Distances between towns are fairly short, and you can sometimes drive from one end of the Napa or Sonoma Valley to the other in less than an hour—if there's no significant traffic. (However, it's not quite as easy as you might think to get between the two valleys, since they're divided by the Mayacamas Mountains.) This may be a relatively rural area, but the usual rush hours still apply, and high-season weekend traffic can be excruciatingly slow, especially on Route 29. ■TIP➜ If you're wine-tasting, either select a designated driver or be very careful of your wine intake. Local cops are quick with DUIs.

Timing

"Crush," the term used to indicate the season when grapes are picked and crushed, usually takes place in September or October, depending on the weather. From September until November the entire Wine Country celebrates its bounty with street fairs and festivals. The Sonoma County Harvest Fair, with its famous grape stomp, is held the first weekend in October. Golf tournaments, wine auctions, and art and food fairs occur throughout the fall.

In season (April through November), Napa Valley draws crowds of tourists, and traffic along Route 29 from St. Helena to Calistoga is often backed up on weekends. The Sonoma Valley, Santa Rosa, and Healdsburg are less crowded. In season and over holiday weekends it's best to book lodging, restaurant, and winery reservations at least a month in advance. Many wineries give tours at specified times and require appointments.

To avoid crowds, visit the Wine Country during the week and get an early start (most wineries open around 10). Because many wineries close as early as 4 or 4:30—and almost none are open past 5—you'll need to get a reasonably early start if you want to fit in more than one or two, especially if you're going to enjoy the leisurely lunch customary in the Wine Country. Summer is usually hot and dry, and autumn can be even hotter, so dress appropriately if you go during these times.

About the Hotels

Napa and Sonoma know the tourism ropes well; their inns and hotels range from low-key to utterly luxurious, and generally maintain high standards. Most of the bed-and-breakfasts are in historic Victorian and Spanish buildings and the breakfast part of the equation often involves fresh local produce. The newer hotels tend to have a more modern, streamlined aesthetic and elaborate, spalike bathrooms. Many hotels and B&Bs have excellent restaurants on their grounds, and those that don't are still just a short car ride away from gastronomic bliss.

However, all of this comes with a hefty price tag. As the cost of vineyards and grapes has risen, so have lodging rates. Santa Rosa, the largest population center in the area, has the widest selection of moderately priced rooms. Try there if you've failed to reserve in advance or have a limited budget. In general, all accommodations in the area often have lower rates on weeknights, and prices are about 20% lower in winter.

On weekends, two- or even three-night minimum stays are commonly required, especially at smaller inns and B&Bs. If you'd prefer to stay a single night, though, innkeepers are usually more flexible in winter. Many B&Bs book up long in advance of the summer and fall seasons, and many of them aren't suitable for children.

About the Restaurants

Star chefs from around the world have come into the Wine Country's orbit, drawn by the area's phenomenal produce, artisanal foods, and wines. These days, many visitors come to Napa and Sonoma as much for the restaurants' tasting menus as for the wineries' tasting rooms.

Although excellent meals can be found virtually everywhere in the region, the small town of Yountville has become a culinary crossroads under the influence of chef Thomas Keller. If a table at Keller's famed French Laundry is out of reach, keep in mind that he's also behind a number of more modest restaurants in town. And the buzzed-about restaurants in Sonoma County, including Cyrus and Farmhouse Inn, offer plenty of mouthwatering options.

Inexpensive eateries include high-end delis serve superb picnic fare, and brunch is a cost-effective strategy at pricey restaurants, as is sitting at the bar and ordering a few appetizers instead of sitting down to a full-blown meal.

With few exceptions (which are noted in individual restaurant listings), dress is informal. Where reservations are indicated as essential, you may need to make them a week or more ahead. In summer and early fall you may need to book several weeks ahead.

19

DINING & LODGING PRICE CATEGORIES

	¢	$	$$	$$$	$$$$
Restaurants	under $10	$10–$14	$15–$22	$23–$30	over $30
Hotels	under $200	$200–$250	$251–$300	$301–$400	over $400

Restaurant prices are per person for a main course at dinner, or for a prix fixe if a set menu is the only option. Hotel prices are for two people in a standard double room in high season.

Updated by
Sharron Wood

Life is good in the California Wine Country. Eating and, above all, drinking are cultivated as high arts. Have you been daydreaming about driving through vineyards, stopping here and there for a wine tasting or a picnic? Well, that fantasy is a common reality here.

It's little wonder that so many visitors to San Francisco take a day or two—or five or six—to unwind in the Napa and Sonoma valleys. They join the locals in the tasting rooms, from serious wine collectors making their annual pilgrimages to wine newbies who don't know the difference between a merlot and mourvèdre but are eager to learn.

The state's wine industry is booming, and the Napa and Sonoma valleys have long led the field. For instance, in 1975 Napa Valley had no more than 20 wineries; today there are more than 275. A recent up-and-comer is the Carneros region, which overlaps Napa and Sonoma counties at the head of the San Francisco Bay. (Chardonnay and pinot noir grapes thrive on its cool, windy hillsides.)

Great dining and wine go hand in hand, and the local viticulture has naturally encouraged a robust passion for food. Several outstanding chefs have taken root here, sealing the area's reputation as one of the best restaurant destinations in the country. The lust for fine food doesn't stop at the doors of the bistros, either. Whether you visit an artisanal olive-oil producer, nibble locally made cheese, or browse the fresh vegetables in the farmers' markets, you'll soon see why Napa and Sonoma are a food-lover's paradise.

Napa and Sonoma counties are also rich in history. In the town of Sonoma, for example, you can explore buildings from California's Spanish and Mexican past. Some wineries, such as Napa Valley's Beringer, have cellars or tasting rooms dating to the late 1800s. The town of Calistoga is a flurry of Steamboat Gothic architecture, gussied up with the fretwork favored by late-19th-century spa goers. Modern architecture is the exception rather than the rule, but one standout example is the postmodern extravaganza of Clos Pegase winery in Calistoga.

Binding all these temptations together is the sheer scenic beauty of the place. Much of Napa Valley's landscape unspools in orderly, densely planted rows of vines. Sonoma's vistas are broken by rolling hills or stands of ancient oak and madrone trees. Even the climate cooperates, as the warm summer days and refreshingly cool evenings that make the area one of the world's best grape-growing regions make perfect weather for traveling, too. If you're inspired to dig further into the Wine Country, grab a copy of *California Wine Country* or the in-depth *Compass American Guide: California Wine Country*.

PLANNING

GETTING HERE AND AROUND

AIR TRAVEL

If you'd like to bypass San Francisco or Oakland, you can fly directly to the small Charles M. Schulz Sonoma County Airport (STS) in Santa Rosa on Horizon Air, which has direct flights from Los Angeles, Portland, Las Vegas, and Seattle. Rental cars are available from Avis, Enterprise, and Hertz at the airport.

BUS TRAVEL

Bus travel is an inconvenient way to explore the Wine Country. Service is infrequent and buses from San Francisco can only get you to Santa Rosa or the town of Vallejo, south of Napa—neither of which is close to the vineyards. Sonoma County Transit offers daily bus service to points all over the county. VINE (Valley Intracity Neighborhood Express) provides bus service within the city of Napa and between other Napa Valley towns.

Bus Lines Greyhound (☎ 800/231–2222). **Sonoma County Transit** (☎ 707/576–7433 or 800/345–7433). **VINE** (☎ 707/251–2800).

CAR TRAVEL

Five major roads cut through the Napa and Sonoma valleys. U.S. 101 and Routes 12 and 121 travel through Sonoma County. Route 29 heads north from Napa. The 25-mi Silverado Trail, which runs parallel to Route 29 north from Napa to Calistoga, is Napa Valley's more scenic, less-crowded alternative to Route 29.

■ TIP→ Remember, if you're wine-tasting, either select a designated driver or be careful of your wine intake. (When you're taking just a sip or two of any given wine, it can be hard to keep track of how much you're drinking.) Also, keep in mind that you'll likely be sharing the road with cyclists; keep a close eye on the shoulder.

When calculating the time it will take you to drive between the Napa and Sonoma valleys, remember that the Mayacamas Mountains are between the two. If it's not too far out of your way, you might want to travel between the two valleys along Highway 12/121 to the south, or along Highway 128 to the north, to avoid the slow, winding drive on the Oakville Grade, which connects Oakville, in Napa, and Glen Ellen, in Sonoma.

From San Francisco to Napa: Cross the Golden Gate Bridge, then go north on U.S. 101. Next go east on Route 37 toward Vallejo, then north on

19

Route 121, also called the Carneros Highway. Turn left (north) when Route 121 runs into Route 29. This should take about 1½ hours when traffic is light.

From San Francisco to Sonoma: Cross the Golden Gate Bridge, then go north on U.S. 101, east on Route 37 toward Vallejo, and north on Route 121, aka the Carneros Highway. When you reach Route 12, take it north. If you're going to any of the Sonoma County destinations north of the valley, take U.S. 101 all the way north through Santa Rosa to Healdsburg. This should take about an hour, not counting substantial traffic.

From Berkeley and other East Bay towns: Take Interstate 80 north to Route 37 west, then on to Route 29 north. To head up the Napa Valley, continue on Route 29; to reach Sonoma County, turn off Route 29 onto Route 121 heading north. Getting from Berkeley to Napa will take at least 45 minutes, from Berkeley to Sonoma at least an hour.

BED-AND-BREAKFAST ASSOCIATIONS

Bed & Breakfast Association of Sonoma Valley ☎ 800/969–4667 ⊕ www. sonomabb.com). **The Wine Country Inns of Sonoma County** (☎ 800/946–3268 ⊕ www.winecountryinns.com).

TOURS

Full-day guided tours of the Wine Country generally include lunch and cost about $60–$100 per person. Reservations are usually required.

Beau Wine Tours (✉ 21707 8th St. E, Sonoma ☎ 707/938–8001 or 800/ 387–2328 ⊕ www.beauwinetours.com) organizes personalized tours of Napa and Sonoma in their limos, vans, and shuttle buses. **Gray Line** (✉ Pier 43½, Embarcadero, San Francisco ☎ 415/434–8687 or 888/428–6937 ⊕ www.grayline.com) has a tour that covers both the southern Napa and Sonoma valleys in a single day, with a stop for lunch in Yountville. **Great Pacific Tour Co.** (✉ 518 Octavia St., Hayes Valley, San Francisco ☎ 415/626–4499 ⊕ www.greatpacifictour.com) operates full-day tours of Napa and Sonoma, including a restaurant or picnic lunch, in passenger vans that seat 14. In addition to renting bikes by the day, **Wine Country Bikes** (✉ 61 Front St., Healdsburg ☎ 707/473–0610 ⊕ www.winecountrybikes.com) organizes both one-day and multiday trips throughout Sonoma County.

THE NAPA VALLEY

When it comes to wine production in the United States, Napa Valley rules the roost, with more than 275 wineries and many of the biggest brands in the business. Vastly diverse soils and microclimates give Napa winemakers the chance to make a tremendous variety of wines. But what's the area like beyond the glossy advertising and boldface names?

The handful of small towns strung along Highway 29 are where wine industry workers live, and they're also where most of the area lodging is. Napa—the valley's largest town—lures with its few cultural attractions and accommodations that are (relatively) reasonably priced. A few miles farther north, compact Yountville is a culinary boomtown, densely packed with top-notch restaurants and hotels, including a few luxury properties. Continuing north, St. Helena teems with elegant boutiques and restaurants; mellow Calistoga, known for spas and hot springs, feels a bit like an Old West frontier town and has a more casual attitude than many Wine Country towns.

ESSENTIALS

Contacts Napa Valley Conference and Visitors Bureau (✉ *1310 Napa Town Center, Napa* ☎ *707/226–7459* ⊕ *www.napavalley.org*).

NAPA

46 mi from San Francisco via I–80 east and north, Rte. 37 west, and Rte. 29 north.

The town of Napa is the valley's largest, and visitors who get a glimpse of the strip malls and big-box stores from Highway 29 often speed right past on the way to the smaller and more seductive Yountville or St. Helena. But Napa doesn't entirely deserve its dowdy reputation. After many years as a blue-collar town that more or less turned its back on the Wine Country scene, Napa has spent the last few years attempting to increase its appeal to visitors, with somewhat mixed results. A walkway that follows the river through town, completed in 2008, makes the city more pedestrian-friendly, and new restaurants and hotels are continually popping up (there are even plans to open a Ritz-Carlton on the river's banks in 2011). But you'll still find a handful of empty storefronts among the wine bars, bookstores, and restaurants, and Napa's biggest tourist attraction, a food-and wine-theme museum and educational center, closed in late 2008.

Many visitors choose to stay in Napa after experiencing hotel sticker shock; prices in Napa are marginally more reasonable than elsewhere. If you set up your home base here, you'll undoubtedly want to spend some time getting out of town and into the beautiful countryside, but don't neglect taking a stroll to see what Napa's least pretentious town has to offer.

19

★ The majestic château of **Domaine Carneros** looks for all the world like it belongs in France, and in fact it does: it's modeled after the Château de la Marquetterie, an 18th-century mansion owned by the Taittinger family near Epernay, France. Carved into the hillside beneath the winery, Domaine Carneros's cellars produce delicate sparkling wines reminiscent of those made by Taittinger, using only grapes grown locally in the Carneros wine district. The winery sells full glasses, flights, and bottles of their wines, which also include still wines like a handful of pinot noirs and a merlot, and serves them with cheese plates or caviar to those seated in the Louis XV–inspired salon or on the terrace overlooking the vineyards. Though this makes a visit here a tad more expensive than some stops on a winery tour, it's also one of the most opulent ways to enjoy the Carneros District, especially on fair days, when the views over the vineyards are spectacular. ✉ *1240 Duhig Rd., Napa*

Continued on page 436

WINE
TASTING *in*
NAPA *and*
SONOMA

The tantalizing pop of a cork. Roads unspooling through hypnotically even rows of vines. Sun glinting through a glass of sparkling wine or ruby colored cabernet. If these are your daydreams, you won't be disappointed when you get to Napa and Sonoma. The vineyard-blanketed hills, shady town squares, and ivy-draped wineries—not to mention the luxurious restaurants, hotels, and spas—really *are* that captivating.

(opposite page) Carneros vineyards in autumn, Napa Valley. (top) Pinot Gris grapes (bottom) Bottles from Far Niente winery.

VISITING WINERIES

Napa and Sonoma are outstanding destinations for both wine newcomers and serious wine buffs. Tasting rooms range from modest to swanky, offering everything from a casual conversation over a few sips of wine to in-depth tours of winemaking facilities and vineyards. And there's a tremendous variety of wines to taste. The one constant is a deep, shared pleasure in the experience of wine tasting.

Wineries in Napa and Sonoma range from faux châteaux with vast gift shops to rustic converted barns where you might have to step over the vintner's dog in the doorway. Many are regularly open to the public, usually daily from around 10 AM to 5 PM. Others require advance reservations to visit, and still others are closed to the public entirely. When in doubt, call ahead.

There are many, many more wineries in Napa and Sonoma than we could possibly include here. Free maps pinpointing most of them are widely available, though; ask the staff at the tasting rooms you visit or look for the ubiquitous free tourist magazines.

Pick a designated driver before setting out for the day. Although wineries rarely advertise it, many will provide a free nonalcoholic drink for the designated driver; it never hurts to ask.

Fees. In the past few years, tasting fees have skyrocketed. Most Napa wineries charge $10 to $20 to taste four or so wines, though $30 or even $40 fees aren't unheard of. Sonoma wineries are often a bit cheaper, in the $5 to $15 range, and you'll still find the occasional freebie.

Some winery tours are free, in which case you're usually required to pay a separate fee if you want to taste the wine. If you've paid a fee for the tour—often $10 to $30—your wine tasting is usually included in that price.

MAKING THE MOST OF YOUR TIME

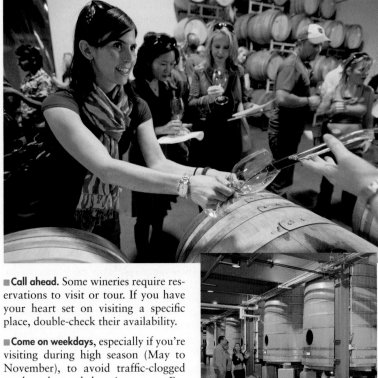

(top) Sipping and swirling in the De Loach tasting room. (bottom) Learning about barrel aging at Robert Mondavi Winery.

■**Call ahead.** Some wineries require reservations to visit or tour. If you have your heart set on visiting a specific place, double-check their availability.

■**Come on weekdays,** especially if you're visiting during high season (May to November), to avoid traffic-clogged roads and crowded tasting rooms. For more info on the best times of year to visit, see this chapter's Planner.

■**Get an early start.** Tasting rooms are often deserted before 11 AM or so, when most visitors are still lingering over a second cup of coffee. If you come early, you'll have the staff's undivided attention. You'll usually encounter the largest crowds between 3 and 5 PM.

■**Consider skipping Napa.** If you've got less than two days to spend in the Wine Country, dip into the Carneros area or the Sonoma Valley rather than Napa Valley or northern Sonoma County. Though you might find fewer big-name wineries and critically acclaimed restau-rants, these regions are only about an hour and half away from the city . . . if you don't hit traffic.

■**Divide your attention.** If you're lucky enough to have three nights or more here, split your overnights between Napa and Sonoma to easily see the best that both counties have to offer.

A tasting at Heitz Cellar.

AT THE BAR

In most tasting rooms, you'll be handed a list of the wines available that day. The wines will be listed in a suggested tasting order, starting with the lightest-bodied whites, progressing to the most intense reds, and ending with dessert wines. If you can't decide which wines to choose, tell the server what types of wines you usually like and ask for a recommendation.

The server will pour you an ounce or so of each wine you select. As you taste it, feel free to take notes or ask questions. Don't be shy—the staff are there to educate you about their wine. If you don't like a wine, or you've simply tasted enough, feel free to pour the rest into one of the dump buckets on the bar.

TOURS

Tours tend to be the most exciting (and the most crowded) in September and October, when the harvest and crush-ing are underway. Tours typically last from 30 minutes to an hour and give you a brief overview of the winemaking process. At some of the older wineries, the tour guide might focus on the history of the property.

■ TIP→ **If you plan to take any tours, wear comfortable shoes, since you might be walking on wet floors or dirt or gravel pathways or stepping over hoses or other equipment.**

MONEY-SAVING TIPS

■ Many hotels and B&Bs distribute coupons for free or discounted tastings to their guests—don't forget to ask.

■ If you and your travel partner don't mind sharing a glass, servers are happy to let you split a tasting.

■ Some wineries will refund all or part of the tasting fee if you buy a bottle, making it so much easier to rationalize buying that $80 bottle of cabernet.

■ Almost all wineries will also waive the fee if you join their wine club program. However, this typically commits you to buying a certain number of bottles of their wine for a period of time, so be sure you really like their wines before signing up.

Preston Vineyards bottles only estate-grown grapes.

TOP 2-DAY ITINERARIES

First-Timer's Napa Tour

Start: Oxbow Public market, Napa. Get underway by browsing the shops selling wines, spices, locally grown produce, and other fine foods, for a taste of what the Wine Country has to offer.

Rubicon Estate, Rutherford. The tour here is a particularly fun way to learn about the

history of Napa wine-making—and you can see the old, atmospheric, ivy-covered château.

Frog's Leap, Rutherford. Friendly, unpretentious, and knowledgeable staff makes this place great for wine newbies. (Make sure

you get that advance reservation lined up.)

Dinner and Overnight: St. Helena. Splurge at Meadowood Resort with dinner at

Domaine Carneros

di Rosa Preserve

Old Sonoma Rd.

Robert Mondav

NAPA COUNTY

Far Niente

Oxbow Public Market
Napa
29

Yountville

Oakville

KEY
First-Timer's Napa Tour
Wine Buff's Tour

Silverado Trail

Stag's Leap Wine Cellars

Wine Buff's Tour

Start: Stag's Leap Wine Cellars, Yountville. Famed for its cabernet sauvignon and Bordeaux blends.

Beaulieu Vineyard, Rutherford. Pony up the extra fee to visit the reserve tasting room to try their flagship cabernet sauvignon.

Caymus Vineyards, Rutherford. The low-key tasting room is a great place to learn more about Rutherford and Napa cabernet artistry. Reserve in advance.

Dinner and Overnight: Yountville. Have dinner at one of the Thomas Keller restaurants. Splurge

at the Villagio Inn & Spa; save at Maison Fleurie.

Next Day: Robert Mondavi, Oakville. Spring for the reserve room tasting so you can sip the top-of-the-line wines, especially the stellar cabernet. Head across Highway 29 to the Oakville Grocery

to pick up a picnic lunch.

Terra. Save at El Bonita Motel with dinner at Taylor's.

Next Day: Poke around St. Helena's shops, then drive to Yountville for lunch.

di Rosa, Napa. Call ahead to book a one- or two-hour tour of the acres of gardens and galleries, which are chock-full of thousands of works of art.

Domaine Carneros, Napa. Toast your trip with a glass of outstanding bubbly.

Sonoma Backroads

0 ———— 4 miles
0 ———— 4 km

Rubicon Estate

St. Helena

Rutherford 128 29

Beaulieu Vineyard

Frog's Leap

Caymus Vineyard

NAPA VALLEY

Far Niente, Oakville. You have to reserve in advance and the fee for the tasting and tour is steep, but the

payoff is an especially intimate winery experience. You'll taste excellent cabernet and chardonnay, then end your trip on a sweet note with a dessert wine.

0 ———— 3 miles
0 ———— 3 km

Start: Iron Horse Vineyards, Russian River Valley.
Soak up a view of vine-covered hills and Mount St. Helena while sipping a sparkling wine or pinot noir at this beautifully rustic spot.

Hartford Family Winery, Russian River Valley.
A terrific source for pinot noir and chardonnay, the stars of this valley.

Dinner and Overnight: Forestville. Splurge at the Applewood Inn and its cozy restaurant, or go all out with a stay at the Farmhouse Inn, whose Michelin-starred restaurant is one of the best in all of Sonoma.

Next Day: Westside Road, Russian River Valley.
This scenic route, which follows the river, is crowded with worthwhile wineries like Gary Farrell and Rochioli—but it's not crowded with visitors. Pinot fans will find a lot to love. Picnic at Rochioli and enjoy the lovely view.

Matanzas Creek Winery, near Santa Rosa.
End on an especially relaxed note with a walk through their lavender fields (best in June).

WINE TASTING 101

TAKE A GOOD LOOK.
Hold your glass by the stem, raise it to the light, and take a close look at the wine. Check for clarity and color. (This is easiest to do if you can hold the glass in front of a white background.) Any tinge of brown usually means that the wine is over the hill or has gone bad.

BREATHE DEEP.
1. Sniff the wine once or twice to see if you can identify any smells.

2. Swirl the wine gently in the glass. Aerating the wine this way releases more of its aromas. (It's called "volatilizing the esters," if you're trying to impress someone.)

3. Take another long sniff. You might notice that experienced wine tasters spend more time sniffing the wine than drinking it. This is because this step is where the magic happens. The number of scents you might detect is almost endless, from berries, apricots, honey, and wildflowers to leather, cedar, or even tar. Does the wine smell good to you? Do you detect any "off" flavors, like wet dog or sulfur?

AT LAST! TAKE A SIP.
1. Swirl the wine around your mouth so that it makes contact with all your taste buds and releases more of its aromas. Think about the way the wine feels in your mouth. Is it watery or rich? Is it crisp or silky? Does it have a bold flavor, or is it subtle? The weight and intensity of a wine are called its body.

2. Hold the wine in your mouth for a few seconds and see if you can identify any developing flavors. More complex wines will reveal many different flavors as you drink them.

SPIT OR SWALLOW.
The pros typically spit, since they want to preserve their palate (and sobriety!) for the wines to come, but you'll find that swallowers far outnumber the spitters in the winery tasting rooms. Whether you spit or swallow, notice the flavor that remains after the wine is gone (the finish).

Swirl

Sniff

Sip

DODGE THE CROWDS

To avoid bumping elbows in the tasting rooms, look for wineries off the main drags of Highway 29 in Napa and Highway 12 in Sonoma. The back roads of the Russian River, Dry Creek, and Alexander valleys, all in Sonoma, are excellent places to explore. In Napa, try the northern end. Also look for wineries that are open by appointment only; they tend to schedule visitors carefully to avoid a big crush at any one time.

HOW WINE IS MADE

1. CRUSHING
Harvested grapes go into a stemmer-crusher, which separates stems from fruit and crushes the grapes to release "free-run" juice.

2. PRESSING
Remaining juice is gently extracted from grapes. Usually done by pressing grapes against the walls of a tank with an inflatable bladder.

3. FERMENTING
Extracted juice (and also grape skins and pulp, when making red wine) goes into stainless-steel tanks or oak barrels to ferment. During fermentation, sugars convert to alcohol.

4. AGING
Wine is stored in stainless-steel or oak casks or barrels to develop flavors.

5. RACKING
Wine is transferred to clean barrels; sediment is removed. Wine may be filtered and fined (clarified) to improve its clarity, color, and sometimes flavor.

6. BOTTLING
Wine is bottled either at the winery or at a special facility, then stored again for bottle-aging.

19

WHAT'S AN APPELLATION?

A specific region with a particular set of grape-growing conditions, such as soil type, climate, and elevation, is called an appellation. What makes things a little confusing is that appellations, which are defined by the Alcohol and Tobacco Tax and Trade Bureau, often overlap. California is an appellation, for example, but so is the Napa Valley. Napa and Sonoma counties are each county appellations, but they, too, are divided into even smaller regions, usually called subappellations or AVAs (American Viticultural Areas). You'll hear a lot about these AVAs from the staff in the tasting rooms; they might explain, for example, why the Russian River Valley AVA is such an excellent place to grow pinot noir grapes. By law, if the label on a bottle of wine lists the name of an appellation, then at least 85% of the grapes in that wine must come from that appellation.

Wine and contemporary art find a home at di Rosa.

☎ 707/257–0101 ⊕ *www.domainecarneros.com* ✉ *Tasting $6.50–$25, tour $25* ☉ *Daily 10–6; tour daily at 11, 1, and 3.*

Fodor's Choice
★ While you're driving along the Carneros Highway on your way to Napa from San Francisco, it would be easy to zip by one of the region's best-kept secrets: **di Rosa**. Metal sculptures of sheep grazing in the grass mark the entrance to this sprawling, art-stuffed property. Thousands of 20th-century artworks by hundreds of Northern California artists crop up everywhere—in galleries, in the former di Rosa residence, on every lawn, in every courtyard, and even on the lake. Some of the works were commissioned especially for the preserve, such as Paul Kos's meditative *Chartres Bleu*, a video installation in a chapel-like setting that replicates a stained-glass window of the cathedral in Chartres, France. If you stop by without a reservation, you'll only gain access to the Gatehouse Gallery, where there's a small collection of riotously colorful figurative and abstract sculpture and painting. ■ TIP→ To see the rest of the property and artwork, you'll have to sign up for one of the various tours of the grounds (from 1 to 2½ hours). Reservations for the tours are recommended, but they can sometimes accommodate walk-ins. ✉ *5200 Sonoma Hwy./Carneros Hwy., Napa* ☎ *707/226–5991* ⊕ *www.dirosaart.org* ✉ *Free, tour $10–$15* ☉ *Wed.–Fri. 9:30–3; Sat. by reservation; call for tour times.*

With its modern, minimalist look in the tasting room, which is dug into a Carneros hilltop, and contemporary sculptures and fountains on the property, **Artesa Vineyards & Winery** is a far cry from the many faux French châteaus and rustic Italian-style villas in the region. Although the Spanish owners once made only sparkling wines, now they produce primarily still wines, mostly chardonnay and pinot noir, but also cabernet sauvignon and a smattering of other limited-release wines such as syrah and albariño. Call ahead to reserve a spot on one of the specialty tours, such as a wine-and-cheese pairing or the walk through the vineyard ($40). ⊠ *1345 Henry Rd., north off Old Sonoma Rd. and Dealy La., Napa* ☎ *707/224–1668* ⊕ *www.artesawinery.com* 🖼 *Tasting $10–$15, tour $20* ⊙ *Daily 10–5; tour daily at 11 and 2.*

Though it's not terribly large, **Oxbow Public Market,** a collection of about 20 small shops, wine bars, and artisanal food producers, is a fun place to begin your introduction to the wealth of food and wine available in the Napa Valley. Swoon over the decadent charcuterie at the Fatted Calf, slurp down some oysters on the half shell at Hog Island Oyster Company, sample a large variety of local olive oils at the Olive Press, or get a whiff of the hard-to-find seasonings at the Whole Spice Company before sitting down to a glass of wine at one of the two wine bars. A branch of the retro fast-food joint Gott's Roadside Tray Gourmet tempts those who prefer hamburgers to duck-liver mousse. ⊠ *610 and 644 1st St., Napa* ☎ *No phone* ⊕ *www.oxbowpublicmarket.com* 🖼 *Free* ⊙ *Generally weekdays 9–7, weekends 10–6, though hrs of some merchants vary.*

Luna Vineyards was established in 1995 by veterans of the Napa wine industry intent on making less-conventional wines, particularly Italian varieties such as sangiovese and pinot grigio. Though these days you're just as likely to taste a merlot or a cabernet blend, it's still well worth visiting its Tuscan-style tasting room with a coffered ceiling, especially for a nip of late-harvest pinto grigio dessert wine called Mille Baci ("a thousand kisses" in Italian). ⊠ *2921 Silverado Trail, Napa* ☎ *707/255–5862* ⊕ *www.lunavineyards.com* 🖼 *Tasting $15–$25* ⊙ *Sun.–Thurs. 10–5, Fri. and Sat. 10–6.*

Austere **Clos du Val** doesn't seduce you with dramatic architecture or lush grounds, but it doesn't have to: the wines, crafted by winemaker John Clews, have a wide following, especially among those who are patient enough to cellar the wines for a number of years. Though Clews's team makes great pinot noir and chardonnay (grown in the nearby Carneros region), the real claim to fame is the intense reserve cabernet, made with fruit from the Stags Leap District. The few picnic tables fill up early on summer weekends, and anyone is welcome to try a hand at the boccie-style French game of pétanque. ⊠ *5330 Silverado Trail, Napa* ☎ *707/259–2200* ⊕ *www.closduval.com* 🖼 *Tasting $10–$20* ⊙ *Daily 10–5; tour by appointment.*

Fodor'sChoice ★ The **Hess Collection Winery and Vineyards** is a delightful discovery on Mt. Veeder, 9 mi northwest of the city of Napa. (Don't give up; the road leading to the winery is long and winding.) The simple limestone structure, rustic from the outside but modern and airy within, contains Swiss owner Donald Hess's personal art collection, including mostly large-scale works by such contemporary European and American artists as Robert Motherwell, Andy Goldsworthy, and Frank Stella. Cabernet sauvignon is the real strength here, though Hess also produces some fine chardonnays. Self-guided tours of the art collection and guided tours

19

Napa Valley

Climbing ivy and lily pads decorate the Hess Collection's rustic exterior.

of the winery's production facilities are both free. ✉ *4411 Redwood Rd., west of Rte. 29, Napa* ☎ *707/255–1144* ⊕ *www.hesscollection. com* ✉ *Tasting $10–$30* ☉ *Daily 10–5:30; guided tours daily, hourly 10:30–3:30.*

WHERE TO EAT AND STAY

$$$ ✕ **Angèle.** An 1890s boathouse with a vaulted wood-beam ceiling sets
FRENCH the scene for romance at this cozy French bistro. Though the style is casual—tables are close together, and the warm, crusty bread is plunked right down on the paper-top tables—the food is always well executed. Look for classic French dishes like beef bourguignonne, a rib-eye steak with red wine sauce and french fries, or a starter of *ris de veau* (veal sweetbreads). In fair weather, ask for one of the charming outdoor tables. ✉ *540 Main St.* ☎ *707/252–8115* ⊕ *www.angelerestaurant.com* ▭ *AE, D, DC, MC, V.*

$ ✕ **BarBersQ.** Hardly a down-home ramshackle barbecue shack, this
AMERICAN temple to meat in the middle of a shopping center has a clean, modern aesthetic, with the black-and-white photos on the wall and brushed aluminum chairs. The menu of barbecue favorites includes a half or full rack of smoked baby back ribs and a Memphis-style pulled pork sandwich, all served with your choice of three different sauces. The supremely juicy fried chicken, made with free-range chicken and served with mashed potatoes and vinegary collard greens, is also popular. If you can save any room, the root-beer float or sweet potato–pecan pie is a fitting end to a homey meal. Outside seating (on a patio facing the parking lot) is available on fair days. ✉ *3900D Bel Aire Plaza* ☎ *707/224–6600* ⊕ *www.barbersqu.com* ▭ *AE, MC, V.*

Where to Eat and Stay in Napa Valley

KEY
- **1** Restaurants
- **1** Hotels

$$$
ITALIAN
★
✕ **Bistro Don Giovanni.** At this lively bistro, the Cal-Italian food is simultaneously inventive and comforting: an excellent fritto misto of onions, fennel, calamari, and plump rock shrimp; risotto with scallops and wild mushrooms; pizza with caramelized onions and Gorgonzola; and tender braised lamb on a bed on fried polenta. Dishes roasted in the wood-burning oven are a specialty. Children are unusually welcome here, catered to with crayons and paper-topped tables and a menu with items like pizza topped with cheese, french fries, and "no green stuff." Fodors.com Forum users suggest snagging a table on the covered patio for a "more intimate and quiet" experience. ⊠ *4110 Howard La./Rte. 29* ☎ *707/224–3300* ⊕ *www.bistrodongiovanni.com* ⊟ *AE, D, DC, MC, V.*

$$
AMERICAN
★
✕ **Bounty Hunter.** A triple threat, Bounty Hunter is a wine store, wine bar, and restaurant in one. You can stop by for just a glass of wine from their impressive list—a frequently changing list with 40 available by the glass in both 2- and 5-ounce pours, and 400 by the bottle—but it's best to come with an appetite. A miniscule kitchen means the menu is also small, but every dish is a standout, including the pulled pork and beef brisket sandwiches served with three types of barbecue sauce, the signature beer-can chicken, and meltingly tender St. Louis–style ribs. The space is whimsically rustic, with stuffed game trophies mounted on the wall and leather saddles standing in for seats at a couple of tables. ■ TIP→ It's open until midnight on Friday and Saturday, making it a popular spot among locals for a late-night bite. At this writing, plans to expand into the space next door were in the works. ⊠ *975 1st St.* ☎ *707/226–3976* ⊕ *www.bountyhunterwinebar.com* ⟝ *Reservations not accepted* ⊟ *AE, MC, V.*

$$$
SPANISH
✕ **ZuZu.** Ocher-color walls, a weathered wood bar, a faded tile floor, and hammered-tin ceiling panels set the scene for a menu composed almost entirely of tapas. These little dishes, so perfect for sharing, and Latin jazz on the stereo help make this place a popular spot for festive get-togethers. Diners down *cava* (Spanish sparkling wine) or sangria with dishes such as white anchovies with endive, ratatouille, and salt cod with garlic croutons. Reservations aren't accepted, so expect a wait on weekends, when local young adults flood the zone. The *bocadillos* (Spanish-style sandwiches) and empanadas available at lunch make it an inexpensive stop for a midday snack. ⊠ *829 Main St.* ☎ *707/224–8555* ⊕ *www.zuzunapa.com* ⟝ *Reservations not accepted* ⊟ *AE, MC, V* ⊗ *No lunch weekends.*

$–$$
🛏 **Blackbird Inn.** Arts and Crafts style infuses this 1905 building, from the lobby's enormous fieldstone fireplace to the lamps that cast a warm glow over the impressive wooden staircase. The style is continued in the attractive guest rooms, with sturdy turn-of-the-20th-century oak beds and matching night tables, which nonetheless are updated with spacious, modern bathrooms, most with spa bathtubs. The inn is within walking distance of Napa's historic, restaurant-rich downtown area. It tends to book up quickly, so reserve well in advance. **Pros:** gorgeous architecture and period furnishings; convenient to downtown Napa; free DVD library. **Cons:** must be booked well in advance; some rooms are on the small side. ⊠ *1755 1st St.* ☎ *707/226–2450 or 888/567–9811*

19

⊕ *www.blackbirdinnnapa.com* ↩ *8 rooms* ⟂ *In-room: a/c, DVD, Wi-Fi. In-hotel: some pets allowed (fee)* ⊟ *AE, D, DC, MC, V* ⊙| *CP.*

$$$$ ⬚ **Carneros Inn.** Freestanding board-and-batten cottages with rocking
Fodor's Choice   chairs on each porch are simultaneously rustic and chic at this luxuri-
★   ous property. Inside, each cottage is flooded with natural light but still
manages to maintain privacy, with windows and French doors leading to a private garden. (The suites are actually two-cottage clusters.)
Wood-burning fireplaces, ethereal beds topped with Italian linens and
pristine white down comforters, and spacious bathrooms with heated
slate floors and large indoor-outdoor showers may make it difficult to
summon the will to leave the cottage and enjoy the hilltop infinity swimming pool and hot tub. The Hilltop Dining Room, with views of the
neighboring vineyards, is open to guests only for breakfast and lunch,
but Boon Fly Cafe and FARM, their public restaurants, are popular
with visitors throughout the Wine Country. **Pros:** cottages have lots
of privacy; beautiful views from the hilltop pool and hot tub; heaters on each private patio encourage lounging outside in the evening.
Cons: a long drive from destinations up-valley; smallish rooms with limited seating options. ⊠ *4048 Sonoma Hwy.* ☎ *707/299–4900* ⊕ *www.
thecarnerosinn.com* ↩ *76 cottages, 10 suites* ⟂ *In-room: a/c, refrigerator, DVD, Internet. In-hotel: 3 restaurants, room service, bar, pool,
gym, spa, laundry service* ⊟ *AE, D, DC, MC, V.*

$$$$ ⬚ **Milliken Creek Inn.** Wine and cheese at sunset set a romantic mood in
the intimate lobby, with its terrace overlooking the Napa River and a
lush lawn. The chic rooms take a page from the stylebook of British-
colonial Asia, with a khaki-and-cream color scheme and gauzy canopies
over the beds in some rooms, alongside hydrotherapy spa tubs and some
of the fluffiest beds in the Wine Country. All but one have a gas-burning
fireplace. A tiny deck overlooking the river is the spot for massages and
private yoga classes. In the serene spa, all the treatment rooms, including one used for popular couple's treatments, have river views. **Pros:**
soft-as-clouds beds; serene hotel-guests-only spa; breakfast delivered
to your room (or wherever you'd like to eat on the grounds); gratuities
are not accepted (except at the spa). **Cons:** expensive; road noise can be
heard from the admittedly beautiful outdoor areas. ⊠ *1815 Silverado
Trail* ☎ *707/255–1197 or 800/835–6112* ⊕ *www.millikencreekinn.com*
↩ *12 rooms* ⟂ *In-room: a/c, safe, refrigerator, DVD, Wi-Fi. In-hotel:
spa, no kids under 18* ⊟ *AE, D, DC, MC, V* ⊙| *CP.*

$$–$$$ ⬚ **Napa River Inn.** Almost everything's close here: this waterfront inn
is part of a complex of restaurants, shops, a gallery, and a spa, all
within easy walking distance of downtown Napa. Guest rooms spread
through three neighboring buildings. Those in the 1884 Hatt Building,
in Victorian style, are arguably the most romantic, with deep-red walls,
original architectural details such as maple hardwood floors, and old-
fashioned slipper tubs. Brighter colors dominate in the rooms of the
Plaza and Embarcadero buildings; many of the rooms have river views.
Baked goods from the neighboring bakery are delivered to your door for
breakfast. **Pros:** a pedestrian walkway connects the hotel to downtown
Napa; unusual pet-friendly policy; wide range of room sizes and prices.
Cons: river views could be more scenic; some rooms get noise from

nearby restaurants. ✉ *500 Main St.* ☎ *707/251–8500 or 877/251–8500* ⊕ *www.napariverinn.com* ⇆ *65 rooms, 1 suite* ⚒ *In-room: a/c, safe, refrigerator, DVD (some), Wi-Fi. In-hotel: 4 restaurants, bar, gym, spa, bicycles, laundry service, Internet terminal, some pets allowed (fee)* ☰ *AE, D, DC, MC, V* ⑩ *CP.*

$$$–$$$$ ⚏ **Westin Verasa.** Across the street from the Wine Train depot and just behind the Oxbow Public Market is this spacious hotel-condo complex, which considerably expanded the city's once-limited options for full-service hotels when it opened in 2008. Although its style is hardly cutting-edge, its look is sophisticated and soothing, all pristine white bedding and furniture in warm earth tones. Gadgets like Xbox 360s, iPod docking stations, and 32-inch flat-screen televisions are a convenient perk for the technologically inclined, while the heated saltwater pool and hot tub and boccie court are there for those who want to unplug. The attached restaurant, Ken Frank's acclaimed La Toque, is one of the best in town. It's open for dinner only, but a more casual café and wine bar is also open for breakfast and lunch. **Pros:** centrally located in downtown Napa; well-equipped kitchenettes; spacious double-headed showers. **Cons:** $20 "amenities fee" charged in addition to room rate. ✉ *1314 Mckinstry St.* ☎ *707/257–1800* ⊕ *www.westin.com/napa* ⇆ *130 rooms, 50 suites* ⚒ *In-room: a/c, safe, kitchen (some), refrigerator (some), DVD, Internet, Wi-Fi. In-hotel: 2 restaurants, room service, bar, pool, gym, laundry service, some pets allowed.* ☰ *AE, D, DC, MC, V.*

MAKING TRACKS IN NAPA

Turn the driving over to someone else—a train conductor. The **Napa Valley Wine Train** (✉ *1275 McKinstry St.* ☎ *707/253–2111 or 800/427–4124* ⊕ *www.winetrain. com*) runs a scenic route between Napa and St. Helena with several restored 1915–17 Pullman railroad cars. The ride often includes a meal, such as brunch or dinner. While it's no bargain (starting at around $90 for lunch, $100 for dinner) and can feel a bit hokey, the train gives you a chance to enjoy the vineyard views without any driving worries.

NIGHTLIFE AND THE ARTS

The interior of the 1879 Italianate Victorian **Napa Valley Opera House** isn't quite as majestic as the facade, but the intimate 500-seat venue is still an excellent place to see all sorts of performances, from Pat Metheny and Mandy Patinkin to various dance and theater companies and, yes, even the occasional opera. ✉ *1030 Main St.* ☎ *707/226–7372* ⊕ *www.napavalleyoperahouse.org.*

SPORTS AND THE OUTDOORS

BICYCLING Thanks to the scenic country roads that wind through the region, bicycling is a practically perfect way to get around the Wine Country. And whether you're interested in an easy spin to a few wineries or a strenuous haul up a mountainside, there's a way to make it happen. ▪TIP→ There are almost no designated bike lanes in the Wine Country, though, so be sure to pay attention to traffic.

19

Napa Valley Bike Tours (✉ *6488 Washington St., Yountville* ☎ *707/944–2953*) will deliver the bikes, which go for $30 to $70 a day, to many hotels in the Napa Valley if you're renting at least two bikes for a full day. One-day guided winery tours are $149.

YOUNTVILLE

13 mi north of the town of Napa on Rte. 29.

These days Yountville is something like Disneyland for food-lovers. It all started with Thomas Keller's French Laundry, one of the best restaurants in the United States. Now Keller is also behind two more casual restaurants a few blocks from his mother ship—and that's only the tip of the iceberg. You could stay here for a week and not exhaust all the options in this tiny town with a big culinary reputation.

Yountville is full of small inns and high-end hotels that cater to those who prefer to walk (not drive) after an extravagant meal. It's also well located for excursions to many big-name Napa wineries, especially those in the Stags Leap District, where big, bold cabernet sauvignons helped put the Napa Valley on the wine-making map.

In between bouts of eating and drinking, you might stop by **V Marketplace** (✉ *6525 Washington St.* ☎ *707/944–2451*). The vine-covered brick complex, which once housed a winery, livery stable, and distillery, contains a smattering of clothing boutiques, art galleries, and gift stores. NapaStyle, a large store, deli, and wine bar, sells cookbooks, luxury food items, and kitchenware, as well as an assortment of prepared foods perfect for picnics. The complex's signature restaurant, Bottega, features the food of celebrity chef Michael Chiarello.

Although it's not worth a long detour, if you need a break from wine tasting you can visit the **Napa Valley Museum** (✉ *55 Presidents Circle* ☎ *707/944–0500* ⊕ *www.napavalleymuseum.org* ▣ *$4.50* �9 *Wed.–Mon. 10–5*) next to Domaine Chandon on the grounds of the town's Veterans Home. Downstairs you'll find exhibits on local history, from the Wappo Indians through the pioneer period to modern wine making, while upstairs are rotating art exhibits.

French-owned **Domaine Chandon** claims one of Yountville's prime pieces of real estate, on a knoll west of downtown where whimsical sculptures sprout out of the lawn and ancient oaks shade the winery. Basic tours of the sleek, modern facilities are available for $12 (not including a tasting), but other tours ($30 each), which focusing on various topics (food-and-wine pairing or pinot production, for example), end with a seated tasting. The top-quality sparklers are made using the laborious *méthode champenoise*. To complete the experience, you can order hors d'oeuvres to accompany the wines in the tasting room, which can be ordered either by tasting flights or by the glass. Although Chandon is best known for its bubblies, still wines like their chardonnay, pinot noir, and roséare also worth a try. ✉ *1 California Dr., west of Rte. 29* ☎ *707/944–2280* ⊕ *www.chandon.com* ▣ *Tasting $5.50–$25 by the glass, $16–$22 by the flight* �9 *Daily 10–6; tours daily at 11, 1, and 3.*

CLOSE UP

Winespeak

Like any activity, wine making and wine tasting have specialized vocabularies, and most of the terms are actually quite helpful, once you have them down. Here are some core terms to know:

American Viticultural Area (AVA). More commonly termed an "appellation," this is a region with unique soil, climate, and other grape-growing conditions. When a label lists an appellation—Napa Valley or Mt. Veeder, for example—at least 75% of the grapes used to make the wine must come from that region.

Aroma and bouquet. Aroma is the fruit-derived scent of young wine. It diminishes with fermentation and becomes a more complex **bouquet** as the wine ages.

Corked. Describes wine that is flawed by the musty, wet-cardboard flavor imparted by cork mold.

Estate bottled. A wine entirely made by one winery at a single facility. The grapes must come from the winery's own vineyards within the same appellation (which must be printed on the label).

Horizontal tasting. A tasting of several different wines of the same vintage.

Library wine. An older vintage that the winery has put aside to sell at a later date.

Méthode champenoise. The traditional, time-consuming method of making sparkling wines that are fermented in individual bottles.

Oaky. A vanilla-woody flavor that develops when wine is aged in oak barrels. Too much overpowers the other flavors.

Reserve wine. Fuzzy term applied by vintners to indicate that a wine is better in some way (through aging, source of the grapes, etc.) than others from their winery.

Table wine. Any wine that has at least 7% but not more than 14% alcohol by volume. The term doesn't necessarily imply anything about the wine's quality or price—both super-premium and jug wines can be labeled as table wine.

Tannins. These natural grape compounds produce a sensation of drying or astringency in the mouth and throat.

Terroir. French for "soil." Typically used to describe the soil and climate conditions that influence the quality and characteristics of grapes and wine.

Varietal. A wine that takes its name from the grape variety from which it is predominantly made. California wines that qualify are almost always labeled with the variety of the source grape.

Vertical tasting. A tasting of several wines of different vintages.

Vinification. Wine making, the process by which grapes are made into wine.

Vintage. The grape harvest of a given year, and the year in which the grapes are harvested. A vintage date on a bottle indicates the year in which the grapes were harvested rather than the year in which the wine was bottled.

Viticulture. The cultivation of grapes.

19

It was the 1973 cabernet sauvignon produced by **Stag's Leap Wine Cellars** that put the winery—and the California wine industry—on the map by placing first in the famous Paris tasting of 1976. A visit to the winery is a no-frills affair; visitors in the tasting room are clearly serious about tasting wine and aren't interested in distractions like a gift shop. It costs $30 to taste the top-of-the-line wines, including their limited-production estate-grown cabernets, a few of which sell for well over $100. If you're interested in more modestly priced wines, try the $15 tasting, which usually includes a sauvignon blanc, chardonnay, merlot, and cabernet. ⊠ *5766 Silverado Trail, Napa* ☎ *707/265–2441* ⊕ *www.cask23.com* ✉ *Tasting $15–$30, tour $40* ☉ *Daily 10–4:30; tour by appointment.*

Robert Sinskey Vineyards makes well-regarded cabernet blends from their all-organic, certified biodynamic vineyards, as well as a dry, refreshing pinot gris, gewürztraminer, Riesling, and pinot blanc blend. However, it's best known for its intense, brambly pinot noirs, grown in the cooler Carneros District, where the grape thrives. The influence of Robert's wife, Maria Helm Sinskey—a chef and cookbook author—is evident during the tastings, which come with a few bites of food paired with each wine (her books and other culinary items are also available in the gift shop, next to the open kitchen). But for the best sense of how Sinskey wines pair with food, reserve a spot on the culinary tour, which ends with local cheeses and charcuterie served with the wines. ⊠ *6320 Silverado Trail, Napa* ☎ *707/944–9090* ⊕ *www.robertsinskey.com* ✉ *Tasting $25, tour $30–$50* ☉ *Daily 10–4:30; tour by appointment.*

WHERE TO EAT AND STAY

$$$$
AMERICAN
Fodor's Choice
★

✕ **Ad Hoc.** When superstar chef Thomas Keller opened this relatively casual spot in 2006, he meant to run it for only six months until he opened a burger joint in the same space—but locals were so charmed by the homey food that they clamored for the stopgap to stay. Now a single, seasonal fixed-price menu ($49) is served nightly, with a slightly less expensive menu but equally hearty meal served for Sunday brunch. The selection might include a juicy pork loin and buttery polenta, served family style, or a delicate *panna cotta* with a citrus glaze. The dining room is warmly low-key, with zinc-top tables, wine served in tumblers, and rock and jazz on the stereo. If you just can't wait to know what's going be served before you visit, you can call a day in advance for the menu. ⊠ *6476 Washington St.* ☎ *707/944–2487* ⊕ *www.adhocrestaurant.com* ▭ *AE, MC, V* ☉ *No lunch Mon.–Sat.; no dinner Tues. and Wed.*

$$$
ITALIAN
Fodor's Choice
★

✕ **Bottega.** At this lively trattoria, the menu is simultaneously soulful and inventive, transforming local ingredients into regional Italian dishes with a twist. The antipasti in particular shine: you can order olives grown on chef Michael Chiarello's own property in St. Helena, house-made charcuterie, or a creamy *burrata,* mozzarella cheese wrapped around a creamy center, which is served with meaty mushrooms and topped with beads of "caviar" made from balsamic vinegar. Potato gnocchi might be served with duck and a chestnut ragu, and hearty main courses like braised short ribs may come on a bed of spinach prepared with preserved lemons. The vibe is more festival than formal, with exposed brick walls, an open kitchen, and paper-topped tables, but service is spot on, and the reasonably priced wine list offers lots of interesting choices from both Italy and California. ⊠ *6525 Washington St.* ☎ *707/945–1050* ⊕ *www.botteganapavalley.com* ▤ *AE, MC, V* ☾ *No lunch Mon.*

$$$
FRENCH

✕ **Bouchon.** The team that brought French Laundry to its current pinnacle is also behind this place, where everything—the lively and crowded zinc bar, the elbow-to-elbow seating, the traditional French onion soup—could have come straight from a Parisian bistro. Roast chicken with mustard greens and fingerling potatoes and steamed mussels served with crispy, addictive *frites* (french fries) are among the hearty dishes served in the high-ceilinged room. ■ TIP➔ Late-night meals from a limited menu are served until 12:30 AM—a rarity in the Wine Country, where it's often difficult to find a place to eat after 10. ⊠ *6534 Washington St.* ☎ *707/944–8037* ⊕ *www.bouchonbistro.com* ▤ *AE, MC, V.*

$$$
AMERICAN

✕ **Étoile.** Housed at Domaine Chandon, this quietly elegant stunner seems built for romance, with delicate orchids on each table and views of the beautiful wooded winery grounds from the large windows. After a few years of being off the radar of many local critics, the restaurant has gotten more attention lately under the young chef Perry Hoffman, who turns out sophisticated California cuisine. Starters like poached lobster with radishes, Asian pear, and pearl barley play with a variety of textures, and luxe ingredients like shavings of black truffle dress up a perfectly cooked beef tenderloin. Four- and six-course tasting menus can be ordered with or without wine pairings. The wine list naturally features plenty of Domaine Chandon sparklers, but it's strong in wines from throughout California as well. ⊠ *1 California Dr.* ☎ *888/242–6366* ⊕ *www.chandon.com/etoile-restaurant* ▤ *AE, D, MC, V* ☾ *Closed Tues. and Wed. and Jan.*

$$$$
AMERICAN
Fodor's Choice
★

✕ **French Laundry.** An old stone building laced with ivy houses the most acclaimed restaurant in Napa Valley—and, indeed, one of the most highly regarded in the country. The restaurant's two prix-fixe menus (both $240), one of which is vegetarian, vary, but "oysters and pearls," a silky dish of pearl tapioca with oysters and white sturgeon caviar, is a signature starter. Some courses rely on luxe ingredients like foie gras, while others take humble foods like fava beans and elevate them to art. Reservations at French Laundry are hard-won, and not accepted more than two months in advance. ■ TIP➔ Call two months ahead to the day at 10 AM on the dot. Didn't get a reservation? Call on the day you'd like to dine here to be considered if there's a cancellation. ⊠ *6640 Washington St.* ☎ *707/944–2380* ⌂ *Reservations essential, jacket required* ⊕ *www.frenchlaundry.com* ▤ *AE, MC, V* ☾ *Closed 1st 2 or 3 wks in Jan. No lunch Mon.–Thurs.*

19

$$
AMERICAN

✕ **Mustards Grill.** There's not an ounce of pretension at Cindy Pawlcyn's longtime Napa favorite, despite the fact that it's filled every day and night with fans of her hearty cuisine. The menu mixes updated renditions of traditional American dishes, such as baby back pork ribs and a lemon-lime tart piled high with browned meringue, with innovative choices such as sweet corn tamales with tomatillo-avocado salsa and pumpkin seeds. A black-and-white marble tile floor and upbeat artwork set a scene that one Fodors.com reader describes as "pure fun, if not fancy." ⊠ *7399 St. Helena Hwy./Rte. 29, 1 mi north of town* ☎ *707/944–2424* ⊕ *www.mustardsgrill.com* ≜ *Reservations essential* ⊟ *AE, D, DC, MC, V.*

$$$$ 🏨 **Bardessono.** Although Bardessono bills itself as the "greenest luxury hotel in America," there's nothing spartan about its large, spare rooms, arranged around four landscaped courtyards, which have luxurious organic white bedding, gas fireplaces, and huge bathrooms with walnut floors. It's got all the high-tech touches you'd expect for a property that opened in 2009—speakers for your iPhone, a flat-panel TV, and fancy spa tubs—and a few you wouldn't, like motion sensors that detect when you're gone and adjust the blinds for energy efficiency. Service is smooth, from the valet who takes your car to those who staff the 75-foot-long rooftop lap pool area April through October, serving food and drinks to those lounging in the cabanas. At the hotel's restaurant, chef Sean O'Toole uses largely local ingredients (some grown by the hotel itself) to concoct a seasonal menu of California fare with an adventurous twist. **Pros:** large rooftop lap pool; exciting restaurant on-site; polished service. **Cons:** expensive. ⊠ *6526 Yount St.* ☎ *707/204–6000* ⊕ *www. bardessono.com* ⇥ *50 rooms, 12 suites* ⚷ *In-room: a/c, safe, Internet, Wi-Fi. In-hotel: restaurant, room service, bar, pool, spa, bicycles, laundry service, some pets allowed (fee)* ⊟ *AE, D, DC, MC, V.*

$$$–$$$$ 🏨 **Hotel Luca.** Although this 20-room newcomer to Yountville just opened in December 2009, the property embodies a rustic Tuscan style through and through, with dark wood furniture and soothing decor in brown and sage. Rooms are clustered around a courtyard, which is warmed by a fireplace when the weather demands it. Uncommonly spacious bathrooms with large tubs and separate showers, warmed by radiant floor heating, invite lingering in the fluffy robes and slippers. A wide variety of spa services are available in the small spa or in your room. The hotel's excellent restaurant, Cantinetta Piero, serves soul-warming Tuscan fare, such as pastas, house-made preserved meats, and thin-crust pizzas from a wood-burning oven. **Pros:** extremely comfortable beds; attentive service; breakfast, included in rates, is served in the restaurant or delivered to your room. **Cons:** rooms are soundproofed, but outdoor areas get some traffic noise. ⊠ *6774 Washington St.* ☎ *707/944–8080* ⊕ *www.hotellucanapa.com* ⇥ *20 rooms* ⚷ *In-room: a/c, refrigerator, safe, Wi-Fi. In-hotel: restaurant, room service, bar, pool, spa, gym, laundry service* ⊟ *AE, D, MC, V.* �🍴 *BP.*

$–$$ 🏨 **Maison Fleurie.** If you'd like to be within easy walking distance of most
★   of Yountville's best restaurants, and possibly score a great bargain, look into this casual, comfortable inn. Rooms share a French country style (picture toile bedspreads, wooden armoires, and trompe-l'oeil paintings on the walls) but vary dramatically in size and amenities. The largest have a private entrance, deck, fireplace, and jetted bathtub big enough for two. ■ TIP→ For a much lower rate, however, you can get one of the tiny but well-kept rooms with a small shower but no bathtub—and save for a French Laundry meal instead. **Pros:** smallest rooms are some of the most affordable in town; free bike rental; refrigerator stocked with free soda. **Cons:** breakfast room can be crowded at peak times; bedding could be

nicer. ⊠ *6529 Yount St.* ☎ *800/788–0369* ⊕ *www.maisonfleurienapa. com* ⤴ *13 rooms* ᐦ *In-room: a/c, refrigerator (some), DVD (some), no TV (some), Wi-Fi. In-hotel: pool, bicycles* ⊟ *AE, D, MC, V* ⦿ *CP.*

¢ ⛭ **Napa Valley Railway Inn.** Budget-minded travelers and those with kids appreciate these basic accommodations just steps away from most of Yountville's best restaurants. Actual railcars, more than a hundred years old, house nine long, narrow rooms that have a bit more charm than your average motel. Most have armoires or other turn-of-the-20th-century furniture, as well as small flat-panel TVs and sparkling-clean bathrooms. A coffee shop in an adjacent railcar sells beverages and pastries. **Pros:** central Yountville location; guests have access to adjacent gym. **Cons:** minimal service, since the office is often unstaffed; rooms on the parking-lot side get some noise. ⊠ *6523 Washington St.* ☎ *707/944–2000* ⊕ *www.napavalleyrailwayinn.com* ⤴ *9 rooms* ᐦ *In-room: no phone, a/c, refrigerator, Wi-Fi* ⊟ *AE, MC, V.*

$$$–$$$$ ⛭ **Villagio Inn & Spa.** The luxury here is quiet and refined, not flashy.
★ Stroll past the fountains and clusters of low buildings to reach the pool, where automated misters cool the sunbathers. Streamlined furnishings, subdued color schemes, and high ceilings enhance a sense of spaciousness in the guest rooms. Each room also has a fireplace and, beyond louvered doors, a balcony or patio. The spa has huge "suites" big enough for small groups, as well as individual treatment rooms, spread out over 13,000 square feet. Rates include afternoon tea, a bottle of wine, and a generous buffet breakfast—and as the hotel is near the town center, you'll be right next to all those outstanding restaurants. **Pros:** amazing buffet breakfast; no extra charge for hotel guests to use the spa facilities; steps away from Yountville's best restaurants. **Cons:** can be bustling with large groups; you can hear the highway from many of the room's balconies or patios. ⊠ *6481 Washington St.* ☎ *707/944–8877 or 800/351–1133* ⊕ *www.villagio.com* ⤴ *86 rooms, 26 suites* ᐦ *In-room: a/c, refrigerator, DVD, Internet, Wi-Fi. In-hotel: room service, bar, tennis courts, pool, spa, bicycles, laundry service,* ⊟ *AE, D, DC, MC, V* ⦿ *CP.*

$$$–$$$$ ⛭ **Vintage Inn.** Rooms in this lavish inn are housed in two-story villas scattered around a lush, landscaped 3½-acre property. French fabrics and plump upholstered chairs outfit the spacious, airy guest rooms. Those on the second floor have vaulted beam ceilings, and all have a private patio or balcony, a fireplace, and a whirlpool tub in the bathroom. Some private patios have vineyard views. Rates include a bottle of wine, a buffet breakfast, and afternoon tea and scones. **Pros:** spacious bathrooms with spa tubs; lavish breakfast buffet; luscious bedding. **Cons:** some exterior rooms get highway noise; pool area is smaller than the one at its sister property, the Villagio Inn & Spa. ⊠ *6541 Washington St.* ☎ *707/944–1112 or 800/351–1133* ⊕ *www.vintageinn.com* ⤴ *68 rooms, 12 suites* ᐦ *In-room: a/c, refrigerator, DVD, Internet, Wi-Fi. In-hotel: room service, bar, tennis courts, pool, bicycles, laundry service, some pets allowed (fee)* ⊟ *AE, D, DC, MC, V* ⦿ *CP.*

19

OAKVILLE

2 mi west of Yountville on Rte. 29.

There are three reasons to visit the town of Oakville: its gourmet grocery store; its scenic mountain road; and its magnificent, highly exclusive wineries.

The **Oakville Grocery** (⊠ *7856 St. Helena Hwy./Rte. 29* ☎ *707/944–8802*), built in 1881 as a general store, now carries a surprisingly wide range of unusual and chichi groceries and prepared foods. Unbearable crowds pack the narrow aisles on weekends, but it's still a fine place to sit on a bench out front and sip an espresso between winery visits.

Along the mountain range that divides Napa and Sonoma, the **Oakville Grade** (⊠ *West of Rte. 29*) is a twisting half-hour route with breathtaking views of both valleys. Although the surface of the road is good, it can be difficult to negotiate at night, and the continual curves mean that it's not ideal for those who suffer from motion sickness.

The combined venture of the late California winemaker Robert Mondavi and the late French baron Philippe de Rothschild, **Opus One** produces only one wine: a big, inky Bordeaux blend that was the first of Napa's ultra-premium wines, fetching unheard-of prices before it was overtaken by cult wines like Screaming Eagle. The winery's futuristic limestone-clad structure, built into the hillside, seems to be pushing itself out of the earth. Although the tour, which focuses on why it costs so much to produce this exceptional wine, can come off as "stuffy" (in the words of one Fodors.com reader), the facilities are undoubtedly impressive, with gilded mirrors, exotic orchids, and a large semicircular cellar modeled on the Château Mouton Rothschild winery in France. You can also taste the current vintage without the tour ($30), as long as you've called ahead for a reservation. ■TIP➔ Take your glass up to the rooftop terrace if you want to appreciate the views out over the vineyards. ⊠ *7900 St. Helena Hwy./Rte. 29* ☎ *707/944–9442* ⊕ *www.opusonewinery.com* ☞ *Tour $35* ☉ *Daily 10–4; tasting and tour by appointment.*

The arch at the center of the sprawling Mission-style building at **Robert Mondavi** perfectly frames the lawn and the vineyard behind, inviting a stroll under the lovely arcades. If you've never been on a winery tour before, the comprehensive 70- to 90-minute tour ($25), followed by a seated tasting, is a good way to learn about enology, as well as the late Robert Mondavi's role in California wine making (shorter tours are also available). You can also head straight for one of the two tasting rooms. Serious wine lovers should definitely consider springing for the $30 reserve-room tasting, where you can enjoy four tastes of Mondavi's top-of-the-line wines, including both the current vintage and several previous vintages of the reserve cabernet that cemented the winery's reputation. Concerts, mostly jazz and R&B, take place in summer on the lawn; call ahead for tickets. ⊠ *7801 St. Helena Hwy./Rte. 29* ☎ *888/766–6328* ⊕ *www.robertmondaviwinery.com* ☞ *Tasting $15–$30, tour $15–$50* ☉ *Daily 10–5; tour times vary.*

Fodor's Choice   Though the fee for the combined tour and tasting is at the high end, **Far**
★   **Niente** is especially worth visiting if you're tired of elbowing your way
through crowded tasting rooms and are looking for a more personal
experience. Here you're welcomed by name and treated to a glimpse
of one of the most beautiful Napa properties. Small groups are shep-
herded through the historic 1885 stone winery, including some of the
40,000 square feet of caves, for a lesson on the labor-intensive method
for making Far Niente's two wines, a cabernet blend and a chardonnay.
(The latter is made without undergoing malolactic fermentation, so it
doesn't have that buttery taste that's characteristic of many California
chards.) The next stop is the Carriage House, where you can see the
founder's gleaming collection of classic cars. The tour ends with a seated
tasting of wines and cheeses, capped by a sip of the spectacular Dolce,
a late-harvest dessert wine made by Far Niente's sister winery. ✉ *1350
Acacia Dr.* ☎ *707/944–2861* ⊕ *www.farniente.com* 💲 *$50* ☉ *Tasting
and tour by appointment.*

In contrast to its snootier neighbors, **PlumpJack** is fun, casual, and sporty.
With its metal chandelier and wall hangings, the tasting room looks like
it could be the stage set for a modern Shakespeare production. (The
name "PlumpJack" is a nod to Shakespeare's Falstaff.) The reserve
chardonnay has a good balance of baked fruit and fresh citrus flavors,
while a merlot is blended with a bit of cabernet sauvignon, giving the
wine enough tannins to ensure it can be aged for another five years or
more. If the tasting room is crowded, take a breather under the shady
arbor on the back patio, where you can enjoy a close-up view of the
vines. ✉ *620 Oakville Cross Rd.* ☎ *707/945–1220* ⊕ *www.plumpjack.
com* 💲 *Tasting $10* ☉ *Daily 10–4.*

RUTHERFORD

19

   2 mi northwest of Oakville on Rte. 29.

From a fast-moving car, Rutherford is a quick blur of vineyards and a
rustic barn or two, but don't speed by this tiny hamlet. With its singular
microclimate and soil, this is an important viticultural center, with more
big-name wineries than you can shake a corkscrew at. Cabernet sauvignon is king here. The well-drained, loamy soil is ideal for those vines,
and since this part of the valley gets plenty of sun, the grapes develop
exceptionally intense flavors. The late, great winemaker André Tchelistcheff claimed that "it takes Rutherford dust to grow great cabernet."

★   It's not all grapevines here—you can switch your fruit focus to olives at
Round Pond. This small farm grows five varieties of Italian olives and three
types of Spanish olives. Within an hour of being handpicked, the olives
are crushed in the mill on the property to produce pungent, peppery oils
that are later blended and sold. Call at least a day or two in advance to
arrange a tour of the mill followed by an informative tasting, during
which you can sample several types of oil, both alone and with Round
Pond's own red-wine vinegars and other tasty foods. ■ TIP→ If you can
arrange to visit between mid-November and the end of December, you might
be lucky enough to see the mill in action. ✉ *877 Rutherford Rd.* ☎ *888/302–
2575* ⊕ *www.roundpond.com* 💲 *Tour $25* ☉ *Tour by appointment.*

Far Niente's wine cellars have a touch of ballroom elegance.

Jack and Dolores Cakebread snapped up the property at **Cakebread Cellars** in 1973, after Jack fell in love with the area while visiting on a photography assignment. Since then, they've been making luscious chardonnays, as well as merlot, a great sauvignon blanc, and a beautifully complex cabernet sauvignon. You must make an appointment for a tasting, which might take place during a stroll through the winery's barrel room and crush pad and past Dolores's kitchen garden, or it could be a seated event in the winery's modern wing, where an elevator is crafted out of a stainless-steel fermentation tank and the ceiling is lined with thousands of corks. ⊠ *8300 St. Helena Hwy.* ☎ *707/963–5221* ⊕ *www.cakebread.com* ✉ *Tasting $10–$30, tour $25* ⊘ *Daily 10–4:30; tasting and tour by appointment.*

It's the house *The Godfather* built. Filmmaker Francis Ford Coppola began his wine-making career in 1975, when he bought part of the historic, renowned Inglenook estate. He eventually reunited the original Inglenook land and snagged the ivy-covered 19th-century château to boot. In 2006 he renamed the property **Rubicon Estate,** intending to focus on his premium wines, including the namesake cabernet sauvignon–based blend. (The less expensive wines are showcased at the Francis Ford Coppola Winery in Sonoma County's Geyserville.) The many tours cover topics that include the history of the estate, the Rutherford climate and geology, and food-and-wine pairings, but many just come to taste in the opulent, high-ceilinged tasting room. ⊠ *1991 St. Helena Hwy./Rte. 29* ☎ *707/963–9099* ⊕ *www.rubiconestate.com* ✉ *$15–$50* ⊘ *Daily 10–5; call for tour times.*

Your instinct may be to enter the beautifully restored 1882 Queen Anne Victorian at **St. Supéry** looking for the tasting room; actually the wines are being poured in the building behind it, a bland, unappealing, officelike structure. But you'll likely forgive the atmospheric lapse once you taste their fine sauvignon blancs, merlots, and chardonnays, as well as a couple of unusual wines that are made primarily of either cabernet franc or petit verdot, both of which are usually used for blending with cabernet

WORD OF MOUTH

"For wineries to visit, Napa is Cab Country. Mondavi, BV, Inglenook (now Rubicon) and Heitz helped put the Napa Valley on the world's wine map. Others now include Silver Oak, Clos du Val, Stag's Leap, Opus One, Groth, and Caymus.... You should take a tour somewhere. Both Mondavi and Groth give good tours about cabernet production."   —Otis_B_Driftwood

sauvignon. An excellent, free self-guided tour also allows you a peek at the barrel and fermentation rooms, as well as a gallery of rotating art exhibits. At the "Smell-a-Vision" station you can test your ability to identify different smells that might be present in wine. ⊠ *8440 St. Helena Hwy. S/Rte. 29* ☎ *707/963–4507* ⊕ *www.stsupery.com* ✉ *Tasting $15–$25* ☯ *Daily 10–5.*

The cabernet sauvignon produced at the ivy-covered **Beaulieu Vineyard** is a benchmark of the Napa Valley. The legendary André Tchelistcheff, who helped define the California style of wine making, worked his magic here from 1938 until his death in 1973. This helps explain why Beaulieu's flagship, the Georges de Latour Private Reserve Cabernet Sauvignon, still garners high marks from major wine publications. The zinfandels, merlots, and chardonnays being poured in the main tasting room are notably good. Still, it's worth paying the extra money to taste that special cabernet in the more luxe, less-crowded reserve tasting room. ⊠ *1960 St. Helena Hwy./Rte. 29* ☎ *707/967–5200* ⊕ *www. bvwines.com* ✉ *Tasting $10–$30* ☯ *Daily 10–5.*

☾ **Fodor's Choice** ★ **Frog's Leap** is the perfect place for wine novices to begin their education. The owner, John Williams, maintains a goofy sense of humor about wine that translates into an entertaining yet informative experience. You'll also find some fine zinfandel, cabernet sauvignon, merlot, chardonnay, sauvignon blanc, rosé, and also their take on the German dessert wine Trockenbeerenauslese. The winery includes a red barn built in 1884, 5 acres of organic gardens, an ecofriendly visitor center, and, naturally, a frog pond topped with lily pads. Tastings accompanied by the highly recommended tour are free, but if you just want a seated tasting of their wines (on a porch overlooking the garden, weather permitting), you pay $15. ⊠ *8815 Conn Creek Rd.* ☎ *707/963–4704* ⊕ *www. frogsleap.com* ✉ *Tasting and tour free; tasting alone, $15* ☯ *Mon.–Sat. 10–4; tour by appointment.*

Caymus Vineyards is run by wine master Chuck Wagner, who started making wine on the property in 1972. His family, however, had been farming in the valley since 1906. Though they make a fine zinfandel and sauvignon blanc, cabernet is the winery's claim to fame, a ripe, powerful wine that's known for its consistently high quality. ■TIP➔ There's

19

Frog's Leap's picturesque country charm extends all the way to the white picket fence.

no tour and you have to reserve to taste, but it's still worth planning ahead to visit, because the low-key seated tasting (limited to 10 guests) is a great opportunity to learn about the valley's cabernet artistry. ⊠ *8700 Conn Creek Rd.* ☎ *707/967–3010* ⊕ *www.caymus.com* ✉ *Tasting $25* ⊗ *Sales daily 10–4; tasting by appointment.*

Mumm Napa is one of California's best-known sparkling-wine producers. But enjoying the bubbly from the light-filled tasting room—available in either single flutes ($8–$15) or by the flight ($16–$20)—isn't the only reason to visit. There's also an excellent photography gallery with 30 Ansel Adams prints and rotating exhibits. You can even take that glass of wonderfully crisp Brut Rosé with you as wander. For a leisurely tasting of a flight of their library wines while seated on their outdoor terrace ($30), reserve in advance. ⊠ *8445 Silverado Trail* ☎ *707/967–7700* ⊕ *www.mummnapa.com* ✉ *Tasting $8–$30, tour free–$20* ⊗ *Daily 10–5; tour daily at 10 (free; tasting not including), 11, 1, and 3 ($20, tasting including).*

Rutherford Hill Winery is a merlot lover's paradise in a cabernet sauvignon world. When the winery's founders were deciding what grapes to plant, they discovered that the climate and soil conditions of their vineyards resembled those of Pomerol, a region of Bordeaux where merlot is king. The wine caves here are some of the most extensive of any California winery—nearly a mile of tunnels and passageways. You can get a glimpse of the tunnels and the 8,000 barrels inside on the tours, then cap your visit with a picnic in their oak, olive, or madrone groves. With views over the valley from a perch high on a hill, the picnic grounds are more charming than many others in Napa, which tend to be rather close to one of the busy thoroughfares. ⊠ *200 Rutherford Hill Rd., east of Silverado Trail* ☎ *707/963–1871* ⊕ *www.rutherfordhill.com* ☑ *Tasting $15–$30, tour $20* ⊙ *Daily 10–5; tour weekdays at 11:30, 1:30, and 3:30, weekends at 11:30, 12:30, 1:30, 2:30, and 3:30.*

WHERE TO STAY

$$$$ 🏨 **Auberge du Soleil.** Taking a cue from the olive-tree-studded landscape, ★ this renowned hotel cultivates a Mediterranean look. It's luxury as simplicity: earth-tone tile floors, heavy wood furniture, and terra-cotta colors. This spare style is backed with lavish amenities, though, such as private terraces and truly grand bathrooms. The Auberge du Soleil restaurant has an impressive wine list and serves a Mediterranean-inflected menu that relies largely on local produce. **Pros:** stunning views over the valley; spectacular pool and spa areas; the most expensive suites are fit for a superstar. **Cons:** stratospheric prices; the two least expensive rooms (in the main house) get some noise from the bar and restaurant. ⊠ *180 Rutherford Hill Rd., off Silverado Trail north of Rte. 128* ☎ *707/963–1211 or 800/348–5406* ⊕ *www.aubergedusoleil.com* ➲ *31 rooms, 21 suites* ⚴ *In-room: a/c, safe, refrigerator, DVD, Internet, Wi-Fi. In-hotel: 2 restaurants, room service, bar, tennis court, pool, gym, spa, laundry service* ▱ *AE, D, DC, MC, V* ⦿ *BP.*

ST. HELENA

2 mi northwest of Oakville on Rte. 29.

Downtown St. Helena is a symbol of how well life can be lived in the Wine Country. Sycamore trees arch over Main Street (Route 29), a funnel of outstanding restaurants and tempting boutiques. At the north end of town looms the hulking stone building of the Culinary Institute of America. Weathered stone and brick buildings from the late 1800s give off that gratifying whiff of history.

By the time pioneer winemaker Charles Krug planted grapes in St. Helena around 1860, quite a few vineyards already existed in the area. Today the town is hemmed in by wineries, and you could easily spend days visiting vintners within a few miles.

The West Coast headquarters of the **Culinary Institute of America,** the country's leading school for chefs, are in the **Greystone Winery,** an imposing building that was the largest stone winery in the world when it was built in 1889. The upper floors are reserved for students and teachers, but on the ground floor you can check out the quirky corkscrew display and shop at a well-stocked culinary store that tempts aspiring chefs with gleaming gadgets and an impressive selection of cookbooks. One-hour cooking demonstrations take place regularly, usually twice a day on weekends and occasionally more often; call or visit the Web site for times and reservations. ⊠ *2555 Main St.* ☎ *707/967–1100* ⊕ *www. ciachef.edu* ☑ *Free, demonstrations $15* ⊙ *Restaurant Sun.–Thurs. 11:30–9, Fri. and Sat. 11:30–10; store and museum daily 10–6.*

Fodor's Choice Although an appointment is required to taste at **Joseph Phelps Vineyards,** ★ it's worth the trouble. In fair weather the casual, self-paced wine tastings are held on the terrace of a huge, modern barnlike building with stunning

19

views down the slopes over oak trees and orderly vines. Though the sauvignon blanc and viognier are good, the blockbuster wines are reds. ⊠ *200 Taplin Rd.* ☎ *707/963–2745* ⊕ *www.jpvwines.com* ✉ *Tasting $20* ☉ *Weekdays 9–5, weekends 9–4; tasting by appointment.*

Arguably the most beautiful winery in Napa Valley, the 1876 **Beringer Vineyards** is also the oldest continuously operating property. In 1884 Frederick and Jacob Beringer built the Rhine House Mansion to serve as Frederick's family home. Today it serves as the reserve tasting room, where you can sample four wines amid the Belgian art-nouveau hand-carved oak and walnut furniture and stained-glass windows, choosing from among wines such as a limited-release chardonnay, a few big but very drinkable cabernets, and a luscious white dessert wine named Nightingale. Another, less expensive tasting takes place in the less atmospheric but also historic original stone winery. ■**TIP**➔ **If you're looking for an undiscovered gem, pass this one by, but first-time visitors to the valley will learn a lot about the history of wine making in the region on the introductory tour.** Longer tours, which might pass through a demonstration vineyard or end with a seated tasting in the wine-aging tunnels, are also offered a few times a day. ⊠ *2000 Main St./Rte. 29* ☎ *707/963–4812* ⊕ *www.beringer.com* ✉ *Tasting $15–$25, tour $15–$40* ☉ *May 30–Oct. 23, daily 10–6; Oct. 24–May 29, daily 10–5; call for tour times.*

The first winery founded in the Napa Valley, **Charles Krug Winery,** opened in 1861 when Count Haraszthy lent Krug a small cider press. Today the Peter Mondavi family runs it. At this writing, tours have been suspended indefinitely because a major earthquake retrofit project is in the works, but you can still come for tastings. Though the tasting room is fairly modest, the knowledgeable and friendly servers ensure a relaxed visit. The winery is best known for its lush red Bordeaux blends, but its zinfandel is also good—or go for something unusual with the New Zealand–style sauvignon blanc. Its zingy flavor of citrus and tropical fruit is rare in wines from this area. ⊠ *2800 N. Main St.* ☎ *707/963–5057* ⊕ *www.charleskrug.com* ✉ *Tasting $10–$20* ☉ *Daily 10:30–5.*

★ Hidden off a winding road behind a security gate, **Spring Mountain Vineyard** has the feeling of a private estate in the countryside, even though it's only a few miles from downtown St. Helena. Though some sauvignon blanc, pinot noir, and syrah is produced, the calling card here is cabernet—big, chewy wines that demand some time in the bottle but promise great things. Tours meander through the beautiful property, from the cellars to the beautifully preserved 1885 mansion. If you're interested in finding out what their wines taste like after years in the bottle, set aside at least an hour and a half for your visit and spring for the $50 reserve tasting, when they'll pour wines of various vintages while you're seated in the mansion's dining room. ⊠ *2805 Spring Mountain Rd.* ☎ *707/967–4188* ⊕ *www.springmtn.com* ✉ *Tour and tasting $25–$50* ☉ *Tour and tasting by appointment.*

WHERE TO EAT

$$
SEAFOOD
★

✕ **Go Fish.** Prolific restaurateur Cindy Pawlcyn is the big name behind one of the few restaurants in the Wine Country to specialize in seafood. You can either sit at the long marble bar and watch the chefs whip up inventive sushi rolls and raw-bar bites, or head into the dining room to study the mouthwatering menu, with listings that include a French-inflected sole almondine and Asian-inspired dishes like miso-marinated black cod. Hearty sandwiches like the bigeye tuna Reuben are popular at lunch. The large, lively space works a modern-chic look, with stainless-steel lamps and comfortable banquettes. ⊠ *641 Main St.* ☎ *707/963–0700* ⊕ *www.gofishrestaurant.net* ▬ *AE, D, DC, MC, V.*

$$$$
AMERICAN

✕ **Martini House.** Beautiful and boisterous, St. Helena's most stylish restaurant fills a converted 1923 Craftsman-style home, where earthy colors are made even warmer by the glow of three fireplaces. Woodsy ingredients such as chanterelles or juniper berries might accompany braised veal sweetbreads or a hearty grilled loin of venison. Inventive salads and delicate desserts such as the blood-orange sorbet demonstrate chef-owner Todd Humphries's range. In warm weather, angle for a table on the patio, where lights sparkle in the trees. If you don't have a reservation, ask for a seat at the bar downstairs, where you can order from either the small (but much less expensive) bar menu or the full menu. ⊠ *1245 Spring St.* ☎ *707/963–2233* ⊕ *www.martinihouse. com* ▬ *AE, DC, MC, V* ⊙ *No lunch Mon.–Thurs.*

$$$$
AMERICAN
Fodor'sChoice
★

✕ **The Restaurant at Meadowood.** Chef Christopher Kostow has garnered rave reviews (and two Michelin stars) for transforming seasonal local products (some grown right on the property) into elaborate, elegant fare. The "composition of carrots," constructed of the tiniest carrots imaginable accompanied by delicate shavings of chocolate, foie gras, and candied tangerine (it sounds odd, but it works) is just one example of Kostow's inventiveness and playfulness. The slow-cooked black cod with chorizo and lamb demonstrates an earthier approach. The chef's menu ($155, $260 with wine pairings), composed of eight or so courses, is the best way to appreciate the experience, but the gracious and well-trained servers provide some of the best service in the valley even if you're ordering a less extravagant three-, four-, or five-course menu. ⊠ *900 Meadowood La.* ☎ *707/967–1205* ⊕ *www.meadowood. com* ▬ *AE, D, DC, MC, V* ⊙ *Closed Sun. No lunch.*

¢–$
AMERICAN
★

✕ **Gott's Roadside Tray Gourmet.** A slick 1950s-style outdoor hamburger stand goes upscale at this hugely popular spot, where locals are willing to brave long lines to order juicy burgers, root-beer floats, and garlic fries. There are also plenty of choices you wouldn't have found 50 years ago, such as the ahi tuna burger and chicken club with pesto mayo. Try to get here early or late for lunch, or all the shaded picnic tables on the lawn might be filled with happy throngs. Lines are usually shorter at the Gott's in downtown Napa's Oxbow Public Market. ⊠ *933 Main St.* ☎ *707/963–3486* ⊕ *www.gottsroadside.com* ▬ *AE, MC, V.*

$$$$
MEDITERRANEAN
★

✕ **Terra.** St. Helena may have newer, flashier, and more dramatic restaurants, but for old-school romance and service, many diners return year after year to this quiet favorite in an 1884 fieldstone building. Since 1988, chef Hiro Sone has been giving unexpected twists to Italian and

19

southern-French cuisine in dishes such as the mussel soup with cara-melized onions and garlic croutons, heavily perfumed with the scent of saffron. A few, like the signature sake-marinated black cod in a *shiso* broth, draw on Sone's Japanese background. Inventive desserts, cour-tesy of Sone's wife, Lissa Doumani, might include a maple bread pud-ding served in a baked apple. The gracious staff unobtrusively attends to every dropped fork or half-full water glass. ⊠ *1345 Railroad Ave.* ☎ *707/963–8931* ⊕ *www.terrarestaurant.com* ♨ *Reservations essential* ▭ *AE, DC, MC, V* ☽ *Closed Tues. and 1st 2 wks in Jan. No lunch.*

$$$ ✕ **Wine Spectator Greystone Restaurant.** The Culinary Institute of America
MEDITERRANEAN runs this place in the handsome old Christian Brothers Winery. Century-old stone walls house a spacious restaurant that bustles at both lunch and dinner, with several cooking stations in full view. On busy nights you might find the hard-at-work chefs (who, incidentally, are gener-ally full-fledged chefs rather than mere students)more entertaining than your dinner partner. On fair days the tables on the terrace, shaded by red umbrellas, are away from the action, but equally appealing. The menu has a Mediterranean spirit and emphasizes locally grown pro-duce. Typical main courses include pan-roasted scallops with spinach and shiitake mushrooms and house-made pasta with a sherry-thyme cream sauce. ⊠ *2555 Main St.* ☎ *707/967–1010* ⊕ *www.ciachef.edu* ▭ *AE, D, DC, MC, V.*

WHERE TO STAY

¢–$ ⌂ **El Bonita Motel.** Only in St. Helena would a basic room in a road-side motel cost around $200 a night in high season. Still, for budget-minded travelers the tidy rooms here are pleasant enough, and the landscaped grounds and picnic tables elevate the property over similar places. There's even a small sauna next to the hot tub and swimming pool, which is heated year-round. ■TIP➜ **Family-friendly pluses include roll-away beds and cribs for a modest charge. Its location right on Route 29 makes it convenient, but light sleepers should ask for rooms farthest from the road. Pros:** cheerful rooms; hot tub; microwaves and mini-refriger-ators. **Cons:** road noise is a problem in some rooms. ⊠ *195 Main St./ Rte. 29* ☎ *707/963–3216 or 800/541–3284* ⊕ *www.elbonita.com* ↴ *38 rooms, 4 suites* ♨ *In-room: a/c, refrigerator, Wi-Fi. In-hotel: pool, Inter-net terminal, some pets allowed (fee)* ▭ *AE, D, DC, MC, V* ¦◎¦ *CP.*

$$$$ ⌂ **Meadowood Resort.** Everything at Meadowood seems to run seam-
Fodor'sChoice lessly, starting with the gatehouse staff who alert the front desk to arriv-
★ als, so that a receptionist is ready for each guest. A rambling lodge and several gray clapboard bungalows are scattered across the sprawling property, giving it the air of an exclusive New England retreat. Guest rooms have views over these wooded grounds from expansive windows. The supremely comfortable beds defy you to get up and pursue the golf, tennis, hiking, croquet, or other activities on offer. In recent years the elegant but unstuffy dining room has won rave reviews, becom-ing a destination restaurant *(see above).* **Pros:** site of one of Napa's best restaurants; lovely hiking trail on the property; the most gracious service in all of Napa. **Cons:** very expensive; most bathrooms are not as extravagant as at other similarly priced resorts. ⊠ *900 Meadowood La.* ☎ *707/963–3646 or 800/458–8080* ⊕ *www.meadowood.com* ↴ *40*

rooms, 45 suites ♿ In-room: a/c, refrigerator, DVD, Internet, Wi-Fi. In-hotel: 2 restaurants, room service, bar, golf course, tennis courts, pools, gym, children's programs (ages 6–12, summer only) ▤ AE, D, DC, MC, V.

$$$–$$$$ 🏨 **Wine Country Inn.** A pastoral landscape of vine-covered hills surrounds this retreat, which was styled after the traditional New England inns its owners liked to visit in the 1970s. Rooms are comfortably done with homey furniture like four-poster beds topped with quilts, and many have a wood-burning or gas fireplace, a large jetted tub, and a patio or balcony overlooking the vineyards. A hearty breakfast is served buffet-style in the sun-splashed common room, and wine and appetizers are available in the afternoon next to the wood-burning cast-iron stove. Though it's not the most stylish lodging in the area, the thoughtful staff and the vineyard views from several rooms encourage many people to return year after year. **Pros:** free shuttle to some restaurants (reserve early); lovely grounds; swimming pool is heated year-round. **Cons:** some rooms let in noise from neighbors; some areas could use updating. ⊠ 1152 Lodi La., east of Rte. 29 ☎ 707/963–7077 ⊕ www. winecountryinn.com ➫ 24 rooms, 5 suites ♿ In-room: a/c, refrigerator (some), no TV, Wi-Fi. In-hotel: pool ▤ MC, V ❝❞ BP.

SHOPPING

Dean & Deluca (⊠ 607 St. Helena Hwy. S/Rte. 29 ☎ 707/967–9980), a branch of the famous Manhattan store, is crammed with everything you need in the kitchen—including terrific produce and deli items—as well as a large wine selection. The **Spice Islands Marketplace** (⊠ Culinary Institute of America, 2555 Main St. ☎ 888/424–2433) is the place to shop for cookbooks, kitchenwares, and everything else related to cooking and preparing food. Elaborate confections handmade on the premises are displayed like miniature works of art at **Woodhouse Chocolate** (⊠ 1367 Main St. ☎ 707/963–8413), a lovely shop that resembles an 18th-century Parisian salon.

19

CALISTOGA

3 mi northwest of St. Helena on Rte. 29.

With false-fronted/Old West–style shops, 19th-century hotels, and unpretentious cafés lining Lincoln Avenue, the town's main drag, Calistoga has a slightly rough-and-tumble feel that's unique in the Napa Valley. It comes across as more down-to-earth than some of the polished towns to the south. And it's easier to find a bargain here, making it a handy home base for exploring the surrounding vineyards and back roads.

Ironically, Calistoga was developed as a swell, tourist-oriented getaway. In 1859, maverick entrepreneur Sam Brannan snapped up 2,000 acres of prime property and laid out a resort, intending to use the area's natural hot springs as the main attraction. Brannan's gamble didn't pay off as he'd hoped, but the hotels and bathhouses won a local following. Many of them are still going, and you can come for an old-school experience of a mud bath or a dip in a warm spring-fed pool.

Floor-to-ceiling stacked bottles are no exaggeration in Schramsberg's cellars.

Indian Springs has welcomed clients to mud baths, mineral pools, and steam rooms, all supplied with mineral water from its three geysers, since 1871. You can choose from the various spa treatments and volcanic-ash mud baths, or soak in the Olympic-size mineral-water pool (kept at 92°F in summer, and a toasty 102°F in winter). Those who visit the spa also get access to a small Zen-inspired garden out back, where you can relax after your treatment. If you're planning several sessions, you might want to overnight in one of the lodge rooms or bungalows ($–$$$). Reservations are recommended for spa treatments. ✉ *1712 Lincoln Ave./Rte. 29* ☎ *707/942–4913* ⊕ *www.indianspringscalistoga. com* ����� *Daily 9–8.*

Fodor's Choice ★ **Schramsberg**, hidden on the hillside near Route 29, is one of Napa's oldest wineries. Founded in the 1860s, it now produces a variety of bubblies made using the traditional méthode champenoise process (which means, among other things, that the wine undergoes a second fermentation in the bottle before being "riddled," or turned every few days over a period of weeks, to nudge the sediment into the neck of the bottle). If you want to taste, you must tour first, but what a tour: in addition to getting a glimpse of the winery's historic architecture, you get to tour the cellars dug in the late 19th century by Chinese laborers, where a mind-boggling 2.5 million bottles are stacked in gravity-defying configurations. The tour fee includes generous pours of several very different sparkling wines. ✉ *1400 Schramsberg Rd.* ☎ *707/942–4558* ⊕ *www.schramsberg.com* ▦ *Tasting and tour $40* ☻ *Tasting and tour by appointment.*

Designed by postmodern architect Michael Graves, the **Clos Pegase** winery is a one-of-a-kind "temple to wine and art" packed with unusual art objects from the collection of owner and publishing entrepreneur Jan Shrem. After tasting the wines, which include a bright sauvignon blanc, fruity chardonnays, and mellow pinot noir, merlot, and cabernet (they're made in a soft, approachable style and meant to be drunk somewhat young), be sure to check out the surrealist paintings near the main tasting room, which include a Jean Dubuffet painting you may have seen on one of their labels. Better yet, bring a picnic and have lunch in the courtyard, where a curvaceous Henry Moore sculpture is one of about two dozen works of art. ⊠ *1060 Dunaweal La.* ☎ *707/942–4981* ⊕ *www.clospegase.com* 🍷 *Tasting $15, tour free* ⊙ *Daily 10:30–5; tour daily at 11:30 and 2.*

Tucked into a rock face in the Mayacamas range, **Storybook Mountain Vineyards** is one of the more beautiful wineries in Napa, with vines rising steeply from the winery in dramatic tiers. Zinfandel is king here, and they even make a Zin Gris, an unusual dry rosé of zinfandel grapes. (In Burgundy, *vin gris*—pale rosé—is made from pinot noir grapes.) Tastings are preceded by a low-key tour, during which you take a short walk up the hillside into the picture-perfect vineyard and then visit the atmospheric tunnels, parts of which have the same rough-hewn look as they did when Chinese laborers painstakingly dug them around 1888. ⊠ *3835 Hwy. 128* ☎ *707/942–5310* ⊕ *www.storybookwines.com* 🍷 *Free* ⊙ *Tour and tasting by appointment.*

Robert Louis Stevenson State Park encompasses the summit of **Mt. St. Helena.** It was here, in the summer of 1880, in an abandoned bunkhouse of the Silverado Mine, that Stevenson and his bride, Fanny Osbourne, spent their honeymoon. This stay inspired the writer's travel memoir *The Silverado Squatters,* and Spyglass Hill in *Treasure Island* is thought to be a portrait of Mt. St. Helena. The park's approximately 3,600 acres are mostly undeveloped except for a trail leading to the site of the bunkhouse—which is marked with a marble memorial in the form of an open book on top of a pedestal—and a fire trail to the summit beyond. ■TIP➔ If you're planning on attempting the hike to the top, a 10-mi round-trip, bring plenty of water and dress appropriately: the trail is steep and lacks shade in spots, but the summit is often cool and breezy. ⊠ *Rte. 29, 7 mi north of Calistoga* ☎ *707/942–4575* ⊕ *www.parks.ca.gov* 🍷 *Free* ⊙ *Daily sunrise–sunset.*

★ Possibly the most astounding sight in Napa Valley is your first glimpse of the **Castello di Amorosa,** which looks for all the world like a medieval castle, complete with drawbridge and moat, chapel, stables, and secret passageways. Some of the 107 rooms contain replicas of 13th-century frescoes, and the dungeon has an actual iron maiden from Nuremberg, Germany. You must pay for the tour to see the most of the extensive eight-level property, though paying for a tasting allows you access to a small portion of the astounding complex, as well as taste several of their excellent Italian-style wines. ■TIP➔ Prices for tastings and tours are $5 higher on Fridays and weekends (a rarity in the Wine Country), so schedule this stop for a weekday, if possible. ⊠ *4045 N. Saint Helena Hwy.* ☎ *707/967–6272* ⊕ *www.castellodiamorosa.com* 🍷 *Tasting $10–$27,*

19

tour $25–$42 ⊙ *Mar.–Nov., daily 9:30–6; Dec.–Feb., daily 9:30–5; tour by appointment.*

♻ The **Petrified Forest** contains the remains of the volcanic eruptions of Mt. St. Helena 3.4 million years ago: petrified giant redwoods. Pick up a brochure before starting off on the leisurely 15-minute walk around the property, which takes you by the largest specimen, "The Queen of the Forest," a 65-by-8-foot petrified log. The site isn't worth a long detour unless you're a geology buff. For the best experience, consider taking a meadow hike, which leads through the woodland until you have a view of Mt. St. Helena. The 45-minute excursion, led by a naturalist, is offered on Sunday at 11 AM and by appointment, weather permitting. ⊠ *4100 Petrified Forest Rd., 5 mi west of Calistoga* ☎ *707/942–6667* ⊕ *www.petrifiedforest.org* ⊡ *$8* ⊙ *Mid-Apr.–mid-Sept., daily 9–7; mid-Sept.–mid-Apr., daily 9–5.*

WHERE TO EAT

$$ ✕ **All Seasons Bistro.** Bistro cuisine takes a California spin in this cheer-
FRENCH   ful sun-filled space, where tables topped with flowers stand on an old-fashioned black-and-white checkerboard floor. The seasonal menu might include seared scallops with a cauliflower puree or fettuccine puttanesca. Homey desserts include crème brûlée and rum-raisin bread pudding. You can order reasonably priced wines from their extensive list, or buy a bottle at the attached wineshop and have it poured at your table. Attentive service contributes to the welcoming atmosphere. ⊠ *1400 Lincoln Ave.* ☎ *707/942–9111* ⊕ *www.allseasonsnapavalley. net* ⊟ *AE, D, MC, V* ⊙ *Closed Mon.*

$$ ✕ **Barolo.** With red-leather seats, artsy light fixtures, and a marble bar
ITALIAN   indoors and café seating out, this Italian-inflected wine bar is a stylish, modern spot for a glass of wine, with many from small producers you probably haven't heard of. Small plates that could have come straight from Tuscany—fried calamari, risotto croquettes, a selection of *salumi*—are great for sharing. A handful of well-executed large plates, like the *pappardelle* with shrimp and veal scaloppine, round out the menu. ⊠ *Mount View Hotel, 1457 Lincoln Ave.* ☎ *707/942–9900* ⊕ *www.barolocalistoga.com* ⊟ *AE, MC, V* ⊙ *No lunch.*

$$$ ✕ **Calistoga Inn Restaurant and Brewery.** On pleasant days this riverside
AMERICAN   restaurant and its sprawling, tree-shaded patio come into their own. At lunchtime, casual plates like a grilled-turkey-and-Brie sandwich or a Chinese chicken salad are light enough to leave some energy for an afternoon of wine tasting. And at night, when there's often live jazz played on the patio during the warm months, you'll find heartier dishes such as braised lamb shank or grilled Sonoma duck breast with a fennel-and-Parmesan stuffing. Service can be a bit lackadaisical, so order one of the house-made brews and enjoy the atmosphere while you're waiting. ⊠ *1250 Lincoln Ave.* ☎ *707/942–4101* ⊕ *www.calistogainn. com* ⊟ *AE, MC, V.*

WHERE TO STAY

¢–$ ⊡ **Brannan Cottage Inn.** The pristine Victorian house with lacy white fretwork, large windows, and a shady porch is the only one of Sam Brannan's 1860 resort cottages still standing on its original site. Each

All it needs is a fair maiden: Castello di Amorosa's recreated castle.

room has individual touches, such as a four-poster bed, a claw-foot tub, or a velvet settee. **Pros:** innkeepers go the extra mile; most rooms have fireplaces; a five-minute walk from most of Calistoga's restaurants. **Cons:** owners' dog may be a problem for those with allergies; beds may be too firm for some. ⊠ *109 Wapoo Ave.* ☎ *707/942–4200* ⊕ *www. brannancottageinn.com* ↘ *6 rooms* ♿ *In-room: no phone, a/c, no TV (some), Wi-Fi. In-hotel: some pets allowed (fee)* ▭ *AE, MC, V* ⊚ *BP.*

19

$$$$
★ ⊞ **Calistoga Ranch.** Spacious cedar-shingle bungalows throughout this posh, wooded property have outdoor living areas, and even the restaurant, spa, and reception area have outdoor seating areas and fireplaces. Though it feels casual and ranchlike, the lodges are still supremely luxurious, with large bathrooms; a large, romantic outdoor shower; beds dressed with down bedding; and a minibar stocked with free drinks and snacks. **Pros:** almost half the cottages have private hot tubs on the deck; lovely hiking trails on the property; guests have reciprocal privileges at Auberge du Soleil. **Cons:** very expensive; innovative indoor-outdoor organization works better in fair weather than in rain or cold; staff, though friendly, sometimes seems inexperienced. ⊠ *580 Lommel Rd.* ☎ *707/254–2800 or 800/942–4220* ⊕ *www.calistogaranch.com* ↘ *46 rooms* ♿ *In-room: a/c, safe, refrigerator, DVD, Internet, Wi-Fi. In-hotel: restaurant, room service, bar, pool, gym, spa, bicycles, laundry service, some pets allowed (fee)* ▭ *AE, D, MC, V.*

$$$
⊞ **Cottage Grove Inn.** A long driveway lined with 16 freestanding cottages, each shaded by elm trees and with rocking chairs on the porch, looks a bit like Main Street, U.S.A., but inside the sky-lighted buildings are all the perks you could want for a romantic weekend away. There are overstuffed chairs in front of a wood-burning fireplace, flat-panel

Best Wine Country Spas

Spas in Napa and Sonoma have two special angles. First, there are the local mud baths and mineral-water sources, concentrated particularly around Calistoga. Admittedly, no one loves dipping into a thick, muddy paste. But once you've had a few minutes to get used to the intense heat and peaty smell, you may never want to leave. Second, there are all those grapes: their seeds, skins, and vines are credited with all sorts of antioxidant and other healthful properties by those who use them in scrubs, lotions, and other spa products.

Below are some of the best spas of the bunch.

■ **Dr. Wilkinson's.** The oldest spa in Calistoga. Although it's the least chic of the bunch, it's still well loved for its reasonable prices and its friendly, unpretentious vibe. Their mud baths are a mix of volcanic ash and peat moss. ✉ *1507 Lincoln Ave., Calistoga* ☎ *707/942–4102* ⊕ *www.drwilkinson. com.*

■ **Fairmont Sonoma Mission Inn & Spa.** The largest such destination in the Wine Country. The vast complex covers every amenity you could want in a spa, including several pools and Jacuzzis fed by local thermal mineral springs. ✉ *100 Boyes Blvd./Rte. 12, Boyes Hot Springs* ☎ *707/938–9000* ⊕ *www.fairmont.com/sonoma.*

■ **Kenwood Inn & Spa.** The prettiest spa setting in the Wine Country, thanks to the vineyards across the road and the Mediterranean style of the inn. The "wine wrap" body wrap is followed by a slathering of lotion made from various grape-seed oils and red-wine extract. ✉ *10400 Sonoma Hwy./Rte. 12, Kenwood* ☎ *707/833–1293* ⊕ *www.kenwoodinn. com.*

■ **Spa at Villagio.** This 13,000-square-foot spa with fieldstone walls and a Mediterranean theme has all the latest gadgets, including men's and women's outdoor hot tubs and showers with an extravagant number of showerheads. Huge spa suites—complete with flat-panel TV screens and wet bars—are perfect for couples and groups. ✉ *6481 Washington St., Yountville* ☎ *707/948–5050.*

TVs, and an extra-deep two-person whirlpool tub. Each cottage also has its own variation on the overall comfy-rustic look, with telltale names like Fly Fishing Cottage and Provence. Spas and restaurants are within walking distance. Rates include afternoon wine and cheese. **Pros:** bicycles available for loan; freestanding cottages offer lots of privacy; bathtubs so big you could swim in them. **Cons:** no pool; decor may seem a bit frumpy for some. ✉ *1711 Lincoln Ave.* ☎ *707/942–8400 or 800/799–2284* ⊕ *www.cottagegrove.com* ⇨ *16 rooms* ⚷ *In-room: a/c, safe, refrigerator, DVD, Internet, Wi-Fi. In-hotel: bicycles, Internet terminal* ▤ *AE, D, DC, MC, V* ⑩*CP.*

$–$$ ⚷ **Indian Springs.** Since 1871, this old-time spa has welcomed clients to ★ its mud baths, mineral pool, and steam room, all of them supplied with mineral water from its four geysers. Rooms in the lodge, though quite small, are beautifully done up a simple Zen style, with Asian-inspired furnishings, Frette linens on the bed, and flat-panel televisions. The cottages dotted around the property have anything from a small kitchenette to a fully equipped kitchen, encouraging longer stays (book well in advance for these). A boccie ball court, shuffleboard, and croquet lawn outside your door provide entertainment when you're not indulging in various spa treatments and volcanic-ash mud baths, or soaking in the toasty Olympic-size mineral-water pool. **Pros:** lovely grounds with outdoor seating areas; stylish for the price; enormous mineral pool. **Cons:** lodge rooms are small; oddly uncomfortable pillows. ⌧ *1712 Lincoln Ave.* ☎ *707/942–4913* ⊕ *www.indianspringscalistoga.com* ⇲ *24 rooms, 17 suites* ⚬ *In room: no phone, kitchen (some), refrigerator (some), Wi-Fi. In-hotel: tennis court, pool, spa* ▭ *D, MC, V.*

$–$$
Fodor'sChoice
★

Meadowlark Country House. Twenty hillside acres just north of downtown Calistoga surround this decidedly laid-back but sophisticated inn. Rooms in the main house and guest wing each have their own charms: one has a deep whirlpool tub looking onto a green hillside, and others have a deck with a view of the mountains. Many rooms have fireplaces, and all but one have whirlpool tubs large enough for two. A spacious two-story guesthouse opens directly onto the clothing-optional pool, hot tub, and sauna area, which is open to all guests and enjoyed by a diverse crowd (the inn is welcoming to all, gay and straight). Fodors. com readers point out that "Kurt and Richard are delightful, helpful hosts." **Pros:** sauna next to the pool and hot tub; welcoming vibe attracts diverse guests; some of the most gracious innkeepers in Napa. **Cons:** clothing-optional pool policy isn't for everyone. ⌧ *601 Petrified Forest Rd.* ☎ *707/942–5651 or 800/942–5651* ⊕ *www.meadowlarkinn. com* ⇲ *5 rooms, 5 suites* ⚬ *In-room: a/c, no phone, kitchen (some), refrigerator (some), DVD (some), Wi-Fi. In-hotel: pool, Internet terminal, some pets allowed* ▭ *AE, MC, V* ⟐ *BP.*

$–$$

Mount View Hotel & Spa. A National Historic Landmark built in 1917 in the Mission revival style, the Mount View nevertheless feels up-to-date, after renovations in 2008 resulted in repainted rooms (some are a dramatic red and black), feather duvets, and high-tech touches like iPod alarm clocks. A full-service spa provides state-of-the-art pampering, and three cottages are each equipped with a private redwood deck, whirlpool tub, and wet bar. The hotel's location on Calistoga's main drag, plus the two excellent restaurants off the lobby, mean you won't need to go far if your spa treatment has left you too indolent to drive. **Pros:** convenient location; excellent spa treatments. **Cons:** ground-floor rooms dark; mediocre continental breakfast; some bathrooms could use updating. ⌧ *1457 Lincoln Ave.* ☎ *707/942–6877 or 800/816–6877* ⊕ *www.mountviewhotel.com* ⇲ *18 rooms, 13 suites* ⚬ *In-room: a/c, refrigerator (some), DVD, Wi-Fi. In-hotel: restaurant, bar, pool, spa* ▭ *AE, D, MC, V* ⟐ *CP.*

$$$$

Solage. A resort for sociable sorts who like to lounge at the bar overlooking the large pool or play a game of boccie after lunch at the excellent indoor-outdoor restaurant, this Calistoga newcomer sprawls over 22 acres. The cottages don't look particularly luxurious from the outside, but inside they flaunt a Napa-Valley-barn-meets-San-Francisco-loft aesthetic, with high ceilings, polished concrete floors, recycled walnut furniture, and all-natural fabrics in soothing muted colors. Sports and fitness are a high priority here: in addition to a large, well-equipped spa

19

UP, UP, AND AWAY

Thought those vineyards were beautiful from the highway? Top that with a bird's-eye view! Several companies offer hot-air ballooning trips over Napa and Sonoma. Rides usually cost between $200 and $250, last about an hour, and include brunch or lunch after the flight. Flights take off at the crack of dawn, literally, and you can watch the huge, rainbow-color balloons inflate as the aircraft is readied. Be sure to dress in layers.

■ **Balloons Above the Valley** (☎ 707/253–2222 or 800/464–6824 ⊕ www.balloonrides.com).

■ **Napa Valley Balloons** (☎ 707/944–0228 or 800/253–2224 ⊕ www.napavalleyballoons.com).

■ **Napa Valley Drifters** ☎ 707/252–7210 or 877/463–7438 ⊕ www.napavalleydrifters.com.

and "mud bar," where you can indulge in mud-bath variations, there's a packed schedule of fitness activities that include yoga, Pilates, and biking and hiking excursions. ■ TIP→ If you want to be in the middle of the action, ask for a room facing the pool. For more seclusion, ask for one of the quieter rooms near the oak grove. **Pros:** great service; bike cruisers parked at every cottage for guests' use; separate pools for kids and adults. **Cons:** new landscaping looks a little bleak; some rooms don't have tubs. ⊠ 755 Silverado Trail ☎ 866/942–7442 ⊕ www.solagecalistoga. com ⏎ 89 rooms ♿ In-room: a/c, safe, refrigerator, DVD, Wi-Fi. In-hotel: restaurant, room service, bar, pools, gym, spa, bicycles, laundry service ☰ AE, D, DC, MC, V.

SPORTS AND THE OUTDOORS

Calistoga Bikeshop (⊠ 1318 Lincoln Ave. ☎ 707/942–9687) offers a self-guided Calistoga Cool Wine Tour package ($79), which includes free tastings at a number of small wineries. Best of all, they'll pick up any wine you purchase along the way if you've bought more than will fit in the handy bottle carrier on your bike.

SHOPPING

Enoteca Wine Shop (⊠ 1348B Lincoln Ave. ☎ 707/942–1117), on Calistoga's main drag, displays almost all of their wines with extensive tasting notes. This makes it easier to choose from among this unusually fine collection, which includes both hard-to-find bottles from Napa and Sonoma and many rare French wines. The **Wine Garage** (⊠ 1020 Hwy. 29 ☎ 707/942–5332) is the stop for bargain hunters, since all their bottles go for $25 or less. It's a great way to discover the work of smaller wineries producing undervalued wines. The unusually helpful staffers are happy to share information on all the wines they stock.

THE SONOMA VALLEY

Although the Sonoma Valley may not have quite the cachet of the neighboring Napa Valley, wineries here entice with their unpretentious attitude and smaller crowds. The Napa-style glitzy tasting rooms with enormous gift shops and $25 tasting fees are the exception here. Sonoma's landscape seduces, too, its roads gently climbing and descending on their way to wineries hidden from the road by trees.

The scenic valley, bounded by the Mayacamas Mountains on the east and Sonoma Mountain on the west, extends north from San Pablo Bay nearly 20 mi to the eastern outskirts of Santa Rosa. The varied terrain, soils, and climate (cooler in the south because of the bay influence and hotter toward the north) allow grape growers to raise cool-weather varietals such as chardonnay and pinot noir as well as merlot, cabernet sauvignon, and other heat-seeking vines. The valley is home to dozens of wineries, many of them on or near Route 12, which runs the length of the valley.

ESSENTIALS

Contacts Sonoma County Tourism Bureau (✉ *3637 Westwind Blvd., Santa Rosa* ☎ *707/522–5800 or 800/576–6662* ⊕ *www.sonomacounty.com*). **Sonoma Valley Visitors Bureau** (✉ *453 1st St. E, Sonoma* ☎ *707/996–1090 or 866/996–1090* ⊕ *www.sonomavalley.com*).

SONOMA

14 mi west of Napa on Rte. 12; 45 mi from San Francisco, north on U.S. 101, east on Rte. 37, and north on Rte. 121/12.

Founded in the early 1800s, Sonoma is the oldest town in the Wine Country, and one of the few where you can find some attractions not related to food and wine. The central **Sonoma Plaza** dates from the Mission era; surrounding it are 19th-century adobes, atmospheric hotels, and the swooping marquee of the 1930s Sebastiani Theatre. On summer days the plaza is a hive of activity, with children blowing off steam in the playground while their folks stock up on picnic supplies and browse the boutiques surrounding the square.

On your way into town from the south, you pass through the Carneros wine district, which straddles the southern sections of Sonoma and Napa counties.

A tree-lined driveway leads to **Lachryma Montis**, which General Mariano G. Vallejo, the last Mexican governor of California, built for his large family in 1852. The Victorian Gothic house, insulated with adobe, represents a blend of Mexican and American cultures. Opulent furnishings, including white-marble fireplaces and a French rosewood piano, are particularly noteworthy. Free tours are occasionally conducted by docents on weekends. ✉ *W. Spain St. near 3rd St.* W ☎ *707/938–9559* 🖃 *$3, tour free* ☉ *Fri.–Wed. 10–5.*

Reminiscent of a Tuscan villa, with ocher-color buildings surrounded by olive trees and colorful flower beds, sprawling **Viansa** focuses on Italian varietals such as sangiovese, nebbiolo, and tocai friulano. Fodor's

19

readers are generally split when summing up the charms of the winery. Some love the market on the premises that sells sandwiches and deli foods to complement the Italian-style wines, as well as a large selection of dinnerware, cookbooks, and condiments. Others find the crowds that tend to congregate here off-putting (it's popular for large parties and weddings). Regardless, the many picnic tables, some of which overlook a wetland preserve below, are a fine place to enjoy a glass of wine while bird-watching (only food and wines sold on the premises are permitted). ⊠ *25200 Arnold Dr.* ☎ *707/935–4700* ⊕ *www.viansa. com* ☒ *Tasting $5–$20, tour $10 (tasting fee additional)* ☉ *Daily 10–5; tour daily at 11, 2, and 3.*

The **Robledo Family Winery,** founded by Reynaldo Robledo Sr., a former migrant worker from Michoacán, Mexico, is truly a family affair. You're likely to encounter one of the charming Robledo sons in the tasting room, where he'll proudly tell you the story of the immigrant family while pouring tastes of their sauvignon blanc, pinot noir, merlot, cabernet sauvignon, and other wines, including a chardonnay that comes from the vineyard right outside the tasting room's door. All seven Robledo sons and two Robledo daughters, as well as matriarch Maria, are involved in the winery operations. If you don't run into them on your visit to the winery, you'll see their names and pictures on the bottles of wine, such as the Dos Hermanas late-harvest dessert wine, or one of the ports dedicated to Maria Robledo. ⊠ *21901 Bonness Rd.* ☎ *707/939–6903* ⊕ *www.robledofamilywinery.com* ☒ *Tasting $5–$10* ☉ *Mon.–Sat. 10–5, Sun. 11–4.*

Although many Carneros wineries specialize in pinot noir and chardonnay, **Cline Cellars** goes its own way by focusing on Rhône varietals, such as syrah, roussanne, and viognier, all grown here in Carneros, as well as mourvèdre and carignane, which are cultivated in Contra Costa County. They're also known for their Ancient Vines Zinfandel, produced from vines that are around 100 years old. The 1850s farmhouse that houses the tasting room has a pleasant wraparound porch for enjoying the weeping willows, ponds, fountains, and thousands of rosebushes on the property. Pack a picnic and plan to stay for a while, if you have the time. ⊠ *24737 Hwy. 121/Arnold Dr.* ☎ *707/940–4030* ⊕ *www.clinecellars.com* ☒ *Tasting free–$1 per reserve wine, tour free* ☉ *Daily 10–6; tour daily at 11, 1, and 3.*

★ Just far enough off the beaten track to feel like a real find, **DeLoach Vineyards** produces a variety of Russian River Valley old-vine zinfandels, chardonnays, and handful of other varietals, but it is best for known for its pinot noir, some of which is made using open-top wood fermentation vats that are uncommon in Sonoma but have been used in France for centuries. (Some think that they intensify a wine's flavor.) Tours focus on the estate vineyards outside the tasting room door, where you can learn about the labor-intensive biodynamic and organic farming methods used here, and take you through their culinary garden. ⊠ *1791 Olivet Rd.* ☎ *707/526–9111* ⊕ *www.deloachvineyards.com* ☒ *Tasting $10, tour free* ☉ *Daily 10–5; tour daily by appointment.*

Buena Vista Carneros Winery is the oldest continually operating winery in California. It was here, in 1857, that Count Agoston Haraszthy de Mokcsa laid the basis for modern California wine making, bucking the conventional wisdom that vines should be planted on well-watered ground by instead planting on well-drained hillsides. Chinese laborers dug tunnels 100 feet into the hillside, and the limestone they extracted was used to build the main house, which is now surrounded by redwood and eucalyptus trees and a picnic area. Their best wines are their chardonnay, pinot noir, syrah, and merlot grown in the Ramal Vineyard in the Carneros District. If you're a bit peckish, reserve ahead for a seated tasting of five wines paired with cheeses or other nibbles. ⊠ *18000 Old Winery Rd., off Napa Rd.* ☎ *800/678–8504* ⊕ *buenavistacarneros.com* 🎫 *Tasting $10–$20* ⊙ *Daily 10–5.*

Ravenswood, whose tasting room is housed in a stone building covered in climbing vines, has a punchy mission statement: "no wimpy wines." They generally succeed, especially with their signature big, bold zinfandels, which are sometimes blended with petit syrah, carignane, or other varietals. Be sure to taste the syrah, early-harvest gewürztraminer, and lightly sparkling moscato, too. Tours that focus on their viticultural practices ($15), held 10:30 daily, include a barrel tasting of wines in progress in the cellar. Another tour, at 11:30 on weekdays from mid-May through September, concludes with wine-and-cheese pairings ($25). Tour reservations are recommended for the former and required for the latter. ⊠ *18701 Gehricke Rd., off E. Spain St.* ☎ *707/938–1960* ⊕ *www.ravenswood-wine.com* 🎫 *Tasting $10–$15, tour $15–$25* ⊙ *Daily 10–4:30; call for tour times.*

Fodor's Choice
★

Although **Bartholomew Park Winery** was founded only in 1994, grapes were grown in some of its vineyards as early as the 1830s. The emphasis here is on handcrafted, single-varietal wines—cabernet, merlot, zinfandel, syrah, and sauvignon blanc. The wines themselves, available only at the winery, make a stop worth it, but another reason to visit is its small museum, with vivid exhibits about the history of the winery and the Sonoma region. Another plus is the beautiful, slightly off-the-beaten-path location in a 375-acre private park about 2 mi from downtown Sonoma. Pack a picnic to enjoy on the woodsy grounds. ⊠ *1000 Vineyard La.* ☎ *707/939–3026* ⊕ *www.bartholomewparkwinery.com* 🎫 *Tasting $5* ⊙ *Daily 11–4:30.*

19

WHERE TO EAT

$$
✕ **Cafe La Haye.** In a postage-stamp-size open kitchen, skillful chefs turn
AMERICAN
★
out about half a dozen main courses that star on a small but worthwhile seasonal menu emphasizing local ingredients. Chicken, beef, pasta, and fish get deluxe treatment without fuss or fanfare. The chicken roasted with rosemary, for instance, and the daily risotto special is always good. Butterscotch pudding is a homey signature dessert. The dining room is also compact, but the friendly owner, who is often there to greet diners, gives it a particularly welcoming vibe. ⊠ *140 E. Napa St.* ☎ *707/935–5994* ⊕ *www.cafelahaye.com* ☰ *MC, V* ⊙ *Closed Sun. and Mon. No lunch.*

$
✕ **Della Santina's.** This longtime favorite, with a charming heated brick
ITALIAN
patio out back, serves the most authentic Italian food in town. (The

Sonoma County

Della Santina family, which has been running the restaurant since 1990, hails from Lucca, Italy.) Daily fish and veal specials join classic northern Italian pastas such as linguine with pesto and lasagna Bolognese. Of special note are the roasted meat dishes and, when available, petrale sole and sand dabs (both are types of flounder). ✉ *133 E. Napa St.* ☎ *707/935–0576* ⊕ *www.dellasantinas.com* 🍴 *AE, D, MC, V.*

WORD OF MOUTH

"No trip to Napa is complete without a side trip to Sonoma, but I am prejudiced. Artesa is gorgeous. Hess is a drive, but the grounds and the jaw dropping art gallery are amazing.... For a fun tour, Frog's Leap. Unpretentious. Touristy, but beautiful and truly unique is Opus One. They do everything by hand. Schedule a tour in advance."   —LlindaCC

$$ ✕ **The Girl & the Fig.** Chef Sondra

FRENCH   Bernstein has turned the historic barroom of the Sonoma Hotel into a hot spot for inventive French cooking. You can always find something with the signature figs in it here, whether it's a fig-and-arugula salad or an aperitif of sparkling wine with a fig liqueur. Also look for duck confit with French lentils, a burger with matchstick fries, or wild boar braised in red wine. The wine list is notable for its emphasis on Rhône varietals, and a counter in the bar area sells artisanal cheese platters for eating here as well as cheese by the pound to go. Sunday brunch brings rib-sticking dishes such as steak and eggs and a Basque frittata with potatoes, onions, and tomatoes. ✉ *Sonoma Hotel, Sonoma Plaza, 110 W. Spain St.* ☎ *707/938–3634* ⊕ *www.thegirlandthefig.com* 🍴 *D, MC, V.*

$$ ✕ **Harvest Moon Cafe.** It's easy to feel like one of the family at this little

AMERICAN   restaurant with an odd, zigzagging layout. Diners seated at one of the

★   two tiny bars chat with the servers like old friends, but the husband-and-wife team in the kitchen is serious about the food, much of which relies on local produce. The daily menu sticks to homey dishes like half a grilled chicken served with polenta and tapenade, rib-eye steak with a red wine sauce, and a marinated-beet-and-leek salad. Everything is so perfectly executed and the vibe so genuinely warm that a visit here is deeply satisfying. In fair weather, a spacious back patio, with seats arranged around a fountain, more than doubles the number of seats. ✉ *487 W. 1st St.* ☎ *707/933–8160* ⊕ *www.harvestmooncafesonoma.com* 🍴 *AE, D, MC, V* ⊙ *No lunch Mon.–Sat.*

$ ✕ **La Casa.** Terra cotta–color tile floors and ceramics on the walls evoke

MEXICAN   Old Mexico at this spot that has been at the edge of Sonoma's plaza for more than four decades. There's bar seating, a patio, and large menu of traditional Mexican favorites, like enchiladas *suizas* (chicken enchiladas with a tomatillo salsa), burritos, and fish tacos. Though the food is fairly standard, the casual, festive atmosphere and margaritas sold by the glass or pitcher make it a popular stop, especially during happy hour (weekdays 4–7). ✉ *121 E. Spain St.* ☎ *707/996–3406* ⊕ *www.lacasarestaurant.com* 🍴 *AE, D, DC, MC, V.*

$$ ✕ **LaSalette.** Chef-owner Manuel Azevedo, born in the Azores and

PORTUGUESE   raised in Sonoma, serves dishes inspired by his native Portugal in this warmly decorated spot, where the best seats are on the patio, along

Who's Who in the Grape World

Well more than 50 varieties of grapes are grown in the California Wine Country. Although you don't need to be on a first-name basis with them all, you'll see the following dozen again and again as you visit the wineries.

WHITES

■ **Chardonnay.** Now as firmly associated with California wine making as it is with Burgundy, where it's used extensively. California chardonnays spent many years chasing big, buttery flavor, but the current trend is toward more restrained wines.

■ **Gewürztraminer.** Cooler California climes such as the Russian River Valley are great for growing this German-Alsatian grape, which is turned into a boldly perfumed, fruity wine.

■ **Riesling.** Also called Johannisberg Riesling or White Riesling, this cool-climate German grape has a sweet rep in America. When made in a dry style, as it more and more often is, it can be crisply refreshing, with lush aromas.

■ **Sauvignon Blanc.** Hails from Bordeaux and the Loire Valley. Wines made from this grape vary widely, from herbaceous to tropical-fruity.

■ **Viognier.** Once rarely planted outside of France's Rhône Valley, it's one of the hottest white-wine varietals in California today. The best viogniers have an intense fruity or floral bouquet; they're usually dry.

REDS

■ **Cabernet Franc.** Most often used in blends, often to add complexity to cabernet sauvignon, this French grape can produce aromatic, soft, and subtle wine.

■ **Cabernet Sauvignon.** The king of California reds, this Bordeaux grape grows best in austere, well-drained soils. At its best, the California version is dark, bold, and tannic, with black-currant notes. It's often blended with cabernet franc, merlot, and other red varieties to soften the resulting wine and make it ready for earlier drinking.

■ **Merlot.** A blue-black Bordeaux variety that in California makes soft, full-bodied wine. Was well on its way to being the most popular red until anti-merlot jokes in the movie *Sideways* and elsewhere damaged its rep... for now.

■ **Pinot Noir.** The darling of grape growers in cooler parts of Napa and Sonoma, such as the Carneros region and the Russian River Valley. At its best it has a subtle but addictive earthy quality.

■ **Sangiovese.** The main red grape of Italy's Chianti District and of much of central Italy. It can be made into vibrant, light- to medium-bodied wines, as well as into long-lived, very complex reds. Increasingly planted in California.

■ **Syrah.** A big red from France's Rhône Valley. With good tannins it can become a full-bodied beauty, but without them it can be flabby and forgettable. Also known as shiraz, particularly when it's grown in Australia.

■ **Zinfandel.** A quintessential California grape. Rich, jammy, and often spicy, zinfandel wines can be quite high in alcohol.

19

a pedestrian alleyway off of Sonoma's plaza. Boldly flavored dishes such as *pork tenderloin recheado*, stuffed with olives and almonds and topped with a port sauce, or one of the daily seafood specials might be followed by a dish of rice pudding with Madeira-braised figs or a port from the varied list. ⊠ *452 E. 1st St.* ☎ *707/938–1927* ⊕ *www.lasalette-restaurant.com* ⊟ *AE, MC, V.*

WORD OF MOUTH

"Napa was nice but much more crowded (a lot of tour groups) and we spent SO much more money in tasting fees. We've stayed in the towns of Sonoma and Healdsburg and really liked both. You can't go wrong either way." —raceloughren

$$$$
AMERICAN
Fodor's Choice
★

✕ **Santé.** Under the leadership of chef de cuisine Andrew Cain, this elegant dining room in the Sonoma Mission Inn has gained a reputation as a destination restaurant through its focus on seasonal and locally sourced ingredients. The room is understated, with drapes in rich earth tones and softly lighted chandeliers, but the food is anything but. Dishes on the frequently changing menu, such as a roasted Sonoma duck breast with braised Swiss chard and duck confit, are complex without being fussy, while some dishes, like the butter-poached Maine lobster with flageolet beans and lardons, are pure decadence. ⊠ *Fairmont Sonoma Mission Inn & Spa, 100 Boyes Blvd./Rte. 12, at Boyes Blvd., 2 mi north of Sonoma, Boyes Hot Springs* ☎ *707/939–2415* ⊟ *AE, D, DC, MC, V* ☾ *No lunch.*

$
AMERICAN

✕ **Sunflower Caffé.** Although you wouldn't realize it as you walk by, this casual breakfast-and-lunch-only café has one of Sonoma's prettiest patios. Equipped with both heating lamps and plenty of shade, it's comfortable in all but the most inclement weather. The menu, composed mostly of salads and sandwiches (as well as omelets and waffles for breakfast), is simple but satisfying, and it relies largely on local ingredients. It's also a comfortable spot to take a quick break with an excellent coffee drink or something from the well-stocked outdoor wine bar. ⊠ *421 W. 1st St.* ☎ *707/996–6645* ⊕ *www.sonomasunflower.com* ⌔ *Reservations not accepted* ⊟ *AE, MC, V* ☾ *No dinner.*

WHERE TO STAY

¢
🏨 **El Dorado Hotel.** Rooms in this remodeled 1843 building strike a spare, modern pose, with rectilinear four-poster beds and pristine white bedding, but the Mexican-tile floors hint at Sonoma's Mission-era past. Rooms are small, but high-tech features like flat-panel TVs and iPod alarm clocks are a nice touch, and each has a small balcony that overlooks the street or the courtyard or El Dorado Kitchen. Though its position (right on Sonoma's plaza and on top of a bustling restaurant and bar) is considered a boon by some, earplugs are advised for all but the hardiest sleepers. **Pros:** stylish for the price; hip restaurant downstairs; central location. **Cons:** rooms could use better lighting; noisy. ⊠ *405 1st St. W* ☎ *707/996–3030* ⊕ *www.eldoradosonoma.com* ⤙ *27 rooms* ⌂ *In-room: a/c, refrigerator, DVD, Wi-Fi. In-hotel: restaurant, bar, pool* ⊟ *AE, MC, V.*

$$$–$$$$
🏨 **The Fairmont Sonoma Mission Inn & Spa.** The real draw at this Mission-style resort is the extensive, swanky spa, easily the biggest in Sonoma. There's a vast array of massages and treatments, some using locally

sourced grape and lavender products. (It's a coed spa, and there are several treatments designed for couples.) The focus on fitness and rejuvenation extends to a 7,087-yard golf course winding through trees and vineyards, a changing schedule of fitness classes, and guided hiking and biking excursions each morning. The guest rooms aren't terribly large but are supremely comfortable; some have fireplaces and patios or balconies. The staff stays on top of every detail. **Pros:** enormous spa; excellent Michelin-starred restaurant on-site; free shuttle to downtown. **Cons:** not as intimate as some similarly priced places. ⊠ *100 Boyes Blvd./Rte. 12, 2 mi north of Sonoma, Boyes Hot Springs* ☎ *707/938–9000* ⊕ *www.fairmont.com/sonoma* ↗ *168 rooms, 60 suites* ⌂ *In-room: a/c, safe, refrigerator, Internet, Wi-Fi. In-hotel: 2 restaurants, room service, bars, golf course, tennis courts, pools, gym, spa, bicycles, laundry service, some pets allowed (fee)* ▤ *AE, D, DC, MC, V.*

¢ ⊡ **Sonoma Creek Inn.** The small but cheerful rooms at this roadside inn with a sunny yellow exterior are individually decorated with painted wooden armoires, cozy quilts, and brightly colored contemporary artwork, elevating this bargain option well above your average motel. Most rooms even have vaulted ceilings, and many have small patios with a little fountain. Free roll-away beds for kids and an independently owned diner attached to the property make it an especially family-friendly option. Pros: clean, well-lighted bathrooms; a lot of charm for the low price. Cons: office not staffed 24 hours a day; slightly out-of-the-way location (about a 10-minute drive from Sonoma's Plaza). ⊠ *239 Boyes Blvd.* ☎ *707/939–9463* ⊕ *www.sonomacreekinn.com* ↗ *16 rooms* ⌂ *In-room: a/c, refrigerator, Wi-Fi. In-hotel: restaurant, some pets allowed (fee)* ▤ *AE, D, MC, V.*

NIGHTLIFE AND THE ARTS

The **Sebastiani Theatre** (⊠ *476 1st St. E* ☎ *707/996–2020*), built on Sonoma's plaza in 1934 by Italian immigrant and entrepreneur Samuele Sebastiani, schedules first-run films, as well as the occasional musical or theatrical performance.

Hit the **Swiss Hotel**'s bar (⊠ *18 W. Spain St.* ☎ *707/938–2884*) to sip a Glariffee, a cold and potent cousin to Irish coffee that's unique to this 19th-century spot.

SHOPPING

Sonoma Plaza is the town's main shopping magnet, with tempting boutiques and specialty food purveyors facing the square or just a block or two away. **Sign of the Bear** (⊠ *Sonoma Plaza, 435 1st St. W* ☎ *707/996–3722*) sells the latest and greatest in kitchenware and cookware, as well as a few Wine Country–theme items, like lazy Susans made from wine barrels.

The **Sonoma Cheese Factory and Deli** (⊠ *Sonoma Plaza, 2 Spain St.* ☎ *707/996–1931*), run by the same family for four generations, makes Sonoma Jack cheese and the tangy Sonoma Teleme. It has everything you need for a picnic.

A block east of Sonoma Plaza, the **Vella Cheese Company** (⊠ *315 2nd St. E* ☎ *707/938–3232*) has been making superb cheeses, such as raw-milk cheddars and several varieties of jack, since 1931.

Where to Eat and Stay in Sonoma County

GLEN ELLEN

7 mi north of Sonoma on Rte. 12.

Craggy Glen Ellen embodies the difference between the Napa and Sonoma valleys. In small Napa towns such as St. Helena well-groomed sidewalks are lined with upscale boutiques and restaurants, but in Glen Ellen the crooked streets are shaded with stands of old oak trees and occasionally bisected by the Sonoma and Calabasas creeks.

FARMERS' MARKET

The Sonoma Farmers' Market overflows with locally farmed produce, artisanal cheeses, and baked goods. It's held year-round at Depot Park, just north of Sonoma Plaza, on Friday from 9 AM to noon. From April through October, it gets extra play on Tuesday evenings 5:30 PM-dusk at Sonoma Plaza.

Jack London, who represents Glen Ellen's rugged spirit, lived in the area for many years; the town commemorates him with place-names and nostalgic establishments.

In the Jack London Village complex, **Figone's Olive Oil Co.** (⊠ *14301 Arnold Dr.* ☎ *707/938–3164*) not only carries many local olive oils, serving bowls, books, and dining accessories, but also presses olives for a number of local growers, usually in late fall. You can taste a selection of olive oils that have surprisingly different flavors.

Built in 1905, the **Jack London Saloon** (⊠ *13740 Arnold Dr.* ☎ *707/996–3100* ⊕ *www.jacklondonlodge.com*) is decorated with photos of London and other London memorabilia.

In the hills above Glen Ellen—known as the Valley of the Moon—lies **Jack London State Historic Park,** where you could easily spend the afternoon hiking along the edge of vineyards and through stands of oak trees. Several of the author's manuscripts and a handful of personal effects are on view at the House of Happy Walls museum, once the home of London's widow. A short hike away from Happy Walls are the ruins of Wolf House. Designed by London, it mysteriously burned down just before he was to move in. Also open to the public are a few restored farm outbuildings. London is buried on the property. ⊠ *2400 London Ranch Rd.* ☎ *707/938–5216* 🖃 *Parking $8, admission to buildings free* ⊙ *Park Sat.–Wed. 10–5. Museum weekends 10–5, Mon.–Wed. 10–4.*

Arrowood Vineyards & Winery is neither as old nor as famous as some of its neighbors (they made their first wines in 1986), but winemakers and critics are quite familiar with the wines produced here by Richard Arrowood, especially the chardonnays, syrahs, and age-worthy cabernets. A wraparound porch with wicker chairs invites you to linger outside the tasting room, built to resemble a New England farmhouse. Tours, offered twice daily by appointment, conclude with a seated tasting. An unusually kid-friendly destination, the winery has a small toy box in the tasting room, and will offer a tasting of nonalcoholic drinks on their tour, if you give them advance notice. ∎TIP→ If you're doing a reserve tasting on a weekend, and you're interested in discovering what **Arrowood** wines taste like after several years in the bottle, ask if they happen to have any library wines open they can pour. ⊠ *14347 Sonoma Hwy./Rte. 12*

Horseback riding tours loop around Jack London State Historic Park.

☎ 707/935–2600 ⊕ *www.arrowoodvineyards.com* ✉ *Tasting $5–$10, tour $25* ☉ *Daily 10–4:30; tour by appointment.*

★ One of the best-known local wineries is **Benziger Family Winery**, on a sprawling estate in a bowl with 360-degree sun exposure. Benziger is noted for its merlot, cabernet sauvignon, chardonnay, and sauvignon blanc. The tram tours here are especially interesting (they're first come, first served). On a ride through the vineyards, guides explain the regional microclimates and geography and give you a glimpse of the extensive cave system. Tours depart several times a day, weather permitting, but are sometimes fully booked during the high season. Reservations are needed for smaller tours that conclude with a seated tasting ($40). ■TIP→ Arrive before lunch for the best shot at joining a tour—and bring a picnic, since the grounds here are lovely. ✉ *1883 London Ranch Rd.* ☎ *707/935–3000* ⊕ *www.benziger.com* ✉ *Tasting $10–$15, tour $15–$40* ☉ *Daily 10–5.*

WHERE TO EAT AND STAY

$$
FRENCH
Fodor's Choice
★

✗ **The Fig Cafe.** Pale sage walls, a high, sloping ceiling, and casual but very warm service set a sunny mood in this little bistro that's run by the same team behind Sonoma's The Girl & the Fig. The restaurant's eponymous fruit shows up in all sorts of places—not only in salads and desserts, but also on thin-crust pizzas piled high with arugula. The small menu focuses on California and French comfort food, like steamed mussels served with terrific crispy fries, and a braised pot roast served with seasonal vegetables. Don't forget to look on the chalkboard for frequently changing desserts, such as butterscotch pots de crème. ■TIP→ The unusual no-corkage-fee policy makes it a great place

19

Hitching a ride on the Benziger Family Winery tram tour.

to drink the wine you just discovered down the road. ⊠ *13690 Arnold Dr.* ☎ *707/938–2130* ⊕ *www.thegirlandthefig.com* ♨ *Reservations not accepted* ⊟ *D, MC, V* ⊙ *No lunch weekdays.*

$$ ✗ **Glen Ellen Inn Oyster Grill & Martini Bar.** This cozy restaurant in a creek-
ECLECTIC   side 1940s cottage exudes romance, especially if you snag a seat in the shady garden or on the patio strung with tiny lights. After taking the edge off your hunger with some oysters on the half shell and an ice-cold martini (or one of their 25 or so variations on the theme), order from the eclectic, frequently changing menu that plucks elements from California, French, and occasionally Asian cuisines. For instance, you might try Dungeness crab pot stickers or a filet mignon with cambozola cheese and wild mushrooms. Desserts tend toward the indulgent; witness the warm pecan bread pudding with a chocolate center that sits in a puddle of brandy sauce. ⊠ *13670 Arnold Dr.* ☎ *707/996–6409* ⊕ *www. glenelleninn.com* ⊟ *AE, MC, V* ⊙ *No lunch Wed. or Thurs.*

¢–$ ▦ **Beltane Ranch.** On a slope of the Mayacamas range a few miles from
★   Glen Ellen, this 1892 ranch house stands in the shade of magnificent oak trees. The charmingly old-fashioned rooms, each individually decorated with antiques and thick old-fashioned bedcovers, have exterior entrances, and some open onto a wraparound balcony ideal for whiling away lazy afternoons. A bountiful breakfast, included in the price, incorporates produce from the gardens here, when it's in season, as well as eggs from their chickens. **Pros:** casual, friendly atmosphere; reasonably priced; beautiful grounds with ancient oak trees. **Cons:** downstairs rooms get some noise from upstairs rooms; cooled with ceiling fans instead of air-conditioning. ⊠ *11775 Sonoma Hwy./Rte. 12* ☎ *707/996–*

6501 ⊕ *www.beltaneranch.com* ⮑ *3 rooms, 3 suites* ⚭ *In-room: no phone, no TV, Wi-Fi. In-hotel: tennis court* ▭ *MC, V* ⦿ *BP.*

$$$–$$$$
Fodor's Choice
★

⊡ **Gaige House.** Gorgeous Asian objets d'art and leather club chairs cozied up to the fireplace in the lobby are just a few of the graceful touches in this luxurious but understated B&B. Rooms in the main house, an 1890 Queen Anne, are mostly done in pale colors, and each has its advantages. One upstairs room has wraparound windows to let in floods of light, for instance, while the lavish creek-side cottages feel Japanese, with massive granite soaking tubs overlooking private atriums. Magnolia trees shade the backyard, where there's a small but idyllic swimming pool and hot tub. Though the staffers are helpful, service never seems fussy, and there's a bottomless jar of cookies in the common area. Although a continental breakfast is included, you can pay a bit more for a full breakfast. **Pros:** beautiful lounge areas; cottages are very private. **Cons:** sound carries in the main house; the least expensive rooms are on the small side. ⊠ *13540 Arnold Dr.* ☎ *707/935–0237 or 800/935–0237* ⊕ *www.gaige.com* ⮑ *10 rooms, 13 suites* ⚭ *In-room: a/c, safe, refrigerator (some), DVD, Wi-Fi. In-hotel: pool, spa, no kids under 12* ▭ *AE, D, DC, MC, V.*

¢   ⊡ **Glenelly Inn and Cottages.** On a quiet side street a few blocks from the town center, this sunny little establishment has a long history as a getaway. It was built as an inn in 1916, and the rooms, each individually decorated, tend toward a simple country style. Many have four-poster beds and touches such as a wood-burning stove or antique oak dresser; some have whirlpool tubs. All have puffy down comforters. Breakfast is served in front of the common room's fireplace, as are cookies or other snacks in the afternoon. ■**TIP**➔ Innkeeper Kristi Hallamore Jeppesen has two children of her own, so this is an unusually kid-friendly inn. **Pros:** children are welcome; quiet location; hot tub in a pretty garden. **Cons:** some may not appreciate the presence of children; less expensive rooms are on the small side. ⊠ *5131 Warm Springs Rd.* ☎ *707/996–6720* ⊕ *www. glenellyinn.com* ⮑ *8 rooms, 2 suites* ⚭ *In-room: a/c (some), no phone (some), refrigerator (some), DVD, Wi-Fi. In-hotel: laundry facilities, some pets allowed* ▭ *AE, D, MC, V* ⦿ *BP.*

19

KENWOOD

3 mi north of Glen Ellen on Rte. 12.

Blink and you might miss tiny Kenwood, which consists of little more than a few restaurants and shops and a historic train depot, now used for private events. But hidden in this pretty landscape of meadows and woods at the north end of Sonoma Valley are several good wineries, most just off the Sonoma Highway.

Many wineries around the Kenwood area are small, so tiny that they don't have tasting rooms of their own. At **Family Wineries** you can sample the output of several such spots. Though the lineup of participating wineries occasionally changes, look for sweet flavored sparklers produced by SL Cellars and still wines from Sonoma producers such as David Noyes and Collier Falls. ⊠ *9380 Sonoma Hwy.* ☎ *888/433–6555* ⊕ *www.familywines.com* ▱ *Tasting $5* ⊙ *Daily 10:30–5.*

On your way into **Kunde Estate Winery & Vineyards** you pass a terrace flanked with fountains, virtually coaxing you to stay for a picnic with views over the vineyard. The tour of the grounds includes its extensive caves, some of which stretch 175 feet below a syrah vineyard. Kunde is perhaps best known for its toasty chardonnays, although tastings might include sauvignon blanc, cabernet sauvignon, and zinfandel as well. If you skip the tour, take a few minutes to wander around the demonstration vineyard outside the tasting room. In the months before crush (usually in September), you can taste the different grapes on the vines and see if you can taste the similarities between the grapes and wines you just tasted. ⊠ *9825 Sonoma Hwy./Rte. 12* ☎ *707/833–5501* ⊕ *www.kunde.com* 🍷 *Tasting $10–$20, tour free* ⊗ *Daily 10:30–4:30; tours weekdays at 11, weekends on the hr 11–3.*

Kenwood Vineyards makes some good value-priced red and white wines, as well as some showier cabernet sauvignons, zinfandels, and merlots, many of which are poured in the tasting room housed in one of the original barns on the property. The best of these come from Jack London's old vineyard, in the Sonoma Mountain appellation, above the fog belt of the Sonoma Valley (Kenwood has an exclusive lease). But the crisp sauvignon blanc is what keeps wine connoisseurs coming back for more. ⊠ *9592 Sonoma Hwy./Rte. 12* ☎ *707/833–5891* ⊕ *www. kenwoodvineyards.com* 🍷 *Tasting $5* ⊗ *Daily 10–4:30.*

★ Named for St. Francis of Assisi, founder of the Franciscan order, which established missions and vineyards throughout California, **St. Francis Winery** has one of the most scenic locations in Sonoma, nestled at the foot of Mt. Hood. The visitor center beautifully replicates the California Mission style, with its red tile roof and dramatic bell tower (a plaque explains that the bell was actually blessed in the Basilica di San Francesco in Assisi, Italy). Out back, a slate patio overlooks vineyards, lavender gardens, and hummingbirds flitting about the flower beds. The charm of the surroundings is matched by the wines, most of them red. Consider paying a bit more ($30) to taste wines paired with artisanal cheeses and charcuterie, served either on the patio or seated in the dining room. ⊠ *100 Pythian Rd.* ☎ *800/543–7713* ⊕ *www.stfranciswinery. com* 🍷 *Tasting $10–$15* ⊗ *Daily 10–5.*

WHERE TO EAT AND STAY

$ ✕ **Café Citti.** Opera tunes in the background and a friendly staff (as well
ITALIAN   as a roaring fire when the weather's cold) keep this no-frills roadside café from feeling too spartan. Order dishes such as roast chicken and slabs of tiramisu from the counter and they're delivered to your table, a few of which are on an outdoor patio. An ample array of prepared salads and sandwiches means they do a brisk business in takeout for picnic packers, but you can also choose pasta made to order, mixing and matching linguine, penne, and other pastas with sauces like pesto or marinara. ⊠ *9049 Sonoma Hwy./Rte. 12* ☎ *707/833–2690* ⊕ *www. cafecitti.com* 🍷 *MC, V.*

$$$$ 🛏 **Kenwood Inn and Spa.** Buildings resembling graceful old haciendas and
★   mature fruit trees shading the courtyards make it seem like this inn has been here for more than a century (it was actually built in 1990). French doors opening onto terraces or balconies, fluffy featherbeds, and wood-

burning fireplaces give the uncommonly spacious guest rooms, many with tile floors, a particularly romantic air. A swimming pool, Jacuzzis, and saunas pepper three atmospheric courtyards, and you could easily spend an afternoon padding from one to another in your robe and slippers. The spa is intimate but well equipped. **Pros:** large rooms; lavish furnishings; extremely romantic. **Cons:** Wi-Fi can be spotty in some areas; the expensive restaurant isn't quite up to the level of the inn. ✉ *10400 Sonoma Hwy.* ☎ *707/833–1293* ⊕ *www.kenwoodinn.com* ↩ *29 rooms* ⚘ *In-room: a/c, no TV, Internet, Wi-Fi. In-hotel: restaurant, bar, pool, spa, laundry service, no kids under 18.* ▭ *AE, MC, V.*

ELSEWHERE IN SONOMA COUNTY

At nearly 1,598 square mi, there's much more to Sonoma County than the day-tripper favorites of Sonoma, Glen Ellen, and Kenwood. To the north is Healdsburg, a lovely small town with a rapidly rising buzz. The national media have latched onto it for its swank hotels and remarkable restaurants, and many Fodors.com readers recommend it as an ideal home base for wine tasting.

Within easy striking distance of Healdsburg are some of the Wine Country's most scenic vineyards, in the Alexander, Dry Creek, and Russian River valleys. And these lookers also happen to produce some of the country's best pinot noir, cabernet sauvignon, zinfandel, and sauvignon blanc. Though these regions are hardly unknown names, their quiet, narrow roads feel a world away from Highway 29 in Napa.

The western stretches of Sonoma County, which reach all the way to the Pacific Ocean, are sparsely populated in comparison to the above destinations, with only the occasional vineyard popping up in between isolated ranches. Guerneville, a popular destination for weekending San Franciscans, who come to canoe down the Russian River, is a convenient place for picking up River Road, then Westside Road, which passes through pinot noir paradise on its way to Healdsburg.

19

SANTA ROSA

8 mi northwest of Kenwood on Rte. 12.

Santa Rosa, the Wine Country's largest city, isn't likely to charm you with its office buildings, department stores, and frequent snarls of traffic along U.S. 101. It is, however, home to a couple of interesting cultural offerings. Its chain motels and hotels are also handy if you're finding that everything else is booked up, especially since Santa Rosa is roughly equidistant from Sonoma, Healdsburg, and the Russian River Valley, three of the most popular wine-tasting destinations.

The **Luther Burbank Home and Gardens** commemorates the great botanist who lived and worked on these grounds and single-handedly developed the modern techniques of hybridization. The 1.6-acre garden and a greenhouse show the results of some of Burbank's experiments to develop spineless cactus, fruit trees, and flowers such as the Shasta daisy. In the music room of his house, a modified Greek Revival structure that was Burbank's home from 1884 to 1906, a dictionary lies open to a page on which the verb "burbank" is defined as "to modify and improve plant life." (To see the house, you'll need to join one of the docent-led tours, which leave from the gift shop every half hour.) ⊠ *Santa Rosa and Sonoma Aves.* ☎ *707/524–5445* ⊕ *www.lutherburbank.org* ⌕ *Gardens free, tour $7* ☉ *Gardens daily 8–dusk; museum and gift shop Apr.–Oct., Tues.–Sun. 10–4.*

Fans of Snoopy and Charlie Brown should head to the **Charles M. Schulz Museum,** dedicated to the cartoonist who lived in Santa Rosa for the last 30 years of his life, until his death in 2000. Permanent installations such as a re-creation of the artist's studio share the space with temporary exhibits, which often focus on a particular theme in Schulz's work. Both children and adults can try their hand at creating cartoons in the Education Room or wander through the labyrinth in the form of Snoopy's head. Check the Web site or call for information about occasional kid-friendly workshops and events. ⊠ *2301 Hardies La.* ☎ *707/579–4452* ⊕ *www.schulzmuseum.org* ⌕ *$10* ☉ *Labor Day–Memorial Day, Wed.– Fri. and Mon. 11–5, weekends 10–5; Memorial Day–Labor Day, weekdays 11–5, weekends 10–5.*

FodorsChoice
★

The visitor center at beautiful **Matanzas Creek Winery** sets itself apart with an understated Japanese aesthetic, with a tranquil fountain and a koi pond. Best of all, huge windows overlook a vast field of lavender plants. ■TIP→ The ideal time to visit is in May and June, when the lavender blooms and perfumes the air. The winery specializes in sauvignon blanc, merlot, and chardonnay, although they also produce a popular dry rosé as well as some syrah, pinot noir, and cabernet. Guided tours range from an hour-long intro to the Bennett Valley, the tiny AVA where the winery is located, to a more expensive one that concludes with a taste of limited-production and library wines paired with artisanal cheeses. ⊠ *6097 Bennett Valley Rd.* ☎ *707/528–6464 or 800/590–6464* ⊕ *www. matanzascreek.com* ⌕ *Tasting $5–$10, tour $10–$35* ☉ *Daily 10–4:30; tour by appointment.*

WHERE TO EAT

$$$
FodorsChoice
★

✕ **Zazu.** A low wooden ceiling, rustic copper tables, and rock music on the stereo create a casual vibe at this roadhouse. It's a few miles from downtown Santa Rosa, but the hearty, soulful cooking of owners Duskie Estes and John Stewart brings passionate fans from all over the Wine Country. Some of the produce for the salads comes from their own garden, and the meats are house-cured, so the antipasto plate or a pizza with house-made pepperoni are both excellent choices. The small seasonal menu—a mix of Italian-influenced dishes and updated American classics—tends toward rich flavors, with choices like rabbit braised in red wine and served with a mushroom risotto. ⊠ *3535 Guerneville Rd.* ☎ *707/523–4814* ⊕ *www.zazurestaurant.com* ⊟ *MC, V.*

RUSSIAN RIVER VALLEY

10 mi northwest of Santa Rosa.

The Russian River flows all the way from Mendocino to the Pacific Ocean, but in terms of wine making, the Russian River Valley is centered on a triangle with points at Healdsburg, Guerneville, and Sebastopol. Tall redwoods shade many of the two-lane roads that access this scenic area, where, thanks to the cooling marine influence, pinot noir and chardonnay are the king and queen of grapes.

ESSENTIALS

Contacts Russian River Wine Road (⊠ *Box 46, Healdsburg* ☎ *707/433–4335 or 800/723–6336* ⊕ *www.wineroad.com*).

At the **J Vineyards and Winery,** behind the bar in the tasting room is a dramatic steel sculpture studded with illuminated chunks of glass that suggests a bottle of bubbly. It's a big clue to what's most important here. The dry sparkling wines, made from pinot noir and chardonnay grapes planted in Russian River vineyards, have wonderfully complex fruit and floral aromas and good acidity. Still best known for its sparklers, J has also begun to make a larger number of fine still wines, often from pinot and chardonnay grapes but also from pinot gris, viognier, and zinfandel. Although you can sample wines on their own at the tasting bar, for a truly indulgent experience make a reservation for the Bubble Room, where you should set aside a couple of hours for a selection of top-end still and sparkling wines served with different foods. Tours are offered twice daily by appointment. ⊠ *11447 Old Redwood Hwy. Healdsburg* ☎ *707/431–3646* ⊕ *www.jwine.com* 🍷 *Tasting $20–$60* ☉ *Daily 11–5; Bubble Room hrs vary.*

Fodor'sChoice
★ **Iron Horse Vineyards** makes a wide variety of sparkling wines, from the bright and austere to the rich and toasty, as well as estate chardonnays and pinot noirs. Three hundred acres of rolling, vine-covered hills, barnlike winery buildings, and a beautifully rustic outdoor tasting area with a view of Mt. St. Helena set it apart from stuffier spots. (Instead of providing buckets for you to dump out the wine you don't want to finish, they ask you to toss it into the grass behind you.) Tours are available by appointment on weekdays at 10 AM. ⊠ *9786 Ross Station Rd., Sebastopol* ☎ *707/887–1507* ⊕ *www.ironhorsevineyards.com* 🍷 *Tasting $10, tour free* ☉ *Daily 10–3:30; tour weekdays at 10 by appointment.*

19

Rochioli Vineyards and Winery claims one of the prettiest picnic sites in the area, with tables overlooking vineyards, which are also visible from the airy little tasting room hung with modern artwork. Production is small—about 12,000 or 13,000 cases annually—and fans on the winery's mailing list snap up most of the bottles, but the wines are still worth a stop. Because of the cool growing conditions in the Russian River Valley, the flavors of their chardonnay and sauvignon blanc are intense and complex. It's their pinot, though, that is largely responsible for the winery's stellar reputation; it helped cement the Russian River's status as a pinot powerhouse. ■TIP➔ Though Rochioli typically pours only a couple of wines for visitors, it's one of the few wineries of its stature that doesn't charge for a tasting. ⊠ *6192 Westside Rd., Healdsburg* ☎ *707/433–2305* ⊕ *www.rochioliwinery.com* 🍷 *Tasting free* ☉ *Thurs.–Mon. 11–4, Tues. and Wed. by appointment; closed mid-Dec.–early Jan.*

Fans of pinot noir will surely want to stop at **Hartford Family Winery,** a surprisingly opulent winery off a meandering country road in Forestville.

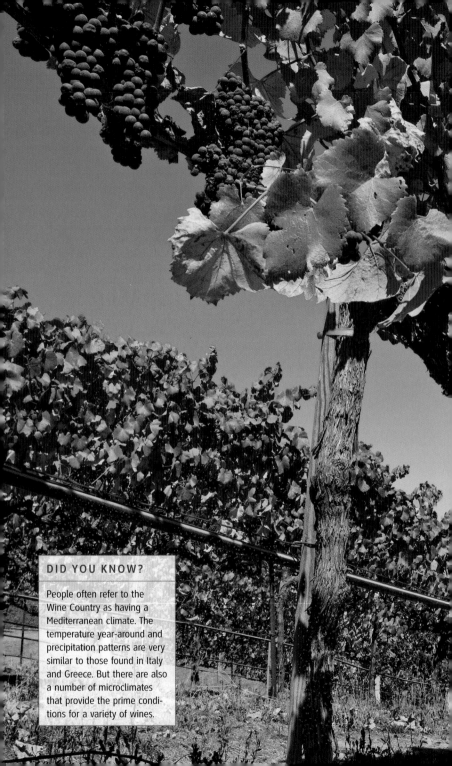

DID YOU KNOW?

People often refer to the Wine Country as having a Mediterranean climate. The temperature year-around and precipitation patterns are very similar to those found in Italy and Greece. But there are also a number of microclimates that provide the prime conditions for a variety of wines.

Here grapes from the cooler areas of the Russian River Valley, Sonoma Coast, and other regions are turned into crisp chardonnays, old-vine zinfandels, and a wide variety of pinots, many of which are single-vineyard wines. ✉ *8075 Martinelli Rd. Forestville* ☎ *707/887–1756* ⊕ *www.hartfordwines.com* ☜ *Tasting $5–$15* ☾ *Daily 10–4:30.*

WORD OF MOUTH

"I like to purchase wine openers or other paraphernalia from the wineries I visit [as souvenirs]. They always have the winery name or logo and they are small [for easy packing]."　　—cabovacation

Pass through an impressive metal gate and wind your way up a steep hill to reach **Gary Farrell Winery,** a spot with knockout views over the rolling hills and vineyards below. Although the winery has changed hands a few times since Farrell sold it in 2004, it has managed to continue producing well-regarded bottles under Susan Reed, who worked alongside him. Though their earthy, full-bodied zinfandels are winners, the winery has built its reputation on its pinot noirs. They also make a fine sauvignon blanc and chardonnay. ✉ *10701 Westside Rd. Healdsburg* ☎ *707/473–2900* ⊕ *www.garyfarrellwines.com* ☜ *Tasting $10–$15, tour $20* ☾ *Daily 10:30–4:30; tour by appointment.*

OFF THE BEATEN PATH

Korbel Champagne Cellars produces several tasty, reasonably priced bubblies and still wines, as well as its own brandy. The wine tour clearly explains the process of making sparkling wine and takes you through the winery's ivy-covered 19th-century buildings. If you've already had the process of wine making explained to you one too many times, a tour of the rose garden, where there are more than 250 varieties of roses, may be a welcome break. Garden tours are given a few times daily Tuesday through Sunday, mid-April through mid-October. ✉ *13250 River Rd., Guerneville* ☎ *707/824–7000* ⊕ *www.korbel.com* ☜ *Tasting and tour free* ☾ *Daily 10–4:30; call for tour times.*

WHERE TO EAT AND STAY

$$$$
FRENCH
Fodor'sChoice
★

✕ **The Farmhouse Inn.** From the personable sommelier who arrives at the table to help you pick wines from the excellent list to the servers who lovingly describe the provenance of the black truffles shaved over your pasta stuffed with salt-roasted pears and Parmesan, the staff match the quality of the outstanding French-inspired cuisine. The signature dish, "rabbit, rabbit, rabbit," a rich trio of confit of leg, rabbit loin wrapped in applewood-smoked bacon, and roasted rack of rabbit with a whole-grain mustard sauce, is typical of the dishes that are both rustic and refined, and the starters often include a seared Sonoma foie gras served with an apple cider sauce. ■ TIP➔ The inn's a favorite of local foodies in the wine industry, who also know that their head sommelier is one of only about a hundred Master Sommeliers working in the United States, so reserve well in advance. ✉ *7871 River Rd., Forestville* ☎ *707/887–3300 or 800/464–6642* ⊕ *www.farmhouseinn.com* ⌕ *Reservations essential* ▭ *AE, D, DC, MC, V* ☾ *Closed Tues. and Wed. No lunch.*

$$–$$$
★

⌂ **Applewood Inn & Restaurant.** On a knoll in the shelter of towering redwoods, this romantic inn has two distinct types of accommodations. The original Belden House, built in 1922, has a river-rock fireplace that encourages loitering in the reception area. Its rooms are smaller than

Annual barrel tasting along Russian River's wine road.

those in the newer buildings, but have charming touches, such as an exposed-brick wall in one or a view of a stand of redwood trees from another. Most of the rooms in the newer buildings are larger and airier, decorated in sage-green and terra-cotta tones. Readers rave about the stellar service, soothing atmosphere, and the earthy Cal-Italian cuisine that's served in the restaurant ($$$), built to recall a French barn. At this writing, new owners had plans for redecorating, adding a small spa, and instituting regional Italian cooking classes, so call ahead or check their Web site for the latest. **Pros:** quiet, secluded location; friendly, homey service. **Cons:** planned improvements may cause some disruption; sounds can carry in the Belden House. ⊠ *13555 Rte. 116, Guerneville* ☎ *707/869–9093 or 800/555–8509* ⊕ *www.applewoodinn.com* ↪ *19 rooms* ⌂ *In-room: a/c (some), Wi-Fi. In-hotel: restaurant, pool, spa* ⊟ *AE, D, MC, V* ⊺⊘ *BP.*

$$$–$$$$
Fodor'sChoice
★

The Farmhouse Inn. This pale yellow 1873 farmhouse and adjacent cottages offer individually decorated rooms with comfortable touches such as down comforters and whirlpool tubs. Most of the cottages have wood-burning fireplaces and even their own private saunas, which make this place especially inviting during the rainy months. The most romantic (and expensive) rooms are those in the newest building, finished in 2009 and built to resemble an old barn that was once on the property. With a chic rustic-farmhouse-meets-modern-loft aesthetic, the spacious rooms have king-size four-poster beds, spa tubs, and patios or balconies overlooking the hillside. It's worth leaving your supremely comfortable bed for the sumptuous breakfasts here. **Pros:** one of Sonoma's best restaurants is on-site; free snacks, games, and movies available; extremely comfortable beds. **Cons:** rooms closest to the street get a bit of road noise. ⊠ *7871 River Rd., Forestville* ☎ *707/887–3300 or 800/464–6642* ⊕ *www.farmhouseinn.com* ⊸ *12 rooms, 6 suites* ⌂ *In-room: a/c, refrigerator, DVD, Wi-Fi. In-hotel: restaurant, pool, spa* ⊟ *AE, D, DC, MC, V* ⍿⊙⍿ *BP.*

¢   ⊡ **Sebastopol Inn.** Simple but cheerful rooms, freshly painted a sunny yellow and equipped with blue-and-white striped curtains, have a spare California country style at this reasonably priced inn. Rooms clustered around a pleasant courtyard are also steps away from an old train station that has been converted into a cluster of cafés and shops. Some of the rooms have microwaves, some have small balconies or patios, and the uncommonly spacious suites (which also have jetted tubs) offer plenty of room for families. **Pros:** friendly staff; just steps from a café, wine bar, and spa. **Cons:** at least a 30-minute drive from most Russian River wineries; some will find the beds too firm. ⊠ *6751 Sebastopol Ave., Sebastopol* ☎ *707/829–2500* ⊕ *www.sebastopolinn.com* ⊸ *29 rooms, 2 suites* ⌂ *In-room: refrigerator, Wi-Fi. In-hotel: restaurant, pool, laundry facilities* ⊟ *AE, D, DC, MC, V.*

SPORTS AND THE OUTDOORS

At **Burke's Canoe Trips** (⊠ *River Rd. and Mirabel Rd., 1 mi north of Forestville* ☎ *707/887–1222*) you can rent a canoe for a leisurely paddle 10 mi downstream to Guerneville. A shuttle bus will return you to your car at the end of the day. Late May through mid-October is the best time for boating.

HEALDSBURG

17 mi north of Santa Rosa on U.S. 101.

Just when it seems that the buzz about Healdsburg couldn't get any bigger, there's another article published in a glossy food or wine magazine about posh properties like the restaurant Cyrus and the ultra-luxe Hôtel Les Mars. But you don't have to be a tycoon to stay here and enjoy the town. For every ritzy restaurant there's a great bakery or relatively modest B&B. A whitewashed bandstand on Healdsburg's plaza hosts free summer concerts, where you might hear anything from bluegrass to Sousa marches. Add to that the fragrant magnolia trees shading the square and the bright flower beds, and the whole thing is as pretty as a Norman Rockwell painting.

The countryside around Healdsburg is the sort you dream about when you're planning a Wine Country vacation. Alongside the relatively untrafficked roads, country stores offer just-plucked fruits and vine-ripened tomatoes. The wineries here are barely visible, since they're tucked behind groves of eucalyptus or hidden high on fog-shrouded hills.

WHERE TO EAT

$$$

AMERICAN

✕ **Barndiva.** This hip joint abandons the homey vibe of so many Wine Country spots for a younger, more urban feel. Electronic music plays quietly in the background while hipster servers ferry inventive seasonal cocktails. The food is as stylish as the well-dressed couples cozying up next to one another on the banquette seats. Make a light meal out of starters like goat-cheese croquettes or "The Works," a bountiful plate of cheeses and charcuterie, or settle in for the evening with crispy lamb cheeks or risotto with seasonal vegetables. During warm weather the patio is the place to be. ✉ *231 Center St.* ☎ *707/431–0100* ⊕ *www.barndiva.com* ⊟ *AE, MC, V* ⊘ *Closed Mon. and Tues.*

$ ✕ **Bovolo.** Husband-and-wife team
ITALIAN   John Stewart and Duskie Estes serve what they call "slow food . . . fast." Though you might pop into this casual café at the back of Copperfield's Books for half an hour, the staff will have spent hours curing the meats that star in the menu of salads, pizzas, pastas, and sandwiches. For instance, the Salumist's Salad mixes a variety of cured meats with greens, white beans, and a tangy vinaigrette; and a thin-crust pizza might come topped with house-made Italian pork sausage and roasted peppers. House-made gelato served with a dark chocolate sauce or *zeppole* (Italian donuts) are a simply perfect ending to a meal. ✉ *106 Matheson St.* ☎ *707/431–2962* ⊕ *www.bovolorestaurant.com* ⌕ *Reservations not accepted* ⊟ *MC, V.*

$$$$ ✕ **Cyrus.** Hailed as the best thing to hit the Wine Country since French
AMERICAN   Laundry, Cyrus has collected lots of awards and many raves from
Fodor's Choice   guests. From the moment you're seated to the minute your dessert
★   plates are whisked away, you'll be carefully tended by gracious servers and an expert sommelier. The formal dining room, with its vaulted Venetian-plaster ceiling, is a suitably plush setting for chef Douglas Keane's creative, subtle cuisine. Each night, diners have their choice of four set menus: five- and eight-course extravaganzas ($102 and $130), for both omnivores and vegetarians. Set aside three hours to work your way from savory starters like the terrine of foie gras with curried apple compote, through fragrant dishes like the truffled wine risotto with Parmesan broth, to desserts such as the hazelnut *dacquoise* (layers of hazelnut and buttercream). If you've failed to make reservations, you can order à la carte at the bar, which also has the best collection of cocktails and spirits in all of the Wine Country. ✉ *29 North St., Healdsburg* ☎ *707/433–3311* ⊕ *www.cyrusrestaurant.com* ⌕ *Reservations essential* ⊟ *AE, DC, MC, V* ⊘ *Closed Tues. and Wed. in winter. No lunch.*

$$ ✕ **Scopa.** At this tiny eatery chef Ari Rosen cooks up rustic Italian spe-
ITALIAN   cialties such as house-made ravioli stuffed with ricotta cheese, braised chicken with greens and polenta, and *polpette Calabrese* (spicy meatballs served with smoked mozzarella in a tomato sauce). Simple thin-crust pizzas are worth ordering, too. Locals love the restaurant for its lack of pretension: wine is served in juice glasses, and the friendly hostess visits guests frequently to make sure all are satisfied. You'll be packed in elbow-to-elbow with your fellow diners, but for a convivial evening over a bottle of nebbiolo, there's no better choice. ✉ *109A Plaza St.* ☎ *707/433–5282* ⊕ *www.scopahealdsburg.com* ⊟ *AE, MC, V* ⊘ *Closed Mon. No lunch.*

WORD OF MOUTH

"Then we started our drive towards Healdsburg. The drive was beautiful...lots of wineries, and green, rolling hills. The azalea trees were blooming. It was 70 degrees in Healdsburg...pure bliss."   —kureiff

19

$$ ✕ **Zin Restaurant and Wine Bar.** Concrete walls and floors and large can-
AMERICAN   vases on the walls make the restaurant casual, industrial, and slightly
artsy. The American cuisine—such as smoked pork chop with home-
made applesauce or the lamb sirloin with mint jelly—is hearty and
highly seasoned. Portions are large, so consider sharing if you hope to
save room for desserts like the brownie sundae with Kahlua chocolate
sauce. As you might have guessed, zinfandel is the drink of choice
here: the varietal makes up roughly half of the 100 or so bottles on
the wine list. ⊠ *344 Center St.* ☎ *707/473–0946* ▭ *AE, MC, V* ⊙ *No
lunch weekends.*

WHERE TO STAY

¢–$ ⊡ **Camellia Inn.** In a well-preserved Victorian constructed in 1869, this
colorful B&B is on a quiet residential street a block from the town's
main square. The parlors downstairs are chockablock with ceramics
and other decorative items, while rooms are individually decorated with
antiques. Each room has its own charms, like a canopy bed, a claw-foot
tub, or a whirlpool bath. ■**TIP**→ **Those on a budget should ask about
the cozy (and popular) budget room with a full-size bed and large private
bath across the hall. Pros:** reasonable rates for the neighborhood; a rare
family-friendly inn; within easy walking distance of dozens of restau-
rants. **Cons:** a few rooms have a shower but no bath; the only TV on the
property is in the common sunroom. ⊠ *211 North St.* ☎ *707/433–8182
or 800/727–8182* ⊕ *www.camelliainn.com* ☞ *8 rooms, 1 suite* ⌂ *In-
room: no phone, a/c, no TV, Wi-Fi. In-hotel: pool, some pets allowed*
▭ *AE, D, MC, V* ⎮⦿⎮ *BP.*

$$$ ⊡ **The Honor Mansion.** Each room is unique at this photogenic 1883
★   Italianate Victorian. Rooms in the main house preserve a sense of the
building's heritage, while the larger suites are comparatively understated. Luxurious touches such as antiques and decanters of sherry are
found in every room, and suites have the advantage of a deck; some even
have private outdoor hot tubs. Fodors.com readers rave about the attentive staff, who "think of things you don't even know you want." **Pros:**
spacious grounds with boccie and tennis courts, a putting green, and
half-court for basketball; homemade sweets available at all hours; spa
pavilions by pool available for massages in fair weather. **Cons:** almost
a mile from Healdsburg's plaza; on a moderately busy street. ⊠ *14891
Grove St.* ☎ *707/433–4277 or 800/554–4667* ⊕ *www.honormansion.
com* ☞ *5 rooms, 8 suites* ⌂ *In-room: a/c, safe (some), refrigerator
(some), DVD (some), Wi-Fi. In-hotel: tennis court, pool, Internet terminal* ▭ *AE, MC, V* ⊙ *Closed 1 wk around Christmas* ⎮⦿⎮ *BP.*

$$$–$$$$ ⊡ **Hotel Healdsburg.** Across the street from Healdsburg's tidy town plaza,
this spare, sophisticated hotel caters to travelers with an urban sensibil-
ity. Unadorned olive-green walls, dark hardwood floors, and clean-line
furniture fill the guest rooms; the beds are some of the most comfort-
able you can find. Spacious bathrooms continue the sleek style with
monochromatic tiles and deep soaking tubs that are all right angles.
The attached restaurant, Dry Creek Kitchen ($$$$), is one of the best in
Healdsburg. Celebrity chef Charlie Palmer is the man behind seasonal
dishes that largely rely on local ingredients, like a spice-crusted Sonoma
duck breast or seared Sonoma foie gras, plus a wine list covering the

best Sonoma vintners. **Pros:** several rooms overlook the town plaza; free valet parking; extremely comfortable beds. **Cons:** least expensive rooms are small; exterior rooms get some street noise. ⊠ *25 Matheson St.* ☎ *707/431–2800 or 800/889–7188* ⊕ *www.hotelhealdsburg.com* ➷ *45 rooms, 10 suites* ♿ *In-room: a/c, safe, refrigerator, DVD, Internet, Wi-Fi. In-hotel: restaurant, room service, bar, pool, gym, spa, laundry service, some pets allowed* ═ *AE, MC, V* ¶○¶ *CP.*

$$$$ 🖼 **Hôtel Les Mars.** In 2005, posh Healdsburg got even more chichi with the opening of this opulent Relais & Châteaux hotel. Guest rooms are spacious and elegant enough for French nobility, with 18th- and 19th-century antiques and reproductions, canopied beds, and gas-burning fireplaces. Most of the gleaming, white-marble bathrooms have spa tubs in addition to enormous showers. Rooms on the third floor have soaring 20-foot ceilings that make them feel particularly large, while the second-floor rooms have a slightly more understated style. Wine and cheese are served every evening in the library, which is sumptuously paneled with hand-carved black walnut, and a continental breakfast is delivered to your room each morning. **Pros:** large rooms; just off Healdsburg's plaza; impeccable service; Bulgari bath products. **Cons:** very expensive. ⊠ *27 North St.* ☎ *707/433–4211* ⊕ *www.lesmarshotel.com* ➷ *16 rooms* ♿ *In-room: a/c, safe, DVD, Internet, Wi-Fi. In-hotel: restaurant, bar, pool, gym, laundry service* ═ *AE, MC, V* ¶○¶ *CP.*

$$$–$$$$ 🖼 **Madrona Manor.** The oldest continuously operating inn in the area, this 1881 Victorian mansion is surrounded by 8 acres of wooded and landscaped grounds. Rooms in the three-story mansion, the carriage house, and the three separate cottages are splendidly ornate, with mirrors in gilt frames and paintings covering every wall. Much of the furniture is even original to the 19th-century house. Candlelight dinners are served in the formal dining rooms nightly except Monday and Tuesday. Chef Jesse Mallgren has earned much praise for his elaborate three-, four-, and five-course menus ($$$$), where luxuries like the a Périgord truffle risotto might precede a bacon-wrapped rabbit loin and a warm chocolate soufflé. ■TIP➔ **For a ridiculously romantic experience, ask for Room 203 or 204. They both have huge balconies that overlook the hotel grounds and beyond.** **Pros:** old-fashioned and romantic; pretty veranda perfect for a cocktail. **Cons:** pool heated May through October only; decor might be too fussy for some. ⊠ *1001 Westside Rd., central Healdsburg exit off U.S. 101, then left on Mill St.* ☎ *707/433–4231 or 800/258–4003* ⊕ *www.madronamanor.com* ➷ *17 rooms, 5 suites* ♿ *In-room: a/c, no TV, Wi-Fi. In-hotel: restaurant, bar, pool* ═ *AE, MC, V* ¶○¶ *BP.*

FARMERS' MARKET

During two weekly **Healdsburg farmers' markets** you can buy locally made goat cheese, fragrant lavender, and olive oil in addition to the usual produce. On Saturday from May through November the market takes place one block west of the town plaza, at the corner of North and Vine streets, from 9 AM to noon. The Tuesday market, which runs from June through October, takes place on the plaza itself from 4 to 6:30 PM.

19

SHOPPING

Oakville Grocery (✉ *124 Matheson St.* ☎ *707/433–3200*) has a bustling Healdsburg branch filled with wine, condiments, and deli items. A terrace with ample seating makes a good place for an impromptu picnic, but you might want to lunch early or late to avoid the worst crowds. You'll have to get in your car to head north on Healdsburg Avenue to **Tip Top Liquor Warehouse** (✉ *90 Dry Creek Rd., Healdsburg* ☎ *707/431–0841*), a nondescript spot that stocks an interesting selection of wines and spirits at fair prices. Though it's strongest in bottles from Sonoma, you'll also find a few Napa wines, including some rare cult cabernets.

DRY CREEK AND ALEXANDER VALLEYS

On the west side of U.S. 101, Dry Creek Valley remains one of the least-developed appellations in Sonoma. Zinfandel grapes flourish on the benchlands, whereas the gravelly, well-drained soil of the valley floor is better known for chardonnay and, in the north, sauvignon blanc. The wineries in this region tend to be smaller, which makes them a good bet on summer weekends, when larger spots and those along the main thoroughfares fill up with tourists.

The Alexander Valley, which lies northeast of Healdsburg, is similarly rustic, and you can see as many folks cycling along Highway 128 here as you can behind the wheel of a car. The largely family-owned wineries often produce zinfandel and chardonnay.

★ Inside the tasting room at **Stryker Sonoma,** vaulted ceilings and seemingly endless walls of windows onto the vineyards suggest you've entered a cathedral to wine. The wines are almost as impressive as the architecture: most of their bottles are single varietals, such as chardonnay, merlot, zinfandel, and cabernet sauvignon. An exception, however, are a few Bordeaux-style blends, including the powerful E1K, which, unfortunately, is not usually poured in the tasting room (though it never hurts to ask whether they have a bottle open). The picnic tables are a particularly lovely way to enjoy the quiet countryside of the Alexander Valley. ✉ *5110 Hwy. 28, Geyserville* ☎ *707/433–1944* ⊕ *www.strykersonoma. com* 🍷 *Tasting free–$10* ☉ *Daily 10:30–5.*

In 2006, filmmaker-winemaker-publisher-hotelier Francis Ford Coppola snapped up a majestic French-style château, formerly Château Souverain and now called **Francis Ford Coppola Winery,** to showcase his less-expensive wines. (His Napa winery, Rubicon Estate, focuses on the high-end vintages). It's still very much a work in progress: at this writing, the property was in full renovation mode, and wines were being poured in a makeshift tasting room. After all the dust settles, however, the winery intends to have a full-service restaurant, a café, and an area for viewing Coppola memorabilia (the desk from *The Godfather* and costumes from *Bram Stoker's Dracula,* for example) that were once housed at Rubicon. Fans of Coppola's wines or movies should check the Web site or call ahead for the latest. ✉ *300 Via Archimedes (formerly Souverain Rd.), Geyserville* ☎ *707/433–8282* ⊕ *www. franciscoppolawinery.com* 🍷 *Tasting free–$8* ☉ *Daily 11–5.*

CLOSE UP

Best Wine Country Festivals

■ **Napa Valley Mustard Festival, Feb.–Mar.** When Napa is at its least crowded, and wild mustard blooms in between the vines, locals celebrate wine, food, and art with exhibitions, auctions, dinners, and cooking competitions. (☎ *707/938–1133* ⊕ *www. mustardfestival.org*)

■ **Wine Road Barrel Tasting Weekends, Mar.** For two weekends in March more than 100 wineries in the Russian River, Dry Creek, and Alexander valleys open their cellars to visitors who want to taste the wine in the barrels, getting a preview of what's to come. (☎ *707/433–4335 or 800/723–6336* ⊕ *www.wineroad.com*)

■ **Hospice du Rhône, early May** This three-day event in Paso Robles is the largest celebration of Rhône varietals in the world. (☎ *805/784–9543* ⊕ *hospicedurhone.org*)

■ **Sonoma Jazz + Festival, late May** Headlining jazz, rock, and world music performers play in a 3,800-person tent in downtown Sonoma, while smaller music, food, and wine events take place around town. (☎ *866/468–8355* ⊕ *www.sonomajazz.org*)

■ **Auction Napa Valley, early June** The world's biggest charity wine auction is one of Napa's glitziest nights. Events hosted by various wineries culminate in an opulent dinner and auction. (☎ *707/963–3388* ⊕ *www. napavintners.com*)

■ **Sonoma County Harvest Fair, early Oct.** This festival celebrates agriculture in Sonoma County, with wine tastings, cooking demos, livestock shows, crafts, carnival rides, and local entertainers filling the Sonoma County Fairgrounds in Santa Rosa. (☎ *707/545–4203* ⊕ *www.harvestfair.org*)

At **Dry Creek Vineyard** fumé blanc is king. Dry Creek also makes well-regarded zinfandels, a zesty dry chenin blanc, a pinot noir, and a handful of cabernet sauvignon blends. Since many of their quality wines go for less than $20 or $30 a bottle, it's a popular stop for those who want to stock their cellars for a reasonable price. After picking up a bottle you might want to picnic on the lawn, next to the flowering magnolia tree. Conveniently, a general store and deli with plenty of picnic fixings is just steps down the road. ⊠ *3770 Lambert Bridge Rd., Healdsburg* ☎ *707/433–1000* ⊕ *www.drycreekvineyard.com* 🍷 *Tasting $5–$10* ⊙ *Daily 10:30–4:30.*

An unassuming winery in a modern wooden barn topped by solar panels, **Quivira** produces some of the most interesting wines in Dry Creek Valley. It's known for its dangerously drinkable reds, including a petite syrah, and a few hearty zinfandel blends. The excellent tour provides information about their biodynamic farming practices and also offers a glimpse of the chickens and goats kept on the property. Redwood and olive trees shade the picnic area. ⊠ *4900 W. Dry Creek Rd., Healdsburg* ☎ *707/431–8333* ⊕ *www.quivirawine.com* 🍷 *Tasting $5, tour $15* ⊙ *Daily 11–5; tour by appointment.*

Fodor's Choice
★ Down a narrow road at the westernmost edge of the Dry Creek Valley, **Michel-Schlumberger** is one of Sonoma's finest producers of cabernet sauvignon, aptly described by the winery's tour guide as a "full, rich big

19

mouthful of wine." The tour is unusually casual and friendly. Weather permitting, you'll wander up a hill on a gravel pathway to the edge of their lovely terraced vineyards before swinging through the barrel room in the California Mission–style building that once served as the home of the winery's founder, Jean-Jacques Michel. To taste older vintages of their cabernet and learn what their wines will taste like after 10 or so years in the bottle, reserve in advance for a vertical tasting. ⊠ *4155 Wine Creek Rd., Healdsburg* ☎ *707/433–7427 or 800/447–3060* ⊕ *www.michelschlumberger.com* ◻ *Tasting $25, tour $15* ☺ *Tours at 11 and 2, by appointment; tasting by appointment.*

Fodor's Choice Once you wind your way down **Preston Vineyards'** long driveway, flanked
★ by vineyards and punctuated by the occasional olive tree, you'll be welcomed by the sight of a few farmhouses encircling a shady yard prowled by several friendly cats. In summer a small selection of organic produce grown in their gardens is sold from an impromptu stand on the front porch, and house-made bread and olive oil are available year-round. Their down-home style is particularly in evidence on Sunday, the only day of the week that tasting-room staffers sell a 3-liter bottle of Guadagni Red, a primarily zinfandel blend filled from the barrel right in front of you. Owners Lou and Susan Preston are committed to organic growing techniques, and use only estate-grown grapes in their wines. ⊠ *9282 W. Dry Creek Rd., Healdsburg* ☎ *707/433–3372* ⊕ *www.prestonvineyards.com* ◻ *$5* ☺ *Daily 11–4:30.*

Travel Smart
San Francisco

WORD OF MOUTH

"Yes, we purchased the 3-day muni passports @$18 each. . . . They were great! . . . They did check the date of the passport on each cable car ride we took, but not on the buses. . . . It was well worth it! We used those passes like crazy!"

—Mommybryant

GETTING HERE AND AROUND

San Francisco encompasses 46.7 square mi. As a major metropolitan hub it has a fantastic public transportation system; however, if you stray from the main thoroughfares public transport can get tricky, and renting a car becomes a more practical option.

All the city's major attractions are easily accessible via Muni (light-rail vehicles), BART (Bay Area Rapid Transit) trains, taxis, and cable cars; or if you have a comfy pair of shoes, you can always walk. It's exactly 8 mi from the west side of the city to the east side. The streets are neatly arranged along two grids that come together at Market Street, and with the area's well-known landmarks—the Golden Gate Bridge (north), Twin Peaks (south), the Bay Bridge (east), and the Pacific Ocean (west)—as a physical compass, it's difficult to lose your way.

The East Bay is also extremely accessible via public transport; BART is a good way to get where you want to go. And the North Bay is only a boat or bike ride away. Both are good choices, depending on the weather. A car only becomes necessary when you want to go farther north, for example, to Napa or Sonoma County. Keep in mind that rush-hour traffic isn't pleasant, so if you do rent a car try to take to the streets between 10 AM and 3 PM, or after 7 PM.

■ AIR TRAVEL

The least expensive airfares to San Francisco are priced for round-trip travel and should be purchased in advance. Airlines generally allow you to change your return date for a fee; most low-fare tickets, however, are nonrefundable. (But if you cancel, you can usually apply the fare to a future trip, within one year, to any destination the airline flies.)

Nonstop flights from New York to San Francisco take about 5½ hours, and with the 3-hour time change, it's possible to leave JFK by 8 AM and be in San Francisco by 10:30 AM. Some flights may require a midway stop, making the total excursion between 8 and 9½ hours. Nonstop times are approximately 1½ hours from Los Angeles, 3 hours from Dallas, 4½ hours from Chicago, 4½ hours from Atlanta, 11 hours from London, 12 hours from Auckland, and 13½ hours from Sydney.

Of the major carriers, Alaska, American, Continental, Delta, Mexicana, Southwest, and United all fly into San Francisco (SFO), Oakland, and San Jose airports. JetBlue, Primaris, and US Airways service Oakland. Frontier, Hawaiian, Horizon Air, and Northwest fly into SFO and San Jose. Virgin Atlantic and the budget-conscious Midwest Express fly into SFO.

Airline Contacts American Airlines (☎ 800/433–7300 ⊕ www.aa.com). **Continental Airlines** (☎ 800/523–3273 for U.S. and Mexico reservations, 800/231–0856 for international reservations ⊕ www.continental.com). **Delta Airlines** (☎ 800/221–1212 for U.S. reservations, 800/241–4141 for international reservations ⊕ www.delta.com). **Southwest Airlines** (☎ 800/435–9792 ⊕ www.southwest.com). **United Airlines** (☎ 800/864–8331 for U.S. reservations, 800/538–2929 for international reservations ⊕ www.united.com).

Smaller Airlines Frontier Airlines (☎ 800/432–1359 ⊕ www.frontierairlines.com). **Midwest Airlines** (☎ 800/452–2022 ⊕ www.midwestairlines.com).

AIRPORTS

The major gateway to San Francisco is San Francisco International Airport (SFO), 15 mi south of the city. It's off U.S. 101 near Millbrae and San Bruno. Oakland International Airport (OAK) is across the bay, not much farther away from downtown San Francisco (via I–80 east and I–880 south), but rush-hour traffic on the Bay Bridge may lengthen travel times considerably. San Jose International

Airport (SJC) is about 40 mi south of San Francisco; travel time depends largely on traffic flow, but plan on an hour and a half with moderate traffic.

Depending on the price difference, you might consider flying into Oakland or San Jose. Oakland's an easy-to-use alternative since there's public transportation between the airport and downtown San Francisco. Getting to San Francisco from San Jose, though, can be time-consuming and costly via public transportation. Heavy fog is infamous for causing chronic delays into and out of San Francisco. If you're heading to the East or South Bay, make every effort to fly into Oakland or San Jose Airport, respectively.

At all three airports security check-in can take 15 to 30 minutes at peak travel times.

■TIP➔ Count yourself lucky if you have a layover at SFO's International Terminal. During its 2005 renovation SFO brought in branches of some top local eateries. The food's far better than standard airport fare; you'll find Italian pastries from Emporio Rulli, burgers from Burger Joint or Lori's Diner, sushi from Ebisu, and much more.

Airport Information **San Francisco International Airport** (*[SFO]* ☎ 800/435–9736 ⊕ www.flysfo.com). **Oakland International Airport** (*[OAK]* ☎ 510/563–3300 ⊕ www. flyoakland.com). **San Jose International Airport** (*[SJC]* ☎ 408/277–4759 ⊕ www.sjc.org).

GROUND TRANSPORTATION FROM SAN FRANCISCO INTERNATIONAL AIRPORT

Transportation signage at the airport is color-coded by type and is quite clear. A taxi ride to downtown costs $35 to $45. Airport shuttles are inexpensive and generally efficient. Lorrie's Airport Service and SuperShuttle both stop at the lower level near baggage claim and take you anywhere within the city limits of San Francisco. They charge $15 to $17, depending on where you're going. Lorrie's also sells tickets online, at a $3 discount each way; you can print them out before leaving home. SuperShuttle offers some discounts for more than one person traveling in the same party ($16 per person), but only if you're traveling to a residential address.

Shuttles to the East Bay, such as BayPorter Express, also depart from the lower level; expect to pay around $35. Inquire about the number of stops a shuttle makes en route to or from the airport; some companies, such as East Bay Express, have nonstop service, but they cost a bit more. Marin Door to Door operates van service to Marin County for $30 to $40 for the first passenger, and $12 for each additional person; you must make reservations by noon the day before travel. Marin Airporter buses cost $20 and require no reservations but stop only at designated stations in Marin; buses leave every 30 minutes, on the half hour and hour, from 5 AM to midnight.

You can take BART directly to downtown San Francisco; the trip takes about 30 minutes and costs less than $5.50. (There are both manned booths and vending machines for ticket purchases.) Trains leave from the international terminal every 15 minutes on weekdays and every 20 minutes on weekends.

Another inexpensive way to get to San Francisco is via two SamTrans buses: No. 292 (55 minutes, $1.50 from SFO, $3 to SFO) and the KX (35 minutes, $4; only one small carry-on bag permitted). Board the SamTrans buses on the lower level.

To drive to downtown San Francisco from the airport, take U.S. 101 north to the Civic Center/9th Street, 7th Street, or 4th Street/Downtown exits. If you're headed to the Embarcadero or Fisherman's Wharf, take I–280 north (the exit is to the right, just north of the airport, off U.S. 101) and get off at the 4th Street/King Street exit. King Street becomes the Embarcadero a few blocks east of the exit. The Embarcadero winds around the waterfront to Fisherman's Wharf.

FROM OAKLAND INTERNATIONAL AIRPORT

A taxi to downtown San Francisco costs $35 to $40. By airport regulations, you must make reservations for shuttle service. BayPorter Express and other shuttles serve major hotels and provide door-to-door service to the East Bay and San Francisco. SuperShuttle operates vans to San Francisco and Oakland. Marin Door to Door serves Marin County for a flat $45 for the first passenger, and $12 for each additional person; make reservations by noon the day before travel.

The best way to get to San Francisco via public transit is to take the AIR BART bus ($3) to the Coliseum/Oakland International Airport BART station (BART fares vary depending on where you're going; the ride to downtown San Francisco from here costs $3.80).

If you're driving from Oakland International Airport, take Hegenberger Road east to I–880 north to I–80 west over the Bay Bridge. This will likely take at least an hour.

FROM SAN JOSE INTERNATIONAL AIRPORT

A taxi to downtown San Jose costs about $15 to $18; a trip to San Francisco runs about $140 to $150. South & East Bay Airport Shuttle transports you to the South Bay and East Bay; a ride to downtown San Jose costs $25 for the first passenger, $6 for each additional, and a van to San Francisco costs $80 for the first passenger, $9 for each additional. Reservations are required to the airport, but not from the airport; call from baggage claim before you collect your luggage. Reservations are also required for VIP Airport Shuttle, which has service to downtown San Francisco for $93 for the first three passengers, $8 for each additional; to downtown San Jose costs $24.

To drive to downtown San Jose from the airport, take Airport Boulevard east to Route 87 south. To get to San Francisco from the airport, take Route 87 south to I–280 north. The trip will take roughly two hours.

At $7.75 for a one-way ticket, there is no question that Caltrain provides the most affordable option for traveling between San Francisco and San Jose's airport. However, the Caltrain station in San Francisco at 4th and Townsend streets is not in a conveniently central location. It's on the eastern side of the South of Market (SoMa) neighborhood and not easily accessible by other public transit. You'll need to take a taxi or walk from the nearest bus line. From San Francisco it takes 90 minutes and costs $7.75 to reach the Santa Clara Caltrain station, from which a free shuttle runs every 15 minutes, whisking you to and from the San Jose International Airport in 15 minutes.

Contacts American Airporter (☎ 415/202–0733 ⊕ www.americanairporter.com). **Bay-Porter Express** (☎ 415/467–1800 ⊕ www.bayporter.com). **Caltrain** (☎ 800/660–4287 ⊕ www.caltrain.com). **East Bay Express Airporter** (☎ 877/526–0304 ⊕ www.eastbaytransportation.com). **Lorrie's Airport Service** (☎ 415/334–9000 ⊕ www.gosfovan.com). **Marin Airporter** (☎ 415/461–4222 ⊕ www.marinairporter.com). **Marin Door to Door** (☎ 415/457–2717 ⊕ www.marindoortodoor.com). **SamTrans** (☎ 800/660–4287 ⊕ www.samtrans.com). **South & East Bay Airport Shuttle** (☎ 800/548–4664 ⊕ www.southandeastbayairportshuttle.com). **SuperShuttle** (☎ 415/558–8500 or 800/258–3826 ⊕ www.supershuttle.com). **VIP Airport Shuttle** (☎ 408/986–6000 or 800/235–8847 ⊕ www.yourairportride.com).

▌ BART TRAVEL

Bay Area Rapid Transit (BART) trains, which run until midnight, travel under the bay via tunnel to connect San Francisco with Oakland, Berkeley, Pittsburgh/Bay Point, Richmond, Fremont, Dublin/Pleasanton, and other small cities and towns in between. Within San Francisco, stations are limited to downtown, the Mission, and a couple of outlying neighborhoods.

Trains travel frequently from early morning until evening on weekdays. After 8 PM weekdays and on weekends there's often a 20-minute wait between trains on the same line. Trains also travel south from San Francisco as far as Millbrae. BART trains connect downtown San Francisco to San Francisco International Airport; a ride is $8.10.

Intracity San Francisco fares are $1.75; intercity fares are $3.10 to $5.95. BART bases its ticket prices on miles traveled and does not offer price breaks by zone. A discounted pass, called a Smart Card, is available for $45 and can be used on BART and on all Muni lines (including cable cars) within city limits. The easy-to-read maps posted in BART stations list fares based on destination, radiating out from your starting point of the current station.

During morning and evening rush hour, trains within the city are crowded—even standing room can be hard to come by. Cars at the far front and back of the train are less likely to be filled to capacity. Smoking, eating, and drinking are prohibited on trains and in stations.

Contacts Bay Area Rapid Transit ([BART] ☎ 415/989–2278 or 650/992–2278 ⊕ www. bart.gov).

▌ BOAT TRAVEL

Several ferry lines run out of San Francisco. Blue & Gold Fleet operates a number of routes, including service to Sausalito ($11 one-way) and Tiburon ($11 one-way). Tickets are sold at Pier 41 (between Fisherman's Wharf and Pier 39), where the boats depart. There are also weekday Blue & Gold commuter ferries to Tiburon ($11) and Vallejo ($13) from the San Francisco Ferry Building. Alcatraz Cruises, owned by Hornblower Yachts, operates the ferries to Alcatraz Island ($26 including audio tour and National Park Service ranger-led programs) from Pier 33, about a half-mile east of Fisherman's Wharf ($3 shuttle buses serve

several area hotels and other locations). Boats leave 10 times a day (14 times a day in summer) and the journey itself is 30 minutes. Allow roughly 2½ hours for a round-trip jaunt. Golden Gate Ferry runs daily to and from Sausalito and Larkspur (each costs $7.85 one-way), leaving from Pier 1, behind the San Francisco Ferry Building. The Alameda/Oakland Ferry operates daily between Alameda's Main Street Ferry Building, Oakland's Jack London Square, and San Francisco's Pier 41 and the Ferry Building ($6.25 one-way); some ferries go only to Pier 41 or the Ferry Building, so ask when you board. Purchase tickets onboard.

Information Alameda/Oakland Ferry (☎ 510/522–3300 ⊕ www.eastbayferry. com). **Alcatraz Cruises** (☎ 415/981–7625 ⊕ www.alcatrazcruises.com). **Blue & Gold Fleet** (☎ 415/705–5555 or 415/705–8200 ⊕ www.blueandgoldfleet.com). **Golden Gate Ferry** (☎ 415/923–2000 ⊕ www. goldengateferry.org). **San Francisco Ferry Building** (⊠ 1 Ferry Bldg., at foot of Market St. on Embarcadero ☎ 415/983–8000 ⊕ www. ferrybuildingmarketplace.com).

▌ CABLE CAR TRAVEL

Don't miss the sensation of moving up and down some of San Francisco's steepest hills in a clattering cable car, the only moving thing listed on the National Register of Historic Places. Jump aboard as it pauses at a designated stop, and wedge yourself into any available space. Then just hold on.

The fare (for one direction) is $5 (Muni Passport holders pay a $1 supplement). You can buy tickets onboard (exact change isn't necessary) or at the kiosks at the cable car turnarounds at Hyde and Beach streets and at Powell and Market streets.

The heavily traveled Powell–Mason and Powell–Hyde lines begin at Powell and Market streets near Union Square and terminate at Fisherman's Wharf; lines for these routes can be long, especially in summer. The California Street line runs east and west from Market and California streets to Van Ness Avenue; there is often no wait to board this route.

■ CAR TRAVEL

Driving in San Francisco can be a challenge because of the one-way streets, snarly traffic, and steep hills. The first two elements can be frustrating enough, but those hills are tough for unfamiliar drivers.

Be sure to leave plenty of room between your car and other vehicles when on a steep slope. This is especially important when you've braked at a stop sign on a steep incline. Whether with a stick shift or an automatic transmission, every car rolls backward for a moment once the brake is released. So don't pull too close to the car ahead of you. When it's time to pull forward, keep your foot on the brake while tapping lightly on the accelerator. Once the engine is engaged, let up on the brake and head uphill.

■TIP➔ Remember to curb your wheels when parking on hills—turn wheels away from the curb when facing uphill, toward the curb when facing downhill. You can get a ticket if you don't do this.

Market Street runs southwest from the Ferry Building, then becomes Portola Drive as it nears Twin Peaks (which lie beneath the giant radio-antennae structure, Sutro Tower). It can be difficult to drive across Market. The major east–west streets north of Market are Geary Boulevard (it's called Geary Street east of Van Ness Avenue), which runs to the Pacific Ocean; Fulton Street, which begins at the back of the Opera House and continues along the north side of Golden Gate Park to Ocean Beach; Oak Street, which runs east from Golden Gate Park toward downtown, then flows into northbound Franklin Street; and Fell Street, the left two lanes of which cut through Golden Gate Park and empty into Lincoln Boulevard, which continues to the ocean.

> ## TRACKING CHEAP GAS
>
> Determined to avoid the worst prices at the pump? Check the Web site ⊕ *www. sanfrangasprices.com*, which tracks the lowest (and highest) gasoline costs in the Bay Area. It's also got a handy price-mapping feature and a master list of local gas stations.

Among the major north–south streets are Divisadero, which becomes Castro Street at Duboce Avenue and continues to just past César Chavez Street; Van Ness Avenue, which becomes South Van Ness Avenue when it crosses Market Street; and Park Presidio Boulevard, which empties into 19th Avenue.

GASOLINE

Gas stations are hard to find in San Francisco; look for the national franchises on major thoroughfares such as Market Street or California Street. Once you find one, prepare for sticker shock—the fuel is notoriously expensive here.

Aside from their limited numbers and high costs, everything else is standard operation at these service stations. All major stations accept credit and ATM cards; self-service pumps are the norm. Most gas stations are open seven days a week until 11 PM or midnight. Many national franchises on well-traveled streets are open 24/7. Local independent stations are likely to close on Sunday or by 9 PM.

PARKING

San Francisco is a terrible city for parking. In the Financial District and Civic Center neighborhoods parking is forbidden on most streets between 4 PM and 6 PM. Check street signs carefully to confirm, because illegally parked cars are towed immediately. Downtown parking lots are often full, and most are expensive. The city-owned Sutter-Stockton, Ellis-O'Farrell, and 5th-and-Mission garages have the most reasonable rates in the downtown area. Large hotels often have parking available, but it doesn't come cheap; many charge in excess of $40 a day for the privilege.

Garages Ellis-O'Farrell Garage (✉ *123 O'Farrell St., at Stockton St., Downtown* ☎ *415/986–4800* ⊕ *www.eofgarage.com*). **Embarcadero Center Garage** (✉ *1–4 Embarcadero Center, between Battery and Drumm Sts., Financial District* ☎ *800/733–6318* ⊕ *www. embarcaderocenter.com*). **5th-and-Mission Garage** (✉ *833 Mission St., at 5th St., SoMa* ☎ *415/982–8522* ⊕ *www.fifthandmission.com*). **Opera Plaza Garage** (✉ *601 Van Ness Ave., at Turk St., Civic Center* ☎ *415/771–4776*). **Pier 39 Garage** (✉ *Embarcadero at Beach St., Fisherman's Wharf* ☎ *415/705–5418* ⊕ *www.pier39. com*). **Portsmouth Square Garage** (✉ *733 Kearny St., at Clay St., Chinatown* ☎ *415/982–6353* ⊕ *www.portsmouthsquaregarage.com*). **766 Vallejo Garage** (✉ *766 Vallejo St., at Powell St., North Beach* ☎ *415/989–4490*). **Sutter-Stockton Garage** (✉ *444 Stockton St., at Sutter St., Downtown* ☎ *415/982–7275*). **Wharf Garage** (✉ *350 Beach St., at Taylor St., Fisherman's Wharf*).

ROAD CONDITIONS

Although rush "hours" are 6–10 AM and 3–7 PM, you can hit gridlock on any day at any time, especially over the Bay Bridge and leaving and/or entering the city from the south. Sunday-afternoon traffic can be heavy as well, especially over the bridges.

The most comprehensive and immediate traffic updates are available through the city's 511 service, either online at ⊕ *www.511.org* (where webcams show you the traffic on your selected route) or by calling 511. On the radio, tune in to an all-news radio station such as KSFO 560 AM, KCBS 740 AM, and KNBR 680/1050 AM.

Be especially wary of non-indicated lane changes. There's a lot of construction going on in the SoMa neighborhood and the waterfront area in the southeast, but this doesn't create too many traffic problems.

San Francisco is the only major American city uncut by freeways. To get from

---

TAKE THE 511

Launched in 2002, the city's 511 service is operated by a partnership of government and public agencies. In this case, several transportation organizations—the Metropolitan Transportation Commission, the California Highway Patrol, the California Department of Transportation, and more—pool their data into a free, one-stop telephone and Web resource for all nine Bay Area counties. It gives the latest info on traffic conditions, route and fare information for all public transit, bicyclist info, and a host of other options. The telephone line can be called 24/7 toll-free.

---

the Bay Bridge to the Golden Gate Bridge, you'll have to take surface streets, specifically Van Ness Avenue, which doubles as U.S. 101 through the city.

RULES OF THE ROAD

To encourage carpooling during heavy traffic times, some freeways have special lanes for so-called high-occupancy vehicles (HOVs)—cars carrying more than one or two passengers. Look for the white-painted diamond in the middle of the lane. Road signs next to or above the lane indicate the hours that carpooling is in effect. If you're stopped by the police because you don't meet the criteria for travel in these lanes, expect a fine of more than $250.

In July 2008 a law passed banning drivers from using handheld mobile telephones while operating a vehicle in California (though that habit has been hard to shake). The use of seat belts in both front and back seats is required in California. The speed limit on city streets is 25 mph unless otherwise posted. A right turn on a red light after stopping is legal unless posted otherwise, as is a left on red at the intersection of two one-way streets. Always strap children under 80 pounds or under age eight into approved child-safety seats.

CAR RENTALS

When you reserve a car, ask about cancellation penalties, taxes, drop-off charges (if you're planning to pick up the car in one city and leave it in another), and surcharges (for being under or over a certain age, for additional drivers, or for driving across state or country borders or beyond a specific distance from your point of rental). All these things can add substantially to your costs. Request car seats and extras such as GPS when you book.

Rates are sometimes—but not always—better if you book in advance or reserve through a rental agency's Web site. There are other reasons to book ahead, though: for popular destinations, during busy times of the year, or to ensure that you get certain types of cars (vans, SUVs, exotic sports cars).

■TIP➔ Make sure that a confirmed reservation guarantees you a car. Agencies sometimes overbook, particularly for busy weekends and holiday periods.

Car-rental costs in San Francisco vary seasonally but generally begin at $30 a day and $150 a week for an economy car with air-conditioning, automatic transmission, and unlimited mileage. This doesn't include tax on car rentals, which is 9.5%. If you dream of driving with the top down, or heading out of town to ski the Sierra, consider renting a specialty vehicle. Most major agencies have a few on hand, but the best overall service is with two locally owned agencies: Specialty Rentals and City Rent-a-Car. The former specializes in high-end vehicles and arranges for airport pickup and drop-off. City Rent-a-Car likewise arranges airport transfers, and also delivers cars to Bay Area hotels. Both agencies also rent standard vehicles at prices competitive with those of the major chains.

In San Francisco you must be at least 20 years old to rent a car, but some agencies won't rent to those under 25; check when you book.

ALTERNATIVE RENTALS

City Car Share and Zipcar are membership organizations for any person over 21 with a valid driver's license who needs a car only for short-term use. You must join their clubs beforehand, which you can do via their Web sites. They're especially useful if you only want to rent a car for part of the day (say four to six hours), find yourself far from the airport, or if you're younger than most rental agencies' 25-years-or-older requirement. The membership fee often allows you to use their service in several metropolitan areas. If using such a service, you can rent a car by the hour as well as by the day.

Two companies, Electric Time Car Rentals and GoCar, rent electric vehicles at Fisherman's Wharf and Union Square. These cars can travel between 25 and 35 mph and are very handy for neighborhood-based sightseeing, but they're not allowed on the Golden Gate Bridge.

Electric Time Car Rentals offers two-seat and four-seat cars with detachable roofs, locked storage boxes, and GPS audio tours of the city. They're located at Anchorage Alley in Fisherman's Wharf. The GoCars are electric, two-seater, three-wheeled, open convertibles with roll bars (so drivers must wear helmets). Their vehicles also have computerized navigation and audio guides. You can pick up a GoCar at two locations: Fisherman's Wharf and Union Square.

Automobile Associations U.S.: **American Automobile Association** (*[AAA]* ☎ *415/565–2141* ⊕ *www.aaa.com*); most contact with the organization is through state and regional members. **National Automobile Club** (☎ *800/622–2136* ⊕ *www.thenac.com*); membership is open to California residents only.

Local Agencies City Car Share (☎ *415/995–8588 or 510/352-0323* ⊕ *www.citycarshare. org*). **City Rent-a-Car** (☎ *415/861–1312 or 415/359–1331* ⊕ *www.cityrentacar.com*). **GoCar** (☎ *800/914–6227* ⊕ *www.gocarsf. com*). **Specialty Rentals** (☎ *800/400–8412* ⊕ *www.specialtyrentals.com*). **Super Cheap**

Car Rental (☎ 650/777–9993 ⊕ www.supercheapcar.com). **Zipcar** (☎ 415/495–7478 ⊕ www.zipcar.com).

Major Agencies Alamo (☎ 800/462–5266 ⊕ www.alamo.com). **Avis** (☎ 800/331–1212 ⊕ www.avis.com). **Budget** (☎ 800/527–0700 ⊕ www.budget.com). **Hertz** (☎ 800/654–3131 ⊕ www.hertz.com). **National Car Rental** (☎ 800/227–7368 ⊕ www.nationalcar.com).

■ MUNI TRAVEL

The San Francisco Municipal Railway, or Muni, operates light-rail vehicles, the historic F-line streetcars along Fisherman's Wharf and Market Street, trolley buses, and the world-famous cable cars. Light rail travels along Market Street to the Mission District and Noe Valley (J line), the Ingleside District (K line), and the Sunset District (L, M, and N lines); during peak hours (Mon.–Fri., 6 AM–9 AM and 3 PM–7 PM) the J line continues around the Embarcadero to the Caltrain station at 4th and King streets. The new T line light rail runs from the Castro, down Market Street, around the Embarcadero, and south past Hunters Point and Monster Park to Sunnydale Avenue and Bayshore Boulevard. Muni provides 24-hour service on select lines to all areas of the city.

On buses and streetcars the fare is $2. Exact change is required, and dollar bills are accepted in the fare boxes. For all Muni vehicles other than cable cars, 90-minute transfers are issued free upon request at the time the fare is paid. These are valid for two additional transfers in any direction. Cable cars cost $5 and include no transfers (see *Cable Car Travel, above*).

One-day ($13), three-day ($20), and seven-day ($26) Passports valid on the entire Muni system can be purchased at several outlets, including the cable-car ticket booth at Powell and Market streets and the visitor information center downstairs in Hallidie Plaza. A monthly ticket, called a Fast Pass, is available for $70 and can be used on all Muni lines (including

WORD OF MOUTH

"I keep this number in my cell phone: 415/673–MUNI. They're great! If I get lost, I just call and I relay to them where I am (or if I don't really know, I tell them what I see around me) and the operator might say, 'Oh, you're on the wrong side. Cross the street and catch the [blank] bus.'"

—MelissaHI

cable cars) and on BART within city limits. The San Francisco CityPass, a discount ticket booklet to several major city attractions, also covers all Muni travel for seven consecutive days.

The San Francisco Municipal Transit and Street Map ($3) is a useful guide to the extensive transportation system. You can buy the map at most bookstores and at the San Francisco Visitor Information Center, on the lower level of Hallidie Plaza at Powell and Market streets.

■ TIP→ During football season Muni runs a special weekend shuttle to Candlestick Park for $10 round-trip.

BUS OPERATORS

Outside the city, AC Transit serves the East Bay, and Golden Gate Transit serves Marin and Sonoma counties.

Bus and Muni Information AC Transit (☎ 510/839–2882 ⊕ www.actransit.org). **Golden Gate Transit** (☎ 415/923–2000 ⊕ www.goldengate.org). **San Francisco Municipal Railway System** ([Muni] ☎ 415/673–6864 ⊕ www.sfmuni.com).

■ TAXI TRAVEL

Taxi service is notoriously bad in San Francisco, and hailing a cab can be frustratingly difficult in some parts of the city, especially on weekends. Popular nightspots such as the Mission, SoMa, North Beach, the Haight, and the Castro have a lot of cabs but a lot of people looking for taxis, too. Midweek, and during the day, you shouldn't have much of a problem—unless it's raining. In a pinch, hotel taxi stands are an option, as is calling for a pickup. But be forewarned: taxi companies frequently don't answer the phone in peak periods. The absolute worst time to find a taxi is Friday afternoon and evening; plan well ahead, and if you're going to the airport, make a reservation or book a shuttle instead. Most taxi companies take advance reservations for airport and out-of-town runs but not in-town transfers.

Taxis in San Francisco charge $3.10 for the first 1/5 mi (one of the highest base rates in the United States), 45¢ for each additional 1/5 mi, and 45¢ per minute in stalled traffic. There is no charge for additional passengers; there is no surcharge for luggage. For trips outside city limits, multiply the metered rate by 1.5.

Taxi Companies **DeSoto Cab** (☎ 415/970–1300). **Luxor Cab** (☎ 415/282–4141). **Veteran's Taxicab** (☎ 415/648–1313). **Yellow Cab** (☎ 415/626–2345).

Complaints **San Francisco Police Department Taxi Detail** (☎ 415/553–1447).

▌ TRAIN TRAVEL

Amtrak trains travel to the Bay Area from some cities in California and the United States. The *Coast Starlight* travels north from Los Angeles to Seattle, passing the Bay Area along the way, but contrary to its name, the train runs inland through the Central Valley for most of its route through Northern California; the most scenic stretch is in Southern California, between San Luis Obispo and Los Angeles. Amtrak also has several routes between San Jose, Oakland, and Sacramento. The *California Zephyr* travels from Chicago to the Bay Area and has spectacular alpine vistas as it crosses the Sierra Nevada mountains. San Francisco doesn't have an Amtrak train station but does have an Amtrak bus station, at the Ferry Building, which provides service to trains in Emeryville, just over the Bay Bridge. Shuttle buses also connect the Emeryville train station with downtown Oakland, the Caltrain station, and other points in downtown San Francisco.

Caltrain connects San Francisco to Palo Alto, San Jose, Santa Clara, and many smaller cities en route. In San Francisco, trains leave from the main depot, at 4th and Townsend streets, and a rail-side stop at 22nd and Pennsylvania streets. One-way fares are $2.50 to $11.25, depending on the number of zones through which your travel tickets are valid for four hours after purchase time. A ticket is $6 from San Francisco to Palo Alto, at least $7.75 to San Jose. You can also buy a day pass ($5–$22.50) for unlimited travel in a 24-hour period. Trips last 1 to 1¾ hours; it's worth waiting for an express train. On weekdays, trains depart three or four times per hour during the morning and evening, twice per hour during daytime non-commute hours, and as little as once per hour in the evening. Weekend trains run once per hour. The system shuts down at midnight. There are no onboard ticket sales. You must buy tickets before boarding the train or risk paying a $250 fine for fare evasion.

INFORMATION

Amtrak (☎ 800/872–7245 ⊕ www.amtrak.com). Caltrain (☎ 800/660–4287 ⊕ www.caltrain.com). **San Francisco Caltrain station** (✉ 700 4th St., at King St., ☎ 800/660–4287).

ESSENTIALS

■ COMMUNICATIONS

INTERNET

These days all public libraries provide Internet access and most hotels have a computer stationed in the lobby with free (if shared) high-speed access for guests. Hotels typically charge $10 a day to provide a high-speed connection in the room. In addition, cafés throughout San Francisco, Marin County, and the East Bay are split, with some offering Wi-Fi free of charge and others charging a $5 to $7 fee. For a list of free Wi-Fi spots in San Francisco, check ⊕ *www.wi-fihotspotlist.com*.

Contacts Cybercafes (⊕ www.cybercafes. com) lists more than 4,000 Internet cafés worldwide.

■ DAY TOURS AND GUIDES

For walking-tour recommendations, see the Experience San Francisco chapter.

BOAT TOURS

Blue & Gold Fleet operates a bay cruise that lasts about an hour. Tickets may be purchased at Pier 39, near Fisherman's Wharf. The tour, on a ferryboat with outside seating on the upper deck, loops around the bay, taking in the Bay Bridge, Alcatraz Island, and the Golden Gate Bridge. An audiotape tells you what you're seeing. Discounts are available for tickets purchased online.

Information Blue & Gold Fleet (☎ 415/705–5555 or 415/705–8200 ⊕ www. blueandgoldfleet.com).

BUS AND VAN TOURS

In addition to bus and van tours of the city, most tour companies run excursions to various Bay Area and Northern California destinations, such as Marin County and the Wine Country, as well as to farther-flung areas, such as Monterey and Yosemite. City tours generally last 3½ hours and cost $45 to $49. The bigger outfits operate large buses, which tend to be roomy. Service is more intimate with the smaller companies, however, because they can fit only about 10 people per vehicle; the vans can be a little tight, but with the driver-guide right in front of you, you're able to ask questions easily and won't have to worry about interrupting someone on a microphone, as is the case with the big companies.

Great Pacific Tours is the best small company and conducts city tours in passenger vans (starting at $49). Super Sightseeing is also locally owned and operates tours in 28- and 50-passenger buses. For $20 to $25 more, both companies can supplement a city tour with a bay cruise. Super Sightseeing can also add a trip to Alcatraz for $22.

Information Great Pacific Tours (☎ 415/626–4499 ⊕ www.greatpacifictour.com). **Super Sightseeing** (☎ 415/777–2288 or 888/868–7788 ⊕ www.supersightseeing.com).

■ MONEY

San Francisco often finds itself near the top of lists rating the most expensive cities in the United States. Don't let that scare you off; those ratings are usually based on the cost of living. Local real-estate prices are out of this world—but a trip here doesn't have to cost the moon.

Payment methods are those standard to major U.S. cities. Plastic is king; hotels and most stores and restaurants accept credit cards. Small, casual restaurants, though, may be cash-only operations. You can easily find ATMs in every neighborhood, either in bank branches (these have security vestibules that are accessed by your bank card), convenience stores, drug stores, supermarkets, and even some Starbucks coffee shops. Some performing-arts venues, hotels, and fine-dining spots will also accept traveler's checks.

Prices throughout this guide are given for adults. Substantially reduced fees are almost always available for children, students, and senior citizens.

CREDIT CARDS

Throughout this guide, the following abbreviations are used: **AE,** American Express; **D,** Discover; **DC,** Diners Club; **MC,** MasterCard; and **V,** Visa.

Reporting Lost Cards American Express (☎ 800/528-4800 in U.S. ⊕ www. americanexpress.com). **Diners Club** (☎ 800/234-6377 in U.S. ⊕ www.dinersclub. com). **Discover** (☎ 800/347-2683 in U.S. ⊕ www.discovercard.com). **MasterCard** (☎ 800/627-8372 in U.S. ⊕ www.mastercard. com). **Visa** (☎ 800/847-2911 in U.S. ⊕ www. visa.com).

▌ SAFETY

San Francisco is generally a safe place for travelers who observe all normal urban precautions. First, avoid looking like a tourist. Dress inconspicuously, remove badges when leaving convention areas, and know the routes to your destination before you set out. Use common sense and, unless you know exactly where you're going, steer clear of certain neighborhoods late at night: the Tenderloin, Civic Center plaza, parts of the Mission (around 14th Street, for example, or south of 24th to César Chavez Street), and the Lower Haight should be avoided, especially if you're walking alone.

Like many larger cities, San Francisco has many homeless people. Although most are no threat, some are more aggressive and can persist in their pleas for cash until it feels like harassment. If you feel uncomfortable, don't reach for your wallet.

▌ VISITOR INFORMATION

The San Francisco Convention and Visitors Bureau can mail you brochures, maps, and festivals and events listings. Once you're in town, you can stop by their info center near Union Square.

Information about the Wine Country, redwood groves, and northwestern California is available at the California Welcome Center on Pier 39.

Contacts San Francisco Convention and Visitors Bureau (⊠ 201 3rd St., Suite 900, San Francisco ☎ 415/391-2000, 415/392-0328 TDD ⊕ www.onlyinsanfrancisco.com). **San Francisco Visitor Information Center** (⊠ Hallidie Plaza, lower level, 900 Market St., Union Sq. ☎ 415/391-2000, 415/392-0328 TDD ⊕ www.onlyinsanfrancisco.com).

ONLINE RESOURCES

Start your search for all things SF by following the links option from **www.sfcity-scape.com.** This comprehensive Web site posts a link to every local publication, cultural institution, and government agency in the Bay Area.

For a snappy view of city trends, with gossip on everything from the city's best ice cream to concerts, check out **www.sfist. com.** For local politics and news, there's the online presence of the major daily newspaper, **www.sfgate.com/chronicle** as well as **www.fogcityjournal.com.** Current arts and cultural events are detailed on the extensive events calendar of **www. sfstation.com** or the San Francisco Chronicle's online entertainment Web site, **www. sfgate.com/eguide.**

You can browse articles from San Francisco, a monthly glossy, at **www.sanfran. com.** The annual summer issues on "bests" (restaurants, activities, and so on) are handy overviews. SF Weekly's site, **www. sfweekly.com,** makes for good browsing.

Where's the Wi-Fi? Although San Francisco's mayor, Gavin Newsom, promised to establish free, citywide wireless Web connections, he hasn't set a deadline. Click on www.wi-fihotspotlist.com to see where you can log on in the Bay Area for free.

INDEX

PHOTO CREDITS

1, Som Vembar, Fodors.com member. 2, Philip Dyer/iStockphoto. 5, travelstock44/Alamy. **Chapter 1: Experience San Francisco:** 8-9, Robert Holmes. 10, Brett Shoaf/Artistic Visuals Photography. 11 (left), elvis santana/iStockphoto. 11 (right), Brett Shoaf/Artistic Visuals Photography. 14-17, Brett Shoaf/Artistic Visuals Photography. 18 (left), Eli Mordechai/Shutterstock. 18 (top right), Andresr/Shutterstock. 18 (bottom center), Rostislav Glinsky/Shutterstock. 18 (bottom right), Chee-Onn Leong/Shutterstock. 19 (top left), Chris Pancewicz/Alamy. 19 (bottom left), FloridaStock/Shutterstock. 19 (right), Klaas Lingbeek- van Kranen/iStockphoto. 20 (left), Robert Holmes. 20 (top right), Aaron Wood/Shutterstock. 20 (bottom right), Brett Shoaf/Artistic Visuals Photography. 21, Lisa M. Hamilton. 22, Brett Shoaf/Artistic Visuals Photography. 23, Hal Bergman/iStockphoto. 25, wili_hybrid /Flickr. 26, Corbis. 27-29, Brett Shoaf/Artistic Visuals Photography. 30, Janet Fullwood. 31, Brett Shoaf/Artistic Visuals Photography. 32, Robert Holmes. 33, travelstock44/Alamy. 35, Brett Shoaf/Artistic Visuals Photography. 36, San Francisco Municipal Railway Historical Archives. **Chapter 2: Union Square & Chinatown:** 37, Rubens Abboud/Alamy. 39, Chee-Onn Leong/Shutterstock. 40, Steve Rosset/Shutterstock. 42, Brett Shoaf/Artistic Visuals Photography. 46, Robert Holmes. 49, Brett Shoaf/Artistic Visuals Photography. 50 (top), Arnold Genthe. 50 (bottom), Library of Congress Prints and Photographs Division. 51 (left), Sandor Balatoni/SFCVB. 51 (right), Detroit Publishing Company Collection, Photography Collection, Miriam and Ira D. Wallach Division of Art, Prints and Photographs, The New York Public Library, Astor, Lenox and Tilden Foundation. 52, Brett Shoaf/Artistic Visuals Photography. 53 (top), Gary Soup/Flickr. 53 (bottom), Albert Cheng/Shutterstock. 54 (top), Sheryl Schindler/SFCVB. 54 (center), Ronen/Shutterstock. 54 (bottom), Robert Holmes. **Chapter 3: SoMa and Civic Center:** 55, Walter Bibikow/age fotostock. 57, Robert Holmes. 58, Rafael Ramirez Lee/Shutterstock. 62, stephenrwalli/Flickr. 64, Brett Shoaf/Artistic Visuals. **Chapter 4: Nob Hill and Russian Hill:** 69, Robert Holmes. 71 and 72, Brett Shoaf/Artistic Visuals Photography. 78-79, POPPERFOTO/Alamy. 80 and 81 (top), Library of Congress Prints and Photographs Division. 81 (bottom), North Wind Picture Archives/Alamy. 82, Library of Congress Prints and Photographs Division. 83, Bettmann/CORBIS. **Chapter 6: On the Waterfront:** 95, Jon Arnold Images/Alamy. 97, Musee Mecanique in San Francisco. 98, Robert Holmes. 107, Lewis Sommer/SFCVB. 108, Daniel DeSlover/Shutterstock. 109 (left), POPPERFOTO/Alamy. 109 (center and right), wikipedia.org. 111, Eliza Snow/iStockphoto. 112, Steve Rosset/Shutterstock. **Chapter 7: The Marina and the Presidio:** 113, Carolina Garcia Aranda/iStockphoto. 115, Brett Shoaf/Artistic Visuals Photography. 116, javarman/Shutterstock. **Chapter 8: The Western Shoreline:** 123 and 125, Robert Holmes. 126, Brett Shoaf/Artistic Visuals Photography. 128, Chee-Onn Leong/Shutterstock. **Chapter 9: Golden Gate Park:** 131, Brett Shoaf/Artistic Visuals Photography. 132, Robert Holmes. 133 and 134 (top), Brett Shoaf/Artistic Visuals Photography. 134 (center), Robert Holmes. 134 (bottom),

Brett Shoaf/Artistic Visuals Photography. 135, Natalia Bratslavsky/iStockphoto. 136, Robert Holmes. 137 (top), Jack Hollingsworth/SFCVB. 137 (center), Robert Holmes. 137 (bottom), Brett Shoaf/Artistic Visuals Photography. 138 (top and bottom), Robert Holmes. 139 (top and bottom), Janet Fullwood. 140 (top), Donna & Andrew/Flickr. 140 (center and bottom), Robert Holmes. **Chapter 10: The Haight, the Castro, and Noe Valley:** 141, Robert Holmes. 143, Brett Shoaf/Artistic Visuals Photography. 144, SFCVB. 145, Brett Shoaf/Artistic Visuals Photography. 149, aprillilacs, Fodors.com member. 151, AP Photo/Noah Berger/Newscom. **Chapter 11: Mission District:** 155 and 157, Robert Holmes. 158, Brett Shoaf/Artistic Visuals Photography. 159, Held Jürgen/Prisma/age fotostock. 162, Robert Holmes. 163, Everett Collection. **Chapter 12: Pacific Heights and Japantown:** 165, Robert Holmes. 167, ryan + sarah/Flickr. 168, Brett Shoaf/Artistic Visuals Photography. 171, Rafael Ramirez Lee/iStockphoto. 175, Robert Holmes. 176 (top), rick/Flickr. 176 (center), Danita Delimont/Alamy. 176 (bottom), iStockphoto. 177 (top), Beata Jancsik/Shutterstock. 177 (center), Rafael Ramirez Lee/Shutterstock. 177 (bottom), Susanne Friedrich/iStockphoto. 178 (top), orphanjones/Flickr. 178 (center), Bruce Damonte. 178 (bottom), Janet Fullwood. **Chapter 13: Where to Eat:** 179 and 180, Lisa M. Hamilton. 185, iStockphoto. 186, Nikolay Bachiyski/Flickr. 187 (top), miss karen/Flickr. 187 (bottom), Audrey Chong/Shutterstock. 188, Atwater Village Newbie/Flickr. 189 (top), Jason Riedy/Flickr. 189 (bottom), Clemson/Flickr. 190, Robert Holmes. 191 (top), Yodel Anecdotal/Flickr. 191 (bottom), SFCVB. 192, Rough Guides/Alamy. 193 (top), Liv friis-larsen/Shutterstock. 193 (bottom), Bill Helsel/Alamy. 194, rick/Flickr. 195 (top), Ei-Lun Tsai/Flickr. 195 (bottom), Cathleen Clapper/Shutterstock. 196, moonlightbulb/Flickr. 197 (top), P_R_/Flickr. 197 (bottom), mashe/Shutterstock. 198, rick/Flickr. 199 (top), mark noak/iStockphoto. 199 (bottom), jessicafm/Flickr. **Chapter 14: Where to Stay:** 245, George Apostolidis/Mandarin Oriental Hotel Group. 246, Clift Hotel. 249, Joie de Vivre Hospitality. 250, Rien van Rijthoven/InterContinental Hotels & Resorts. 256 (top), George Apostolidis/Mandarin Oriental Hotel Group. 256 (bottom), David Phelps/Argonaut Hotel. 264 (top), The Ritz-Carlton, San Francisco. 264 (center left), Joie de Vivre Hospitality. 264 (center right), Queen Anne Hotel. 264 (bottom), Cris Ford/Union Street Inn. 271 (top), Rien van Rijthoven/InterContinental Hotels & Resorts. 269 (bottom left), Starwood Hotels & Resorts. 269 (bottom right), Joie de Vivre Hospitality. 280 (top), Hotel Nikko San Francisco. 280 (bottom left), Orchard Hotel. 280 (bottom right), Hotel Monaco. **Chapter 15: Nightlife and the Arts:** 285, irene./Flickr. 286, Robert Holmes. 295, Evanne Grate/rick/Flickr. 309, Rough Guides/Alamy. **Chapter 16: Sports and the Outdoors:** 319, Jack Hollingsworth/SFCVB. 320, Robert Holmes. **Chapter 17: Shopping:** 333 and 334, Robert Holmes. 349, besighyawn/Flickr. 356, Lisa M. Hamilton. 369, besighyawn/Flickr. **Chapter 18: Marin County, Berkeley, and Oakland:** 371, Robert Holmes. 372, Jyeshern Cheng/iStockphoto. 373, Robert Holmes. 375, Brett Shoaf/Artistic Visuals Photography. 378, Robert Holmes. 391, Mark Rasmussen/iStockphoto. 393, Robert Holmes. 398, S. Greg Panosian/iStockphoto. 405 and 415, Robert Holmes. **Chapter 19: The Wine Country:** 419, Robert Holmes. 420, iStockphoto. 421 and 423, Robert Holmes. 424, Warren H. White. 428, Robert Holmes. 429 (top), kevin miller/iStockphoto. 429 (bottom), Far Niente+Dolce+Nickel & Nickel. 430 (top and bottom) and 431 (top), Robert Holmes. 431 (bottom), star5112/Flickr. 432 (top left), Rubicon Estate. 432 (top right and bottom) and 433 (top and bottom), Robert Holmes. 434 (top), *Philippe Roy/Alamy*. 434 (center), *Agence Images/Alamy*. 434 (bottom), *Cephas Picture Library/Alamy*. 435 (top), *Napa Valley Conference Bureau*. 435 (second and third from top), *Wild Horse Winery (Forrest L. Doud)*. 435 (fourth from top), *Napa Valley Conference Bureau*. 435 (fifth from top), *Panther Creek Cellars (Ron Kaplan)*. 435 (sixth from top), *Clos du Val (Marvin Collins)*. 435 (seventh from top), *Panther Creek Cellars (Ron Kaplan)*. 435 (bottom), Warren H. White. 436 and 439, Robert Holmes. 452, Far Niente+Dolce+Nickel & Nickel. 454, Terry Joanis/Frog's Leap. 460, Chuck Honek/Schramsberg Vineyard. 463, Castello di Amorosa. 479, 480, 486-487, and 489, Robert Holmes.

ABOUT OUR WRITERS

A veteran Fodor's writer, Berkeley-based writer and editor Denise M. Leto roams the city out of sheer love for SF, peeking down overgrown alleyways and exploring tucked-away corners from the Tenderloin to the Richmond, often with her two homeschooled sons in tow. She updated all the neighborhood chapters and the Experience chapter in this edition. She also wrote our special features on cable cars, Chinatown, Golden Gate Park, and Alcatraz.

Fiona G. Parrott is a freelance writer who was born and raised in Mill Valley, California. She spent her childhood exploring the raw wilderness of Marin County and her later years exploring the culinary and musical delights of San Francisco, Berkeley, and Oakland. At present she divides her adventure time between wilderness and cityscape, researching and writing about the Bay Area's cutting-edge hotspots. She's been a veterinarian, actor, bartender, watermelon picker, latrine builder and university lecturer, but writing for Fodor's has been one of her most exciting jobs. She's updated the Sports Outdoors, Shopping, and Marin, Berkel & Oakland chapters, as well as the Trav Smart San Francisco chapter. In rece years Fiona also contributed to Fodo Scotland and Fodor's Great Britain.

A longtime Fodor's contributor, Sharr Wood simply adores San Francisco, fro its flourishing food, wine, and cockt culture to its perpetually perfect weathe When she's not exploring the Wine Cou try, she's writing about the city's nightli editing cookbooks, developing recipes, plying her friends with cocktails in h Mission District apartment.

Bay Area writer Sura Wood lost her hea in San Francisco when she was eight, a she's never stopped loving the city. arts journalist for the last fifteen yea she's written with gusto about San Fra cisco's food, fashion, hotels, nightlife, a and architecture for the Fodor's Web si She updated our Where to Stay, Where Eat, and Nightlife & the Arts chapte and Eye on Architecture feature for th year's guide.